WINTER SOLDIERS

An Oral History of the Vietnam Veterans Against the War

WINTER SOLDIERS

An Oral History of the Vietnam Veterans Against the War

RICHARD STACEWICZ

Haymarket Books
Chicago, Illinois

First published in 1997 by Twayne Publishers
Copyright © 1997 Richard Stacewicz
First paperback edition published in 2008 by Haymarket Books

Haymarket Books
P.O. Box 180165
Chicago, IL 60618
773-583-7884
info@haymarketbooks.org
www.haymarketbooks.org

Cover image of Vietnam Veteran's Against the War's takeover of the Statue of Liberty in 1976.
Photo courtesy VVAW.
Cover design by Rachel Wilsey

Trade distribution:
In the U.S. through Consortium Book Sales and Distribution, www.cbsd.com
In the UK, Turnaround Publisher Services, www.turnaround-psl.com
In Australia, Palgrave MacMillan, www.palgravemacmillan.com.au
All other countries, Publishers Group Worldwide, www.pgw.com/home/worldwide.aspx

Special discounts are available for bulk purchases by organizations and institutions. Please contact
Haymarket Books for more information at 773-583-7884 or info@haymarketbooks.org.

Printed in Canada by union labor on recycled paper containing 50 percent post-consumer waste in ac-
cordance with the guidelines of the Green Press Initiative, www.greenpressinitiative.org

ISBN-13: 978-1931859-60-8

Library of Congress Cataloging-in-Publication Data is available

10 9 8 7 6 5 4 3 2 1

For Maria, who gave me a third shot at life;
for my wife, Ann, my son, Johnny, and my daughter Sophie
whom I will always cherish;
and for the Vietnam Veterans Against the War,
who continue to struggle for peace and justice

Contents

Preface

Winter Soldiers, the title of this book, was a term coined—and adopted—during the Vietnam war by the Vietnam Veterans Against the War. It was derived from a famous passage by Thomas Paine, in his pamphlet *The Crisis,* written during the first winter of the American Revolution:

> These are the times that try men's souls. The summer soldier and the sunshine patriot will, in crisis, shrink from the service of their country, but he that stands it now, deserves the thanks of man and woman. Tyranny, like hell, is not easily conquered; yet we have this consolation with us that, the harder the conflict, the more glorious the triumph. . . . 'Tis the business of little minds to shrink, but he whose heart is firm and whose conscience approves his conduct will pursue his principles unto death.

This oral history of Vietnam Veterans Against the War (VVAW) is an attempt to provide a heretofore neglected perspective on another crisis, the Vietnam war—and on the debate that erupted during the war and that still persists among academics and politicians and in popular culture. The Vietnam war and the antiwar movement, perhaps more than any other event of the twentieth century, opened a rift in American society. The debate over the war focused not only on the war itself but also on broader issues: the status of American democracy, the meaning of patriotism, and the role of the United States in the global arena. In all these issues, both sides of the debate claimed to be acting in the best interest of American society and in concert with the nation's democratic heritage. Although this debate reached its peak during the war and has now become part of our history, its influence is still strong: how our nation interprets the history of the Vietnam war will have a decided impact on our foreign and domestic policies today and in the future.

Of course, numerous studies have been written about the history of the war, about its effects on Vietnam and the United States, about the GIs charged with carrying out the nation's military policies on the ground, and about the antiwar movement. But until recently, historians and the creators of popular culture have tended to neglect the VVAW—a veterans' organization that, for the first time in American history, provided a forum for veterans to speak out against a war from which they had just returned. Their experiences in Vietnam as well as in the war at home provide a unique view of an era in American history that continues to haunt us.

For my own study, I began by searching out and examining written documents pertinent to the history of VVAW. Its files had been deposited in an archive in Madison, Wisconsin, but I found them incomplete and woefully inadequate for gaining an understanding of veterans' motivations for speaking out against the war. I realized that such understanding, and a more detailed account of the organization's activities, could be gained only through interviews with surviving members. My first contact—which took place in 1991, at the time of the Persian Gulf war—was with Barry Romo, a national coordinator for VVAW, and it was through this contact that I was able to begin the interviews contained in this book.

Over the course of a year, I conducted more than 30 interviews with former and current members of VVAW. My initial plan was simply to use bits and pieces of the interviews to construct my own interpretation of the history of VVAW. As I transcribed the interviews, however, I realized that these veterans and their supporters had eloquent and powerful voices, and that they should speak for themselves. I therefore decided to develop an oral history in which the story of VVAW would be told primarily through their narratives.

I have edited the narratives, deleting repetition and less relevant material, but I have always tried to keep the spirit of the individual speakers, letting them describe in their own words the development of the consciousness of VVAW and its members. Before conducting the interviews, I had gone through the VVAW archives, and through FBI files and the records of the Nixon administration that referred to VVAW, and I found that the speakers' narratives correlated well with the surviving written records—and with each other.

I have tried to place the events described in this work within their historical context by providing a chronology at the beginning of the book, and by giving a brief introduction to each chapter. In these chapter introductions, I sketch the mood of the nation, the history of American involvement in Indochina and Vietnam, and the "other war"—the war that was fought at home in response to this involvement.

As a historian, I have tried to present the narratives, and my own expositions, as objectively as possible. However, I believe it is also appropriate—and important—for me to offer my own conclusions. This I have done in the Epilogue.

Here, I will say only that I am indebted to the men and women whose voices fill these pages. They welcomed me into their homes and their lives. We spent countless hours together, talking, drinking, laughing, and crying; and I came to respect their courage and their commitment to democratic ideals. I have completed this study not only for its historical value, but also for their sake, so that their voices would not be forgotten, or would not be only a faint whisper from the past.

In this regard, a special acknowledgment is due to Barry Romo, since my encounter with him started me on the path that led to this project. The story of our first meeting, and the circumstances surrounding it, is also told in the Epilogue.

I must, in addition, thank the numerous teachers and mentors who have challenged me and supported my work on this project. I want especially to acknowledge Buzz Alexander at the University of Michigan, who stands out as one of the finest teachers I have had the pleasure to know. His teaching style and his perspective on the Vietnam war challenged my assumptions about it and inspired me to learn more about it. Leo Schelbert, Marion Miller, Robert Messer, and Richard Fried at the University of Illinois at Chicago have also provided constant support and guidance throughout this project; their dedication to the students who have had the honor to work with them is truly remarkable.

My editors at Twayne, Donald Ritchie and Mark Zadrozny, provided valuable insights which have helped me shape this oral history. I am especially indebted to Susan Gamer for her critical comments and superb editing skills. Her contributions to this book have been invaluable.

I would also like to acknowledge the many friends who have given my wife and me support and encouragement during times when we struggled to balance our family life with work and illness. In particular, I would like to thank Earl Silbar for his unshakable friendship and support. I am also grateful to John Knox, who played a critical role in bringing my work to the attention of Mark Zadrozny at Twayne.

Finally, I would like to thank my parents, John and Lucia Stacewicz, who have taught me how to be a survivor and how to care; my sister, Maria Bajor, to whom I am greatly indebted and forever grateful for having donated a kidney to me when I was ill; and my wife, Ann Goethals, who has stood by me in sickness and in health. She and my son Johnny and my daughter Sophie have been a constant inspiration and have given me unimaginable love and joy.

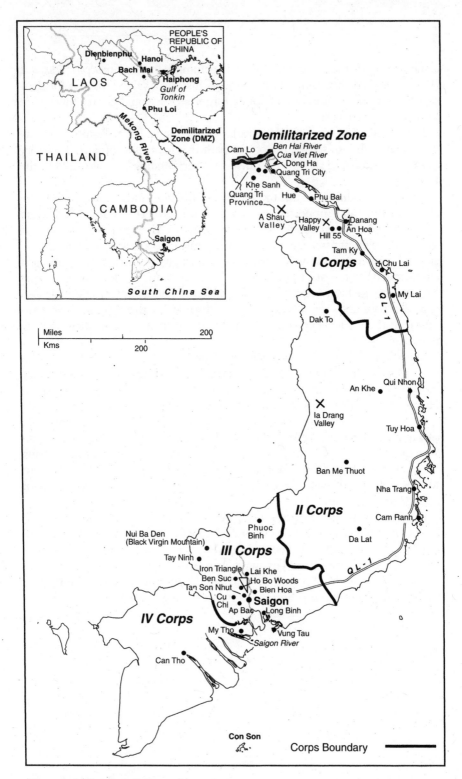

Vietnam at the time of the war.
(Map by Richard J. Thompson, Jr., and Donald S. Frazier.)

Introduction

On a rainy day in April 1967, at a time when American involvement in the war in Vietnam was escalating sharply, thousands of protesters gathered in Central Park in New York to march in an antiwar demonstration. These civilians were joined by a small group of Vietnam veterans, marching under a banner borrowed from Veterans for Peace, an organization of antiwar veterans of World War II and the Korean war. Written across the banner were the words "Vietnam Veterans Against the War."

Although the marchers in Central Park were not yet aware of it, many other Vietnam veterans across the nation were lending their voices to the antiwar chorus. These veterans were speaking out as citizens who believed that the war revealed, and reflected, a corruption of democracy, and that it was their duty to inform the American public. The attitude of these veterans—including the narrators of this oral history—is represented by John

The antiwar march in New York, April 15, 1967.

1

Kniffin, a former Marine who served three tours in Vietnam between 1965 and 1968: "We had taken an oath to defend the government of the United States and the Constitution. What do you do when the government of the United States is the enemy of the Constitution? Where does your allegiance lie?" Kniffin and many other veterans were motivated to speak and act against the war by an unshaken faith in the American people and in what they saw as American ideals.

While these veterans were on active duty in Vietnam—or even earlier, while they were preparing for active duty—many of them had come to believe that they themselves, the American public, and the Constitution had been betrayed by the nation's leaders. The betrayal they perceived is captured by Jack McCloskey: "It was a combination of seeing the war itself and . . . the other part of it . . . was the shattering of the American dream."

In Vietnam, many soldiers saw a war that conflicted with ideals they had been taught to cherish and protect. Most had been raised as children of the cold war, and many had been told, or had assumed, that they were going to Vietnam to protect the Vietnamese from an onslaught of godless communism, which had to be stopped there, before it could engulf the United States. Some had grown up in the aftermath—and the shadow—of the Second World War; and they often believed or hoped that they were going off, like their fathers, to fight a "good war." They had, for the most part, come of age in a society that seemed to be living up to its promises—a society in which the majority of citizens were achieving the "American dream." They were, typically, inclined to believe their leaders because little in their direct experience had given them reason for doubt.

Shortly after landing in Vietnam, however, many of them came to believe that, in the words of the veteran Jan Barry, they had been sent there to "act as the palace guard in this police state"; in other words, they realized that the Vietnamese government they had been sent to defend was far from democratic. During their tours of duty and later, when they returned to "the world," they decided that the American public was being misled by the media and by those charged with prosecuting the war—the accounts of the war that came out of Washington and through the media did not correspond to what they had experienced in Vietnam.

Their concept of the "shattering of the American dream" was partly a result of this ideological clash, but it was also partly a result of their growing sense that the nation's leaders, civilian and military, cared as little for the well-being of American troops as for the Vietnamese. Many of them had come of age in an environment where military heroes had been respected, or even idolized.[1] In the service, though, they encountered abusive and incompetent commanders who cared more about their professional careers than about the young men whose lives they held in their hands. That, of course, can happen in any war; but in this case it seemed obvious that American GIs were poorly

2

equipped and were being placed in situations where their lives were at risk for no clear strategic advantage. There was another factor as well: when these veterans returned home, they discovered that they were often shunned, even by some of those who had sent them to war.

While many veterans participated in the antiwar movement nationwide, it was the dozen or so on that rainy April day in New York who formed the Vietnam Veterans Against the War—the VVAW—and it was the VVAW that became the primary vehicle for veterans' antiwar protests. The founders believed that by speaking out as veterans, they could more effectively challenge the "official" picture of the war—the war as portrayed by Lyndon Johnson's administration and then by Richard Nixon's—and thus persuade the public to bring the war to an end through democratic processes. Throughout the duration of the war, these veterans remained committed to nonviolence. Their weapon in their effort to end the war was their *voice,* and they felt that their voice would be unimpeachable because what they were saying was grounded in experience.

It is important to note that, by and large, the veterans who became the most vociferous advocates for withdrawal from Vietnam were those who had served on the front lines. Of the veterans who joined VVAW, 57 percent had been in combat in Vietnam.[2] In this war, of course, as in most modern wars, the vast majority of people in the armed services were support personnel, but those actually in combat more directly confronted the contradictions it represented.[3] Their experiences, then, could give their voices greater authority: these veterans were men who had been in the belly of the beast and had emerged to share their knowledge. This is not to say that people "in the rear with the gear" could not reach the same conclusions about the war; many, in fact, could and did. However, it is useful to understand that often the urge to speak out against the war was motivated, in large part, by ideological, emotional, and physical trauma.

It is also important to try to understand what such trauma implies. Most Americans have never experienced combat and have never even been caught up in warfare as civilians. Thus it is hard for most of us to grasp the effect of combat duty—of continual danger and anxiety—on the human body and the human mind. Many of us may never fully know what it must feel like to face death in a situation, other than illness, over which we have little if any control. Nor will most of us know how it must feel to sense that our lives are considered expendable, as these veterans felt they were considered dispensable by the people managing the war. Most of us have not experienced the kind of affection that develops among combat troops who are charged with protecting each other, or the kind of despair that descends when comrades die needlessly. Finally, most of us can never fully comprehend the anxiety experienced by anyone who is required to kill other human beings, particularly when the ideological justification for such killing has been been undermined.

To understand these veterans' reactions to the war in Vietnam, then—to understand the narrators of this history—it is important to put ourselves in their shoes. John Shay, who has analyzed the psychological impact of the Vietnam war, gives some advice that is also relevant here. In *Achilles in Vietnam,* Shay asks his readers to "respond emotionally to the reality of combat danger in order to make rational sense of the injury inflicted when those in charge violate 'what's right.'"[4]

The antiwar veterans, of course, constituted a relatively small percentage of all veterans of Vietnam. Thus it is important, as well, to consider how these dissenting veterans, including the narrators of this history, were like most other veterans of this conflict and how they were, in certain ways, distinct. The disillusionment and anger these veterans experienced while they were in Vietnam and when they returned to civilian life was widespread. Numerous studies have shown the degree to which American soldiers in Vietnam exhibited their growing unease with the war; in fact, in 1971 Colonel Robert Heinl asserted that the armed forces in Vietnam were nearing a state of complete collapse.[5] Vast numbers of veterans returned home from Vietnam feeling confused and embittered, and they had a high rate of posttraumatic stress disorder (PTSD)—partly as a result of the cognitive dissonance they had experienced.[6] Also, the narrators here, like many other veterans, had engaged in covert acts of resistance to military authority while they were in the service. They had disobeyed orders, become involved in antiwar activism while still on duty, and at times contemplated killing or actually attempted to kill an officer who seemed to be needlessly risking their lives.[7]

But whereas most veterans tried to put the war behind them when they returned home, the members of VVAW felt compelled, at that point, to speak out—as they saw it, in defense of the principles of American democracy. They were impelled to describe the nature of the war they had experienced, and what they believed it revealed about the American nation and its foreign policy. A second way in which these antiwar veterans were distinct had to do with the communities to which they returned. These men, in general, came home to areas of the country where the civilian antiwar movement was active and well-organized. Some of them had mixed feelings about civilian antiwar activists, but for most, the antiwar community provided a haven within a larger society that would have preferred to forget them. Civilian activists who accepted the veterans into their groups and engaged in dialogue with them provided an alternative analysis of the war, an analysis that corresponded to the veterans' own experience.

Another important consideration is the antiwar veterans' concept of the citizen-soldier—and the winter soldier. The term "citizen-soldier" has been used to describe citizens' duty to protect the freedoms conferred upon them by a democratic system. It has its roots in the late eighteenth century, during the American and French revolutions, when groups of farmers, artisans, and other ordinary people banded together and formed militias to defend their new independence from tyranny. In fact, the founders of the American republic, who were wary of large standing armies, viewed citizens as the principal defenders of democracy.[8] To the Vietnam veterans who became antiwar activists, this was a significant concept; they saw themselves as having become citizen-soldiers when they went to war, and as risking their lives for the same ideals on which the nation had been founded and which its first citizen-soldiers had fought to defend. They also saw their antiwar protests—their attempts to reach the public in an effort to change the course of American foreign and domestic policy—as part of the duty of citizen-soldiers and even, perhaps, as "above and beyond the call of duty."

The term "winter soldiers" was created by VVAW members, who first adopted the name in 1971, during hearings held to investigate possible war crimes committed by American troops and their allies; the VVAW claimed that such abuses were not aberrations but were part of the standard operating procedure in Vietnam.[9] They had created the term by inverting Thomas Paine's well-known words about "summer soldiers": "The summer soldier and the sunshine patriot will, in crisis, shrink from the service of their country . . ."[10] Paine had been writing to encourage Americans—a ragtag army of citizen-soldiers—to confront the most powerful military force in the world, in order to protect their newly won independence and their democratic ideals; and the antiwar veterans saw an analogy with their own situation.

This analogy was suggested by Mike McCain, a former Marine who served in Vietnam during the year of the Tet offensive, the bloodiest year of the war:

> We started understanding, as a group of people, [that] it was easier to be a soldier than it was to be a critic of the government, of the state, of the society, but that if we were to be true citizens, that's what we had to do. You can't accept things at face value; you have to be a member of society. You have to argue. You have to decide whether or not something is right or wrong, and then once you've made that decision, act upon it.

In addition, therefore, it is important to understand how, in the process of speaking out against the war and reaching out to their fellow veterans and the public, the antiwar veterans broadened their analysis of the war and American society. They had a growing sense that the war in Vietnam was a symptom of deeper-seated problems afflicting the republic, and they expanded the role of their organization to address more general needs of veterans and the communties in which they lived and worked.

Finally, it is important to realize that in speaking out, these veterans—not surprisingly—opened themselves up to attack, not only from individuals who felt differently but also from the government, which viewed the antiwar movement as a threat to national security and, specifically, to the nation's ability to prosecute the war. The VVAW thus became a target of the Nixon administration, which sought to destroy it and to discedit antiwar veterans.

In the narratives that follow, veterans and civilian members of VVAW discuss their reasons for going to war as well as their reasons for opposing it. They describe their first efforts at speaking out and their first attempts to build an antiwar veterans' organization. They detail the roadblocks they encountered as they tried to educate the public about the nature of the military and the war as they had experienced it. They also discuss the legacy of VVAW and its impact, not only on the participants but on American society.

This is, then, not only a history of Vietnam Veterans Against the War but also the story of these veterans' developing political consciousness. In telling both stories, the narrators offer a unique perspective on the war and the antiwar movement. Their experiences shed new light on our nation's armed forces and its democratic institutions during the latter half of the twentieth century.

Chronology

1858   September. French capture Danang and gain a foothold in southeast Asia.

1874   March. Treaty of Saigon is signed, acknowledging French sovereignty over Cochin China (the southernmost region of Vietnam).

1883   August. French gain control of Annam and Tonkin (the middle and northern regions of Vietnam).

1911   Ho Chi Minh leaves Vietnam as a cook's apprentice on a French ocean liner, not to return until 1941.

1919   Following World War I, Ho Chi Minh, now living in Paris, presents a petition to the Allies at the peace conference, demanding independence for Vietnam. (The next year, he will be one of the founders of the French Communist Party.)

1930   February. Vietnamese Communist Party is formed by Ho Chi Minh, now in Hong Kong, and other advocates of independence.

1940   June. France falls to Germany; thereafter, Japan and France cooperate in Vietnam.

1941   February 14. Ho Chi Minh returns to Vietnam from Hong Kong, after a 30-year absence.

        May 10. Vietminh (Front for Independence of Vietnam) is founded to fight for Vietnamese independence.

1943   From 1943 to 1945, Office of Strategic Services (OSS) helps fund Vietminh in its struggle against Japanese forces; OSS agents provide assistance in espionage and sabotage.

1945   August 15. Japan surrenders.

        September 2. Ho Chi Minh declares Vietnam's independence and founds the Democratic Republic of Vietnam. That same month, the French move in to reestablish control.

1946   December 19. After a yearlong effort by France to regain its former colony, Ho Chi Minh calls for resistance; war breaks out.

1950   May 8. United States begins to provide overt military and economic aid to the French.

August 3. Thirty-five American advisers from the Military Assistance Advisory Group (MAAG) arrive in Vietnam to train troops receiving American weapons.

1951   September 7. United States provides direct aid to South Vietnam.

1954   April. French forces come under heavy attack at Dienbienphu; President Eisenhower propounds the "domino theory" as a rationale for continuing to support the French.

May 7. Two-month battle at Dienbienphu ends in defeat of the French.

May–July. Geneva conference on Vietnam. The country is partitioned as the French withdraw from North Vietnam, which is controlled by the Vietminh; however, Vietnam is supposed to be reunified in 1956.

July 7. Ngo Dinh Diem appointed premier of South Vietnam.

July 21. General Walter Bedell Smith, an American observer in Geneva, announces that the United States will not act to prevent implementation of accords.

October 24. United States pledges support to Diem and agrees to send $100 million to build up the military forces of South Vietnam.

1955   January 1. Direct aid from the United States to South Vietnam begins.

October 23–26. Diem wins (rigged) election and deposes Bao Dai; Diem announces a new Republic of Vietnam (RVN), which is immediately recognized by the United States.

1956   January 11. Diem announces Ordinance 6, providing for the arrest and detention of anyone thought to be dangerous to the security of South Vietnam.

July. Diem refuses to participate in elections to reunify Vietnam as stipulated by the Geneva accords; the United States supports him.

1957   May 8. Diem visits the United States. He is praised by Eisenhower (and much of the press) as a democrat seeking to save Vietnam.

October. Civil war breaks out in South Vietnam between Diem's forces and Vietminh who remained in the south after the partition of Vietnam.

1959   April 4. In a speech, Eisenhower says that the United States has a national interest in preserving a noncommunist Vietnam.

May 6. Law 10/59 in South Vietnam establishes special tribunals and provides for the imprisonment and execution of those deemed dangerous to its security.

July. Two Americans are killed at Bien Hoa.

1960 December 20. National Liberation Front (NLF) established in South Vietnam to organize and direct the growing insurgency against Diem's regime. Diem coins the (derogatory) term "Vietcong"—short for Viet Cong San, "Vietnamese communists"—to refer to his opponents.

December. Nine hundred American military advisers are in South Vietnam.

1961 May. President Kennedy sends Special Forces troops into South Vietnam, approves clandestine warfare against North Vietnam, and starts a secret war in Laos, which borders on Vietnam.

December. By the end of the year, 3,200 American advisers are in Vietnam.

1962 January. Air Force begins Operation Ranch Hand, the spraying of herbicides (including Agent Orange) as defoliants; this is meant to destroy the jungle cover of NLF forces, and to destroy their crops.

February 8. Military Assistance Command, Vietnam (MACV) is created, under General Paul D. Harkins.

April. "Strategic Hamlet" program is developed and implemented.

December. By the end of 1962, 11,000 American military personnel and advisers are in Vietnam; 109 Americans have been killed or wounded this year.

1963 January 2. Army of the Republic of Vietnam (ARVN) Seventh Division numbering about 10,000, equipped with American weapons and advised by American military personnel, cannot defeat a small force of 300 NLF fighters.

May 8. In Hue, 20,000 Buddhists demonstrate against the Diem regime and are fired on by government forces.

June 11. A Buddhist monk, Thich Quang Duc, immolates himself on a street in Saigon street to protest Diem's actions against Buddhists. Diem's sister-in-law, Madame Nhu, refers to the immolation as a "barbecue" and offers to provide gasoline and matches for more.

June 27. Henry Cabot Lodge is appointed United States ambassador to the Republic of (South) Vietnam.

August. First organized demonstrations against American involvement in Vietnam take place in New York, Philadelphia, and other cities. Small protests will continue to take place throughout the duration of the United States' advisory role in Vietnam.

August 21. Diem declares martial law and has 1,400 Buddhist monks arrested.

November 1. Diem is ousted in a military coup led by General Duong Van Minh and other officers, who are supported by the Kennedy administration. Minh establishes a military "directorate."

November 22. President Kennedy is assassinated; Lyndon Johnson takes office.

December. By the end of 1963, there are 16,500 Americans in Vietnam; during the year, 489 Americans were killed or wounded.

1964 January 30. General Nguyen Khanh overthrows Minh in a bloodless coup.

March 8–12. Secretary of Defense Robert McNamara tours South Vietnam and reaffirms American support.

April. Units of the North Vietnamese Army (NVA) begin to enter South Vietnam.

June 20. General William Westmoreland succeeds General Harkins as commander of MACV.

July 2. General Maxwell Taylor replaces Lodge as American ambassador to South Vietnam.

August 2–4. United States claims that North Vietnamese patrol boats in the Gulf of Tonkin have carried out an unprovoked attack on American vessels.

August 7. Congress passes the Gulf of Tonkin resolution, giving President Johnson power to take "all necessary measures to repel any armed attack" against United States forces.

December. By the end of 1964, there are about 23,000 American military personnel in South Vietnam engaged more directly in the war. During this year, 1,278 Americans were killed or injured.

1965 February 7. NLF attacks American base at Pleiku. Johnson orders air strikes against North Vietnam.

March 8. First American combat troops arrive in South Vietnam.

March 24. First "teach-in" on Vietnam is held, at the University of Michigan.

April 6. Johnson authorizes United States forces to take the offensive in support of ARVN.

June 19. Air Marshall Ky becomes premier of Vietnam. His is the eighth government since the ouster of Diem in 1963.

June 28–30. United States forces carry out the first major American offensive in the war, near Saigon.

July 28–30. Fifty thousand American troops are sent to Vietnam; the draft is increased to 35,000 each month; the air war against North Vietnam is expanded.

September. Master Sergeant Donald Duncan of the Fifth Special Forces Group, First Special Forces, quits the Green Berets and becomes the first soldier to speak out against the war.

October 15–16. First International Days of Protest are held in cities across the United States.

October 23–November 20. American forces engage in the largest battle of the war to date, in Ia Drang Valley, defeating NVA forces.

December 27. Three American antiwar activists—Tom Hayden, Staughton Lynd, and Herbert Aptheker—visit Hanoi.

December. Johnson announces a temporary halt in the bombing of North Vietnam. By the end of 1965, 184,000 American troops are in Vietnam; during this year 1,369 were killed and more than 5,000 wounded.

1966   January 31. American air strikes against North Vietnam are resumed after a one-month cessation.

March 6. "White paper" issued by United States State Department, characterizing American involvement in Vietnam as legal under the Constitution and international law.

March 10. Protests by students and Buddhists against the South Vietnamese government begin in Hue and Danang.

June 16. ARVN troops are sent into Hue to stop the protests.

June 30. Privates James Johnson, Dennis Mora, and David Samas—the "Fort Hood Three"—announce that they cannot participate in an immoral war.

October. An Army doctor, Howard Levy, refuses to train Green Beret medics at Fort Jackson, South Carolina, claiming that Special Forces troops are committing atrocities in Vietnam.

December. By the end of 1966, 385,000 Americans are stationed in Vietnam; during the year 5,008 were killed and 30,000 wounded.

1967   February 23–April 1. Operation Junction City, the largest American offensive in the war thus far, involving 34 battalions, takes place near the Cambodian border.

April 15. A dozen Vietnam veterans gather with thousands of civilian protestors in Central Park in New York to demonstrate against the war. Soon thereafter, these veterans will lay the foundations for Vietnam Veterans Against the War (VVAW).

June. VVAW is formed.

July 30. Gallup poll shows that 52 percent of Americans disapprove of Johnson's policies in Vietnam.

September. Nguyen Van Thieu is elected president of South Vietnam.

October 16–21. Antidraft demonstrations are held across the United States.

October 21–23. Fifty thousand antiwar activists gather in Washington, D.C., to protest against the war. Although VVAW members participate, the organization refuses to endorse the march.

October 25. American bombing of targets near Hanoi and Haiphong in North Vietnam is increased.

November 3–22. One of the bloodiest battles of the war takes place at Dak To.

November 22. General William Westmoreland returns home to assure Americans that the United States and South Vietnam are winning the war.

November 30. Senator Eugene McCarthy announces his candidacy for the presidency.

December. By the end of 1967, there are 500,000 American troops in Vietnam; during the year 9,353 have been killed and almost 100,000 wounded.

1968   January 20–April 14. Seige of Khe Sanh, an American Marine base in I Corps, takes place in conjunction with the Tet offensive.

January 30–31. Tet offensive begins. NLF and NVA forces overrun numerous military bases, cities, and towns throughout South Vietnam. In Hue, NLF and NVA troops gain control of the Citadel (the center of town; this was the former capital of the kingdom of Annam). The battle to retake Hue lasts several weeks and is one of the worst of the war. Afterward, the bodies of several thousand Vietnamese, thought to have been executed by NVA and NLF forces, are found buried around Hue. Although the United States regains control of the contested areas, the attack stuns the American press and the public, who had been told that victory was at hand.

March 12. Senator Eugene McCarthy makes a strong showing in the New Hampshire Democratic primary, losing narrowly to Johnson.

March 16. Hundreds of unarmed villagers in My Lai are slaughtered by American troops under the command of Lieutenant William Calley. Robert Kennedy announces that he will run for the presidency.

March 31. President Johnson announces that he will not seek renomination for the presidency.

May 3. United States and North Vietnam agree to begin formal negotiations.

August 5–8. Republican convention in Miami nominates Richard Nixon for president. Republicans call for "Vietnamization" of the war, and a negotiated settlement.

August 26–29. Democratic convention is held in Chicago; Hubert Humphrey is nominated for president. Thousands of antiwar activists, including VVAW members, converge on Chicago. On August 28, they are attacked by the Chicago police department and the National Guard.

October 31. President Johnson announces a halt to the bombing of North Vietnam.

November 5. Richard Nixon is elected president.

December. By the end of 1968, although Johnson has begun the "Vietnamization" of the war, 500,000 Americans remain in Vietnam; during the year 14,314 were killed and 150,000 wounded. This has been (and will remain) the bloodiest year of the war.

1969   March 18. President Nixon orders secret bombings of communist base camps in Cambodia.

May 10–20. Fierce battles for Hamburger Hill take place.

June 8. President Nixon announces the withdrawal of 25,000 American troops.

June 10. NLF forms the Provisional Revolutionary Government (PRG) to challenge the Thieu regime.

August 4. Henry Kissinger and Xuan Thuy of North Vietnam begin secret negotiations in Paris.

August 17–26. American troops refuse to engage in combat during a major battle with the NVA in Queson valley.

September 3. Ho Chi Minh dies (of natural causes), age seventy-nine.

September 23. Trial of eight antiwar activists involved in organizing demonstrations at the Democratic convention begins in Chicago.

October 15. The largest antiwar demonstrations in American history take place in many cities across the country.

November 15. In Washington, D.C., 250,000 demonstrators gather to protest the war. VVAW members rekindle the organization after nearly a year of inactivity following the Democratic national convention of 1968. Vietnam veterans begin to attend antiwar rallies across the nation.

December. At the end of 1969, 479,000 American troops remain in Vietnam; during the year 9,414 Americans were killed and 70,216 wounded.

1970 April 20. President Nixon promises to withdraw 150,000 American troops this year.

April 30. American forces enter Cambodia, expanding the ground war in southeast Asia.

May 4. Six students are killed by police and the National Guard during antiwar protests at Kent State University (Ohio) and Jackson State College (Mississippi).

May 6–20. Hundreds of antiwar demonstrations are held at universities and colleges across the country in response to the invasion of Cambodia and the killings at Kent State and Jackson State.

May 8–20. Construction workers attack demonstrators on Wall Street in New York City.

June 24. Senate repeals Gulf of Tonkin resolution. President Nixon, however, claims that he has authority as president to continue the war to protect American troops in Vietnam.

September 4–7. Operation Rapid American Withdrawal (RAW) is carried out by VVAW; 120 members march from Morristown, New Jersey, to Valley Forge.

December. By the end of 1970, 335,000 American troops remain in Vietnam; during the year, 4,221 have been killed and 30,643 wounded.

1971 January 1. Congress acts to block use of American ground forces in Cambodia and Laos.

January 31– February 2. VVAW holds "Winter soldier" hearings in Detroit, during which members acknowledge their participation in and knowledge of war crimes by American and Vietnamese forces in Vietnam.

April 19–23. Operation Dewey Canyon III is held in Washington, D.C.: 1,500 VVAW members gather to demonstrate, lobby, and engage in acts of civil disobedience; 700 of them discard their combat ribbons on the steps of the Capitol.

April 24. Half a million demonstrators, including the May Day Tribe, converge on Washington, D.C., to protest and shut down the city.

June 13. *New York Times* begins to publish the Pentagon Papers.

July 15. Nixon administration announces planned trips to China.

October 3. Thieu is reelected as president of RVN, no one having run against him.

December 26–30. Operation Peace on Earth is initiated by VVAW chapters across the country in response to the Nixon administration's escalation of the air war in Vietnam.

December. By the end of 1971, 156,000 American troops are still in Vietnam; during the year, 1,380 have been killed and 8,936 wounded.

1972   February 21–27. Nixon visits China.

March 30. People's Army of (North) Vietnam begins a major offensive in South Vietnam, along the demilitarized zone (DMZ).

April 10. Nixon administration intensifies air war throughout North and South Vietnam.

May 8. Nixon announces the mining of ports in North Vietnam.

May 20. Nixon visits Moscow for summit meeting with Leonid Brezhnev, president of the Soviet Union.

June 28. Nixon administration announces that no more draftees will be sent to Vietnam.

July 7. "Gainsville Eight" are indicted by Justice Department; they are charged with conspiring to incite and participate in rioting at the forthcoming Republican National Convention in Miami Beach, Florida.

August 11. The last American combat unit leaves Vietnam, but 44,000 Americans remain in-country.

October 8–11. Henry Kissinger and Le Duc Tho (the negotiator for North Vietnam) hold secret meetings in Paris and develop a tentative peace agreement.

November 7. President Nixon wins reelection, partly by having promised to bring "peace with honor" in Vietnam.

December 14. United States breaks off talks with North Vietnam.

December 18–23. United States resumes bombing of North Vietnam; this is the most intense bombing of the war.

December. At the end of 1972, 24,000 American military personnel remain in Vietnam; during the year, 312 have been killed and 1,221 wounded.

1973   January 8–18. Henry Kissinger and Le Duc Tho develop a second peace agreement, identical to the one they worked out in October 1972.

January 23. President Nixon announces that "peace with honor" has been achieved and a cease-fire will be in effect as of January 27.

January 27. The United States ends its direct participation in the war in Vietnam. The draft ends in the United States.

February–March. Five hundred ninety American prisoners of war (POWs) come home.

March 29. The last American troops leave Vietnam. Heavy fighting continues in the South, where 150,000 NVA soldiers remain.

August. Congress prohibits any further combat role for the United States in southeast Asia.

December. At the end of 1973, the war continues in Vietnam. During the year, 237 Americans have been killed and 60 wounded.

1974   May 9. House Judiciary Committee begins impeachment hearings.

July 4. During Operation Dewey Canyon IV, VVAW activists march on Washington, D.C., demanding jobs, treatment for posttraumatic stress disorder, and benefits for veterans.

August 5. Congress cuts American aid to South Vietnam.

August 9. Nixon resigns the presidency.

December. In 1974, the war has continued to exact a heavy toll on the Vietnamese people; during the year, more than 80,000 combatants and civilians have been killed.

1975   January 6. NLF/NVA forces capture Phouc Long province.

March 25. Hue falls to communist forces. Hanoi launches the final major offensive of the war.

April 1. Americans begin to evacuate Saigon.

April 29–30. The last Americans, with some of their South Vietnamese supporters, are evacuated from South Vietnam.

April 30. The communists take Saigon. The war is over.

During the war, 3,330,000 American military personnel have served in Vietnam; 58,183 have been killed and 303,713 wounded. Of South Vietnamese military personnel, 223,748 have been killed and 570,600 wounded. Of North Vietnamese military personnel, it is estimated that 660,000 have been killed (no data are available on the wounded). Of North and South Vietnamese civilians, it is estimated that 600,000 have been killed and 3 million wounded.

Glossary

AFSC	American Friends Service Committee; "Friends" refers to the Quakers.
AIT	Advanced infantry training, usually following basic training.
AK-47	Russian and Chinese assault rifle.
amtraks	Armor-clad amphibious vehicles, used to transport troops and materiel.
AP	Air Police.
APC	Armored personnel carrier.
Article 15	Provision in Uniform Code of Military Justice for punishment of enlisted men by commanding officers.
ARVN	Army of the Republic of Vietnam.
ASA	Army Security Agency; group responsible for intercepting enemy transmissions and maintaining the secrecy of Army signal and electronic intelligence.
AWOL	Absent without leave.
BLT	Battalion landing team.
bouncing Betty	Mine that explodes at groin-level.
butter bar	Second lieutenant (who wears a single gold bar).
BX	base exchange; Air Force equivalent of post exchange (PX).
CALC	Clergy and Laity Concerned.
CAMP	Chicago Area Military Project.
CAT	Combat Assistance Team.
cav	Helicopter-borne air cavalry.
Charlie	GI slang for the Vietcong.
CIA	Central Intelligence Agency.
CID	Criminal Investigations Division.

CO	Commanding officer; also, conscientious objector.
comm	Refers to communications.
Conex	Large (8- by 8- by 8-foot) metal shipping container for supplies and equipment (from the commercial name "Continental Exchange").
CP	Communist Party.
CW	Continuous-wave radio.
DAV	Disabled American Veterans.
defcon 2 alert	"Defensive concentration," nuclear-weapons alert (defcon 1 would be nuclear war).
DI	Drill instructor.
DMZ	Demilitarized zone; boundary between North and South Vietnam.
DRV	Democratic Republic of Vietnam; North Vietnam.
E-5, E-6, etc.	Ranks or grades of enlisted men.
EM	Enlisted man.
EM club	Enlisted men's club.
FBI	Federal Bureau of Investigation.
FO	Forward observer; person responsible for calling in artillery fire.
frag	Fragmentation grenade; this term (as a verb) is also used to indicate trying to kill a superior officer.
FSM	Free Speech Movement.
grunt	Foot soldier in the Army or Marines.
hootch, hootches	Living quarters (GI term).
HUAC	House Un-American Activities Committee
in-country	In Vietnam.
jefe	Boss (Spanish).
K-bar	Combat knife.
KIA	Killed in action.
klick	Kilometer.
LBJ	Lyndon Baines Johnson.
lifer	Enlisted man who is in the military as a career.
LSD	Landing ship dock; a ship used to transport smaller landing craft.

LZ	Landing zone.
MACV	Military Assistance Command, Vietnam.
MDM	Movement for a Democratic Military.
Medcap	Medical Civilian Air Patrol; an Army and Marine program in which medics accompanied armed patrols and gave medical assistance to villagers.
Medevac	Medical evacuation by helicopter.
MI	Military intelligence.
MIA	Missing in action.
MOBE	National Mobilization to End the War in Vietnam.
MOS	Military occupational specialty.
MP	Military police.
M-60	Machine gun.
NAACP	National Association for the Advancement of Colored People.
NCO	Noncommissioned officer.
NLF	National Liberation Front.
NVA	North Vietnamese Army.
OCS	Officer candidate school.
OD	Olive drab.
OSS	Office of Strategic Services (forerunner of the CIA).
O2 spotter	Light observation aircraft.
PAVN	People's Army of (North) Vietnam.
PL	Progressive Labor Party.
POW	Prisoner of war.
PRG	Provisional Revolutionary Government.
PTSD	Posttraumatic stress disorder.
PVS	Post-Vietnam syndrome; term coined by VVAW members to refer to the psychological maladies suffered by many Vietnam veterans.
PX	Post exchange; store on a base that sells merchandise to military and some civilian personnel.
QC	South Vietnamese national police force.
R and R	Rest and relaxation.
RAW	Rapid American Withdrawal; name of a VVAW march.
RCP	Revolutionary Communist Party, formerly Revolutionary Union (RU).

recon	Reconnaissance.
retcons	Units of exposure to radiation.
RF	Regional Forces; South Vietnamese provincial militia.
RSB	Revolutionary Student Brigade, branch of RU/RCP.
RTO	Radiotelephone operator.
RU	Revolutionary Union.
RVN	Republic of Vietnam (South Vietnam).
RYM	Revolutionary Youth Movement.
S-2	Chief intelligence officer on a battalion or brigade staff.
SDS	Students for a Democratic Society.
six-six	Misconduct charge.
SMC	Student Mobilization Committee.
Spec-4	Enlisted men's rank.
strak troops	Neat, clean, professional, obedient soldiers (slang).
SLA	Symbionese Liberation Army.
SWP	Socialist Workers Party.
SEALs	Elite commando troops in the Navy (acronym for "sea-air-land").
Tet	Vietnamese lunar new year; the country's most important holiday.
tiger cages	Small cells in which political prisoners were held by the South Vietnamese government.
VA	Veterans Administration.
VC	Vietcong.
VFP	Vets for Peace, antiwar organization made up predominantly of veterans of Korean and World War II; also, name adopted by many Vietnam veterans' antiwar groups.
VFW	Veterans of Foreign Wars.
WRL	War Resisters League.
WSO	Winter Soldier Organization.
YAF	Young Americans for Freedom.
YSA	Young Socialist Alliance.

I

MOLDING THE CITIZEN-SOLDIER

With the war ended, history decided, he would explain to her why he had let himself go to war. Not because of strong convictions, but because he didn't know. He didn't know who was right, or what was right; he didn't know if it was a war of self-determination or self-destruction, outright aggression or national liberation; he didn't know who really started the war, or why, or when, or with what motives. . . . He went to the war because it was expected. . . . Because, not knowing, he saw no reason to distrust those with more experience. Because he loved his country and, more than that, he trusted it.

Tim O'Brien, *Going After Cacciato*[1]

We felt it was absolutely imperative to let the American people know how the motivation to carry out the criminal policy is developed through dehumanization. . . . The crimes against humanity, the war itself, might not have occurred, if we, all of us, had not been brought up in a country permeated with racism, obsessed with communism and convinced beyond a shadow of a doubt that we are good and most other countries are inherently evil.

Al Hubbard[2]

A Time of Hope and Fear

The young men who went off to war in Vietnam and returned to challenge their leaders' portrayal of that war had grown up in a nation at the height of its international power. They had been raised in an era of unprecedented economic growth that many Americans thought would last forever. Americans were especially proud of their victory in World War II, which had propelled the nation to its new prosperity and strength. They were, however, uneasy about the state of the world and about the cold war, which dominated the foreign policy of the United States.

World War II had fundamentally altered the global landscape. While the United States emerged from the war as the world's leading economic, industrial, and military power, its prewar economic rivals had seen their fortunes decline. Europe and Japan were devastated, and the colonial empires that had still existed before the war crumbled after it: the war unleashed a wave of independence movements. Between the end of World War II and the 1960s, dozens of nations achieved their freedom from colonial rule.

These developments gave American foreign policy makers an opportunity to grasp the reins of world leadership and develop a global community committed to democracy and free trade. Although Europe remained the primary concern of the United States' foreign policy elite, the emerging nations of the third world became increasingly dominant in its agenda during the postwar years.

In the aftermath of the war, the United States publicly supported independence movements in the third world in two ways. First, it played a leading role in the creation of the United Nations, whose second article of incorporation proclaimed every nation's right to self-determination. Second, as the world's leading democracy, which had made a decisive contribution in defeating fascism, the United States proclaimed its own interest in spreading its democratic heritage worldwide.

Not coincidentally, American foreign policy makers also encouraged third world leaders to open their doors to American trade and investment. In fact, that policy was pursued zealously; for example, in March 1947, George C. McGhee, assistant secretary of state, remarked, "Our tradition of free enterprise . . . has become so thoroughly ingrained in our economic thinking that it amounts with us to almost a religion. . . . We are perfectly sincere in our conviction that it would be in the best interests of other nations to follow our example."[3]

The nation's foreign policy community argued that American global leadership would usher in an era without destructive conflicts, an era in which no peoples would wear the yoke of colonialism and all would be allowed to achieve the prosperity promised by free enterprise. This attitude was captured in a speech to Congress by former secretary of state Cordell Hull as early as 1943, while the war was still going on: "There will no longer be a need for spheres of influence, for alliance, for balance of power, or any other special arrangements through which, in the unhappy past, the nations strove to insure their security or to promote their interests."[4]

American corporations seized this opportunity to project their influence around the globe. By the end of the war the United States was already the world's leading exporter, and by 1957 the value of its overseas exports had doubled.[5] Foreign investment also increased dramatically, rising from $7.2 billion in 1946 to $49.3 billion in 1965. Third world markets proved to be especially profitable for American investors, who sometimes tripled the return on their investments.[6] Moreover, in the postwar era American industries relied on foreign sources for nearly 50 percent of their raw materials,[7] and American foreign policy makers wanted to maintain stability worldwide to ensure access to these raw materials. Thus the expansion of America's global trade was considered vital to the nation's economic health. As one assistant secretary of state commented, "Any serious failure to maintain this flow would put millions of American businessmen, farmers, and workers out of business."[8]

The economic supremacy of the United States in the postwar years brought an end to the long depression at home and began a period of impressive material well-being. Jobs were plentiful and well-paying. Labor unions were at the height of their strength and were able to win long-term contracts that provided benefits and economic security for their members. Government programs also contributed to the nation's overall sense of well-being. Social welfare programs protected the neediest of Americans and a generous GI Bill offered millions of working-class veterans an opportunity to buy homes and attend institutions of higher learning.[9] These veterans were in general proud of their military service overseas and delighted with the new prosperity their service had given them.

In fact, Americans as a whole engaged in a buying spree that would last well into the 1960s. They bought larger and more powerful automobiles and new appliances that promised to ease the drudgery of everyday life. For the first time in human history, a large segment of the working class had a level of comfort and stability that had previously been reserved for the middle and upper classes. The United States seemed to be living up to its promise; the American dream seemed to be a reality.

Americans were convinced, by and large, that their economic vigor and technological prowess would lead to a future of boundless growth and opportunity. For young Americans of the baby-boom generation, opportunities to surpass their parents' achievements seemed limitless. In the mid-1950s, the nation's shift from a predominantly industrial economy to a service-sector economy opened up new occupations for young working-class people—they no longer expected to follow their fathers' footsteps into the ranks of the industrial workforce. Working-class parents who had unsatisfying dead-end jobs in industry—even though they too were sharing in the nation's wealth— urged their children to get a good education and move up the economic ladder.[10] Most teenagers were no longer required to contribute to the family finances and so were free to postpone entering the workforce: unprecedented numbers of them completed high school and went on to higher education. By 1960, 95 percent of American teenagers were enrolled in high school, and nearly 50 percent of those were going to college.[11]

The mood of the nation was tempered, however, by the cold war. Although World War II had severely damaged America's economic competitors, it had not destroyed the Soviet Union or the ideological challenge of communism. The Soviet Union called on the world not only to embrace communism but to reject free trade and close its doors to American capital.

The United States reacted to this threat in several ways. During the Truman administration, foreign policy makers created a national security apparatus in Washington, D.C., that had a domestic as well as an international focus.[12] At home, the cold war was waged by a variety of governmental agencies intent upon weeding out perceived communist subversion in government offices, schools, and cultural institutions. The House Committee on Un-American Activities (HUAC), for example, carried out numerous public hearings in which suspected communists were accused of spying for the Soviet Union. Countless Americans, including civil servants, educators, and writers, were harassed and blacklisted because of their left-wing affiliations.[13]

Also, National Security Council Directive 68 called for a buildup of the armed forces to protect the "vital interests" of the United States. American presidents from Truman to Nixon developed a massive military bureaucracy, vastly expanded military spending, erected dozens of bases, entered into numerous mutual-defense treaties, and provided military and economic aid to nearly 100 nations in the first two decades of the cold war.[14] In 1948, President Truman established the nation's first peacetime conscription, to staff American military outposts across the globe. However, thousands of young men did not wait to be drafted: they volunteered for service, no doubt to some extent from a sense of pride and duty, but also to learn valuable technical skills; the armed forces were seen by many young Americans as a vast training school for a high-tech economy. By the end of 1948, the Army had 140,000 troops stationed in the far east; 100,000 in Europe; and 155,000 across the United States. By the late 1950s, there were 3 million servicemen and -women, half of them stationed overseas.[15]

In addition, the National Security Council and the Central Intelligence Agency (CIA), which was under its command, carried out numerous clandestine foreign policy initiatives. The CIA trained foreign police forces and engaged in espionage to support friendly governments and to undermine governments that were deemed to be a threat. The National Security Council also developed and implemented a number of publicity—or propaganda—campaigns to persuade Americans to support the increased military spending and send their sons off as servicemen.[16]

Throughout the cold war—except, perhaps, during its final years—anticommunism dominated political discourse in the United States. American leaders tended to envision a world divided into two alternative and mutually incompatible ways of life. On one side stood the Soviet Union, which was depicted as an aggressive, godless empire intent on destroying freedom and subjugating the people of the world. On the other side stood the United States, which was described as an altruistic democracy, dedicated to individual freedom and committed to protect the free world. President Kennedy echoed this view in his inaugural address: "Only a few generations have been granted the role of defending freedom in its hour of maximum danger," Kennedy said, and he urged Americans to "pay any price, bear any burden, and meet any hardship" in the "struggle against the common enemies of man: tyranny, poverty, and war itself."[17]

Although politicians led the anticommunist crusade, many American social and cultural institutions also promoted the doctrines of the cold war. The mass media, in particular, played a leading role. By the 1950s, Americans had come to rely on television, radio, and the popular press for information about, and analysis of, the world and their place in it.[18] The news media in general adhered consistently to the dominant cold war ideology and served as a conduit for politicians.[19] The film and television industries also contributed to the ideology—and the tensions—of the cold war and legitimized the use of force to combat communism. On Saturday mornings, all across the nation, the baby-boom generation filled movie theaters; at home, every evening, they and their elders turned on their newly acquired television sets. In both settings, they were presented with a plethora of combat films and westerns that portrayed American military forces as "all-conquering, all powerful, always right."[20] Young men who were bored with their own lives and longed for heroism were especially attracted to these films and television programs. For many people, in fact, it was an actor—John Wayne—who best conveyed the image of the American fighting man. Wayne was tall and rugged-looking, and he nearly always got the woman, even when he was too preoccupied with his military duties to attend to her needs. Wayne's characters, in westerns as well as World War II films, engaged in violence only when they were compelled to do so by a threat to their lives, the lives of their loved ones, or the nation. They seemed to be the quintessence of American individuality, decency, and bravery.[21] The opponent, by contrast, was usually stereotyped as an aggressor who sought to undermine the American way of life. In many westerns, for instance, the hero confronted wild-eyed whooping Indians who indiscriminately killed innocent settlers. Many war films conveyed a similar message, with perpetually screaming Japanese soldiers.[22] Even popular science fiction and horror films had an effect, suggesting that alien forces threatened the nation.

In addition to the media, American educational institutions played an important role in disseminating the doctrines of the cold war. The most important part of the educational arsenal was the history and social studies curriculum. Through these school subjects, American youth was provided with a shared identity and a national purpose—a context for America's response to the world. American history texts reflected the new emphasis on the United States as the leader of the world, and on the threat represented by communism. By the 1950s, these texts focused much of their attention on the nation's rise to power and on how it was "taking up our responsibilities" in a world threatened by communism and poverty.[23] The 1955 edition of *The*

Story of Democracy, one of the most popular high school history texts, depicted the Soviet Union as a "police state" that hindered individual expression, enforced conformity, and severely circumscribed public dialogue—in contrast to the United States, which was characterized as a pillar of democracy and as holding sacred individuality and freedom of expression.[24] The authors of this textbook concluded by reminding young Americans of their duty to protect the nation and its principles by serving in the military when called on.

As a supplement to classroom study, school administrators developed extracurricular activities to introduce young Americans to participatory democracy. School officials "urged students to reject complacency and accept the responsibilities of world leaders."[25] Right-wing organizations, such as the Young Americans for Freedom, founded by William F. Buckley, opened chapters in schools, promoting cold war doctrine and enlisting students in their political programs.[26]

Some religious organizations also supported, and worked for, the cold war agenda. Many religious leaders espoused the objectives of American foreign policy objectives and urged their followers to participate actively in the crusade against communism. The Catholic church and the growing evangelical element of Protestantism can be seen as examples. Many Christians were taught that communism, which was officially atheistic, posed an enormous threat to a deeply religious nation. American intervention in third world nations, for instance, was frequently characterized as a "messianic one: to save as much of the world as possible from Communism and to help its peoples establish the American way of life."[27] In fact, some of the clergy and some laypeople viewed the communists as Satan incarnate, and any action undertaken by the United States to thwart their advance as justified.

It must be granted that many international developments during the cold war seemed to vindicate this preoccupation with communist aggression. Although the Soviet Union had been an ally of the United States during World War II and as such was entitled to its share of the spoils of war, Americans viewed its postwar incursions into eastern Europe as aggressive. Also, by the early 1960s, the Soviet Union had built up an imposing nuclear arsenal. It had, furthermore, suppressed a revolt in Hungary, launched a satellite (Sputnik), and erected the Berlin Wall. And left-wing insurgencies had broken out in Cuba (in 1959) and in various regions of the third world; Americans saw these as inspired and controlled by the Soviet Union. Most Americans came to view such developments as threats to the nation's security. Public opinion polls taken in 1964 show that although Americans wanted to avoid war, they were also committed to standing up to international communism, building a strong defense, and "maintaining respect for the United States in other countries."[28]

While the cold war concerned Americans and dominated discourse on foreign policy, domestic discontent also bubbled to the surface of social consciousness in the late 1950s, exposing cracks in the national veneer. The civil rights movement reminded the nation that not all Americans had equal access to its economic promise or its democratic institutions. By the early 1960s, this movement had grown and gained the attention of the nation and the world. If most Americans assumed that racial problems were confined to the south, that idea was dispelled when discontent in northern urban areas— where blacks had been concentrated in racial ghettos—exploded into a riot in Watts in 1964. By 1967, rioting had spread throughout many American cities, and a more militant African-American movement for equality and justice had developed.

During this time, a youth culture also emerged, challenging the older generation's concept of domestic tranquillity. The huge increase in school enrollments during the 1950s had brought together urban teenagers from a broad spectrum of the American populace. Middle-class white students mingled with working-class students and black students who had migrated to the north and west during the 1940s and 1950s. Working-class teenagers had always had something of a reputation for "delinquency," and by the late 1950s and early 1960s, middle-class young people had also begun to adopt the dress and mannerisms of the working class, and those of the black teenagers they were now meeting in their schools and neighborhoods.[29] White teenagers were introduced to new musical and cultural forms that offered an exciting alternative to their parents' seemingly boring, conformist world. This was, after all, the generation that writhed to shocking new rhythms, defied dress codes, increasingly flouted sexual taboos, and demanded equality and freedom of expression.

This rebellion took as its target the hypocrisies teenagers perceived at home, at school, and in their society. Although high school textbooks and popular culture decried communistic conformity, for example, young people could see the "organization man" leaving his suburban home in the morning, dressed like all his neighbors, and heading off to work, where all his coworkers were just like him. School administrators also seemed hypocritical: they gave lip service to participation in democratic processes, and yet they imposed strict dress codes and rules of behavior in which their students had no say. In general, then, young people reacted against the growing conformity of a service-centered, consumer-driven, middle-class society—they wanted to carve out their own individuality and to be treated as adults.[30]

Ironically, though, their rebellion was aided and abetted by the consumer-driven society they found so stultifying. Prosperity filtered down to young Americans, and it also turned their rebellion into a commercial success. Hollywood and the recording industry responded to young people's desires and gave them any number of movies and records that reflected their growing alienation from American society. Two hugely popular stars—Marlon Brando and James Dean, the "Rebel Without a Cause"—perhaps best expressed this sense of alienation.

Discontent with the nature of American society and its political system emerged significantly among college students. Young, serious, mostly white middle-class students, energized by President Kennedy's plea to "ask not what your country can do for you but what you can do for your country" and concerned with the inequities exposed by the civil rights activists, participated in freedom rides and boycotts. Some became involved in a small but active campaign against nuclear weapons.[31] By 1964, student activism targeted college and university administrations and eventually the war in Vietnam.

Of course, rebellious young people did not confront all these contractions at the same time. Also, many young Americans, conforming to the wishes of their elders—or following their own inclinations—simply worked hard in school and participated in various extracurricular activities in their schools and communities. But whether or not they took part in the rebellion, young Americans felt its influence.

Heeding the Call to Arms

The men and women whose voices follow were affected by, and express, the tensions of growing up in a time of consensus and rebellion. Those who went to war did so with attitudes and ideas that had been inculcated by schools, religious organizations, the mass media, and their families.

New York Yankee

JAN BARRY CRUMB

Jan Barry enlisted in the Army in the spring of 1962, spent 10 months in Vietnam before going on to West Point, and left the service in May 1965. He was interviewed at his home in Montclair, New Jersey.

My name is Jan Barry Crumb. I use Jan Barry as my pen name. I was born in Ithaca, New York, in January 1943. I was a stereotypical kid in a rural area. I was in the Boy Scouts, worked on farms, worked in gas stations, worked for a veterinarian all the way through high school, delivered newspapers from the time I was eleven. I did very well academically, played three sports, played in the band. I was in class plays. I did everything in a small town that you could do. To that degree, I grew up in a society in which I didn't realize that there were any limitations.

I was steeped in all the World War II battles and Korean battles and the World War I battles and the Civil War battles. I knew all this stuff as well as a teenager could understand it. I wanted to make a career of the military at a young age. I had this romantic fixation on West Point and a military career.

I was attracted to this because my father had been in the Navy in World War II, as a whole generation was in the military. There was also a television show called *Long Gray Line* or something like that, that I watched during the 1950s, about life in West Point—in a very romanticized way, but it's what I wanted. To say you wanted to go to West Point gave a sense to adults that you were a really serious kid who knows where he wants to go. That happened to be something that was a highly favored goal for a young person. If I wanted to dream that I could go to West Point, I could get there. There was nothing to suggest that I couldn't.

One of the reasons I think I was attracted to having this as a goal was that I was this shrimpy little kid until late in high school. [I] was like the smallest boy in my class. It appeared to me that I could be this big powerful soldier; not just a soldier but a general; not just a general but a famous one—like all the famous graduates of West Point, right? By having that as a goal, there were very clear things that you understood you needed to do to prepare. You had to be a good athlete, good in academics, lead an upstanding life.

I went from being this shrimpy kid to a star football player by my senior year in high school. I had grown a little more and learned through four years of being batted around the field how to play this game. I managed also to get by in baseball and basketball, without any spectacular skills but by learning the basics. I learned to work hard at reaching a goal that was a step on the way to where I ultimately wanted to get. I graduated from a local rural high school in Interlochen, New York, in 1961.

Were you aware, at that point, of American involvement in Vietnam?

Vaguely. I knew that there was something going on there—Special Forces, the beginning of something—but it didn't impress me as anything more than an adventure in Asia. I wasn't particularly focused on Vietnam; I was waiting for World War III, with the Russians. That was what the whole focus of the training was, and that was the whole thinking of this country. I was simply attuned to the enemy of the day. When you grew up in the 1950s, the enemy was Russia. These other, smaller places were sideshows: interesting, but not where the main action was going to be. Laos had been in the news in the late 1950s; we had sent troops to Lebanon in 1958 or whatever it was. . . . I mean, Vietnam was so low on the scale of anything, [that] there was like a rumor that it even existed, and I end up there. [Laughs.]

One of the things that's so difficult to describe after the late 1960s is what it was like before that time. Even the movies about the 1950s can't do justice to the deadening effect of the culture of this country. Education was indoctrination. Nobody used the word, but that's what it was. When I graduated from high school in 1961, we had no idea you could question anything. No matter what government did, there wasn't even the thought that you could question whatever it was. The civil rights movement wasn't even on the horizon as far as most people's recognition or understanding. These issues weren't there. They were created by groups which gave voice to something we didn't even know you could voice out loud or even think about.

I did not get an appointment [to West Point] from high school through the congressional route, and I went to Syracuse University; and [during] my first year I was involved in ROTC, sports, goofing off, and was practically flunking out. I figured I was wasting my time. In fact, I thought everybody on this campus was wasting their time. They didn't know what they were doing there. They were in college because they were told: You're smart; you should go to college. In the spring I just walked downtown one day and enlisted in the Army. I assumed that if I joined the Army, the Army would see what a good soldier I was and send me to West Point. This was the spring of 1962.

"Rite of Passage"

JACK McCLOSKEY

Jack McCloskey served as a medic in the Army from 1962 to 1965, spending part of that time in Santo Domingo. He was recalled in July 1967 while on active reserve, spent the next year in Vietnam, and was discharged in July 1969. He was interviewed in his apartment in San Francisco, California.

I come from a very heavy Irish-Italian Catholic background. I grew up basically lower-middle-class, raised in the projects. My mother died when I was fourteen, and my father had been at sea since he was about thirteen. He just couldn't handle it, so I went into an orphanage for four years.

Everybody in my neighborhood, all my relatives, all my uncles, my father, everybody was in the military during the Second World War. My uncle Danny was a career Marine. He had lots of stories of what that was like. My uncle Joe, from my mother's side, was a machine gunner in the Army. My father was in the merchant marine. My uncle Ray was an officer in the Army. My uncle Bobby was in the Navy with the Pacific fleet. My uncle Bill was in the Marines. Every uncle I could think of—all of them had military backgrounds.

Part of my upbringing is that if you were a male, there was an obligation—not just to get out of the ghetto, but as part of a way of life—that you went into the service. This was part of becoming a man. It was part of the transference from adolescence to adulthood.

In Pennsylvania, the law says that once you turn eighteen, you can sign yourself out of the orphanage or an institution like that. Two months after I turned eighteen in November, they give me restriction or something and I said, "Fuck this, I'm eighteen," and I split. I signed myself out of the orphanage. I kicked around for about a year and a half. I was a dishwasher, waiter, busboy. Then I joined the service when I was nineteen. I went in in 1962.

My older brother Bobby joined the Navy, was a medic, a corpsman, and except for Great Lakes boot camp and Great Lakes Naval Corps School, he was stationed at Philadelphia Naval Hospital. For him, it was like a job, eight to five. I saw my brother being a corpsman, so I wanted to be a medic also. That was the big factor [in] why I chose to be a medic. I went into the Navy. I enlisted for four years.

Had you heard of Vietnam when you enlisted?

I had never heard of Vietnam in my life. For me, you know, there was no war going on. There was definitely a cold war. There was always that thing of communism and all this bullshit. I grew up with a "kill a commie for Christ" background: communism was wrong. I went to this school in west Phillie called Our Lady of Victory, which is a Catholic grammar school. When you walked into the auditorium of the school, there was a big picture of Iwo Jima, the Marines raising the flag. I remember growing up and going under our desks during air-raid drills, that type of shit.

I remember when I first got stationed in Camp LeJeune in 1962 or 1963, getting off the bus and seeing a sign that actually said, "Colored here and white there." It was bizarre shit. You've got to remember that when I was in the service [for the first time] you had a lot of civil rights stuff coming in. I really was for it. I thought it was great. When I look back, one of the things I feel, along with the orphanage and neighborhood, my father had some Native American blood in him. I was taught not to be racist.

Boot camp for me was very easy, a snap. I didn't have any problems with discipline. I didn't have any problems with adjusting, because of the orphanage background. The orphanage was like a mini–boot camp. I knew how to make a bed. I knew how to have things neat. You had to learn to adjust to different people and give them space. I learned at an early age how to live and get along with a group of males. I didn't have that cultural shock of going from my own bedroom to sharing a fucking room with 200 other guys. So in a way I think it was easier for me.

In 1965, when I was stationed at Camp LeJeune, they sent the Marines down to the Dominican Republic. Although they had snipers coming at us, that to me was a laugh. It wasn't really combat when I compare it to my Vietnam experience. It was like a cakewalk. You didn't have the mass weaponry

31

over there. One side of the street was theirs, the other side was ours. I remember that there was a big yellow school bus in the middle of the street. It was a whorehouse, and certain times we used it and certain times the rebels would use it. This was right in Santo Domingo, the city, so it was areas I was used to. It was not like when I went to Vietnam in the jungles. I mean, I'm from the city; I never saw a fucking cow in my life until I was fifteen years old. [Laughs.]

I got out in January of 1966. When I got out of the service, I was not political at all. I had a good time in the service the first time. I had stayed in active reserve. I became a meter reader. I started auditing classes at the University of Pennsylvania.

I got a telegram—I'll never forget this—on July 4th, 1967, saying: "You have been reactivated. Report to the Philadelphia Naval Shipyard." I was twenty-three, twenty-four. At this time I had been going through changes. The change started happening for me in June of 1967. I had heard of Vietnam. I had been tending bar right across the street from the University of Pennsylvania. Most of the kids coming to the bar were college kids. There were some demonstrations and there were some talks, and one time this young woman walked into the bar, and I courted her. She came from an upper-middle-class background, totally different from mine. She happened to be between her junior and senior years at Vassar. She happened to have a Quaker background. We happened to fall in love. She happened, later on, to become my wife.

She talked about the war. She talked about her Quaker background. Lydia, my ex-wife, really opened my eyes, not just to Vietnam but to the world at large. I mean, my world began to expand when I met her. Although we're divorced now, we're still very good friends. I owe her a lot.

I remember that July 4th, getting that telegram and agonizing with myself. By this time, I looked at politics differently. I felt that the war was wrong. What should I do? Should I go AWOL [absent without leave]? Should I just ignore them and say I never got it? Should I report? I reported. Even though I was against the war, there was a part of me that wanted to go to Vietnam. I had to test myself. Am I going to be a coward? I think every male has that.

"Going to Save My Catholic Brothers"

BARRY ROMO

Barry Romo enlisted in the Army in January 1966, received his commission as a second lieutenant in January 1967, served in Vietnam from July 1967 to April 1968; and was discharged in July 1969. He was interviewed in his apartment in Chicago, Illinois.

Barry Romo, newly inducted: "... the rugged soldier. He looks a little fat, but it's just his baggy pants—but note carefully the broad shoulders, rough red face, and clean-shaven head."

I grew up in a black neighborhood, and I'm Mexican. My family moved to California in 1834, when it was still Mexico, so they greeted the gringos when they came to take it over. [Laughs.] My parents were Catholics. I went to an all-boy Catholic high school. The great side of Catholicism, of us all being one universal Catholic church, all of us with souls, all of us equal before God—I absolutely, to the core of my soul, believed it at a very early age.

My mom was a World War II British war bride. It really makes me mixed up. My mom one day would make enchiladas and the next day make steak and kidney pie. My mom was absolutely antiracist. She just would not allow it. My family would say they were Spanish, and my mom would laugh, "Yeah, right. Spaniards don't work picking oranges. We're Mexican." [Laughter.] She raised me to be vehemently proud of our Mexican heritage.

My father was a very respectful person. He never could bring himself to call black people Negroes and really couldn't call them black. Black people were "colored," and that was respect. He loved our black neighbors. Just a very respectful kind of guy, and that's what I was raised with—respect, pride.

My father always voted Democratic. My father was proud because he voted against Nixon more than anyone else. We lived in his congressional district, so he got to vote against him when he ran for Congress, the Senate, vice president, and every time he ran for president. [My father] just hated Nixon.

My father was a working-class Mexican meat cutter. He started out as an agricultural worker, spoke Spanish, and learned to speak English as a second language. My father had to pay to become a meat cutter. He knew he had to get out of the fields. He went to a guy who owned a store who told him that if he cleaned up the store, he would teach my father how to cut meat. This must have been around 1919. He then worked in a slaughterhouse and finally became a butcher. He belonged to a union for 50 years. He got married and had two kids, got a divorce, and got drafted—World War II.

He was forty-some years old and they had passed a law saying you couldn't draft anyone over thirty-five. My father said, "I'm in already, what the hell, I don't like Hitler," and being the good trade unionist that he was, he went to Europe. My father was a cook, the sergeant in charge of the mess hall, because he was a meat cutter. They called him "old man" and made fun of him.

My brother was already in the Army because the activation had already started in 1940. He was a Ranger. He fought in New Guinea and the Philippines.

What impact did your parents' views have on you?

I always had black friends. I was just so disgusted with every racial thing that you could see on TV. My first thought about the Kennedy assassination was that the Klan killed him. They killed him because he was Catholic and because he loved black people. You couldn't shake that. Most of my friends believed that.

I was president of the Junior Republican club. I worked for Barry Goldwater. I belonged to Young Americans for Freedom. I'd worked on electioneering around open housing, and although I was a Republican for Barry Goldwater, I was always antiracist, pro–civil rights, always had a philosophy of human rights over property rights.

I enlisted in the service to go to Vietnam.

Why?

I thought I was going to Vietnam to save my Catholic brothers and kill communists, who were the new Nazis in the world. My republicanism was based on Catholic anticommunism. [I] read Dr. Tom Dooley's books, which were, of course, CIA . . . mandatory reading.[32]

My dad couldn't afford to send me to college, so I could get the GI bill and prove my manhood. I could fulfill everything in the world in one fell swoop.

I went into the service, and my father was sixty-six years old. He sat me on his lap and he cried. He said, "This country wasn't worth it," and that "we had relatives in Canada and I would rather that you left." And I said, "Dad, you fought in the Second World War, and I'm just fighting in my war." My dad said that was a war to defeat fascists, Nazis, and he said that made sense. He said, "You're just going to go over and fight some poor son of a gun. That's all you're going to do. It's not worth it. I didn't raise you to die; I don't want you to die." I thought he was stupid and didn't understand the world situation. I had finished Catholic school and he only had a sixth-grade education. I was smarter.

My brother was extremely proud. He saw it as my rite of passage. He's twenty-some years older than me, and his son is only one month younger than me. He was my brother, but I never treated him like a brother. His kids and I were like brothers. Anyway, my brother did all those brotherly things. He told me to use a rubber if I slept with a woman, and you always had to wash your peepee. He had been in the jungles of New Guinea, and the worst thing you could get is jungle rot, so always wash your crotch.

I went into the service in January 1966.

"Told to Believe Everything on Faith"

JOE URGO

Joe Urgo enlisted in the Air Force in May 1966, served in Vietnam for a year (from December 1967 to December 1968), and was discharged in September 1969. He lives in New York City and was interviewed at several locations there.

I was born in Brooklyn, New York. My family is middle-class, second-generation Italian. My parents moved from a small apartment to a small house to a larger house, a version of the middle-class American dream. I was raised in middle-class neighborhood in Queens, with mostly small businessmen, shops, and store owners, and Irish, Jewish, and Italian second-generation people.

The only thing I can remember in particular that my father impressed on me was that any kind of discrimination against people based on religion was wrong, because the neighborhood we were living in had Jews in it. We always were talking to the Jewish neighbors. I came up with some very rock-hard principles on that.

I went to the local Catholic grammar school. I went to four years of Catholic high school and one year of Catholic college, Saint Francis College of Brooklyn. My ambitions were essentially what 95 percent of Catholic boys want to be. You either want to be a priest, a cop, or an FBI [Federal Bureau of Investigation] agent.

I was an altar boy, but even there, as an altar boy, I grappled with the contradictions. I grappled with the pastor who came every Sunday and asked him why he drove a Cadillac around. He said, "It's from donations." I said, "Well, why don't you sell it and give it to the poor?" "Well, I can't do that." He gave me some bullshit excuse. A priest that I served a lot under was a drunk, and he was always hitting my elbow and getting me to pour a lot more wine into his cup. So these priests were what was held up to me as the typical Catholic church.

I can remember in high school in particular, Mr. Gavigan and Mr. Murphy, two history teachers. They were conservative. Mr. Murphy, in particular, was a racist. He'd tell black racist jokes when one of the only two black kids in school wasn't in class, and then when he wasn't doing that, he'd have a map up on the wall, showing communism taking over the earth . . . this red thing. So I was raised in this atmosphere. Brother Faber was my religion teacher one year, and he did a whole thing about communism. I can remember asking a question in class: "Well, I don't understand. Communists say everything has to be shared by the people and here you are, and Jesus said that too" . . . and Brother Faber looked very seriously and said, "Yes, but what Jesus was talking about was communism with a small *c*. What's in Russia is Communism with a big *C*." I sat down, sort of like—oooh, like I was supposed to grasp some point. I didn't really get it.

You were told to believe everything on faith, and yet their actions didn't measure up to what they said. There were contradictions. I couldn't go anywhere with them, but they never left me; I always remembered them. All this would be seeds of what was later to come.

In 1960, John Kennedy came to Queens on a visit, and I went out to see him on the campaign trail. That was the first time I can remember ever doing anything political. The killing of Kennedy had an enormous effect on me. I can remember crying all night long on my swing in the backyard and really anguishing over how this happened. It really represented an enormous torment in terms of hopes dying. None of this seemed in contradiction to the Goldwater stuff later on. When I was for Goldwater, it was never like I hated Kennedy; this was all one seamless thing here, and it had to do with hopes and the future.

In 1964, the World's Fair came to New York City and settled down in this area of Queens about 2 miles from my house. I went to the World's Fair and was really amazed at the portrayal of the future, of this good life we have. All the science and technology was going to build this better life for people. I spent my whole summer at that fair.

I was reading a lot, but what happened was: The only intellectual stimulation that one could get at that time, that was challenging, and that fit this middle-class, white, Catholic background was in the conservative movement. I went looking for political ideas and ended up in the Young Americans for Freedom, the YAF, which is a reactionary, conservative organization. I was getting new literature and wearing their pin and all this kind of stuff.

Then I ended up working for Barry Goldwater in the New York City campaign office after school in 1964. I read all his position papers. I thought I was well versed on the contradictions as they were present in the society, and this conservative Goldwater really had the angle on what needed to be done. In the Goldwater office, several things stand out. One is sitting in the Goldwater office and arguing with old woman who was telling me the Holocaust didn't happen. I'm telling her, "Hey, lady, you're stupid; what are you talking about?" So it made me start thinking: Who am I friends with here?

I got all caught up in this, worked for Goldwater, then got into William Buckley. I used to watch his TV show, read *National Review.* I got all these position papers. I worked for him when he ran for mayor in 1965, after Goldwater lost. I was not really raised as a macho kid, so all this was very much an intellectual pursuit.

I did grow up on a very steady and protracted diet of horror movies and war movies. Every Saturday it was the horror movies, and on television every weekend it was *Twelve O'Clock High, Purple Heart,* one after another. I must have seen *Purple Heart* a dozen times. But I also liked, and was very moved by, *To Kill a Mockingbird,* the Harper Lee novel and film. [That] was very critical in my consciousness too. I watched that at least a dozen times. There were two sides that were battling within me. There was the humaneness and antiracism in *To Kill a Mockingbird,* and then there was this patriotic non-thinkingness.

Were you aware of the war in Vietnam?

As it was building in intensity, I was becoming more aware. I was for the war in Vietnam because we had to stop communism. I remember reading a story about how the Vietcong stopped this bus of schoolchildren and cut a finger off of all the kids on the bus. I'm thinking, God, these people got to be stopped.

I went to a demonstration against the war in 1965. It was the first demonstration by the Vietnam Peace Parade Committee. I went to support the war, and I stood on the sidelines. I can remember thinking that they didn't understand what I understood. At one point, some Nazis came by handing stickers out that said, "Niggers Back to Africa." They were on our side, booing the people on the street. So I said, This is who's on my side? Then I saw another guy who looked to me like he was probably a Korean war vet, and he's standing in uniform out in the middle of the street as the women and children and men are walking by, he's going, "Fuck you, fuck you, fuck you," and he's got his finger up. I'm thinking, What are these people? This is my side? This is the intellectual argument? I was a little dismayed by this.

So I was going to these different things. I was grappling with all these questions. I was seeing a whole lot of hypocrisy on the side I was on, but I didn't fundamentally change. I still supported the war.

While I was still in college, I decided that I didn't want to be a priest, because that didn't make any sense to me, and a cop seemed too mundane, so I was going to be an FBI agent. It looked so authoritarian and official. It was sort of like an ideal from my boring youth. I wrote letters to J. Edgar Hoover, and I went on a family trip to Washington. I took a tour through the FBI building, and I read all his books on communism, wrote him all these letters, and I wanted more literature on communism and that kind of thing.

They wrote me back, and [said,] "Well, first you need a college degree." Then when I failed out of college, the way to get it was [that you would] actually be a clerk or something. So I actually went to the FBI building here in New York and filled out an application to be a clerk. I filled out a twenty-page document or something and submitted this thing. I never heard from them.

When I failed out of college, I got a draft notice. I decided that I really had to face the choice: Am I going to get drafted and let them do with me what they want, or am I going to find something to do with my life? I'm going to go into the Air Force. And I'm not just going to go into the Air Force to be anybody, I'm going to go in and go into air intelligence, photo mapping, photo reading—you know, something that's going to give me a skill, give me an occupation, give me something I can do with my life, something that looks challenging and bold and everything else. I also didn't want to miss my generation's war.

I enlisted in the Air Force in May of 1966 at the Times Square recruiting station over here in Manhattan. The recruiter promised me everything under the sun.

"I Believed in What We Were Doing"

BOB HANSON

Bob Hanson enlisted in the Army in the fall of 1966, went to Vietnam in February 1967, and served there until October 1968; he was discharged in August 1969. The interview took place in San Francisco, at the office of Swords to Plowshares, where he works.

I was born October 15th, 1947. I was born in Harlem, raised in Harlem and a suburb of the city—Mount Vernon, New York, in southern Westchester county.

I grew up in a multicultural environment in New York City—the public schools—and in Mount Vernon. I went to a consolidated high school for the city of Mount Vernon, which was a city of 100,000 people. It was a one-story suburban high school with a varied population, some working-class, some middle-class. Lots and lots of kids had their own cars. I grew up in a black middle-class environment.

I could have avoided going into the military by going to see a shrink and having him certify that I couldn't function. I didn't do that. I know people who did do that. That was their choice; I made my choice. I believed in what we were doing. I used to watch the news all the time. I read the *New York Times* all the time, so it was not like I didn't know what was going on. I was sort of rah-rah American. I had friends who were in the antiwar movement, but I wasn't. I didn't think any less of anybody who opposed the war. For me, it was just a personal choice.

One of the pluses of living in New York state is that at eighteen years old, you can drink legally. I had turned eighteen years old in 1965, and I used to disappear down to Greenwich Village every weekend, from about late 1965 on. I was fighting more and more with my parents, and I didn't like school, so at the end of the school year of 1966—I knew I was eighteen, I was going to be drafted anyhow, so I enlisted for the Army, to get away from my parents and just to do something exciting. I enlisted [as] "Airborne unassigned."

I took basic training at Fort Gordon, Georgia—Military Police Training, which is what they decided I was going to be in the Army. I got my orders to Vietnam on Friday the 13th, January 1967, and arrived in Vietnam the beginning of February 1967.

A Lifer's Son

MIKE McCAIN

Mike McCain enlisted in the Marine Corps in May 1966, served in Vietnam from May 1967 to October 1968, and was discharged in April 1969. He was interviewed in his home in Country Club Hills, Illinois, a suburb of Chicago.

I was born in 1946 in Champaign-Urbana, Illinois, on the military base down there. I grew up in the Air Force. My father was a lifer in the Air Force, a World War II fighter pilot and one of the original members of the Air Force. After that, there was such a glut that he had to move on to something else, so he started to get into communications and electronics.

I grew up all over the world, spent most of grammar school in Europe. I went to eight different schools in 12 years before I finally graduated from high school down in Louisiana, which was, once again, at the foot of a runway.

Because it was all I knew, that's what I thought everything was. I mean, it was a totally integrated community by the time I was old enough to be conscious about it. I always went to school with Hispanics, blacks, Italians, whatever. One of the real strengths about living in other places of the world besides the United States was the viewpoint that people were just people—there's no difference between anybody in the whole world. Everybody wants a decent place to live, food on the table, being warm in the wintertime, and clothes and education for their children. That's what reality was.

We were Methodist. We went to church very regularly. I don't myself, now. One of the experiences I had was, a group of us used to go to five churches every week. It was all kids. It must have been around my freshman year in high school. One of the things I noticed is that everybody said the same thing. Except they said, "We're the only ones who are right. The rest of these guys aren't right." The experience was that you can't all be right; therefore, I'll take the best of what each of you says and make it myself.

We always lived in the country. I had grown up with hunting. I remember I was twelve or thirteen years old when I first got a shotgun. I went through the NRA [National Rifle Association] safety classes, learned how to shoot pellet guns, BB guns, and then moved up to handguns and then rifles and then shotguns as a part of the rite of passage of childhood. I grew up with weapons. I knew how to handle them properly. It was a way of life.

I was basically an extremely bright student. I didn't have to work very hard in high school. I was president of the National Honors Society; I was president of the state organization of French clubs; I was student body treasurer; I was captain of the debate team. I'd get up when the math teacher couldn't explain the calculus problems to the rest of the class and explain it so that people could get it and understand it.

I was a voracious reader, better informed than just about everybody I was around because I had been to so many places and done so many things and had so many interests. So what I could bring to a composition in English class or to a discussion in social studies or history class, or whatever the hell it was, was broader than most people's range. It was my mother and grandmother that really raised us, and education was very important in our household. We didn't have television at all in the 1950s. We listened to radio, and we had music.

My parents had gotten divorced my senior year of high school. My father, to a certain extent, just split and abandoned us and then later filed for divorce, which was the same time he retired from the military.

I graduated from high school in 1964, and we had absolutely no money. Although I was a National Merit Scholar and stuff, we were totally ignorant and naive about how to go to college.

I moved to California with my father, who I had just reestablished relationships with. I went to work full time for the telephone company to save up money to go to school. I entered college in the fall of 1965 and proceeded to figure out that I didn't have to do anything even then. I was going to Yuba City College up in Marysville in northern California. The first year of college was a repeat of high school. So I went and took tests and would ace all the tests. I majored in physics and electrical engineering. It was a piece of cake, but then they kicked me out for not attending class. Because I was out of state, I got drafted by my local draft board in Louisiana.

I got my draft notice, and there wasn't anything I could do. I mean, I could say I'm in college, but it doesn't matter. That's what their response was:

You're eligible for the draft. Because I was a student, they encouraged me to enter Officer Candidate School. I knew enough about the military to know that I didn't consider the Army much of a fighting unit, and one of the advantages of growing up in the military is knowing what second lieutenants are for—it's fodder. So I knew I didn't want to be a second lieutenant and go to Vietnam, because they were going to kill my ass.

The Marine Corps was the only branch of the service which said, "We'd like you to go to OCS [Officer Candidate School], but if you choose not to, fine."

What did you know about Vietnam?

Not much, hardly anything at all. I knew it was somewhere west of San Francisco. I knew vaguely where it was. I thought I was a fairly well informed young person. But looking back, there were two things I didn't know. One was the civil rights movement, and the other was the international politics of what we were doing in Vietnam. I did know about Dienbienphu, that the French had been defeated there, because I was living in France at just about that time. I was aware of Vietnam from that, but from 1954, 1955, 1956, to 1966, I had no knowledge of it at all.

What did you think the war was about?

I bought the program, that it was about the containment of the spread of communism. That was the ideology I had grown up with. It was very pro-capitalist, pro-American, very knee-jerk reaction to anything that was different. There wasn't that much critical discussion of it, because there wasn't much information. I don't remember internal discussions in the family about it.

I went into the Marines to feel like I had some control. I already knew that I didn't have the eyesight to be a pilot, and the analysis of the time was that if you're going to go to war, you may as well go with the best. To this day, and throughout their history, the Marine Corps [has] been the best, the absolute best. I figured that was where the best opportunity for survival lay.

I went in in May 1966.

"Good Old West Texas Boys"

JOHN KNIFFIN, TERRY DuBOSE, TOM WETZLER

John Kniffin and Terry DuBose (of Austin, Texas) and Tom Wetzler (of San Antonio) were interviewed together in Austin, at the home of Terry DuBose. John Kniffin first served in the Marine Corps from 1960 to 1963. He reenlisted in February 1965 and landed in Vietnam in March 1965; he served three tours of duty there before being discharged in the fall of 1968. Terry DuBose enlisted in the Army in August 1966 and was discharged in July 1969. Tom Wetzler enlisted in the Army in 1968 and served as a medic in Vietnam until his discharge in 1969.

John Kniffin (JK): Terry and I share a common heritage; we're both good old west Texas boys. We grew up believing devoutly in our country. I volunteered in 1965 to go over there because I seriously believed that we needed to stop communism.

Terry DuBose (TDB): I volunteered too, in 1966.

JK: I was brought up to believe that the communists were the Antichrist; you know—they were going to destroy western civilization. The worst thing in the world was a red.

TDB: It was a mental disease; it wasn't a political party.

Where did this come from?

JK: Church, school . . .

TDB: I grew up in west Texas in Brownsville, went to school there, and went to school in Abeline, at a Baptist College. There was a whole movement of

Terry DuBose as a student at Hardin-Simmons College, 1966.

speakers who came around. They had an organization that was connected with the John Birch society, Americans for Freedom or something. . . .

Tom Wetzler (TW): The Freedom Lobby.

TDB: They went around to high school auditoriums and had these speakers that told these horror stories, most of it bullshit, I think. There were these essay writing contests where kids got to go to Washington. The essays that were chosen were those that were the most anticommunist and pro-American. It was feeding on itself during the McCarthy era. It continued right up to the war.

I worked as a delivery guy in a flower shop. I remember the guy I worked for joined the John Birch society. He had all this literature he would share with me.

I graduated from Hardin-Simmons and couldn't get a job in 1966. I had good credentials at the college. I interviewed every company that came. The only job offer that I got was from the Treasury Department, watching the border for illegal aliens coming across.

Firestone, General Motors—all these big companies that interviewed the seniors—had this pat set of questions: "What's your military status?" "Can you get in a national guard unit?" There was a three- or four-year waiting list: I don't know how Dan Quayle did it. They said, "Come back and see us in two years." I mean a college graduate, male, without a deferment or medical problem, could not get a job with a serious company.

So I went home to the same summer job. Got real depressed, and by August [1966], I enlisted. I was real naive when I volunteered to go over there. I think it was the propaganda that convinced me to go. I volunteered when Barry Sadler was singing his song, "Green Berets."

JK: My dad was a veteran. He really didn't talk about his military experience that much, but growing up in Texas in the fifties—I mean, my favorite movie was *Battle Cry.* I loved the book and loved the movie. I think every Texas boy thought about being like Audie Murphy at one time.

I remember having a discussion with a friend of mine while we were in high school about joining the military. If you go off to combat and get killed, oh, well. If you don't get killed and win all these medals, your life is fixed forever, like Audie Murphy.

TDB: Of course, you're never the one who's going to get shot. I never believed that.

JK: Another part of it was Kennedy's challenge: "Ask not what your country could do for you, ask what you could do for your country." A lot of us thought that maybe military service was one answer to that. Even though I was going to A&M when Kennedy was assassinated, and even though there was a lot of redneck hatred of Kennedy, the archtraitor, still, the assassination of the president of the United States affected all of us.

But why join the Marine Corps?

JK: As I said, *Battle Cry* was my favorite movie. . . . [The others are smiling.] OK, I'll get to the real reason. Being a midget [JK is about 5 feet 6 inches tall], you always had this image of Marines as being these big 6-foot giants. In reality, you'll find out most Marines are about my stature. I guess I needed to prove that I could go in with the baddest and cope with it.

Did you assume you were going to go to Vietnam?

TDB: No. I didn't. I didn't know where Vietnam was, essentially. I was just getting it out of the way so that I could get a job.

JK: As a matter of fact, when I was in staging, fixing to go to southeast Asia, I thought I was going to Watts, because that was right around the time Malcolm X was killed and they were having the riots there and we were all on standby. I had heard a lot about Laos and Cambodia. I knew about Vietnam in the 1950s during the French-Indochina war and that the communists had attacked and over run Dienbienphu. I knew essentially about it.

TW: I remember studying in high school history that the difference between the American Army and the Europeans was that the Americans would be told to do something and then have to be told why in order for them to justify it. That was one of the saving factors about the United States military. I was attracted to some aspects of the romanticized idea when I was a kid.

I assumed that I would be going into the Army if I wanted to continue my education past high school—I needed the GI Bill. I also wanted to live out my adolescent fantasy and I also felt that I had something to give back to my country. I didn't have a character—I was still developing one—to have convictions. I saw that as a good life move. It was a good thing to do to set me up for my life. I wanted to see what the war was about.

I got involved with counterculture activities and lifestyle. I was challenged by a lot of friends of mine who would ask me questions I had no answers for. My stock answer was: You can't be all right and our government's all wrong. I wasn't ready to believe that everything I had learned about America, growing up in the 1950s and 1960s, was wrong. I wouldn't admit that I didn't have the answers to the questions, and I thought that I'd find the answers myself. I got answers different from what I expected, and not what I hoped for. I mean, I hoped that I would find something to justify my faith that what the United States was doing was right and just and good, that the people in Vietnam would like us being there.

The day after my eighteenth birthday, I went down to enlist. I enlisted in 1968.

A Patriotic Young American

DANNY FRIEDMAN

Danny Friedman (of Brooklyn, New York) was drafted by the Army in May 1967, landed in Vietnam in November 1967, served a year there, and was discharged in May 1969. He was interviewed at a restaurant in New York City.

[I was] born and bred in Brooklyn. My father was in his thirties during World War II, and he had some sort of medical exemption. He was involved in civil defense. He had his own business. He sold and installed restaurant and bar equipment. He worked six days a week. Some years he wouldn't even take vacation. I remember he would get two weeks' vacation a year, and he would

Danny Friedman, Fort Gordon, Georgia, June 1967.

only take it every other year. My mother also worked full time. She worked for the telephone company.

My parents always worked hard and saved their money. They wanted their own home and eventually got their own home when I was about six years old. They liked to spend their money on themselves a little bit too. They traveled a little bit when they took their vacations.

They were patriotic people. They were more political than I was. I guess they'd say they were liberal. I remember my mother hated Nixon, and my mother hated Nixon because you couldn't trust him. You couldn't trust him in the 1950s, and you couldn't trust him in the 1960s; you sure as hell can't trust him in the 1970s. I remember arguing with her in 1969, when he first got elected, that he was going to be a great president, that he was going to win the war. Yeah, sure. [Sarcastically.] They were Democrats all the way. They never voted Republican in their life. Maybe John Lindsay, that's about it. They were strong Zionists, though. They were actively involved in Jewish organizations like B'Nai B'Rith, the Hadassah, the men's club of the local synagogue, the sisterhood of the local synagogue.

I went to James Madison High School. I played football in high school. I guess I was about as patriotic a young American as you could ask for. I didn't know anything about politics and grew up watching John Wayne movies and bred on TV shows like all the westerns and *Combat* with Sergeant Saunders, and spent every nonschool hour playing soldier or cowboy or something, the way any average American kid grows up without a consciousness . . . the TV generation, the John Wayne mystique.

What is the John Wayne mystique?

The John Wayne mystique is: You've got to do the right thing. Yours is not to question why; yours is to kick ass on the commies and win the pretty girl. I wasn't unique. This was what most people thought.

I remember "duck and tuck" during the Cuban missile crisis, and all I could think about during all of those exercises is, "If this is for real, we were going to get the blond in the first row." That's all we talked about underneath the desks, not the missiles. We said, "She's beautiful and we don't want her to die a virgin and we certainly don't want to die a virgin." [Laughs.] That was about the extent of our political consciousness.

I graduated from high school in 1965. The war was going on. I remember there was a guy on the football team that graduated a year before me, and he enlisted in the Marine Corps. That was something I really envied him for. I thought it was great man, enlisted in the Marine Corps, going to Vietnam. It was terrific. I couldn't wait to do that. It was a war. It was a chance for glory. The communists were trying to take over the world, and we were going to stop them. We were going to stop them in Vietnam before we had to stop them in New York. That was enough for me.

Some people had brains back then, but I didn't. I had them, but the thought process was clouded with eighteen years of propaganda. Safety wasn't part of my vocabulary. I was very reckless. I risked my life in many ways, many times, for a lot less reasons than national security.

I remember my mother saying something to the effect that, "If you're drafted, we'll take you to Canada." I said, "No you won't." I didn't enlist, actually. I went to college. Even though I was as patriotic as I was, I wasn't right-wing gung ho or anything, I considered myself a cool dude and everything, but also going to college and going out with girls was cool too. It seemed like more fun.

I wasn't very much of a studious student. I was more into partying and hanging out and stuff. I wasn't getting good grades, and after three semesters I dropped out of college. I got a job on Wall Street, and I got drafted. As a matter of fact, I got turned in by one of my teachers. I had an economics professor who failed me one semester, and I took it again and ended up getting the same teacher. I gave him a hard time because he allowed some SDS [Students for a Democratic Society] types in the class time to speak in class on one occasion. I thought they were no-good communists and that kind of stuff. If you don't like this country, you ought to get the hell out of here.

When I dropped out of school, he notified my draft board. In one week I got a letter changing my exemption from 2-S to 1-A, and the week after that I got the notice to report in 1967.

To Learn a Skill

BILL BRANSON

Bill Branson enlisted in the Army in March 1966; spent 18 months in Panama and then 14 months in Vietnam; and was discharged in May 1969. He was interviewed at his apartment in Chicago.

I was born in Bethany, Missouri, in 1947. My father was going to watch-making school, so they moved to Saint Paul, Minnesota. I spent a few years there. Then we went to California because my father got certified there as a watchmaker, so he moved out to a chain of jewelry stores in California and started working. I grew up in southern California, in San Bernardino.

We moved from one part of town to the other, kind of stayed in the homes that were on the new fringes that they were just building. That's where the less expensive homes were. We always had a house. We were working-class, but you could have a family of three then and a three-bedroom house on one person's salary and a little six-cylinder station wagon and not be too bad off.

47

My mother was Catholic and my father was a Protestant, but he believed that kids should just take a sample of whatever they wanted and you could make up your own mind later. So he was pretty open-minded in some senses around that. He was never a bigot or anything religiously. In the jewelry business, he worked with Jews all the time. [There were] a few gentiles, a couple of Mexican-Americans that they had there to speak Spanish and stuff.

The education out there was just fantastic compared to nowadays. I went through the school system there and then started junior college. I was never the big macho-type jock or anything. I didn't do well at sports. If it was an individual sport like handball, I could get into it. We had all had the big indoctrination about communism over the years, and so what had happened was that I had read a couple of books that had a significant influence. I read *The Rise and Fall of the Third Reich* [by William Shirer], and I read *Masters of Deceit* by J. Edgar Hoover. I read a bunch of other books, but *Masters of Deceit* was a decisive book because it had every propaganda technique that ever was in it. It told you how to recognize them.

I was armed with this knowledge. So when I was in high school, I went to pep rallies and I almost got sick to my stomach. They looked just like Nazi rallies to me. It pissed me off big-time. I tried to get out of it. I just asked, and it was like, "Who the fuck are you, asshole?" OK, I had to go, but I wouldn't participate. I was more of an individualist. Group sports and stuff didn't turn me on. In scholastic stuff, I was pretty good. I was above average.

I graduated from high school in 1965. The family wasn't rich. I was never under the impression that I would be put through school. I had a job working in the jewelry store as a stock clerk, helper, and whatnot for money. I went to junior college. The tuition was nothing. Books were the main thing. I lived at home, so I didn't have any expenses. But I knew that when I got to state college, it was going to cost a lot of money. I didn't know where that was going to come from. I had planned on going through school and graduating. I didn't do too badly, but I had a math course that I fucked up pretty good. I thought about it and said, I'm not ready for this.

I really hadn't been raised with much independence, so I really didn't handle junior college well. I wasn't mature enough to deal with it. Everything was planned for you, everything was done, everybody was into coddling kids, everything had to be squeaky-clean, individualism was not encouraged.

I got to the end of that rope, and I felt like breaking away. I was tired of fucking being around the house. I'd be out at school, and you couldn't do anything. So I said, fuck this. The only way for me to break loose is to go in the service.

There was a huge Air Force base there, Norton. It was a big repair center and math center. Lots of people I grew up with were all Air Force people. Everybody had a vet real close. Both my parents were veterans. My father was in World War II as a B-29 mechanic in the Pacific. My mother was an officer in the Army. She was a nurse and was in charge of some ward in some hospital. She also flew light aircraft, Piper Cubs and stuff.

I always got lots of war stories. It's hard to classify it all, but generally, there's good times and there's bad times, and it's just something every growing boy should do, especially if there's a war on.

We had many veterans, and they were more respected. You'd proven yourself. You went in, and you had VA care your whole life. They never had to worry. You could even be put up if you had no place to live. Their retirement from the service was good. When you came out, you may have a skill. They were mostly technical people.

That was what people said: Get yourself some technical thing. You can come out and get a job. Well, fuck, that was the mid-1960s, and you could get a job. There was no reason why you couldn't get a job if you're white, educated—there was never a question of starving or anything, as long as you were decent help.

I had a cousin who had gone in the service and got out after I had gone in, but he went to Fort Juachuca in the Army and sat on this fucking base for two years. It was no big deal for him. He was able to come home on the train every once in a while. So, it was, yeah, in basic you got to do this and that and you can be a man, prove you're a man, but it's no big thing.

I went down to the recruiter and got talked into the ASA [Army Security Agency]. I wanted to be a helicopter pilot, but my eyes were just a little bit bad. I really wasn't prepared for a sense of wanting to be a killer. I didn't want to do that. I wanted to be a technician. I knew that I was smarter. I had a better education, but I didn't want to be an officer, that wasn't my role. So I said, "What do you got that's technical?" They said, "Gee, you passed all these tests and did wonderful, so we're going to send you to ASA." I went for it. It was four years. What's four years when you're eighteen? You don't know any different.

My mother wasn't really happy with me going in the service but didn't really resist it. My father wasn't happy either, because he started thinking more about the other side of things as I got closer to doing it. He knew what it was like to sit on an island and have the Japanese maybe 20 feet away in the middle of the night ready to cut your throat.

What did you know about Vietnam when you enlisted?

Well, you had the newsreels and you had the popular songs, you know, "Green Berets." I was anticommunist. I thought they were evil and whatnot. I loved it when our politicians gave it to them. I believed the domino theory. I believed we were going to free those people and we should. That was our role in the world. This was our generation's war—I didn't want to miss it. I went down and deliberately enlisted.

Off I went. I was in the service on March 18, 1966.

"Kill a Commie for Mommie"

JOHN LINDQUIST

John Lindquist enlisted in the Marine Corps in 1967 and served in Vietnam for a year, from May 1968 to May 1969; he was discharged in August 1969. He was interviewed at home in Milwaukee, Wisconsin, with Annie Bailey; they have lived together for the past 25 years.

I was born in 1948. I grew up on the west side of Milwaukee in a white, quiet, working-class neighborhood on the western side of the Jewish community. We were working-class. We didn't own a car or nothing, but the house was great. The first vacation we had together as a family was when I was twelve.

My father was an airmail sorter. My mother's side of the family was Norwegian. They were farmers. She had to beg her father to send her to school beyond the fourth grade because girls didn't need to learn more than the fourth grade. My father's Swedish side of the family were lumberjacks from Minnesota. He left Hibbing and wanted to go into the Army Air Corps in 1920.

Did he talk about his experiences?

None. When he was found to be color-blind, they didn't allow him to fly. I later found out from my mother that he was pretty bitter about that. When my sister and I were born, my father had a heart attack, and then he had two more. The third heart attack killed him, when I was twelve. He was sixty-three when he died.

My father never went to church. My mother took us to church. I used to think it was kind of neat at first. I joined the church choir. I bought this rap. You know, I'd be falling asleep, and then I'd wake up and say Jesus!—like God would get me for falling asleep. I figured out that it wasn't for real by the time my father died. When I was fourteen, I told my mother that I wasn't going to go to church anymore.

For three or four years I was in a youth group, marching band, toured Europe and all this shit. It was to keep me off the streets. There were 149 kids, so it actually turned out to be fun. I was a skateboarder. We had Milwaukee's first skateboard club. I was into surfer magazines and rock and roll.

I had an identity, and that was going to work. When I was twelve, I got my first job. I was a paperboy. Then I washed cars. Then I was an usher in a movie theater. After that, I worked as a clerk in a store stocking groceries and other part-time jobs.

My dad was already dead. I had three sisters and my mother. I was already 6-foot and was fairly independent, but I had enough respect for my mother that if she said be in at such and such a time, I would be home. I learned respect and manners and how to treat women.

Annie Bailey (AB): I've seen some of those home movies at Christmastime, and John's over there in the corner with his hands clasped in front of him, and the expression on his face is terror. If you move, you're going to get beat . . . He was raised in a very stern environment. You get it or you got beat.

John Lindquist (JL): We had rules and regulations. My mother didn't beat me, but my father did before he died. That's just the way I grew up.

I went to Washington High School. I wasn't tracked in high school. I did OK. I was learning. If I would have applied myself more, I would have done better. I had the hardest time in English classes, so I spent seven summers in summer school.

Did you know anything about Vietnam before enlisting?

JL: Yeah. I knew it was better to be dead than red. I read the *U.S. News and World Report* every week. I read *Newsweek.* We had debates in school, and I used to always be on the "better dead than red" side. I used to take quotes from the *U.S. News and Business Report,* doing my research and getting ready for it. I followed the progression of fighting the commies on TV with the news. That's what I knew, and I equated it all to World War II. I had grown up on all those World War II movies. . . .

AB: Back to Bataan was his favorite movie. [Laughs.] He went out on a date. I met this girl, just a couple of years ago, as a matter of fact—first girl he ever went on a date with. He took her to the movies to see *The Guns of Navarone.* It was over, and he goes, "Wow, you want to see it again?" and she sat with him through it again. What a nice girl. I would have said, "Fuck you."

JL: When I was learning how to read, I was sent down to the library to get my first books, so where do I go? I go to the war section. My first book that I read, I think I read it seven times, was *Guadalcanal Diary* [by Richard Tregaskis].

What did you like about that?

JL: Patriotism, you know, and fighting for your country. That was before TV. Then after TV, I was seeing all those movies for the first time. I was enthralled by it. By the time I was eleven or twelve, I wanted to be a Marine. When I got to be the age, the draft was no worry; I was going to enlist.

What did you think you were going to do in the armed forces?

JL: I enlisted in the Marine Corps because I wanted to kill communists. I was such a rabid anticommunist that I thought [Joe] McCarthy was my kind of guy. I was willing to do anything to stop communism. I was going to do at least 20 years. I was going to be a combat engineer. I might even make sergeant-major. It was totally unrealistic. At the same time, I thought that was a good way to earn respect—you know, kill a commie for mommie. My mother did not track me into that. I mean she didn't even want me to go into the service. No way.

Why not?

JL: She wanted nothing to do with war. She had nobody in her family that had anything to do with war. I was eighteen, and even though she was not excited about me going, there was no way she could have stopped me.

I graduate in 1966. Right out of high school, me and my buddy went to England to treat ourselves and see the Rolling Stones. I didn't ever get to see them. We used to go to the London School of Economics and shit like this, and they'd say, "You're what? You're going to enlist in the fucking Marine Corps?"

Taking a year off in England, farting around and listening to Jimi Hendrix and all that shit, was fun, but at the same time I still wanted to go kill communists.

I met this girl at the disco. . . .

AB: The only girl that would dance with him . . . because he's such a nerd. . . .

JL: She was the only girl that would dance with me. We go to Carnaby Street. We got short hair. We buy all these bizarre-looking clothes with stripes and checks and flowers and black, you know, and we go down to the fucking local disco. . . . "Hey, will you dance with me?" . . . You know. [We're all laughing.] . . . And I'm talking about short hair. Man, they fucking laughed at us. So finally this girl takes pity on us and says she'll dance with me. It turns out she's an American. . . . Anyway, to make a long story short, we married and purposely got ourselves pregnant so I could have a baby to carry on the family name.

I joined the Marine Corps in 1967.

The Marines Will Make a Man Out of You

JOEL GREENBERG

Joel Greenberg enlisted in the Army in September 1966, went to Vietnam in November 1967, and was discharged in June 1969. He was interviewed at home in Chicago, with his companion, Annie Luginbill.

Joel Greenberg (JG): I grew up in Queens, New York. My parents were both, in their own ways, progressive. My mother had been with the CP [Communist Party] during the McCarthy period. My father was very strongly pro-union. He had been a union organizer. My grandfather had been CP on my father's side.

Annie Luginbill (AL): He's a red diaper baby.

JG: I know what it's like to have the FBI knocking at your door, checking around and questioning, stuff like that. I remember the May Day demonstrations in the early 1950s, when I was very young. My parents would get dressed in their uniforms, go down Fifth Avenue in New York, and have tomatoes and shit thrown at the people in the parade. That's when they changed May Day to a communist holiday. Even then, veterans were put right up in the front ranks to show we were patriotic—right, they were supposed to get hit by tomatoes.

They were both veterans of World War II. Both had been overseas in the Pacific. As far as my mother was concerned, it [her wartime experience] was very positive. My father was a fuck-off and didn't give a shit about anything. My father was a medic and my mother was a nurse. They were both stationed in Hawaii. My mother had been in Guam as well. She was part of that layer of nurses when they first got commissioned to put them in the province of officers. She still has this thing that came out of Congress. It says, "By act of Congress, you are now an officer and a gentleman." [Laughs.]

I was brought up in a way that we were free to make whatever decisions we wanted to, as long as we could justify it. My parents wanted us to go to a specialty high school, and I wanted to go to a local neighborhood high school where my friends were going. They may not have agreed with that, but they respected that decision, and it was the same thing going into the Army.

We had a high school where we were on two shifts. There were over 2,000 students in my graduating class, and it was pretty well mixed. My group of friends in high school were pretty tight. We were pretty badass. Before we graduated, about seven or eight of us all went down to the Marine recruiters in 1965 and said, "If you guarantee we can stick together, you can take us all." We were going to join the military. The only thing that I ever heard a recruiter say that was truthful was, "I can't guarantee you'd be together after basic." So we said, "Forget it." But one by one, we all went in.

It had nothing to do with politics in the sense of any consciousness. I wasn't pro-anything. My background was basically one of apolitical, myself. I had always wanted to go in the Marines. It was a reflection of having grown up with Vic Morrow, *Combat,* the John Wayne movies, Sergeant Rock of Easy Company, Marine advertisements—the propaganda. You know, "The Marines will make a man out of you." It was more growing up with the macho image and being lost and floundering, in terms of not having a direction in life.

AL: It was just macho.

JG: The only college that accepted me right out of high school was the University of Florida at Jacksonville. I was all set to go, but just before graduation my father had a heart attack. That eliminated that, and I ended up going to Manhattan Community College at night. That was about the only thing I could get into. I wasn't a great student. I didn't know what I wanted. I was floundering with no real direction, so what do you do? You go into the military. At least when I get out, I'll be a man. If I go to Vietnam, I go to Vietnam. You don't think about it. You do what you've got to do. It was no big deal.

What did you know about Vietnam?

JG: I knew Vietnam existed. I knew there was a war going on, and I knew that my parents were willing to send me to Canada if I wanted to go.

The night before I was going to enlist, I had an uncle who was over, and he had been a paratrooper in World War II. He told me about jumping. The next day I went into the Army and enlisted: "Airborne unassigned." That's why I wound up in the Army. I found out later on that the Marines went to the same jump school as the Army did. I went in in September of 1966.

Seeds of Doubt

LEE THORN

After receiving a draft notice, Lee Thorn enlisted in the Navy reserve. He spent 10 months on an aircraft carrier in the Gulf of Tonkin—from December 1965 to September 1966, when he was discharged. He was interviewed at his home in San Francisco.

I was born in Kansas City in 1943. My father was an accountant and my mother was a nurse—middle-class. My grandfather had been a Seventh Day Adventist pacifist [and] had gone to Canada during World War I but came back. His father's prize role had been as a Marine, so he didn't want his father to know. [He] went to boot camp and he died. There was a big influenza outbreak during World War I. My father had enlisted in the Army Air Corps while he was in college, and went in in 1941 and got medically discharged for asthma, and then he was drafted into the Marine Corps after he was medically discharged—so he was in Guanaco when I was born.

I had gone to school at Berkeley. The draft board was corresponding with me, and I had thrown away all their stuff. I dropped out of school and I didn't pay any attention to it. . . . Stupid. I knew I was going to be drafted.

Lee Thorn in 1957, age fourteen.

It [the Vietnam war] was not much in my consciousness. I think I vaguely knew there was something wrong over there. I was a little bit concerned. I knew I didn't want to be on the ground. I figured I'd have to do it, especially because I had dropped out of school; but I didn't want any part of the ground forces, so I enlisted in the Navy reserve. They told me I could go to Chinese language school. That's great, so I did it. It was like this long boot camp. I got out of Chinese language school [and] they said, "No problem—just sign up for an extra two years." I didn't know what to do.

I got out in June. I was pissed. I was ready to go back to school and come back as an officer, but I almost starved to death. I couldn't find a job because of my draft status and because everybody asked what your military status was. I tried to get a job at Bob's Big Boy, which is a chain restaurant, and they wouldn't give me a job because of my age. So—back into the Navy in September of 1964, and I ended up washing dishes for 14 weeks on 12-hour shifts. That wasn't too much fun.

I was at Seal Beach, California. I'd met a couple of personnel people and they said, "What do you want to do?" and I said, "I want to go up to personnel," and they said, "Where do you want to go?" and not knowing how to get these things, I said, "The bigger the ship, the better," because I knew I'd get seasick. So, "How about a carrier?" and they said, "What coast do you want to go to?" I said the east coast, and they said, "Sure, we'll try to get you on a ship." Well, I ended up getting orders to the airborne early-warning squadron in San Diego. But then I started getting into trouble because I'd gone to Berkeley and all my friends were still in Berkeley. That's when the free speech movement started. I told these guys, "I want to go up to Berkeley and see what's going on."

I wanted a 72-hour leave to go to a free speech movement, so they gave me a 72-hour lecture. [Laughs.] Most of my friends were involved in it. I supported it and I also wanted to see what was going on, but I was stuck in San Diego, so they wouldn't give me leave.

"Do What You've Got to Do"

DAVE CLINE

Dave Cline was drafted into the Army in January 1967 and was sent to Vietnam in July of that year. He remained there until December 1967, when he was wounded for the second time and was sent back to the United States.

I was born in Buffalo, New York, grew up there, and then moved to the suburbs outside of Buffalo. I joined the Boy Scouts, church choir, all that stuff. My parents were just regular people, German and Irish background. They went to church—Lutheran church, Evangelical and Reformed.

My father was a World War II veteran. After World War II, they encouraged a lot of people coming home to start their own businesses because they had a lot of these loans. He started a business where they'd take these treadle sewing machines and put them in a box—you know, a carrying case—and make them electric sewing machines. He used to travel all up and down western New York and northern Pennsylvania doing that, and then that went bankrupt. He went back to working in the auto plants and the steel mills. He was involved in organizing the UAW-CIO prior to the war, when he was a machinist in Buffalo. He's always been a unionist.

Prior to going into the military, I didn't pay much attention to politics, [but] I had some awareness of what was going on. There was really not too much talk of politics in my household. The only time I can remember politics being discussed at any time was when Eisenhower ran for president. My father was big on him; I think that had to do with the World War II thing. You know—a lot of guys got behind Eisenhower because he had been the commander in the war.

We used to have arguments a lot with my father around racial issues, because our family had moved from Buffalo to the suburb of Eden. He wasn't a Klansman, but he reflected a lot of the prejudices that a lot of people reflected at that time. The area had been a German area, and it turned to black. A lot of people would say, "Look how the blacks are wrecking the area" and stuff like that.

I was aware of the civil rights movement and sympathetic to the efforts of the civil rights movement. I never was involved in anything, but I was aware of the activities. They had the freedom summers, and people were going.

What made you sympathetic to the civil rights movement?

When I was a little kid in Buffalo, I had contact with black people. Also, where I lived was near an Indian reservation. I had two girlfriends who were Native American women, and I used to catch a lot of flak from my friends for going out with Indian women. It was not black, but it was prejudice, you know. I used to look at it like this: I got a girlfriend, I'm getting laid, and these guys are fucking sitting home at night. [Laughs.] That's how I looked at it.

So there was that connection, but I think it was the basic appeal to justice that anyone can identify with if you don't have an emotional attachment to racism. There was a positive thrust of fighting for what the ideals of America are supposed to be—you know, freedom and all that good stuff. You've got to remember that in them days, Kennedy and all this stuff is coming up. All of that was putting out a sense of a movement to fulfill ideals or fulfill dreams. There was a sentiment out there, even in Bob Dylan's songs.

When I was sixteen, my brother and I started playing guitar, and through the course of listening to music, I became aware of Bob Dylan's music. I got *Freewheelin' Bob Dylan.* We had our bedroom in the basement. We had the record player there. We put the record on. We're listening to him, and my brother and I say, "This guy sounds like shit, man; he can't sing for nothing." My father was upstairs yelling, "Turn that shit down." Of course, we're fighting with our father—you know, the generation gap—so we cranked it up. After that, we liked Bob Dylan. [Laughs.] Dylan's message was to question things.

Then, in the course of things, I one time had heard Dick Gregory. I think he ran for president, and he had gone around campaigning on the Peace and Freedom ticket, or something like that, and I had gone to hear him speak. He was critical of the war.

I was out of high school and working. While my parents wanted me to go to college, I really didn't lean in that direction. I really didn't have any direction in my life. I was into partying, girls, rock and roll, drinking beer, and stuff like that.

I turned twenty on January 8th. I got drafted on January 15, 1967. The reason I got drafted when I was twenty was because I got my leg broke when I was eighteen. I got hit by a car, and I had a full-length cast on it for a long time. Up in Buffalo, they were grabbing you at nineteen. I got a six-month deferment because of the broken leg. In fact, I thought the broken leg would stop me from being sent to the war because it healed slightly shorter than the other, but no such luck.

When I got drafted, I was half thinking, hoping, that we are going to Vietnam to help these people fight communist aggression. That's what it was about, fighting for people's freedom, sort of the World War II [idea]—go into France and drive out the foreigners. My father had been a vet. They looked at it as, basically, you've got to serve the country when you're drafted.

I recall thinking, I know that there's people saying it ain't right and stuff like that, but at the same time, I really didn't think that I was in a position to make that judgment. There's that tradition leaning on the one side [World War II, maleness] and then there was people saying this was fucked up on the other. I guess the tradition was stronger, or at least I deferred the decision. When I went in, I said that I don't know if it's right or wrong, but I'm going to do what you've got to do. I got myself pumped up, though. We were going over to help the people. I'm going to be the good guy. I'm going to be one of the good Americans helping the villagers and shit like that.

Skeptic

MIKE GOLD

Mike Gold was drafted by the Army in December 1965, served in Germany from June 1967 to April 1968, and was discharged in March 1969. He was interviewed in New York City, at the Office of Veterans Affairs at the City University of New York, where he was the director.

I'm first-generation American. My mother and father were born in Russia and Poland. My brothers and I were born here. My father died when I was one year old. It was just my mother and my older brothers. My brothers got me into things.

My two older brothers were veterans. My oldest brother, Ed, was in during Korea, and he was interested in politics. He used to do work for the local block captain and the Democratic Party. At that time, the district that I lived in in Brooklyn was a real powerhouse. It was the Seneca Democratic Club. They had the leadership position of the Democrats in the legislature of the state. When I was eight, I was handing out literature for [Adlai] Stevenson. I was early into politics.

Before being drafted, I was a college student in my first year at Brooklyn College. I was active in the civil rights movement in high school, and in college in the New York end of the civil rights movement. I thought Johnson was doing a very progressive domestic agenda and was doing a lot about civil rights, the so-called "great society."

I left college because I had a full-time job in the mayoral campaign of John Lindsay. He had been a Republican congressman. His campaign was kind of a fusion campaign, a hybrid Democrat-Republican, to try and sort of sweep the city clean. He was supposed to be a breath of fresh air. I was a major in political science and history, and that kind of job was right up my alley. I started it in the summer of 1965, and it lasted until the election in November of 1965.

I stayed out that fall semester, and my draft board—which was the largest in the country at the time, in the center of Brooklyn—caught me for being on leave. I lost my 2-S. They took it away. The school wrote them that I was going back in January, but they wouldn't listen to anything. I got my notice in December [1965].

I thought about not going in, because I was real disappointed about not going to college. The antiwar protests started in New York. The people who were doing it were the hippies in the Village—you know, the poets and the artists were out there against the war. I had heard negative things about the war, and I thought they might be right; but I hadn't quite made up my mind, because of the disinformation we were getting, supposedly fighting for democracy and all that stuff. I believed a lot of malarkey. I thought they were doing the draft from twenty-six down to eighteen. When I took my time off to work, I thought I'd never be drafted. I was eighteen, but you popped to the top of the list when your deferment changed. There I was. The only alternative I knew about was going to jail. I didn't think that was productive.

I had inklings of some other things. . . . When I was being drafted, this guy next to me was sticking his arm full of holes. . . . People had knowledge of faking psychological and medical disorders to get out. . . . On reflection, many things could have worked. . . . To me, it was out of the question. . . . I couldn't fake being what I wasn't.

I didn't fully associate the Vietnamese with being like the Russian communists and stuff like that. I knew something was different there. They were indigenous people. I had more sympathy for them. It was an undeveloped country. I knew we were doing something wrong bringing all this death machinery to them. I didn't know much about fighting going into the war.

Conscientious Objector

RON SABLE

Ron Sable was drafted into the Army as a conscientious objector in 1968. He served as a medic in Vietnam from May 1969 to June 1970. He was interviewed in his office at Cook County Hospital in Chicago.

I grew up in a fairly sort of middle-class background. My father was a building subcontractor and my mother worked after we got in school. We lived in Kansas City.

I was a Methodist and a Boy Scout and Eagle Scout, and all that kind of stuff—very involved, actually, as a youth in church youth activities. I was sort of a liberal, you know. My family's ethical values came out of fairly traditional religious notions about fairness and equity.

I went to what was considered even then sort of a center-city or inner-city high school that was stably integrated. It was not a particularly college-oriented environment, although my family always expected me to go to college. I was student body president—made an address at my graduation and talked about racial violence and racial harmony. I don't think it was particularly radical, but it was quite a startling message for a high school graduating audience in 1963.

I went to undergraduate school at the University of Kansas, which was about as big as my horizon was at that time. I was president of my fraternity and very involved in interfraternity activities. I belonged to a fraternity that had originated from the south, where there was still a blackball system in place. I and a series of local presidents were unsuccessful in getting the national organization to abandon that at the time. I actually, essentially, left the fraternity after I left college because of the frustration with that thinly veiled racist policy that they had. I was very involved in school political activities. I was a student body president in my senior year.

It was 1968 when I graduated. I ended up being drafted as a conscientious objector in the Army.

How did you come to the point of being a conscientious objector?

Well, it was a personal examination about how I felt about killing. It was based on my religious upbringing.

My draft board had not faced many CO [conscientious objector] applications. They were not very sophisticated in it. They had a sort of standard notion that you had to be some kind of religious fanatic to seek this in Kansas City. But the fact that I checked off this box saying that I was going to serve, even though I had this list of reasons that were far more politically oriented than they would have accepted, was all that they needed, really. They didn't really care what I thought. Had I applied for exemption as a CO—in other words, to do alternative service—I'm sure they never would have granted that. Otherwise, I would have been faced with going to jail.

I had long discussions with my family about that. At the time, I thought that I was prepared to face it. The more that I've known, having worked in jails and know[ing] about prisons, that probably would have been a mistake. I don't know if I ever considered seriously leaving the country. I knew people who did that as well. I guess I was just ambivalent, as many of us are, about the United States and its role in the world. I couldn't conceive of leaving.

I think that in retrospect, to serve in the military, having those feelings, was a mistake. I'm not sure there was any position that didn't have compromises in it. Over there, I never carried a gun, but other people pulled guard duty and sort of killed on my behalf, if you will, in a very direct way. Now, I don't think it's a very tenable position. It was a way of serving but at the same time not doing something that I thought was fundamentally wrong in terms of killing other people.

What was your impression of Vietnam?

I didn't know lots and lots. I read some, but I actually learned a lot more when I was there. I went through this funny basic training where you do everything else except the weapons training and virtually everybody is assigned to the medical corps.

Antiwar Officer

PETE ZASTROW

Pete Zastrow went through the ROTC program at Dartmouth College; later, after working as a desk officer, he served a year in Vietnam, from December 1968 to December 1969, when he was discharged. He was interviewed at home in Chicago.

I was born on Long Island in 1939. My father being in the telephone company, we moved from place to place and ended up in a suburb of Cincinnati—Fort Thomas, Kentucky—after which I went off to college and graduated from Dartmouth college in 1961. At the same time, I was commissioned as a second lieutenant in the Army, having gone through ROTC at Dartmouth.

Why did you join the ROTC?

Well, actually, the first thing that intrigued me about it was that the best history professor at Dartmouth taught military history, which was the first course you took in ROTC. He was a Dartmouth legend. His course was tremendous. That's what got me started, and I guess once I began, there was just no reason to stop.

This was 1957. Vietnam wasn't happening. I realized something was going on. But it was a nonwar period. There were no protests. There were a few people who threw water balloons at the ROTC parade when I graduated. [Laughs.] It wasn't so much protest as much as the whole concept of the military that they didn't like. It was no confrontation—it wasn't that kind of time, and it wasn't that kind of place. It was not that era. So friends of mine who got out at the same time ended up spending a couple of years in Germany and at various military bases throughout the United States.

I went on to graduate school at Indiana University for six years. I finished all the course work [and] took the qualifying exams for the Ph.D. I reached a point where I had gone through all of the stuff I was going to go through. I had the thesis proposal accepted. I had filed everything on little cards and color-coded them all. I had presented one paper to a group of graduate students on the same subject. I was teaching freshman literature and composition for four years at a small Catholic college in Cincinnati.

It was kind of understood when I went into the ROTC that you would receive defers for four years; and usually, if you needed another two years, particularly if you were teaching, most likely you could get it. Six years was usually the limit on it. Each year, sometime in the spring, I would receive a form from the military saying, "If you wish to be deferred for another year, you have to fill out a form" and go get a physical exam showing that you were still physically capable of being in the military. Each year I would go faithfully and do that. Then, I got the notice in January of 1968 that I was supposed to report, so I did.

I was following the news all along, and I was, of course, aware that I was going to go into the military at some point. But I was a student, and students don't care about that sort of thing. [Sarcastically.] But at some point along there—it must have been around October or November of 1967—I had been doing a lot of reading about Vietnam, and I had sent a letter to the local newspaper stating that it seemed to me the war was immoral, illegal, stupid. You're paying $323,000 to kill each enemy; why don't you just give them each $323,000, and the war would stop? You know, the whole line about the wrong war, the wrong place, and the wrong enemy. The moral issues were a little more difficult, because we had not yet seen the immorality of what American troops were doing. It was a general feeling of, What are we doing interfering in another country, without a general political base for that?—just feeling that it wasn't right. So anyway, I wrote that this war was wrong and if I were sent to Vietnam, I wouldn't go. It caused a great stir. Readers sent in all kinds of letters about my article.

I went into infantry officers training school in Fort Benning, Georgia, in January. From there I was sent to Fort Leavenworth, the home of the Command and General Staff College. On the top floor of the college was this weird little office called the Institute for Combined Arms and Support, which had 69 career officers. I was there after my first two months in the military.

They did essentially three things: they wrote field manuals, they did planning for operations 15 to 20 years in the future, and they wrote tables of organizational equipment, which is something only the military worries about. TOE the military calls it. Initially, they made me an editor of field manuals.

Field manuals were just immensely tedious. You would go through an old field manual and then send it to all the branches to have someone read it and say what should be changed; get it back; make all the changes; and send it out again—so that it would take about a year and a half to get all these things changed. Then you would have to sit down with all these experts and go through it, word by word by tedious word. Eventually you would get it printed. All the army manuals were constantly being revised.

They wanted me to do this field manual, a study of Vietnam about munitions. How many rounds did a rifle fire of what kind of ammunition in a jungle at night? etc., etc. What that amounted to was having the people in the field in Vietnam, particularly the artillery people, fill out these little forms, which they all religiously did because their generals told them they had to—I'm sure totally false—and they were all chucked into this room at RAC headquarters in Langley, Virginia, which was the Research Analysis Corporation, a research organization funded privately and off budget by Congress.

They used to fly me there regularly to go to conferences. You'd walk down these halls and there would be a retired general, a retired admiral, one right after another. We'd sit in these meetings and talk about this blithering idiocy. I'd be sitting in these rooms with people who were so far above me in terms of rank—I mean, they had aides who were higher-ranking than I was.

My feelings [about the war] hadn't changed; I would fight with all my superiors about it. It was a very social group, and I was the only eligible bachelor that these people's wives knew. They all had marriageable daughters. It was very much a party atmosphere. I can remember champagne brunches which were absolutely mind-boggling. We'd go on ten-thirty on Sunday morning and drink champagne with eggs and ham until four, when people would have to crawl home. All of these people were getting promoted, so there was promotion party after promotion party, and the booze flowed freely.

I'd go to these parties, and we would just fight tooth and nail. I remember it was the time of the Democratic convention. I remember watching that at one of the parties with these people and just really fighting it out. Because, of course, they thought it was the best thing in the world to be clubbing these people insensible. I didn't. After two or three drinks, who cared? I have to say, they loved it. They liked to have somebody to argue with, because I didn't know anything, so what the hell? We had a good time.

Eventually, I had finished the revisions of this horrible field manual, and they wanted me to write the field manual of the tactical use of nuclear weapons. Because of that, they did security clearances, and when they did security clearances they found that I had written a letter saying I wouldn't go to Vietnam. I was therefore a security risk. That's when all these folks got together and sat down with me. We had this long long afternoon discussion for five hours at least, of generals and colonels of the base, the historian, and the base morale officer, the chaplain, all of these people sitting around this poor little first lieutenant. I had done my homework. I knew what I was talking about, and they couldn't understand me. I didn't know what they were talking about. The assumptions are so different that you really can't carry on a conversation.

These people were all Vietnam veterans. Some of them were running companies and more often battalions, or various staff jobs. A week or so later I said I would go to Vietnam if I were ordered to do so, based on the stupid idea that these people had all been there, so how could I talk about it until I had seen it for myself? It was probably just the easy way out, but it must have been a difficult decision at the time. In retrospect, I don't regret it, although I wish I had a better basis on which to have made the decision.

When my orders came for Vietnam, my immediate superior, who was a colonel about to retire—a great old man, actually—said, "I'm letting you go because I think it would be good for you to see what the Army is really about, though I certainly know enough people in Washington to get these orders changed and keep you, which I would like to do, but I think for your good . . ." I think he was quite sincere. I think he was full of shit, but he was sincere.

Antiwar Activist

DAVID EWING

David Ewing was drafted into the Army in September 1970 and served in Germany from April 1971 to April 1972, when he was discharged. He was interviewed in San Francisco, in his office at Swords to Plowshares.

I was born in Trenton, New Jersey, and my dad was a city fireman. He retired from the fire department in 1955. He only had an eighth-grade education, so he had difficulty finding another job. He worked as a security guard for RCA in Princeton, New Jersey.

That had a big impact on my family, because that's the time when Einstein was working in the lab [the Institute for Advanced Study at Princeton] and a lot of the great luminaries of American physics worked there. My dad was actually the security guard at the lab who sat at the door. Every morning Einstein would come in, so my dad was the guy who had to recognize him visually. My family just worshipped Einstein and the physicists, especially my dad, with an eighth-grade education. He really had a love of learning for a guy with poor education. He was a self-educated guy. My family was not religious, so we had like this secular worship of science and learning that substituted for religion.

My father tended to be Republican, but my mom was more liberal. I think she thought of herself as an Eisenhower Republican. Right around this time, some of the physicists were being called before HUAC. My dad was a conservative, but he felt this was very unfair, that these leading physicists were being charged with being communists. He was very confused by that.

I was kind of a quiet guy, kept to myself a lot. I was a lousy athlete. I was on the high school chess team. We were undefeated the year I was on the team. So it was kind of this academic thing. I wasn't very popular. I was kind of offbeat. The 1960s were a great time to be offbeat, much easier than it is today.

In 1964, 1965, I didn't know where Vietnam was, but then I heard about the demonstrations and I immediately started following it. I remember hearing about it and talking about it in school and being really interested. I was interested in philosophy, I guess, but I didn't become actively political until I was a junior in high school. In 1968 especially, the year I graduated, that was the Columbia strike. It was just such a dramatic thing, that kids my age could tear down a university. You see these high school and college kids just running rampant and destroying things, hijacking trains, and driving all over the country and creating chaos. It looked great to me. It was liberating, a whole new wonderful sense of power, because a lot of people feel dispossessed. I immediately joined SDS, as soon as I could.

I was eighteen in 1968, so I was just the right age for everything to start breaking loose. The alternative to the system that we were all bored with meant looking at what was happening in the socialist countries [and] the revolutionary movements around. I really had a strong academic interest in Russian history while I was in high school. A friend of mine and I on the bus would debate about the different factions of the Bolshevik party. Looking at "what ifs" and stuff like that. It was just a fascinating thing. Even the cultural revolution in China was such a dramatic thing for me.

My dad died in 1963, five years before I finished high school. We owned our own home in the suburbs, but my family lived on social security payments for the children, and my mom would get commodities—you know, peanut butter. It's like a depression story. Times were hard, and I never had anything fancy. I mean, we had food and everything basic. It was a time when you didn't have to be stylish. Kids didn't have to have a $300 pair of Reeboks. You could blend in, so I never really felt deprived.

I graduated from school, and my family had no money. I couldn't go to a good school, so I went to a local community college in Pennsylvania, about 30 miles north of Philadelphia and about 10 miles from Trenton. I started the SDS chapter in that school.

I knew what was happening in SDS. I had a tremendous interest in understanding the different political perspectives of the left movement. My views were more extreme than other students'. A group I was associated with, the hardest-line Maoist faction, was called the Progressive Labor Party. They were fanatically pro-China. They're the ones who seized control of the SDS resources and office after the convention. I thought that the PL people were more serious. They had no quick promises. It was a long haul, and it was going to be working people. We're going to have to organize vast numbers. We were going to have to convince people that there needs to be change. I was with them, and I was a Maoist. I was definitely not a pacifist. I was ready to fight for what I thought was right.

The country was very polarized, and the school was very polarized, about the Vietnam war. There were actually debates held one time at a public assembly, where professors debated the war. It was really a remarkable thing. The professor they had who was defending the government's position gave this rap about patriotism and the need to do what you were told and that kind of thing. It was very unconvincing for the audience. Then, the guy who gave the liberal view was a history professor who talked about the history of Vietnam. He was very convincing. He didn't use appeals to patriotism or nationalism, nothing like that. It was just sort of like: These are the facts, and if you look at Ho Chi Minh, this is what he did, and he said this—you know, it was a completely different thing. So that was eye-opening and very encouraging, to think the truth mattered. For a young person to think that the truth counts is very refreshing. I think young people get confronted with hypocrisy. For me, that was a moment that I've always remembered.

I was fighting with my mom, as all teenagers do, and I couldn't stand living at home any more. She disapproved of my girlfriend, so in a huff, I moved out of the house one day and had to get a job to support myself. I rented a room near the college for $15 a week and I got a job in a factory. I couldn't finish the semester. I ran out of money. I lost my 2-F deferment. I was confronted with—you know: I could leave the country, I could wait around and get drafted, or I could enlist. I really couldn't bring myself to enlist, because that would have been three years.

PL [Progressive Labor Party] was organizing in the military, and I was just the right age to be drafted anyway, so my PL friends convinced me to join them in this Army organizing project, to organize in Vietnam against the war. So instead of enlisting, I just waited for my draft notice and when it came, I went in.

I was just in the right place, and I knew the history of other wars where communists had done this: in Germany against the Nazis, [and] Americans fought in the Spanish Civil War. So there was quite a long tradition of doing this kind of thing. I was very familiar [with the fact] that it had happened before. It seemed like a hard thing to do, but it seemed like the thing I had to do. So I just bit the bullet and did it.

The movie *Doctor Zhivago* must have come out in 1966 or 1967. [The actual date was 1965.] There's this one scene where there's a bolshevik organizer in the streets when it was announced that the war had begun. There's throngs, thousands and thousands of cheering Russian men running to the recruiter's office, and he's there running with them, but he had this smirk on his face. Then there was his narrative about stuff that he was doing. He was saying stuff like, "They're laughing now. They think this is a big party. Wait till they find out what imperialist war is really like." So I saw myself as that smirking bolshevik good guy. I thought that the United States would tire of the imperialist war. I hoped the soldiers would. That was one of the clear images in my mind—a Hollywood image, you know.

I was inducted in the Philadelphia induction center on September 17, 1970.

The Women in VVAW

Women, although they were not combat veterans, became active and significant members of VVAW. The women who speak here came from backgrounds similar to the men's; but they tended to be less willing to accept dogma uncritically. The reason for this difference may have something to do with different expectations for men and women. Because women were not considered fit for combat, they were not subject to the same hyperpatriotism as men, or to a magnified male image or the concept of military service as a rite of passage. In fact, their descriptions of growing up in the United States during the cold war provide insights into the power of the dominant ideology over their male counterparts—young working-class men.

Women of this generation grew up on the cusp of the women's movement. They were starting to demand more of themselves, and they looked up to mothers, grandmothers, and other women who had been strongly outspoken and individualistic. Older women like these could open a young woman's eyes to social hypocrisy, and particulary to sexism and racism. Moreover, having experienced life as a second-class citizen, an older woman could often understand oppression, and might counsel young women to be strong and to become involved in society. That is precisely what many younger women did.

ANNIE LUGINBILL

Annie Luginbill became involved with Vietnam Veterans Against the War after having worked with the Chicago Area Military Project. She was interviewed with Joel Greenberg at their home in Chicago.

I'm a Chicago native. My parents are, I would have to say, very independent people who live in one of the most Republican counties in the country, Du Page County, and who have always been very independent. My father votes Libertarian when he's pissed off, so I came from a very liberal—I will not say progressive, but liberal—family. I worked for Kennedy in 1960, for Johnson in 1964, and was gassed in the streets of Chicago in 1968.

Women of VVAW, Wisconsin, 1981: Annie Luginbill *(standing)* and Annie Bailey *(seated)*.

I was in the eighth grade, and I was going door to door in a Republican county working for Kennedy because he seemed to make the most sense at that point in time. It was what he promised to do for the world, as much as anything, because it was, "Ask not what your country, yada, yada." I mean, it was the whole very forward-looking, "let's all hold hands and make the world nice" philosophy, which I didn't see coming out of anybody else. It came out of my family and upbringing. My father would send money to India supporting families because when he was in World War II, he was stationed in India and Burma. So he had a sense of the world. He came out of the experience knowing that there were people a lot less well off than we. That's something that we always grew up with, so it just kind of played into going on into political activity. I just wanted to see the world a nice place. That's how it always has been.

I started college in the fall of 1966. I went to Elmhurst College and met black people for the first time. I met people from New York for the first time. I thought New York was a foreign country. I still do. [Laughs.]

I got very involved in college politics. I was in an early SDS chapter at Elmhurst college, another very Republican area. It [SDS] was the only game in town. I was certainly not going to join the Young Republicans if I didn't like them enough to work for their presidential candidates. SDS made sense. People shared a common goal, a common hope. We're talking democratic politics; we're talking a good world for the world. It was very basic and simple and very New Left. We were touchy-feely. It was a whole era. It's hard to describe the 1960s to someone who really wasn't immersed in it. Working with SDS led to an even broader understanding of the world.

How so?

In terms of the role the United States government played. One of the most formative books in my thinking was a book called *The Enemy* [Felix Greene, *The Enemy: What Americans Should Know about Imperialism* (New York, Random House, 1970)] which just generally relayed all the facts and figures behind everything the government was doing: money it sends here, it's not really sending it here, it's putting it into a bank account for somebody's kids to go to a Swiss school, or something like that.

SDS was a place where I found people who read the same kinds of books, pamphlets, newspapers; had the same kind of understanding; and wanted people not to be hurt. It's not easy to explain. People just didn't want there to be suffering. Coming out of the civil rights struggle, as so much of the New Left did, there was a lot of suffering that went down, and people really didn't want to see that.

I dropped out of college, worked, went back to college, stayed active and in touch with people. SDS, at least in my college, got involved in draft counseling. I was involved in doing that for a while. Then I thought to myself: You know, what I don't want to really be about is telling students how to keep their deferments so young working-class guys get drafted to go off and die. That does not make a lot of sense; let's rethink this.

I thought about it and thought that what I really don't want to do is what I am doing now. I looked around and discovered that people were actually doing work with active-duty GIs. OK, we're telling you guys how to get legally out of a situation in which you are, so you don't have to die. That just leaves a big gap there.

SDS folks were doing the draft counseling. I looked beyond that. I had volunteered at the American Friends Service Committee [AFSC] switchboard during the convention of 1968. We were right down the hall from the Student Mobilization. So people were running in and out of the offices, and one of the groups of people that was doing GI work and having counseling training sessions was CAMP [Chicago Area Military Project], using the AFSC facilities. They did one training session and I was doing the switchboard, and then they did another training session, and I went away from the switchboard to sit in on the training. I thought: This is what I want to do. It just makes a lot more sense. Yes, you have to learn fucking rules and regulations, and there's a lot more about the uniform code of military injustice that I've learned that I never wanted to learn; but that seemed to make the most sense. That's how I got involved in doing GI work.

ANN HIRSCHMAN

Ann Hirschman became active in VVAW as a result of her work with the Medical Committee on Human Rights. She was interviewed in her home in Cranbury, New Jersey.

I grew up on Staten Island in New York. Staten Island is a Republican stronghold to the point where they didn't even go for Roosevelt any of the four times, OK? I mean, we are talking about somewhere to the right of John Birch. Anticommunism on Staten Island was a religious tenet. It went with going to mass on Sunday. These people think Democrats are a communist plot. I was fairly used to being outside the mainstream in that sense.

I was raised in the Jewish religion and also grew up in a very ecumenical family. We were taken to the house of worship of every possible available faith. I've been to mosques, I've been to tent revivals, I've been to Buddhist temples. I was a granddaughter and daughter of progressive people.

My grandmother, for instance, was an early advocate of birth control. She personally knew Margaret Sanger and was very willing to tell me when I was a young girl, like ten, that she knew Margaret Sanger and that if I ever felt uncomfortable about talking to my mother about the need for birth control, I should by all means come to her. She was the type of woman who when asked about homosexuality would mention that she never met an orgasm that she didn't like. [Laughs.]

My grandfather, my grandmother, and my father's parents all did what they thought was right and the hell with what the neighbors thought. I don't remember whether it was my mother or one of my grandmothers who, when confronted with "Well, what will the neighbors think?" said, "Think? That would be very refreshing." [Laughs.] So, I was raised to believe that it was perfectly OK to be unembarassed to do what you felt was right.

What was right based on?

Right was based on: All people are created equal, and that there is no more worth in the queen of England than there is in your garbage collector on any kind of level, and that most human beings are about 79 cents worth of chemicals, and their actions prove what they have inside them.

My dad was more conservative than my mother. He was more traditional as far as duty, honor, country. He went to military high school. He was in the Air Force in World War II. My mom did work for the secret service as a secretary during World War II—for the OSS then—which she has never spoken about. But when the civil rights movement began, and we began hearing things in like 1962, 1963, 1964, about what was going on in the south, my dad, even though he was very militaristic on some levels, was absolutely adamant that there should be no Jim Crow laws.

In 1963 I was sixteen. I went to the march on Washington [and] saw the "I have a dream" speech. I went with a bunch of friends from Staten Island. We had read about Martin Luther King. We knew there was a march on Washington, and we wanted to be a part of it and hear what was going on.

While I was not a "pink diaper baby"—there weren't any communist organizers in my house, no union people—my family was very unafraid. Nobody should be afraid of ideas. Nobody should ever censor a book. That was another big tenet of our faith, right up there with "Orgasms are a good idea." Ideas are good. Even to the point of learning about Nazis and how they thought, or learning about the KKK, or racists, or whatever. We were supposed to learn about them and understand them so that we didn't hate them. They thought, "If you understood it, you wouldn't go kill it." I'm real lucky.

Communism was not a threat in my household. My mom, early on—like in the 1950s— worked for HIP, Health Insurance Plan of New York. That was considered a communist organization. People were called before the Senate investigating committee.

Most of our neighbors, because of the economics of it, were blue-collar workers and were union. Half of them got called before HUAC. This was more like a mark of distinction [laughs] than it was a stigma in our house. "Oh, he went before HUAC. He must be a real brave person." It was never like, "He must have been a criminal."

Mom kept us out of school to watch the Army-McCarthy hearings, to watch the country get back in order. She thought that [Joe] McCarthy was the biggest danger that had come down the pike. She was not at all afraid of Russians under the bed, because she knew Russians and they weren't under the bed. She was pretty terrified of this stupid senator somewhere out of the midwest.

In high school . . . we're talking 1959 to 1963 . . . I went to the United Nations every day because there was a program in the New York City high schools whereby a couple of students from each borough each year were chosen to participate in a program where we worked for the United States Association for the United Nations with the likes of Eleanor Roosevelt and Adlai Stevenson and folks like that.

I got a sense of a worldview. I used to sit in at World Health Organization and UNICEF [meetings]. World Health was dealing with the effects of war. Not only the stuff that everyone knows about, like bullet holes and burn wounds, which I learned about in a more intimate sense when I was dealing with vets, but the aftereffects of war on the civilian population, which has always been a focus of mine . . . the epidemics, lack of access to medical care, how much access to medical care a war uses up.

Our teachers were people like Eleanor Roosevelt, and she was real clear. Those of us who weren't seeing it right away got hit in the face with her shovel, and if you didn't get it right off, she'd make you hurt. [Laughs.] Pain is a very good teacher. I stayed in this program my last three years in high school.

After high school, I went to college for a year and decided I was really interested in being a nurse and I went to nursing school. During that time, during vacations, I would be at civil rights demonstrations and stuff like that. I immediately got to be a medic because I knew first aid, in Mississippi, Alabama, wherever. [I] taught people to read, watched people get shot, got beat up, the whole thing. Good friends of mine got hurt and died later. [Takes a breath.] After that it was like the antiwar movement was a logical extension of that for everybody from Doctor King to Malcolm.

When did you become aware of Vietnam as an issue?

In 1965. Dave Dellinger. Vietnam Peace Parade Committee. I was in nursing school and started hearing about peace stuff while working with the Medical Committee for Human Rights, which I had connected with in the south. You heard about this stuff, and people were actually doing stuff.

I was against the war on principle because we were intervening in a civil war, which—again, having a worldview which came from the likes of Eleanor Roosevelt, there was a clear difference between civil war and international war. I was a lot more sophisticated, from that experience, than your average sixteen-, seventeen-, eighteen-year-old was in those years.

The first actions that I actually was involved with against Vietnam were 1967, the Pentagon, and [I] started getting involved with antiwar activists and came back and started working with the Vietnam Peace Parade Committee, Norma Becker, Dave Dellinger—good friends I still have from that era. I worked with SDS a little bit around the Columbia thing. I worked in the public health service in 1967. That was where I first met vets. We parted company because they kicked me out around 1969. I had sassed a colonel.

ANNIE BAILEY

Annie Bailey had already been active in the antiwar movement before joining VVAW in 1971. She was interviewed with John Lindquist at their home in Milwaukee, Wisconsin.

I was born in Cincinnati and raised in Milwaukee. My dad was an industrial designer and my mother did trade show coordinating and other advertising stuff. They were well-educated working-class.

The thing that was most important, on a consistent basis, was that the family spend time together doing something fun and learning something at the same time. We went to museums. We went to the art center. We went driving out into the country. My father would take us out to these historic buildings just to look at. My father always said, "Keep your eyes wide open. Never focus on one thing; you'll miss something. Hold your head up. Always look around you. It only goes by once."

My mother lived by Doctor Spock. They had very good instincts. They knew what they didn't want.

What do you mean?

Well, sort of uptight, never question authority, never speak to your parents about money, never question their judgment, they're the adults, you're the kid. . . .

They allowed that?

We'd get into it, but we had four rules. They never changed: You treat everybody like you want to be treated; don't touch anybody else's stuff without permission; do what you're told if you don't know any better; and always tell the truth. If you broke one of those rules, there were serious consequences. It wasn't beating, although occasionally we did get spanked. The punishments were more like a lecture. My father could go on and on and on forever. He would make you sit there and listen. To make sure you were listening, he'd make you repeat it back to him. He was intense.

We started out being religious. We went to North Shore Congregational. I was already into the civil rights movement in the early 1960s. Our church was involved in going down to Selma and Montgomery for the civil rights stuff. Jim Groppi was here and he was a priest here who had a big parish in the inner city, and he was plugged into the civil rights movement and he started the open-housing marches back in 1963. Politics crept into our church, and a bunch of families left when they fired our minister for ragging on rich people about filling the plate on Sundays and then going to their defense-contract corporations. The whole family walked out. That was it for organized religion. That was the start of my politicization.

I also have an uncle who's a communist. He gave me my first subversive literature on Eugene Debs in junior high school. He was a college professor. He came to visit my folks and he found me moping. He says, "What's the matter?" "I have to do a book report and don't even have a fucking book." He throws me this little paperback, a biography of Eugene Debs. He came through. I got into reading about stuff.

At the time when I first started participating, it was just to get into circulation with people who were away from my community that I was in. Whitefish Bay was very closed and affluent. My parents spent a lot of time trying to keep up with the Joneses. At that time, they believed there was a middle class. They understand now that that was all an illusion. But they bought into it hook, line, and sinker. My mother used to tell me to go to college and get a rich husband and you'll never have to work a day in your life. She regrets that now.

When I went to school they were saying: Just be glad because you're going to be a lawyer or a doctor. I'd say, "No way! I'm not going to college, I hate school." I loved to read. I loved to learn, but you had to go through so much bullshit to get to that point. That's what I didn't like. The rules and regulations, but also the flimflam teachers who didn't really give a shit, and the administrators who would screw things up, or the other students who were making what you were wearing and how big your tits were more important than what was in your head. If you didn't go with their line, then you were rejected. You were a misfit. You were an outcast. That happened to me, and I just wore it like a badge. The daydreams they were trying to sell me at Whitefish Bay high school were not real to me.

I moved away from my family and found something else to do. I started "straying" [sarcastically] when I was about fourteen. I was attracted to older kids. I lived in group houses, collectively. Everybody contributed whatever they could. I started hanging around the city—rock and roll, antiwar, open housing—and all that stuff was real to me.

What was real about it?

Well, because it was multicultural and there's a lot of guys [laughs], and girls love guys—especially older guys, college guys. Of course, I never stopped there, I went down to Northwestern train station on Friday nights looking for sailors from Great Lakes. During those times when I wasn't with my family, there were a lot of things that they had told me that proved to be true countless times. Those kinds of things helped me, when I was away from them, to make better judgments. Their growth tied into my growth. When I left the family fold and went out on my own, they opened themselves up to my ideas and my lifestyle. They didn't like it, but they really tried hard to learn what I was experiencing.

How did all of this tie in to Vietnam?

I had a really good friend who was a black guy from Cleveland who was stationed at Great Lakes. He was my first official date. I didn't tell my parents he was black. I had him come to pick me up at my house. I just wanted to see what they would do. They were great. They were fine about it. But two days after he turned eighteen, they sent him to Vietnam. He was killed about three months later. I lost my first friend in Vietnam in 1963. It was the summer before I was going into high school.

I knew war sucked. I knew how unnecessary it was. My dad was antiwar from just having been in World War II. He was a master sergeant. I'd say, "What did you do in the war, Daddy?" And he'd say, "I don't want to talk about it." My father had already told me it never solved anything, and it brings out the worst in people. He saw Americans abusing German prisoners. He saw what happened in little Italian towns. You go in, you find the best house in town, kick everybody out. You take it over, trash it, and do whatever you want with it. When I lost my first friend in Vietnam, we started discussing the implications of the war.

The antiwar movement and the civil rights movement were so mixed up together. I hung on every word from Dr. King all the time, and he was antiwar. Then good old Muhammad Ali . . . Cassius Clay changed his name and refused induction. I went to an antiwar demonstration at UWM [University of Wisconsin at Milwaukee] and met Groppi and some other people.

All this kind of stuff was going on and influencing me. The fair-housing marches were going on in the mid-1960s, SDS was forming on our campus here, and it was all kind of mixed up together. I got into the social whirl of the community. I went to demonstrations, and once I was there I was into it, but I wasn't an active person on planning committees and things like that. But I was also active in other ways. We were smuggling draft resisters from Chicago to Detroit and through Windsor into Canada. Because I was younger, I couldn't be charged with a federal crime. When you were underage, you had to do a little more underground stuff. You had to take more risks.

My attraction to veterans was less political; it was more practical. I was tired of having my boyfriends ripped away from me, being drafted and killed, gone and never seen again.

JEANNE FRIEDMAN

Jeanne Friedman became active in the civil rights movement while she was in high school and in the antiwar movement while she was a graduate student at Stanford University in Palo Alto, California. She became actively involved with Veterans for Peace (an independent organization of antiwar Vietnam veterans) in San Bernardino, California, in 1969. She was interviewed in a coffee shop in Chicago.

I grew up in New York City. I came from a pretty poor working-class family. My father put in window glass and my mother was a dressmaker who worked in the textile industry. I was raised as an orthodox Jew. My family was very religious. As I got older, I became less and less religious.

My parents were both union members, and I was taught early on to never cross a picket line. We would die before we would do that. All my aunts and uncles were union members—furriers, a butcher, and garment workers. Every member of my family and all our neighbors in the Bronx were Democrats. My first political activity was stuffing envelopes for Adlai Stevenson's presidential campaign. I didn't know there was a Republican Party until I was in junior high school.

I went to an all-girl junior high school which was fairly well integrated. Actually, one of the most important things that ever happened was my junior high school graduation. I was in the color guard because I was very tall. My best friend, whose name was April, was a black young woman. She was my first black friend—we met in the color guard. After graduation ceremonies—this would be 1956—the color guard went out with our teacher to celebrate at a local ice cream parlor: three white girls, one white teacher, and April, all dressed in white uniforms with blue ties. And they wouldn't serve us. After we just sat there for awhile, the teacher said, "We have to go now." We asked her why, and she couldn't explain it to us. I was absolutely shocked. A few years later, there was picketing of this store by civil rights groups, and I joined the picket line.

Being raised in a working-class environment, I thought everyone was in pretty much the same boat, and I had no familiarity with any kind of "left" analysis or politics until I got to high school and college.

I went to Bronx High School of Science. It was like a different world—for the first time, I met kids from all over New York City, kids who came from homes of great wealth and included the sons and daughters of New York intellectuals. Among them were kids who had very definite political ideas. I made friends with people who lived in Greenwich Village, who were into the jazz and folk scene. I started hanging out with those kids because they were the most interesting.

My two main high school activities were the school paper and working with the High School Committee for the United Nations, which I really believed in. I helped put out their newsletter and spent a lot of time at the UN [United Nations]. The civil rights movement was targeting several stores and restaurants in New York. When Woolworth's in the south would not serve black people, there were picket lines at Woolworth's in the north. There was also picketing of Schrafft's, the restaurant chain that wouldn't serve my junior high school color guard. I did that.

I went to City College of New York, which was located in Harlem. Some decades earlier, CCNY had the reputation of being the "little red schoolhouse." City College had served generations of immigrants' children and was one of the best colleges in the country. It was completely free. I was there from 1959 to 1963. And since there were a lot of students who were "red diaper babies," there were some overtly political campus groups—there was a

W. E. B. DuBois Club on campus, and they invited Malcolm X to speak every semester. I think I went to hear him every time he spoke.

The civil rights movement was the most important activity in the country, and there were several groups on campus that were active in bringing speakers, raising money, and recruiting. I joined picket lines around the city, which were usually solidarity pickets, and I wanted to go to the south. My parents were positive that I would be killed and absolutely refused to let me go.

What I didn't know at that time was what had happened to a cousin who was a few years older and in graduate school. Because of his research, he tried to get a security clearance and was denied because of his parents' activities. My aunt and uncle had joined an organization in support of Republican Spain, and the group was a Communist Party front group. So my family was pretty freaked out about any kind of political activity outside of the Democratic party. The legacy of McCarthy and fears for my safety were behind their objections to my going south.

Instead I launched into Fair Play for Cuba. I signed petitions, and when Fidel came to speak in Central Park after the victory of the Cuban revolution, I went to hear him. I didn't know very much about Cuba, but I knew enough to be against Batista. Initially, people talked about the Cuban revolution as a populist revolution, not a communist one. And what I was learning in school was that the United States often supported dictators. But my initial support for Castro was based on democratic values. I went to hear all kinds of speakers throughout New York. These were things I could do that my parents didn't know about.

When I graduated from college in 1963, I applied for a career position with the United States foreign service. My major had been in international relations; I was still very interested in the work of the UN; I wanted to travel; and I wanted the United States to make better foreign policy decisions than supporting dictators, which I thought I could influence. I passed the written exam and I flunked the oral. I was turned down because I was a woman—that's what the guy told me. He said, "What will happen is we'll do all this training and then you'll marry some other foreign service career officer and we will have lost all this training." So then I decided to go to graduate school. I went to Stanford.

Stanford was a very bizarre choice for me. When one of my teachers at City College suggested it, I thought he was talking about a school in Connecticut. At first, I didn't know it was in California. Stanford was at that time changing their predominantly western student population, and they were admitting more graduate students from the east and midwest. Coming from New York, Stanford was a complete shock. In 1963, it felt odd to be dark-haired on that campus—everyone else seemed to be blond-haired and blue-eyed. [Laughs.]

From the time I started graduate school, I was a teaching assistant. That's how my tuition was paid. One of my students was this young blond boy from Texas and he had never met a Jew before. He told me that one day after class. Just as a joke, I asked if he wanted to feel my horns. He said he would really like to. He was a really sweet kid, just a product of his upbringing. [Laughs.]

To be studying political science in 1963 was amazing. The country and world were on fire—the civil rights movement, the assassination of President Kennedy, a year later the Free Speech Movement at Berkeley, and the escalation of American involvement in Indochina. So this was a very radicalizing time to be a graduate student studying the forces of change. And Stanford was a good place to be in the sense that you got a very clear idea of what the opposing forces were. For the first time, I met people who espoused a political ethic that I didn't agree with in terms of international affairs and United States foreign policy.

My first year, I worked really hard, and in June they gave me a master's. I wasn't sure I wanted to continue with graduate school, but I liked being in California and I was moving to a little cabin in the woods, where other hippie-radical graduate students lived. Through one of my professors, I got a research job on a disarmament project at the Hoover Institution, probably the most conservative place on campus. Although my degree was finished, I was still able to take classes, and I was trying to save some money and figure out what to do next. Working at the Hoover was really the culmination of my political transition from liberal to radical. I was wearing my "Part of the Way with LBJ" button on election day, riding in the elevator with the head of the Hoover, who was an advisor to Goldwater.

When I left college, I didn't believe in the notion of a ruling class. At Stanford, I could see the links for myself. I came out of college as a liberal but within a couple of years began to identify myself as a radical.

In December of 1964, while I was at the Hoover, the Free Speech Movement in Berkeley exploded. Some Stanford students went up to Berkeley to find out what was going on. We felt that the press the FSM was getting was completely false, so we decided to put out a leaflet for Stanford students. The leaflet was called "The Truth About Berkeley." And at the bottom of this one-page flier we invited interested people to come to a support meeting. We were totally surprised when lots of people showed up.

We formed an ad hoc group of primarily graduate students and started doing solidarity work on the Stanford campus. We went up to Berkeley all the time, to sit in on meetings and to demonstrate. And we brought as much information back to Stanford as we could—published a regular newsletter and spoke at various forums on campus. We took the name of our group from a group at Berkeley. We began by being interested only in the issue of free speech but soon were swept into the beginnings of the antiwar movement—the Vietnam Day Committee. And when information about American involvement in Indochina began to spread around Stanford, there was the beginning of what would become a very strong antiwar movement.

It was clear to me as a graduate student that the most important thing I should be doing was working in that movement. My job at the Hoover wasn't what I had hoped, and I finished out my one-year contract. In a time of campus ferment, it seemed that graduate school was exactly the right place to be, so in the fall of 1965 I reentered Stanford.

Why did you object to American involvement in Vietnam?

I think it was for all the right reasons. By that time, I was much more sophisticated about Cuba and the history of American imperialism. There were these huge teach-ins at Berkeley and at Stanford. We were hearing from people like Bob Scheer, Noam Chomsky, Dave Dellinger—and I was reading. By that time, I had a very well-identified anti-imperialist position. My model for that position was Vietnam, and I was adamant that the Vietnamese people ought to be able to elect the government that they wanted. Because the United States government wasn't letting them do that, I began to see myself in opposition to the U.S. government. From 1966 to 1969 I pretty much did nothing except teach my classes and organize against the war.

LINDA ALBAND

Linda Alband grew up in a fairly conservative environment and became involved with right-wing political organizations in high school, though she did not consider herself a "hidebound conservative." She became an active member of VVAW in the fall of 1971. She was interviewed in a coffee shop in San Francisco, along with another member of VVAW, Sheldon Ramsdell.

My parents weren't involved in anything, so it was [a] rather nebulous background. In high school, I was involved in conservative politics, pro-Goldwater. We set up a group called Youth for Political Action, which was essentially Young Republicans, only we didn't call ourselves that. We wanted to appear like we weren't biased, even though we were. We didn't do much of anything, but we did sponsor some speakers and we were Republican-oriented.

I never was accepted in high school. I got a job at the Federal Reserve Bank out of high school because I didn't have enough money to go to college and people my age never accepted me. I ended up finally figuring out that the problem with acceptance wasn't me; it was them. I found friends elsewhere. And throughout the process of finding friends and meeting people, my ideas about a lot of things changed. So I don't think I was really a hidebound conservative. It was—there were certain things about Goldwater and that whole era that I thought were good things at the time that I was in high school. I never did trust LBJ [Lyndon Baines Johnson]. I mean, I always thought LBJ was a liar. You know, in some ways I trusted George Wallace more than a lot of other politicians, because if you're dealing with somebody out front you know how to deal with it. I think that's the whole rationale with supporting Goldwater and being a conservative at that point—a matter of knowing what's going on rather than having to deal with a pack of lies.

Interestingly enough, I wrote an antiwar term paper when I was a senior in high school, and I didn't even know it was antiwar. I had a copy, and I read it like a number of years later and thought: God, this is—you know—criticizing the war, and I hadn't even realized it at the time. It's just based on newspaper accounts, and so I was thinking, you know: All these politicians running for office, like Ed Muskie, say they didn't have enough information to critique the war at that point, when they had a hell of a lot more than I did. And I wrote something that critiqued the war, you know, just as a little high school student that didn't know what they were doing.

2

THE CITIZEN-SOLDIER GOES TO WAR

We had taken an oath to defend the government of the United States and the Constitution. What do you do when the government of the United States is the enemy of the Constitution? Where does your allegiance lie?

John Kniffin

Someone once said, "How could you change so quickly?" I said, "Well, it wasn't a question of changing quickly; it was a question of being in shock over taking the blinders off. When you take sunglasses off, the sun shines in: it doesn't trickle in, it doesn't take time, it all becomes bright." That's the same thing that happens once you get rid of the mythology that chains you down. You can see things because you're free. The contradictions were raised by people who had discussions with me—people who didn't spit on me, and who didn't call me baby-killer. It wouldn't have happened otherwise. I would have probably drank.

Barry Romo

The United States in Vietnam

It can be argued that Vietnam became a focus of American foreign policy makers during the first 25 years of the cold war because of the path to independence the Vietnamese people chose to follow. On this argument, the world of the cold war was bipolar—a struggle between the United States and the Soviet Union—and each nation had to choose sides; any nation that did not choose to remain in the American orbit would be considered an ally of the Soviet Union and thus a threat to the global interests of the United States.

On a global scale, then, Vietnam meant little, in and of itself, to those managing the war. Each administration involved in prosecuting the war confirmed this by stating, repeatedly, that the real issue in Vietnam was America's prestige. In 1964, to take just one instance, Walt Rostow, an adviser to President Johnson, said, "It is on this spot that we have to break the liberation war. If we don't break it here we shall have to face it again in Thailand, Venezuela, elsewhere. Viet Nam is a clear testing ground for our policy in the world."[1]

This, of course, is an example of the famous "domino theory." The free or uncommitted nations of the world were seen as a line of standing dominos; if any one of them was allowed to "fall" to communism, the next would also fall, and then the next, eventually bringing down the entire line. The mechanism operating here might be seen as a progressive weakening, or as each "fallen" nation becoming a model for others. Thus, American foreign policy makers would have felt that Vietnam could not be allowed, by falling to communism, to weaken the line of dominoes or to set an example for other third world countries. Whatever the reasoning, though, Vietnam became a formidable opponent—unlike, say, Guatemala, Nicaragua, Iran, or Indonesia, where the United States had been able to exert control during the postwar years by supporting proxy governments or by using clandestine operations to unseat governments considered "unfriendly."[2] One reason why Vietnam proved so resistant was, undoubtedly, that throughout its history it had fought off foreign powers seeking to dominate it. Centuries of resistance to foreign intervention had led to a strong anticolonial sentiment among the Vietnamese people, who came to view the United States, allied with South Vietnam, as simply another attempt at domination by a colonial power.[3]

The United States first became involved in Vietnam during the Second World War, when it supported Vietnamese efforts to expel the Japanese invaders. Although Vietnam had been a French colony since the 1860s, World War II had loosened the grip of the French: after France was invaded by Germany in 1940, Japan had quickly moved into Indochina. The Japanese occupation of Vietnam worsened the conditions of the Vietnamese, which were already deplorable, and was an impetus for the development of a well-organized resistance movement that included various segments of the population.

The struggle against Japanese control was led by Ho Chi Minh and the Vietminh—the Vietnamese Communist Party—which had been formally organized in 1941 to fight for independence. Ho Chi Minh and other Vietnamese leaders had previously been active against French colonialism, and they used that experience in their efforts to dislodge the Japanese. American agents of the Office of Strategic Services (OSS)—the forerunner of the CIA—were sent to Vietnam to provide covert assistance. However, these attempts did not succeed, and Vietnam did not become independent until after the war ended, in August 1945, with the surrender of Japan.

On September 2, 1945, Ho Chi Minh, as leader of the Vietminh, proclaimed Vietnam's independence in Hanoi, before a throng that included

American military personnel who were attending the festivities. Ho began his speech by paraphrasing from America's Declaration of Independence: "We hold truths that all men are created equal, that they are endowed by their Creator with certain unalienable Rights, among these are Life, Liberty, and the pursuit of Happiness."[4] Like many third world leaders of his generation, Ho was moved by the democratic ideals in the Declaration of Independence. He looked forward to developing a close relationship with President Truman and hoped that the Americans would support an independent Vietnam—a hope that was based not only on the aid the United States had provided during the war but also on its anticolonial rhetoric when the hostilities ceased.

The OSS agents who had developed close ties to the Vietminh now urged the State Department to cooperate with the new government in Vietnam. One agent, Major Archimedes Patti, who had worked with Ho Chi Minh during the war, sent a cable to the American embassy in Chunking, stating that Ho was not "a starry-eyed revolutionary or flaming radical, given to clichés and mouthing the party line." Patti said that his own aim was "to attain American support for a free Vietnam," but he found that nothing was done about his communiqué; he would say later, "All the information that people in the field passed to Washington ended in a dry well."[5]

What happened instead was that, despite Ho Chi Minh's expressed willingness to cooperate with the United States, the Truman administration refused to acknowledge Vietnamese independence. This was because of America's interest in supporting France:[6] before the end of World War II, French leaders had expressed an intention to regain control of Vietnam after the war, and American foreign policy makers wanted to support this attempt in order to ensure that the French would become part of the United States' efforts to rebuild an anticommunist Europe.[7]

From 1946 to 1954, then, the United States provided covert and overt aid to the French in Vietnam. But the attempts by France to reclaim Vietnam as a colony met with stiff resistance from a reinvigorated Vietnamese independence movement. During these eight years, although the French were able to maintain control of the southern region, they were never able to gain dominance over the northern half of the country, where the Vietminh held power. Despite financial support from the United States, France pulled out of Vietnam after suffering a decisive defeat at the hands of the Vietminh and their supporters at Dienbienphu in 1954.

This left Vietnam divided along the 17th parallel, with the Vietminh in control of the north while several factions vied for control of the south. The peace accord signed by the French and the Vietnamese in Geneva in July 1954 stipulated that national elections were to be held in 1956 and that Vietnam was to be reunified under a single head of state. The elections, however, were never held.

American foreign policy makers, who feared that Ho Chi Minh would win such an election handily, moved into Vietnam to forestall his victory: they should not, they believed, allow an avowed communist to take control of Vietnam. Also, although they had no evidence of any links between the Vietminh and the Soviet Union, American leaders assumed that Ho Chi Minh was a Soviet puppet intent upon fomenting revolution throughout southeast Asia.[8]

Essentially, it was to thwart Ho Chi Minh that United States created the government of South Vietnam, under the leadership of Ngo Dinh Diem, in 1954 and thereafter supported it: the Americans provided military, financial, and technical assistance to Diem in the hope that South Vietnam would become a strong anticommunist ally. Under Diem's control, the South Vietnamese government violated the Geneva treaty by refusing to participate in elections. As a result, Vietnam remained divided throughout the years of direct American involvement.

Diem's regime proved to be far from democratic. Diem, who was a Catholic in a predominantly Buddhist nation, had little support among the Vietnamese. He effectively destroyed the nation's traditional political processes by putting his relatives and cronies into positions of power; and he repressed opponents who viewed his rule as illegitimate and publicly called for his ouster. American economic support for Diem's government created corruption and commercialization in and around Saigon—the capital—while the majority of Vietnamese, who lived in the countryside, became further impoverished.[9]

Diem's unpopularity strengthened the anticolonial movement in Vietnam. By 1960, the National Liberation Front (NLF) had been formed to coordinate the political and military efforts of the opposition. The NLF was made up of diverse sectors of the Vietnamese population and was dominated, though not necessarily controlled, by Vietminh who had remained in the south after 1954.[10]

In response to the efforts to unseat Diem, American foreign policy makers increased their military and economic support for him—despite a growing sense among Americans on the ground that he and his government were corrupt and beyond redemption.[11] In public, the Kennedy administration continued to laud Diem for his commitment to democracy and his willingness to stand up to communist aggression. After visiting Vietnam in 1961 to assess American progress, Vice President Lyndon Johnson called Diem "the Winston Churchill of southeast Asia."[12]

An American military advisory force had been charged with training the Army of South Vietnam (ARVN). As insurgency against Diem spread, the size of this advisory force was increased. By 1961, 3,000 American advisors—who were authorized to fire back on NLF forces if attacked—were stationed in Vietnam. By the end of 1963, there were 16,500 American troops in Vietnam. President Kennedy also extended the war into North Vietnam in May 1961, by sending Special Forces troops north to carry out various espionage activities against Ho Chi Minh's government.[13]

Despite the increases in American aid and tactical support, the ARVN continued to lose the struggle against the NLF, which, although poorly equipped, was a highly motivated guerrilla force. The ARVN suffered a humiliating defeat at Ap Bac in January 1962; and in November 1963, the American foreign policy command—disturbed by the poor showing of the ARVN and by Diem's corruption, and embarrassed by the escalation of public protests against Diem among the South Vietnamese (these protests had included the immolation of a Buddhist monk)—supported a coup against the Diem government. Rather than questioning its policy in Vietnam, then, the United States persisted, believing that a change in personnel would solve these problems.

By mid-1964, the American role in Vietnam had changed dramatically. The Johnson administration, aware of the fact that American policies had been failing, was looking for a way to increase military involvement without seeming to contradict Johnson's campaign promise to keep the nation out of a "hot war" in Vietnam. Although Americans were, on the whole, deeply concerned with the cold war, they were unwilling to send American troops to the far reaches of the globe unless the security of the nation was threatened. Thus Johnson needed to present the war in Vietnam as a defensive measure, and he found a way to do this in August 1964, when United States naval cruisers in the Gulf of Tonkin were attacked—or were said to have been attacked (there was little if any evidence that the attacks actually took place). Johnson characterized the alleged attacks as an assault on American sovereignty, and Congress thereupon gave his administration what amounted to a blank check, the "Tonkin Gulf resolution": the American military presence in Vietnam could be escalated without any formal declaration of war.[14] As a result, the war entered a new and much more dangerous phase.

With this new mandate in hand—and the election behind him—Johnson began a bombing campaign called "Rolling Thunder" in the spring of 1965. Both North and South Vietnam were bombed, although until then direct military involvement by the North Vietnamese had been negligible. Along with this dramatic increase in the air war, there was also an increase in American ground personnel. American ground forces charged with actually engaging in battle had been introduced into the country in March 1965. With the massive buildup in troop strength that followed, the United States began to rely on citizen-soldiers. In the summer of 1965, Johnson authorized the conscription of 35,000 men monthly. The escalation of United States forces continued without interruption during the next three years, so that by the end of 1967, about 500,000 Americans were stationed in Vietnam. The average age of the American conscripts was nineteen.

To wage the war in Vietnam, the American military command relied on technological and military superiority. The air war initiated by Johnson, which would continue throughout the war, pulverized the country, indiscriminately destroying crops, animals, and people. Napalm, Agent Orange, and a variety of deadly antipersonnel weapons were developed and used in Vietnam. American ground troops also engaged in tactics that devasted the countryside: search-and-destroy missions, interdiction, harassment, and others. All this did not undermine the Vietnamese liberation movement, though; in fact, the increased American military involvement drew the North Vietnamese into a more direct role in the fighting.

Meanwhile, Americans were continually told that victory was at hand. President Johnson and the military commanders assured them that the United States would prevail against the poorly equipped communist-led insurgents. In 1968, however, this optimism was shattered by the Tet offensive.

On January 30, 1968, during a cease-fire to commemorate Tet—the lunar new year, Vietnam's most important holiday—forces of the North Vietnamese Army (NVA) and the NLF attacked dozens of South Vietnamese towns and military bases, taking the Americans and the ARVN by surprise. During the fierce fighting that ensued, considerable territory came under communist control: enemy forces even took the American embassy in Saigon and held it for a time—though only briefly—before it was retaken by American troops. Although the Americans were able to regain control of the areas seized during the Tet campaign, and although they inflicted heavy losses on the enemy, the unexpected outcome of the communists' initial assault convinced many Americans that the war in Vietnam was unwinnable.

By this point, American troops in Vietnam were increasingly disillusioned with the war—both its nature and the way it was being conducted—and civilian protesters at home were intensifying their attacks on Johnson's policies. As a result of this crisis in confidence, Johnson halted the bombing of North Vietnam and refused a request by General Westmoreland for further increases in military personnel.

Johnson also decided not to run for reelection; and Richard Nixon, who campaigned on a promise to end the war, narrowly won the presidential election in November 1968. Nixon assumed control of the war when he took office in January 1969. In the summer of 1969, he announced his "Vietnamization" policy: American ground troops were to be gradually withdrawn, and the United States would return to its earlier policy of giving the South Vietnamese forces financial assistance, training, and air support.[15] By January 1973, direct American military engagement in Vietnam was halted.

The Citizen-Soldier on the Road to Disillusionment

The antiwar veterans' accounts of their military experience cover virtually every phase of the war, every branch of service, every military rank, every geo-

graphical region in Vietnam, and various other American bases overseas. Thus their perspectives on the war represent an overarching critique of the military as well as the war itself. A veteran's transformation from an uncritical supporter of American foreign policy to a thoughtful critic of the war in Vietnam was, typically, a gradual process: it began in boot camp, was sharpened in Vietnam, and became fully developed only after the return home. For those few who had already questioned the United States' role in Vietnam before entering the armed forces, or had held strong views against the war, their military experiences only confirmed their deepest fears and served to strengthen their antiwar commitment.

"We're Backing the Wrong Side"

JAN BARRY

As a child in upstate New York, Jan Barry was steeped in military history and dreamed of going to West Point and making a career in the Army. He was well aware of the cold war and was ready to take up arms against the Soviet Union if that became necessary. He enlisted in the spring of 1962, as a step toward achieving his goals.

Jan Barry as an inductee.

In basic training, and then in radio school in Fort Benning [Georgia], my focus was entirely on how you get into West Point. At the end of radio school, everyone else in this class was sent to Germany or Panama; two of us were on orders to Vietnam.

When I got the assignment in 1962, I went to a library and couldn't find any book about Vietnam. Everything was in reference to French Indochina. When I got to Saigon, Tan Son Nhut Airport, the reception area was a bunch of World War II tents in a palm tree grove that looked exactly like a south sea island setting in World War II. There was no propaganda or no training, so people were thrown out into this country and had to find out for themselves what was going on.

The headquarters of my unit was in Nha Trang. It was an aviation unit that flies Canadian De Havilland bush pilot planes that land and take off in a very short space. It was also the Special Forces headquarters. We were the air force, in essence, for many of their operations.

I was to keep the radios working, which is not what I was trained to do. I was trained in infantry radios. Typical Army—you train in the infantry and they send you to an aviation unit. So I had on-the-job training.

Airplanes were held together with spit, baling wire, and chewing gum. People flew them until they crashed. You also realized that we were left with all the leftover equipment. You had helicopters, the banana-shaped helicopters from Korea, that literally came apart in midair, crashed, and killed people. We were using bombers left over from World War II that crashed because the wings came off in these dives. The most sturdy planes in this crazy arsenal were these little bush pilot planes that were not designed for military use.

This unit had airplanes stationed on airfields all over South Vietnam and in Thailand. They flew in and out of the airfields for repairs, R and R, beer runs. It was a combination of half serious military missions and totally frivolous things like beer runs and taking nurses up for rides with officers. In the middle of all that, people like me, who are enlisted men, have to pull night guard duty to supposedly protect all these people.

You had orders that you couldn't keep any ammunition in your rifle. They [the rifles] were locked up because I was told that guys had previously gotten drunk on Saturday nights and got into shoot-outs in the barracks. They never said this, but what became clear was they were afraid we would shoot the officers. Somebody almost did one night. I think they were also afraid that somebody would shoot a civilian and it would be an international incident. So there was some practical reason, but there was also the problem of being in a war zone and not having access to your weapons.

You were in this ridiculous Mickey Mouse situation, like play-acting, in which you're on guard duty but your weapon isn't loaded. This is an M-1, by the way. This is a World War II rifle.

We got blown out of bed one night, about three A.M. It turned out that they [the NLF] had come through the wire and were blowing up airplanes. There were Vietnamese guards outside the perimeter and American guards on the interior perimeter where our airplanes were. All the guards started shooting like crazy, although they had no idea what they were shooting at. It sounded like you were in the middle of World War II. We couldn't get access to our weapons because it was Saturday night and the person who had the key to the conex box—which was a big steel box where all the weapons were locked up—was downtown shacked up with his girlfriend.

What was your impression of the Vietnamese?

We referred to the Vietnamese as "mama-san" and "papa-san," which is from occupation duty in Japan. We referred to them as gooks, which is even further back, in reference to Chinese or other Asians. There was nothing really to refer to Vietnam in and of itself.

Most GIs I was with could not have found the place on a map or, further-more, could have cared less. They go where they're sent. They had no idea how we had come to have a relationship with this country. It was kind of like: We must have taken over this place sometime in the past and kind of forgot about it, and now it's gotten out of hand. Nobody had enough sense of his-tory to put any of this together.

A lot of us really liked the Vietnamese who we met [and] we got to become friends with. In some cases, you got invited to homes, you met larger fami-lies. There was an interpreter in our unit, who—because several of us were treating him friendly—took us home and told us a lot. This guy spoke French, German, Chinese. This guy had been an interpreter for a lot of dif-ferent people coming through. [Laughs.] They were all scared to death of the Saigon government. This was supposed to be our arsenal of democracy. You began to realize what it feels like for these people to live in a police state. They say the wrong thing, they disappear.

Then we had our allies, the South Vietnamese Army, who—even before it had happened to me—I had been told would turn around and shoot at you. Indeed, when they had martial law declared after the Buddhist demonstra-tions began in May of 1963, on two occasions, guards leveled their weapons at me and other GIs that I was with. I think they were mad because Ameri-cans were going out with their women.

We were told that Madame Nhu [Diem's sister-in-law], representing the government, had said all kinds of nasty things to Americans in Saigon, imply-ing that she didn't think that we should have anything to do with their peo-ple socially. We were under some kind of orders not to fraternize with the women, which everybody broke. We particularly were not supposed to dance with them. You could go to a bar where you could pick up all kinds of pros-titutes, but you couldn't dance with them.

What was your impression of the enemy?

The only thing the Vietcong had were old French rifles [and] crossbows. Every once in a while, they would find a helicopter had crashed because it had been hit by an arrow. When they got their first machine gun, I think it was around May of 1963, everyone was laughing in the operations room. They put an X on the map on some mountaintop way the hell out there. Everybody was, "Yeah, sure, they got their first machine gun, hah, hah, hah! Right!" Nobody took them seriously as a military force. There was no sense of dire danger. It was a big fucking adventure.

It became clear at a certain point that if we didn't bother the NLF, they didn't bother us. There was no real danger that somebody was going to knock you off unless you went out there and continued to press it. If we started pushing it, they came in and blew up our airplanes.

I spent an awful lot of time talking to officers and sergeants about the military. Here I am with people who were through some of the worst shit in World War II and Korea. The top professionals the military's got to send out to this end of the world are shaking and scratching their heads. This was crazy. This did not make any sense compared to their previous experience.

The ones who were the real gung-ho professionals, who were out there pressing it, came back very disillusioned. They kept saying, "We're backing the wrong side. The other side is raising the right issues on behalf of the people here, and the side we're backing is a dictatorship." One day, I was speaking to a Special Forces sergeant, and he said, "I been out there; we're supporting the wrong side." He said, "These [NLF forces] out there, who are from the south, that didn't come from anyplace else, are responding to these legitimate grievances that these people have against the Saigon government." He explained the whole thing to me. He put the pieces together. He says, "When you go out there, these villagers' only protection is the NLF against this police state in Saigon. What we're here for is the palace guard of a police state." He did not like to be a protector of a police state, which was the first time anybody ever said that in so many words. I had enough understanding of things to understand that part of it, and you could see for yourself that in essence, we were supporting this rotten dictatorship.

It became very clear that what was being claimed in Washington and out of Saigon headquarters had nothing to do with what we could see for ourselves. McNamara [Robert McNamara, secretary of defense] and various other VIPs would come through, and there were warnings that no one was to tell these people what was really going on. I had also heard from people who had been stationed in South Korea, Turkey, and other places that this was not unusual, that we had two different agendas: one for the public and what the real agenda was.

Slowly, one by one by one, everything was undermined as to the presumed reasons we were there. We were devastating the shit out of these little people, for what purpose? After some of them became your friends, you had to think about what was your purpose. We weren't in any way helping these people.

So you say, Wait a minute—what is it that I'm supposed to be doing as a military professional, being honest with the public and protecting this country, or playing subterranean games that have other agendas that most people are not aware of? If they can't tell the public, I'm suspicious of what's going on here. I had no other context in which to put any of this. There wasn't a book around you could get a hold of and read any of this stuff. I didn't know there was a peace movement. I had to make a decision as a twenty-year-old person in the middle of a military culture. This didn't make sense in my life. When I got a hold of *Catch-22* [by Joseph Heller] sometime during that period, maybe when I got out, I said, "That's it! That's the way it is."

I spent ten months [in Vietnam] until somebody discovered that I had been selected for preparatory school for West Point. I didn't change my mind about going to West Point until I got to West Point. I'm twenty-one years old; not only isn't it what I expected, I had questions I never expected in my life to have.

I wore a combat patch on my right arm. If you've been in a war, you get to wear one of these things. It was highly unusual at that time and place for a PFC to be given a medal for the work I did in Vietnam. When people saw me wearing this thing, they would say, "Where the hell did you get that? What war have you been in?" I remember a colonel stopping me and saying, "Son, what war you been in? Vietnam? We're fighting over there?" They had no idea back here, even in the military, of what was going on in that part of the world. I was always asking how this fit together strategically. I began to realize that there was no strategic vision. It just didn't make sense, what the military was doing. If the real threat was the Russians, why are we escalating the war in Vietnam?

They were also expecting a much bigger war. They told the class of 1968 that I was in that "you would be leading platoons in combat in Vietnam; prepare for it now." That was not being told to the American public. This was the summer of 1964, when Johnson was saying he's the peace candidate.

I had to really think hard about the consequences of continuing to be a professional soldier. The first thought that came vividly to my mind is that [if] I go back as a platoon leader, I've got 40 young kids to keep alive in a situation that didn't make sense for the professional. My thought of trying to keep them alive was that this was an impossible situation. To what purpose?

I thought, Do I want to spend another 30 years of my life being involved in things where we can't tell the public the truth?—where you're out in the field and can't tell superior officers what's really going on, where the people with the most experience say it's crazy. And when you're at a place like West Point, where I thought the idea was to examine the military closely and learn better, they don't even want to know what the details are in Vietnam. They'll take care of it when they get over there. Sure did—right. The disaster, in my mind, was not nearly as big as it turned out to be.

But if they were communists?

So what? I was at least sufficiently aware that we were not making this same crazy assault on eastern Europe, where there was a real communist oppression going on. This wasn't dealing with the Russians as the main threat. It wasn't resolving any of the problems in southeast Asia, by the way. People were dying of bubonic plague right outside our barbed wire, and we did nothing to mount a public health campaign.

In Vietnam you had what clearly was a civil war in the south. North Vietnam could just disappear from everybody's mind at that point. It was not even a factor, for all the rhetoric. It was a homegrown rebellion with weapons that they could use or grab. They dug up the rifles from the previous war, or stole them. They weren't being supplied from the north. In fact, a friend of mine was with an advisory unit in the delta in 1964. He said after the Gulf of Tonkin craziness, they got supplied in retaliation.

In the fall of that same year, an upperclassman comes to me and says, "Mr. Crumb, what do you think about the North Vietnamese attacking our warships?" I thought to myself, I don't believe that it happened. They had more sense. They were fighting a guerrilla war. There was no way that they were going to go out in these tiny boats and attack these huge warships. I didn't say it to this guy. I didn't really know him, and I didn't have any basis other than my own experience, but I didn't believe this was the real story.

By that time it had become clear to me that our relationship to Vietnam was inauthentic in a number of ways, [rather] than what was claimed officially. When they made various official claims, by that time, I'm saying, yeah, sure. But I couldn't say that in the setting. I was caught in a situation in which I could have these interior thoughts and they kept building up.

The other factor that turned me off from West Point was: They told that incoming class that hazing had been outlawed; anybody who was subjected to any kind of hazing was to turn in anybody who did it. Well, one of the people that I knew very well in the Army was hazed. He reported it, as he was supposed to. The upperclassmen all lied, and he was thrown out.

There was super-harassment and stupid petty things like memorizing all kinds of trivial bullshit. They would trip you up because you couldn't possibly memorize all this bullshit. There was something called "beast barracks" that was really heavy harassment. You'd have to do all this changing into uniforms five times in five minutes, walking around with a rifle on your shoulder for hours at a time; you had to march around the classes in this bracy way; you had to march into the eating areas and get harassed the whole time you're eating; and on and on and on. None of this was teaching anyone to be a soldier. What they were doing was psychologically breaking people, but they couldn't break down people who had already been in the military several years.

I had an ulcer attack walking out of this dining hall one night while they were screaming at me. They did some tests and determined it was an ulcer. I was in the infirmary a couple of days. This doctor comes in, who looked rather strange for an Army doctor. He says to me in this very indirect way, "Well, I know a man who used to take his wife for Sunday drives and have picnics along the road to Da Lat," which is way the hell out in the country in Vietnam. It's a resort area for the Saigon elite. He said enough other kinds of things to make me realize he was talking about himself. He had already been in Vietnam.

He said, "And then there was this young fellow who wants to go to West Point. He gets his whole town behind him and letters of recommendation. He gets there and it's not the right place for him. He can't stomach this. He literally can't stomach it." He tells this story. A parable. He realized exactly the situation I was in. I was in the wrong place and couldn't even realize that I had a choice. I didn't have to stay there.

I instantly knew what he was telling me. You have a choice. You don't have to take this shit. I mulled that over, submitted my resignation, and got the response: You can't resign. Another colonel tells me, "We've invested too much in you. You're one of the people we're pushing at the top of this class. You're on the fast track here."

I said, "I'm leaving." I started doing in essence what was a sit-down in some kind of fashion, without knowing a thing about the civil rights movement. I no longer braced, for example. No one was going to mess with me anymore.

Where did your questioning attitude come from?

I grew up in a typical small town in upstate New York, which is close to New England values—where individuals are not lockstep automatons. . . . George Washington's soldiers questioned him closely. When they didn't like things, they rebelled, whether it was that they weren't getting paid, or fed, or whatever. So I grew up with both traditions of the military as this great American tradition and, on the other hand, you rebel when you're mistreated or even on behalf of everybody being mistreated. You say no. I'm not going to participate.

I was the tenth in that group of 50 [Vietnam veterans] to resign. It wasn't just my own impression that there was something wrong with West Point's training of cadets. [But] I had to make that [decision] in total isolation, not knowing that nine other people had made the same individual decision.

I had been told since I was in high school by various teachers, "You should be a writer." It's something I never took seriously. It's something I did for myself. At that point, it became: I'll write the story that reveals all of this. So what I said in my official resignation was that I was resigning to become a writer.

I left in November [1964]. I still have to go back in the Army and finish my enlistment. I ended up at Fort Rucker, Alabama, from December through May of 1965, in an infantry unit being utilized to work out the helicopter assault tactics in Vietnam. Vietnam was definitely heating up. In March of 1965, the first big Marine units went in to secure a beachhead around Danang. These guys were being readied to go to Vietnam in the bigger assault units. Of course, they didn't want to hear about anything. I had no intention of going back. I was getting out in May.

All of a sudden, they sent troops into Santo Domingo. These guys in this unit are breaking out illegal guns, Swedish K's and machine guns they're not supposed to have, all looking forward to rushing into another country where there's a war going on. They don't even know what the hell the issues are. I think, Oh, God, how soon do I get out of here? I've got one more month, this is going on, and I could end up in this craziness.

My commanding officer says, "You're sure you don't want to stay in the Army? I'll make you a sergeant." It was, like, I'm leaving it. Good-bye, folks.

"It Was a Horror Show"

LEE THORN

Lee Thorn received his draft notice shortly after he had dropped out of college. He went into the Navy, but he had already developed questions about the nature of the war, after having spent some time with friends in Berkeley who had come to oppose it.

I was in a squadron with 1,400 guys. I had the worst evaluations of anybody in the whole squadron because of the political shit. They didn't trust me. I didn't have a great attitude. I hated it the minute I got in.

What was it about the Navy that turned you off?

I was a little older than most of the guys. I felt like they were trying to take my identity away from me, trying to turn me into a number, so I tried to resist them. I got into some trouble.

I had been assigned to a goodwill tour to go around to the far east, Australia, Thailand. The next thing I know I got pulled off of that and put on the *Ranger* [an aircraft carrier], which is on its way to the Gulf of Tonkin. I had written Christmas cards to my family and other people, saying that I was going to Vietnam, with "Peace on earth; goodwill toward men." I was serious. That's how little I knew.

I go over there in December of 1965. I didn't really do personnel once I got on the ship. I started working nights. I was there till we came home September 1st, 1966. So it's like 10 months.

I got there, and they immediately detached me from the Airborne Early Warning Corps—which is these radar planes—to A-4 Squad, which is a bomber squad. I was the radio monitor for that squad, so it was my job to pass information that came through the comm from the CO of the ship to CO of the bomber squad.

We were there about maybe six weeks; then the first guy from my squad died. I hated it. The first guy that died was the guy I had gotten to know; I'd heard about his family—so I decided not to get to know people.

Then the second guy died and then a third guy died. He got cut in half at the waist. So then I stopped going out on the hangar deck. I got in big trouble, so they put me on the flight deck, in the bomb loader. The flight deck is the most dangerous place to work in the world. More guys die there. Just about everybody that works there regularly gets hurt. I was up on the flight deck when these guys missed the flight deck right off the side. I watched those guys drown. So I stopped going on the flight deck.

We ended up participating in the firebombing of Haiphong. This was like in May or June. This was a really big deal. There were B52s coming in from Guam and Thailand, tactical bombers coming in from everywhere—from South Vietnam and Thailand, and also from the ships. I showed the movie of what we did to Haiphong. It was part of my job. It was to show the pilots how they'd done. After seeing what we did, I just totally couldn't take it. [Shifts in his seat and looks increasingly uncomfortable and agitated.]

What was it about that movie that horrified you?

It was just the horror of it. It was brutal. This was a terror attack against the city. We set firestorms. It was like Nagasaki, you know—like firestorms where the air burns. The oxygen gets burned up because it's such intense heat from so many bombs dropped in one area. It was also obvious that someone had made a decision. . . . They didn't give a fuck about who we killed or what the military significance was. I could not ignore the fact that this war was just about killing. It was a horror show.

Things had sort of been building up. When the first guy died it was like . . . [Bangs his fist on the table next to his chair.] By that time you I couldn't ignore what I was involved in. We were in hell.

I know a lot of guys were numbing out. The pilots weren't all that enthusiastic about it. Most of them were trying not to go to primary targets, except unless they were doing tactical support to troops. This is really hard—I have

PTSD, officially 30 percent. [That is, 30 percent disabled.] I get disability . . . [Struggling to continue.]

Anyway, I got out and two weeks later I was back on Berkeley campus. It was in the fall of 1966. I was totally antiwar.

"I Made Promises to Dead People"

JACK McCLOSKEY

Jack McCloskey served as an Army medic between 1962 and 1966; in 1965, he was sent to Santo Domingo. He was recalled from the active reserves in July of 1967 for duty in Vietnam. By this time, he had met a woman with strong antiwar convictions and had developed serious reservations about the war; nonetheless, he reported for service.

I remember going to Camp LeJeune in North Carolina. They tried to send me through field medical service school again. In the morning you learned about first aid and all that shit, and in the afternoons it was like Marine Corps boot camp. Every Navy corpsman that's attached to the Marines gets intensive weapons training. The first time I went through, in 1963, I learned how to shoot an M-14. I learned how to shoot a .45; I learned all that bullshit.

During the second time, when it came to picking up a rifle, I refused. I said, "No, I can't do this." I got called a coward. I got kicked out of field medical service school and they cut me orders for Vietnam.

I had one week here before I went to Travis Air Force Base. I remember coming to San Francisco at the end of the summer of love and walking around with a Marine Corps haircut and meeting some people, letting them know I was in the service, walking on Haight Street, and some people saying, "You shouldn't go," and other people sharing joints with me. I remember that feeling of that week, and even though it was the hard time, I loved it. There was a part of me that said, Well, maybe I'll stay here. But again there was that other part of me. So I went. I got there at the end of September 1967.

What were your first impressions in Vietnam?

There was a lot of racial shit in Vietnam—in the rear especially. We'd go into Danang, and we'd see rebel flags and this bullshit. In the field, at least in my company, there was no racial tension whatsoever. I'd say 60 percent of my company was third world, Hispanic or black, and Native American. The rest were poor whites.

I was in an outfit that saw a lot of combat, from the day I got there to basically the day I left. My first six months we operated right outside of Danang, this place called Nano Bridge; then Hill 55 and a lot of operations into Happy Valley—these types of places. Lots of combat.

What was that experience like? How did it affect you?

I remember the first guy I treated [voice cracks; tears in eyes]—a nineteen-year-old Marine who stepped on a bouncing betty. I remember running up and him saying, "Doc, doc, I'm going to live, ain't I?" I said, "Sure, babe," and he died. I remember crying, holding his hand, and crying. I cried at the next one, I cried at the next one, and I cried at the next one, until I got to a point where I wanted to either jump up and shoot myself or shut down.

Inevitably you get close to people in Vietnam. I got close to people, and they got killed. At that point, Vietnam had robbed me of one of the greatest human dignities a person can have—that's the ability to cry; that's the ability to feel. It got to a point where I didn't want to know where guys were from in the company. I didn't want to know their backgrounds. If they get hurt, I'll treat them; just don't talk to me.

There was also, though, in Vietnam . . . [Breaks down.] I have never, ever, in my life, had a family like that, and that family was destroyed. When you're on the line like that, sharing like that, when your life depends on the other person and his life depends on you, you become so close. If I could gain that feeling now, that tightness that I had in Vietnam, I would do anything for that; but I can't get it anymore back here, and that's where the love-hate relationship comes in.

Even to this day—I'm almost fifty years old, and I still have a problem with intimacy. My ex-wife told me that it was easier for me to love a Vietnam veteran than it was to love her. I'm not talking about the sexual end; I'm talking about being close.

I think my hardest time in Vietnam was in this one operation called Allenbrook. We got literally wiped out. What sticks out in my mind after the battle is putting people in body bags.

There were three of us who used to hang around together, all three of us medics: this guy Casey from a little town in New Jersey, and this black guy named Allen from Birmingham, Alabama. The three of us were tight, and we all had nicknames. I was Plastic Man, Casey was Mike the Mongoose, and Allen was Super Chuck. Both of them got killed. Casey got killed during Allenbrook, and then two weeks later Allen got killed. Both of their deaths hit me hard. It was not death in the sense of death, because I saw that all the time. It was—when Casey got it, a part of me died. When Allen got it, another part of me died.

I got hit twice. I got hit right below my knee, and I got shrapnel in my face and arms. When I got hit in the knee, I left the field for about a week. When

I got hit in the head, I didn't leave the field until we pulled back from the operation.

In February or March, right before the Tet offensive, I came to Hawaii for R and R and Lydia [his wife] met me there. Because of her Quaker background and connections, I could have gone to Sweden, Canada, France, come back to the states, gone underground. I remember the last night, she and I had a big fight about this. I had to go back to Vietnam, even though I was against the war.

Why?

This had become my family. By the time I returned to Vietnam, I was the senior medic in the company. There was a part of you that was God in Vietnam. You had to choose who would live and who would die. I went back because I thought I could make a better choice. I sometimes feel that was arrogance on my part. I felt that I was a very good medic. I did everything from tracheotomies to suturing people.

My last six months in Nam were with a helicopter assault battalion. We never had a base camp. We were aboard this ship called the *USS Tripoli,* and we would go all over, from Danang up to the DMZ, from three days to 30 days. We never knew where the fuck we were going. I remember being back on ship, never in the field that much. I'd start thinking of Casey and Allen, remembering the good times, and I'd start shaking. I started using morphine. As a medic, I had an unlimited supply. I never mainlined; it was always in the asscheek or arm. Under that medication, I was able to remember the good times we had. I could get away from the horror. I could get away from their deaths.

I got out in 1968. I had been highly decorated—I got a Silver Star, Bronze Star, and Purple Hearts in Vietnam. I had seven months of active duty left. I was stationed at Hunter's Point naval shipyard [in California]. There was only about 250 military personnel; the rest were all civilian shit workers.

I started to let my hair grow a little bit long. I remember every Friday we'd have an inspection and the Navy commander of the shipyard would come by and shake his head, saying, "McCloskey, get a haircut." "Sure, captain, never." [Laughs.]

I had been back less than two weeks and they had this big antiwar march in October of 1968. I marched in that. I was tired of the horror of war. I had made promises to dead people that this shit wouldn't happen again. I remember getting up on the podium and people getting up before the podium and saying, "Killer, killer, killer." Right then and there, the antiwar movement totally turned me off.

I'd say from July of 1969, when I got out of the service, to September 1969, I never talked to anybody. Nobody. I then went to school at City College here [New York City], getting my A.A. degree [an associate's degree]. I never mentioned to anybody in school that I was a Vietnam veteran. Until I got involved, all I would do was go to school and get drunk, go to school and get drunk. I was not involved in anything. It wasn't until Kent State and Cambodia that I started getting active again. When they turned the guns against their own people here at Kent State, when I saw American people believing the lies about Cambodia, that was it.

What compelled you to speak out? Why not just go on with your life?

When you're in Vietnam, you dream—dream about your girlfriend, dream about your wife—but you're dreaming of what it was before you left. When we came back to the world, it wasn't the world we left: your girlfriend's changed, you've changed—even though you don't think you've changed—so you go through this psychological "Hey, what the fuck is this back here in the world? This is the world I fought for?" I come back. I don't understand it; it doesn't understand me.

In Vietnam you came back as an individual. Seventy-two hours before, you're in combat. Seventy-two hours later, you're here in the world. What you learned for survival in Vietnam are not the norms for survival back here in the world. The Vietnam vet came back to a society, most especially to those among our own peer group, that in a lot places in a lot of ways rejected them.

What do you do if you're eighteen or nineteen and you're from Harlem, you're a good machine gunner, you're a good medic, you're a good squad leader, you're a good mine-detector person, you're a good this, you're a good that? What do you do? For the first time in your life, you've been given responsibility, and you do a good job—and even if that good job means killing people, you've done a good job. [Then] you come back home, and you're just another nigger again?

You have to remember [that] the anger, the frustration, the alienation, that a lot of veterans came back with, to me are signs of sanity, not insanity. How else could you react to that situation?

This is why I'm very very proud that a lot of vets didn't fucking go off, didn't come back and start killing people, even as hurt and as painful as it was for them, they came back and didn't take their revenge out on the American public. In fact, they came back trying to change it.

You've got to remember that we were promised that if we go fight this war, we've got all this shit—we've got education, all these jobs waiting for us when we come home. What did it turn out to be? Bullshit.[16] So I think it was a combination of seeing the war itself and understanding what that was about, and the other part of it, I think, for most white veterans that joined VVAW, was the shattering of the American dream. "I was given all these promises. I come home and they're not there."

I remember, when I first came back from Vietnam, trying to talk to my father, who had served in the Second World War; trying to talk to my uncles, who had all served—but when I questioned my war, they thought I was questioning their war. They didn't want to hear it. I'm saying to them, "I'm not questioning your war. What you taught me, believing in America, believing in the Bill of Rights, I still believe in. The difference is [that] now I know my country can be wrong, and because I love my country, I want my country to start looking at that Bill of Rights." We did what we did because we loved our country and wanted our country to realize that it made mistakes. I am just as patriotic as my father or my uncle or anybody.

"It Was a Process"

JOHN KNIFFIN, TERRY DuBOSE, TOM WETZLER

John Kniffin—who was interviewed with Terry DuBose and Tom Wetzler in Austin, Texas—grew up in west Texas and was attracted to the heroic image of the soldier, especially as portrayed in the movies by Audie Murphy; in fact, he joined the Marines not only to serve his country but because he wanted to be like Murphy.

John Kniffin (JK): My first tour was kind of an accident. I was assigned to teach officers [at] basic tank school at Camp Del Mar [part of Camp Pendleton in California], and I have a problem with officers. I ended up getting in trouble and I was given a choice. I could join the Fifth Marine Division, which was forming up, or I could go to classroom instruction. I figured being in a tank with four of those idiots was bad enough; being in a classroom with 73 of them would be intolerable. I think I'll opt for the Fifth Marine Division. It's a boot outfit; all I'll have to do is walk around with a coffee cup in my hand and supervise while all the recruits do all the work. Sounds like a plan.

I come in from leave half drunk one night; everybody's packing shit in seabags. I said, "What's going on?" "I don't know, sarge. They say get all your shit together and get on the tracks." Next thing I know, we're on the boat and sailing over to the land of the setting sun.

We went in in March 1965. I'm going in with the Third Battalion, Ninth Marines; part of what the Marine Corps calls BLT, battalion landing team. We're sitting off the coast of Vietnam. When we got the order that we were going in to hit the beach at Danang, all our lifers are giving us all this shit about, "This is where we're going to find out about whether or not your Marine Corps training took. It's not going to be any joke."

We're sitting there, heads facing our machine guns, checking our weapons for the three-millionth time. We're watching from the deck of the LSD [landing ship dock] with binoculars, don't see any firefight going on, don't really see anything going on. Nothing seems to be happening.

The tanks were the last to hit the beach. We move the tanks in, and there's all these Vietnamese civilians there selling soda pop, candy, their sisters; girls with flowers; and a big banner that says, "Welcome American Heroes," crap like that. We're looking at the lifers, saying, "You paranoid fucks, what's the matter with you?"

It was a big joke initially. It seemed like the NLF or VC [Vietcong] or NVA did not want to screw with the Americans initially. In general, they seemed to hope that if they left us alone, we would just go home. Then they decided that we were not going to go away and they were going to have to deal with us. It wasn't until August and Operation Starlite that there was any heavy action. [This was first major American operation using armor, August 1965.]

Initially, I was there during the "hearts and minds" phase, and I left during the "you get them by the balls and their hearts and minds will follow" phase. Our mission initially was to protect the Danang Air Force Base. We were doing good things. We'd go into the villages, set up regional defense forces, Medcap programs, build hospitals and clinics, help ensure sanitation, give them soap, give them medicine, and stuff like that. All of us were involved in it. That was the nature of Marine Corps involvement in the early phase.

How did you feel about that? Was this what you figured a Marine would be doing, giving out toothpaste?

JK: I didn't have any problem with it; I thought it was kind of neat. We were over there generally trying to help these people in this poor primitive nation that's about 2,000 years older than ours. [Sarcastically.]

Then Westmoreland's theory was that the Marine Corps didn't get any kill ratios going on in I Corps. We needed to get kill numbers up and kill figures back to Washington. Our tactical areas of responsibility started expanding, getting bigger and bigger and bigger. The combat during 1965 was mostly boring until August, and then things started to get heavy. Then 1966 was pretty serious and 1967 was even more serious and Tet in 1968 was terrorizing.

There was also some kind of shit originally in 1965, where your mail franking privileges and your combat pay were established by being outside an established firebase for at least seven days a month or some shit like that. Like the Air Force dudes at Danang didn't get combat pay because they weren't in a hostile area. If you were outside the wire, you did get it. My platoon commander wanted us outside the wire so that we got the extra money and the mail franking privileges. So we'd go on little missions and take S-2 scouts on the tanks and run around looking for trouble. Sometimes we'd find it, sometimes we wouldn't.

My first firefight is a big joke. We got fired on by two kids with a bolt-action French rifle left over from World War I. You've got to understand, an adult Vietnamese looked like he was about fifteen years old, and a fifteen-year-old looked like he was about nine. That's what we were seeing. We ended up expending 12 rounds of 90-millimeter and 5,500 rounds of subcaliber—that's 50-caliber and 30-caliber. We got one confirmed kill, and the tank ran over that. That was a big joke in I Corps.

How did that make you feel?

JK: Made me feel bad. Made me feel even worse the more I saw it. I mean, we're killing babies over there.

What if they're communists?

Terry DuBose and Tom Wetzler joined John Kniffin in answering this question. Terry DuBose had gone into the armed forces after finishing college, because he could not find a job—he found that many companies were unwilling to hire and train draft-age men. Unlike John Kniffin, he was not a front-line soldier; he served in III Corps, spending most of his time "in the rear with the gear." Tom Wetzler served as a medic.

Terry DuBose (TDB): I didn't see any communists.

Tom Wetzler (TW): They didn't look like the commies we had seen in the movies. They looked different. The commies in the movies have beards. They have a sinister look about them. . . .

JK: You know what Karl Marx looks like—come on. [Laughter.] They're drooling. They got a baby on the end of their bayonet.

But some of the political ramifications affected me more than the combat. Our initial mission was to go in with these Medcap programs and CAT [Combat Assistance Team] programs, but then we received word that the Vietnamese people need to have confidence in their own government. Therefore, we can't deal directly with them; we have to deal with local province administrators, which were generally ARVN colonels and shit like that.

That meant that all of a sudden, we weren't building hospitals and clinics; we were building villas for some scumbag. The C rations that we were giving were in turn being sold back to the Vietnamese people.

They were clearing areas for free-fire zones. We were relocating people from areas where they had been farming for generations and telling them, "If you come back, you will be shot"; and they would put them in concentration camps at Cam Lo and places like that, feed them some rations, and let them sit around in tarpaper shacks, watch the trucks go by, have their women turn into prostitutes and their kids turned into beggars. It was fucking stupid. The strategic hamlet approach. That's what we started doing, and more and more it started bothering me.

I was over there for 33 months. I sort of look at it as a three-phase thing. I went over there to save the world from communism—for freedom and democracy, you know. That lasted for a while. It wore off. That really wasn't what I was doing there. So I was just marking time till I could go on R and R. That lasted for a while until somebody real close to me got killed. Then I was over there for revenge. That's the way it was till the end. I just wanted to fucking kick ass and take dinks who were busy shooting at me.

The last year I went ahead and extended in 1967 for six months because I had a little more than a year to do in the Marine Corps. If I came back with less than six months to do, then I would be discharged upon returning to the states. If I came back with a year to do, I'd probably be busted and go out as a private.

Why would you get busted?

JK: Because of my attitude. I was a good field Marine. I was a shitty garrison Marine. I didn't fit in with the program.

TW: A lot of people, myself included, were very uneasy [in the rear]. . . . It was just too easy to come out of the field, go in the rear, get real annoyed at the petty bullshit, and take on behavior that was self-destructive.

JK: They had junk on the bunk, things on the springs. Everything you owned, your basic issue, would all have to be laid out in a prescribed manner as per the Marine Corps guidebook, you know? Scivvy drawers, khaki pants, green fatigue pants, all laid out, all marked, all perfectly in order. All your field gear, your rifle would be clean and immaculate, all this crap going on. Screw that. I'd rather be in the bush when I'm rolling around in a tank. I don't want to put up with this bullshit.

TW: Most people that spent time in the field did not do well in the rear. They no longer had the personality or the patience to put up with being in the military. You're not in a combat situation, but you're not out of the military either. You're in a never-never land with incredible nonsense.

Didn't you think such drills made you a better Marine?

JK: I didn't. I thought it was largely irrelevant and silly.

TW: You kept your equipment clean and yourself healthy. Outside of that, nothing matters. I think there were an awful lot of people that had nothing better to do than to go around caring about these things. It was Army bull-shit. That's what the Army does. Lifers are like flies: eat shit and bother peo-ple. That's what their purpose in life is. It was hard to deal with people who were so regimented and wanted you to be that way, while the same people would also think nothing of throwing teargas grenades at some kids at the dump who were just trying to scavenge some food. It seemed like the folks who were the most interested in being strak troops were also the biggest jerks. It seemed to me we were supposed to be helping these folks.

JK: My feeling was that I wasn't exactly sure what a VC was. One definition was: If he's dead, he's a confirmed VC. But I did have a gut-level feeling that if I allowed my people to fuck over a Vietnamese, that if he wasn't a VC, the next time I come through that area, he would be. I didn't see any point in that. I didn't feel that [it] was the mission of the Marine Corps to harass these people, but there were a lot of people that enjoyed that. There were a lot of people that really liked to beat the shit out of some poor teenager that they caught without an adequate explanation as to why he wasn't in the Viet-namese military.

First operation I was telling you about, we come back in, got this kid on the back of the tank. We throw him off at S-2 headquarters. They're supposed to notify the ARVNs, and I guess they go torture everybody in his family and find out what the fuck he's doing. We throw him off the track, and all these clowns come running out of the tent. They all got their helmets and their rifles and their flak jackets, and they're standing over this body like Frank Buck, you know, getting their picture taken to show the folks back home what a great time they had. I'm getting fucking livid and about to unload on them with the 50-caliber, and my lieutenant's trying to get me back in the tank.

You have wanna-bes and you have people who are getting shot at. The peo-ple that are getting shot at see no reason to fuck over people [voice rising to an angry pitch], because that's just going to make more people to shoot at you.

You mentioned earlier that you came back to Vietnam in 1967 because you could get out early by extending. How did you make sense of this if you were already becoming disillusioned?

JK: It's like you come back to the states and it's still going on. You're hearing about your buddies are now KIA [killed in action]. So you've got to go back. You're a man.

As Tet started, I was just coming back into country. I flew back in-country the 26th of January. I was initially at Quang Tri firebase outside of Quang Tri City. The Fourth Marines had been moved up to the mouth of the Cua Viet river. I was assigned to a provisional rifle company made up of anybody they could find, including Seabees. Then when the offensive started in Hue in February, a tank commander was killed, so they pulled me into Hue. Toward the end of the Tet offensive, our platoon was part of Operation Pegasus to try to get into Khe Sanh.

You'll notice that nobody said anything about the Hue massacres until the Calley business came out. Then all of a sudden, there was this mass grave that was found in Hue. I don't accept the massacre story, for a couple of reasons. First, supposedly they massacred the people to gain their support. That's what we were doing, and it wasn't working for us, and I think the Vietnamese were a little smarter than that. Secondly, Hue has a history of being in rebellion against the Saigon government. There was an uprising in Hue during the Tet offensive, and the year before when the military Region 1 commander was in revolt against the Ky government in Saigon. The Marine Corps was in the interesting position of sitting between two friendly forces, one on the north of us and one coming up from the south.

There's a big church that sits just as you're coming into the town. It's got a big steeple on it. We had orders to take that church under fire with tanks. . . . We pounded the shit out of Hue. We're the ones that did all of the damage.

Terry, can you tell me about your experiences?

TDB: I went to jump school at Benning and then to Vietnam. I never got the assignment I wanted. I thought I was going to be with an Alpha team. I don't know what happened. I ended up in a supply unit. I was one of those folks in

Second Lieutenant Terry DuBose, Fort Benning, Georgia, 1967.

an office. It was a high standard of living. It was plush. We didn't get hit very often.

I was real green. I was the junior officer in the whole headquarters. I was expecting spit and polish, and it didn't work that way in Vietnam. I was lucky they weren't carrying weapons; I probably would have gotten fragged in the first three months.

Most of the clerks I had working for me were ex-artillery. They had been out in I Corps or II Corps or someplace with artillery units and had either hurt their hearing or had freaked out. They weren't excited about the spit-and-polish thing. I remember one incident where the colonel from head-quarters called in and said he wanted a footlocker. I hung up the phone and was hollering at Don to get the keys for the truck, somebody else to go down and unlock the conex, "Get this footlocker up there!"

About that time, this guy I was telling to get the keys to the conex box comes through the front door; he's singing "There's a place in the sun where there's room for everyone." I was shouting the orders, and he was totally ignoring me. [Laughter all around.] I fell in behind him, saying, "God damn it! Go get the keys!" He was headed in that direction. He gets to the back-door. He's still singing, so I yell, "Shut up!" He turns around and says, "Lieu-tenant, that's not a military order. I don't understand 'shut up.' If you want me to be quiet, you should say 'at ease.'" I walked off, but the next thing I know, they deliver the footlocker and it's all cool. It took me about six months before I got over that sort of syndrome.

What happened during those six months?

TDB: I lost a couple of friends. It just took on a different feeling. I started traveling the Mekong inventorying supplies more. The Vietnamese didn't look like communists. They looked like farmers. I came from an agrarian community. It didn't make any sense.

Tom, how did your situation compare with John's and Terry's?

TW: I thought that I could do it all as a medic—the humanitarian gig, see the war, and serve my country. I was with the First Infantry Division. We were in III Corps northwest of Saigon, in the Iron Triangle area out of Lai Khe.

When I went in, I wanted to see some proof of what I had learned; I wanted to see if the faith I had was to be verified. But all the experiences I had in the military showed me the opposite. The military was not led by people who were particularly smart or had any kind of decent ethics that I liked. When we were in Vietnam, we weren't doing anything I was raised to think this country was about. I was getting different answers than I hoped for. There was a certain disillusionment.

Do you have any specific examples?

TW: I thought the officers would have a clue about what was going on, and it became clear that people were just following orders blindly. I just kept on meeting people who kept on telling me what to do and didn't want to tell me why, and I had this nasty habit of asking *why* all the time. I found out that they didn't know why either; and when they didn't know why, it pissed me off. When they couldn't tell me why my friend was dead here, that pissed me off even more.

JK: I'd like to say something about officers. One of the problems in the Marine Corps—the officer was considered professional; we were transient. So an officer's tour of combat was generally 50 percent in the field and then the remaining back in a village. What it meant to the enlisted man is that about the time they gain the experience and not get your butt killed, they get sucked back in the rear with the gear, and you get a brand-new butter bar and you have to go through the whole process again.

You realize they really aren't Jesus Christ. They don't have the answers, and they need to listen to somebody who's been there longer than them. That's why some of us came out with real strong feelings against officers. We met some real fine people, but we also met a lot of jerks who were never allowed to develop the experience. There was nothing an enlisted man could say to them. They were the leaders. They were in charge. It created a real sense of friction for us.

TW: There was a tendency to see what it was doing to people's lives there too. The first guy that I medivaced out turned out to be the last guy I medivaced out 10 months later. He was sent back to a hospital in the states and then they sent his butt back.

I had to look around and see who was in this infantry platoon with me. It was mostly black faces or real stupid white boys. . . .

JK: Thanks, Tom. [Laughter.] That's one thing that I did notice—the closer you got to the front, the colors changed. The Remington Raiders back in the rear with the gear were predominantly anglos, while the Marines on the line were either stupid white boys or blacks and Hispanics. The blacks saw through it. They had no illusions at all. "Well [sounding like a naive white boy], what are you over here for?" "You jive motherfucker, what are you, some kind of psycho?" They were sitting there telling you in 1966 and 1967: This is the same shit that's going down in Watts and in Chicago; it's just over here against little yellow people rather than black people. I mean, they knew it. It was dumb people like me who had to be taught the hard way.

TW: I found that we started to admire people who were not strongly in favor of the war or the military, folks who expressed misgivings and doubt about our role. I mean somebody only had to look around to see that we were destroying this place.

It had been an agricultural area. I'm a city kid, so I didn't have particular empathy for farmers, but I could see areas where people had had villages and towns that no longer existed. You could see roads that just went to splotches in the forest and whole sections of what had been growing areas had been knocked over or cleared. It was clear that we were destroying land. I did feel something about that.

I was struck by the Vietnamese as well. We'd go through bodies to see what they were carrying. We'd pull out pictures of their families. . . . I remember one prisoner, after we blew an ambush on three Vietnamese. . . . This one guy was left alive and he just squatted with his hands over his head, just shaking with fear. He was terrified, in a state of semishock, like we were after this thing too. We were all sort of shaking and looking at each other for a while. . . . I could be mad at moments or I could be scared at moments, but I could never work up too much hatred. . . . I didn't feel like I could hate these people who weren't doing anything to me that I could hate them for. I was pissed off that friends of mine were killed, but I understood why.

It seemed that the country people had a dignity about them that we were destroying little by little. I could see the rampant poverty around and that people had no choice but to turn to prostitution or theft. The Vietnamese weren't excited by us, and I didn't begrudge them. I had to ask myself, What would I be doing if I were Vietnamese? What side would I be on? I had visions of World War II—entering Paris, liberation sort of thing. I thought we were supposed to be helping people, and it was clear that they didn't think we were. I didn't see the "welcome to the village smiles" on the people; I just saw fear or contempt or loathing.

While I met a lot of Vietnamese who were nice, there was always that wall which was hard for me to bridge. Of course, I was standing there with a uniform and rifle in someone else's country.

As time went on, it also became clear that the people we were fighting against—either the NLF or North Vietnamese—were just much better than the ARVNs, who were supposed to be our allies. I established a real strong respect for people who with very small supplies endured so much to keep on resisting us, while our allies, who were fairly well equipped, seemed to be more interested in ripping off their own population. That made no sense to me whatsoever.

You realized this while you were in Vietnam?

TW: It was there to be seen. You could not *not* see it. We were creating these little islands of American consumerism on the bases with beer halls and steak things and a miniature golf course, for God's sake. When I went back to the rear, it was like some bizarre Disneyland kind of thing.

There was a cartoon passed around which said, "I'm anti-killing and anti-war, but I'm also pro staying alive, so I'll do what I need to do."

So did the troops discuss these feelings?

TW: All the time.

TDB: We were just interested in getting drunk.

JK: In the beginning we were going to carry out our mission. Toward the end, after the Tet offensive and the release of Khe Sanh, we were going to stay alive. When I was there, we didn't want to directly confront the military when they'd send us out on night patrol or something like that. It was a little more subtle. We'd go outside of the wire to a nice safe place where we wouldn't get into any trouble and just ford up.

I remember one experience. I was asked by my lieutenant commander if I was at my ambush location. I says, "Yes." He says, "Fire a flare." They were starting to suspect what we were doing. I said, "Say what?" He said, "Fire a flare." I said, "For what purpose?" He says, "So I know you're where you're supposed to be." I says, "Yeah, right, so will everybody else. I'm not going to do that." I was getting pretty salty then.

We were talking earlier about not screwing over the people, because if they weren't VC and you screwed them over, they became VC. Generally I think the edge was with us because we had the technology and the firepower; but there were two occasions where clearly the edge was with them, and they cut me some slack.

On one occasion, I was on unauthorized liberty in Hue with another Marine. We were way back in the walled city where we weren't supposed to be. The QC [South Vietnamese national police force] and MP [military police] came to this house. They [the Vietnamese] put us in this chicken coop thing behind the house. We're out there talking, and a few minutes later two guys come in wearing black pajamas and carrying rifles. They're over there talking. Joe and I are over there talking. Joe looks over at one of them and says, "You RF [regional forces]?" Guy looks at us, says "No." "AF [allied forces]?" "No." I said, "Don't ask them any more questions, Joe."

We're out there for few minutes; mama-san comes out there and talks to them in Vietnamese; they nod their heads, walk on off; she tells us, "Let's go back in the house." We go back in the house. We're unarmed because policy is: Marines on liberty don't carry weapons in town. They're armed. They could have taken us out if they wanted to. I could see why they didn't, but they could have.

How did all these experiences lead you to get involved in opposing the war when you got back? Wouldn't it have been easier to just go on with your lives?

109

JK: I had lost a lot of good friends over there, and some of the finest human beings I'd known came back in black body bags—and the people here in the United States not only didn't give a shit; they thought I was fucking stupid · for going over there in the first place. We don't want you former professional killers here. What did you expect?

Was this a feeling you got from the antiwar movement, or was it more general?

TDB: By 1970, it was definitely general. In fact, everybody I know, as soon as we got off the plane in California, put on civvies. You didn't want to travel in your uniform like they did after World War II.

JK: We had to sneak back into the country again. I was told at El Toro [Marine Corps Air Station, Santa Ana, California], when I was processing out a story about some woman that was all upset because her kid had been killed in Vietnam, so she blew away the first GI she saw returning from Vietnam.

I came back feeling there was something definitely wrong in that [after] World War II and Korea everybody was welcomed home, and [after] Vietnam, "Oh, you're back. Where've you been?" And they didn't really want to talk about it. There was nobody I really could talk about it to until Terry. Nobody understood. Terry was the first person.

We [Marines] were also disproportionately represented in the casualty figures. The Marine Corps was in military Region 1, just south of the DMZ. We were not messing with VC; we were messing with North Vietnamese regulars for the most part and taking heavy, heavy casualties. Those of us who came back [and] took an antiwar position were very, very pissed. We felt very betrayed by the government.

Why?

JK: Lyndon Johnson did not want to have another Dienbienphu at Khe Sanh, so they held out [under] siege for 77 days, took tremendous casualties. We took tremendous casualties trying to fight our way through there to get to them, and then they blew up the firebase and abandoned it. They could have airlifted those people out at any time, because the North Vietnamese never established air superiority in the south. They could have taken them out at any time. There was a political statement to be made to stay there and to hold.

At another point in the war . . . Second Battalion, Ninth Marines, was on an operation north of the Ben Hai river. It was called a recon force. They went up with a battalion and came back with less than a platoon. Our tanks were bringing back dead Marine bodies stacked on the back of the fucking tracks like cordwood [angry]—that's why.

TDB: They were the angriest of VVAW, the Marines that served in I Corps.

When I got back, the first people I made contact with were old college friends who were in graduate school by that time and they had huge questions about the war and what was going on. Why in Vietnam? Why did you volunteer? I couldn't answer. I didn't understand myself. There was no legitimate answer. There was no Hitler. From all outward appearances, we were killing rice farmers. I came from a cotton farmer family. It just didn't feel right. The mood of the country didn't make you feel any better about it, especially on a campus like this [University of Texas, Austin]. There were a lot of protests.

Before I went over there, I barely knew where Vietnam was, much less where Can Tho, or Phu Loi, or My Tho, or any of those places were. As I started reading the newspaper accounts here, the things I was hearing about those places I knew, that were no longer just places on a map, but real places—it wasn't accurate. What I was seeing in the paper was not what I remembered being reality. You could listen to a news report about a place much differently once you've been to a place; and more and more, it was bullshit. That's when I started going to antiwar demonstrations.

Why go to antiwar demonstrations?

TDB: Probably guilt as much as anything else, and because I volunteered.

JK: The first antiwar demonstration I attempted to be a part of was the National Student Mobilization Committee to end the war in Vietnam, in 1969. I was living in Houston, working for the phone company. I went over to the house where the demonstration headquarters were. I didn't realize they were a bunch of Trots [Trotskyites].

I told them that I had just returned from Vietnam. I had some photographs, principally of Hue, which were taken before we destroyed it during Tet in 1968—when *Life* had done a big spread of what it looked like after Tet in 1968, particularly of the Citadel. I said, "If you want them, you're more than welcome to use these photographs to illustrate your point." I was told that they didn't want any professional killers in their antiwar demonstration. I said, "Fine. You've got all the answers; go do your thing."

I was pissed off at the protesters. I questioned their motivation, but I couldn't say they were wrong. I knew some of the things we were doing over there was wrong.

I went back to the phone company. My wife started in the State Hospital here in Austin. I was just hiding out. If anybody asked me, "I don't know." It went that way until I met Terry, and that was such a fucking relief because this was the first man I could talk to who had any understanding whatsoever about what I was feeling. Through Terry I met other people and then realized, shit, I'm not as crazy as I think I am, or if I am, at least there's a lot of other crazy fuckers out there.

I still believe that a lot of these campus radicals that we were working with, they had no moral qualms about the right and wrong position of the war in Vietnam; they just didn't want their butts to get blown away. I'm still cynical about that. They wanted to stay here and make a lot of money just like our Senator Phil Gramm, who's sitting up there on student deferment at A&M and then on a critical-occupation exemption because he's teaching economics at Aggie. That's where I'm coming from.

· The Kent State thing went down, and I started to have the disturbing feeling that what went on in Vietnam was going to happen here in the United States—that cordon and search operations were going to go on here. Our country was going to be a military dictatorship, and the same kind of crap that I participated in was going to come home to roost. That scared the shit out of me.

TDB: Kent State did me, too. I felt like that was wrong. I was already having doubts about the war and what was going on. That was too close to home.

JK: Besides, we had taken an oath to defend the government of the United States and the Constitution. What do you do when the government of the United States is the enemy of the Constitution? Where does your allegiance lie? I knew there was something wrong. I didn't have a political analysis, because I wasn't a political person. I wasn't a political person until I was exposed to all this rhetoric.

TDB: It's like I said the other night: it was a process.

"A Crisis of Faith"

BARRY ROMO

Barry Romo had a strong Catholic upbringing. He enlisted in January of 1966, determined to go to Vietnam to "save his Catholic brothers" from the communists.

I went through basic training. Then I went to advanced infantry training, and then I went to officer candidate school. I got my commission on January 19th, 1967, second lieutenant. I became an officer at nineteen.

112

Barry Romo in Vietnam, at a firebase near Tam Ky, with General Koster *(right)*.

I went to Vietnam [in] the early part of July. I came into the country in Bien Hoa around Saigon and then waited for orders and got assigned to the 196th Light Infantry Brigade. I was flown to Chu Lai and went through a three-day or five-day orientation. I was then assigned to a company as a weapons platoon leader, which is mortars. I was only at that for about three days. A platoon leader got blown up, so I got sent right out.

What were your feelings about being in Vietnam?

My fear was that I was going to fuck up. I wasn't afraid of dying. I was absolutely convinced I wasn't going to get wounded. It may sound strange, but I wasn't afraid of that at all. I was worried how I was going to lead. Luckily, because I was so young, and knew I was so young, when I was assigned to a platoon, I didn't come in like I was some officer sent from God. I knew that the question of leading wasn't a question of just giving orders but was a combination of learning and developing respect from your men.

I flew out to the platoon. There was a big operation going on in a place south of the San Trebong river, which is just north of My Lai. I met the platoon sergeant, who was about a twenty-four- or twenty-five-year-old E-6. He introduced himself and took me around to meet people. We walked around, and he showed me body parts from combat. Right away he wanted me to see what war was. It sounds really stupid, but I expected combat was people being shot and body parts. I found it interesting. It didn't seem real either. It might have been a plaster of paris cast or something you'd find in a joke shop. It had a very dreamlike quality to it—a combination of being able to impose your will, and things just being so much out of your control.

We ran around on the APCs, almost like hot-rodding. They were trying to keep this road open. There was an operation going on at the other end. So at night, the armored personnel carriers would drive back and forth on the road, shooting indiscriminately so that they [the Vietcong] couldn't put any mines in the road, and during the day [we] could bring heavy equipment over. The Vietcong crawled up and found the area where the APCs [armored personnel carriers] were meeting and turning around like this [motions in a circle], and they dug in that area and put a 500-pound bomb in overnight. The next morning we pulled out and they blew up the lead track, set it on fire, Americans died, and the Koreans—we were working with Koreans— went into the village and killed everybody. Men, women, children. That was my real introduction to death in Vietnam.

Then I remember going someplace. I had to walk down the road and walked to a roadblock. There were GIs abusing Vietnamese as they were patting them down and really messing with them, slapping them around, going through their baskets, and throwing their food around and everything. I told them to stop and they said, "Who are you?" I carried my rank in my pocket, because you never wore it; you'd be an idiot to wear it. So I reached into my pocket, took it out and said, "Look, I'm an officer. Stop cursing these people; stop messing with these people. Do your job." I had gone over to help the people, and I wasn't a racist. I changed, because I became like them [the other Americans] within a few months.

Why? How did you feel about this behavior?

I felt confusion, because this stuff doesn't happen. There's majors and captains around, and they ain't stopping nobody, and I'm only a second lieutenant in-country less than a week. They don't care. But the thing is that you don't feel like you have alternatives. At least I didn't.

When I first got there, we were mostly in more stable positions in comparatively stable areas. We were mostly making sure that the North Vietnamese and Vietcong didn't sneak up on Chu Lai and drop in mortars and rockets. It was just interdiction. Then we started going on longer operations. At first, we would only go on a-couple-of-day operations. Then we started doing 40-day operations where you would just go out and stay out. You would then come back for two days, three days, and then be sent back out for another 40 days.

What happened was: You take casualties, and you stop caring about the people because the people you care about are the people who speak English, who are wearing the uniform you're wearing, who sit beside you, who show you the letters home, who are going to go back to the states. That's who you start caring about. It's a question of developing familiar—as in "family"—relations with your fellow comrade GIs. That becomes all-powerful, to the point where I care about these people. I'm going to get these people back.

The reason that develops is, one, you can't speak the same language [as the Vietnamese], but more important, it's a question of racism: We value life; they don't value life. It's also a question of: They don't want you there. You know, if people were different and you go into their village and they're throwing flowers at you and "yeah, GI, we love you so much," then that's one thing. It's another thing when you go into their village and they stare at the ground or look at the sky and say bad things to you if they've got the guts. And if there's a field and they go walking and they know there's a mine there, you go walking and they could say stop, but they don't say stop, and an American dies or gets his legs blown off. So what happens is, basically, fuck them.

You were aware of this while you were in Vietnam?

I was partially conscious of that, but for the most part, not very much. There were too many things going on. There wasn't time for reflection. Combat is not all this "stiff upper lip," "right on" kind of shit. If you got caught in a firefight, they did not bring you back; you stayed right where you were, doing an operation for another three weeks. And then next week you get blown up, and you go on another operation for two more weeks. And you're down to 18 men from 40 men. They don't pull you out; you just keep going. You don't sit around listening to radios and watching TV.

You move all day, and move all day, and move all day, and do whatever you're doing. If nothing happens, then you're walking and walking and walking and walking. Then at night, you work in shifts. You sit down and cook some C rations, and you stay awake and go to sleep and stay awake and go to sleep and stay awake and go to sleep. You get up, eat some breakfast, and you move.

Think about how you would be after a month of this. You don't have reflections. You're planning where you're going. You're looking at the hills. You're reading a map. You got tasks. You got to make sure that your men dig in. You got to make sure you got flanking out. And when you're going into a night situation, you got to make sure you set up prepositioned artillery so that if something happens, you just got to call it in.

You have to contend with individuals who still have wants and needs and pain and sorrow. These are fucking teenagers who have got fucking guns. They're running around a jungle. It's hard for coaches to keep a team together for an hour on a football field or basketball court. You're saying, Keep these people together for 30 days at a time in a situation where they're cooking their own food, shitting their own pants, and getting letters from home saying, "Dear Johnny, I'm nineteen years old and I hope you're all right, but I found somebody else."

Then you're dealing with a racial mix of Puerto Ricans and blacks and whites at a time when racism was the order of the day in the United States. You're dealing with the fact that for the most part, we were from the lower working class. So you got all these things in play. It's funny watching movies, because for the most part they're idiotic. Maybe in the heat of a battle you scream at people like you see in the movies, but for the most part, you got to cajole. You got to get the job done, and the job takes on all kinds of other dimensions.

We were running around out in the jungles—as opposed to rice paddies or the mountains—the foothills and the jungles. One time we were going up a ravine and walked in upon a jungle base camp. The banana leaves were all green, . . . fires were still going, and wet footprints were on the rocks. We're walking through this. . . . By this point I increased my platoon firepower from where you have normally two M-60s. . . . I begged, borrowed, and stole to where I had three—one M-60 per squad. I had tons of firepower.

Anyway, I had an arrow with three arrowheads up front. We're going up a ravine . . . it was a 40- or 50-degree angle with jungle along the side . . . and we get to a slight waterfall—a cascading waterfall. The minute we get there, they were right on the other side. It was brilliant on their part because you couldn't climb over it. They opened up on us and we shoot back, and my company commander turns around and runs to the rear and does it so fast he slips on a rock and his feet kick up—it looked like 6 feet in the air—and falls on his fucking ass. Meanwhile, I'm maneuvering my people to get a broad front. . . . I'm doing that. . . . He pulls the fucking other two platoons out of the area, leaves me there, calls in artillery. The artillery is now landing between the other two platoons and me. So I got the Vietcong here, or what-ever; and friendly fire here; and he's fucking running down the hill.

We fight our way out of that. . . . They pull me back. Within a week we're back at a base camp. Now I'm doing a slow fuse, and I can't hold alcohol. Lieutenant Fox, who was the FO with the company, and Lieutenant Archuletta and I are drinking. We went over to the officers' club . . . and you buy booze by your rank. . . . See, you could be fifty years old, be an E-5, and been in World War II, and all you could buy was beer; but you could be nine-teen years old and a lieutenant, and you get to buy Johnny Walker Red because you could hold your liquor. [Sarcastically.] So we went and each of us had a bottle of something, and we got drunk.

The more I drank, the more it came out. By the end of the bottle we are screaming . . . really loud: "Motherfucking coward. . . . Kiss ass. . . . Did you see what he did?" We're talking about him like he's a dog. He's three beds down from us . . . we're almost sitting at his feet . . . we're drunk; we're also armed. . . . And I just said, If that motherfucker ever puts me in that situation again, I'm going to kill him. I was absolutely serious about it.

I was in the field, the first time, from July until December. Then in December, I was moved to battalion headquarters. I was made a battalion S-2, which was a captain's job. I didn't know what the fuck I was doing. I had no college, and now I'm supposed to be a staff officer. So they gave me an NCO [noncommissioned officer] who taught me what to do.

I would get debriefings and supposedly help pick sites where the companies would have operations in the battalion. I'd have a helicopter maybe an hour or two hours a day and I would fly over the areas, just looking. I would be sent out to be with the Vietnamese units, not as an advisor, not as a commander, but to report back to our battalion on where the Vietnamese unit was. Also, people would capture a prisoner and I'd fly out to the area, pick them up, and bring them to a rear area to be held.

I did that until February or March. I asked to go back into the field. I told the battalion commander, a lieutenant colonel, that I didn't enjoy being in battalion, that I didn't feel comfortable. We had a company wiped out while I was with battalion headquarters, and I had asked to be assigned as platoon leader. Then the 11th Brigade had come over—you know, that's Calley's brigade.

When the 11th came in, they had whole units where not one single person had combat experience. They had a program called infusion where they would take senior NCOs and junior officers and send them to the 11th. Then they would take these new people and send them to the 196th, so that you had some kind of cadre with combat experience. So we were sent down to the 11th from the 196th, and I was real happy about that.

We went to division headquarters in Chu Lai. We're getting briefed. A colonel told us, "This is where you're going to be; this is the layout of the area; this is the kind of enemy you're going to face; just because the 11th Brigade is brand-new in-country, don't think these guys aren't any good"—this whole rap—"they're really kicking ass. This one task force, task force Baker, turned in a body count of 370-some"—I can't remember exactly—"they just kicked commie ass."

I'm there with a couple of other of my lieutenant friends who are getting transferred at the same time. I'm thinking: If these guys got 300 and some people, then they got 300 and some American casualties. One of us in our little group said, "Well, how many American casualties?" The guy said, "One, and he shot himself in the foot." We're looking around thinking, What's going on here? I asked, "How many weapons did they capture?" The guy says, "Three." Well, three could be three hand grenades; it could mean a rifle, a bayonet, and a hand grenade—which means one VC. One of us said, "Hey, they're killing civilians." We knew it. Anybody who had been in combat knows you don't get 300 and some casualties, one American casualty, and capture three weapons! So we said, "They're killing civilians." The guy ended the briefing right there.

We got assigned to our units. We're going, "What the fuck are these people about?" We stayed drunk because—Jesus, did we make the wrong decision?

You didn't think killing civilians was right?

Fuck, no! No way!

When I was a battalion S-2, I went back to my old company to pick up some prisoners. This platoon sergeant—who I absolutely dislike—from the Third Platoon is taking his K-bar and cutting the kneecap off of a prisoner—a live prisoner. I said, "Stop it." He said, "Hey, I got to find out my information." I said, "Stop it." So the guy stopped it, and then he went over and kicked a pregnant woman in the stomach. I said, "Don't ever do that again." I went over to his platoon leader. I said, "I'm in battalion, if I ever see that happening again, I will guarantee you that he gets court-martialed." It's kind of funny—everybody gets one chance, right? So the guy goes, "Aw, he's really a good guy. We been taking casualties, and stuff's hard." I said, "Stuff gets hard, but if he ever does it again . . ." I was real adamant. . . . It was the sickest I'd ever been.

There's a difference between torturing a captured prisoner, kicking a pregnant woman, and other stuff. I mean, I burned villages, took every bit of rice we could find and destroyed it, or kicked people in the butt. I'm not saying I didn't knock people to the ground. One time, some of my men grabbed a farmer and put him in a pond, holding his head underwater—but, one, I knew they weren't going to kill him; and, two, it wasn't permanent damage. It was still torture, but to take a knife and carve out part of a person's body, to kick a pregnant woman, that's just beyond anything. There's nothing soldierly or manly in these concepts there.

While I was their platoon leader I only had two people killed, but there were tons and tons of casualties. The first Bronze Star—I think we took at least 12 casualties in one day. The day before we took eight casualties and then the very next day took 12 more, so out of 40 people I had lost 20 in two days. We would take casualties like that. Sometimes it would be one or two, sometimes more; but those casualties were unfortunate because they were a combination of friendly fire and intense Vietcong fire.

One time what happened was—We had walked through an area, walked onto some VC and had killed them. We discovered a giant rice cache and stripped this whole area of its food. They were waiting and they were angry, and even though they only had light machine guns, they stayed and fought. They didn't run away at all. I can't imagine the kind of anger these people had.

What did you think about the enemy?

I had the utmost respect for them. . . . Next to us, these guys were the best soldiers in the world. How come they'd fight to the death? When they ran out of bullets they'd throw fucking rocks and kick your fucking butts. Saigon troops ran away, sold drugs, sold their sisters into prostitution, were lazy, were cowards. Why were we fighting for people who wouldn't fight for themselves?

When did you realize this?

Within a week of being in-country. That's how come I started to change. People without armor and airplanes and helicopters were fighting you real bad, and your buddy's selling drugs and women.

Everybody hated the ARVN. Everybody thought the ARVN were sissies. Everybody thought the ARVN couldn't fight. Everybody thought the ARVN were a bunch of pimps. You developed affectionate names for your enemy—Charlie, Mr. Charlie—and you hated your damn allies. When I meet people now who tell me "Oh, yes, our ARVN friends who fought well," I go, "Where the hell were you? Don't give me that fucking shit."

I was called on the radio and told to report to where the helipad area was with all my gear. I was happy this time to get out of the field. I had 45 days left. At this point I thought, I'm finally going to make it home. A guy had a handwritten sheet of paper: "Your nephew has been killed along the DMZ. Your brother wishes you . . ." (He didn't even verbally say, Your brother wishes you to be the body escort.) ". . . Do you want to escort the body?" My nephew was in the 196th Brigade and in the post–Tet offensive in May. He was shot in the throat and died in his own blood. I was utterly devastated. I got on the helicopter. I wanted to throw the fucking rifle out of the helicopter.

I get to the rear area, fill out some paperwork, and start thinking about extending. I'll go home, I'll bury my nephew, and I'll come back here for another six months. My friends, who I transferred down with, were at the base camp where I was flown to. They found out what happened; then they threatened to break my fingers. They said, "We're not going to allow you to extend. You've been blessed. You're going home. Sorry about your nephew, but you're not coming back; and if you try, we will break your hands." They were absolutely serious. At this point, people were killers. That's not talk. So I said, "You're probably right"—not that I was afraid of them, but I figured that if they were going to do that to me, they were probably right and I just wasn't thinking correctly.

Less than 24 hours later I was at Travis Air Force base and was driven by bus to Oakland Army Terminal. Then I saw my family. My parents were ecstatically happy and sad that my nephew was dead. My brother and sister-in-law were sad that my nephew was dead, but happy that I was home. I felt cheated. I didn't get to have a happy homecoming. I felt guilty for being happy for being home [when] my nephew was dead. We buried my nephew and then had a gigantic funeral and party.

I was back from Vietnam, [back from] killing people. People looked peaked. People looked strange. People were silly. People didn't know what was going on. People had sugar to put in their coffee. People had refrigerators with cold beer in it. People were driving cars and not worried about getting blown up, and they thought they knew what was going on because they watched the news. They knew nothing.

I got home in time for Robert Kennedy's assassination. Go to Fort Ord, and Martin Luther King gets killed. Fuck. I'm coming home, and people are being killed! What is this? It's fucking madness. What am I coming home to? The war's over there—the war's not here.

I've got eight more months. I go to Fort Ord, a company commander, not even twenty-one yet, a first lieutenant, in a special AIT company [advanced infantry training]; 99.9 percent of everybody is going to Vietnam. I was in charge of the company, and I enjoyed that. Here was 300 men and they were mine. They called me sir and saluted me. They performed for me. I would be up before any of them were up, with a clean set of fatigues. I would always change fatigues two or three times a day so they were always starched. I would run [the men] every morning. I would take them out to the field most of the time. I ended up having the lowest rates of desertion and AWOL. I never gave discipline my whole time in the military, even in Vietnam. I never gave an Article 15.

I was proud of what I was doing, my leadership and stuff. I had a real good relationship with my battalion commander—a good guy, smart guy, not like my captains in Vietnam. He was constantly pumping me, "Come on, you're going to extend. What the hell else is out there? How are you going to make money like this at twenty-one?" I was thinking about extending because if I extended for one year, I would make captain.

I went and checked out different things. I really didn't have a girlfriend. I had no money, coming from a working-class background; and if I did another year, I could put tons of money away, and get the GI Bill, have a new car, be totally set for college, and wouldn't have to skimp or work. So it was looking attractive to me.

I had a doofus for a mess sergeant. He had like nineteen years, and he didn't even know what his name was. The deputy post commander, who was a brigadier general, was coming through and checking my company out. My sergeant got confused and said the potatoes in Mermite containers were the meat, and the meat was the vegetables—you know. He just became all flustered because this guy was a general. The general ordered me to demote him. I said, "Sir, this guy's been here 19 years. Sir, I'm not going to do it. He cooks; the place is clean. He does his job. I'm not going to ruin him." I had to fill out that much paperwork on the guy to say he was good and smart—to keep him from getting busted. When that happened, I said: If they can do that to him, they can do that to me. I'm getting out. This is ridiculous. This is insane. What am I doing?

In the meantime, like a good Catholic, I had a crisis of faith. Stuff was beginning to unravel. I never missed mass or communion. I went to mass in this same period, and watching the priest put on his vestments, with a giant stained-glass window that had either Christ the Lamb or Christ the Shepherd in a base church behind him. . . . The guy's putting this stuff on . . . I'm looking . . . Christ here . . . the Cross . . . thou shall not kill . . . and I said, None of it makes sense. It's a pile of crap. I stood up and walked out. I went back to my bachelor officer's quarters and became physically ill. I knew I was right not to be there. This was all a crock. Fuck them. That was it for the military and that was it for religion.

I got out, and I actually figured I wasn't going to get into college. It was like 10 days before the semester started. So I look for a job. The first job they send me to, they hire me. They go, "Leadership—you were an officer," so they were going to put me in training management at the Bank of America or something. I said, "What does that mean?" And they said, "Well, you start out repossessing." So I said no.

Then I went over to my friend's house and I said, "Jeez, can you believe that? I get back from Vietnam and I'm going to get killed repossessing someone's car because they're unemployed!" And so Mr. Ashton [a family friend] goes, "Why don't you go to school? I'll help you." He got my paperwork through and got me courses with teachers that he knew. I went back to school and really had a good time. That was my one time, I think, of really having a great time. I was at San Bernardino Valley Community College.

I then went back to the Catholic church where I grew up, and the priest was a guy named Father Kaiserhauer who had spent 30 years in Brazil. He was a wonderful man. He had been in Germany during the rise of Hitler. I came back to see him, and he would say, "I think the United States is going fascist," and he wasn't talking about the protesters either. He says, "I see the same stuff in terms of the government." He says, "The corporations are all corrupt and this stuff is really, really terrible." He says, "Barry, I want you to teach again. Christian doctrine." I said, "Father, I don't believe anymore; Vietnam really kicked my ass." So he says, "What do you believe in?" I said, "Social justice," but I couldn't bring myself to say the war was wrong.

I remember going to a poli-sci class and the guy ended up being pretty right-wing, but he was antiwar. And he would ask questions . . . never called me a baby-killer . . . asked questions, and I couldn't answer them. My friends, who were antiwar, Mr. Ashton, and the whole Ashton family asked questions, and I just couldn't answer them.

What kinds of questions?

"We've got to pull out of Vietnam, Barry, it's not worth it." We can't pull out, there will be a bloodbath. "Isn't B-52 bombing a bloodbath? So why should we commit the bloodbath?" I had never seen a bloodbath by the Vietcong, but I wasn't thinking back on my own experience. My whole Vietnam experience was up there, and I was back arguing Republican nonsense out of a book. They were making me face my own contradictions. They don't change because you burn a flag; they don't change because you spit on them. They change because you confront them with the contradictions of their own life, and that's why people change.

Someone once said, "How could you change so quickly?" I said, "Well, it wasn't a question of changing quickly; it was a question of being in shock over taking the blinders off. When you take sunglasses off, the sun shines in: it doesn't trickle in, it doesn't take time, it all becomes bright." That's the same thing that happens once you get rid of the mythology that chains you down. You can see things because you're free. It wouldn't have happened otherwise. I would have probably drank.

I remember being at home drinking wine with Jeff—who had been with the 101st Airborne and been shot in the throat in Vietnam—when Nixon announced the invasion [of Cambodia]. We looked at each other and we said it was all a lie. The United States is getting out of Vietnam, you know. Nixon got elected; he said, "I'm pulling you out; I've got a secret plan," and the first thing the motherfucker does is invade everybody he can invade. The war wasn't over. He was going to invade every other country, domino theory in reverse. So we got our fatigues on—starched fatigues, right—got our medals out, put on black armbands, went down to the campus, and joined the antidraft rally. Turned in our medals. It was all downhill from then, because once you open your eyes, the minute you break with everything, it's like you see the world and the world becomes much clearer.

Why protest? What did you think you could accomplish?

We have a voice that could end the war. They had to listen. They could put blacks aside, they could put old women aside, they could put World War II vets aside. How are they not going to listen to vets when they say the war's wrong? We're veterans. The American public respects us. We've seen all the movies. They always tell us they love us and respect us. We're going to get up there and tell them the truth, and we're going to change—really change—the war. The war's going to end. It's going to work.

During the antiwar movement [I] found out that 50 percent of the males were vets. I think we were two-thirds combat [and] a high proportion of people who joined versus [being] drafted because we believed. People who got drafted didn't go in with any preconceived notions, so that the fall from grace was smaller. Those of us that enlisted in the service to prove our manhood and fight for democracy went in believing it and came out and had to do something to change it, because the fall was greater.

"Chickenshit"

JOE URGO

Joe Urgo enlisted in order to gain some control over his life. He saw his enlistment as a step to future employment, but at the same time he shared the anti-communist sentiment of his Catholic community and the Republican Party.

I enlisted in May of 1966, in the Air Force, and was assigned to basic training. I was not very athletic, so I had a lot of problems with just the physical training stuff; but more than that, it bothered me the abuse that they put everybody through. All I saw from around me was this stupid abuse by the drill instructors against everybody and everything. It was all part of this intimidation. I didn't think it was necessary to treat people that way to get them to do what they wanted.

Then when it came time for assignments, I was told that I couldn't get air intelligence, because you have to be in four years. You have to be in your second enlistment. That week in basic training they needed air policemen. So most of the people in my flight were put into air police. I graduated from air police school in August.

I was assigned to Langley Air Force Base in Virginia. They had a detachment of F-106 nuclear loaded fighter interceptors in Richmond, Virginia. It was a very small installation, no more than 150 people. My job for the next 16 months was to guard the nuclear-loaded aircraft and nuclear weapons in the bunkers on this little installation.

What we were doing on the base was filled with so much stupidity, pettiness, hypocrisy, manipulation, and meanness that I wanted to get out of there. They had a real problem at this time because they were getting a whole bunch of us that were dedicated. We would do what they wanted to do, and we would do it right and very scientifically.

We would run tests that were supposed to work a certain way. They put you on this alarm panel board and they tell you it's going to work this way. Then they run a test: The nuclear bomb has gone off and the wind keeps shifting. Nobody can figure out which way the wind direction is going. This captain keeps sending the troops out to guard the weapons, but you would get the maximum dosage of retcons in 10 minutes, so everybody dies during the test. I said to him, "Sarge, in an hour, everybody you got here is dead. Why are you doing this?" He said, "Just keep quiet." I said, "But in an hour, theoretically, everybody's dead. All that has to happen is [for] somebody [to] wait an hour."

I actually thought that they were serious. What I realized is that nobody actually believed in what they were doing, but they were doing it because this is what they were trained to do. It was filled with all this macho power and authority, but they would never figure out what the problem was and solve it—because to solve it meant you had to challenge authority; you had to change the structure.

I got totally frustrated and I said, Fuck it; I'm volunteering for Nam. I got my first application in as soon as I could. I was notified in August of 1967 that I'd be going to Nam in December. So in December of 1967, I came home on my pass and left the day after Christmas in 1967.

I ended up on the security police night shift at Tan Son Nhut. I worked midnights most of the time, Charlie Flight. I was there from 11:30 to the early morning. I worked all Echo Sector, which was the west perimeter of the base.

I was green. I wanted to do what they wanted me to do. Every night, [when] we're going out to post, they start in with petty harassment. They're fighting with us to shine our boots on the night shift. I thought, This is stupid. Nobody sees us, but they've got to have this discipline. I thought, This is chickenshit, man. The shit starts all over again.

You didn't think that was important for discipline and . . . ?

No, because I was gung-ho. I was ready to do what they wanted me to do, but I didn't see why it made a difference that I had to have my boots shined on the night shift. Every night they would come to us and tell us we were going to be attacked. After a while, nobody believed it anymore. Oh, yeah, we're going to be attacked. [Sarcastically.] Maybe we really should get attacked; then this chickenshit will stop. We need a good fight to settle things out. We need to do what we came here to do.

The night before Tet, I turned twenty-one. Intelligence that night was really scary. They're coming. Something's going to happen. The next night, we got worse intelligence. We go to post, and about three o'clock in the morning the radio starts to go crazy. They're telling us something's going to happen. Then the radio's quiet. Then it all starts.

The Vietnamese massed off the perimeter of the west end and attacked. I was about 100 yards in and to the south of where it was. I was guarding the construction area, Red Horse Area. I could see Tangle One. I could see another tower. I knew the people in the 051 bunker [a large bunker located right at the west end of the base].

My friend in Tangle 4, Del Tucker, comes on the radio and says, "They're coming through. They're coming through." They hit the 051 with a B-40 rocket and on tape you can hear one of the guys, either Fisher or somebody, come on and say, "My legs are gone. They're coming. We need help. We need help." The guy on the radio is telling them, "Hold on, hold on." Later on I was to find out that no one knew where the west end of the base was, which is why the teams didn't respond earlier. So four of the five guys died in the bunker. The fifth guy, Coggins—black guy—actually walked off the bunker the next morning. The word that we had was that he lost it.

They came through the base. They came up the flight line. Then some fighting engaged. Some teams came down. This whole huge attack took place throughout the night as soon as the helicopters could respond. Helicopters with the gunships, all night long, just raked that end of the airbase. From my position, what I could see was hundreds of thousands of rounds, shooting down into this west end of the base.

I sat up all night and watched this whole thing take place, listened to the transmissions on the radio, listened to all kinds of people get lost. Nobody knew what they were doing. There was this one captain, Denezio, who later got an award, because he actually had some grasp of the thing—of tactics— and he deployed some people. Then they were able to fight the Vietnamese.

I'm on post for 40 hours. I'm really upset at what's going on. I sat out there, and I couldn't figure this out. What had these guys died for? I was really confused. I can remember sitting on this post about three or four o'clock in the morning and just breaking down. All these emotions, the pettiness, the chickenshit, the harassment, now this.

This is what I was hoping would happen, and now it happened. We got attacked, and this is not what I expected. The reality hit me hard. That experience, the incompetence that I saw on every level, and why these guys died— that is what changed me.

I asked questions; nobody could give me answers. I tried to get a report of the attack; I couldn't get a report. I went and found a friend of mine who was on day shift, and he said there was a tape recording. I got a copy of the tape recording. I listened to it.

I went into the base headquarters, found out there was this previous attack, and researched the previous attack. They said that one of the things we need on the west end of the base, at Echo Sector, is the grass needs to be cut, and good lighting needs to be installed. The grass was never cut. Good lighting was never installed. Why didn't they do this? Why did these guys die? I could have been on that bunker that night.

I knew them well enough to be friends with them—Fisher and everyone else. One guy was just going to have a baby. His wife was pregnant. One guy had another month to go. This then became a quest. For the next 11 months, this is what I did in Vietnam. I went through the steps of this attack. I worked up a whole analysis. I questioned everybody in my unit. I got all these bits and pieces and stories, and the whole picture that I got was that nobody believed in what they were doing. Nobody cared. Nobody was gung-ho as I thought we should be. Then, what that did—that ideological ripping opened me up to a whole series of other things.

Our gun area was near the officers' barracks, and the officers were complaining because we're cleaning our machine guns too loudly while they're sleeping in their air-conditioned barracks, right? Then I go to the base exchange in the morning, and there's these officers rolling refrigerators and stereos and cartons of beer out to their air-conditioned hootches. Every morning, that BX [base exchange] was stacked with millions of cans of beer and soda, and stereos, and refrigerators. Every day, they'd move out, and new stuff would come in. Somebody's making a lot of money off this war. So I go from the money angle to the incompetence, death—all kinds of shit started to come out.

The other thing that happened was: I became friends with some of the black guys when I took on the racism question. The way it really got sharp is when the movie was shown every night on the base, the flag would come up, and the black guys wouldn't salute the flag anymore. So this huge argument broke out about saluting the flag. I argued with them about, "Why don't you . . . ? That's our flag." One guy said, "Ain't my flag, man. Ain't done nothing for me. You take a look at my people." The next thing you know, me and Matthews were the first whites to refuse to salute the flag. After all my years of flag-waving and being patriotic, this is the first time I came to oppose the flag.

Then I start looking around: everything's gook this, gook that. This one guy I remember one day said, "I'm going to go get some gook food. Look at that gook kid." I thought, This is stupid. Then I realized I didn't know anything about these people.

Had you ever talked to any Vietnamese people?

I was never open to it. I never actually went downtown and tried to meet families and people like that. To the degree I was able to do things, I spent one night talking to an ARVN soldier at my post. This guy just hated the government. He hated Thieu and Ky and all these guys. I started getting this experience—they don't like what they're doing either. What am I doing here?

Curfew would end at six A.M. in the morning. The Vietnamese would come down the road [and] we had this game of shooting slap flares. You hit the flare and it shoots out. We would shoot them, kind of like over their heads. But one night, I lowered my hand too much and almost killed a couple of people, an old man and a little boy. It went right by them, real close. That shook me up because I didn't want to kill these people.

I'm continuing to pursue why these guys had died, all this kind of thing, one thing leading to another. I'm now becoming very rebellious, disruptive. I'm losing my morale. I don't dress right. I wasn't reliable to the security

police anymore. I spent all night asleep. I was not carrying ammunition anymore. I decided: If the shit gets hot again, I'm running; I'm not going to kill.
By the end of the year, I wasn't believing it anymore.

The attitude among the troops was so rebellious that nobody was wearing
their helmets anymore. We weren't saluting the officers. The base police were
given orders to write up all the guys coming off the night shift if they did not
have their helmets on and if they didn't salute the officers. Now this is really
great. Now we're going to take the chickenshit to a new level. Nobody's
going to tell me why my friends died, but they are going to write me up
because I'm not going to salute this asshole.

In September or October, I got late copies of the *Daily News* with the 1968
[Democratic] convention laid out all across the pages. I can remember walking up and down the barracks when everybody was in there and holding up
the centerfold of the *Daily News* that showed the police beating people, and
saying, "This is what we're in Vietnam protecting?"

I organized a whole lot of people to vote for Nixon, because I thought
Nixon was going to end the war. I just turned twenty-one, so that was the
first time I ever voted. It was all part of our protest to end the war. It was like
we had an antiwar mood growing in the barracks. I can tell you, it got so serious—the harassment—that there was a discussion about killing one sergeant.
That's always been amazing to me. We were not a line unit, an infantry unit,
[where] killing was normal, but we discussed whether we should kill them. It
was that kind of atmosphere. Fragging. It was an incredible experience. It
changed my life. I can remember actually thinking that that twenty-first
birthday was the first day that I can remember that I wanted to mark things
from.

I came back the day before Christmas in 1968, totally stressed out and
anguished. I came back and dressed up in my uniform and went to midnight
mass with the family because I wanted that attention, respect, acknowledgment. I still wanted something to be proud of. Stuff never goes away like
that. At midnight mass, all the priest talked about was grace. I can remember
leaving the church in a new level of anger because people were dying—this
asshole doesn't say anything about what's going on in the world. This is the
kind of shit that got us there. It's ignorance. That's essentially the last time I
went to the Catholic church.

I got 17 months left. Now I was a sergeant in the Air Force. I was assigned
to an installation at Atlantic City, New Jersey, right behind the Atlantic City
airport. Essentially, I did 14 of them. . . . Then I got out three months early.

For six months I was pretty numb. I went through this period of just trying to figure out what was going on. Now I'm doing the same bullshit. I
don't give a shit. It's eight hours of boring duty. Most of the guys have been
to Nam. We're rebellious. We weren't cleaning our rooms the way they
wanted [us] to. We were putting posters up on the wall. They're harassing us.
This little tit-for-tat fighting is going on all the time. One of the maintenance

guys had a poster on the wall, and they made a big deal about it. So everybody starts putting things up. You want to fuck with him? Fuck with all of us.

On my breaks I would come up to New York and go to antiwar demonstrations. I was collecting literature. I'd be riding the bus back to Atlantic City carrying stacks of the *East Village Other* and all of these alternative newspapers. They're talking about revolution! I can't believe this! People actually talking about revolution! It was the first time I was ever introduced to Mao Tse-tung. I'm reading this stuff. I remembered all those years of all that right-wing stuff that I had about how many millions Mao killed. Then I read the *Little Red Book,* and I said, "This guy didn't kill millions. This is tremendous, what he's saying here. This guy's not going to kill millions of people with this kind of philosophy."

It started with the three priests in the Catholic church; everybody in authority that you held up to any kind of test did not measure up. Nobody, no law, no structure, no government, no official, no priest, no sergeant, nobody held up to the test of what they were supposed to be. Essentially, once you rip with that, what you do is say: I'm going to look for something else. I'm going to look for where the truth is. I'm going to look for who's going to be honest and true, and reflect reality, and actually be right.

The same time, in August of 1969, Woodstock was happening. I was thinking about going up there, but then I didn't. But the Atlantic City rock festival had Janis Joplin. So I said, "Gee, this sounds interesting. I'm young. This is where the young people are. I want to check this out." I bought these tickets to the Atlantic City rock festival.

Well, wouldn't you know it, we go to post one night and this master sergeant comes to post and tells us that he's getting ready to cancel all vacations and leaves because the Atlantic City rock festival is coming and he thinks the communists are organizing it. The thinking was that we were going to put out people with shotguns to protect the perimeter of the base so that the communists don't come there.

I'm standing there. [Laughs.] Absurdity wasn't even the word. What zoo am I in? What circus is this? This is insane. I said to him, "Sarge, I just want you to know that I'm going to that rock festival, and if they make one move toward this base, I'm going to get out in front and lead them here." I didn't give a shit.

Then, between the moratoriums we went into a defcon 2 alert. We went one stage before nuclear war. Normally we have two nuclear-loaded aircraft in the hangers; right—they now put two nuclear-loaded aircraft outside the hangers in addition to the two. The pilots are all walking around with pistols. We're on 12 hours on, 12 hours off. All leaves are canceled indefinitely. We are on the highest stage of alert I have ever seen. I'm scared shitless. I don't know what's going on. They tell us nothing.

I learned to call home by dialing through the Watts line to a base in upstate New York and then having the operator there place a phone call. So on my post one night, I get by a phone and I called the AP [Associated Press]. I'm speaking to this guy on night duty. I said, "Look, I'm calling from an Air Force base, and we're on alert getting ready for a nuclear war. Can you tell me why? What's going on?" It's like I woke him up or something. He goes, "What're you talking about?" He says, "There's nothing going on, man." Now I'm really scared. This was real.

I never found out what it was until I went to see Ellsberg speak. [Daniel Ellsberg, who leaked the Pentagon Papers.] He talks about how Nixon was going to nuke Hanoi between the moratoriums. All the United States forces went on worldwide alert, getting ready to move into defcon 1, which is nuclear war. Kissinger talks about it in the book Seymour Hersh wrote on Kissinger [*The Price of Power*, 1983].

The point of all this was that I realized that these motherfuckers are insane. They're going to nuke people for all this madness. The fact that they scared me became an emboldening thing. Now I was more rebellious than ever before.

The Air Force came down with an early out. They wanted to cut the budget, and I believe the early out was really linked to getting rid of a whole lot of resistance. In September, we were let out three months early. All the troublemakers got out.

I can remember just before we got out, this whole new load of guys came in, and they'd just come from Nam. This one guy, this Italian kid—I'll never forget it—I help him with his bags and take him up to his room. He puts his bag on the floor, reaches over, and slaps his antiwar poster up on the wall. They're not just getting rid of us; they're getting some worse people. This guy didn't wait for nothing. He's putting his poster up as the very first act he's going to do.

By March of 1970, I'm going to all the demonstrations in New York city as I can. I'm not working. I'm using the couple of thousands of dollars that I saved from Vietnam to support myself while I come into New York every day and do all these different things. I'm looking for a vets' group.

What did you hope to accomplish? Why not just go on with your life, get a job?

The driving force initially, I think, came out of that betrayal of ideals—and manipulation. For a long time, vengeance—anger—was the answer. They're going to pay for trying to get us killed. Not only for trying to get us killed—they're going to pay for what we did to the people.

They were going to keep on doing this shit to people. They were going to keep on selling new lies to the youth. If you hide out, they get to keep doing it forever and ever and ever. So you've got to come out and tell people the truth. I felt that responsibility very heavily. I think a lot of people did. It's really based, I think, in a real fundamental belief in people: faith in people.

"A Big Letdown"

JOEL GREENBERG

Joel Greenberg was a "red diaper baby" but considered himself apolitical as a young man. He enlisted in the Marine Corps because he was attracted to the Marines' advertisements, promising to make men out of enlistees. He was interviewed with his companion, Annie Luginbill.

I enlisted in September of 1966. I ended up in California at Fort Ord for basic. I was there for basic, went to Fort Gordon for radio-teletype, and then Campbell.

In reception you take a battery of tests. I passed everyone except for writing. They reviewed them and said, "What do you want to do? You can be anything but a translator." My attitude was: I'm still looking for the elite kind of thing, so I want to go Special Forces. You're eighteen-nine [eighteen years, nine months old]. Special Forces doesn't take anyone less than nineteen-six. So what can I take that will get me into Special Forces? Well, they look for three things: medic, communications, or light weapons infantry. I was never too good at first aid. Whether I was intimidated because both my parents had gone that way, I don't know. I didn't want to be infantry. So that left signals. So I'm in signals.

When I was in Gordon for radio-teletype they had openings for OCS [officer candidate school]. I had a year of college, which was more than most. So I filed for OCS. They said, "What are you being trained for?" I said, "Signal." They said, "You don't have the knowledge and experience for signal." They wanted people with electrical engineering degrees or degrees in communications, stuff like that. "But if you want, we'll send you to OCS as infantry, armor, or artillery"—you know, the combat arms. I had enough sense to know I didn't want that. So I was a radio-teletype operator.

I got to the unit in May of 1967. We were stationed at Campbell. A platoon sergeant picked up a picture of the platoon and said, "I will keep this and I'll go crossing off whatever percentage of you guys are going to get killed because you didn't listen to me while you were here."

There were aspects of basic that I liked, but there was a lot of things I didn't like about the military. All in all I wasn't really satisfied with the military. It was a big letdown from what I anticipated.

How so?

Too much chickenshit nonsense. It didn't seem real or tangible. Go to the motor pool and clean the jeeps. You go out on a field exercise—shit, I had been in the Boy Scouts; it's camping. You have to get up at six in the morn-

Joel Greenberg in Vietnam: aloft, with *(left)* Ben Rudd and *(right)* George McField; and two other views.

ing and shave in cold water. This is part of why I was discouraged with the military. Things that I wanted, I wasn't getting. I wasn't getting the glory out of it. It's one of these things that when you're looking at something from afar, it's never the same when you go through it.

I put in a 1049, a request for a personal transfer. I requested to be sent to Vietnam. It came back and was turned down. I didn't know why at the time, but a couple of weeks later the whole division came down with orders.

I ended up going to Vietnam in November of 1967. I was part of the advance party down in Bien Hoa, cleaning hootches and getting things ready for when the division came over. Then we got into the area [where] we were going to be billeted. A couple of us were assigned to a barracks to clean it. It wasn't anything very glorified. That was the first couple of weeks after we got there. We then convoyed out to an area called Phuoc Binh, a little northeast of Bien Hoa. Basically that's where I was for six months.

What was your duty?

Radio-teletype. Within my platoon, we had three radio-teletype teams: one E-5, two Spec-4s or PFCs. They changed periodically. We provided backup to comm centers. We had the ability to communicate with voice, CW [continuous wave radio], and teletype. There were very few times where we served as the primary source of communication.

When we first got in-country, it was a month before we could communicate with the people we were supposed to communicate with, because we came over with new equipment and they still had old equipment. Even though it was all AM radio—we were on the same frequency—but it was like a half a millisecond difference. It was just off enough that we couldn't communicate.

During the time we were at Phuoc Binh, each team had a day on the rig, which meant an eight-hour shift every three days. The rest of it was details. It was three police calls a day, filling sandbags, and details, details, and details. Then they took the E-5s out of the picture and put us on 12-hour shifts. I didn't see any combat the entire time I was in-country.

I tried getting out. I filed a 1049 for infantry. It came back rejected. My unit would not let me go because I was needed. Why am I needed? We're not doing anything here. We're just sitting here. I'm getting fed up with this bullshit. It's all details. Got nothing to do but fill sandbags.

The sergeant talked to me and said, "You really don't want to go into infantry. Stay here. When we get a chance to send a radio-teletype team to the field, I'll send you; don't worry." At each juncture, they kept on putting the brakes on.

After six months, we wound up moving to the central highlands. We were there for about a month and some change. From there we went up to a Special Forces camp in Dak Pen, which was right across from the Laotian border. We spent a week or so there and then the brigade went south. I stayed with an infantry battalion. We stayed there for a few weeks. Then I went down to Cu Chi. I was there for a couple of months. I was in the field a lot. The field represented anything from Camp Evans, which was Third Brigade headquarters, and then later on into the A Shau, basically at Firebase Birchess Garden. When I came back to battalion headquarters, beginning in September and October, late 1967 into early 1968, the replacements that we were getting were people who were drafted, compared to most of us who first joined in 1966. Now we had people who were more aware of Vietnam—as well as changes taking place within the antiwar movement in the country being reflected in the attitudes of the people coming in.

At the end of the first year, they had what they called the "Mad Grenadier" running around battalion headquarters at Camp Eagle. This was somebody or somebodies who were throwing grenades and claymores at the officers. We were the only battalion that I know of that had to wear flak jackets and sealed pots in the company area. We had MPs patrolling the area.

As time went on, you started questioning more directly. My parents and my brother sent things, including things like C. Wright Mills's *The Power Elite;* Lenny Bruce's book, *How to Talk Dirty and Influence People;* and [Eldridge] Cleaver's *Soul on Ice.* I left all of them because they were paperback, except *Soul on Ice.*

I never considered myself to be a hippie, but when I came back from leave, I bought some Day-Glo paint and black lights and did up our hootch. Drugs by that time were more prevalent. Another thing was the racist attitude of things, and the contradictions.

What do you mean by racist attitudes and contradictions?

I had a real interesting experience fairly early on. Still back in Bien Hoa, I was in-country about two weeks and they gave us a day off. We went into town. First Vietnamese we get to meet were the bar girls. I asked one, "What do you think about the Americans being here?" The answer was, "Just bullshit." It's like some white person going into the ghetto and saying, "What do you think about white folks?"

The Vietnamese I met were those who had something to gain from the Americans' being there, whether it was prostitutes, mama-san, papa-san, or whoever it was. You never really got to meet Vietnamese on a one-to-one basis where they would say the Vietcong were right. We met people who worked on the base, women who came in to do the laundry and clean the hootches.

Within our platoon, we had three guys who I considered kids. I was nineteen and I turned twenty in December. We had one kid from Florida who lied to the recruiters about his age to get in when he was sixteen. There was a certain naiveness, openness, and honesty that they had that most of us didn't. Mike Cordon was one of them, and he developed a relationship with this girl—Suzie, one of the girls that worked at the EM [enlisted man] club—to the point where he wanted to get married.

Suzie's family came from the north when the Catholics left the north. Her father was politically affiliated with the powers that be in Vietnam. They were a good Catholic family. So you would think that this was somebody who you would say: Great; this isn't some little floozy that somebody's getting attached to. But he ran into all kinds of problems, up to and including his brother.

133

His brother had two tours in Vietnam at that point. He was Special Forces. He had three years or something like that. He had a special job lined up at the Pentagon after another six months in-country. They told him that "If your brother marries this girl, we can't give you clearance for this job. You go talk to him." His brother was cool and told him he would deal with whatever came down.

Here was a case where, if these were our friends and we're fighting for their liberation and all the other propaganda shit, and here's a girl that you think would typify the best that this country has, then why would they be so opposed and hostile?

One thing that I had no use for was racism of any sort. That was part of the way I was brought up. Regardless of what I said earlier, one thing we had no choice in was, we were dragged to Washington for King's civil rights march in 1963. We did go. The area that I grew up in was basically an all-white neighborhood. It was mixed in that there were Jews and Catholics. My mother was involved in desegregating the apartment complex that we lived in. Most of the houses were single-family, but there were apartment buildings there. She worked with the NAACP [National Association for the Advancement of Colored People]. My oldest friend, in terms of longevity, is someone I went to nursery school with. It was a black family that was parallel to ours. They had a kid my age and a younger kid who was my brother's age. We still maintain contact.

Gooks and all this other shit—I was very well aware of what those code words meant. I would not refer to them in any derogatory way. If you were there defending these people . . . ? The contradictions became clearer and clearer over time.

It's funny, when I was clearing [being discharged], you go through these lines: "If you got any shit [imitating officer on duty], get rid of it now and no questions will be asked." Some of the other guys and I split a nickel bag and I filled up a tube of toothpaste and hair dressing with grass. It's not a whole lot. I thought I'd give it to my brother. So I'm worried about that because everywhere you go, "If you got anything, we're going to find it." So I got my suitcase ready to go through the line, and this black AP is the one that winds up checking my bag. It wasn't planned—it was just a fluke that as soon as he opened up the suitcase, there's *Soul on Ice*, right on top. The guy looks at the book, he looks at me, looks at the book, looks at me, closes the suitcase and [says], "Get out of here."

I got out in June of 1969. I came back with the attitude that the United States shouldn't be there. We weren't really wanted there. The war was wrong. It wasn't very well thought out. It was about five or six months after I got out before I did anything.

What did you do after you got out?

I drank. The first demonstration I went to was in October 1969 up in Poughkeepsie. It was the moratorium. It was to build up regional demonstra-

134

tions before the big demonstration in November. I went to see what was going on. I wasn't active by any means, but I wasn't hostile toward the activists.

Were people aware that you were a veteran?

Yeah.

Were they hostile to you?

No, not at all. Some of the pro-war students were, because I was antiwar. I got in a confrontation with one of the teachers who was coaching the golf team. He was out there. He was not a vet, but very right-wing. We were trying to lower the flag, and he had his boys out there with their golf clubs to defend the flag.

Then I went to the moratorium in D.C. Again, I went down mainly as an observer [rather] than a participant. One of the things that impressed me about it was the number of veterans that I saw. When I got back to New York, I got in touch with Vets for Peace [VFP] and through working with them, they eventually channeled me into VVAW.

Why switch from VFP to VVAW?

It was more our generation. The older vets, according to us, were more straitlaced.

"Any Illusions I Had Were Blown Away"

DAVE CLINE

When Dave Cline was drafted in January 1967, he had read the speeches of Martin Luther King and others opposing American involvement in Vietnam and had developed his own misgivings about it. But because of the strong influence of his upbringing, and the influence of cultural values regarding the war and his own role as a young American, he was unable to take a clear position.

I went to basic training at Fort Dix. Then I went to advanced infantry training at Fort Polk, Louisiana, Tiger Land, which is one of the training spots for Vietnam.

Down there, they used to give you basically two raps on why you were going to Vietnam. One was that rap about we're going to help the heroic South Vietnamese people. We're going to go fight for freedom [and repel] communist aggression. They'd show you the maps and stuff, the domino theory, the Red Chinese are trying to engulf all of southeast Asia. The other rap was: killing communists was your duty. It was a killing thing. I couldn't identify at all with that one because I was brought up in a Christian background—thou shall not kill, you know. I mean, I didn't even like hunting, and where I came from, a lot of people hunt. I always found that a little sick.

They shipped us up to Fort Lewis, and they sent us down to Fort Ord, and then they shipped us to Vietnam on troopships from there. I went over there in July of 1967. We were almost three weeks sailing across the Pacific. There was a guy named Wilkerson, who was from Tennessee; a guy named Chingary, who was from Woodbridge, New Jersey; and a guy named Warner, who was from upstate [New York]. We hung around together. I can remember standing out on deck at night having these discussions around are we going there to help the people, or is this a fraud? We would have discussions about it because we'd be reading the paper, and there was the beginning of protest and people challenging it.

In the Army PXs [post exchanges], they used to carry magazines. One of the magazines they carried was *Ramparts,* which was a left-liberal magazine in them days. I started reading that magazine. I read Martin Luther King's speech, "Why I Oppose the War in Vietnam," in that magazine while I was at Fort Polk, Louisiana.

We'd sit around and discuss it. It wasn't like we were saying we're not going to go. I didn't have a support network of people fighting it. I didn't feel confident to make that call.

We stopped in the Philippines one night on the way to Vietnam, at Subic Bay. That was the only time we got off the ship. That was the first time I ever saw any third world country. I still recall crossing the bridge into town, and there was these kids on little rafts under the bridge begging for money. You throw the money off into the water and they'd dive for it. That was the first time I ever saw such abject poverty. Then in Vietnam, it was that same thing, the abject poverty. You see people begging and eating out of garbage and stuff like that. You felt definitely like, What am I doing here?

The boat came into Danang, and then they flew us from Danang to Cu Chi. I remember it was humid and hot and smelled. First thing you do when you get in-country is, they give you these indoctrination classes and they say, "Forget all that shit they told; you can't trust any of these people. They're not really people anyway; they're gooks." They teach you about booby traps: "The prostitutes got razor blades in their vaginas; the Coca-Cola's got ground glass." They'd tell you all that stuff. In other words: You see anyone with slant eyes, that's your potential enemy—don't trust them. That sort of blows away any "help the people" thing.

I was in infantry, 11 Bravo, so it wasn't like I was in one of these civic action teams. The area I was assigned to at Cu Chi, right by the Ho Bo woods, was called the Iron Triangle. That was considered to be a Vietcong area, or what they would call a liberated area, going back prior to the French war. That's always been one of the strongholds of NLF, Vietcong activities. In the time I was in Vietnam, we operated in Cu Chi, and then they moved us to Tay Ninh, which is also considered a liberated zone, up by Nui Ba Den—the Black Virgin Mountain—and going all the way over to Cambodia. So [in] both of the areas I operated in, the civilians you ran into were basically all Vietcong or Vietcong sympathizers. Any illusions I had were blown away.

What did you think about your role, since your illusions were blown away?

I have these letters I wrote from Vietnam; I still have them. For a long time, I couldn't remember a lot of things, you know; and I got these letters from my parents and read them over. There was a lot of shit in there I had forgotten all about. A lot of people getting killed I had forgotten about. Actually, reading them letters—I was like writing these antiwar tracts from Vietnam. There were pretty heavy-duty things about racism and blacks and whites fighting together, and how America has to deal with blacks as equals because we're equal here and shit like that. But I was operating on the basic idea that you're stuck here and you have to survive. It was fucked up. I was just going to stay alive and get out of this shit. The idea that I was just going to refuse to go out there was something I didn't even think about.

Did you have any contact with the Vietnamese there?

Communication was not too hot between people. They'd know a little English and you'd know a little Vietnamese. The main connection I had with the Vietnamese was either with the ARVNs, who I used to really think were shitheads, and mainly the whores.

I can remember one time we were going out on an operation and we were moving past one of their camps, and they [ARVN] were trying to pimp their wives or their girlfriends to us at the time. I thought, What a bunch of sleazebags. I used to know some of the girls. You come in, you get to know a couple of them. I used to think they were nice.

During the interview, Dave Cline pulled out some of the letters he had written home. He showed them to me and read some aloud.

[Reading.] "August 17, 1967—Hi, everyone. How's everything going? We haven't been doing much here. They have everything screwed up. We've just been monkeying around. . . . I have 328 days over here. . . . I think this stuff stinks. You're always dirty because it's hard to take a shower here. It's always muddy. . . . Lately I been thinking about the problems Americans got. We get *Time* and *Newsweek* here, and I been reading about the riots in the cities. Over here we don't have any racial tensions. Everyone hangs around

137

together. There's just a few white and colored guys who hate each other, but there's only a few of them. I've been reading about the riots. . . . One writer said it was the formal destruction of discrimination. The masses are less patient in their quest for equality. I believe this. We're over here fighting for 'freedom.' Whether all of us support or believe this is doubtful. But when we come home, everyone figures that they gave their sweat and blood for whites and blacks; and if people mess with anyone about his worth, people here won't take it. When this thing ends, either the cooperation or equality we have here will come back with us or America will be a house on fire. . . . I have to close now because we have to put sandbag walls around the barracks in case of mortar attacks."

What were your impressions of the military?

[Returning to his narrative.] It was fucked up, the way they treated people. There was a young black guy from Chicago in my unit. Every time we would get in a firefight, he would just break down. The first time it happened, he broke down crying. Another time, they sent him out on patrol and the patrol got ambushed. He took his rifle and just started beating it on a tree, bent it right around a tree. They refused to take him out of the field. The sergeants and the officers kept telling him they were going to make a man out of him, he's a pussy, and all that stuff. The kid was useless in combat because when the bullets started flying, he'd just start crying.

I got shot on two different occasions. The first time I got shot was over by the Saigon river, doing sweeps into the Ho Bo woods. I got shot in the back. They landed us in this rice paddy area and we were doing a sweep up to the river. This was an area where the Vietcong used to bring supplies through, so they would sweep through this area on a monthly basis. The Vietcong found out what the schedule of sweeps was, so they built concrete bunkers in a horseshoe shape all around the LZ [landing zone]. They knew the whole thing. When they brought in the first wave, they started shooting at them. Then they brought in the second wave. We were on the third wave. You could see the tracer rounds shooting in front of the helicopters as you were coming in. We were bailing out of the helicopters. It was all in rice paddies. We were running along these rice paddies and this kid I mentioned, this black kid, he was loaded down with bandoliers of machine-gun bullets. He slipped off the dike into the rice and started sinking in the mud. He was just standing there crying. So I turned around and kneeled on the edge of the dike, trying to pull him out of the mud, and I got hit right in the upper back. It hit me, came through my back, hit a rib, and then came out through my lower back on the other side.

I got reported dead at that time, actually. What happened was, my left lung got filled up with blood and I fell in a rice paddy. They tried to get me out. They brought a helicopter in. The medic went to open the door and got a bullet through his hand. He jumped back in the ship and they took off. So I lay there for almost an hour. I had leeches all over me. They gave me two hits of morphine, so after a while I wasn't feeling no pain. Then they reported I was dead. I was sent to Vung Tau hospital. Two months later I was back in combat.

[Reading from another letter.] "August 31, 1967—Don't worry when I tell you this, but I got shot yesterday. . . . All together we had eight killed and 44 wounded. . . . I know almost all the dead or wounded, and I'm sick about the fight. They sent us out there and we got slaughtered. . . . What I saw out there yesterday was the most terrible thing in my life. I ain't going out there ever again. It scares me just to think about it. This place is hell."

[Returning to his narrative.] My friends—Warner, Chingary, and Wilkerson—had been told I was dead. They came in from the field. They got drunk. A lot of times, that's how guys would mourn their friends and remember them. A lot of times they wouldn't even have memorial services when guys got killed. It was just, either the guy got killed or he went home, but he's gone. They used to tell you over there, "Don't make any friends, because then you won't feel bad if they get killed." Then they found out I was alive. They came down to see me at the hospital, which was pretty heavy duty.

[Reading from another letter.] "October 17, 1967—I don't know if I told you, but the battalion went into a hospital the other day. They got all kinds of medical equipment there. In our orderly room they got a banner they took from there that says, "People of Vietnam Unite for Peace" in Vietnamese. If Charlie really wants to do that, there ain't no one here who would complain. In our battalion, some of the guys are signing up for two more years in the Army to get off the line—that's how bad it is out there. If it's real bad by Tay Ninh, I might do that. I hope I get shot out there and it isn't serious, because if you get two Purple Hearts, you're off the line. . . . Over here our guys and Charlie are killing each other and it ain't proving a thing. When we lost those nine men the other day, they found 15 dead Charlies, but that isn't any satisfaction. . . . Most of the guys here don't want to kill nobody. They just fight to keep alive. I heard they had a walkout on McNamara and they had signs that say, "Support Our Boys in Vietnam but Not the People Who Send Them There." Need I say more? I have 264 days to go."

[Returning to his narrative.] Then they moved us up to Tay Ninh. This was just prior to the Tet offensive. We were out chasing NVA regulars out in the bush by the Cambodian border. We'd find out they had these permanent base camps set up all over.

They had us stop in this field and told us to dig foxholes, but it was real hard ground so we could only dig shallow holes. They [NVA] were out there in the jungle at night. It was really freaky. They'd be yelling, "Fuck you, fuck you," out to you in the jungle at night. They started mortaring us, and we were in real shallow holes. They walked a mortar round right up to the foxhole. The round blew up and killed the sergeant. He was a nice guy. A guy named Walker from Georgia. He got hit in the head with shrapnel. The lieutenant's throat got cut. The radio got smashed, and I got one piece in the shoulder.

Then they started mortaring us again. It was right in the middle of this big fucking anthill. The ants are coming all on us, the mortar rounds—it was real insane. That was the only night I really ever wanted to fight in all of Vietnam. I was ready to kick ass that night. I didn't even want to go in from the field. They ordered me from the helicopter to come back. When I got in from the field, they treated me for the wound, pulled out the shrapnel, put a patch on it, and tried to send me back. I disappeared for a week. I went AWOL. I was hanging out downtown at the whorehouses and sneaking back at night. They finally caught me and sent me back in the field.

Why did you go AWOL?

I didn't know where to go. I was just partying, getting fucked up. I was smoking pot at the time. I wasn't even thinking about going AWOL; I was just thinking about the next minute. You know what they say in AA, "Live a day at a time." Vietnam was the downside of that expression. You weren't thinking about anything. You were just trying to keep alive. That was what I was trying to do. I just thought, Fuck it, man—until they get me I'm just going to keep on doing this.

I got wounded the last time out near the Cambodian border. This happened on December 20, 1967. Again, we were doing these sweeps and we were overrun about two in the morning. The North Vietnamese launched a massive human wave attack. We could hear them yelling orders maybe 25, 30 feet away, and these guys were charging. That was the only time in Vietnam I thought I was dead for sure. It was really crazy. It was like that scene at the end of *Platoon* [Oliver Stone's film of 1986].

A guy came running up to my foxhole. We saw him coming from the next hole over and we didn't know if it was an American retreating over to us or a Vietnamese, because it was two in the morning. So we didn't shoot him.

I was sitting there with my rifle waiting to see, and all of a sudden he stuck his rifle in. I saw the front side of an AK-47 and a muzzle flash, and then I pulled my trigger. I shot him through his chest. I blacked out initially, but then I came to and found a round went right through my knee. They threw me in a foxhole and gave me a bottle of Darvons. I lay there until the battle ended. In the morning they medivaced me out.

They carried me over to this guy I had shot. He was sitting up against this tree stump. He was just sitting there with his rifle across his lap. He was dead. The sergeant started giving me this pep talk, "Here's the gook you killed!" In my unit they had a big thing about confirmed kills. If you had a confirmed kill and the person had an automatic weapon, then you were supposed to get a three-day in-country pass. The confirmed kill was to your credit, but the weapon was what determined whether you got a pass. While I was in a number of firefights and may have shot a number of people, this was the only person I could say was a confirmed kill of mine.

This kid looked about the same age as me. The first thing I started thinking was, Why is he dead and I'm alive? The only reason he's dead and I'm alive is that he had his gun pointing where my knee was and I had mine pointing where his chest was. It could have been him or me. It was just fate or coincidence or luck, or whatever. When I first went there, I used to pray a lot to God: Don't let me get shot. But I kept on getting shot, so I sort of stopped believing in that sort of attitude.

Then after going into the hospital, I started thinking about that guy. I wonder if his mother knows he's dead? I wonder if he had a girlfriend? Looking back, I think I was retaining the sense that he was a human being. Part of the act of killing is to dehumanize the person. What I was doing, though I didn't realize it at the time, was [realizing] that he was a human that I killed and dealing with that act.

[Reading from a letter.] "December 24, 1967—Here it is, Christmas eve in Vietnam. I got a great present for Christmas. I got off the line. On December 20th I got shot in the knee. . . . When I got hit, it was two in the morning. The North Vietnamese hit us with a human wave attack. Charlie ran up and stuck his weapon in my hole and started shooting. I had to shoot him. When they kept charging, I thought we were all going to die. It was the most terrible experience in my life. . . . I hope you pray for peace on Christmas and I hope this war ends in 1968."

[Returning to his narrative.] I was sent to a hospital in Camp Zomo in Japan. When I was in the hospital, I went to the Army library there. I found a book by Donald Duncan called *The New Legions* [1967]. It was at that time that I began to develop a political understanding of the war. Previous to that, I thought the war was fucked up, but it was sort of like: The politicians are fucked up; let Lyndon Johnson and Ho Chi Minh fight. In reading that book, I began to get a sense that these people had a cause that they were fighting for. I mean, I understood that they were better fighters than us . . . not that they were better fighters, but that they were more motivated than us. We wouldn't keep charging like them.

I said, When I get back, I'm going to do something to stop other people from getting sent to this craziness. A lot of guys, when they get back from the war, pretend it didn't happen—you know, like, "Where you been for a year?" "I been in Nam and got a new car." You know.

My brother Bruce was a year younger than me, and I thought they were going to try to get him next. When I got back, I was sent to the hospital at Fort Dix and on a medical recuperation leave for a couple of months. They sent my brother Bruce a draft notice, and he was trying to determine what he should do. He considered the idea of going to Canada and becoming an exile. He went up to Montreal and met with these groups of people who were draft dodgers up there, and he decided that that wasn't for him. He hooked up with this group called the Buffalo Draft Resistance Union. Bruce and Bruce Byers, another fellow, refused to be inducted into the military. They took sanctuary in a Unitarian Church in Buffalo. They held a vigil every night and they had all the different peace groups. While I was home on convalescent leave, I went down and stayed in the church with them and made public statements opposing the war in Vietnam. I was in the papers saying, I just got back; I'm supporting my brother.

I was opposed to the war and supported the demonstrators. You got to take a stand, you know. I also thought at the time that the people would get behind us because we were the guys who fought the war. They're going to listen to us because we're their sons. I was a little naive, but that was what I was thinking.

"I Started Learning the Real History of Vietnam"

MIKE McCAIN

Mike McCain was the son of a lifer in the Air Force. He joined the Marines after having received his draft notice, because he believed that the Marines offered "the best opportunity for survival." He also wanted to be with the "best of the best."

I enlisted in the Marine Corps May 24th, 1966. It was still what they called the "old Corps" where they could touch you and be up in your face. I mean, just intense. I personally got whaled on every single day for three months. Sergeant Bolton, our gunnery sergeant, would just walk up and, boom, cold-cock you while he was asking you a question. I figured I'm going to learn how to fight and survive. I got other things that I want to do afterward.

One basis of boot camp is to get you physically fit; the other is emotional, the ability to be able to react when told to without having to be critical. You're broken down psychologically and then rebuilt in the mold which can respond when the need arises, especially during wartime. There's nothing like the threat of death to focus your mind.

How did they prepare you for Vietnam?

We were getting straight propaganda. We got there the story of how poor little General Ky and Thieu were just standing facing these onslaughts of North Vietnamese hordes. They had asked us if we could come and help them out in any way. Of course, the United States government, being the kind and wonderful people that we are, said, Listen, we'll try and figure out something we can do to help.

You believed that?

Yes. I had no other basis of belief.

I was a radio operator. You carry this very peculiarly shaped package on your back and an antennae up in the air; the second lieutenant is standing next to you [laughs], so I got one of the few jobs that had less of a life expectancy than second lieutenants. My MOS [military occupational specialty] was 2533. I could operate any piece of radio gear the military had, AM-FM, single-sideband, radio-relay, cryptology stuff. I graduated first in my class in radio school, which is one of the most intense schools in the military.

Then I got sent to Defense Language Institute. There was an experimental class set up in the Defense Language Institute up in Monterey at the Naval War College where they took a 12-month language class and compressed it into 90 days. I was there with officers and enlisted people from every branch in the service. I graduated first in my class there too.

Pfc. Mike McCain receiving the *Leatherneck Magazine* Award.

Every time I graduated, I got promoted. When I got out of boot camp I got PFC because I was the series honor man; I got the Leatherneck Dress Blues Award; I got every single award the Marine Corps could give you coming out of boot camp. Out of radio school, I was made lance corporal. Out of language school, I was made corporal. So I was an E-4 at the end of a year in the Marine Corps. I was an E-4 when I got out too. [Laughs.] I came close to sergeant, but by then I had an attitude.

I got offered to go to OCS then, and embassy school. I was the perfect size for going to embassy school. When I graduated from boot camp, I was 210 pounds of solid muscle with a 28-inch waist. I was bright and articulate and I looked good in uniform. They loved people like me. I had all the bases covered, but I said no. I had already enlisted for three years and in order to do either one of those things, I would have had to have increased my time in the military. I already knew I didn't want to do that.

I had already grown up in it. There were some problems of being a lifer in the military, and there was nothing that could be done about that. The class structure is rigid. I mean the guy that's the colonel could be the stupidest thing alive, but he's still the colonel. There's no future in being an enlisted man with 30 years in the Marine Corps, being an E-9 and knowing how to do everything and talking to some shave-ass lieutenant and calling him sir. I would have told them to fuck off. I turned all that down, knowing that the only alternative was going to Vietnam.

I got to Vietnam on May 28th, 1967. I was in the First Marine Division, Headquarters Battalion, Com Company Radio Platoon, in Danang. We were the ones that ran the first Marine Division Com center. We went on every operation that the Marine Corps was involved in. I did convoy duty and I did operations. For not being a grunt, I was in combat about as much as it was possible to be, which is about 50 percent of the time.

What do you mean by combat?

Actually being in a position to get shot at and having to shoot back. Most combat veterans will say that the most intense periods of their lives were those wartime experiences. It was insane—flashes of intense terror and fright coupled with incredible moments of quiet and tenderness. You're never nearly as alive as you are except when your ass is on the line. Either somebody's shooting at you, or you're shooting at somebody else. Everything is on. All your senses are alert. You feel everything. You smell everything. Sex doesn't have anywhere near the immersion of sensation that combat does.

In Danang, you had a few rockets come in now and then, but you walked around in a bathing suit and flip-flops, smoked dope and drank beer at the club, paid $5 to get laid, and stuff like that. It was like being in a resort.

We were living on the highest point of Danang harbor, which is one of the most beautiful natural harbors in the world. Our hootch in Danang was pretty cool. We had hustled mattresses. We had sheets. We had blankets and pillows. We had cantilevered porches built down the side of the mountain to hang out on. We had these huge stereo sound systems. We had cold water to drink. They're very comfortable. But then of course, when you're out in the bush, it wasn't like that at all.

As soon as I got over there, as a goof, I started going around and asking people that I would meet, you know, the mama-sans that would come in to work around us, "Ay, which one of you guys invited us over here?" I started learning the real history of Vietnam and the war and the struggle of the French against the Vietnamese from the Vietnamese.

There are Marines there who are telling me, "Don't believe anything you heard, man; this place is fucked." It was like this, "Hey, new kid, what they just told you, you been lied to, asshole. They're fucking with you." These are Marines telling me this.

One story was being told in the United States, and people who had been there for a while knew what that story was, but that was not the reality of what was going on. I mean these great advances and military victories and all that were being reported in the United States papers, people were telling me were just not true at all. "No, man, that's bullshit. They kicked our ass."

How did this strike you?

It was like an epiphany. It was like, Wow, what's going on here? So I started asking. There wasn't any putting it together at that point. The conscious analysis didn't happen until much much later, not until after Tet in 1968, after I had been there for a long time, that I started really questioning and understanding the politics of what was going on. But that was just the beginning of it. It didn't reach completion for years after I got out of the military and did antiwar work, because I had to study the history. There was just this feeling that there was some problem here.

Did you ever personally experience the problems you had heard of?

Oh, yeah. The experience with the ARVN was that. The ARVN was as much our enemy as the NVA or PRG [Provisional Revolutionary Government]. That was the first real clue, because these people were supposed to be fighting for their own country and there was no way in hell they were.

They were just a bunch of crooks. They would steal anything they saw that they wanted. If they saw a young woman who was particularly good-looking, she would get raped by all of them. Somebody had a piece of meat or some food they wanted, it would be taken. They couldn't be counted on for anything. They were worthless. They were a drain on the society as a whole. This is what I saw. They didn't act like the soldiers who were supposed to be try-ing to free the people.

The military is always supposed to be in the service of the people. This is what I thought then; this is what I think now. I'm not antimilitary, not at all. There are rules that you have to abide by. Neither the ARVN nor the United States military functioned in a way that I thought was right. I mean, there was always prostitutes around. They institutionalized prostitution around military bases. You could get laid for five bucks or a case of C rats. That, I felt, was fundamentally wrong.

There was another problem in that the United States military was not intel-lectually capable of understanding what was going on in Vietnam. One of the things that was going on then was that we would take places in the daytime; then move out at night; it would be taken over; and then go out and go through the same fight the next morning. We weren't educated about this hill as a strategic position; we were just told: Kill—go kill!

I had a constant struggle with officers. Most of the officers didn't have a clue about what was going on, nor did they know how to lead, which I was already learning how to do. I was active in sports in high school; and grow-ing up in the military, I knew what chain of command was, I knew what teamwork was. We're all in this shit together. Very seldom was there that rela-tionship with officers.

One of my nicknames was "The Man." The Man was the guy who made sure you came back. I was always a squad leader or platoon leader, and nobody that was ever with me died—and we were in some pretty difficult places. I had a sense . . . I knew when something was about to happen. I'd wake up from a dead sleep in our hootch and tell everyone to move and get in the bunker, and we'd get in the bunker and the first round would hit. Nobody would have survived.

You don't let ignorance rule just because it's wearing a bar. You don't allow yourself to be killed because some asshole says go do something. I mean the lieutenants in Vietnam had to be brought along. That's where fragging was involved. When push came to shove, if your only choice was to die yourself or getting rid of this dude who was going to put you in a position where you were going to be killed, the choice was reasonably simple.

The other thing was the callousness of the military itself that I found out about very quickly. If you got office hours, your punishment was to work in the mess hall. So people were doing disgustingly gross shit with the food because it was their punishment, right? Once you find that out, you say, "I don't think I want to go there anymore. I don't like this guy beating off into my coleslaw, pissing in the spaghetti, or whatever it was." [Laughs.]

We wrote to Senator McGovern, Kennedy, and the guy from Oregon [Sen-ator Wayne Morse] who voted against the Tonkin Gulf [resolution], saying, Listen, we think we got a bad situation here and we don't think the Marine

Corps should be doing this. We had already talked to our own officers and stuff and said, This is not such a good idea, guys; we all like to eat.

That was the first time I got in trouble. I got called up before very high brass. "How dare you tell somebody else that there's something wrong with our Marine Corps? You should have come to us first." Our response was, We tried. Nobody would pay any attention to us. "Well, you must have not done it right." It became totally our fault. We became the ones who had done something wrong. We had circumvented the chain of command, which is a deadly sin. We refused to accept it. They were wrong.

I was bucking authority. They were doing two o'clock in the morning inspections and shit like that. I told them, This is real stupid, man. I had grown up in a family that said you should always fight for what's right. Your bosses are supposed to take care of you, all of this shit. I've always been an uppity sort of guy. I've always been willing to accept that people might be smarter than I was, but they damn well better take my opinion into consideration because I was just like anybody else. Our society is supposed to be about that kind of stuff.

Very few people would argue, if they'd been there very long, about the correctness of what we were doing. It just wasn't an argument that held a lot of water. It was always talked about, but there were always people who didn't want to admit it. Because then it means, What's my life about? What's my country about? Questions like that are hard to deal with. Most people don't want to raise the questions.

At one point, my commanding officer decided that the way to deal with me and that phenomenon was by getting rid of me. I was made the commanding general's bodyguard of Task Force X-Ray, which was the unit that was in Hue City. It was Brigadier General Foster Carr Lahugh, a graduate of VMI [Virginia Military Institute], straight, traditional, old Corps. I couldn't leave the boy's side. I was like connected with an umbilical chord with this guy.

We moved up to Phu Bai, which was a combined Army and Marine Corps unit. It was either the 101st or 82nd Airborne. We were the ones who had to go into Hue the 30th or 31st of January when Tet started.

The first night of Tet, when I was in Phu Bai, the CIA officer in Hue City came through the lines and walked into the command center totally unannounced. He and his Vietnamese radioman got through our lines and just walked into the commanding general's bunker to make their report. These guys were tripped out to the fucking nines. They're dressed in solid black. They got weapons I'd never seen before. They had the highest-quality, most brand-new radios that existed—weighed half as much as I had, twice the battery life. They had stuff that I would have given my eyeteeth to have.

He came in and he just gave the list of names of thousands of people that the CIA thought were sympathetic to the north. As far as I know, all the reports of the NVA coming in to Hue and killing all these people and burying them in mass graves was not done by them at all, but was done by the United States military.

I quit carrying bullets after that. I didn't carry bullets the last six months I was in Vietnam.

What about that experience made you stop carrying bullets?

I had already had the Vietnamese do several things for me, like I'd be out in the ville having dinner with people and somebody leaves the room and comes back a few minutes later and says, "There's a sweep coming through here; you'll have to come hide." I'd get put in a cellar or tunnel or something; and there'd be me—this big old white boy—and a couple of other Vietnamese, who I later figured out had to be the PRG or NVA because I could talk Vietnamese. So we'd talk.

They talked about their families and their life and what they wanted to do, just like I did. It was the most elemental of political discussions. "Are you married? Got any kids? My daughter's in high school now. She's doing pretty good. I'm worried about this guy she's going out with." I felt that they were all good people. They were just like anybody else.

As soon as Tet was over, the general got reassigned to the states, and I got sent back to radio platoon and was even more of a jefe than when I left because I had been up in Hue. When I got back to Danang at the end of February, we had this big party. That's when I found out about all the guys that died up on 337, which is the radio hill.

It's the most painful [holding back tears] . . . having your friends die. It's the most difficult thing next to your wife and children. The only comparison is family. . . . It's not really a comparison—that's what they really are, is family.

How did you make sense of their deaths?

I didn't. I smoked reefers [and] drank to numb it, because there was no mechanism. My first introduction to drugs was in Vietnam. I started smoking reefers there, speed, barbituates, because there were times on operations where you didn't want to go to sleep, so the corpsman would give us a thousand-tab jar of 10-milligram straight meth amphetamine. We'd take that out with us.

A political consciousness is growing in the entire military by that point. We started to occasionally get glimpses of an alternative analysis of what we were doing there. There were active-duty GI projects in some of the places around the world. People in Vietnam were starting to wear peace symbols on their helmets. "Vietnam for the Vietnamese." "Get the GIs Out of Here." "Peace Now." All those kinds of things.

I was there when Martin Luther King Jr. was assassinated. The MPs were almost all white. The cats were just happy—very, very happy. They thought

that was the coolest thing since white bread. I mean, it was all that traditional shit. "Thank god the nigger's dead. He deserved it." That sort of
shit. They came across the street mouthing off. We had a couple of black
people in our platoon, and we locked and loaded on them. Said, "Motherfucker, get your ass out here, or you will die. I don't want to hear that shit
anymore."

One of the guys I was involved with was from Chicago, "Honey Bear." He
had been telling us about the Black Panther Party. He had been getting the
newspaper from them. We were all reading it. We read anything.

There was an underground system of radio stations. The last operation I
was on was the first incursion into Cambodia trying to break the Ho Chi
Minh trail. So I'm sitting on top of the highest point in South Vietnam,
which is a hill called Ba Nai . . . I think it was Hill 1327. We were a mile or
so up. After midnight, all these underground radio stations would start coming on the air. The entire country was connected from top to bottom with
this underground system. You'd have the guys from Detroit with the
Motown show and the guys from Texas would be doing the country-and-
western bit. There'd be a salsa show and rock and roll, and all of this was
interspersed with news about what was actually going on. That was the first
time we actually started hearing about the mutinies in the Army. Of course,
we had done the same things in the Marine Corps already.

What do you mean?

You know, "I want you, Joe, to take your platoon out here. I want you to
make a perimeter. You go out three klicks to this point, head east, then do
this, and this whole thing. . . ." "Yeah, right." [Sarcastically.] You go out like
half a mile, find yourself a nice place, sit down all fucking day and come back
at night. "Yeah, I checked everything out and it's fine." That had been going
on for a long time.

The stupidity of the—you know—"Go out and take a hill during the day
and come back at night and give it up to the enemy" was the start of that.
There was a futility to anything we were doing. People just said, "If there isn't
any reason for it, what the fuck am I going to do it for?"

You discussed this . . . ?

Absolutely. A major topic of discussion, particularly after Tet. I mean, Tet's
the epiphany. That's where everybody got their eyes opened. That was an
eye-opener. "How did these little motherfuckers do this? How could this
possibly have happened?"

We had not been told the truth. What Westmoreland was doing was a
denial of the reality for so long that we didn't understand what had happened. We didn't realize that after Tet, the war was over. We destroyed huge

percentages of the infrastructure of the PRG and NVA. They were decimated, but we didn't perceive that at the time.

Tet starts the end of January, is over by the end of February, and I left country at the end of October of 1968. I had gotten my flight date, and like in 10 days before I was supposed to go home, I got busted for possession of a tenth of a gram of marijuana. My platoon commanding officer walked into the hootch and caught me with it. Within seconds of him walking in the door, people came in both doors of the hootch behind him, covered both doors, locked and loaded, and would have killed him on the spot if I had said, Do it. After he busted me, people were lining up to take him out because of the respect and position that I had in my unit, and I said, "No, you can't do that. It's wrong." He got transferred very shortly thereafter. Somebody made a phone call and he got sent to Fifth Marines in An Hoa, which was not a fun place to be. He was killed within two weeks of getting there with an M-60.

Because there was no longer any witnesses, I went from general court-martial to summary court-martial, where you have one officer who's judge, jury, defense, prosecuting attorney, and everything. It ended up being this hippie captain, a graduate in history from Berkeley. We talked about the great quantity of marijuana in Vietnam for an hour or so. He fills out the form, "not guilty," and I was on a plane in 48 hours and I was gone, but that took almost six months. I ended up doing almost 18 months in-country.

I got out late fall of 1968. Got transferred to Cherry Point Marine Corps Air Station in North Carolina, and basically did not do anything. I went to another school, to microwave relay school, where I learned how to work with microwave transmission. I then got an early out and was released on April 1, 1969.

I was still married to my first wife, Elaine. We packed the car. Sean was born then. We drove in a Volkswagen van from North Carolina to Los Angeles. Her family was in Los Angeles. I went to college. I was a straight-A student. I started studying political science, history, economics—trying to learn the history of what I had just been involved in.

Then Jackson State and Kent State and the invasion of Cambodia happened in early 1970, and I just got to where I felt I had to do something. I didn't know what it was I was supposed to do; I just felt that there was something I was supposed to do.

The military was killing our babies. You don't send the military into your schools. That was wrong. That's what we had done. We knew it. It was a gut reaction. There wasn't any analysis. There was just this overwhelming sense that what had just happened was very, very wrong. Something had to be done. We didn't know what.

So the killing at Kent State was what motivated you . . . ?

We came home with nightmares about . . . [Chokes up.] I did some stuff over there that I still refuse to talk about. I did stuff to children and women that I don't even want to think about, that I did in the heat of being in war, that I think is totally wrong. There's too much pain. That's part of what got me looking at stuff. There's no excuse for it. It's wrong. You get to thinking, Is there some other way to do things? The answer is yes, but it's a lot harder to do those than it is to kill people.

"Killing Them to Protect Them from Communism"

DANNY FRIEDMAN

Although Danny had been "a patriotic young American," he did not enlist. Instead, he attended college and worked. When he had difficulties in school, he was drafted. He was an irreverent young man who rarely took anything seriously.

I got my physical on May 11, 1967, in the morning, at Fort Hamilton; and I was off to train in Fort Jackson, South Carolina, for indoctrination and processing, and then Fort Gordon, Georgia, for basic training.

I went to armored cavalry advanced infantry training after basics at Fort Knox, Kentucky. I graduated. Just before we were scheduled to go in, they called us all together and said, "We got enough cavalry officers for a while, so we're closing down the OCS school temporarily." They gave us three choices. We could cancel our OCS application and continue our two-year tour; we could elect a different OCS, like infantry; or we could elect to have our OCS application put on hold and we would be scheduled for the next OCS class after it reopens.

I elected to withdraw the OCS application. I figured, I already got four months in. I don't know if I want to do another two and a half years of this. Most of the guys opted to be available for the next class. Within two months, the guys that withdrew the application got orders for Vietnam. The guys that elected to be put on hold got orders to Germany. I guess they figured these guys were smart and they wanted to keep them alive. [Laughs.] I guess they thought it would be more convenient to recall somebody from Germany than from Vietnam. Once somebody got a taste of Vietnam, they would be unmanageable in OCS. They were right.

Did you hear anything about Vietnam, or did anybody talk about it while you were in basic?

They were talking about Vietnam all the time. We got a lot of indoctrination. Most of the NCOs and sergeants were back from Vietnam. "You wouldn't last in Vietnam more than five minutes, boy!" [In a southern

151

drawl.] They talked about, "You got to watch out for the women; they put razor blades in their cunts." "They ain't human. Gooks and slopes." A lot of that. We saw a lot of propaganda films about why we were in Vietnam, about the communist threat, [and] the domino theory.

I graduated AIT and then I got orders to Vietnam. I remember going home on leave. I had two weeks' leave. Everybody bought me beer and stuff like that. It was great. I wished I could make a career out of it. It was very exciting. It was like going off on this grand adventure. I had no fear, no anxiety. I was oblivious to what the reality of it was. It was just like I was going to play war, except this time I got real guns. This is going to be fun.

Waiting on line to get on an airplane to go to Vietnam in San Francisco at Travis Air Force Base, a bunch of us bought this cavalry rope that you wore on your shoulder and we put them on our khaki uniforms. Some officer came up to us and said, "You're not authorized to wear that!" I said, "I got cavalry armor, cavalry brass; this is a cavalry rope." He says [loud singsong voice], "That is not authorized to wear outside your own unit!" I got really intimidated by this crazy officer. He was drunk, really drunk. He was really belligerent. Then it dawned on me. I said, "What the fuck you going to do, sir, send me to Vietnam?" Here I am, waiting on line to go to Vietnam, where I might be killed, and this guy's hassling me about the stupid rope I'm wearing. It was the first time I ever spoke back to an officer, sergeant, or anything. I was always a very "play by the rules" type of guy. I couldn't believe this guy was flipping out over this stupid rope. He got very flustered, blew off some steam, but eventually just walked away. Everybody was cracking up on line. They were cheering and stuff.

We were on a Braniff International Airways flight. It was a regular airliner with stewardesses and everything. They were being nice to us. As we got closer and closer to Vietnam, the stewardesses started acting differently. Less nicer.

We're coming in, and the next thing we knew, the pilot was saying, "Bien Hoa Air Base is currently under attack, so we'll be making a rather direct approach." The plane was like this [hand inclined at a 90-degree angle] and like this [down and stop]. Everybody left their stomachs at 20,000 feet. MPs come on the plane and say, "Everybody off the plane double-time. Follow us. We're being mortared; we got to go to the bunkers." We hear poof, poof, outside, so I say to the stewardess, "Please don't let them take me. What kind of girl are you, anyway?" [Laughs.] They're smiling, saying, "Please step this way, sir." To this day, that Braniff airplane is sitting somewhere with my fingernail marks on the side of the fuselage. That was my first political statement, I guess.

It was November 1967 when I landed in southeast Asia. We got assigned to our units. I was assigned to 199th Light Infantry Brigade. The nickname of the unit was Red Catcher—you know, Got to get the reds. We were assigned for two days with Red Catcher, where we got weapons assigned, got qualified on our weapons, got oriented on various Vietnam things like crossing rivers and firing M-72 rockets, and stuff like that. That all took about two days. That left the rest of the week for details. I wasn't much for details.

I hooked up with this other guy. He was a Chicano. This was his second time around. He said, "Man, we don't need this shit. After reveille, when it's still pretty dark, hang out with me." So I hang out with him.

We were in Long Binh, right outside of Bien Hoa, and it was pretty much a safe town at that point. He says, "You got your PX card?" You were issued ration cards for the PX, which allows you to buy x amount of cigarettes a month, like one or two radios, one TV, two watches. They had things that they marked off so that you didn't buy a whole lot of stuff and sell it on the black market, you know. I said, "Yeah, I got my ration card."

We just walk right outside the base. There we are, no weapons or nothing. We're just walking outside the base, two GIs in jungle fatigues. He hailed a cab. This old beat-up Mercedes picked us up. He says, "Papa-san, take number one GI to PX." Papa-san says, "Number one, oh, yes, yes." He knew this whole thing.

Most of these cabdrivers were black market hustlers, and what they did was: They'd take our ration cards, they'd put grease on them, take us to the PX, we'd buy a bunch of stuff, they'd stamp it, then the papa-san would take a rag, wipe the grease off, take us to another PX. We bought all this stuff for papa-san and he gave us a markup on it, and by about halfway through the day we had our pants full of money. We went to Bien Hoa. We had a good

Danny Friedman at firebase Camp Smoke, May 3, 1968: "My old 32 track Jumpin' Jo before she was turned in for a new diesel track."

meal, massage, steam bath, got all pipes cleaned, and number one baby-sans. It was great. After two days, we got some number one reefers.

They never missed us. That lasted for almost a week. Then we got assigned to a unit. The platoon I was assigned to was in base camp at the time. I got there the day before the platoon came in. They totaled a track. They hit a mine. The crew had been killed. That was my first inkling of, Ay, this ain't all fun and games. Everybody was crowding around it. It was very solemn and stuff. They had all the personal possessions of the guys who were killed laid out on the ground.

I got assigned to my unit. D Troop 17th Cav was an armored cavalry unit with armored personnel carriers. Basically, what I found out was that we were being used in southern Vietnam in lieu of tanks because we could go through the rice paddies—tanks were too heavy and got bogged down. They used us as tanks, but we didn't have the armor of tanks, so we got ripped up a lot.

We got to go and look for the VC and kill them. We were considered armored reconnaissance. My MOS was armored recon specialist. Recon sort of like alludes to sleuth, right? When you're going around in a noisy gasoline or diesel 13-ton armored personnel carrier, it's not sneaking around. They kind of like hear you coming 16 miles away. Basically, we were the guinea pigs. We were the bait. We're supposed to go around till someone shoots at us, and then we call in air strikes. It was recon by getting shot at.

We saw a lot of shit. We were involved in a lot of operations, from Tet on down. We were in a lot of firefights. It was pretty hot and heavy. We'd have people hit and pinned down. Then we'd withdraw and call in air strikes. We'd sit back and watch like four hours of air strikes. Shit, that got them all. Nothings's alive in there, you know. Half of us dismount from the tracks and go look at the bodies. As soon as we all got in the nipa palms, Charlie jumped out of the tunnels and started blowing us away.

I saw people die. There was this guy, James Thornton, a black guy from Philadelphia. I got pretty friendly with him. We got ambushed and his track took a rocket and he got killed. I used to think about him a lot. I visit him on the wall.

I had some good times. We hauled a lot of beer around with us. We used to throw away C rations, but we made sure we had room for beer. There was a situation . . . It began where one of the tracks took a rocket. Everybody on the track got killed that time. It was like a Mexican standoff. We lined all the tracks up outside the nipa palms. Our track commander, this guy Wild Bill from Illinois, loved his beer and he loved his Skol. He had a buddy on another track, Elmer from Alabama.

He goes, "Hey, Elmer, this here's Wild Bill. You got any cold ones?" "Yeah." "Mind if I come over and get me some?" "No, you can come over and visit for a while. Have yourself a cold one." So he says, "OK. In about 10 seconds, I'm going to start heading over there, so lay me down some cover fire." He says, "Hey, Jew"—that was my nickname; I was the only one they ever knew, so—

"Hey, Jew, come up here on the 50-caliber and give me some support." I said, "Well, if you bring me back one I will." He says, "Yeah, OK."

It was a funny scene. He had like no shirt on. Beer gut hanging over. This is a guy in his early twenties, but he was like an old man to us. He had fatigue pants rolled up and he was wearing thongs. In the middle of this combat, right, we were taking fire and he's trying to run over to this other track.

It was a real hot day. It was the dry season and the paddy was all dried up. It was just clumps of dried-up mud. There's like dried-up clumps of mud with space in between them. It's sort of like trying to run on cobblestones with deep grooves in them with thongs on. It was one of the hardest things to walk on, much less run on. He's doing this duck step. You see pops of dust kicking up where bullets were landing around him, and he tried to run on this stuff. It was one of the funniest things in the world, considering that people were shooting at him. . . . All this to get a beer.

He made it. Pretty soon, he's calling me back on the radio. "Hey, Jew. This is your daddy. I'm coming home. Lay me down support fire." I say, "Wait one. You got me a cold one?" He goes, "Negative. Elmer wouldn't give any orders to go." I said, "I don't see how you're going to get back." He said, "Wait a minute. You saying you're not going to give me no cover fire?" "Let me see the cold beer in your hand first." It was like silence for a little while, and then he said, "Okay, old Elmer said he'd let you have one this time, but he's going to get you back for it." I said, "You tell Elmer that would be just fine with me." He's got two beers in his hand trying to negotiate this mud and shit. It was the funniest thing. It was like a bit of humor in a day of hell.

What was your impression of the Vietnamese? What kind of contact did you have with them?

A lot of times, we go through a village and harass the villagers and stuff like that. Nothing like My Lai, or even *Platoon*. For the most part, anybody that pulled some shit got in trouble.

We had what they called Kit Carson scouts. They were the Vietnamese interpreters. Some were former VC or Chieu Hoi [defectors]. This one was a regular ARVN who was assigned to us. We used to beat the shit out of the guy. One time, I seen him rifle-butt a guy in the head. We walked over and kicked the shit out of him. The other guy was tied up with his hands behind the back, and this guy hits him with a rifle butt. It doesn't seem right. You don't do that shit.

We didn't really respect the ARVNs very much. When I first got there, we had a brother unit, the Fifth ARVN Rangers, and we actually wore their patch. After Tet, they punked out. The unit commander was so pissed off that he ordered everyone to take their patches off our uniforms. Our view of the ARVN was that they were punks who didn't want to fight. On reflection, there were maybe political reasons for why they didn't want to fight. The VC had more reason to fight. I mean, they're the same people, so it couldn't have been a cultural thing. They were political things. We didn't realize that, of course.

One time, we were sitting there with a Vietnamese guy—he wasn't our regular interpreter; he was somebody else who was just traveling with us. He was telling us how his family fled from the north and came to the south, how his village got burned by the ARVNs, this and that. He got recruited when he was thirteen years old and shit. It was sort of like a passing bit of philosophy. I realized that we aren't really helping these people much.

It was sort of like a night of drinking beer and reflecting. It's something you can't really think a lot about and try to stay alive. You got to justify the mission because you have to stay alive. But from that point on, there was kind of an undercurrent of realization that all was not what it's cracked up to be.

We got *Stars and Stripes*. We got news about the demonstrators, the riots in Detroit . . . the National Guard troops, which we referred to as draft dodgers, shooting up our cities, while we were here fighting the war.

In fact, some stateside reporters from newspaper or TV came on our unit and put microphones to one of the guys, it might have been Wild Bill. . . . "Students are burning and protesting against the war back home." . . . He says, "Hell, if I was back home, I'd be right alongside with them."

It really surprised me, but I laughed. I didn't have the awareness to like totally agree with it. I thought it was funny. I wasn't offended. That's the key. I didn't get pissed off and jump on this guy. That was an important realization.

The rest of the time in Vietnam, I got shot once—I took a bullet in the neck during an ambush. I recovered, got sent back to my unit. There was some real scary shit during Tet. We were expecting to be overrun. We got last rites during Tet. I was a Jewish boy; I took it anyway. We had pretty heavy mortar attack, but we weren't overrun. They actually bypassed us and went right to Long Binh.

When I was home from Vietnam, I stopped at Travis. I was going to meet a guy I grew up with, my best friend who was in the Air Force, stationed in southern California. I was going to stop off and hang out with him for a couple of days before I went home.

I got to Los Angeles, and I wanted to rent a car to drive out to Victorville. The guy at the counter says, "Do you have a major credit card, sir?" This is 1968. I don't think I even knew what a credit card was at that point. He says, "We can't rent you a car unless you have a major credit card." I said, "I just got back from Vietnam. You want a deposit?" I had a pocketful of money. I said, "I'll give you whatever you want." The rental car was like $30 a week. He says, "I'm sorry sir, you have to have a major credit card."

So I bought a bus ticket to fucking Victorville. I tried to call my friend, and he says, "Don't take the bus; I'll come get you." I said, "All right, I'll be in the bar at the bus terminal."

He shows up. I was half shitfaced. I say, "Let's go cash in my ticket." There was a girl on line in front of me, and she was buying a ticket for Bakersfield, which was the next town from Victorville. I said, "Excuse me, miss, you don't have to buy a ticket; we can give you a ride. We're going there." I was being nice.

There was an elderly woman behind the counter selling tickets. She says, "You goddamned GIs think you can come here and do anything. This is a decent lady and don't you dare talk to her. I'm going to have you arrested." Fucking shit, man. I'm just back from Vietnam, fighting for your country, and you want to have me arrested. I can die for your country, but I can't talk to your women? My friend had to drag me away. I was crazy.

When I was home on leave before I got to Fort Knox, in November or December of 1968, I was still wearing my uniform, and I went to visit friends at Hunter College in the cafeteria. This, I would have to say, was one of the turning points. They were kidding around with me, "Hey, there are people outside in the hallway with tables, and they're communists. Why don't you go over there, show them your uniform, and tell them what the world is really like?" They were kind of like me, except they didn't have any experiences. They were just into football, girls, having a good time, and partying and stuff. They got off on egging me on and getting off on me reacting.

So I go up to these girls at a literature table. I go, "How can you do this? You're supporting the communists. Don't you know why we're in Vietnam?" So I started telling them why we were in Vietnam. About halfway through, something clicks in my head. I just realized that I was reciting all the propaganda I learned in basic and AIT. Everything I was saying was based on what I was told before going to Vietnam and not based on my experiences in Vietnam. It was directly contradictory to my experience in Vietnam. All this flashed in my head instantaneously.

What was the experience that contradicted the propaganda?

Basically, that we were there to help the Vietnamese, protect them from the communists. We were fighting the people we were supposed to be protecting. That was the contradiction. We were fighting the South Vietnamese. There were NVA up north there, but they were still Vietnamese. We were killing them to protect them from communism. It hit me that what I was saying was based on what I was told, not what I experienced. I was stunned.

It was like when I was shot. I didn't realize I was shot. I thought somebody superstrong just hit me as hard as they possibly could with a fist in the neck. That's what it felt like. Then the blood started spouting. With this though, it was like somebody hit me in the head, but inside the brain. It was just like this incredible awareness. It shocked me.

I sort of like shut up, stared at them, and I remember just walking away back to the cafeteria. I just sat down and people were asking me what was going on, making jokes and shit, but I was dead serious then. I got over it. I never stay serious too long.

I went to Fort Knox. I still had a bullet in me from when I was shot. The second day with the unit, I reported sick call. I ended up going to the hospital and getting the bullet out, getting a lot of convalescence leave, and doing a lot of soft time during the rest of my tour at Fort Knox. I just didn't care about anything anymore. I was just doing my time. I worked in the weapons pool, drank a lot of beer, got fat. I got out in May of 1969.

When I got out I took my old job back on Wall Street and went to college. I was back at Kingsborough at night. I was working in the Stock Exchange at the time of Kent State and the Wall Street riots. They kept us inside during the actual riot, but they let us out for lunchtime. Everything had chilled out, mostly; and there was some construction workers around, some cops around, and I was just talking to somebody about shit. I forgot what I was saying, but basically, "Hey, the students got a right to protest. I can see where they're coming from. The war is fucked up." At this point, I had bushy hair, sideburns, a mustache.

A construction worker comes up to me and knocks me down. He says, "You draft card–burning, welfare-collecting hippie. You goddamn better love this country or leave it." There was all these cops standing around laughing. This one cop must have been like a deputy commissioner. He had all sorts of gold braid on and stuff. He was laughing. I walked over and said, "You going to do something about this shit?" He says, "I didn't see nothing." Okay, fine. I kicked the guy in the fucking balls. I grab him and say, "You son of a bitch, I just got back from Vietnam two months ago, don't give me any fucking shit. I probably pay more taxes than you earn in a month. Don't tell me about welfare either." [Laughs.] I was pissed off. I smashed him in the face. Then the cops grab me, but I got away. I had my ID and just ran back into the stock exchange. They tried to follow me, but people there were pretty good about hiding me.

Then, I went to college that night. There were student strikes and stuff at Kingsborough. Some guy got up and said he was in Vietnam and he was talking against the war. Oh, that's right on, man. It was a guy I had grown up like around the corner from. I was talking to him afterward, and he says, "First of all, it's like what I feel; and second of all, the chicks love it." So I tried it. College kids loved it. We got a Vietnam veteran who's against the war. This is fantastic.

I was actually speaking out against the war for several reasons. A, I thought the war was wrong. B, I thought, if someone's going to say the war was wrong, it should be someone who fought in the war. And C, it was great to get laid. [Laughs.]

This is a very infantile analogy, but from where I grew up, this was great to have pretty girls with no bras who wanted to fuck me just because I was in Vietnam. I mean I got fucked because I was in Vietnam, but this was the first time anyone wanted to fuck me, you know. [Laughs.] It was great. It was better than I got treated when I first got home.

"The Shit We Were Harassed With"

BILL BRANSON

Bill Branson enlisted in 1966 because he had wanted to "break away" from home. He saw miltary service as a way to get a skill and lifelong security, as many of those in his community in San Bernardino, California, had done.

I went into ASA and spent eight months at school in Fort Devins. I got my—quote—"technical education," which didn't amount to shit, but it was difficult nonetheless. The ASA was the unit that had a real high percentage of college-educated people in it. You had to be intelligent. It was really difficult to learn Morse Code like in three days. We had our share of idiots and fools like anybody, but we had people who had been in college and were a little older and had gone into the service into this, rather than go to Vietnam.

I went to Panama for 18 months and then went to Vietnam for 14 months. In Panama, I saw a lot of shit that I hadn't seen before. I saw slums and the way people lived there. When they had elections, everybody would arm to the teeth and they would send armored units to cruise up and down the canal highway. They had a dividing line in Panama City. It was like a razor cut. There was the American zone. They defended that zone with machine guns. I'd see all that stuff. When I was there, I really learned to hate the military too, because of a lot of shit that went on.

When I came there, I still had some naiveté about it. I thought if I worked hard, I'd get somewhere. So I worked and worked and worked for months and months and I didn't even make PFC for a long time. Finally, I got PFC and wanted to be Spec-4 because everybody else there was a Spec-4. I just worked my ass off. So one day, one of the guys who had been around longer took me aside and said, "You know, you work so fucking hard, they're never going to let you off this position or promote you, because as long as they got you hungry, they're going to get all this work out of you." I thought about it for a couple days, and the guy was right. So I started working less.

We had NCOs that had nothing better to do than to make your life miserable. They came down on us for all kinds of idiotic stuff. It was like someone I heard years later talk about prison. It isn't the big things that get you; it's the little things. It's like not being able to have a chair or a transistor radio, or any little thing.

I could go on and on with the shit we were harassed with. I absolutely fiercely hated the military. When I was outside the base or downtown, it was different. I drank a lot; most people did. You'd go downtown, get wasted, come back. It was binge kind of drinking. Fortunately, I didn't become an alcoholic.

We had this one sergeant who started putting me through all kinds of shit. I hated his ass. He tried to get me court-martialed over a haircut. I went to the lawyers and I defied the CO by refusing an Article 15. I had been tipped off that they had a big problem. The general had come in and said, "You're not allowed to send anyone up for court-martials. I'm tired of you guys court-martialing people, you company commanders and battalion commanders; you handle this shit." They had so many guys they were sending into the brig in every unit there, not just ours. The general probably summed up wisely that these guys were just passing on all their problems and jacking people around instead of solving their problems. So, hell, I refused it, which you had a right to do. I demanded a court-martial. The CO knew he'd been fucked. I got in some other trouble and here was me, the introverted little kid, and I'm getting in all this trouble. All it amounts to is that I don't want to be fucked with.

Did you want to get out?

I wanted out so bad I could taste it. I hated it so fucking bad. I was incredibly frustrated and was actually not very happy with Vietnam. I just felt like there was something wrong going on there. I had friends who were much more opposed to it. They played Joan Baez records and all that shit all the time.

My 18 months is up. The Army decided they didn't want people going native anymore, so they wanted to rotate much more. What they did was, they wouldn't let you extend unless you're some unbelievable person and everyone wanted you there. We had a number of choices available and it seemed like everybody was going to this airborne base in Kentucky, Fort Campbell. Well, I had been in the Army for a while, and I knew the ropes a little bit, so I computed the odds and picked the places I figured no one else would want, anything to get me out of Fort Campbell. So I picked Peshawar, Pakistan. . . . Vietnam was my last choice. [Laughs.] Vietnam was the magic thing. They wanted people real bad. I found out later that they had a directive, and the only way you could stop someone in ASA from going to Vietnam was if they'd fucking been court-martialed or something. It was like you had to be a serial killer. Otherwise, you're gone.

I landed in Long Binh in Saigon. I got settled in at Phu Bai, and I was there the whole time. I was considered an expert intercept operator. I was pretty damned good because Panama was one of the most difficult stations in the world. I ended up monitoring the local area, what we called Area 1, right around Hue.

The base had several thousand people on it. It had Marines and Navy and every fucking kind of shit in the world. We had cushy lives. We had air-conditioned barracks. We had to have an air-conditioned place to work because the radios used to have vacuum tubes. We didn't have KP. By that time I was an E-4 with tons of seniority. Eventually I got promoted to E-5. E-5s are exempt from any kind of shit deal except filling sandbags and whatnot.

We would work 12 hours and come off and fill sandbags for three or four hours. Then we'd go drink for a while then go back to sleep and work 12 more hours. I met a lot of good people there, and we used to get a harmonica and a guitar and sit and play Bob Dylan songs and peace songs and have little hootenannies on the barracks steps.

It sounds like a good life. What was the problem?

When you get in a big bureaucracy you get so you hate it so bad. The Army was just as fucked-up as anyplace. I saw so many incompetent fools as officers and NCOs. It's like you don't know what's going on. It's just wrong. Not necessarily morally wrong, just fucked-up wrong, just incompetently wrong. They just mistreat people.

Do you mean mistreat American soldiers or Vietnamese?

Everybody. They—whoever the "they" was—was fucking everybody, and it was very apparent that the Vietnamese were not getting anything out of this.

You could see how incompetent they [commanders] were. What a criminal waste it was—so close to your face, you know—unless you just turned yourself off to it. I didn't have to worry about being in combat and having to turn myself off, although it was mind-numbing being there. We got hit with rockets and stuff about 22 times. It wasn't that big of a deal, but it was enough to keep you nervous.

I at least thought that this was a combat zone, they're going to relax some of the stuff; but it was worse, the harassment and stuff. Whenever they thought they might get their ass kicked by the Vietnamese, they eased up a little bit. It was like clockwork. When we had a few rocket attacks things would ease up, and then they would gradually tighten the clamps.

They wouldn't issue grenades to anyone on that post. We had no explosives. We had weapons and two magazines apiece. That's 40 rounds. That's all we had.

It was really difficult to get off post. You could go a couple places. You could go to the PX next door, which was the [24th] headquarters; or you could go, if we took a weapon, to Camp Eagle, which was about a kilometer or two up the road. I went out in the field, but unofficially.

We had a unit at Camp Eagle. That was the 101st Airborne base. I knew a bunch of the guys who worked in the motor pool. I got to be friends with them. I would go up and exchange shirts with one of them, put on a flak jacket, trade my M-14 for an M-16, and go out in this jeep. We'd take off and go to Birchess Garden or we'd go to fucking Saigon, and we went to Hue. That's the only way I got to see anything. I went out in the countryside and drove around. I learned something about the Vietnamese in Hue and Saigon.

What did you learn from going out like that?

What an adventure! Everything was like a picture postcard in the country-side. It was green, with these beautiful temples and these incredibly peaceful settings in rice paddies.

Hue was really strange. Every fucking wall in that city had holes in it, bullet holes. It wasn't that long after the Tet. The place was a fucking ruin but everybody was conducting business.

We went into a section that was still VC. It was like the baddest section. There were lots of Army vehicles going through, and everybody got real nervous. There was a place you could clip your weapons upside-down on the jeep by the front windshield. I pulled that fucking weapon off and locked and loaded, man, because those people were not friendly. A lot of the older men would sit there and just fucking glare at me. It was a heavy aura. It took some balls to glare at a GI over there.

The base had an orphanage that we sponsored in Hue. I heard about it and said, Fuck it, I got to get out of this goddamn place, and here is another way to do it. I volunteered to go in and do whatever. It really didn't amount to much except you gave a few bucks and you got to go in there and visit it once in a while and talk to them.

We drove to the orphanage on this electrical service truck. I recognized this area of the town, and I'm going, "Holy shit, do you realize this is in the middle of the fucking VC stronghold?"

We drove in there right up to the fucking orphanage and started unloading. A guy comes, meets us, and says, "I'm sorry, but you can't take your weapons inside the orphanage." It's like a religious shrine, Catholic or something. The guy that was in charge says, "OK, fuck it, I'm going to leave a couple guys out here. Don't worry, nobody is going to fuck with us or this truck, because we're here at the orphanage." We left a couple guys to guard the truck and we went inside.

Little kids [were] everywhere. They were really nice. They had tea and stuff. These were all educated people there with university degrees and they're speaking English, which wasn't easy. It was like us speaking Vietnamese, which we didn't even bother to attempt. We're sitting there drinking tea and they kind of rounded up a couple of us off to the side, and this young Vietnamese guy starts rapping to us. He talked about why all those kids were there and what the fuck is going on here. It wasn't really blatant like "Join the NLF," but it was a lot of thought-provoking stuff about the war. He was risking his life to say that.

When I was down in Saigon, we'd driven passed what they called the race-track. In the 1968 Tet they [NLF, NVA] came in and fortified that and held it for days. They were having air strikes on it and they couldn't get them out of there. I saw that fucker, that son of a bitch is like one block here. It wasn't nothing. They fought like fucking tigers for days. Those were some tough sons of bitches, man.

Was that your general experience with the Vietnamese?

We had house girls that did all the cleaning. We always gave them gifts, but it was hard for them to get it off post. You had to give a note. One time I had to literally go down there while they were searching them. What a sight that was. I was really offended by it.

I thought they treated them like fucking cattle. Slapping them around, fucking pushing them, and—shit, I mean they went through hell every day to get on and off that post.

The guys in the 101st unit I used to visit put in a huge MI [military intelligence] compound inside the base with its own fortifications and everything. It was dug into the hills and it had its own helicopter pad, holding pens, the whole bit. I used to hear the screams at night from the fucking guys they were torturing over there. That was a little upsetting. It wasn't like a full-blown understanding or anything. It was like: This war sucks, and I'm going to do whatever to get through.

Were you aware of the antiwar movement at that time?

Oh, yeah, very much. I remember later on when they were circulating a picture of the riots all over the country in the United States. I saw a picture of a guy with an M-60 on the steps of the Capitol with smoke in the background. I remember ranting and raving for hours: "They're beating the shit out of these fucking people, they're killing people at home, they got to have GIs on the steps of the Capitol, and what the fuck are we·doing here? Hey, man, something is seriously wrong here."

I extended for two months to get a five-month early out. The Army was having such severe problems with the Vietnam vets returning, they released all the requirements. At first, to get early out you had to be signed up for college and everything. Then it was, Get the fuck out of here and don't talk to me.

I got out in October 1969 and bummed around for a while. I went through San Francisco and jumped on a plane for home in San Bernardino. [I] hung around there for a while and then I got a motorcycle and rode around lots and lots. Then I signed up back to the same junior college, because I had the GI Bill.

We were older by centuries than everybody else there. You'd seen all this shit. I'd seen shit in Panama. I'd seen shit in Vietnam. I had some pretty severe stress problems and no way to let it out except drinking.

I got back into school and jumped in and started kicking ass. I was really into it, but I couldn't hide from the contradictions. The war was still going, and I had friends over there. There was an active peace movement on the campus of the school I was going to. Kent State happened, and I think that threw me for a loop.

Why?

I could not deal with having these fucking scum beat people up and shoot them down. I knew right away what happened. It was very clear to me that they had just fired into this fucking crowd. I'd been in the military, and I knew what it takes to shoot at people. I said, "Man, there is no way that they didn't do that on purpose. There is no way that you should open up on some kids throwing rocks." I just couldn't deal with that anymore. Everything came home. I can't get away. These fuckers are pushing me from all sides.

I agonized over it for a few days and started asking around. I found out they were doing stuff over at the student center. I just walked in there one day and said, "Hi, I want to join up and do whatever. I don't give a fuck what it is." I identified myself as a veteran. I started doing different stuff like passing out literature. I felt like this has got to be done and I can't do anything else. It was an irresistible force.

"I Turned 180 Degrees at That Instant"

JOHN LINDQUIST

John Lindquist had wanted a military career since he was a young boy. Like many of his peers, he had been captivated by the image of the military in movies and on television; he joined the Marines to be with the "baddest" branch of the armed forces. He was interviewed with Annie Bailey, his companion for 25 years.

I get off the bus in boot camp. The staff sergeant gets on the bus and says we have a minute to get off the bus, "Five seconds are over; now move." Everybody starts scrambling. He already grabbed the first guy by the hair and threw him out the door. We're all asshole and elbows out the door to go out and stand on the yellow footprints, and the guy next to me started picking his nose. So he [the sergeant] walked up and decked the guy. He knocked him out. I'm not shitting you. I didn't move a muscle. He was waiting for me to move a muscle because he was going to deck me too. I didn't say nothing. I didn't do nothing. I didn't move. I already know things are kind of fucked-up.

It was like a bubble, a membrane, in front of my brain went. [Grunts, mimicking an explosion with hands moving apart and outward from a clenched position.] I thought, What the fuck did I do? I turned 180 degrees at that instant. At that moment I changed my mind. I'm not bullshitting you. I says, Holy shit, I fucked up.

What about that experience had such an impact on you?

It was like: All those debates in debate class and these raps and arguments from kids who were already antiwar and against the draft—I'm calling it communist propaganda, and they're true. Everything they said all of a sudden came back at me. I'm not kidding you. I knew that I messed up and it was too late. Then I also at the same time thought, Holy shit, I'm married; my wife is pregnant; I'm making $96 a month; and I'm going to Vietnam. I knew it wouldn't do any good to resist. I'm stuck. I'm at least man enough to know I got to live up to what I did.

Man, we had a spastic platoon. They [the Marines] were offering two-year enlistments, same as the Army in the draft period, getting all these esprit de corps dudes, especially younger dudes. There were a lot of seventeen-year-olds and some a little bit over eighteen. I'd say we had 25 percent who were seventeen. Project 100,000 was on during that time period. [The "One Hundred Thousand Program" was established to broaden draft eligibility.] There were guys in that unit who had never worn shoes, never brushed their teeth in their life. They just threw the dregs of society in there. A good third of us were there on court order. It was such a fucked-up unit.

There'd be this inner competition for events. One was the rifle range. We were last. We must have had 18 guys out of 80 who didn't even qualify. We won the ribbon on general inspection. We were the best house cleaners. [Laughter.] Man, the DI [drill instructor] was pissed off. The DIs just get the shit razzed out of them by the other DIs. Oh, God, we did four hours of full-out PT, all of us did—you know, jumping jacks and push-ups to the point where you're doing 250 and you can't get your knees up off the ground and they're coming around and hitting you upside the head.

I never stopped PT no matter how much it hurt. They wanted you to hate them so much that you weren't going to give up unless you passed out. Dudes would pass out. We'd pick them up and say, "That's OK, man, you passed out, that's OK." At least they didn't give up. We didn't know it, but that's what they were trying to get us to do.

I was in great shape. You go to AIT and staging and all you do is run and march. I weighed 148 when I came in and 184 when I got out. I grew an inch. I was a badass dude. By the time you get to Vietnam, you're in great shape; and your whole tour in Nam, you're just falling apart. By the time I got back from Vietnam, I was 128 pounds, jungle rot all over my body, and all this shit, gingivitis in my mouth . . . my breath stinks. . . . My mother says, "Ooh, what the hell happened to you?" I'm just rotting, that's all.

One guy [a sergeant], the meanest dude, had pins in his ankle, walked with a limp, did two tours in Vietnam, and hated fucking gooks. That's all he'd talk about, "Hate them fucking gooks"—you know, the whole racist indoctrination. You call them Vietnamese, you got hit. This dude would do it. At the end of that cycle he was so frustrated with us. We just weren't together. They rushed us through.

So I hang out and do the best I can and get my ass kicked and all kinds of bullshit. Meanwhile my wife is going fucking nuts, schizophrenic, right? She comes down while I'm in boot camp. I didn't even know she was in town. She checks in at the rescue mission, comes to the base, sits on the colonel's car, the colonel freaks, [and] she freaks out on the colonel.

They hit the roof. They got me standing in front of the staff sergeant's desk. They're all over me. You've seen those movies where they're in your face. [He mimics fast-talking in-your-face style.] You know—and at the same time, you're seeing your wife who wants to be assured by you that you can take care of this, and at the same time you're freaking out. There's nothing I can fucking take care of. I can't even give her affection.

I went to Vietnam in May of 1968 and left in May of 1969, so I caught the end of the Tet offensive. I flew into Danang. Forty-five guys went to Khe Sanh and four of us went to Dong Ha. Dong Ha is just down the DMZ from Khe Sanh, maybe like 20-some miles.

I landed in the middle of the battle for Dong Ha city. They're dropping napalm on the line in broad daylight as I'm getting off the plane, tossing all the gear out the back door, the plane's leaving already, turning around and splitting. It didn't even stop. There's a battle going on. Holy shit. What the fuck did I get into? I just got here and the shit's hitting the fan.

I was told the next day that I was going to leave; I was going up north. I said, "What do you mean I'm going up north? How far fucking north can you go?" "You're going up to Cua Viet."

So I got on the riverboat to go to Cua Viet, which sits on the mouth of the Cua Viet river, which comes out of Quang Tri and empties into the South China Sea about four miles below the DMZ. We get up to Cua Viet, and it's this beautiful white sand beach, almost naked of everything, with a fuel farm with a plywood hut and no bunker. It looked like the surface of the moon up there too. What a trip.

What were your duties there? What did you do?

Cua Viet was a forward fuel base. All the fuel that came into northern I Corps, Quang Tri, Khe Sanh, all of it, came right to the base camp, so that we were targeted all the time for incoming artillery. We had numerous field fires.

John Lindquist in Vietnam: at his quarters with Seventh Motors at Quang Tri; in a bunker (blast wall in front of the radio corner); and making the peace sign, on R and R in Dong Ha.

We had a battalion of amtraks. There was only four of us running communications for the bulk fuel unit. We couldn't do any patrolling, because you have to do six-hour shifts. We participated in the off-loading of all the fuel, whether it was a Navy auxiliary oiler tanker or civilian tankers. Once in a while, we'd get Shell oil tankers. That was kind of an eye-opener. These dudes would be getting $1,200 a month, and I'm getting 16 cents an hour, you know?

I didn't get the first half-day off until I was there 10 1/2 months. That's how much work there is to do. The war's going on, rain or whatever. When the monsoon comes, the rain's fucking up to here [holds arm up to chest], plus you got to move equipment, and drive trucks—ah, man, it's the pits. So you work.

The vast majority of the people thought the Marine Corps sucked. We did our job because we had to protect one another, survive, and go home.

Was this a topic of discussion among you?

There were some political arguments about the war and that, but generally we stayed away from it. We generally didn't like it and just wanted to remain friends. We'd do our job and then come home and get as blasted as we could and listen to rock and roll. By the time I was there, marijuana was starting to become fairly prevalent. The shit's really good. You've got to remember, drugs are much more prevalent as the war goes on. Usually dudes don't take it out to the field, just because you got to be so alert. The grunts would use it back in the base camp.

Annie Bailey (AB): [John] managed to eke out a handle. His handle was hippie. He had some sunglasses and he took the red filters off the Navy flashlight and put them in there and looked at the world through rose-colored lenses. He wore his beads and he kept his M-14 poster up on the wall. The "Milwaukee Fourteen" were some draft resisters who broke into the Milwaukee induction center and pulled a bunch of files out onto this meridian in the road and poured blood on them.

John Lindquist (JL): I was against the war already. Antiwar stuff was already there. I read *Rolling Stone.* I subscribed to *Avant Garde.* You could get anything in the mail you wanted. We even considered reproducing a leaflet that was in *Avant Garde.* We got to the idea stage and that's about it, you know. It would be a real risk anyway. What the fuck would you get for it anyway, besides a six-six and a bad discharge? So piss on it; let's get stoned.

On what basis were you against the war?

JL: Number one, before I went to Vietnam, it was what I heard in school. After that, it was what I read, the *Avant Garde,* the *LA Free Press;* I was reading all this stuff in Vietnam.

It was also the amount of firepower. It was the conditions of the Vietnamese people, the racist crap from the guys, [and] the sexual conduct of some of the troops. I mean, I wouldn't even consider having sexual relations with a twelve-year-old girl, but people talked about it and girls would offer themselves to you. I was married, and I wasn't into that. I didn't do any of that for 17 months.

Besides the nickname "hippie," it was "the gook lover." It was fucked-up. A lot of people would consciously revel in the gore. When the ARVNs would kill some VC and string them out between Dong Ha and Quang Tri, other guys would be gawking and getting their cameras out. I just didn't want to get into it, revel in it. I would purposefully say, "I seen that; I ain't going to look at it." "Aw, come on, hippie," you know, "you're a fucking gook lover." I'd say, "Shoot them and bury them." That was the ARVNs. Christ, they [NVA, NLF] used to do it too. That's the thing, they're not without blemish on the other side . . . mutilations and torture, just like we did to them, so it's fucked-up all around.

AB: The thing about John is that he is not cruel, and that war was cruel.

JL: I did four months at Cua Viet. The lieutenant finally pulled me out. Said the last time he visited me, all I did was shake from the incoming. I didn't notice it. It was nothing like Khe Sanh. You might go 10 days without incoming, then you get five days with 30 rounds, 50 rounds, 114 rounds.

Then they sent me back to Dong Ha and put me on convoys. Usually on pace truck, which was the first one to run over a mine. When you would leave Dong Ha, all the way to Cam Lo, it was rice paddy with some trees and stuff like that. But as you left Cam Lo and climbed into the mountains, just toward when you got to Camp Carroll, the jungle would actually brush by your face. It's not triple-canopy jungle, but it's dense. The road just cut through it. It was an old French highway. You couldn't see nothing except jungle on either side of you. It was fucking scary. Someone could reach out and place a fucking grenade in the truck . . . that's what you felt like. Then they defoliated and Rome-plowed 200 meters on each side. We loved it. We didn't think nothing about Agent Orange. We used to think it was cool.

I got out of Nam in May of 1969. I'm still married to my first wife, Lisa, who's in a mental hospital in England. I get sent to England, get a "Dear John" within nine days, go back into the Marine Corps, process through for a hardship discharge, and then leave. I came back here after I got discharged [and] I burned my uniform. I wanted to burn my ribbons too, but my nephew talked me out of it. I gave them to him.

I hang out for a half year and work a little. I got a job painting walls for a Navy captain, and I was telling him why the war sucked while I worked for him; and, man, did he hit the roof.

Did you have a lot of support at home for your views?

JL: No, almost none. I go out to northern California, come back, and start the GI Bill. I met other vets who were either fed up with the war or against the war. I was already speaking out against the war. I was the most antiwar of the bunch, but they were all pissed off. They might not have been able to verbalize their feelings; but when the first moratorium came, 17 of us attended in Milwaukee. Then I met Annie in March of 1970.

AB: We were introduced by a professor.

JL: I saw the VVAW ad in the February [1971] issue of *Playboy,* showed Annie, and said, "We got to find these people."

Why? What was it about the ad that made you want to join VVAW?

JL: Number one, the ad itself—maybe you've seen it—an American flag draped over a coffin, and it gave the number of people either dead or wounded. Also, this was an organization that could have a lot more impact.

"What I'd Seen Was Evil"

BOB HANSON

Bob Hanson grew in the New York City area. He thought that he had a good grasp of what was happening in Vietnam, having kept up with developments by reading newspapers, magazines, and so on. He joined the armed forces to find some excitement and to get away from his family.

I got my orders to Vietnam on Friday the 13th, January 1967. I had 15 days on leave and then I came to San Francisco Bay area, to the Oakland Army Terminal. I arrived in Vietnam around the beginning of February of 1967.

When I got to Vietnam, I sort of lucked out because I was put in a unit that was different than most military police units. We guarded communication sites that were on the top of mountains throughout Vietnam, so we were sort of isolated from most of the higher authorities. We were on our own. I lived on top of this mountain right by the South China Sea right on the coast for over a year. The site was so scenic that people used to come from miles around just to photograph the view. We were about 15 miles south of a major Army base, Tuy Hoa, which was right on the coast. In increments, I'd say of three months, things would get significantly better.

The first three months—February, March, April—we lived in tents, it rained all the time, and we ate C rations. Then the rains ended; we got a road in and a mess hall. So the next three months were significantly better. I did really well. In fact, that year on top of the mountain, nothing ever happened. When Tet happened, we were on top of this mountain and it was like a light show for us.

So you had an easy time?

The first year, yes. I was in Vietnam for 19 months. I extended for six months to avoid being put in an MP company in a southern base, which was usually what happened to you. I extended for six months in order to pick where I was going to go next and also for some excitement.

I went home for all of March 1968. Just watching the TV at home, you could see there was a lot more antiwar activity. The night before I was supposed to leave the states to go back to Vietnam, I was at Fort Dix, in a USO sort of a building for entertaining the soldiers. Here's LBJ coming on TV saying, I'm not going to run; and everybody was cheering because they thought the war was going to be over in a couple months. [Laughter.]

I came back and I had extended for six months to be a helicopter door gunner, which I thought was going to be fun. I wanted some excitement. In a sort of perverse way, it was. I wanted to be part of a unit that was going to be in a lot of combat, so I picked the First Cav.

Why?

From before I went into the Army, they [First Cavalry Division] were always featured on the news. I was right. They were in the shit all the time.

I found out my company had screwed up my orders, probably on purpose to keep me in the same company. It took me about three months to get out of the company I was in and eventually get to the First Cav. During those three months, I was stationed in Saigon. This was April, May, and half of June 1968. We were attached to the First Signal Brigade. What I was doing was, I was guarding first brigade headquarters. There were about eight of us who were doing this on a rotating basis. We lived in a big four-man room with an overhead fan, a TV, and a refrigerator and a woman who would come in and sweep up. We were on a ground floor of a three-story villa that the army had rented. At night, we would grill steaks on the third story. I lived real well. That sort of changed my attitude toward all that I was seeing.

The reason that that was so was that being an MP means you're a cop in the Army, so people don't fuck with you except your own cadre. I could eat wherever I wanted to. I used to eat in officers' open messes. I used to listen to them talk about their life in the Army. I would watch them every day. For a lot of these guys who were captains and majors and colonels in the Army, the Army was a corporation. They all worked at MACV headquarters. They all lived real well. They were going up the corporate ladder. They really didn't give a shit about these people.

During that time, there was a mini-Tet offensive. The Vietcong had taken over part of the area I had lived in, and the 11th Armored Cav and the ARVN were attempting to take it back. We were in the middle of this. You had supersonic tactical aircraft making runs on multistory buildings with people inside, who were civilians, for at least a week. You had point-blank tank fire on the same buildings.

I watched the Air Force make bombing runs on these multistory buildings with civilians in them, and then all the smoke cleared and we were allowed to run around the city again. Along this road, which was called Plantation Road—a big, wide boulevard—there was this block-long line of military dump trucks. Each dump truck was heaped to the top with bodies, all of which were civilians, like so much cordwood.

I remember passing this scene, and just at the entrance of Tan Son Nhut, I saw this little girl try to run across the street, decide she couldn't make it, and then try to run back across the street. In the process, she was hit by a civilian vehicle. Everybody saw this. I jumped off the bus, and the first vehicle out of Tan Son Nhut was an American military ambulance. I stopped the guy and told him this little girl had been hit right up the road. The military hospital was in the same direction. I said, "This little girl has been hit up the road. Why don't you take her to the hospital?" The guy said, "Fuck her." That attitude changed my whole opinion about the war.

So there are guys who said, "Fuck her," and there's you.

I never called people gooks. People always to me were people. I grew up in a multicultural environment in New York City. Because I was an MP, I could go where I wanted. I used to travel around the city a lot. You would see gigantic refugee camps with tens of thousands of people. I used to see, in front of the various PXs for military personnel, kids sell themselves to survive. Slowly it started to dawn on me that this wasn't right, that we had no business being here.

About the middle of June I got my orders to go to the First Cav. At this time, the whole First Cav was in I Corps, Quang Tri province, Khe Sanh, Dong Ha, that whole part of Vietnam. My feelings about the war were changing, but I was happy I was going to do my duty and I did do it.

So here I am, a helicopter door gunner for three months—July, August, and September, and the first week of October 1968.

The helicopters in an Army division, especially in an air cav division, are flying trucks. One day you could be flying down to Danang to pick up beer for the company; the next day you could be flying a Special Forces team deep into Laos. I did all of that.

The way it would work when you were taking a team into Laos was: You would fly there in the morning. You would sign one of these papers saying you wouldn't talk about what you were doing. You took three ships: one ship carried the team; two other teams flew along to be there in case there were any problems. Besides the three ships, there were two Cobra gunships, an Air Force O2 spotter; besides that you had a couple of Air Force prop-driven aircraft that were fighter-bombers. This is like the circus flying across the sky.

We fueled at a Marine corps refueling point, LZ Stud; then you flew through the Khe Sanh valley, turned left, gained altitude to 7,000 feet; the two high ships would circle the low ship with the team that would land; then we go back to base. Coming back from the morning insertion, you'd land,

and there'd be nothing to do for hours. We played all day, then we'd fly somewhere else in the afternoon to pick up another team.

In Quang Tri province, in the summer of 1968 when I was there, you saw Air America aircraft all over the province. All the time you were there, you'd constantly see aircraft taking off and landing, both those labeled Air America and, say, a C-47 that was camouflaged with no lettering, no numbers, no nothing. I am absolutely convinced that the CIA's military arm was Green Berets, Special Forces: they were like this. [Crossing his fingers.]

One of the two times I did that, flying back to their base camp, I saw this heap of burlap sacks right by the runway. Having nothing to do, I walked over to the sacks, and this Green Beret sergeant walks up to me and says, "This is none of your business." I said, "You bet, sarge" and walked back to the ship. An hour later, two SAG helicopters—they were CH-34 Choctaw helicopters with Asian crews—landed. The sacks were thrown on the ship, and zip, off they went. A couple of years later, I saw this book called *The Politics of Heroin in Southeast Asia* [by Alfred McCoy, 1992], and there were pictures in the middle of the book. One of the pictures was of a typical burlap sack, and that's what I saw. Three months after I get back to New York, there's this gigantic junkie epidemic in New York City. So you could see exactly where it came from.

One of the things about being in an aviation unit in a cav was that you did all kinds of things, and one of the things you did was you took the battalion commander above his people—and they're like these little dots and he's playing chess master. Lots of these guys were incompetent. There was one guy that we were afraid to fly with—everybody in the company—because his own people had tried to shoot him down already.

In the cav, you flew until the day you went home. I went home four days late, so it was pissing me off. Because they sent me home four days late, the day I left, I was supposed to fly another combat mission. That morning, the first sergeant comes in and says, "Hanson, you're not flying; you're going home." Within an hour, I'm out of the company, on a helicopter to Hue; then I get a flight to An Khe, which was rear division headquarters for the First Cav; zip, zip, another hour I get rid of my stuff and I'm on another plane to Cam Ranh Bay. Within three hours I'm on another plane going back to the states. This was October 5, 1968.

The flight took 24 hours. We stopped at Midway Island. We landed at about three-thirty in the morning at Fort Lewis, Washington. They gave us a steak and eggs breakfast. I took a cab to Tacoma, Washington. I checked into a hotel, and I slept for 36 hours straight. That was my welcome home.

Instead of flying back to New York immediately, I took a bus down to San Francisco, just to decompress. From there I flew back to New York.

I had nine more months to do in the Army. I did it all in Germany. I decided to do more traveling. I got out of Germany two days before Woodstock. I didn't know anything about it. I knew people who were going. I did not go. That's my only regret in life.

I very quickly became antiwar.

What made you antiwar?

I thought all of what I'd seen was very evil. Lots and lots of guys in VVAW did it out of some kind of personal guilt. I never did. I never did anything to have motivated myself to be in the antiwar movement based on some kind of guilt. It was all of this evil that I saw, especially in Saigon—more than anything else, what was done to the people of Vietnam.

"Avoiding the Enemy"

PETE ZASTROW

Pete Zastrow had been in the ROTC as a college student and kept on getting deferments until he had left graduate school. By the time he went into the armed forces, as an officer with a desk job, he was already convinced that the war was wrong. But despite his antiwar convictions, he decided to yield to pressure from his superiors to "experience Vietnam."

I went on December 5th of 1968. I was at Fort Leavenworth for eight months. I was in the Infantry Officers Basic School at Fort Benning, where you're even more isolated than you are at a college campus, in that you had no idea what the news was. It was a very closed community. Here we are going through this training, and we didn't even know Tet was going on. It was a very collegiate setup. You went to classes all day and drank all night. You paid very little attention to the outside world.

We had classes that were geared toward jungle warfare. I remember some utterly fascist British major who came and told us all about how they'd killed all of the gooks in Singapore and saved all of these areas for British rule back in the old days and how we were going to be able to do the same thing in Vietnam. God, I hated him. I found some of those classes incredibly difficult to deal with. They never got much into the great world picture.

We had classes on how to be a real officer, and you learned officers' manners. You know, why you shouldn't carry an umbrella, how to open doors for women, and how to introduce women or behave when you were being introduced. I still remember being amazed by the way you dealt with women. Women were either the lowest of sluts and whores or, on the other hand, to be put way up on this pedestal. All this stuff that was fed into the lectures. You were in a totally male environment.

You get to Vietnam and spend a day, two days, three days, not very long, at Transportation Headquarters at Long Binh, long enough for them to process the paperwork and decide where to send you. In my case I was assigned to First Cavalry Division Air Mobile.

We sat in this big airplane hangar to get our first official briefing in-country. Right in the middle of this group of scared United States troops were two Vietnamese women, squatting down the way Vietnamese women do, with their dustpans and their brooms, sweeping the floor. The people who were talking to us did not see them at all. They were so much a part of the furniture. They were irrelevant. I thought at the time, Something is really wrong with the way this war is being done. How are we ever going to win a war when they have the ability to put someone right here where all these troops are and nobody even sees them? I don't know if other people were struck the same way. I don't think I ever told anyone that story before.

I was sent to the First Cavalry Division because they were getting killed off in large numbers. The First Cavalry Division was known for its 438 helicopters. Only half of them ever worked at one time, but [what] we were able to do was move large groups of people into foreign territory very quickly.

The cav worked on the theory of being able to surprise people. So you have what we called our Charlie-Alpha, or combat assault, and you'd just lift up a company and set them someplace—the idea being that they would then filter out about the area and come into contact with any bad guys that were around. If there were a lot of them, then the cav would put in another company, or two more and five more. In some places, before I got there, up north in the A Shau Valley, they just got slaughtered. They would keep doing that, sending people in, and they would keep getting killed. I'm happy to say that I never saw that.

What they did was to go out and see where all the trails were, where all the bad guys were, finding that they used bicycles and elephants and all sorts of horrible creatures of war to move troops and supplies down to resupply people for what every American intelligence officer thought was going to be the final attack on San Yan. They [the cav] were to build a firebase in the middle of one of these trails, so they couldn't use this trail.

In the course of doing this, the normal course of avoiding the enemy and keeping out of major firefights kind of got violated by mistake, because nobody knew where anyone else was. So a lot of people got killed—us and them both—which is why they suddenly needed a lot of people. I was fortunate enough to be one of them.

You mentioned that troops made an effort to stay out of contact with the enemy in the normal course of things.

Yeah. We walked around in circles, which is what most of the companies in the camp were doing. It's not something that officers sat down and discussed, but I had a feeling that there was a whole lot of that going on. I felt the same way. I liked people who were in-country and I didn't want to see any of them get killed.

I have an equal feeling that the Vietnamese were doing exactly the same thing. I'm pretty sure from my reading that they were, because they didn't want to get into a firefight with the Americans. By the time I got there, the bad guys pretty much knew how we were operating, and they could get around us.

How did the troops feel about this avoidance?

I'm not really sure what the people in the company felt. In that kind of position, you are there as a company commander. You're God. If I decide to have these troops go off and fight this enemy, I have the ability to make them do that, and they have to. It's a terrible responsibility. The system works against getting close enough to really know what the troops think.

I was not aggressive enough, so I ended up in the information office. I was a brigade information officer. The information office seemed to be the place where they sent the misfits. Some of that time I spent in the rear as an executive officer, because I was made captain while I was there. I never should have been a captain. I got there because while I was being deferred, I was also being promoted. By the time you're a captain, you should be on your way to a military career.

For nine months I went regularly to a brigade briefing every night designed for the information office. We'd hear all kinds of things—troop movements, numbers needed in a certain territory—but the most important figure always focused on was the number of kills. We had the theory that if we shot enough of them, they would give up the war. It was a stupid theory. It was never going to work, but we still kept it up. When some other brigade in the division was known to have a high hostile kill, and we didn't, bad news! The brigade commander did not like that because it did not make him look good.

It seemed to some of us at the time that they worked very hard to make sure their body count was correct. They checked and they rechecked and wanted to make sure you didn't count a body twice and that people saw it. This was on the battalion level, so that body count levels were probably not so far off. We found out later on that at each level up the line, they'd been upped. I'm sure you heard the figures that each Vietnamese citizen was killed a number of times over, and somehow they still kept coming.

In the information office we had two functions from a military view, one of which was to publicize the events of the people we were working with, which really means to make our commander look good. And the second job is to shepherd around journalists, or to make our commander look good, which is very easy when you have control of the helicopters, which is the only way to get around in the area.

I was very good at what I did. We went out to the field. We had two groups of troops who were information specialists who were supposed to write our articles, and our photographers. They would take their cameras, rush off into the jungles and take pictures of people fighting a war. But their real function was to spend time in the rear taking pictures of people going home, award ceremonies, and promotions, so that stuff could be sent home and so it could be given to the people who were doing it so that you could receive some immediate gratification because they'll give you something before you go.

The Army actually runs an information school at Fort Benjamin Harrison, and they teach people to write little newspaper articles for hometown newspapers. "Private So and So has been assigned to such and such a place where he is a valued member of such and such a company and is serving his country with valor and distinction." This would appear in a soldier's hometown newspaper. There's a form for that. Everybody who goes into the military is supposed to fill one of those out. The official information officer fills it out according to an official formula and then sends it out to the hometown newspaper.

This was considered a nice job. We could sleep in beds. We ate better. We got to the PXs and bought everything up. My troops thought they had died and gone to heaven.

It sounds like the good life. Were there any problems there?

You were always aware of two things. One, that you never wanted to get close to anybody because they might be dead tomorrow; and you were aware consistently that you were not at home. You were always aware when you were in the field, but even in the rear, that it would be an unusual night if there were not shells dropping on top of you. This was also the very end of 1968 and almost all of 1969. The discontent was huge. One of the first things I saw when I was transferred to the information office was a group of troops who were out in back of one of the buildings. They were essentially collecting money to give to the person who would shoot someone. One of my troops told me about it later. They had collected $750 or something, a tidy little sum, to get rid of some asshole. We were in one place where we had two brigades, and one of the two commanders couldn't stay in his office because people kept on opening his door and throwing grenades under his desk.

I used to, for reasons of my own, act as a green-line guard. I'd sit in one of the observation posts along the green line, which was around every base. One of the defenses would be to send out patrols of maybe five to 10 people to go out 1,000 meters in front so that if the bad guys were to come, these people would be there to alert the base that they were coming. I knew damn well that they would go out here [pointing] and come around the base and come in here [pointing]. They weren't out there. Why the hell should they be? We were all aware that they were doing this. They were only out there as an alarm. It was a stupid thing to do.

Your war is not worth putting my life on the line for in a stupid situation. All the reasons that we were given for fighting that war, we saw to be untrue. I think a lot of it came from firsthand experience. It was very pragmatic and very concrete. But I still marvel at how little we talked about the war. And this was among a group of people where the dominant sentiment was that this war sucked from the beginning to the end.

How did you deal with this realization, and with still having to be there?

We smoked a lot of dope. I told my troops I'd provide the money, but they had to buy it. I'd also keep it, because nobody was going to go through our camp and investigate my footlocker because I was a captain. We would go to the PX, buy cigars, empty out the tobacco, and fill them with Vietnamese or Cambodian Red. When you bought marijuana, the little old ladies would give you a vial of opium, and you'd paint that on the outside of the cigar. You'd stand out there and you'd smoke that, and boy could you play pinochle.

I went home to Cincinnati just before Christmas . . . December 5, 1969. Immediately after I got out, I saw an ad for it [VVAW] in a newspaper someplace in early 1970. I signed the papers and paid my $5, joined, and did absolutely nothing about it. I went out to the west coast instead.

When I was out on the west coast, I spent a lot of time with people who were very much involved in progressive movements. I started reading all the literature of Carl Rogers and a whole series of things. I got involved in Earth Day things and riots at Stanford over the Cambodian invasion, and very upset over Kent State and feeling a real need to try to do something.

"The Army Was Rampant with Personal Vendettas."

MIKE GOLD

Mike Gold grew up in New York, where he was raised by his immigrant mother and his older brothers after his father's death. As a young boy, he was active in the Democratic Party, along with his brothers. While he was in college, he took a semester off to work on John Lindsay's mayoral campaign; this made him eligible for the draft, and he could not bring himself to avoid it, although he had doubts about American involvement in Vietnam.

178

I went to Fort Jackson, South Carolina. I did basic there. We were confined to the tank hill because there was spinal meningitis on the base. We stayed there drinking 3.2 beer, smoking cheap cigarettes.

My company commander, this young lieutenant who hadn't been to Vietnam . . . We used to be doing PT and calisthenics and he'd say, "Man, you got to hurt now or you're going to hurt in Vietnam." They pushed us pretty hard.

Then I was shipped out to Fort Leonard Wood, Missouri, where I was being trained as a combat engineer. I did that . . . building bridges and roads and blowing them up. I had scored very well on the tests in basic, and one day they called me in AIT and told me I had an option to be an officer. They were building up officer candidate schools. I was held there for four months, since they decided to assign me to one of the officers on base, the motor pool officer. I was in the motor pool for most of that time, learning motor pool operations.

One of my platoon sergeants went after me, and I don't exactly know what he was accusing me of, but he sent me for psychological evaluation, just because of this New York thing and being different, so different from him. I forgot where he was from, but he was a real redneck. I walked into this thing, and this doctor says to me, "How are you?" I said, "I'm fine. Everything's OK." That was the end of it. He threw it right out.

The army was rampant with personal vendettas. You see that in *An Officer and a Gentleman* [film of 1982]. Lou Gosset plays the kind of platoon sergeant that I ran into. He was like my platoon sergeant. They try to break you and try to make you over. They don't have time to do everybody at once. They pick a few, and they're really on their case. The DIs would call the guys from California "surfers," and the people from New York would be "hoods." Being Jewish and small of stature, you know—I'm short and thin, healthy; I mean, I could always do all the stuff—but it was easy to be picked on. I was real different. In basic and AIT . . . if I wanted to go to services Friday night it was a big deal. I'd be the only one asking.

The guys that went to AIT with me went to Fort Campbell, Kentucky, and became part of the 27th Engineers that went to Vietnam. I was held to go to OCS. My motto was to be chairborne, not airborne. I had applied to, like, adjutant general, OCS finance, stuff like that. When it came down, I went into artillery. It was only combat arms available. I went to Fort Sill in artillery OCS. We were hearing about artillery officers. Your first job is forward observer for an infantry unit, and they said FOs were dying off like flies.

I had a couple of friends there who had all been in college. . . . We used to sit around talking and we came to a conclusion on the reason for being where we were. . . . We were hired killers. We're in the Army and being paid for it. If we're killers, we should volunteer to go to Vietnam, to do what the Army's all about.

179

How did you feel about the fact that you were hired killers?

We accepted that; it was a philosophical discussion. . . . We were prepared to do what we were told to do. . . . The alternatives still seem the same. . . . If you wanted to leave, you'd have to go to jail.

They had dream sheets of where you wanted to be assigned. Myself and several other guys volunteered to go to Nam. On the day that orders came down, the G's and H's in that section of the alphabet went to Germany, no matter what we put down.

I was stationed in the Third Armored Division north of Frankfurt. I was in the First Brigade. It was one of the biggest brigades in the Army. My unit was levied to go to Vietnam. I wasn't levied because I had just got there. That was June 1967. The unit was levied again. That was a year later. I had less than a year, so I didn't go again.

What was the experience like in Germany?

It was crazy. There was a lot of unrest on the base. There were lots of fights in the enlisted men's clubs. Also, there was racial stuff going on. We had some real yahoo battalion commanders. . . . We had one guy . . . he was the mech-infantry battalion commander, and he had a great rivalry with the tank guys. He wanted to be the best battalion. He wanted his guys to be real aggressive infantrymen. They used to have raids on one another with baseball bats, empty M-14s, to go bust heads in another battalion. He had his guys going out busting heads.

I was also very aware of the European peace movement. That's where my thing started. Nine of us had this house in a nearby town. We lived off base. There were demonstrations. We met German students. We used to get information about what was going on in Vietnam from them. It was very compelling, what they were telling us. We were getting the other side of the propaganda that we were getting from the United States military and the media. We heard now about large opposition in the United States. The Europeans had more information than the Americans.

You believed them?

There were officers and NCOs who had been to Vietnam. There were various kinds of complaints that it wasn't being run well. . . . It was situation fucked-up. Most of the guys were not career officers. All of them had some college. These were thinking guys.

There were also personal experiences. . . . I had to do a lot of court-martials and being the new officer in my battalion, I was given the orders to be defense council for guys. Most of the guys in trouble in my battalion ended up being black. I had to defend them. I was giving my commanding officer fits because I knew the guys on my board intimately because they were my fellow officers. I would challenge the ones off the board that I knew they were racists. One or two of these things were thrown out because I got enough guys thrown off the board to make it illegal.

When I was a first lieutenant, then I became a prosecutor. When you're a prosecutor, you get to investigate the charges. It was a real stacked deck. They gave me the UCMJ [Uniform Code of Military Justice] and I read it. The Army became a game of reading the book. I was going to make them follow it to the letter. I would be investigating charges and throwing them out. . . . That was the thing.

I got out in April of 1969 and stayed in Europe for a year. I got out on the day I would have been promoted to captain. I was interested in becoming a foreign service officer. When I went in to different countries, I went into the embassy. I was asking those people what it was like. I was hearing some interesting things. These were people working for our government. That was the time that United States embassies were being demonstrated in front of. People were telling me how Americans were being perceived by Europeans. They had studied international affairs, and they felt powerless. It had a big effect on me. My conclusion was that this wasn't a way to change things, because they were in it and they couldn't do much about it.

What do you mean by "change things"? Change what and why?

This war in Vietnam was wrong, and how could we get out of it? We were there for all the wrong reasons. Guys were getting killed for nothing. We weren't bringing democracy to Vietnam. . . . We heard all the stuff about the rotten governments in Vietnam, propping up of dictators. It was an idealistic position.

I came back in April of 1970. I went back to college almost immediately. I went to get my benefits in the office. . . . There were a couple of vets working for the director. I started asking about getting touch with the other veterans. The student body seemed younger and rather alien to me.

We started talking about organizing a group . . . getting the veterans together and seeing what they needed. When I first started the GI Bill, we got about $100 a month. We needed to work part-time and go to school. I was doing the census and going to college. We were having a lot of trouble with the VA and our benefits. They delayed. There were issues about jobs and housing, readjustment problems.

We organized this veterans' group. Then I met people like Danny Friedman. . . . We were all going to Brooklyn College. They were in VVAW and brought me to a meeting. I joined VVAW and have been a member ever since.

Conscientious Objector

RON SABLE

Ron Sable went into the military as a conscientious objector; he was opposed to the war on religious grounds. As a result of his position, he became a medic.

The training, the propaganda of the Army was crude, almost to be laughable. For those of us that were college grads, this sort of rhetorical 1950s anti-communist stuff was sort of a joke. But they were serious about it, and these kids who were seventeen or eighteen, or whatever, had no broader experience, or no information to deal with that. I think a lot of people went over there thinking that the Vietnamese would welcome us with open arms, that they were courageous allies in this fight—and none of that proved to be true.

I went May 1st of 1969 and was there through June 5th of 1970. It was a fairly quiet Tet year. I was attached to an engineer battalion. There were about 10 medics and a bunch of construction people who laid fuel pipeline and built roads along QO1 highway on the coast.

The first night on my home base, we got hit. We got hit about once a month. There was activity in the area, although generally the area around Qui Nhon and the valley were secure. There were handful of casualties each time. On a day-to-day basis you never felt so threatened. This was a noncombat secure area.

There was actually a book that came into my possession during the time I was there. In fact, it was through the PX. We'd get books every month, and almost nobody paid any attention to them. So I had the run of this library that came into the post office there. There was a book by two scholars, historians, from an eastern school. It was a documentary history of Vietnam, and it went back to pre–World War II.[17] It was so clear, reading this stuff, that we didn't belong. We had essentially sided with the wrong side, had played a very pernicious and awful role in it.

That, and then the concrete experience of what it felt like . . . what US imperialism is all about to people in other countries . . . had an impact on me. One of the stories that I often tell, a remarkable example to a lot of GIs about what the Vietnamese really thought, was that Ho Chi Minh died during my tour of duty and all of these Vietnamese, including the ones that worked for us, were mourning his death. That was a very startling experience to all of these GIs. So I think that learning a lot historically about what had gone on and my concrete experiences confirmed all of my worst suspicions about what's happening.

I extended a month to get out early. I spent a total of 19 months in the Army, including the 13 months spent in Vietnam. Just as I got out in 1970,

I went to visit some people in Berkeley who were friends. They were mostly people who were against the war. They were doing antiwar talks.

Seymour Hersh's story about My Lai in the *Atlantic* was just breaking at that point. The thing that was startling to me was that the people were saying that this sort of thing can't be true. American boys can't do this sort of thing. I was shocked at their naiveté. I never doubted for a moment that there could be this brutality. You saw this kind of viciousness toward Vietnamese on a daily basis. Not that they were shot, but certainly physically abused—and nobody talked about them as anything but gooks. All officers and enlisted people did. That kind of racist dehumanizing notion about these people clearly led people under adverse circumstances to commit a lot of atrocities.

Some people felt personally betrayed. For me, the experience confirmed all of my worst suspicions and gave me a clear picture of what was wrong with the way the United States behaved in the world. That had to be changed.

But you're back. You're working, going to school. Why do this?

For me, it comes out of a sort of a notion that you have the responsibility to make things better. . . . People were still dying . . . and the key role that the veteran could play in [stopping] that . . . their credibility could not be undermined. It's the perfect foil for the reactionary veterans' movement.

"Trying to Organize the Troops"

DAVID EWING

David Ewing went into the military intending to organize troops as part of efforts by the Progressive Labor Party—a faction of Students for a Democratic Society—to create a resistance movement within the Army. He saw his work in the Army as a logical extension of his antiwar work as a civilian.

I was inducted in the Philadelphia Induction Center on September 17, 1970. I was stationed at Fort Dix, New Jersey. I thought what I would do is just keep my head down and get through basic training. The plan was that you just keep your mouth shut until you get to Vietnam, because if they figure out you're in PL, you're fucked. Friends of mine who had done it before were all caught. When I went in, they [PL] immediately lost track of me. My letters were screwed up. I couldn't write people.

When you go in, on the first day, they give you these tests. It seemed to me that doing well on the test would be inconsistent with going to Vietnam

183

organizing grunts, but I found it very difficult, psychologically, not to do well on a test. It really was a dilemma for me, and I didn't know what to do, so I did the best I could on the test. I thought the tests were really pretty easy, actually.

Within a day or two they herd all draftees into one room and offered us no combat if you take an extra year. They isolated the draftees from enlistees. I wanted to go into combat, so I wasn't going to do that. I guess two-thirds of the guys took the offer. That sort of narrowed down the group. I became a grunt.

It was still a pretty tough basic training. People were psychologically broken very, very quickly. People who are ungainly, uncoordinated, or nerds were just brutally dealt with by the drill sergeants. A lot of young people were broken by the experience. One guy in my company committed suicide, hanged himself in the barracks on the weekend. I was twenty. I was one of the oldest people, certainly the most mature of pretty much anybody.

It was a crazy scene in the military. It's like living with 20 armed ten-year-olds or sixteen-year-olds. There's all the emotional range of craziness and very immature people with access to big weapons.

People were very disgruntled, and I would feed into that. I would run down the military and suggest people resist in little ways, but never any communism. The authorities never realized I was doing it. I was never distinguished from any other complainer.

The hard thing for me was a day about six weeks through. Part of the training is not to permit you to sleep. It's important to mold people. If you don't let them sleep, it breaks their resistance. I hadn't slept in about six weeks. I was really tired. We had to go see the propaganda movie about Vietnam, and the company commander told his personal stories about Vietnam, all these great things like how you could have sex with prostitutes. I was just appalled by the whole thing. My worst images of Vietnam and reasons for doing this were all being confirmed by my company commander. Then they showed a film about Ho Chi Minh that just trashed Ho Chi Minh. He was probably the person I most admired in the world. It really shook me up. I think I became emotional because of not sleeping. I was on the edge. Walking back from the film, I almost tore my uniform off. If someone had just poked me, or said something about Ho Chi Minh, I would have ripped that uniform right off. That was the only time I was really furious. But I held it together.

Everybody is waiting for their orders to see where you're going to go for your next training. I fully expected AIT. During the last couple days of basic training, I got my orders to Fort Monmouth, New Jersey. I remember looking at it: I knew it wasn't infantry, but I didn't know what it was. I talked to other guys, and a guy in my unit said, "You lucky asshole. I signed up for that; this is the greatest job in the army." It was Signal Corps. It was a very privileged job. I just laughed.

It turned out that the training at Fort Monmouth was to be a microwave radio technician, which was a Vietnam MOS. I was 26-Lima-10, which is the tactical microwave repairman and operator.

All the instructors in the training program at Fort Monmouth, New Jersey, had been to Vietnam. I watched classes graduate. Every single class that graduated, every single person went to Vietnam. There was no question that I was going to make it. We went through. Finally, when my class graduated, April 1971, we got our orders. My orders were to Germany. Two-thirds of my class went to Germany and one-third went to Vietnam.

It was such a mixed feeling. You couldn't help but thinking, God, I'm going to live, and then feeling like I had failed in my duty. It was a really difficult thing. At that time, there was tremendous GI resistance in Germany. That was part of the peak resistance by black soldiers. American soldiers were concentrated in really large units in Germany, so there were great opportunities for organizing.

I was shipped out to Germany and sent to Heidelberg, [which] was Signal Corps headquarters. After you're there, they decide where to put you. It could be anywhere, basically, in Europe or the Middle East. I got my orders for the north coast of Germany. It was extremely remote. There were very few soldiers.

In the British zone, the nuclear weapon defense was coordinated by the Americans. They were using the 26-Lima-10 people to operate microwave stations to coordinate the nuclear battlefield. The United States in the 1960s was planning a war to stop Soviet armored advance. The Soviets had heavy tank formations. They were relying on tactical nuclear weapons to stop the advance. So what they did was, they set up lines of tactical missiles every 20 miles with a 1-megaton nuclear warhead. I was on one of the lines. My job was to kill the missile base and the Soviet armor and all the Germans in the town 20 miles east of us. I knew the war message. I just wouldn't have told my commander.

I was ready to try to do my organizing. The problem was, the biggest base I was on had 50 soldiers. Unless you were lucky, you would never find anybody. There were small numbers of black people and large numbers of whites, so there was never enough critical mass for blacks to do anything about their horrible situation, the discrimination they were facing.

I tried, but I was very ineffective. I would try to set an example of resistance, so I wouldn't iron my uniform; I would disobey orders. I had my SDS jacket, a denim jacket with a big red fist stenciled on the back. I used to wear that all the time off duty. I'd tell people stories about the student movement. Soldiers were interested, but people would identify me right away as a problem guy.

Once the Army figured out I was a problem, I was transferred virtually every month. It was such an awful thing to be transferred in the military. [You had to] pack up all your gear, lose all your friends.

We got to this little base with the 10 guys. It was just out of control. There's no officers, just these 10 guys. They had their own bar. People would run bar tabs to $200 and $300 a month. I wasn't that much of a drinker, and I didn't use any drugs. All the other soldiers used drugs heavily, especially at that base. People did unbelievable amounts of hashish. You walk in barracks, you just couldn't see, there was so much smoke. I had no idea what this was about; it was completely alien to me. It was part of the gap between me and the other soldiers. I was really put off by those guys. People played pinochle and smoke hashish and listened to Jethro Tull and these really weird hippie albums. I couldn't figure it out.

I was always trying to encourage people to break things. We had our own fleet of vehicles that we could drive anywhere we wanted. We had Army pickup trucks and a car. As a matter of principle, I would never use the clutch when I drove the stick shift. Just fucking slam it! I destroyed trucks on purpose, but the other soldiers, who were drunk, would destroy them too. They were much more effective. They would destroy them unintentionally. We would destroy a vehicle every single month. I told all the soldiers that I was fucking with them and I did it. It created a big problem, and the other soldiers told that I did it. I got in trouble for that.

We got word one day that the captain was coming out for inspection, which was very unusual. So I took blue paint and painted my boots blue, not on the surface, but on the edge. Then I was ordered to cut the lawn. So I took the lawn mower and cut the letters FTA [fuck the Army], like 20 feet in size.

The captain comes out and there's a gigantic FTA to greet him. I'm wearing these blue boots. The guy is looking at me like he just can't believe it. He doesn't say a word, though. The sergeant is in so much trouble. It's just incredible. He's really under scrutiny now. They bring people out to check out on the sergeant.

Then it became serious. It wasn't fun anymore. They were really determined to get me. They determined I was a communist or some kind of big problem. Then they fucked with me immediately.

First thing, they offered me an Article 15, which is the nonjudicial punishment, the lowest form of punishment. It saves the Army a lot of time because they don't have to argue in a court-martial, where you have rights. You can accept the Article 15 or decline it. Theoretically, if you're offered the Article 15 and you think it's unfair, you can request a court-martial by your peers. I was determined to fight anything, but you could also accept and write an explanation.

So I accepted it, but I wrote an explanation explaining my conduct, which incriminated the sergeant in committing crimes and incriminated my company commander too in being a party to some of the crimes—things they had done that I knew were illegal, knowing that the appeal would be to his commander. I was hoping that he would see that and back off, which he did.

The sergeant called me in and said, "Ewing, we decided to withdraw yours and we're going to give you another chance." This guy was apoplectic. The company commander was really pissed at me for doing this to him. He was livid. They decided they were really going to get me. My sergeant told me that he was going to see me in Leavenworth.

They were constantly watching me, looking for things, but I wasn't the only problem. There were other people there with drug problems or who were criminals. There were other problems he had to contend with; it wasn't just me.

I was really under a lot of psychological strain by this point. I was the only soldier in my unit who didn't use drugs. They brought these drug-sniffing dogs into my room. It was about three o'clock in the morning. The doors kicked open, the lights are on, the dogs are barking, the guards are running around pulling my closet open, kicking my footlocker open, the dogs are sniffing everywhere. But the dogs didn't find anything. The next time I knew that that meant that they were going to plant heroin on me. That would be a super-serious bust.

Just at this time, Nixon ordered troop cuts in Europe. Everybody with five months or less was immediately let out. I had like six months left. So all of a sudden, I had 30 days to go. They just gave up.

My old company commander had been replaced by a West Point guy who hated me even more. He was going to screw me on my discharge. I knew he was going to give me an undesirable or something. The actual day I left the unit, the company commander was away, so the company clerk typed up my papers for me. The guy gave me real good paper. The guy was really nice.

It's funny. During that year, they kept promoting me. We made rank so fast during the war that I was E-4 within one year.

I got out in April of 1972, and all of a sudden I was back on campus. I went back to a different school, Towson State College, where my girlfriend had gone to school. I joined the SDS chapter. I was the most experienced person in the chapter, so I immediately was a chapter leader. This was the height of the antiwar stuff. I found myself leading really mass demonstrations involving thousands and thousands of students.

3

FROM CITIZEN-SOLDIERS TO WINTER SOLDIERS

*That was the bottom line. America, your sons have come home and are
telling you, hey, wake up and smell the roses. This is what really
happened over there. We're not no college professors or commies.
We're the guys that were there. We were working-class kids:
the sons of America who fought the war and came back.*

Danny Friedman

*We did what we did because we loved our country and wanted
our country to realize that it made mistakes. I am just as
patriotic as my father or my uncle or anybody.*

Jack McCloskey

A Nation in Turmoil

Antiwar veterans, most of whom were released from military duty after
1967, returned to a nation in turmoil. The public was divided not only over
the war but also over the civil rights movement and the growing women's
movement; and these movements were themselves embroiled in factional
struggles, which were exacerbated and sometimes even instigated by
increased governmental secrecy and clandestine activity. Civil strife had broken out in many American cities. Two of the most revered leaders of the era,
on whom many young Americans had pinned their hopes for peace and
equality—Martin Luther King Jr. and Robert Kennedy—were assassinated
within a short period in 1968. Veterans had to navigate through this turbu-
lence as they sought to build their antiwar organization.

Antiwar veterans were motivated to speak out because of their belief in the
democratic system and in the ability of citizens to affect change. As Jan Barry

put it, "None of us had a degree in political science. We had the same general sense as most people: You change the public attitude in this country, things change." In order to change the public attitude, veterans had to find ways to reach the American people. They naturally gravitated toward the antiwar community, which had already captured the attention of the media, the public, and politicians.

The antiwar movement had emerged in the early 1960s in response to the escalation of American involvement in Vietnam. Before 1965, the movement was made up predominantly of pacifists and left-wing activists who had cut their teeth on two causes of the late 1950s and early 1960s: the civil rights movement and the protests against nuclear weapons. These early antiwar activists had remained on the margins until the United States dramatically increased its military intervention in Vietnam in the spring of 1965. As a result of that increase, though, their movement began to attract new adherents.[1]

The first major antiwar rallies were held in New York, and teach-ins were held in universities across the nation in the spring of 1965, in response to the escalation of the war and the draft. These antiwar protests drew a variety of Americans from all walks of life, including homemakers, veterans of other wars, students, and active-duty servicemen.[2] Between 1965 and 1967, the movement grew in numbers and expanded its activities. Rallies were held in New York, San Francisco, Washington, and other cities across the country, often with hundreds or thousands of participants. Their aim at this point was to change public opinion and government policy through nonviolent protest.

Nonviolent protests, however, seemed to have little if any effect on foreign policy makers, who continued to intensify American military activity in Vietnam. As a result, a segment of the movement became increasingly frustrated and turned toward active resistance, and this new level of activism damaged the shaky coalitions that had been formed during the preceding years. Thus by the time the dissenting veterans began to form Vietnam Veterans Against the War, the larger antiwar movement had split into factions. Left-wing groups and religious groups, for example, disagreed over tactics and the degree to which they should support the NLF and Vietnamese independence. Tensions were also increased by the emergence of a counterculture within the antiwar community. By 1967, Yippies (a term dervied from Youth International Party) and zippies, as well as a number of other marginal groups within the movement, had also attracted the attention of the media. Much of that attention, however, was unfavorable: they were often criticized—even by Americans who shared their antiwar convictions—for their flamboyant behavior, acerbic language, and disdain for convention.[3]

Frustration and factionalism also developed in other areas of public dissent. Civil rights activists, in particular, seeing little progress in racial politics, had become more militant, and the peaceful nonviolent methods of the early 1960s gave way to the more militant rhetoric of the Black Panther Party. This affected the antiwar movement: leaders within the African American community began to openly criticize the Vietnam war; some even linked their own struggle for justice with that of the Vietnamese. Muhammad Ali's refusal to serve, Martin Luther King, Jr.'s outspoken opposition, and the growing militancy of the Black Panther Party contributed to antiwar activists' sense that American foreign policy was inherently racist; and these factors also contributed to the rising tensions within American society over the war.

The women's movement that took shape during the mid-1960s added a new dimension to antiwar criticism: the impact of the war on women in Vietnam and the United States. Also, some activists within the women's movement—and within the African American community—disassociated themselves from male activists; thus more cracks in the edifice of dissent were exposed.

Despite this growing divisiveness, antiwar activity in the United States and across the world continued to grow. In 1968, antiwar rallies were held in Paris, London, Rome, and other capitals. Although activists felt that they were ignored by their political leaders, this increased dissent actually did profoundly affect the politicians who were managing the war.[4]

In the Johnson administration, the cold war consensus began to crumble as a number of civilian advisers privately questioned the efficacy of the United States' military tactics in Vietnam. Even the chief architect of the war, Robert McNamara—the secretary of defense—began to worry about the impact of the antiwar movement on the nation's ability to prosecute the conflict succesfully. Still, on the whole, he and others in power who were becoming disillusioned remained silent about their doubts and publicly supported Johnson's policies. Their unwillingness to reveal any discomfort, it has been argued, was due to their fear of undermining American credibility in the global order they had sought to construct.[5] Another apparent factor, of course, was party unity: 1968 was an election year.

For whatever reasons, then, the administration did not reassess its policies in Vietnam. Rather, administration officials increasingly tried to conceal their activities from the public, and they stepped up their campaign to counter the claims of the antiwar movement that the war was immoral, illegal, and unwinnable. As early as 1965, State Department officials had traveled the country, publicly debating antiwar advocates and attempting to frame the war in terms consistent with traditional American principles. In 1967, Johnson authorized the creation of a Committee for Peace and Freedom in Vietnam and an Information Group in the White House to keep track of antiwar activity and to disseminate the administration's version of events. This version was given to the press and to the administration's allies in Congress, to be passed on to the American public.[6]

The Johnson administration also expanded the scope of efforts by intelligence agencies to discredit and destroy the antiwar movement. The FBI, various branches of military intelligence, and local "red squads" engaged in activities that would in effect curtail Americans' freedom of speech.[7] (The impact of such activities on VVAW is detailed in Chapter 5.) In addition, Johnson directed the CIA to undertake an operation (code-named CHAOS) to infiltrate the antiwar community and find its presumed links with international communism. In such activities, the national security agencies undoubtedly overstepped their legal mandates.[8]

Although these efforts were occasionally successful, the Johnson administration could not stifle the growing dissent within its own party; nor could it change the reality of the war that was revealed by the Tet offensive in early 1968. For years, the American public had been told, consistently, that victory was at hand; to many Americans, Tet exposed that promise as a lie.

The cracks within the Democratic Party widened during the presidential primaries in the spring of 1968. Lyndon Johnson, the incumbent, was nearly defeated in New Hampshire by the antiwar candidate, Eugene McCarthy—an outcome that not only revealed a growing antiwar sentiment among Democrats but signaled the end of Johnson's presidency. Antiwar activists increased their attacks on the administration; and shortly after the New Hampshire primary, Johnson, weary of the struggle—or perhaps convinced that he could not win—withdrew from the campaign.

Antiwar Democrats then pushed for the nomination of an antiwar candidate for president at the national party convention in Chicago. Although some critics of the war were skeptical about ending it through democratic channels and had therefore shunned electoral politics, many activists now supported McCarthy and Robert Kennedy, viewing Kennedy, in particular, as the last best hope for peace.

The assassination of Robert Kennedy and Martin Luther King, Jr., as well as the notorious events of the Democratic national convention (which had seemed to be rigged and had been accompanied by protests that were forcibly subdued by the police), sent shock waves through the antiwar community. Thereafter, angry and frustrated antiwar activists looked for new ways to change society. Some dropped out of the movement, believing that the American political system was compromised beyond redemption. Others began to call for revolution.

In the election, Richard Nixon, the Republican candidate, defeated the Democrat Hubert Humphrey, no doubt partly because of the debacle at the Democratic convention, but also partly because Nixon campaigned on a promise to end the war quickly. When he took office, however, Nixon continued to follow the policies of the previous administration; he too concealed his plans in Vietnam from the public and used both rhetoric and intimidation against his opponents.[9]

Nixon avowed an interest in pursuing peace and did introduce a policy of "Vietnamization" of the war—that is, phasing out American forces so that actual combat would be conducted by the Vietnamese. But at the same time he was increasing the use of air power in Vietnam, and he engaged the military command in his efforts to widen the war in secret. The undisclosed invasions of Laos and Cambodia were part of these efforts.[10]

The rhetorical attacks on the antiwar movement were led by Nixon's vice president, Spiro Agnew, who made a series of vitriolic speeches not only against the movement but also against the press, although much of the press had been friendly to the Nixon administration. When the largest demonstrations in American history were held across the nation in October 1969, Agnew called the leaders an "effete corps of impudent snobs who characterized themselves as intellectuals" and described them as "hard-core dissidents and professional anarchists."[11] (In fact, though, the movement was led by a variety of groups that reflected the diverse nature of American society.)

Nixon and his staff continued their attempts to discredit the antiwar community and derail the movement, but antiwar activism persisted. Protests increased even further when it was revealed that in March 1968 hundreds of Vietnamese civilians in the villages of My Lai and My Khe had been killed by American troops; when Nixon announced that Cambodia had been invaded; and when four student protesters at Kent State University were killed by the National Guard in May 1970.

Nixon stepped up the attacks on his opponents by greatly increasing various clandestine activities by members of his White House staff, the FBI, the CIA, and other branches of the Defense Intelligence Agency. In June 1970, he developed a plan—called the Huston plan—to coordinate and control these agencies' activities from the White House. The Huston plan called for the creation of an overarching Interagency Group, which was essentially authorized to violate civil liberties. As Johnathan Schell has commented, "The White House would be, in effect, empowered to commit a wide variety of crimes against the members of any group that it suspected of being subversive."[12] As it happened, the Huston plan was never implemented, because the agencies involved did not want to relinquish control,[13] but Nixon did form his own group of individuals to perform the same function.

Meanwhile, troops still in Vietnam, especially after 1968—the year of the Tet offensive—continued to be dissatisfied with the war, as our narrators' accounts of their experiences in Vietnam have shown. Desertion, AWOL, insubordination, fraggings, and drug abuse among GIs increased dramatically after 1968, and the antiwar movement spread throughout the military. GIs published antiwar papers, formed antiwar organizations, and set up antiwar coffeehouses in an effort to help focus this growing dissatisfaction and make it consciously antimilitarist, anti-imperialist, and antiracist.[14]

Back in the World: Veterans and the VVAW

Antiwar veterans who spoke out were not immune to the prevailing fragmentation, deception, and chaos. The stories they tell on the following pages reveal the difficulties they encountered during this time of turmoil. Nonetheless, they attended peace rallies where they encountered other veterans and began the process of linking up with their comrades, believing they would have a stronger voice, and that their testimony would carry greater legitimacy, if they openly acknowledged their status as veterans. The entity they created— the VVAW—was the first antiwar organization in American history consisting of veterans who were protesting against a war from which they had just returned.

Perhaps the most striking aspect of the interviews here is the veterans' pride in the fact that VVAW and other veterans' groups across the nation chose to make their protest nonviolently. These were, after all, men who had been trained to fight and kill. For some, the commitment to nonviolence was ideological and was based on their own intimacy with violence: they were horrified by what they had experienced as servicemen, and sometimes by what they had done in the name of their country. For others, nonviolence was more pragmatic: it was based on their understanding that the federal government had the power to destroy their efforts if they resorted to violent tactics. Regardless of their motivations, though, they continued to adhere strictly to nonviolent protest.

In the following narratives, antiwar veterans describe how they tried to reach the public and their elected representatives, how they went about building VVAW, and how they were received by their fellow citizens and by the people who were prosecuting the war. Their experiences reveal the difficulties they encountered in trying to build a democratic resistance movement in a climate that was often undemocratic, and the roadblocks they had to surmount or circumvent in order to get their voices heard.

The Roots of VVAW

JAN BARRY, ANN HIRSCHMAN, SHELDON RAMSDELL

Jan Barry (JB): When I got out of the Army, in May of 1965, [I] flew back to upstate New York and immediately came to New Jersey. There was a girl here I had been writing to and therefore decided to come to this region looking for a job. I ended up getting a job for a newspaper that I'm actually working for now, in the library.

She went to a peace demonstration either in 1965 or early 1966 in New York. I wasn't in any way interested in going to this peace demonstration. She came back. I asked what happened, and she said some news person came up and asked why she was there and she really didn't have anything much to say. I remember being mad at her. "Well, why didn't you know why you were there? Why couldn't you say why you were there? Why couldn't you say what's wrong with the war?"

At that point, my sympathies were to research what was going on. I researched everything, from reading Mao Tse-tung in the original to what's behind their side of it, and whatever else I could get my hands on. I was taking college classes on Saturday, and I took economics. I did research into our economic relationship with South Vietnam. Out of this I learned that we were, in essence, turning it into an economic colony, turning a rice-exporting region into a place [where] we sell them rice. There were lots of articles in *Fortune* magazine and other kinds of places about these great deals that were being done.

I talked to people. Reporters started telling me they'd go out and interview the ones just coming back from Vietnam, [in] late 1965, early 1966, from the first larger wave that went in there, and "These guys are more bitter than you are."

At one point, I ran into one of these guys, and he was extremely bitter. He was the only survivor in a unit that was wiped out. He said, "Why the hell should I prop up this rotten society?" He disappeared and no one ever heard from him again.

That was the thing that propelled me to organize something, realizing that there were all these angry guys out there, so turned off from their own society that it was frightening. Somebody had to articulate why that anger was there, what that bitterness was about. I didn't know how, but I had to learn how to do that.

I remember toward the end of 1966 I had finally reached a point of frustration. I decided to move to Manhattan and start looking for more compatible people. I didn't think [of] a peace movement. There were lots of people who were asking questions. They were thinking about raising the questions. None of these questions were visible in the news media that we worked for.

Things like "Johnson Goes on Peace Parley" would be the headline. You'd read the story, and it had nothing to do with a peace parley; it was a war parley. Everything was out of a Washington perspective. Even if the reporter from the *New York Times* or whatever was reporting from Saigon, the story got twisted around to be a Washington perspective. You learned how to read between the lines. The editors were doubting their own reporters in Vietnam. That was very clear to me. It all added up to: The American public has no idea whatsoever of the reality. How do you convey that reality when everything seems to be closed up?

I walked into the New York Public Library main branch one day, asked for the personnel office, and said, "I'd like to work here." I took a pay cut and took the job, filing things and all the rest of the stuff.

I discovered there were all these students from all the various colleges in New York who worked there, and they were talking about something [that] was going to happen in the spring. They were so out of it. We're talking about young students who had no idea about anything. This didn't lead me to want to get involved with them until I saw an advertisement in the *New York Times Book Review* from the Veterans for Peace, saying, "If North Vietnam stops bombing us . . . we'll be ready to negotiate" or something like that. It turned the whole thing around. They weren't bombing us. They weren't threatening us. "Join us, April 15th," I think it said, "at Central Park for the start of this march"—which was the first time, place, and invitation that I felt, Ah-hah, that appeals to me. I liked the way they turned the issue around, a twist on reality.

I went with a friend [and] several people from New Jersey. There was this mob scene. There was a huge number of people at Central Park, from Columbus Circle all the way back as far as you could see. One of the stories of the peace movement that still hasn't really been told was the diversity. It wasn't just this hippie image that has determined the legend. This demonstration that I'm seeing for the first time was full of families in their Sunday best and younger people. This was pre-hippie. People in 1967 still had straight, narrow ties. Look at all the civil rights people and the peace movement people of the time: suits and ties, short hair. I went there wearing a suit and tie and a raincoat.

As we're standing there wondering what to do next, there's this big cry, "Vietnam veterans to the front!" There's this huge group of disciplined people marching, wearing Veterans for Peace hats. At the beginning of this group of veterans someone had provided a banner, hoping some Vietnam veterans would show up. It said, "Vietnam Veterans Against the War." There were some guys already carrying the banner and there were some guys behind them. I just joined that group.

There were some young guys in parts of uniform, or suits and ties, and some women and children. I don't think there were more than a dozen Vietnam veterans and some family members; but behind them—which to me at the time was far more impressive—was like a regimental size, I think 2,000 guys, marching in military formation wearing Veterans for Peace hats.

When we proceeded out of the park and down through Fifth Avenue and through the various other streets, people were ready to lynch, howling and screaming and throwing things. First they see a little group of dignitaries, which apparently included Martin Luther King, Jr., Dave Dellinger, A. J. Muste, and a couple of other people carrying an American flag. They're way out there by themselves taking all this abuse. Then, there's this little band of people carrying a sign, "Vietnam Veterans Against the War." You heard this sea change in the crowd. "What is this? Is that for real? [Angry tone.] It can't even be for real. This has got to be a joke." Then behind that, this group that clearly is veterans. "What!" I mean, this isn't what they expected. "Who are these people? If they're involved, I've got to rethink my opposition to all these people, hollering and screaming at them." You literally could feel and hear a change in these sidewalk crowds. Of course, behind that came a crowd that was so huge [that] they filled up all the streets in midtown Manhattan over to the UN and blocked all the traffic. The entire plaza in front of the UN was filled. All the side streets were filled, and people were still coming.

The march on April 15, 1967, brought together numerous pacifist and left-wing organizations to form the first mass mobilization against the war. It was estimated that between 200,000 and 400,000 people marched in the rain in New York, while another 50,000 marched in San Francisco. As Charles De Benedetti has commented in his book An American Ordeal, *"Thousands of people found a way to express unity beyond the divisions."[15] The media, though, tended to focus on the newly emerging counterculture in the movement, rather than on the kinds of people—evidently the majority—described by Jan Barry.*

JB: Then everybody left. I started asking around, "What happened to that veterans' group?" I found out when Veterans for Peace had a meeting, went to that meeting, and I discovered that there was no Vietnam veterans' group. They initially said, "You should join us." I thought that we would make more of an impression upon people, we'd have a better ability to articulate to people what's going on in Vietnam, if we stand as a Vietnam veterans' organization. I simply started asking where any other Vietnam veterans were.

By June 1st . . . we actually had our first organization meeting. I had names of maybe two dozen people. We formed an organization utilizing the same name that was on the banner. Dave Braum designed the logo, which we talked about. "Let's take that patch that has the sword going through the

**UNDER THIS SYMBOL
55,000 AMERICAN SOLDIERS
HAVE DIED**

**UNDER THIS SYMBOL
MORE THAN 317,000
CAN BE BROUGHT HOME
ALIVE**

One of the original VVAW flyers. At left is the official logo of the U.S. Military Assistance Command, Vietnam, symbolizing American military might (the sword) against the communist threat (the Great Wall of China). At right is the insignia of VVAW.

Great Wall of China and put the rifle with the helmet on it, which symbolized a dead GI. We're filling the Great Wall of China with dead GIs!" There was symbolism!

We started off with a structure that had officers and bylaws and very few people. The only titles we had were for the paperwork: president, vice president, secretary, treasurer. I didn't utilize that in most of the organizing. I would just say I was a member of the national executive committee. I did this deliberately so that somebody couldn't decide they could pop me off. I had seen a few assassinations going on. I thought, I'm not going to be a target. Somebody thinks they could just kill me and that's the end of the organization. In addition, my own sense of organizing was that these guys don't want one person telling them what to do. What they need is a process in which empowerment takes place.

One of the things that I find astounding about this whole process is, I think, that this society provides these ready-made forms of democracy that are there if you want to use them. So without even thinking about it, we formed a democratic organization rather than an autocratic organization.

Our first office was a desk in the corner of the Fifth Avenue Peace Parade Committee. We had support from Veterans for Peace. Many of us went to their meetings. They utilized their fund-raising network to raise money and get us off the ground. It was a lot of money. By 1968, we took an office of our own on Fifth Avenue.

The VVAW in New York received financial support from various organizations and individuals who saw the group as pivotal in the antiwar movement. For example, George Ball—a former adviser to President Johnson—was one of the first contributors, donating $100.[16]

How did you get along with the peace movement?

JB: In the peace movement, you ran into attitudes that ranged from not knowing what to do with us to people who wanted to manipulate us in various ways. One of the first times I walked into the Peace Parade Committee, some woman who looked very much like my mother said, "And how many babies did you kill?"

The socialist groups were always trying to manipulate us, [to] get you to join their organization. Certain things would happen, but we were so unsophisticated or inexperienced that you didn't even realize that a number had just been run on you. You just knew that something was funny.

You go to a coalition meeting; somebody from some really radical black group says, "Fuck the Vietcong—I don't care about those Vietnamese. They never did nothing for me." Jerry Rubin is doing crazy things that have absolutely nothing to do with Vietnam but addressing his ego. Over in the other corner is somebody else who is babbling that the whole problem is sexism. That isn't keeping those people from dying every day to say that. What are we here for? This is a peace movement coalition meeting, right?

The whole point was to focus on what this crazy coalition was going to do for its next spring or fall offensive. That's what we do in the peace movement, because it used the students. It took six months to organize these monsters. They thought, Well, if we could get 100,000 people in Washington, that will end the war. If we get 200,000 people . . . if we get 500,000 people . . . then the moratoriums would get 1 million people to surround the White House, it will end the war.

I was much more interested in: Where can I go and talk to two, or three, or four conservatives, and change their minds? In the middle of all this, you had a group of veterans, who psychologically and politically were bouncing all over the place.

Ann Hirschman (AH): A lot of the peace movement people tended to be Quaker [quiet tone], *and then there were the vets!* [Loudly, laughing.] These people were not always comfortable with each other.

Early on, Dave Dellinger, Norma Becker, Vietnam Peace Parade Committee, and the pacifist crew from Lafayette Street, WRL [War Resisters League], were very comfortable [with VVAW]. Norma and Dave were very uncomfortable with this group in the movement.

> *Ann Hirschman was referring to the counterculture types. Jan Barry also expresssed a dislike of the growing counterculture wing of the movement when he refused to endorse the October 1967 march on the Pentagon. He did not want the organization to be associated with this new contingent, fearing that its activities would alienate Americans rather than making them more receptive to the antiwar community.[17]*

AH: VVAW never had anyone that I met who was just an event freak. They were not pointless partiers. They were not Tom Forsad and the zippies.

JB: One of the reasons I felt so strongly about forming VVAW was to provide a forum for people to come to and utilize a platform. Other people came for all kinds of other reasons. What I found most remarkable is: Even with all these various places that people were coming from, it still grew to be fairly basic VVAW philosophy that we're going to do this nonviolently, which is remarkable. You're talking about people who had all been trained to kill people. Many of them did, repeatedly.[18]

We were going to level with the American people and tell them things, even if they didn't want to hear about them, like war crimes. We discovered early on, when going around speaking, that you couldn't even touch on the subject [war crimes]. People didn't want to hear that. "There's no way that American boys would ever do something like that!" Everybody—liberals,

Photo collage by Sheldon Ramsdell, 1967–1968. *Left to right, across top:* David Braum, Jan Barry Crumb, and Don Weiss at a debate in Valley Stream, Long Island (New York) on January 26, 1968; crowd at an antiwar rally in Union Square (New York City) on Veterans Day, 1967; and David Braum speaking at that rally. *Across middle:* Stephen Greene at the Union Square rally; Carl Rogers, David Susskind, and David Braum on the set of Susskind's television show, October 22, 1967, and *(below)* Senator Gruening of Alaska with Carl Rogers; Francis Rocks and Stephen Greene at Union Square. *Across bottom:* Jan Barry Crumb speaking at the debate in Valley Stream; students at the debate; Carl Rogers with Rev. Martin Luther King, Jr.

conservatives—just cut it right off. You felt stunned. This is what had been the reality over there. You're simply reporting the reality, and people say, "No, it couldn't have happened."

We constantly talked about how you turn things around, imagewise. We didn't use the word "jujitsu," but it was the same kind of principle: to turn around a lot of these things so people would turn around and say, "Wait a minute. What? What did you just say?" Get them to think about it.

Sheldon—Shelly—Ramsdell grew up in Algonquin, Maine. He joined the Navy in 1954; served on an aircraft carrier patrolling the waters around the Philippines, Indonesia, and southeast Asia; and was discharged in 1958. He was interviewed in a coffee shop in San Francisco.

Sheldon Ramsdell (SR): One day—a Sunday, I think—there was a draft-card burning in Union Square [in] 1967, and I went down out of curiosity. I'm suit and tie; red, white, blue; I think I even had an American flag pin on. There was Carl Rogers and Jan [Barry] Crumb and David Braum standing there, and they had signs that said VVAW.

I got very angry and upset and went over there and talked to Carl and said, "You guys for real? I mean what the fuck is this? What's going on here? I don't believe this. Why would they be burning draft cards anyway? They'd already served!"

He says, "I was a chaplain's assistant in Vietnam, and what about you?"

I says, "I've been in the Navy, but I got out in 1958, for crying out loud."

He says, "Well, you're a Vietnam vet."

I says, "I'd been overseas on a carrier and we'd been doing border reconnaissance bombing and I was processing gun camera film." I didn't ask what we were blowing up or who we were bombing. Apparently it was Laos. The Pentagon Papers explained it to me, finally, but I was never convinced that I was actually a Vietnam vet until Carl had insisted.

So I said, "Jesus, I've been looking for you. I've been pissed off at Johnson and all this bullshit—the lying, the deception. This war should have been won long ago."

He says, "Exactly."

Then I met Jan [Barry] and we got together and had little meetings up on the West Side. There were three or four, maybe six of us at the most. I said, "We've got to do media. I've been trained in it in the military and at Union Carbide." I studied it at Carnegie Endowment. I had a job in public relations, and I had studied photography. I had all of that behind me, and so I said, "Let's put it to work against this war policy."

JB: When we first started out, there was a small number of people in VVAW, so it made sense that we go on television and talk programs and talk anyplace we could find an audience. Our goals were to educate the public to the reality of what was going on in Vietnam so a better decision could be made. We were calling for—I think the tag line of the thing was—"Save our buddies now; withdraw them now." No one else should die in a war that the American public didn't vote for. This wasn't really clear to people. There had been no vote on this war.

In that first several months, well into the beginning of 1968, our whole goal was to utilize those people we could get motivated, to do their research and speak. The average GI doesn't know all these facts. You can't simply say, "I was out there, but I don't know anything about the Geneva Convention; I don't really know about Ho Chi Minh; I don't really know about how we got into Vietnam." We insisted . . . that you get educated.

If the people knew the reality of Vietnam, what would they do?

JB: They would be talking to other people, and ultimately there would be a change in policy. None of us had a degree in political science. We had the same general sense as most people. You change the public attitude in this country, things change. It wasn't any grander than that.

To give you a sense of strategy . . . When we first started, we wore suits and ties. [It was] a conscious decision that we're going to show people that we're serious. At that time in American society, if you were a serious person, you wore a suit and tie to do serious business.

We had a big debate about whether or not to wear our uniform, because it was against the law to wear a uniform after you were no longer on active duty. I think the first demonstration that we all decided that yes indeed, if you wanted to do it, you could do it, was in April of 1968 in New York. Some people showed up in dress uniforms. We're not talking about the grungy jungle shit. Full-dress uniforms. There's a couple of pictures around with guys standing with VVAW banners and flags in full-dress uniforms. You can imagine the effect this had upon cops and lots of other people. Holy shit! These people are for real—a whole bunch of medals.

We researched the Geneva accords. We went out and debated people from the State Department and said, "You made an agreement with everybody that in 1956 there would be these elections. What happened to these elections?"

The amazing thing was, in 1967, the White House was so conscious of this, they would send someone out from the State Department to debate people in teaching kinds of situations. On one occasion, it was a Democratic Party gathering in Long Island. I can remember Paul O'Dwyer, who later became the City Council president, was at this meeting on the dais. A congressman representing LBJ shows up drunk. When I had finished speaking, he ran off—literally jabbering, howling, and screaming—off the stage. He didn't know what the hell he was talking about. He hadn't been to Vietnam. He had none of the facts.

On another occasion I was asked to speak at the New York State Maritime Academy in a teach-in to the cadets. The other speaker was a major in the Marine Corps from the Pentagon. Same thing happened. He hadn't been in Vietnam. He didn't have his facts straight. I stood there correcting him about what the Marines did on which dates in Vietnam.

We would go anywhere that we can get an invitation. I did radio and television programs in New York, Philadelphia, [and] upstate New York. I did speaking engagements as far north as Boston and later on in Wisconsin. As far as most of us were concerned, every audience at whatever age was an important audience.

We went on radio programs, which were just like today: most of them were right-wing radio programs. We'd show up and start debating these people. They would bait us. As an example, someone would say, "We're going to get you. We've got files on you people," which scared a couple of people. I didn't see anything in my life that I was worried about. There were some people who were closet gays who did get a little worried. So the people who did have something to be concerned about got a little shaky when somebody said, "We've got files on you."

On another occasion, it was a television program, David Frost. At the commercial break, the guy next to me turns and says, "Why don't you go back to Russia where you came from?" I said, "I don't come from Russia. . . . My mother's one of your greatest admirers." This was some religious nut. You never knew who you were going to be put into a debate situation with. It was great. I could care less who I was debating.

SR: In the beginning, we were a media group, doing a thing on morality. Carl, David, and Jan did the David Susskind show. Susskind was very, very good at this. We did it twice, in fact. I was selling oranges all of a sudden. It was a product. I went and listened and said, "Great, great, but who's going to believe it? Who even believes that these guys are veterans that have been in the war at all?" You can talk your head off and nobody would listen.

We went to Long Island, to Hofstra University, for example. We had rocks thrown at us, chased out of town, police escorts. We were communists and all this shit. I'm outraged. They'd never even heard that these guys were in Vietnam, or even that I served, for Christ's sake. It devalued us, and I really felt like we really didn't have a message for anybody here.

The earliest members of the organization, like Sheldon Ramsdell, felt frustrated by the disregard and disrespect they seemed to be getting. They had tried to engage the public through established channels but found their way blocked by many Americans' inability to hear what they were saying. The cold war consensus was so strong in some quarters that, rather than listening to those who had served, various segments of the public attacked VVAW mem-

bers as communists or malcontents. Nonetheless, VVAW persevered. In 1967, VVAW slowly grew, attracting the attention of other veterans, and civilians as well. As VVAW began to coalesce as an organization, more women began to provide support for the veterans as office workers, counselors, and support personnel.

How did you get hooked up with VVAW? ·

AH: Well, mostly through MCHR [Medical Committee on Human Rights], the old MCHR cadres and contingents. I started working with VVAW as an entity in the middle of 1968.

They started being in marches and they got asked to do security. It was like, there's beef. [Laughs.] VVAW was instant security. It's still going on. If you have a demonstration, they will ask the vets to do security.

One of the first guys I actually worked one-on-one with was Jim Duffy, one of the New York vets. He went off one night. We were in the Lion's Head bar in the Village. This was my baptism by fire on what you do with a vet who is not sure who, where, or what he is. I was pretty good with people who slipped their cogs—I'm a nurse—but I had never been with people who slipped their cogs and wanted to kill people.

He flashed back to Danang around drink three. He's an Agent Orange victim and he doesn't tolerate alcohol very well. He thought he was in Danang. You can't find the Bronx at all well when you think you're in Danang. And for someone who thinks he's in Danang, tunnels are not a good idea. You don't want to send them in the subway. I lived within walking distance, so Norma [Becker] said, "Ann, take him home." So I did. I spent the rest of the night with a 6-foot crazy person and didn't die of it.

I then started working in the office. It was all men. If they noticed you were female, they treated you very well. After about three days, they stopped noticing that I was female. These guys, even then, were trying to clean up their act on their complete, total, and unbelievable sexism. I got accepted and by being accepted, I started being of use to people in medical ways and just as someone to talk to who wasn't a vet.

What was your impression of these men?

AH: Here was a group of incredibly sexist guys who were incredibly needy and incredibly vulnerable. I was very protective. I wanted to be their mother. They really needed help. After a couple of weeks, I realized that wasn't going to work, and I started listening and talking and hearing what they had to say. Pete Mahoney and Bill Ehrhardt were able to get through to me. This was also a really intense place. It was truly amazing. They also had a tremendous amount of pure physical courage, which I admire.

A Brief Hiatus—And a Resurgence

SHELDON RAMSDELL AND JAN BARRY

During the presidential election of 1968, various members of VVAW worked on the campaigns of Robert Kennedy and Eugene McCarthy. As a result, VVAW effectively disbanded during the spring and summer of that year, since many veterans felt that their time and energy could be best used by helping to elect an antiwar candidate. After Kennedy's assassination, antiwar veterans overwhelmingly supported McCarthy for the Democratic nomination.

Sheldon Ramsdell (SR): Carl would drag me off to Washington, and we would meet with Senator Fulbright, Ernest Gruening, Edith Green, all of the antiwar senator types. Then McCarthy popped up, and Carl called me and said, "I got a ticket for you for Manchester [New Hampshire]. Fly up with a group of veterans to work with Gene McCarthy." I said, "Terrific."

[I] flew up there to Concord, and before you know it I was a press agent for the senator and I had to be with him. I worked all the primaries, traveled with him, flew everywhere with him. Wonderful. We wound up in Chicago at the convention, and it was an atrocity. Daley [the mayor of Chicago] was running the show. Everybody was beaten up. We were teargassed. The rooms were raided. We were totally disenfranchised. After McCarthy, I was burned out and didn't want to be involved in any politics.

Jan Barry (JB): Coming out of the Democratic convention in Chicago, Carl Rogers and I called a meeting of VVAW in New York, and nobody came. That's how low the morale was after the Democratic convention in Chicago. People went out there, saw what happened, and said, "The hell with it. If this is the way things are going in this country, I'm not going to participate." A lot of people dropped out. I dropped out a few times. It [the organization] disappeared altogether for a while. One group stayed active in California because they were completely isolated from all of the rest of us and continued organizing. Carl Rogers decided that he was going to go in the direction of forming LINK, which was a servicemen's link to peace, to connect the GI movement with the peace movement.

Veterans involved in Eugene McCarthy's campaign were shocked by the violence directed against antiwar protesters at the Democratic convention in Chicago—violence committed by the Chicago police under the direction of Mayor Daley. They were also shocked by the machinations of the Democratic Party bosses, who effectively shut out the party's antiwar factions. In fact, the debacle of Chicago alienated many antiwar veterans from the democratic process—and, of course, many civilians as well.

On the west coast, the Los Angeles chapter, which had been coordinated by James Boggio, became frustrated with the genteel tactics of the group in New York. Boggio, along with other members of the Los Angeles contingent, called for a much more radical approach, directed against those in power who continued to prosecute the war. In a letter to the national office in New York, he wrote, "I am hoping that this letter will entice you to join with me in revolution. Having served (or wasted) the past year as coordinator for Viet-Nam Veterans Against the War—and after having participated in the Chicago Uprisings—it occurred to many of us Yippiescommiesfaggotspeaceniks that the times they are a-changin'. . . . When I bellow for revolution I'm merely suggesting that our dear ol' Viet-Nam Vets group reinvigorate, degenerate, scramble, and mutilate its archaic format of the past (i.e., holding stuffy little meetings in stuffy little rooms) . . . and that we begin RIGHT NOW *to do our thing where it's at!"[19] Boggio's letter reflects the growing anger and disillusionment of many citizen-soldiers who felt they were still without a voice. Their actual activities remain unclear, because from then on there was little communiction between them and VVAW in New York, but their sentiments reflect the feelings of many of those who returned from Vietnam after 1968.*

Nevertheless, the organization experienced a resurgence in the fall of 1969, after almost a year of inactivity, when the My Lai massacre was revealed. My Lai gave antiwar veterans greater legitimacy and a new incentive to speak out.

JB: Around September or October of 1969, the first My Lai story came out. The first moratorium was in October. It was like breaking a dam. I got this phone call from somebody from the Vietnam Moratorium who said, "We have all these veterans here and don't know what to do with them. Didn't you used to have an organization?" So I went back into reconstituting this organization.

SR: The real beginning was in 1969 in New York. Adam Allinsky, David Hawk, and Sam Brown, who was instrumental in setting up VMC [Vietnam Moratorium Committee] at that time, said, "Shelly, we're going to give you a phone and a desk, and you get the list of the veterans." They funded us. Jan [Barry] Crumb had the list. It all was there. We sat down, got on the phone, we did mailings. We ran that ad in the *New York Times* with the signatures and the ranks.[20]

The Vietnam Moratorium Committee held rallies throughout the nation in October of 1969, when hundreds of thousands of Americans gathered in different sites to protest peacefully against the war. After the moratorium, the White House—Nixon was then president—attacked the demonstrators, labeling them as anti-American and calling their activities detrimental to the peace process. In reaction, liberal antiwar leaders, such as David Hawk and Sam

Brown, urged veterans to participate in massive demonstrations in Washington, D.C., planned for mid-November in conjunction with the National Mobilization to End the War in Vietnam (MOBE), which was led by more militant members of the movement.[21]

Now that Democratic Party was out of office, its antiwar wing could more openly criticize American policies in Vietnam. Liberal antiwar Democrats saw VVAW as an organization that could be used to discredit Nixon's policies and propel the Democrats back into the White House in the next election. Since 1968, a significant segment of the corporate community had also begun to turn against the war; and as inflation began to spiral upward during the summer of 1969, businesspeople increasingly saw the war as a drain on the economy and on their own firms. Business leaders were also worried about an impending tax increase and—like most Americans—about rioting and the general unrest caused by disillusionment with the war.[22] With the help of these Democrats and business leaders, VVAW went back into action.

New Blood

JOE URGO

I'm going to the moratorium. I'm going to all these groups and saying, "Is there a vets' group here?" I knew that I had to find a way to express myself as a vet. They told me about a group named VVAW, but I couldn't find anybody from it. Then somebody told me about Vets for Peace. So I go to the local Vets for Peace chapter and I meet the local head of it. Essentially, I work for him for a while; but he was a Korean War vet, and he was so mainstream in his approach. Besides, he wasn't coming through this Vietnam experience.

Then I started actually sitting at that VVAW desk, [at] 156 Fifth Avenue, waiting for someone to come in. Jan Barry comes in, Kevin Kelly came in, Scott Moore started coming every day, then this guy Al Hubbard started coming in every day. I met Madelyn Moore. I started coming every day. That was the beginning of the change in VVAW, the resurgence.

Next thing you know, some plans are being made. Jan, maybe, is talked to. It wasn't a coup d'état. It was just a shifting out of some people and a shifting in of some people. At this point, and for actually most of the time in VVAW, I was not one of the people that was in the apartments at night, sitting down with people, making the plans. I was the guy who came in the office every day at nine o'clock, stayed there until nine o'clock at night, took all the mail, set up the mailing lists. I coded everything; I organized everything. Hubbard, Moore, and [Mike] Oliver, and some other people, would go up to Scott Moore's mother's apartment and do all this strategizing.

Madelyn Moore was the woman that came in and kept us all in line. She had all these skills. She was a secretary to a general or something, and she had all this experience in the service herself. She was against the war—with her husband, who was one of the vice presidents of American Can.

There was no plan at this moment because we were doing something that was never done before. I learned later on that there was this history of resistance that we could connect to, but none of that was handed to us. We had to do it all ourselves and learn this all anew. It led to an in-house breeding of values and reaching out to people. When we reached out to people, if they were honest with us, we would work with them. We learned how to talk about the war through all these debates and train new guys coming in. Once our word started getting out, through the different things we'd talk about, then you'd see 15 to 20 vets come through every day.

When vets came in, I'd say, "Look, can you do this?" I put people to work. These guys come in [with] all their anger; you have to talk to them, you have to bond with them, you also have to give them a vision about what we're about. This is what we're doing.

What was your vision or overall goal? Where did you want the organization to go?

Essentially what it was, for three years, was a very quiet, intellectual protest group. It went to the 1968 convention. They went to demonstrations and held banners up, petitioned people, and they went on the David Susskind show and they debated things. It was very much historical and analytical in its approach. It wasn't up in their face. I wasn't an up in their face kind of kid, but that's what I wanted.

We had an experience that no one else had and that no one knows about. We have to tell the people the truth. I think that we understood that we had been lied to and brainwashed and used. If we'd been lied to, they'd been lied to. So in that kind of situation, the compelling thing is to find a way to tell the truth. We had this experience that was rich with truth and was powerful.

It was a very powerful thing to go to an Ethical Culture meeting [Society for Ethical Culture, in New York] or to go to a group of antiwar people, or whatever, and be able to say, "Let me tell you about what's going on in Vietnam, what we did to the people." The people didn't know this. It would be very moving—the degree to which people were open to hearing us and were glad that we came. The more that we put things in the sharpest and clearest terms, the more strength that we gave to people and got from people.

We gave a jolt to the antiwar movement, and we were welcomed with open arms by the great majority of people. They were very afraid of us in some places at first because the only vets they knew were the American Legion and the VFW [Veterans of Foreign Wars]—the reactionary old World War II and

Korean vets, who were proud of what they did. Once it was clear that we were different kind of vets, then people welcomed us.

I have one really sharp example that I have never forgotten. In 1970, after Kent State, Nixon had organized, through Peter Brennan, an attack on a demonstration in the Wall Street area. They mobilized these construction workers to march into a demonstration and beat up a couple of hundred youths that were at the demonstration. As VVAW was building the organization in the city, different vets are coming into the groups, and as they are telling their stories about what made them join, between 10 and 15 of these guys were in Wall Street working down there when the kids were getting beat up by the construction workers. They jumped in on the side of the youth. They were the youth just like us.[23]

That generational thing, that unity between us, speaks more about what the times were like than the way a lot of the revisionist history is doing today, trying to make it look like the antiwar movement attacked us and hated us and everything else. We dreamed up this little old lady that goes from airport to airport calling vets baby-killers, and she was, actually, one of our friends.

BOB HANSON

The way I found out about VVAW was that I used to watch the Dick Cavett show all the time. One night, Jane Fonda and Mark Lane were on the Dick Cavett show. They mentioned in passing VVAW. So I called the MOBE [National Mobilization to End the War in Vietnam]: "Have you ever heard of them?" "Yeah." They gave me the address, and that's how it started. I showed up at the office.

What was your first impression of this group?

Most of the guys came from working-class backgrounds. Lots were working out their guilt. There was no real perception of how the war would end, what our real contribution was; it was a lot of agonizing all the time.

Were there other black vets in VVAW besides you and Al Hubbard?

No, not really. I don't know why. It's just not their thing. Most came from working-class environments, from projects or small towns. They were antiwar, but they didn't do anything overt about it.

I remember in the cav, some units were 50 percent black. The day after the three runners did the [black] power salute at the Olympics, all over the LZ the guys were giving me the sign. I think a lot of black combat vets went into the Panthers all over the country. Lots and lots and lots. Of course, I came from a middle-class background. It was a different perspective.[24]

What was it like to be involved with all these veterans?

I was in the New York office from July of 1970 to the end of May 1971. I was just a flunky, never any authority position in all of my years with VVAW. I did mostly fund-raising—which was on a daily basis, more so on weekends—setting up a table somewhere around Washington Square Park, and sometimes we'd go to other locations, like Fifth Avenue near Rockefeller Center, just hitting people up all the time. It was fun and amazing. We did raise a lot of money.

The people I was doing the fund-raising with were the people in my life. They became the bulk of my friends because I was removed from anyone I knew from high school.

Did you raise money in other ways?

Scott Moore's family was a fairly affluent family; they provided a lot of funds. And wherever you'd go, there'd be politically committed people who would give us money. There was this famous happening in 1971 at Grace Church that Norman Mailer and other people held. We were a significant focus for dollars that came out of this thing.

What was happening [in the VVAW office] was the preparation for this Labor Day thing—the three-day thing from Morristown, New Jersey, to Valley Forge. I arrived in the middle of that as the membership is exploding.

BOBBY MULLER

Bobby Muller grew up in Great Neck, New York. He enlisted in the Platoon Leaders Corps in college, spent 10 weeks in Quantico (a Marine training facility in Virginia), and was commissioned as a lieutenant in the Marine Corps in January 1968. He went to Vietnam in September 1968 and was injured in April 1969. He lost the use of his legs as a result of this injury and gets around in a wheelchair. He was interviewed in a restaurant in Washington, D.C., where he lives.

I got active in 1970 because my hospital and my ward was the centerpiece of a cover story in *Life* magazine on May 20, 1970. I was the spokesman for the ward when all the media came around following up on the *Life* magazine story, because I said the VA hospitals suck. I stopped shaving. I had a beard and long hair. If you're going to treat me like an animal, all right, I'll look like one. [Laughs.]

There was an outrage. It triggered congressional hearings. I did a lot of media because we really triggered off a hell of a national scandal about what was going on.

Off of that, VVAW guys came into the hospital and said, "We just saw you on TV. We want you to know about the organization."

That's when my understanding really started to go through changes, because I was in the hospital for almost a year and I thought that I basically just had a bummer of an experience in Vietnam. I figured that I just had a lousy trip. It was through the process of talking with some other guys that I realized, Hey, wait a minute; it wasn't just me; the whole thing was fucked-up. Everybody had similar experiences to me, and I really started putting the pieces of the puzzle together and then became an active spokesman against the war.

I did a lot of national media for VVAW. Back in 1970, 1971, I did the Dick Cavett show a couple of times. I did David Susskind. But I never joined VVAW. I represented VVAW. I'm making a technical point. I just wasn't joining anything, even VVAW. That's how I think a lot of us operated. VVAW was, "Anarchists unite."

The thing that was beautiful about VVAW is that when we had a protest or we had a rally, you didn't have to tell guys, "This is what you say." You didn't have to tell them what the party line was. You just say, "Hey, what's your experience, brother?" Each guy would tell his story, and it was just understood that the war was ridiculous. We never had guys on the other side of that issue. There were a handful, but they were political hacks that had gotten recruited by the right-wing elements.

I think the public related to VVAW, obviously, in terms of its politics, as an antiwar organization. But I think for those of us who were involved in VVAW, it was much more the camaraderie, brotherhood, and a form of therapy, to just be able to work through all of what we needed to work through, sharing our experiences.

What I came to understand, years later, was really how much of the exception those of us in VVAW were. That when you talk about Vietnam veterans across the country, I realized that we were really, really, really the exception. The majority of Vietnam veterans by 1979 had never talked about their Vietnam experience. This was documented in surveys that the VA contracted with Lou Harris to conduct. It was also confirmed through surveys that Egindorf and Company conducted for the VA. In other words, they came back, got out of their uniforms, came back to their society, people may say, "Hey, were you gone?" "I don't want to talk about it. Let's get on with it." That was the majority.

What made you different? What was the element or elements that made you different?

We were east coast. We were big city. It's a lot different coming of age in Boston or New York than it is out in the godforsaken rest of this country, politically. I mean, you go back to Rah-rahville, the idea of guys coming together and going against their local American Legion, VFW . . . there just wasn't the catalyst.

Leadership counts. There does need to be people showing the way a little bit, being the ones who precipitate action, movement, and consciousness-raising. It wasn't everywhere. The majority of guys simply never talked about it.

MIKE GOLD

I was tremendously active. I was in VVAW. I was an officer of the veterans' group in Brooklyn College. We found out there were about 1,100 veterans at Brooklyn College. We became mainly interested in organizing the veterans' club at the college to make it a VVAW chapter.

We sent out a mailing, and 40 or 50 guys came to a meeting. We decided to be a veterans' organization . . . but not all the guys wanted to be in VVAW. In fact, it never became a VVAW chapter. It became about the rights of veterans.

We found out that there was the Emergency Employment Act and the university was offered by the city to have jobs, and we heard that they turned it down. We wrote a grant and we got 40 part-time jobs for veterans. . . . We found out about these grants for veterans' counseling work that the federal government was offering. We set up a counseling program, a rap group, with the guys who had been in Vietnam. . . . Then we got psychologists to work with us; . . . we hooked up with a drug counselor; . . . we were doing things with guys who were incarcerated. . . . We found veterans were out of school and needed tutoring and special academic work, so we started a program for that. We helped them get their GEDs [high school equivalency diplomas]. We sought professors that would teach the history of Vietnam, social sciences, literature, English; and we did that.

We were sensitizing the administration about what we were all about. They were used to working with young kids leaving home and going to college. We found ourselves different. Our friends were the Puerto Rican Student Alliance and the Black Student Union.

JAN BARRY

We were constantly trying to recruit people and get chapters formed through the Vets for Peace groups. There were groups who had other names, GIs and reservists against the war in Vietnam, or unaffiliated vets who didn't belong to any group. They were just active with whatever local committee there was. We would suggest to them that it would also make sense to identify themselves as veterans.

As VVAW was expanding its membership base across the northeast, into Ohio, Michigan, and several other midwestern states, President Nixon, in a nationally televised speech on April 30, 1970, announced the invasion of Cambodia by American troops. Nixon's speech and the protests that erupted in its aftermath—these were the protests in which students were killed by the National Guard at Kent State and Jackson State universities—impelled veterans across the country to join the antiwar movement,[25] although many had been protesting against the war as individuals or in small isolated groups since 1965. This infusion of new members provided the start of VVAW's expansion into a national organization.

"Vets for Peace"

The veterans who now became active in various Vets for Peace groups across the nation brought a heightened sense of urgency. They were angrier than their counterparts on the east coast—the veterans who had founded VVAW. Joe Urgo reflected the attitude of these new members when he said, "I wasn't an up in their face kind of kid, but that's what I wanted."

Those who had became active before 1968, like Jan Barry, tended to remain more skeptical about the antiwar movement. What distinguished later members from earlier members was their age, their social class, and the nature of the war they had experienced. The veterans who protested against the war after 1970—after the shootings at Kent State—were younger and tended to be from working-class backgrounds. Most had been grunts who served in combat; and for the most part, they had experienced warfare on a much larger, more brutal scale than their predecessors in VVAW who had served before 1967. Many had lived through the fierce fighting of the Tet campaigns, had experienced the bloodiest year of the war—1968—and had been exposed to the growing resistance in the armed forces.[26] Typically, these new veterans had come to their antiwar stance not through an intellectual understanding of American foreign policy but out of a heartfelt sense of having been used and discarded.

Not only had these new veterans served in a different war; they had also returned to a changed nation. On their return home, they encountered a much more vociferous antiwar community, some segments of which had come to embrace confrontational tactics and revolutionary ideology. Years of polite protest had failed to change the nation's course in Vietnam, and veteran and civilian antiwar protesters alike felt frustrated. Thus melding the new antiwar veteran into VVAW would prove to be a challenge for leaders of the organization.

On the west coast, from San Francisco to San Bernardino, veterans began to join antiwar demonstrations. Others, in all regions of the nation, began to form their own groups. In doing so, they also expanded the scope of veterans' antiwar activity, making links with active-duty GIs and contributing to a breakdown of morale in the military. They also worked more closely with certain elements of the antiwar community and third world organizations like the Black Panthers, which itself included many veterans.

Each of these disparate groups worked independently to bring the reality of the war to the public. The commitment to using democratic channels was evident among all veterans' organizations.

California

LEE THORN, JACK McCLOSKEY, BARRY ROMO, JEANNE FRIEDMAN, BILL BRANSON, MIKE McCAIN

Lee Thorn (LT): I got out of there [the Navy] in the fall of 1966, and two weeks later I was back on Berkeley campus. I was totally antiwar. There were 27,000 students on the campus, but there weren't that many vets. We started recognizing each other, so we started to get together by the early part of 1967. We didn't know what other vets' groups were doing, but we knew we

Lee Thorn in the spring of 1967, age twenty-three: "About two months after organizing Vets for Peace at UC Berkeley, six months after returning from Vietnam."

were all antiwar. We also knew we couldn't relate to the antiwar movement in general.

What made you feel that way?

LT: For one thing, when they made speeches, they talked about baby-killers. Secondly, these guys always talk about the working class, but they would not go off this campus. Vets used to laugh. They felt like this was bullshit. I was really exceptional to the vets' movement, coming from a middle-class background; most everybody else was [from] a working-class background. And third, for me—and this was true for quite a few of us—they [students] were a little bit romantic about violence.

We'd all been out for just a matter of months. We had a fairly good view of what was going on in the war, a lot better than we had when we were in it. I was beginning to sense that the violence I had been involved in had changed me almost viscerally, almost on a cellular level. These kids were talking about violence as if, you know, you just go do it. That's it. No problem. They had no sense of how it would affect you, what it does to people. They took it too lightly, like "off the pigs." It was stupid.

We knew we could kill; there was no question about that. We were nonviolent, but we weren't that way by nature. We had chosen to be nonviolent. In order to pull off nonviolence, we had to vent some, so we used to vent out all these little fantasies. We talked about blowing up fucking train tracks, but we didn't do it.

By the spring of 1967 we called ourselves Veterans for Peace. By 1969, there were seven or so Veterans for Peace activists working. There was one at City College, there was one in Daly City, one in Chico, Freemont, and Davis. They came to us. We gave them organizing materials. I met Jack [McCloskey], like a week after he got to San Francisco, at a Vets for Peace meeting in Berkeley. He said he was interested in doing something. We gave him materials.

By 1970, Vets for Peace was pretty big in Berkeley—somewhere between 50 and 100 members and maybe 30 to 35 activists. We were speaking everywhere—high schools, seminaries, churches—especially to kids. We didn't want them to go into the military. It was the same kind of feeling we had in fighting to end the war: we wanted to bring these guys home because we didn't want them to die.

Was it a moral or a political objection?

LT: It was both. It was a moral issue for me especially. It was mainly a vehicle to vent our anger. We had gotten used, and we knew it.

We also coordinated the training of 250 draft counselors. We were very well organized. It's like New York and here, maybe Massachusetts, were the best organized. We were into activism. When Cambodia hit, that was like an extreme time.

Jack McCloskey (JMC): After Kent State, there started being a lot of antiwar demonstrations at City College here in San Francisco. I started going to them, started looking at guys at demonstrations—some of them wearing fatigues, a little bit older than the students—started talking to some of them. About four of us started a group called Veterans for Peace.

There was a natural drawing together of these veterans. In Nam there was a bonding that happened. I think for a lot of Vietnam vets, when they went to Vietnam, that was their first lesson of what it means to be intimate.

I was operating from City College with another guy named Rob Bodelin, a guy named Jim O'Donnell, and a guy named Carlos Melendrez, who was a Chicano Vietnam-era veteran. I considered him my mentor. Then we met Lee Thorn.

I met Carlos, and then two days later I'm speaking before 5,000 people. It blew my mind away. I said, "I'm a Vietnam veteran. I think the war is wrong. These are the reasons why it is wrong. It's unwinnable. We shouldn't be there. It's basically a civil war." I talked about the Vietnamese constitution almost being word for word out of the American constitution. By this time I had done some reading.

LT: In 1970, we opened a GI coffeehouse in Oakland called the Pentagon. The Oakland Army base was right there, and that was the debarkation point for people.

What was the reason for opening up a coffeehouse? What did you hope to accomplish?

JMC: This was a place where GIs could come in and we would talk to them about things like KP, guard duty, foxholes, shit like that. Our goals were to basically to educate young men going to Vietnam. Our role was to humanize. People were trained that the enemy you're fighting is lesser than you. One of our jobs in coffeehouse was saying to them, "Hey, these are mothers, these are fathers, these are sons, these are daughters; this is who you're going to be shooting at. They're no different than you."

We never talked about how we would approach these people. It just came natural. We didn't have meetings and say, Hey, we're going to talk to these folks about KP, or whatever; that never happened. It just happened that all of us that were involved in this came from the same approach. We were operating out of feelings.

We never tried to make up their minds for them. We knew where they were coming from. We had been in their position. If they wanted things, if they wanted a lawyer, if they wanted a safe house, if they wanted to go AWOL, sure, we would help them. But we never pushed. We let them make their decisions.

We helped a lot of guys, even the guys that went to Vietnam. We taught them something. We taught them how to survive and not to unnecessarily take other people's lives. You have to remember, a lot of these guys had misgivings by this time; this was in 1970. The antiwar movement was becoming bigger and bigger and bigger, and these are eighteen- and nineteen-year-old kids. Some of them draftees, some of them joined. There was a difference when I went into the service and when these guys went into the service. They knew about Vietnam. I mean who the fuck wants to be the last person to be killed in Vietnam? For what?

We weren't open during the day, except on weekends, but every night, from four o'clock to about twelve midnight, we would have veterans there. It was all veterans doing this. We would have some entertainment for them. We would have folk music, shit like that. We would have cake and cookies. It was like an antiwar USO. That's the flavor I remember. A lot of them were curious, and I'm sure a lot of them were the Man. I'm sure a lot of them were also very lonely.

Did you worry about the Man—law enforcement agencies—coming in?

JMC: No, no. We were always up front of where we were coming from. From the beginning, even before we became VVAW, our line was: We are nonviolent. I don't mean our line in the sense that this was something we talked about. This is individually where we came from. We had seen enough violence. We knew what violence did. I don't consider myself a pacifist. I mean if somebody fucks with me or my children, I'm going to defend myself. I just don't believe in violence. I don't believe that war's a solution for anything. That's where Lee, myself, all of us came from.

The coffeehouse worked until we started getting Berkeley radicals talking to people about imperialism, capitalism, [and] all that bullshit. These were people who were upper-middle-class, spouting Maoists, Leninists, Stalinists, or whatever their line was. I knew what they meant—I had done a lot of reading—but I also knew that you don't approach people like that. It was patronizing, condescending. It just wasn't working.

Here's this fucking white kid coming in that's been spoon-fed all his life, and he's going to tell this kid how to run his life. I think a lot of the Berkeley radicals and the left chased these guys away. You can't ram shit down people's throats. We got so fed up with the Berkeley radicals that we were spending more and more of our time fighting them than doing the work. We felt it was becoming detrimental.

The Pentagon closed down in 1972.

LT: The other thing we did was work with guys on the *Coral Sea,* [a carrier] based in Alameda. There was a bunch of guys on there that had been supported by Up Against the Bulkhead Guys and Vets for Peace people, who were organizing against the war. When the *Coral Sea* went out, the vets were the ones who created the Peace Navy deal, where we had guys who had access to small boats who'd go out there and get turned over by the wake of the ships trying to stop them. [Laughs.] When they couldn't organize to get the ship from leaving, they tried to organize everybody jumping off the ship. I was involved with setting up sanctuary in churches in Berkeley.

Then my wife and I went to Hawaii, because a bunch of guys were jumping in Hawaii. There's a GI coffeehouse in Honolulu which we worked out of. I helped set up the safe houses for guys that jumped in Hawaii.

I met a guy in Hawaii. We were talking about dud bombs, and this guy says, "Well, I tell you how you dud bombs: you just put Kool-Aid in the trigger mechanism. It corrodes the wires and it won't go off." There's all this Kool-Aid in the military. The word got around; it was on every carrier within three months. Everybody knew how to dud bombs.

By 1971 they were putting stickers, "Repaired by SOS," on A-4s and A-6S—you know, on the sides of bombers—and then the pilots wouldn't fly. It was great.[27]

JMC: We worked a lot with the Farm Workers. We worked a lot with the Black Panthers, although we never got into their trips with weapons. A lot of them happened to be Vietnam vets. We marched with them in some big demonstrations. We helped with breakfasts. I think for a lot of the third world veterans, Vietnam was just another foot of the oppressor on them. So there was a different perspective. They were able to accept us more than they accepted most white groups, because of our backgrounds. We were not people coming in and telling them about their lives. There were more similarities, I think, between the lives of the Vietnam vets against the war and the lives of the people that joined the Black Panthers than there was between people who joined VVAW and the peace movement.

We did guerrilla theater. We used a lot of the things that we were taught in Vietnam. We learned very quickly: visibility. We had credibility. So they couldn't fuck with us in that sense. You also have to realize how painful it was for me to get up and say this war was wrong.

In what sense was it painful?

JMC: Because of our buddies' deaths. If you're saying this is wrong, then my buddy died for nothing. But again, we made promises to dead people. The only way we could justify the deaths of our buddies over there was by saying, "We've got to stop it." We've got to stop it. Stop the killing. Stop the killing.

[Tearfully.] Here in San Francisco, that was the chant I remember hearing the most, "Stop the killing, stop the killing, stop the killing."

Barry Romo (BR): The first thing we did [in San Bernardino] was, we joined the local antiwar group.

We gravitated instantly toward speaking out. When churches and schools found out that there were combat vets who were against the war, [there was a] gigantic demand, talking at churches and youth groups, telling the kids the war's wrong and telling them not to go.

We gravitated right toward the GI Project and working with GIs at coffee-houses, drop-in centers; working with the GIs at Norton Air Force Base and Edwards Air Force Base; helping to publish newspapers; distributing the papers; having barbecues with the GIs; providing the network that they couldn't have because they were in the service, to do the organizing that they wanted to do. These were tied in with the MDM [Movement for a Democratic Military] projects, which were down in San Diego.[28]

We would sneak on base. In fact, one time we got the old Black Panther movie, *Bang, Bang, Piggy, Pig You're Dead.* We brought it on base and had a guerrilla movie. We had bunches of people all over the base driving around, and the APs were chasing them, and we had another group of guys who were showing that Black Panther movie on the side of barracks. [Laughs.] They'd show it to guys who'd come out; then they'd take off, show it at the side of another barracks, until they got caught.

How did the active servicemen react to this?

BR: We were fucking GIs [animatedly], mostly enlisted men, and mostly combat too.

They all wanted to be like us. "I want to be alive, out of the service, with long hair. I don't want to have my hair cut, some stupid-ass fucking cracker telling me what to do, and be separated from rock and roll." Fuck, everyone wanted to be like us.

These were Air Force guys. What are they going to say? [Laughs.] They're fucking Boy Scouts compared to us. If someone hassled us, we'd say, "What have you done? I know the medals you haven't got there. What is the highest thing you got? A good conduct medal. You don't have anything for bravery."[29]

It really was fun. It was very anarchical. We were young, going to college; I was getting a 3.7, 3.8, and working—steam-cleaning Edison company trucks. You didn't have to sleep much then. It was still the adrenaline from Vietnam. You could fucking go for 20-some hours.

I became very radical very quick, because of political pressures and stuff. I got involved very quickly in Black Panther support work, in police repression work in the black and Hispanic community. I was in La Raza Unida. The question of racism was top in our minds.

There was a sense of: We were accomplishing something. There was a sense that we were part of something. There was a sense that, in fact, we were going to bring people back alive. We could make a difference.

Jeanne Friedman (JF): I left Stanford in June of 1969 and signed a contract to teach at the University of Redlands, an extremely conservative Baptist university in the heart of southern California. It was like another country in another era. I got there in the fall of 1969.

I first met antiwar vets at a demonstration against Ronald Reagan at the Rose Bowl. Leland Lubinsky was a Vietnam vet living in San Bernardino. He had helped to organize a Vets for Peace group at San Bernardino City College and knew Barry Romo. Leland was very active in San Bernardino, working with all the traditional peace groups. We became great friends after our first meeting, and it was through Leland that I met all the other vets.

I was in touch with the student antiwar activists on my campus and hooked them up with the vets. Together we opened a draft counseling center in downtown Redlands. At the same time we were doing that, the first GI organizing project was beginning at Camp Pendleton, in Oceanside. It was called The Green Machine—Movement for a Democratic Military. The first two civilian staff people were from Stanford, Kent Hudson and Pat Sumi. Sometime in the fall of 1969, I went to Oceanside to visit the project. I spent one afternoon on the streets of Oceanside leafleting GIs and was completely hooked. I thought this was the most important antiwar work I could be doing.

Why?

JF: Talking to the GIs, you really felt you were at the center of where change needed to come. These were Marines who could refuse to go to Vietnam or provide a lot of information when they were there. These were people who were open. They were scared to death. They were these young guys who didn't know what was going on. All they heard was Marine propaganda. Everything we said was just a startling revelation.

We talked a lot about the racism in the military, which struck a very deep chord with the African American Marines. Everything about the Marines was racist to the core, so these guys were already very skeptical about what they were being told. A lot of Marines, both black and white, didn't want to go to Vietnam. The civilian support staff found attorneys from LA, San Diego, or wherever, who could help them.

Not only did I meet people who were going, but also people who had come back. Talking to them was just amazing. What was most startling for me, coming out of the civilian antiwar movement, was that these were people who you didn't have to do a lot of arguing with, because they knew what you were talking about. With civilians, particularly students, you had to convince them that the United States military was there for a reason in the rest of the world, and that reason was economic. You didn't have to do that with a GI—they got it. They saw all the stuff that was part and parcel of the United States' military machine.

After that one day at Oceanside, I came back and said, "We've got to start a GI project in San Bernardino." We did.

Bill Branson (BB): There was a bunch of us [in San Bernardino]. We used to get together socially. That was the place that I wanted to be, with other veterans, where we could sit around, get messed up, and talk.

We were against the war continuing for even a minute further, and we were against fucking over the Vietnamese at that time. We hated pigs by this time; we started to identify the establishment. There was talk of imperialism and stuff like that. We had a better idea of who the enemy really was. It was fucking rich people.

I didn't enjoy getting up in front of a bunch of people and being exposed. I always felt like the eye had stayed on me because I had lived with this whole McCarthy thing—anybody that was unusual was blacklisted in that whole era. You knew instinctually you had to defend yourself for being unusual, whether it was the length of your hair or whatever. So I didn't enjoy it that much, and it was a lot of stress and a tough life.

We did some wild stuff. We did a lot in conjunction with the peace movement there, everything from marching around distributing leaflets to picket signs and starting guerrilla theater.

We infiltrated people into this huge shopping mall [for example]. We were at the side entrance with our watches synchronized. All us vets came in wearing fatigues and carrying toy guns and stuff. It was incredible. We started grabbing people out of the crowds and started pushing them, shoving them, and calling them names. We drug them all down and threw them in a big group and pretended to machine-gun them. We threw fake blood all over the place. We had people come in with posters and leaflets telling people what we were really there for. The whole place was in a total uproar.

The cops put out an automatic weapons call. They're all coming from everywhere, and this one security guard is trying to keep us from leaving. All of us ran out in the parking lot except Barry. He gets arrested like always. We all stuck together. They took our licenses and consulted, and finally they just let us all go except for a couple people. Barry went to trial and he lost. It was no big deal.

What was the purpose of that?

BB: We wanted to show Americans what it was like to be Vietnamese. To have fucking armed guys doing this shit. It was jar people out of their complacency and to show a real lesson at the same time—not just to turn off the lights, pull some terrorist thing, or just fuck with people's heads. People were really shocked. We sure drew their attention to the war.

We made definite gains. When we spoke, there were always a few people that really indicated that we changed their lives. If we met reactionaries, I thought we set a pretty good example of how to deal with those assholes. We were one group of people they had trouble dealing with. For one thing, we wouldn't back down. We were tougher than they were. We had just finished killing people, and we weren't afraid to fight them. We could always deal with them verbally better, just because they hadn't been there. At that point in time the most right-wing veteran you would meet from Vietnam was confused and asking questions. They thought the people with peace signs were breaking the law. When they realized we were veterans, it was all right. Our line was: Veterans have done a lot of stuff in Vietnam, and this is what we have to do to pay back for what we did. We stuck our necks out a lot. We organized and organized and had a large group of people.

Mike McCain (MMC): I was going to Los Angeles Valley College in Van Nuys. There was this little group of people who said they were SDS. There was a couple of veterans. We got together with people in southern California, Barry Romo and others. We started a chapter in Los Angeles. In the summer of 1970, it really picked up and jumped off.

We started talking, doing these educational things; student strikes are going on; educational forums and seminars are happening everywhere. Then we started organizing vets all throughout southern California. We just started talking to each other. It evolved into an organization just from the discussion. There was no clear leadership. It was anarchy. Part of the military experience was that you learned how to function in groups.

We started doing fund-raisers, and we paid for an office, rent, bought our first Gestetner [a ditto copier], and learned how to do this for days and days and days at a time. We started learning about the power of media and ink.

But what began to happen was, we had begun to have this analysis of the role of the country. One of the most interesting things, one of the most correct things in serendipity, was the connection with Thomas Paine and the whole idea of the winter soldier and the sunshine patriot that became a fundamental tenet of the organization. We started understanding as a group of people [that] it was easier to be a soldier than it was to be a critic of the government, of the state, of the society; but that if we were to be true citizens, that's what we had to do. You can't accept things at face value. You have to be a member of society. You have to argue. You have to decide whether or not something is right or wrong, and then once you've made that decision, act upon it. That was the biggest thing we did as an organization, and that's why so many people are alive today. I could easily be one of the people that was dead from a drug overdose or something else. If it wasn't for activism, it wouldn't have happened.

How did activism do that?

MMC: By the late 1960s and 1970s, Vietnam vets were already viewed as the bad guys in many many ways because of what was seen on the media all the time. It wasn't seen as a direct result of what our government had told us to do. It was seen as these individual terrible things the people had done.[30]

In World War II, they had victory parties. They were thanked by the communities for what they had done. We were not. We were ostracized. We were kept isolated. I don't even remember if there was a band playing when we got off the plane at El Toro. I mean, there were planeloads of people coming back and forth every day. They just let us off and loaded up with fresh green to go over there.

So we had to make our own community in order to survive. The organization saved a lot of people's lives.

We were very bright, articulate people, all of us. No matter from where we came, even if we didn't have the education, we got it. We became self-educated. Some of the changes that people went through, from the first stumbling efforts at public speaking and trying to explain themselves, were remarkable.

When Ron Kovic [Kovic wrote *Born on the Fourth of July,* 1976] and I went up for that first time that either one of us had been in public, we were scared shitless. Here I come pushing him up and there's hundreds of people out there, and we start to talking and they start responding; and as the evening wore on, we got more and more comfortable. By the time it's over, people are coming up and glad-handing us, telling us how great we are. "Oh, I think there is something interesting about this." [Laughs.] We're getting invited to dinner and, "Here, you want to fuck my daughter?" I mean, it was pretty amazing.

Texas

DAVE CLINE, JOHN KNIFFIN, TERRY DuBOSE, TOM WETZLER

Dave Cline (DC): I'm still on active duty. I went down to Fort Hood, and I'm obviously on their shit list. At Fort Hood, it was about half Vietnam returnees. It was also the riot control center for the midwest. Troops from Fort Hood were sent to Chicago during the rebellion following Martin Luther King, Jr.'s assassination.

They had a GI coffeehouse at Fort Hood, a place called the Oleo Strut. The Oleo Strut is actually a shock absorber on a helicopter, so that was the idea of what the thing was supposed to be, like a shock absorber for the military. The GI movement started at Fort Hood—the Fort Hood Three, years before I got there, guys who refused to go to Vietnam.[31] That began to plant the seed. The soil was fertile because the reality was that the government was lying to us. Most people are decent people. They don't want to go kill people and engage in brutality.

I went down there and got involved in publishing an underground news-paper called the *Fatigue Press*. We were putting out literature against the war and against the military and for GI rights and against racism. The way we would distribute literature is: We'd go on hits through the base and go through the barracks late at night and put them on wall lockers, put the papers on bunks, and stuff like that. We'd do hits and do an area and get through quick. We handed them out at gates and in the town.

Then they said that we were going to go to Chicago, and they started mobilizing. [The military was developing a riot control operation for the 1968 Democratic convention in Chicago, Operation Garden Plot.] We started a campaign of organizing against the riot control. There was this big meeting right on the baseball diamond on the base. There were 100 or 150 guys from different units. It was a pretty broad spectrum of people, because in them days there were all kinds of things happening. There were black guys who wouldn't talk to white guys on principle because they were nationalists. There was freaks. Fort Hood used to be called Fort Head. There was a lot of drugs going on there. There were lots of different people and different views. We got all these different people together opposed to riot control.

There was a lot of sentiment that we just fought the Vietnamese; now they want us to fight the Americans. A lot of blacks looked at it like they were going to fight their own people. There was a number of guys who identified with the demonstrators from a counterculture point of view. It was like the madness was getting worse.

We adopted a pretty simple plan. We decided to get a sticker printed up. It was a black hand in a peace sign, and we were going to distribute the stickers to everybody who was opposed to being used in riot control. If we were put on the streets, we were going to put the stickers on our helmets as a sign of opposition to the riot control and a sign of solidarity with the protesters.

They must have had infiltrators, because they had a good idea of who was at the meeting. Everybody at the meeting was removed from the roster. They weren't sent to Chicago. We were identified as subversives. People were sub-jected to harassment and interrogations by military intelligence and CID [Criminal Investigations Division].

I was questioned by military intelligence on a number of occasions. They would do wall locker searches. You could have anything you wanted in your locker. I had all sorts of shit . . . *LA Free Press,* underground papers, a book on

Buddhism, radical books, stuff like that. We had posters like this. [Points to a poster on his dining-room wall.] This was made to the dimensions of a Fort Hood wall locker. If they found more than one piece of literature in your wall locker, they could charge you with distribution of literature.

My commanding officer had been this guy who had been a sergeant in Germany. He had been picked [as] the best soldier in Germany. They used him as the guy who posed for pictures for the manual on how to do the manual of arms and then they sent him to OCS. He became a captain. He went to Vietnam and became the commander of an ARVN unit in Vietnam. Then he came back and was in charge of my unit. So this guy was so gung-ho that his asshole was OD [olive drab] green, you know? I got more medals than him. I got Bronze Star, Purple Hearts, and he didn't have half that shit.

So one day they came into the barracks. I was in there and they called us to attention. He came over to do a wall locker search. They had issued these guys Winchester 12-gauge pump shotguns with a 20-inch barrel. They're a special weapon. The bayonet that comes with them is not a blade bayonet; it's a spike bayonet. This guy had it on the gun, and him and the sergeant came in and searched my wall locker. The guy's got his fucking gun with his bayonet in my face.

I'm standing at attention and he's telling me shit like he hopes he sees me when he gets out of the service. I was responding, but in a way that I couldn't get in trouble. I said, "I hope I see you too, sir." He started talking about the

June 1969: GIs expressing their political opinions while drilling at Fort Dix; the V sign was flashed for the photographer Barbara Rothkrug of Liberation News Service.

Vietcong. I said, "I fought the Vietcong, sir. I was wounded on several occasions." I wasn't going to give him an inch on the thing, but he was trying to fuck me up. He's waving the bayonet in my face. I knew he wasn't going to stab me, because there were witnesses. He eventually turned and stormed out because they couldn't find more than one copy of any of the literature. We were careful about that. We were organizers, man.

On May 16, 1970, Armed Forces Day, that was the first big effort we did where we held demonstrations throughout the country. We called it Armed Farces Day. We had about 1,000 guys march at Fort Hood. We had coordinated demonstrations against the war, calling for justice for the students who were killed at Kent State, Jackson State, and in Augusta, Georgia, and calling for freedom for Bobby Seale and all political prisoners. That's something. It's a movement.

The day of the march [in May 1970], all the stores in Killeen closed up and boarded up their windows because they thought there was going to be a riot. The whole fucking town shut down. I'd never seen a whole military town shut down. It was unbelievable. There was no riot.

The continuation of it was VVAW. When you got out of the service, there was something to go into. Veterans became a major force in the antiwar movement.

Terry DuBose (TDB): I came back [to Austin, after having traveled around the west coast] and met people in Direct Action, and every Sunday afternoon we'd get together and have potluck lunches. These were people who believed in protesting and breaking the law—civil disobedience. We were in a meeting and a guy from Madison, Wisconsin, who was in the Air Force here had become disillusioned and wanted out. He didn't realize that there were two people here at Bergstrom [Air Force base] who had started underground papers. Within three months after the first issue had hit the streets, they got out; they were discharged. So he was the third one to bring up this reincarnation of it. He came to a Direct Action meeting asking if anyone would help him distribute the newspaper at the gate because there were just a small group of people with him. They needed to cover all the gates at five o'clock when people left. I said, "What you need is the veterans' antiwar group." The student body president said, "Well, unfortunately, on this campus there is no organized veterans against the war."

I said, "I served in Vietnam." So he and I got together and talked to this guy who was student body president. He told us what to do to get recognized on campus. We had to get a faculty sponsor. We got Dr. Donner, the head of the RTF program here. He introduced me to his secretary and said, "Anything he needs for antiwar protest, you give it to him." So she typed up this announcement for a meeting. The only place I knew of to describe was this big oak tree east of the tennis courts, so we set up under this big oak tree in this park right across the street from the campus. I had always silk-screened, so I silk-screened these sandwich boards for "Vets for Peace." That

Terry DuBose with his sandwich board.

was the name we chose because it expressed the sentiment of what we were trying to do.

I got the flyers, put on this sandwich board, and just got out on the mall and started passing them out to people.

John Kniffin (JK): I saw Terry one day and came to the meeting held under the oak tree.

TDB: We had a meeting there and then started having meetings on campus. Alvin Glick came and said, "If you guys would shave and clean up, maybe someone would listen to you." [Laughter.]

We had a meeting about whether it made a difference or not if we had long hair. I mean it was hard for a white boy from west Texas to be identified with an antigovernment thing. It was the only outward manifestation you could take that made a political statement to say to hell with the establishment.

JK: I was working for the phone company, and I was listening to all this shit from the rednecks in the phone company about goddamn hippie communist queer bastards who don't work, don't take baths, believe in free love, and shit like that. So I tried a little experiment. I let my hair get longer and longer. All of a sudden I discovered I was a communist hippie queer bastard that didn't believe in his country, didn't bathe, and didn't work. It was interesting the way attitudes changed.

In the earlier demonstrations we had, we put the first few sentences of the Declaration of Independence on our flyer and started asking people if they agreed with the sentiments. We found out most of them didn't. They thought it was communist literature.

Tom Wetzler (TW): I got involved with VVAW when I was still a GI at Fort Sam [Houston]. I was working on the *Military Left,* the paper, when we got information on the RAW [Rapid American Withdrawal] march from one of the press services we subscribed to. Sometime later, I was given Terry's number by the national office. I called him, and he invited me to a meeting being held up in UT [University of Texas].

We have lots of military bases in Texas. You got Fort Hood north of here, bases in San Antonio . . .

JK: . . . Lackland, Kelly, Randolph, Fort Sam Houston, Fort Hood, Fort Bliss—Texas is just one big military base. It was natural that that would be the focus of a lot of our energy. We seriously wanted to end the war, and the best way to do it is talk to people who are fixing to go over and fight it. In general, I think we had a receptive audience. The enlisted men supported us; they thought it was great.

TDB: We were going to Bergstrom and other bases. We wanted to support antiwar GIs. [We did] silk-screening, helped them get out the press.

The Oleo Strut was real strong in Killeen, and Dave Ziegert with the Serviceman's Union and Terry Ford and John Harris were really up against it. You talk about someone who paid their dues. Every day when they got up, they had a cloud over their heads because they couldn't do a thing. While we were smoking pot down at the beer garden, at Shultze's, they weren't even allowed into their house, because they couldn't take a chance. It was oppressive.

DC: We had a lot of rules, like you couldn't smoke pot, because we were always under constant surveillance and they were always trying to bust us. Besides that, we had opposition from two groups.

There was an active Klan group that we had an active fight with. One time they opened up on us. We were driving down to a rally in Houston and there was a Klan group out of Houston that was active against an underground newspaper called the *Space City News.* We were driving in a convoy of six or seven cars filled with GIs, and all of a sudden this guy comes zooming by and starts shooting at the front tire of the front car. He hit the oil filter, so we broke down in the middle of nowhere. We sent one guy back to get all our guns. We were armed back then. We had a lot of guns.

Two weeks later we caught the guy that did it up in Waco and fucked him up bad, right in the street. We beat the shit out of them.

The local Legion was opposed to us. We called them the goat ropers. They broke the front windows. One time they held a demonstration where they drove up a gasoline truck: "Free gasoline for any protester who wants to make the supreme sacrifice."

TDB: We would go up there to a coffee house and have the GIs down here. They would come and sleep on our couches and stuff because the ones in the military didn't have any support up there.

JK: As Terry says, we're dope-smoking hippies. To the people at the Strut house, we weren't serious revolutionaries, because if we were serious revolutionaries, we would forgo drugs. There was kind of a schism.

We felt that they were working against their stated purpose because their officers were already telling the GIs that the Oleo Strut was a hotbed of communist activity. As soon as a GI walks in there, someone tries to give them a Mao button or a copy of the Little Red Book—you know, they're just going to reinforce that. And some of us are saying maybe you need to reach GIs where they are, instead of assuming everyone's thinking the way you are just because they're disenchanted with the military. That was always a source of friction.

I still have a problem with communists. I didn't view myself as a communist. I was an anarchist, and maybe a little distrustful sometimes. These people were Maoists and Marxists.

Did you want the GIs to resist actively?

TW: We felt it was up to individual GIs to make their move. It was our job to support them.

JK: And if they did get busted, that it wouldn't be in a vacuum. There'd be people out there who knew what was going on, what the true story was, and attempt to get that information out.

TW: We provided information on military laws; we provided information about CO status, medical information, legal information, and any other counseling that was available to give GIs the ability to broaden their options and answer whatever questions.

TDB: That's where I first came up with the discussion with them that if you're going to worry about the politics of the Vietnam war, you've got to do it before you deploy—because once you get over there, there's no politics. It's shoot or be shot.

What we were also doing was just trying to get the media's attention. Protest was a media thing. It served a real purpose if you had the eye of the media. That was the only way we could communicate with anybody. We couldn't buy attention. So we had to generate these situations to grab their attention.

JK: In a way, it was easy, because antiwar veterans were a kind of unique phenomenon. If we had a bunch of them, then the media would pay attention. The only problem was keeping someone like me from putting my foot in my mouth.

What did you think protesting would do?

JK: Nixon kept on talking about the silent majority, right? I think a lot of us felt that the silent majority were an unenlightened majority, that if they knew what was going on, and they knew it was wrong, then the people of the United States would stop it. That's supposedly the way a democracy works. If your government is doing something that's against the will of the people, the people say stop it, and the government stops it. A naive position, admittedly, but we believed it.

TW: We had faith in that idea.

You hadn't lost faith as a result of your service in Vietnam?

TW: We had lost faith in some things, but we didn't have anything left to have faith in except that other people around us would be willing to stop the war if we gave them the information they needed. There was nothing else left to have faith in.

You hear about people talking about alienation when returning from the war. I think a lot of us felt that there wasn't a society worth relating to—people whose whole life seemed to be based around collecting money and stuff. There was still this basic desire and need to have faith in our fellow citizens and people in our community.

JK: We wanted the war stopped in any way possible. We didn't want any more people killed. We weren't buying into Black Panther rhetoric, you know: If you're not part of the solution, you're part of the problem. At the same time, we weren't buying into the Trot [Trotskyite] rhetoric, that if you violate the law, you're an agent provocateur. We were more like Thoreau. Sometimes you have to violate the law for conscience.

Operation RAW

JOE URGO, JOEL GREENBERG, BOB HANSON, SHELDON RAMSDELL

As veterans across the country became more actively opposed to the war in the summer of 1970, VVAW in New York continued to look for ways to expand its access to the press and the growing community of antiwar veterans. As new members on the east coast and elsewhere joined VVAW, the organization expanded its activities, becoming more "up in your face," as Joe Urgo had put it. New methods of protest had to be developed if the organization was to attract attention and shake the public out of its seeming complacency. After President Nixon announced the invasion of Cambodia, he tried to gain the upper hand over his antiwar opponents by labeling them as "bums"—and by promising a quick withdrawal of American troops from Cambodia.[32] Some of the American public was placated for a short while and was willing to give Nixon the benefit of the doubt; the antiwar veterans, however, were not.

In an effort to "bring the war home" to the American public, VVAW—like other veterans' groups across the country—borrowed from civilian antiwar organizations the idea of guerrilla theater. Operation Rapid American With-drawal (RAW) was a staged attack on an American village by American sol-diers who acted as they had in Vietnam. This action took place during the Labor Day weekend in September of 1970.

Joe Urgo (JU): In this period of early 1970, after Kent State, the organization was mainly putting tables out and trying to reach out that way, trying to do anything to get publicity. So all that summer of 1970, we were out there with leaflets sending out packets, meeting vets out on the streets, taking names, building the organization, and getting, I would say, a couple of hundred names through this process. Essentially, what was needed was something to put us out there on the map.

Operation RAW [Rapid American Withdrawal] was an attempt by VVAW to have a protest that brought home the reality of what we were about and what we did. It was something that would shape people and something that was going to build an organization.

Some of the people of the VVAW leadership thought up this simulated search-and-destroy mission through a section of New Jersey and into Penn-sylvania from Morristown to Valley Forge. We marched for three days through these towns and villages doing simulated search-and-destroy mis-sions. It was a very powerful experience. About 100 or so vets joined it.

Joel Greenberg (JG): Every day and every mile, we continued to grow. People just came flocking to it.

Bob Hanson (BH): We did things where we acted in a way an American unit would act when they came into a Vietnamese village.

Sheldon Ramsdell (SR): We were taking prisoners along the way and wearing khakis and had little plastic M-16s, which the feds inspected thoroughly in the boxes before we marched. A man actually came out of his farmhouse with a gun to head us off. We all hid in the bushes. Combat vets were lying there, going like this with these little toy guns [waving them in the air above their heads], saying, "This ain't real."

JU: Some vets forgot that they were not in Vietnam and went over the line in some of the ways they were trying to torture people.

How did you handle that kind of thing?

JU: Talking—"Oh, hold on, Bob; Bob, slow down." Struggle with the guy to let go a little on the choke chain he had or the way he was using the rubber knife. Anybody who witnessed this grasped the reality of how brutal we had been to the Vietnamese people, and we tried to make that point to people.

Guerrilla theater groups joined us many times. We handed out leaflets saying, "If you were Vietcong, we would do all these things to you."

What was the reaction to this march?

BH: People were amazed that there were Vietnam veterans against the war. Lots of people who had participated had only come back from Vietnam months before; others had been back for, say, a year or two. Those that had been back a year or two had let their hair grow out, and they looked like hippies. People were amazed to see that those that looked like hippies were actually veterans.

JU: The only opposition we got was from the American Legion, which stood on the sidelines shouting that God was our savior and that we weren't really vets.

JG: I still have nothing to do with the VFW or the American Legion, and it's not because of their national policies today, but because of where they stood back then and the treatment they treated us with. The American Legion didn't want us because we were losers and drug addicts. VFW didn't want us because Vietnam wasn't a foreign war.

Whether you agree or disagree, my attitude even within the vets' movement, among Vietnam vets, is: We share a common experience, a common bond. If we disagree, let's talk about, let's argue it out. I respect your rights; you respect mine. If we're not going to respect each other's rights, then the battle lines are drawn.

JU: We received a lot of help along the way. People met us with food and different things; and at night, farmers would let us use land that they weren't using.

BH: We would use the land that belonged to some Quaker family to sleep at night or conduct some kind of specific guerrilla theater.

JU: At night, we sat down with the campfires, and people from VVAW had come with a set of proposed objectives of the organization. There had been some objectives handed out before, but this is the first time that they were being put out to people in a mass way. They'd say, "What do you think of it? Let's vote on it."

We had to debate and reach unity, and it was a very protracted, difficult process. It was a very moving experience because I sat down with people I didn't know, debating this and that point about this objective: How do we say this, and how do we say that?

What was hammered out through several nights of political struggle over campfires were these first nine objectives, one of which was to remove the CIA and all United States military from every country in the world.

JG: It was great. The camaraderie, the shared experience. . . . One of the big things about any kind of demonstration is that it brings people together and out of their isolation. You're together with other people who share the same thinking. We do have something to present to this country, something to teach them.

JU: This group of vets was the seed of what was going to be a bigger VVAW. The seed wanted to rid itself of a whole lot of our brainwashing process. We didn't want to kill the people of the world. We don't want to be racist. We don't want to be sexist. There was a whole orientation about remolding and changing ourselves. I think that people were affected by the whole experience of the 1960s, by millions of people in this country going up against imperialism, by the black liberation movement, the national liberation struggles around the world, the Chinese cultural revolution.

There was a lot that we knew nothing about. We went back into the books and started reading all these histories—you know, reading different books about Vietnamese history and talking about the Geneva talks.

We got to Valley Forge, [where] a lot of people were waiting for us. We set ourselves up on this hill and marched down the hill in line formation, making it look like this was an assault—and this crowd was at the bottom welcoming us, cheering. There was a rally. Jane Fonda spoke, John Kerry spoke, and Donald Sutherland spoke. Fonda was becoming very well known at that point for her support of the GI movement. She and Donald Sutherland had been going around GI bases for a while with the FTA show. ["Fuck the Army," a spoof of USO shows, was performed just outside of bases.]

This was a very moving day. Donald Sutherland was tremendous, and I think Jane Fonda's contributions were good overall. She wanted to join up with us. We were the vets. We're the ones who have the right to speak. She scheduled a nationwide tour of college campuses. She asked VVAW to go along. Hubbard went with her, so that everyplace she spoke, Hubbard spoke and built a chapter in that college town. The colleges were filled with thousands of vets coming back.

Chapters were being built. The organization is beginning to grow, not just in one area but nationwide. We're beginning to make links and ties to many vets. We're looking for vets anywhere and everywhere. While all this is going on, there's a GI movement that's been building for years on the GI bases, in coffeehouses, in Vietnam, and in bases and ships all over the world. Now these guys are getting out of the service, and we're trying to make headway into that. What they did on the GI bases was tremendous, so much so that by 1971, Colonel [Robert] Heinl would write his famous article saying the military was in a state of collapse.

The Winter Soldier Hearings

JAN BARRY, JOE URGO, BARRY ROMO

After the killings at Kent State, and after the invasion of Cambodia became public, Veterans had been increasingly speaking out against the war and building antiwar organizations across the nation. Some of these, which were geographically closer to the east coast, became VVAW chapters, as in Ohio. Others remained independent until a series of VVAW actions brought the organization more national attention and members on the east coast consciously sought to build the organization nationally. The two major actions that had attracted new members and brought the previously independent groups into VVAW were the "winter soldier" hearings and Dewey Canyon III.

From 1967 to 1970, Jan Barry and various other VVAW members had corresponded with William Fulbright and other senators on the Foreign Relations Committee, pleading with them to include Vietnam veterans in the Senate hearings on the war. During those three years, the antiwar veterans received numerous responses, ranging from outright contempt to sympathetic disregard.[33]

In the fall of 1969, the My Lai massacre—which had taken place in 1968—became public knowledge. For several years, VVAW members had been revealing their own knowledge of such atrocities, and the brutality of the war in general; they had received little attention until the My Lai story broke, but then VVAW was inundated with calls from reporters who wanted to follow up on the story. At this point the VVAW office in New York—which was frustrated at having received no support from the Foreign Relations committee—decided to hold its own hearings, hoping to attract the attention of the press and force the committee to deal with veterans' allegations. In a sense, My Lai had legitimized these previous claims.

Throughout 1970, veterans held a series of local "winter soldier" investigations in 13 cities across the northeast and midwest, for the purpose of exposing war crimes committed by American forces and their allies in Vietnam.[34] These events received attention locally, but the antiwar veterans also wanted to reach the nation. They therefore organized a hearing in Detroit, Michigan, in which 150 veterans from across the country described war crimes they had participated in or seen in Vietnam. This hearing was held from January 31 to February 2, 1971. The winter soldier hearings, more than any other actions by VVAW to that point, challenged the morality and conduct of the war.

It should be noted that some of the veterans who spoke out during these hearings experienced flashbacks and other trauma as a result of their testimony. They were willing to risk this because they felt a strong need to reveal the truth.

Jan Barry (JB): Congressional hearings were going on and they were being publicized, and they had everybody except for people who carried out the policy. What we suggested was: Why don't you hear from some of the people who have carried out the policy? The general didn't carry out the policy.

Jan Barry speaking at the winter soldier hearings in Detroit, January–February, 1971.

Men who had been in Special Forces units, as an example, could testify to exactly what went on, what the policies were. We had put together a package of people who could present a wide variety of personal experience. At one point, we had three or four people who wrote a Special Forces history of internal operations willing to testify.

The senator from Alaska, [Ernest] Gruening, met with us a couple of times and said he really wanted to promote this. William Fulbright was his friend, but he still couldn't pull it off. Somebody told me that he was afraid we'd be blown away politically. We weren't worried about that. John Kerry was the first person to testify before any congressional committee from that perspective. That was in April of 1971, when we had that whole week of demonstrations in Washington. It took that long, and that demonstration, and that amount of favorable media attention for Fulbright to have the courage, or whatever else it took. They didn't blow away John Kerry, and there were plenty of other articulate people who could have appeared.

After the My Lai story broke, we were inundated with newspapers, and particularly magazines for men—I can't remember the titles, like "Macho Guy": "Tell us the most gory horror stories you can tell us." I kept on saying, "That isn't the point. The things that were done were done because they were part of a policy to do them." We weren't going to just line people up to tell them horror stories. We were going to line people up to demonstrate why these things happened.

Joe Urgo (JU): In the fall of 1969, there was a discussion in VVAW around this question of Calley and war crimes, and what we realized is that Calley was a scapegoat. What he did is what was done on an everyday basis all over Vietnam by every unit. We knew from our own experiences that this was just normal operating procedure.

There was another group that was in the same building as us that had been around for a year or more. It came out of the [Bertrand] Russell Tribunal. It was called the Citizens Commission of Inquiry into United States War crimes (CCI). The Citizens Commission had been doing hearings around the country, but their method of doing the hearings is that they would bring vets in and vets would testify to some press. They would get some publicity around them and then they would use that to do another one of those, but they were not about organizing vets. They were about organizing this process of carrying on their own agenda and raising money to do another one of these things.

JB: At first, I was the only Vietnam veteran representative [in CCI]. A lot of veterans didn't want to touch this with a 10-foot pole for those negative reactions, number one. And number two, a lot of people felt badly for having participated in what they participated in. It took about six months, well into

1970, for people in VVAW to warm up to the idea. Once they warmed up to it, VVAW embraced the idea.

JU: We were the largest source of vets in the country. We were the ones actu-ally organizing vets with a conscious program and objectives and a method to our work that had the potential to build it into a huge organization. So we linked up with them [CCI] and Fonda and started promoting the idea of win-ter soldier investigations.

CCI people wanted it in Washington, and Fonda wanted it in Detroit. For the VVAW leadership it was a struggle. What it really came down to was, in Detroit it could be broadcast into Canada, and Vietnamese could come tes-tify in Canada about what was done to them, on a closed-circuit TV hookup. Detroit was also the heart of the industrial working class, and some people in the organization wanted to do something that rooted it more in the back-ground of the working class.

I was all over the place on this. At first I was for Washington because I thought that if you want media, you go where the media is, and the media's in Washington. CCI wanted it in Washington because they wanted to appeal to the legislators. They were going for congressional hearings, you see—that was their agenda—and so if you're going to do it in Washington, there's got to be a focus toward the government. Then I thought Detroit. The reason for going to Detroit was to go to the people.

Well, two things happened. One is that Mark Lane had allied himself with us, and CCI said they didn't want to have anything to do with him because they didn't trust him. Lane was doing a book on war crimes [*Conversations with Americans,* 1970] and he never checked with the VVAW people to put his vets through our process of checking out their story. Essentially what he did was, he printed a book that was full of flaws.

The *New York Times* decided to tear this book apart on the front page of the book review. So here's Mark Lane linked up with us because he's into war crimes. The struggle of how to work with Mark Lane and when not to work with him became the focus of the animosity and rivalries. The lesson is that we'd better do our work right. We'd better talk to these vets and weed out the bullshitters so that we can't get set up, because we're going to come under attack. We're going to do this right.

JB: There was this split between some of the staff members and some of the veterans on how to approach this. Because of the split, particularly midwest organizers of VVAW said, "No; we should do it in the midwest, in the mid-dle of the country." I said, "Let's do them both." I attempted to be the bridge between the two and got torn apart. My arms were being ripped apart in both directions. You learn so much about how movements fragment. I've watched this in movement after movement after movement. There will be two different tendencies, and people will insist: You go this way or that way;

you can't go with both of them; you've got to choose. It drives me up the wall. Coalitions to begin with are tenuous, but if you don't have a coalition, what have you got? There was a lot of hostility there.

Jeremy Rifkin [of CCI] is an example. He was not a veteran and yet went around bossing veterans. A lot of veterans didn't like this. "Who the hell is he to tell them what to do, when to do it, how to do it, where to do it?" Secondly, Rifkin, I think, was miffed because he was very good at making connections. He was the one that made the connection with Jane Fonda. So he started bad-mouthing Jane Fonda right at the point when she's going out on a nationwide speaking tour to raise money for VVAW. [That was after the RAW march.]

When the split happened, VVAW, Jane Fonda, and certain other people went in this direction. Jeremy Rifkin, other Vietnam veterans, and supporters went in the other direction.

The CCI hearing was held in December of 1970. As far as the media coverage, it was zip. Therefore, it gave us even more impetus to have the winter soldier hearing be well organized. Somehow we [had to] break through this media grip.

JU: We knew we were going into some heavy shit and we had to do this right. What we were doing in the winter soldier investigation, which was very conscious from the beginning, was that in order to not allow another scapegoat to develop, we had to prove that what was done in Vietnam—in terms of the torture, murder, massacres, rape—was not individual decisions by individual GIs but in fact policy that had been worked out by the centers of the United States government, through its think tanks, war colleges, Pentagon, and various other ways that these policies were determined.

How do you lay the blame at the very bowels of the United States government and say this is where the murder and massacre and torture was directed, planned, centered?

How did you manage all that?

JU: Phone calls, letters, and finding people in the same unit at the same time who could confirm that they knew something. The vets in Detroit—Bill Crandle, Tim Butz, Mike Oliver, and Scott Moore—drafted a set of questions that were very good at making sure that we were not getting bullshitted and lied to. These are mostly vets that have been in combat. We had to know the language and know what forces were in what place at what time and what policies were worked out. Some guy came in and claimed that his unit did something, and it didn't jibe. We tried to rely on at least a double confirmation and then sometimes a triple confirmation that the story had to check out.

The way we did it was by organizing the vets into unions so that a panel of the First Marine Division would testify, from the earliest guy to the latest;

the Third Marine Division, the earliest to the latest; First Infantry Division, the earliest to the latest. We would show the continuity within the units across the years. Here's this guy from the First Marine Division—he was there in 1967—talking about this and this and this. Here's a guy who was there just three months ago, just came home: he's doing the same thing. They were doing it in this corps and that corps. They were doing it in every unit in Vietnam, every corps we were in, through the whole time we were there.

Now, within this there's a guy all the time who's saying, "Wait a minute. I was in this division, and we didn't do that. I was there a whole year; I didn't see any of this." We said, "OK, that's true. Maybe you had an officer that enacted a different policy. All of that's going on around you. Other units were doing it. Did you ever use free-fire zones in the area?" "Yeah, we used free-fire zones all the time." "Well, did you know that's a war crime?" "It is?" "Did you ever do H and I—harassment and interdiction—through a village at night?" "Oh, yeah, we did that all the time." "Well, that's a war crime. You were killing civilians sleeping in their villages at night in their hootches." "Well, we were just trying to get some testimony out of them, so we had to knock them round a bit." "Oh, yeah? What else did you do?" "Well, you know, some of them were thrown out of choppers." "Oh. What do you think about that?"

A lot of guys didn't think these things were war crimes. So people came and didn't think they had testimony.

JB: It [the winter soldier hearing in Detroit] was so well organized. They'd [veterans] come from all over the country [and] poured their souls out. There were two, three, four people talking about the same situation, who hadn't seen each other since they were there. People had to show their documentation, in as many cases as possible, [and] come up with a second person, sometimes more—because once they started networking, more people said, "Yeah, I want to come to Detroit. I'll back you up." [We asked,] "So you said you were in this unit. Where's your DD-214?" It was double-checking to make sure that nobody could, as they tried to do, say these veterans didn't even serve in Vietnam.

Barry Romo (BR): I heard there was going to be a war crimes conference of just GIs in Detroit. I had given lots of speeches, and [in] one of the speeches I told about the Koreans beating babies against walls and stuff. One of the people that heard it said, "Hey, there's this conference. Would you go?" And I said, "Yeah, I might." So they said, "They'd pay the way." I said, "Sure." So I went there.

Originally, they [VVAW office in New York] were going to charter a plane, but they didn't do it. They had all these schemes of getting the Playboy plane and all these things, and they didn't get them. So we had to buy the tickets, and when they bought the tickets at the last moment, you don't get the rates. And so I had to call up well over a 125 people that were going to go. I almost didn't go. I was burned out from calling all these people and telling them they couldn't go. I said, "Fuck no. I've lied to all these people; these people all want to go, and the national office fucking does this to me."

This Asian woman—I can't remember her name, but she was like a college grad— she says, "Hey, you've got to go," and gave me this little rap: "You don't run from struggle; you go to struggle. You struggle in, you struggle out." You know, life's a struggle. She gave this Marxist thing. OK, makes sense to me. I wasn't overly stratified in my thinking. I was open still at that point.

I didn't know anybody. They didn't have an organized force on the west coast, really. They found out I was an officer and in the AMERICAL division, and that made me the coordinator for the AMERICAL panel.

[I] watched people freak out right and left. This was the first time I had seen post-Vietnam syndrome: delayed stress. Horrible things happened.

JB: We were talking about all these things, and this woman gets up and says, "This is all horrendous, talking about all these rapes and killings. You're all male chauvinist pigs!" I said, "Lady, you're right, and we're working on changing it." Which I think was the bottom line of VVAW. We weren't people who started out saying, "We're better than thou." We said, "We did these things and it shouldn't be done. We're part of this and it shouldn't be continued."

BR: Finally, we had a third world revolt. I was the only Hispanic there, and [I] united with the only Native American and the blacks. We all formed a panel. We demanded a panel on racism alone. We held the panel on what racism was to the Vietnamese, which was starting to come out, but also the question of racism against servicemen in the military. That was the first revolt against a sort of a more liberal antiwar view.

I was disturbed by their [the organizers'] liberalness in the context that people were allowed to take the blame as an individual rather than take the blame as a society. That really bothered me, because I saw guys near suicide. I knew that was not the way it was supposed to be. [I] didn't have a clear viewpoint or anything but knew that was wrong. And secondly, [I] knew that unless we exposed how the service trained us and how society used us, we couldn't defeat it, because it wouldn't be redirected toward the government—it would be directed down toward the GIs, servicemen, and lower-ranking officers.

Did anyone ask you to name names?

BR: Some of the newsmen did. We refused, saying we wouldn't allow the scapegoating to take place unless you guarantee us that the officers will be put on trial . . . all the superior officers, like Westmoreland, the division commanders. . . . We said: Otherwise, if it's going to be like Lieutenant Calley—put Lieutenant Calley on trial but you let General Koster and Westmoreland off—then we won't do it.

At the end of winter soldier, we were supposed to go into Windsor [Ontario] and meet with Vietcong and North Vietnamese soldiers. Nixon placed incredible pressure on the Canadians, which stopped the visas for those guys. We still met with the Vietnamese, but we didn't get to meet with actual soldiers.

JB: We got some coverage. They sent CBS cameras out there and never used the material. A *New York Times* reporter was there for the whole time, and they only had one story, which really didn't say that much. What did happen on the first day is, the *Detroit News* went after us and said, This is all a bunch of bullshit. The Pentagon says they don't even have any information that these people are real veterans. [After the first day] there was better coverage in Detroit, Chicago, and the midwest—some really fantastic coverage.

One of the first things that came out of there was Dewey Canyon I, which was a secret Marine raid into Laos. Well, the next thing that happens was: The reporters were provided names of other veterans around the country who were on the same mission, and out comes the story—that they interviewed these people across the country who said, "Yeah, I was there." Dewey Canyon I would have been a secret piece of military history. Coincidentally, as we are there in Detroit, the news comes out that Dewey Canyon II is taking place right now in Laos. Only we knew what that meant. Dewey Canyon II meant that there really was a Dewey Canyon I. [Laughs.] It was confirming, by using the same code words, that what we were saying there not only was true, but they were continuing to recycle it.

Coming out of it, the vets there got mad because they could see how the media, outside of the middle west, ignored this story or deliberately buried it. People were muttering at this meeting, "What are we going to do next?" John Kerry proposed, "Why don't we go to Washington and take the story right to Congress?" Other people were saying other things, but that really was the genesis. I loved this—you know, the creative thing that happens when people come together. Out of that, the mind-set started Dewey Canyon III, which was a limited incursion into the country of Congress. By that time

[1971], we could organize an action that was our own action [and] had nationwide draw, national significance to what we were doing.

Dewey Canyon III:
"A Limited Incursion into the Country of Congress"

BARRY ROMO, JAN BARRY, BILL BRANSON, SHELDON RAMSDELL, TERRY DuBOSE

Vietnam veterans, dissatisfied with the lack of press coverage received by the winter soldier hearings, decided to take their stories directly to Congress. On April 18, 1971, 1,500 antiwar veterans and their supporters converged on Washington, D.C., to engage in four days of protest. The following narratives

Dewey Canyon III: VVAW members on the silent march to the White House.

describe how veterans organized the event, what they hoped to accomplish, and how they were received by their representatives and the press.

Barry Romo (BR): After winter soldier, I was asked if I wanted to be the organizer on the west coast. [I] came back, and they called me up and said, "We're building up this demonstration, this march on Washington; we'll pay your way out to New York." [I] flew out to New York.

[We] fought for three days [in February of 1971]. We hammered out a basis of unity for a national organization, which was really ultraleft for the time. There was infighting over what we were going to do at the demonstration. We came up there with the idea of throwing our medals away. We came up with all the stuff we were going to do ahead of time.

[I] remember there was an argument for hours on what we were going to call the demonstration. As a joke, I told people, "Fuck it. Call it Dewey Canyon III. Why? Dewey Canyon I was a secret invasion of Laos, Dewey Canyon II was whatever, and Dewey Canyon III is the vets' invasion of Washington."[35] And people said, "Hey, that's funny." It was an offhand joke. You know how you sit around a meeting drinking coffee, people have drank too much, cigarette smoke, 50 people, 50 very powerful views, and getting tired and making an offhand joke. And then, "We'll use it." People got into it. By saying Dewey Canyon, we can expose that we had a secret invasion: Dewey Canyon I. That's cool. let's do it.

Jan Barry (JB): We went from being a handful of people to doing a demonstration on the Mall in Washington that was better organized than we probably organized things in the military. For Washington in particular, there were working committees. It was a huge enterprise to do. There had to be fund-raising done. There was a fund-raising committee. We went to Boston one time with John Kerry and a couple of other people to talk to somebody like Marty Peretz, who now owns the *New Republic*. I don't know whether he contributed or not, but we were talking to people of this caliber who put the money up for this to take place.

According to an FBI memorandum from the Washington office dated April 13, 1971, "VVAW had received fifty thousand dollars from United States Senators McGovern and Hatfield, who . . . obtained the money from an unknown New York source."[36] Although VVAW did receive this relatively large infusion of cash, its resources were limited and were spent predominantly on advertising the event.

JB: This guy [Kerry] was born to this. His family is part of that whole circle. I had no insight, even, into this life, but I didn't put it down, while other people are saying, "Why do we have people like this in VVAW?" There were these class resentments. A lot of guys were enlisted people. "Why do we have officers being prominent?" One of the things I could get away with was, I never became an officer. I told West Point what they could do with that. Enlisted people appreciate that.

When we got to Dewey Canyon, the very first night—like a Sunday night—I got down to Washington. There were people pulling in and there was like a staging area, and some small group of people arrived from California and said something really rude and curt to me. I had no idea why they were saying that.

BR: [We] went to Washington. The national office of the headquarters where we were all coming into the first night's camp for Dewey Canyon III had a flag flying. This was like the night before we started. It was like an assembly area. We refused to register until they took the flag down. We then got the reputation as the radicals of the organization, but then a lot of people agreed with us.

Bill Branson (BB): We went to Washington—the big problem there is, we didn't have enough money to send all the people coming from California. They dicked around at the national headquarters, and we could have rented buses for all the money we spent. We could only send a few. I got to go because I had done a lot of organizing. It was my first big action.

We were incredibly militant. We figured if we were going to go all the way out there to Washington, to the belly of the beast, we were going to kick some ass. And we did. The leadership of the VVAW at the time . . . were from a different strata of society, like Kerry and those guys. They convinced a few people like Hubbard and others to take a conservative light on what we should do, like just basically be there and bear witness or some stupid thing. The vets who came were not in that mood.

We didn't want to tear the place apart, but we definitely wanted to make an impression. We were not there to do anything halfway. As we got together in bigger and bigger groups, we became more and more militant. The service had taught us: When you're with your comrades, you just fit right in.

When we got there, it seemed pretty damned organized. People picked us up and we got a van ride in there. At first we were on the Anacostia Flats. We weren't on the Mall. We started camping there.

We started a struggle immediately. When we got there—we were one of the first groups—there was this fucking garrison flag flying over the place, and we made them take it down. We got into quite a bit of face-to-face struggles over that, and we almost got into fights. But we weren't going to go that far. We definitely made them take that fucking flag down.

JB: We had the first mass meeting on Monday evening. Things were a little chaotic and hadn't come together as they had been organized, and everybody was milling around. We started this meeting and I started speaking. Somebody started hollering and screaming and saying nasty and rude things from the audience. Clearly this was organized to try to drown me out. I could see that there was some kind of organized business going on to try to discredit me and Hubbard and then right down the line, whoever appeared to be the leader of the moment.

So I figured the easiest tactic was to turn the meeting over to somebody else, which is what I did. I got up and sat down right in the middle of these people. The other person I left the meeting to was a little flustered, but I knew that people could pick up on this.

Some members in the Washington action wanted to move the encampment from the Anacostia Flats, relatively far from the seats of political power, to the Mall, directly in the center of the political establishment.

BB: We were supposed to be making the decision on whether we were going to fucking take over the Mall. Barry and some people were running around dragging people to this meeting where all this was being decided. There we are at this historic meeting. It turned out to be a heavy debate whether we should just go for it and whether the cops would attack us. Barry was arguing and others were arguing, "Fuck this; we're not staying here."

People had been talking about what were we going to do. There were original plans on what we were supposed to do. I don't remember what all they were, but it didn't involve taking over the Mall. It was mostly like a lobbying thing and stuff. People said, "Fuck this. We don't mind lobbying, but we're not going to sit down here near where the World War I vets were fucking slaughtered and have them do what they want to us on the side." It wasn't spontaneous; it was a decision that was made.

The next morning we took all our shit and packed it up and threw it on the trucks. We all got into this giant march. All these veterans staggered onto the road and marched up Pennsylvania Avenue. We had banners and stuff. People worked on banners all night. It was just buzz, buzz, buzz; no one got any fucking sleep. People got wired on the incredible amount of energy, pulsing energy, to the point of being manic.

It wasn't too hard to tell what we were all about. We marched up Pennsylvania Avenue and people came out everywhere. Buildings emptied; all the windows went up. I looked up and there were people everywhere. There were lots and lots of tourists there, and they were fucking cheering. We had people running out shaking hands. I had never seen a march like this.

There was cops along the sides of the street, but they stayed away from us. I can guarantee you, if they had attacked us then, there would have been guerrilla warfare in the streets. They knew better, which was good. They wouldn't have been able to stop us. Guys were not going to put up with a lot of shit.

What was the point of going to the Mall?

BB: I was for anything that was going to kick ass. I really didn't care what it was. I wasn't going to set anything on fire. Short of that, I was there to make an impression. I felt like Washington was full of assholes that sent us there and I was prepared to spit in their eye, amongst other things. I didn't have a highly developed line on propaganda, but all of us instinctually knew that we were in a historical situation. We talked about it a lot. We were there to do as much as we could. We weren't going to be told to be good boys and go home.

Was the discussion the night before causing tension between the national office and different people around the country, or was it pretty much consensus and everyone agreed after the decision and every one went along with it?

BB: I think as it became apparent that it was the right thing to do, they went along with it. They couldn't have done otherwise.

There was a definite force from the national to tone things down. Constantly. In fact, they tried to gather all our plastic guns and we said, "No, you're not." "Oh, no, you're going to get us shot at." "No, we're not. If they shoot at us, the world won't end tomorrow."

They were trying to get us to be conservative, and it just wasn't getting over. Your average guys there felt like they had been shafted. All those people had already had a chance to be fucked by the conservative people who were still in charge of society here that treated us as outcasts and shit. They had no jobs. We felt an intense kinship with the people still in Vietnam. We felt the war was wrong and it was going to go on forever if we didn't do something about it ourselves. It was time for us to make a statement. We made it in our typical fashion. We tended to be almost instinctively organized in everything that we did. We didn't take any shit, and we were smart in almost everything that we did. We were not conservative, so we got in arguments constantly with the leadership. I think almost immediately, as we started pouring in, they got scared.

I think they were afraid of us. I remember getting in a shouting match with Hubbard. He's telling us a lot of bullshit—that if you act this way you're going to get thrown out. We're telling him, "Fuck you, you're a jerk-off, why the fuck won't you talk to us like human beings, we're not fucking kids, we're part of this thing, you ain't shit, and who elected you anyway?"

JB: I stayed pretty much on the site. I went with Kerry on one occasion to the State Department. We gave a briefing to State Department people in a briefing room. It blew my mind. They wanted to know why we were there! We had a list of demands that I read on the steps of Congress which in essence became a legislative model for several different things that were proposed in the following years, pointed toward the VA and various other directions.

Then it was like getting us through a week in which a lot of improvising went on. Something came up, like they refused to allow the group into the cemetery the first day. I had nothing to do with the decision that was made. Somebody, whatever number it was, decided that the solution was to go to the Pentagon and offer to turn themselves in as war criminals, which blew the Pentagon's mind. "What do we do with these people? We'd better let them into the cemetery."

BB: A bunch of guys from California went down to the Pentagon and tried to turn in a bunch of guys as war criminals. We took over everything—the Lincoln Memorial, the Rotunda—we walked in the streets. Nobody stopped us.

JB: When Nixon was quoted as saying he didn't think these were real Vietnam veterans, one group decided they were going to go parade at night around the White House with the flag upside down. It was tremendously dramatic.

Sheldon Ramsdell (SR): Ron Ziegler had said, from Nixon, that this was just a bunch of hippies. A woman came down to the Mall from the AP or UPI, [and] collected nearly 1,000 combat cards—you know, military service cards (DD-214s). She put that in the paper the next day. Nixon was totally discredited.

Terry DuBose (TDB): It was exhilarating. Incredible camaraderie. They had these tables with food laid out from people in the community. You could have anything you wanted. We all wore our fatigues, and if you went out on the curb and stuck your thumb out, a taxi would pick you up and take you where you wanted to go for free. They were all sympathetic.

Did you lobby?

TDB: Yeah. In fact, John Tower [senator from Texas] refused to talk to us. He returned to Texas because there was a flood in south Texas. Eckardt [also a senator from Texas] gave us a phone and a little closet to set up operations so that we could get press releases back to Austin. He was real supportive. [Philip] Hart, from Michigan, had a room there. They always had cookies and milk. Anybody could go there; it was a congregating point. His staff was real supportive. It was a great feeling. There was news media all over the place.

BR: We lobbied; all of us lobbied. I didn't believe in lobbying at this point. I thought they [elected officials] were all scum. They would only move when we forced them to move. But we were going to lobby, so we went lobbying. We went and saw our congressmen and stuff. We decided lobbying just wasn't enough. It just wasn't dramatic enough.

We got up one morning and sat in at the Supreme Court. That wasn't planned. Some of the national people got mad: Mike Oliver, Jan Barry, Scott Moore, and Al Hubbard said, "You're going to ruin the demonstration by doing this." We said, "No, we're not." We got arrested and it made great news. Rather than be a detriment, it was good. The media loved it.

Why do these kinds of media-grabbing events?

BR: They [the American public] saw the war on TV. They had to see us on TV. People's experience was not being in a rice paddy, but watching someone in a rice paddy. We had to interrupt their seeing war on TV with their seeing veterans demonstrating against the war on TV. We had to fucking interfere with their fucking lines of thoughts, and that was the only way to do it. We know, and they don't. We're telling you that what you see on TV is not it. It's part of it, but it's not it, and it's wrong and you've got to bring people home.

After the veterans decided to move their encampment, Justice Warren Burger upheld an order by the Justice Department that they were to be removed from the Mall at night. They were told that they would not be allowed to sleep in the park at night; it was illegal. One of the most critical debates among veterans took place as a result of this ruling.[37]

BR: We came back [from the Supreme Court], and the Department of Justice said we can't go to sleep in the park. I think it was Mike Oliver [who] got up and made a speech: "We won't sleep; we won't break the law. We're going to stay here and demonstrate till the end of the week; we'll take speed to stay awake so they can't arrest us; we'll stay awake for the next three days." One of the guys, Sam Shorr from California, got up, and he said, "These guys are crazy. One, no one told us where we could sleep in Vietnam. Two, ain't nobody going to tell us as Vietnam vets that we can't sleep in our park. Fuck them. We are going to sleep in the park. If they're going to arrest us, they'll arrest us. We're not going to take drugs; drugs are destroying the country." People went back and had heartfelt discussions, and we won the vote. The overwhelming majority of people who lost the vote stayed, even though they didn't want to get arrested.

JB: It was a huge discussion. It was a close vote, which everybody had sort of pushed aside. It was like 480 to 400 [to stay]. I had a telephone line to the outside so I could call and say, We're now being arrested. It was a special line that had been put in so they could round up all the lawyers and the rest of it. I'm sitting there on a camp stool, and I think it's Urgo that came up and said,

"Well, what are you going to do if they [the park police] come in?" I said, "I'm just going to stay."

I was torn. I was always a very conservative person when it came to tweaking the nose of the law. I saw no purpose in spending any time in jail whatsoever. I thought it was lost time, number one. Civil disobedience was a tactic to me and not a lifestyle. For a lot of people, it was their life. You do this and to hell with whether or not you accomplish anything, but you feel good. I wanted to know what we were accomplishing. I mean, what's the purpose of going to jail?

We [also] have a right to be here on this place, camping. They can't just arbitrarily take this right away from us. But there was this debate, which Kerry and Hubbard led, where people stood up in the crowd and argued this and that side of it, and then they voted. It was real democracy in action. It was astounding. Once the vote went 480 to stay, then the consensus was: Well, if you're staying, then I'm staying.

BR: We got our sleeping bags out, supremely confident that we were going to get arrested, smiles on our faces. [We] got into our sleeping bags—we hadn't been sleeping in them before—got in them because, by God, we were going to sleep there.

I remember Ron Dellums came to our delegation because he was a California congressman; [he] wore his medals. Ron Dellums stayed with our contingent overnight and said that if they arrest you, they're arresting me. They're not arresting me as a congressman but as a veteran. We loved the man. No publicity here. "I'm here, I go to jail with you."

JB: Edward Kennedy was there most of that night in a tent talking with veterans. You never knew who you were going to run into. I turn around and bump into somebody who's a member of Congress.

BR: We're in the bags; the park police start walking through and they looked down at us. This lieutenant or captain, this old chubby white guy, looks down at us and goes, "I don't see anybody sleeping. [Laughs.] Nobody sleeping here. You guys don't have to worry about nothing because we don't see anything and we're not going to do anything." So we all laughed. And Dellums stayed until about two in the morning and said, "Well, they aren't going to bust, so I'm going to go home." We said that's all right. He was there.

We got up in the morning and we beat them. That made it "Vets Overrule the Supreme Court."[38] It was a crisis in the national government, with Burger convinced that this was a communist march on Washington. He was the one that ordered us to be arrested on the Supreme Court steps, and the other justices are going, "What are you doing?" If you read *The Brethren* [by Bob Woodward and Scott Armstrong, 1979], you read how all the other Supreme Court justices think Burger has gone butt-fuck. This guy was having flashbacks to: MacArthur was right when he killed the Bonus Marchers. He wanted us killed and driven out of the city. He thought that was so just.

Despite the efforts by the Nixon administration to have the veterans evicted from the Mall—with which the Supreme Court had cooperated—John Dean sent out a directive ordering the park police not to arrest veterans. At this point, Nixon's aides did not want a confrontation that would arouse public sympathy for the veterans, who had been receiving a great deal of media attention. The veterans, however, did not know of this directive.[39]

JB: The original intent of the Friday [event] was to take all the medals and throw them into a body bag and to take the body bag to the Capitol. People got mad because they put this fence across the steps of Congress. "What are they putting this up for? It's fencing us out." So on the spot, there was this mumbling and grumbling, and someone said, "Let's throw the medals over the goddamned fence."[40]

BR: Getting ready to throw our medals away, [there] was a fight with Kerry. Kerry wanted us to put them in a body bag. [Kerry argued] that it would be disrespectful to throw them away; people wouldn't understand. That was the only fight I ever remember having with Kerry. I said, "Fuck you. God damn it, we decided this months before; at every point you want to change shit. The only way we're going to wake the public up is to do dramatic events, and we got these medals. . . . We're making a statement that they can't ignore," and stuff like that. People handily decided to throw their medals away. I don't think Kerry did. Then we went and lined up and just threw the medals away. [It was] one of the heaviest things.

On April 23, 1971, about 700 veterans and their supporters gathered outside the fence erected by the Nixon administration at the west steps of the Capitol. They lined up, approached the fence one by one, and announced their names and ranks and the awards they had received while serving their country. They then threw their medals over the fence—back to those who had conferred these honors on them.

JB: A lot of what I was doing was keeping the threads of a security operation going. People consulted with me about this problem and that problem. There were people doing all kinds of strange, weird things, trying to screw things up.

There was a television report that [Al] Hubbard wasn't who he claimed to be.[41] All of a sudden, they bring Hubbard, looking like he'd been destroyed. We go into a truck trailer in this little huddle. Everybody's like: Should we strangle him or . . . ? [Laughs.] At this point, you don't know if he is part of something that was deliberately done to discredit us. Did he do it because,

Who's going to listen to a sergeant? If you say you were a captain, you get listened to. We didn't have any way of knowing. Everybody's standing around, and I said, "What has been done has been done. I suggest we just go right outside right now, hold a press conference, and say: He made a mistake, he's suffering the consequence of it, and that's the end of it."

SR: I was in the studio during Dewey Canyon. John Kerry went on the show and Al demanded to be on the show and elevated himself to captain. [Laughs.] He was a sergeant and there's nothing wrong with that, but John [Kerry] was a lieutenant or something. . . . [Al Hubbard] went on the show. . . . After the show I'm in the office in Washington. . . . The phone didn't stop . . . live talk shows are calling up saying, "What's with this Al Hubbard lying about his rank?" I said, "It's not important." I was pretty honest. I knew the issue was a matter of race and elitism and Hubbard was not going to sit down and take it.

JB: After we had really reached a peak, we heard there were also soldiers on active duty ready to be sent in to do whatever they were ordered to do, as in the 1932 march. There was a big story in the Washington papers, recalling all those events in which they turned soldiers on their own companions of World War I. One of those evenings, this young guy arrives in the middle of the camp and says, "I'm from the 82nd Airborne" or something. He said, "They order us to come in here, we're not coming. You guys are our only hope that we don't have to get sent to Vietnam, or back to Vietnam." We got pieces of that kind of information all week long, plus this overwhelming support of people just coming with food, and money, and donations.

It [Dewey Canyon III] was overwhelmingly successful in several different ways. We had the five o'clock follies, which was our take on press conferences in Vietnam. These news media people lapped this all up, because we did this parody of a military news conference. One of those evenings, at five o'clock, this guy comes over to me, hands me this thing, and he says, "This is what Walter Cronkite is going to be reading tonight at six o'clock." It was very positive and made this a major nationwide and international news story, because the Cronk was it. Cronk says, Take notice of this, America. This was the guy who had written what the Cronk was to read, and he rushed over there to hand it to us. At that point, I knew that the White House had lost the public on this issue.

There was a *Time* magazine retrospective that said this was probably the most memorable or most important demonstration of the peace movement. Everybody had forgotten that that kind of statement was made about it. But I think that it had that effect because the peace movement by this time was exhausted.

SR: CBS had a truck down there. Cronkite has us on every single night. We had a logo [VVAW insignia] on the back of his head every single night for the rest of that week. It all changed, just like that. Look how far we had to go to get any kind of credibility at all. A reporter from a news service collected our cards, and suddenly we're real. What the hell's been going on all this time? Nobody's been wanting to believe it!

JB: At some point after that, I did get some feedback from a friend of mine who still was in the military as an officer. He said that in the Pentagon, VVAW's demonstration shook the whole place up. Captains and majors were screaming at colonels and generals that they better fucking wake up: "Those veterans out there were right." People who did two or three tours were not going to go back again to save the assholes of these people who screwed it all up. It set off within the military establishment, apparently, this vicious debate.

What impact did Dewey Canyon III have on the organization?

JB: There were groups that came out of this that decided that what they wanted to work on was the legislative aspect of making things happen. Other groups decided what they wanted to work on was the psychological—what became the rap group direction. Other groups decided they wanted to work on community organizing when they went back to where they were going back to. Other people decided that what they were going to do was to go back into the academic world, get that degree that gave you the credentials; and they went and did that. Other people, like John Kerry, decided that politics was where they wanted to go. They went there and they got there.

They turned mainly conservative guys into radicals overnight with the way the government reacted. These guys came here thinking they were going to talk to their congressman and be listened to. That was the original intention. We'd go to Congress and lobby them like everybody else does and get listened to. When they slammed doors in our faces and threatened us everyplace we turned, these guys got radicalized.

4

LEFT FACE

The process of radicalization within VVAW was very, very quick, and very intense. I started, like I think a lot of us did, simply saying: The war is wrong. Then going to: Wait a second—it wasn't that the war was the problem, but the war was a symptom of a problem. The problem was this society, the government, the thinking and the institutions, the educational system—and click, click, click, you rapidly went through this evolution of consciousness from what you first thought was the problem to becoming what was symptomatic of much deeper problems.

Bobby Muller

It [VVAW] was ultrademocratic, which led to some of its problems. There was a lot of folks and every one of them had an attitude. Every one of them had an agenda and felt that their opinion had a right to be heard. Meetings would go on and on and on. Women and other nonveterans had joined the organization, and they demanded a right to be heard.

Mike McCain

Swimming Against the Tide

Dewey Canyon III was, by all accounts, VVAW's most successful event, in terms of gaining the attention of the media. Yet veterans who had tried to lobby their congressmen were for the most part unsuccessful. Most echoed Jan Barry's sentiments, saying that doors in the halls of Congress had been "slammed in their faces." These were men who had given a great deal for their nation, and for democracy. They had risked their lives in Vietnam, and they had come home to share what they had seen there with the American public and its representatives. They had hoped that through the democratic process, they could bring the war to an end. Yet it became evident to many of them that—except for a few sympathetic leaders in Congress—those who held power in Washington were not interested in veterans' perspectives on the war. Veterans had given the political process their best efforts and still had not reached their goal.

The national attention received by Dewey Canyon III did bring veterans, GIs, and civilians from across the country into VVAW. From the summer of 1971 through 1972, the organization grew dramatically, signing up roughly 50,000 new members.[1] During this period, though, VVAW had to struggle to find new ways to keep the war in the forefront of the public's attention. And despite its increased numbers, its efforts were hampered by continued splintering of the civilian antiwar movement, by the fact that a significant portion of the public remained detached from the war and from antiwar protests, and by the ability of the Nixon administration to dominate much of the discourse on the war and to deflect attention onto other foreign policy issues.

Dewey Canyon III also rekindled the disintegrating antiwar coalitions, but only briefly. Following the veterans' weeklong encampment, between 200,000 and 500,000 protesters from numerous organizations, including labor and civil rights activists, converged on Washington during the weekend of April 24, 1971. (The government's estimate was 200,000; the coalition's estimate was 500,000.) *Time* magazine reported that the gathering was peaceful and orderly, a demonstration that even "cops could have brought their children to."[2] Throughout the week, protesters lobbied their representatives and carried out several acts of civil disobedience. Meanwhile, in San Francisco, 125,000 people gathered in the largest antiwar demonstration ever held on the west coast.

But then, on May 3, several thousand members of the "May Day Collective" came to Washington for a "day of disruption." These demonstrators planned to bring the capital to a halt by direct, though nonviolent, actions that would close down buildings, block traffic, and impede the flow of many everyday activities. They warned those in power to "end the war or face social chaos."[3] The administration, however, was well prepared for May Day. National troops and the police rounded up 7,000 protesters and held them in Robert F. Kennedy Stadium to await hearings. (Most were eventually released without ever going to trial.)

This swift response from the Nixon administration not only quelled the May Day protest but irreparably damaged the radical wing of antiwar activism. Although a majority of Americans wanted to see an end to the war, they did not condone these protesters' attempt to shut down the government; and some Americans had grown tired of the war and protesters alike.[4] Also, the May Day Tribe—a small subgroup of anarchists—alienated the liberal wing of the antiwar community, leading to more crumbling of the already tenuous antiwar coalitions.

Thus large segments of the antiwar movement had become deeply frustrated by their inability to influence the Washington establishment, and deeply cynical about the democratic process. Many dropped out of the movement, convinced that their efforts were fruitless. This attitude seemed to be vindicated in June 1971, when Congress failed to pass bills which would have set a deadline (December 31 of that year) for the withdrawal of American troops from Vietnam.[5] Even though the Democrats had gained control of both the House and the Senate in the elections of 1970, and even though the majority of Americans wanted the war ended, the legislators were reluctant to force Nixon's hand.

Some parts of the antiwar community, especially people who had come to view the war as a symptom of deeper-seated problems, turned their attention to other issues: racism, sexism, and economic ills. Some decided that the democratic process was so flawed that no less a remedy than revolution was necessary to bring about significant changes in the nation. They gravitated to various splinter organizations that had emerged in the preceding years, including the Revolutionary Union, the Progressive Labor Party, and sectarian groups committed to Marxism-Leninism, Maoism, Stalinism, or a number of other revolutionary ideologies.

Liberals, who had not yet lost faith in the two-party system, refocused their energies in an attempt to promote change through the Democratic Party. After its infamous nominating convention and its defeat at the polls in 1968, the party had become more open to progressive ideas, and as the presidential election of 1972 approached, many progressives began to work for the Democrats, supporting the candidacy of Senator George McGovern, who had long been an outspoken critic of the war.

Antiwar activism was kept alive by pacifists, and by religious organizations that continued to address the immorality of American intervention in Vietnam, yet even those who remained active became increasingly frustrated by their lack of progress during the remainder of 1971 and into 1972. One leader of Clergy and Laity Concerned (CALC), an organization of religious dissenters, reflected a widespread feeling when he commented, "In 1965 the American people knew there was a war, and we had to convince them that it was wrong. In 1972, people know the war is wrong, but we have to convince them that there is a war."[6]

There were several reasons why Americans had to be convinced that there was a war. For one thing, the administration continued to portray President Nixon as a man of peace who was committed to a swift conclusion of the war—a characterization that seemed to be confirmed by Nixon's troop withdrawals, which continued during 1971 and 1972. In 1968, 500,000 American troops had been stationed in Vietnam. By the end of 1971, this figure was down to 175,000, with only 75,000 of these engaged in combat[7] By the end of 1972, only 24,000 American troops remained in Vietnam. Second, as the number of troops was reduced, media coverage of the war declined. One newspaper editor commented that, with fewer and fewer Americans engaged on the ground in Vietnam, "it's hard to justify front page coverage." As the war disappeared from the front pages of the nation's newspapers, and from television screens, it also diminished in the public consciousness. By December of 1971, according to one poll, only 15 percent of Americans believed that Vietnam continued to be the nation's most pressing problem.[8] Americans now tended to be more concerned with domestic issues, such as school busing, crime, and the declining economy.

The effect of the economy, in particular, needs to be understood. The unprecedented economic vigor of the years following World War II had peaked by the mid-1960s, and thereafter inflation was on the rise but growth was stagnant. In fact, by the early 1970s a new term, "stagflation," was coined to describe this phenomenon. America's industrial cities had been the epicenters of this decline: their infrastructures began to sag, their crime rates rose, and the contours of their ghettos became, seemingly, permanent. These economic woes resulted, at least in part, from the enormous financial burden of the war and the reemergence of foreign competition, especially in Japan and Europe.

In August 1971, in an attempt to reverse the slide, Nixon imposed wage and price controls and "severed the dollar from the gold standard."[9] Although he did not cut into the budget for Vietnam, he did begin to cut back the "great society" programs initiated during the administration of his predecessor, Lyndon Johnson. Nixon also defined himself as a "law and order" president—that is, one who would crack down on lawlessness and disorder.

During the late 1960s and early 1970s, working-class Americans, distressed by the declining economy, engaged in a wave of wildcat strikes. Yet they also became increasingly concerned with the rise in the crime rate and the disorder associated with the war and the antiwar protests. By the late 1960s, many of them saw a link between their own problems and a general rise in lawlessness, which they attributed to urban ghettos, student protesters, and the permissiveness of American society—especially of American liberals, who seemed to be catering to the African-American community and the antiwar community. As noted above, after its disastrous convention of 1968 the Democratic Party had amended its rules, giving a stronger voice to those who had previously been shut out of its policy making, such as blacks and antiwar dissenters. But even before the party became more "liberal," working-class disaffection with it had already become evident: in the election of 1968, a large segment of the working class voted for the third-party candidate, George Wallace.

Given the state of the economy, then, and given other pressing domestic concerns—and because more and more American troops were coming home and the war seemed to be winding down—Vietnam tended to drop out of sight.

But despite the prevailing impression that the war was winding down, the Nixon administration had dramatically escalated the air war. It was true that

American forces were being withdrawn and that the fighting was increasingly being turned over to the ARVN forces; but as this happened, the North Vietnamese and NLF forces increased their efforts to topple the Thieu regime. The Nixon administration countered the communist advances in 1971 and 1972 by increasing aerial bombardment of both South and North Vietnam. In fact, from December 26, 1971, when the Nixon administration inititated Operation Proud Deep Alpha, to the spring of 1972, the United States engaged in the most intense air attacks since the beginning of direct American involvement in Vietnam. When Nixon inaugurated the spring attacks, he told his aides, "The bastards have never been bombed like they're going to be bombed this time."[10] Throughout the spring, American jets indiscriminately bombed both civilian and military targets in North and South Vietnam, and Nixon had North Vietnamese ports mined. All this was an effort to salvage the "Vietnamization" program.[11] The administration argued that the escalation of the air war was defensive, to protect the American troops still in Vietnam and to force the Vietnamese to the bargaining table. (However, the Vietnamese had been seeking peace for some time, and peace talks had been started during the Johnson administration.)

This drastic intensification of the war shocked a wide spectrum of American journalists, politicians, and academics, some of whom had so far refused (at least in public) to criticize the Nixon administration with regard to Vietnam. Critics of the bombing argued that Nixon had overstepped his constitutional mandate and was threatening the nation's democratic system— a charge that VVAW had been making for several years. One journalist, Tom Wicker, described Nixon an "unchecked Caesar."[12] Despite the outcry, though, antiwar activism was muted, and Nixon held firm in his resolve to prosecute the air war throughout the rest of the year.

In the face of the increased criticism, some Americans rallied to the president, as public opinion polls revealed. In November 1971, 65 percent of Americans had said that the war was morally repugnant; but in September 1972—a year after the war had entered its most brutal phase, and shortly before the presidential election—59 percent of Americans said that Nixon was "more sincere, believable" than his Democratic opponent, George McGovern. They also said that they believed Nixon was more likely to bring peace (by 61 to 22 percent).[13]

Evidently, Nixon gained the support of a significant percentage of Americans by contending that the air war was a defensive measure. His administration had also diverted public attention away from Vietnam by focusing on domestic issues that more directly affected Americans. And he had enhanced his status as a peacemaker throughout 1971 and 1972 through highly publicized diplomatic missions to China and the Soviet Union.

In the summer of 1971, the Pentagon Papers were published, exposing the deceptions of the Johnson administration over its Vietnam policies and supporting the antiwar activists' claim that the war had undermined democracy at home. Shortly after this—in July 1971—Nixon announced that Henry Kissinger had visited China in order to enlist the Chinese in an effort to bring about an end to the war in Vietnam, and an end to the cold war. He also announced his own intention to visit China, and during the spring of 1972 he did visit not only China but also the Soviet Union. These diplomatic efforts captured the attention of the media and the nation and were generally approved by all quarters of American society. The president had, in the words of Jonathan Schell, used "his power to dominate the airwaves and the news columns with his words, his deeds, and his image of himself, of the country, and of the world."[14]

One purpose of Nixon's high-profile diplomacy was political: he was running for reelection. But numerous clandestine efforts were also being made to ensure his victory in the presidential election of 1972, by the White House and the Committee for the Re-Election of the President (CREEP). These clandestine measures were directed largely against his opponents—not only his political rivals but, more significantly, dissident citizens.

Although surveillance and infiltration of the antiwar community had taken place since the outset of activism, the Nixon administration drastically increased these tactics and expanded their scope during the summer of 1971. Nixon and his aides felt that the United States "was at war externally and internally,"[15] and that this state of war justified their use of new and intensified secret measures.

One of the first episodes in this clandestine war at home had to do with the Pentagon Papers. After having failed to block publication of the papers through the courts, the Nixon administration went after Daniel Ellsberg, the former Defense Department intelligence analyst who had compiled the papers and had released them to the *New York Times*. In July of 1971, the Nixon White House organized an undercover operation under the leadership of E. Howard Hunt—a former CIA agent who wrote spy novels—to discredit Ellsberg.[16] The aim was to paint Ellsberg, and the antiwar movement as a whole, as psychologically unstable, even deranged. To this end, in September the operatives broke into the office of Ellsberg's psychiatrist in Los Angeles, hoping to find the evidence that would impugn Ellsberg; Hunt (wearing a red wig) carried out this burglary himself. No damaging evidence was found, but by then the Nixon administration had embarked on other strategies.

During the following year, White House operatives engaged in numerous illegal and deceptive activities, including hiring thugs to attack Ellsberg during his public appearances; creating and disseminating phony campaign literature attributed to Edmund Muskie, Nixon's strongest Democratic rival, in an effort to defame Muskie and divide the Democrats; publishing false polling data purporting to show that Americans supported Nixon's policies in Vietnam; and, of course, breaking into the Democratic Party's headquarters in the Watergate Hotel in June 1972.[17]

Thus the war at home as well as the war in Vietnam had reached a new height during 1971 and 1972. But while the war in Vietnam had become much more mechanized and more destructive, Nixon was to a considerable extent still able to portray himself as a man of peace. And while his administration became increasingly involved in illegal efforts to destroy the opposition, Nixon was still announcing that he wanted to heal the wounds of war, bring the nation back together, and uphold law and order.

New Directions for the VVAW:
The War at Home

During this period, as the war continued to rage in Vietnam, the public became increasingly concerned with domestic issues and the antiwar community became increasingly frustrated and ineffectual. In this somewhat surrealistic atmosphere, Vietnam Veterans Against the War attempted to build a national organization and to change the nation. Veterans were not, of course, immune to the maladies that were infecting the United States. In the following narratives, they reveal the degree to which they were affected by the events that swirled around them, how they tried to keep the war in the forefront of the public mind after their march on Washington in April 1971, and how they were greeted.

The Radicalization of Veterans

JAN BARRY

I had told people months before this [Dewey Canyon III] that I was getting out. I was burned out. I said, "One more event, and that's it. I'll stay with VVAW to get us through this event, and then it's good-bye as of June 1st."

Everybody was frustrated. Here we gave it our best shot, and it didn't even slow the war down. Shortly after that, there was all this ideological business. I didn't want to be part of it and thought it was ridiculous. We had been face to face with communism as GIs in Vietnam.

People were not wrong, in an ideological sense, to want to broaden the focus and take on the capitalist system or take on, however you want to frame it, a larger system. That's exactly what needed to be understood. The disagreement I had was that it was totally inapplicable to utilize rhetoric of a previous time and place to address where we were and what we needed to address. It was clearly applicable to China at a time and place. It was going to turn off most of your audience. They didn't want to hear that.

258

JOE URGO

Jan and the old leadership ran out of ideas. They stopped hanging around. They didn't know what to do. What was required was more of an analysis.

SHELDON RAMSDELL

We were not communist. At that time, if you read Carl Rogers's stuff—this is Mr. *Esquire* magazine, *GQ*, you understand? This guy is not a political radical. None of us were. We were just pissed off.

I think from the beginning, the main interest in the back of our minds was problems at home. Things were happening that made you pay attention to issues. I read the Malcolm X book . . . King being killed. You realized there is more here involved than we've been saying. There's more involved than just stopping the war. It's working-class kids, coming home totally fucked-up, [who] can't believe their government anymore. . . . I mean, we want them to believe in something. Some kind of system that's going to help you live.

BOBBY MULLER

The process of radicalization within VVAW was very, very quick, and very intense. I started, like I think a lot of us did, simply saying: The war is wrong. Then going to: Wait a second—it wasn't that the war was the problem, but the war was a symptom of a problem. The problem was this society, the government, the thinking and the institutions, the educational system—and click, click, click, you rapidly went through this evolution of consciousness from what you first thought was the problem to becoming what was symptomatic of much deeper problems.

Where at first you were concerned about what happened to the Americans—you know, my guys—it didn't take very long until you understood: My God, look at the conduct of the war; look at how we whacked these people. We had to speak—we all did—about the racism of the war, in that they're gooks, they're dinks, they're slopes, and all of that stuff, and show the indifference to the people.

BARRY ROMO

I considered myself a Marxist, but very vulgar. I hadn't done very much reading. It's more a question of siding against imperialism, of knowing what bombers do to people, of seeing inequities, of seeing racism, of people calling me a commie when I was antiwar. It didn't scare me. It had the opposite effect. It made me think: Wait a minute—are all the commies antiwar? [Laughs.]

I remember going on a march against the Nazis in Marquette Park [in Chicago]. We went to bars and talked and argued with people about why they should be antifascist. The Nazis are screaming, and they go, "There's whites with the niggers; there's whites with the niggers. They're communists. Communists have been race mixers and for niggers' rights forever." OK, if it's a choice between you and people marching with black people, the choice is easy. [Laughs.]

MIKE McCAIN

You start learning history. I read the biography of Kim Il Sung, the history of the Labor Party of Albania, and all of Marx, all of Mao, all of Lenin and Emma Goldman. We also read Locke and Galbraith. That was a way of understanding what was going on and what we were supposed to do. Everything is connected.

MIKE GOLD

We became more political. We were reading more stuff. If you went to college, you were studying Marxism and socialism. But we didn't think America was ready for revolution. We had seen the belly of the beast—the military. We knew how difficult it would be to change. We knew about the preponderance of force and what it could do.

Some guys started to talk about violence, and that's what we were targets for . . . to get us violent as crazy vets. But the guys I knew in VVAW were tremendously constructive . . . wanted to build rather than destroy. A lot of guys wanted to go back to Vietnam and help rebuild. We wanted to do things in the community. There was an overwhelming sense of that kind of stuff.

We understood that as veterans, we had something to say. . . . Recognizing the United States as an imperialist power, we knew that there were going to be other situations we would have to stop. We felt the way to do that was by organizing veterans by doing something. That's what we did do.

DANNY FRIEDMAN

I started getting political, but not in a serious way. It was more like a glorious adventure. I met some girl, and she was more serious about politics. She would read Mao to me in bed and shit like that. I thought the Red Book was kind of cool, but I never got into serious study groups or anything. I had a general awareness that socialism—communism—is like an ideal situation that isn't practiced in Russia or China; but philosophically, it's better than what's happening today.

I was the angry young man that embraced any and every cause, even the Palestinians, who I was sympathetic toward. I got into class struggle and support of national liberation struggles and stuff like that.

JOHN LINDQUIST

There was an honest element in VVAW that was becoming leftist and anti-imperialist. . . . Not all of us. I mean you could sit up and argue with me, and I don't want to hear the word revolution. I'd be holding my ears. I'm not kidding you. So you've got to realize, I represent a whole segment of the organization that didn't want to hear this stuff.

Spontaneous Combustion

JOE URGO

We broke through the media wall, and there was interest in putting us out there because we served some bigger interests—but it also meant thousands of vets now saw VVAW. New chapters were forming all over the place and people were independently doing all kinds of different things. Winter soldiers [hearings], demonstrations, and guerrilla theaters were happening all over the country.

SHELDON RAMSDELL

We didn't organize. We didn't have the money to, but the word would get out. Little chapters grew up . . . all over the country, and they'd tell us after the fact.

MIKE McCAIN

After Dewey Canyon III, people just started walking in saying, "My name is Joe Schmuck; I'm a Vietnam vet. I want to do something too. What can I do?" It was exponential growth. The membership of the organization was growing by leaps and bounds. We had a 50,000-member mailing list by 1972. They weren't necessarily people who came to chapter meetings, but people who came to fund-raisers and marches and events. There were some chapters that had 10 or 15 people, but there were some chapters that had 100 people in them. We could mobilize more people than anyone else in the United States at that point.

New York and the National Office

DANNY FRIEDMAN, ANN HIRSCHMAN, SHELDON RAMSDELL, MIKE GOLD

Danny Friedman (DF): I went with some friends of mine to Florida for spring break around Easter 1971. I started to hear on the news about the vets in Washington throwing the medals. When I heard about these guys in Washington, it just occurred to me that that was the greatest thing in the world to be doing. It made absolute sense.

As soon as I got back, I wrote down the phone number, from the radio, of VVAW. I went to the offices on Fifth Avenue. I walked in, and it was like a little cubbyhole of an office. Most of the guys were already in Washington. Madelyn Moore, Scott Moore, Joe Cheslio, Robby Dunne, Joe Hirsch, a lot of volunteers, girls, young people, older women were doing a lot of stuff. I just said, "Hey, I want to help. I'm a Vietnam vet." They said, "Welcome." I was like a leader all of a sudden.

John Kerry, Al Hubbard, Mike Oliver, and Jan [Barry] Crumb all came back. I started doing stuff with them. I was a full-time staff person for the national office. They gave us $50 a week for living expenses. We organized a Brooklyn chapter, and other chapters got started.

Ann Hirschman (AH): Vets were coming home, literally following you into VVAW, seeking out VVAW. We were starting to get guys who had heard of antiwar vets while they were still in Vietnam.

Being able to help somebody was the single most therapeutic thing that ever happened to any vet who came back. I'm convinced that first being heard and taken seriously, without shock, and then being able to help somebody else—I think that healed all the guys that ever get healed. I watched it happen. I was seeing guys like Dan and Eddie, the guys who had started out in the office, beginning to help the new guys. That was like a total kick for the guys who had already healed most of the obvious bleeding emotional wounds, to have guys come back that they knew they could help. This was wonderful. It's like leadership suddenly happened. Kaboom!

DF: We knew about PTSD before there was such a word. It was called post-Vietnam syndrome. We had rap groups with Arthur Egendorf. I'd sit in on some of those groups, but then I got tired of them. I said, "Ah, I ain't got no problems. I'll just kick some cop's ass; then I'll feel good." [Laughs.] I had a reputation of being a little bit of a rowdy guy, not exactly a pacifist.

Most of the guys I know who saw heavy combat and who were involved in VVAW early on did not have any serious PTSD problems, because there was a dealing with it up front; it was healing—while most of the people that I observed who did have serious PTSD problems are the kind of guys who came back and believed they were never there. They tried to get on with their lives, and years later the shit came back on them. They turned into heavy drinkers [and] druggies.

Sheldon Ramsdell (SR): We visited hospitals. Vets were coming home to lousy hospitals and lousy care, and that really became a big issue. We really got very pissed off.

DF: We took the VA over once in 1972, the first time—the same week that we took over the Statue of Liberty. Then in 1974 we did it again.

> *Why did you take over the Veterans Administration? What was the purpose of that?*

DF: The VA is supposed to be the advocate of the veterans. They weren't helping veterans.

> *Why not just call the director and say, Help us out?*

DF: Well, we met with the director. He blew us off.

    Both times, I orchestrated the strategic part of it. They knew we were coming, and we were still able to get in there because we did a lot of diversionary stuff. We had a list of demands: jobs and training, this and that. . . . We got busted on those takeovers.

Mike Gold (MG): We were doing draft counseling and selective service counseling.

DF: We had winter soldier investigations. We were doing guerrilla theater in the streets. We had marches through Brooklyn, Queens, Long Island. We had all sorts of hassles getting into Veterans Day parades [and] Memorial Day

Danny Friedman with a friend in Albany, New York, Thanksgiving 1972. The occasion was an antiwar fast, protest, and march: "Twenty-two inches of snow."

parades. They wouldn't let us march in the Veterans Day parades. They turned their backs on us. It was like we were outcasts—like we lost the war, you know. We're not real veterans. We had long hair and beards. I had very long, bushy hair and a very thick, heavy full beard. I used to wear a fatigue hat turned sideways with the flap up with a VVAW button on it right at the front.

MG: We marched in a Veterans Day parade in Astoria and got spit on.

AH: We started demonstrating at the United Nations frequently. They were about to debate Vietnam, and the vets thought they had some insight. So these guys want to meet with George Bush, who was then ambassador to the United Nations. We tried for two weeks to see George Bush. He would not talk to us.

DF: We had a formal position that the United States government had gone insane and we wanted the UN to take the United States government into custodianship.

VVAW members in the New York area tried for several weeks to meet with George Bush and the secretary general of the United Nations. After having been rebuffed numerous times, they took action to force Bush and the UN bureaucracy to listen to their demands. They chained themselves to the doors of the UN, took over some offices there, and held vigils in the offices they had seized. In each case, they were arrested and thrown off UN property.[18]

AH: After two weeks at the United Nations, the guys found out that there was going to be a dinner at the UN Association. It was a black-tie soup-and-fish affair at the Riverdale School in the Bronx, which is a very private school with a ballroom. So five of us decided that we would go have dinner with George.

The good thing about working with VVAW is that these guys were in the military; they knew how to plan an action. If you wanted to get busted, you planned to get busted. If you didn't want to get busted, you didn't get busted.

Me, Danny, Brian, Mark, and Pete got about five pints of blood [and] put it in plastic bags.

DF: We all piled into my little red Maverick. We drove around the school and checked it out. We figured out what we were going to do. The school was set up like on top of a hill. We parked the car at the bottom of the hill off the road and walked up to the back of the school. We met the students. They hid us in their dormitory building, which is next to the main building. It was inside a locked compound.

AH: We had been at the school all afternoon . . . hung out in the lounge and watched soap operas all afternoon with the guys and girls. There was a demonstration outside that was planned as a diversion.

DF: The cops were all outside . . . surrounding the building, and all the doors were chained from the inside. We were already inside. Then, when the dinner was starting to happen, . . . we went from the dormitory, through the basements, through a courtyard, through the kitchen of the other building, and came up inside the chained doors. We just walked right inside. There was Bush in his tuxedo and all these women in mink coats sitting at the dais.

AH: We didn't dress. When we arrived, they knew somebody different had come in, but that was OK—there was no security inside the hall. We came to dinner in a sedate and dignified way: "Yo, George, either you talk to Vietnam veterans about the war in Vietnam or the blood of these people will be on your head." We threw blood at him.

DF: They [the plastic bags] splattered against the wall, splattered all over Bush and the minks and everything.

What was the reaction?

AH: Shock. How dare we! Rich people don't move when they're in shock. Nobody had ever threatened them in that way before. We knew they weren't going to hurt us. These were rich people. As Danny said, "They're fairly ineffective."

Why do that?

AH: To get attention. We knew that we were never going to be able to affect George Bush's debate in the UN, but he was never going to be able to pretend that the United States was unanimous about this war.

DF: Then we just cut out of there, went back down the hill the way we came. We were back in the VVAW offices on 26th Street before anybody knew what happened. It was the greatest operation ever.
  We were also supporting all kinds of stuff. There were squatters' movements, the Young Lords Party, the Black Panther Party. . . . The Black Panthers had their own little subgroup of veterans up in Harlem. We used to meet with them and support their things.

AH: This was a time when the Panthers were having their free breakfast programs, and a lot of people were saying, "Yeah, we're trying to end the war, but what are we doing on our block? What are we doing in our community?"

We found that there was a huge problem in our neighborhood where the Brooklyn office was, which is where I lived. A lot of the kids had lead-poisoning problems. The city wanted to do something about it but was not acting.

Our community action consisted of testing every kid we could lay our hands on for blood lead. The Brooklyn chapter did it. We just recruited all these neighborhood teenagers who were a little scared of, and a little in awe of—in a healthy sense—these big veterans. The kids started hanging out, and we tried to help them. We had a fairly successful rate of testing. The teenagers adored these guys, and we said, "We need all the little kids," so they went home and got all their brothers and sisters and friends.

Why go into community action when this was a veterans' organization?

MG: Guys were altruistic. . . . I think it was also to do service and make a real connection with people in the community—to be trusted.

California

BARRY ROMO AND BILL BRANSON: SAN BERNARDINO
LEE THORN, JACK McCLOSKEY, AND BOB HANSON: SAN FRANCISCO

Barry Romo (BR): After Dewey Canyon III, we went to the airport. Our tickets didn't take us out till the next day. We were so hyped, we said, "All right, we'll sleep right here in the damn airport. We slept on the Mall; we'll sleep here!"

The head of whatever airline it was goes, "Well, come on, boys. I think I can help you. . . . There's a 747 leaving and there's extra seats; we'll put you on that. . . . We ended up in business section or something. There's all these businessmen, and we're just grungy. [They're] buying us drinks, giving us money, saying, "You guys are the best. You guys are the best goddamn things that are happening." It reinforced everything we had thought we were doing.

I get off the plane, and VVAW just mushroomed. After we threw our medals away, everybody wanted to belong to VVAW. I think we had about 600 people on the mailing list before we got to Dewey Canyon, and it grew to thousands.

We'd go on campuses and stick up leaflets saying we're going to be here. Teachers would sponsor us. People would contact us. It was spontaneous. You get four leaflets, you go on campus and pass the four of them out, and 200 people came to your fucking meeting.

[I] started organizing, going up and down the state, organizing and organizing about 20 hours a day, going places, showing movies—and having your eyes opened, because you came from San Bernardino, and even though you've been off to a war in a third world country, meeting people: you know, black people whose husbands are in jail on trumped-up charges, meeting Asian people. . . . I remember meeting one woman who's ill, and she goes, "I hate you and I love you at the same time." No sexual or boy-girl thing—just friends. And she goes, "I'm repelled because of what you've done to Asian people, but I love you because of what you're doing now." Things like that. Being opened up to all kinds of experiences. It was amazing.

Then, you had other experiences. I was kicked out of the school district in San Diego because I was a "bad" Vietnam vet, not like the "good" Vietnam vets. I went to a high school and rapped to them about Vietnam. I told people not to go in. A bunch of people came up afterward and said, "What can we do to mess the machine up?" So I said, "Well, if you're a girl, all you have to do is call up the draft board or write a letter, and say: Hi, my name is Jay, instead of Janet, and I'm eighteen years old, and I'm not going to register for the draft." I said, "You're not doing anything illegal, but they have to investigate it."

The John Birch society organized against me, and I get a call later in San Bernardino: "Barry, they're threatening to fire this teacher because of your speaking out against the war, and they're going to have a well organized parents' meeting to confront this whole issue. Would you come back and meet them?"

So I came back to the thing and gave the rap that I gave to them. I showed the movie I showed to them. It was a short version of the winter soldier film. [*Winter Soldier* was a film about the hearings, produced for VVAW in 1972 by an independent filmmaker.]

This teacher stands up, and they're all sort of quiet, and says, "Mr. Such-and-Such, why don't you speak up?" Mr. Such-and-Such had 20-some years in the Marine Corps—retired math teacher. He got up and he goes, "I went to Vietnam, but I was in logistics. I didn't see anything Mr. Romo is talking about because I was never in combat. I heard what Mr. Romo had to say, and there are two other vets besides myself who are on campus." He says, "I can't contradict Mr. Romo's line because he's said the truth."

They applauded and they fired the teacher. They treated me and this young woman teacher like a dog. I walked out and I cried. There was so much hate. They couldn't deal with the truth.

How did you keep on going in the face of abuse?

BR: The Vietnamese. They were being slaughtered. They were being killed day in and day out. They couldn't get away from the bombs, couldn't get away from people who wanted to cut their ears, couldn't get away from the rapists, and they couldn't get away from the war. No matter how nice the life was for us, I knew that they were dying.

Bill Branson (BB): We came back with this incredible feeling of unity. We were a collective in southern California. We lived together and worked together, but it was amorphous. It wasn't a Stalinist organization, but we could see the need for something.

There was an organization formed in California with regional coordinators. I was regional coordinator for a while. There was shit going on everywhere. We produced tons of literature and participated in all kinds of coalitions all throughout California.

We got involved in Gary Lawton.[19] We were involved in freeing Angela Davis. We bodyguarded the guy who put up the bond for Angela Davis. A bunch of the guys in the LA chapter drove around with him. They had M-16s and stuff, a ton of guns.

Lee Thorn (LT): I raised some money and got together a bunch of people in my house in September or October of 1971. I developed a strategy for organizing the west coast. First, we had to find out who was the chief architect of Dewey Canyon III and pay him and steal him. Nobody from the Bay Area that we knew of had gone to that. It turned out that there were a few guys from LA who had gone to it, so they had already organized a VVAW chapter down there, but we didn't know it until I went back and heard about it.

Jack McCloskey (JMC): We heard about VVAW, but no way were we going to buy into them until we checked them out. Because of our own experience with the Pentagon and the Berkeley peace movement, which I think was much more radical and dogmatic than most parts of the country, we had a fear. We sent Lee Thorn to New York to find out what this fucking organization was about.

Lee went to New York and came back with information about VVAW. We decided then that our Vets for Peace chapter would become a chapter of VVAW. VVAW was a national organization and it would give us more credibility. We wanted to learn. These guys had been at it a little longer. They had some experience. We brought Mike Oliver and Bob Hanson out here.

LT: They came out, and we set up a strategy to organize from Washington, Oregon, northern California, Arizona, Hawaii, and Alaska. We decided we were going to have a demo so that we could get in the papers. That would be a way to get the vets out of the woodwork and join VVAW. We needed publicity. We knew there were a lot of vets who wanted to do shit, especially after Dewey Canyon III.

First thing we did was we got ourselves in the Veterans Day parade in 1971.

JMC: We had two legal permits to march in the Veterans Day parade here in San Francisco.

Bob Hanson: The whole march was devoted to Vietnam veterans. We were in the march as VVAW. We were at the end of the march, riding in a flatbed truck.

LT: There's all these PL [Progressive Labor Party] guys on the truck, who of course weren't telling us they were on the truck. They got everybody yelling "Ho, Ho, Ho Chi Minh is going to win," and we're in the middle of a Veterans Day Parade . . . really pissed me off. The cops are like half Vietnam vets, right? Pissing everybody off.

We just got off the truck in front of the reviewing stand. Jack was going to run up to the reviewing stand and grab the microphone. I don't remember what the hell he was going to say, but first we had to get into ranks so we had some kind of order so that [if] we had to deal with some cops, we would be in a position to do it. They had all kinds of cops there. I had the bullhorn. I was in front, and I couldn't get the line straight. I said, "Let's go." When I started moving up . . . this guy over here [pointing to the right], who it turns out was a cop, was surging.

Anyway, this captain had this other cop run at me. He started from about 20 yards away, ran at me, jumped me, and came down on my head with his club. He was trying to kill my ass. So I go down. Mike Oliver, who's got shrapnel all up and down his back, jumps over on top of me and protects me. They start hitting Mike on the back. Most of the people split. Jack and Jim O'Donnell stayed, and they distract the cops away from Mike. Mike carries me off to the side, and then Hanson takes them all on. What a horrible film [this episode was filmed by a news team] of Hanson on his back, kicking like this. [Demonstrates.] . . . There's six cops on him. We got beat up.

JMC: Myself, Mike Oliver, Lee Thorn, Jim O'Donnell, Bob Hanson got the shit beat out of us. About four or five of us had to go to the hospital. Each individual did what they had to do. I started to struggle. I'm not going to stand there and let some cop beat my fucking head. We never took it. I know there were some cops who wanted to kick our ass, but there were other cops who were very reluctant.

LT: Finally, this black sergeant comes along and calls them off. Meantime, I'm bleeding like a pig, I got a concussion, and I'm thinking to myself: Boy, this is going to be great TV.

[To Jack McCloskey.] What was your reaction to this?

JMC: We expected to have more respect because we were veterans. All it did was strengthen us. We sued the police department and we won. We settled out of court, and we should have taken them all the way. But the next year we had over 250 Vietnam Veterans that marched under the VVAW banner legitimately in the parade. [They] didn't fuck with us at all.

LT: All of a sudden, all these vets came out of the woodwork because we got a lot of publicity. By December we used to have like 30 guys at a meeting here in San Francisco, and at that time we had coordinators. I raised enough money that we could actually pay people. So we paid them, four or six people, like $300 a month.

JMC: Our first office was in this place called Project One at Tenth and Howard, which is four blocks away from the Tenderloin district in San Francisco.

We got guys coming in off the streets. We got guys coming back from Vietnam looking for us. They heard about us by word of mouth, by them seeing us in demonstrations. They'd read about us. We got a lot of good publicity by friendly reporters that were Vietnam veterans.

How did you keep all those people together?

JMC: That led to discussion, incredible discussions. That was part of the beauty of it—people threatening to throw each other out windows, people coming from the heart. . . . Some people were against the war because they saw it as a waste of people. Others were against it because of some political reasons. Others were against it because they saw their buddies being killed for nothing. We were talking about what our experiences were in Vietnam, how fucked it was, how we didn't want to see other people going through that experience, how we saw ourselves being treated when we got home.

LT: The local meetings were always heated. It was not so much ideological battles as tactical battles. I was probably one of the more moderate people. The range wasn't so large, and it was left all the way. I knew it was a civil war we had no business in. I believed that "imperialist" was probably the correct terminology, but I didn't think that using those terms in public statements was a good idea. That made me "right."

We almost always drank during meetings and smoked dope. So it could get pretty hot. We tried to work on a consensus basis.

JMC: We started working more closely with the peace movement. But the peace movement always wanted us to lead demonstrations, so again, we were put on point. Why the fuck are they telling us to go up front? Because of our visibility? Because of our credibility? Or because if shit happens, we're the ones that get it again? [Laughs.] So we always had that mixed feeling.

We were not only involved in stopping the war, but we started getting more involved in the political consciousness. . . . You can't stop the war unless you change the way people look at things. I was involved here at City College and started working with Asians, Chicanos, blacks, women, and gays at the college. I remember one thing we did was not to have teachers hired unless we had input into the hiring. I remember going up before the board and talking about the problems of black people. Joselyn Wong, a young nineteen- or twenty-year-old Asian woman, going up and talking about the problems of Vietnam veterans. Charlie Smith, who was black, talking about the problems of gays, and Charlie was a straight black male. It blew their minds.

I started doing the counseling, what we called "rap groups." At this point, I was getting my degree in psychology. I saw these guys coming to meetings drunk, punching each other out, punching their wives and partners out.

We started rap groups here in January of 1971 with Vets for Peace. When we started the rap groups, we started with basically left-wing veterans that had problems readjusting.

Did you ever approach the VA or other groups to start counseling programs?

JMC: Yeah—fuck, yeah—we approached the VA. We were told to fuck off. The VA was not offering that. They didn't want us to exist.

A lot of these psychologists and psychiatrists that were working for the Veterans Administration would freak out. They couldn't grasp some of these stories that Vietnam veterans were telling them, of killing, of slaughter. These were people that got college deferments and then went to graduate school and got their degrees. They didn't understand Vietnam. They were afraid of us in the sense that they thought we'd go off in any second, which I blame on the media. The image that was put on us was: Here's all these crazy, psyched-out, doped-up Vietnam veterans that are slaughterers. The rap groups got so good that we started showing how fucked-up the mental health system in the VA was.

Then I formed, with Rob Bodelin and David Harris, a group called Twice Born Men. We got our name from a letter Phillip Berrigan wrote, talking about people going through the prison or military system and coming through that system facing their fears and working themselves through those fears, being twice born.

We had a farm right outside of Fresno called Raisin City. We had 60 acres of land. Joan Baez donated a prefabricated house to us that a lot of Vietnam veterans and ex-cons came up and helped build. The farm was a catharsis. We would bring all these Vietnam veterans, all these ex-cons, and then we would start bringing juvenile [offenders] up, and we would grow things. The catharsis was these people had all this trauma in their lives, and they would plant things and see this shit grow. We had the farm for about four years, but we lost the farm because none of us knew about management. But the farm was successful in the sense that it got all these veterans and all these ex-cons and all these kids getting back in touch with themselves. Instead of destruction, seeing construction. That's what Twice Born Men was about.

Then in 1974 , there was five guys working out here through what they called VISTA. Four of them were Vietnam vets. Three of them happened to be old VVAW members. They were all interns through the VA, and part of their training was to have different community organizations. So I came in and did a talk about Twice Born Men. Three weeks later they quit the VA and they asked me and I went in with them, and we started Swords to Plowshares.

The rap groups came out of VVAW; Twice Born Men came out of the rap groups; Swords to Plowshares came out of Twice Born Men and the ex-members of VVAW that were working for the VA.

Swords to Plowshares was developed as a full-service organization aiding veterans by offering counseling, job placement services, and a variety of other programs. It still functions in San Francisco.

Oregon

LINDA ALBAND

The word would get out and people would write in—which is how I got involved in Oregon, because Michael [McCusker] had a whole box of letters from people that never got answered. People would write to him because he was very charismatic, but he's not an organizer. . . . These were guys that were totally isolated. People were suffering really severe sleep disorders. Some of these dudes were so bad, you couldn't like tap them on the shoulders when they needed to be woken up without the fear of maybe getting strangled.

Things really took off in Oregon during the People's Army Jamboree, because that's where we were prominent. People donated money for the People's Army Jamboree, so there was some equipment and stuff that was purchased, like a printing press; but there was no structure, there was no office, there was no money. We didn't have an office or anything. We just did it.

Oregon was pretty small. We had people in Ashland, Eugene, Springfield, and Portland. And then we had contacts with the scattered vets who lived out in eastern Oregon. I think the chapter in Eugene, for a while, was involved in Democratic Party politics. One of the chapters was involved in setting up some sort of rap groups among themselves. We worked with a chapter in Vancouver, Washington, who were pretty heavily involved with vocations for social change . . . and we worked with people in Seattle. We just worked with whoever was there. We worked in a lot of different areas.

Wisconsin

ANNIE BAILEY AND JOHN LINDQUIST

Annie Bailey (AB): We were active in VVAW since May 1971. Right away, we picked up on the alienation between a lot of vets and their families—guys who were married, came back, and were having a lot of problems with their wives, or with their families. That's where we started, right from the very beginning. Within six months of forming VVAW, we had a family night.

John Lindquist (JL): I started being a veterans' counselor in 1972. I worked with vets on the street to make 20 hours a week as my part-time city job as a student under the Nixon Emergency Employment Act, the Veterans Aiding Veterans program. They give me 5- by 7-inch cards with names and return addresses of people. I called them, rang their doorbells, and explained their benefits to them; [I'd] see if they have any problems and refer them.

AB: He also wore his VVAW button everywhere.

JL: And recruited a bunch of people; but I didn't care, though, whether I recruited them or not. You could tell when you ran into some right-wing dudes. I just wouldn't talk politics with them.

AB: We discovered early on that Vietnam veterans were militantly antiorganization. The more organized you wanted to be, the less response you got.

JL: It's a flow-through organization. Vets come in, have a good time, do some demos, find it too political, and leave; or vets come in to do their thing and leave. Some come in and stay for a long time and become leadership. We don't care what you want to do. You put in what you feel comfortable with. That's our model, at least here.

You're seeing the flavor of Milwaukee. It's been like an extended family. The strength of this chapter for the longest time was its "extended family-ness."

What else were you doing?

JL: We were doing every antiwar demo; guerrilla theater; there was a speakers' bureau, a slide show, discharge upgrading, . . . rap groups. . . . VVAW had already started the first rap groups with Lifton. McCloskey suggested that we consolidate a national clearinghouse on PVS [post-Vietnam syndrome], so I compiled the PVS library. At the same time I was putting together the library, Jack was putting together rap groups in San Francisco . . . and Jack played an instrumental role in the DSM III printing of this as a disability.

> *DSM III was the Diagnostic and Statistical Manual of Mental Disorders, Third Edition (1980), published by the American Psychiatric Association (APA). It was in this edition that APA first officially recognized posttraumatic stress disorder as affecting combat veterans.*

AB: We declared war on the VA. The war on the VA was our shining light.

JL: We took over the VA about every other month. . . . We were in the newspaper and on television more often than the mayor.

> *Why take over the VA?*

JL: Because the treatment was so bad. We didn't even have methadone for people who were strung out on heroin.

Takeover of a VA facility in Chicago, 1975. Annie Bailey is seated in front (chin in hand).

Nobody else was saying anything about these issues?

JL: Not locally. Not the traditional vets. There was no other Vietnam veterans' organization. There were all the traditional ones.

Texas

TERRY DuBOSE, JOHN KNIFFIN, TOM WETZLER, DAVE CLINE

Terry DuBose (TDB): Washington brought people out of the woodwork. Right after Dewey Canyon III we got back here and the LBJ Library dedication had been announced. Westmoreland was coming, Nixon was coming, Johnson was here, everybody who was anybody was going to be here. So we started planning this protest and we started using the name VVAW, but we didn't have a charter with them. They thought we were SMC and Vets for Peace. They said, "You can't use our name." We said, "Why?" "Because we don't deal with SMC and YSA [Young Socialist Alliance]."[20] We said, "We're not SMC or YSA." We finally convinced them that if we gave up Vets for Peace, we would use VVAW. At that point we switched.

John Kniffin (JK): We had 40 or 50 who were all vets.

Tom Wetzler (TW): There was guerrilla theater going on periodically in places, following up with flyers. You know: "An American infantry platoon just passed through your town. If you were Vietnamese, XYZ would have happened to you."

TDB: And there were a lot of churches, the Unitarian churches, and of course American Friends, who brought food. We saw a lot of support, but there were people who drove by and threw bottles too.

TW: The first action I ever did was the RAW March from Fort Worth to Dallas. [RAW stands for "Rapid American Withdrawal." The march took place on Labor Day 1971.] The American Nazi Party blocked the street at one point.

JK: I think there were three of them with a big banner that said "Death to the Red Scum." So first we said, "Let's kick their ass." Then we said, "No, let's just laugh at them." So we marched out of this park, past these Nazis, singing Hava Nagila.

Dave Cline: We tried to work with family members of GIs. Married people were living off base. There was this one trailer court that they were living in that was really substandard housing—rats and everything. We attempted to organize a tenants' union.

One of the features of GI organizing that was constantly frustrating is that, since it's not a permanent constituency, people were constantly being discharged; you'd get to a certain level and then fall back. There was not an organization that could be built. In a sense, you ended up planting seeds rather than building an organization.

Ohio ·

PETE ZASTROW: CINCINNATI
BILL DAVIS: COLUMBUS

Pete Zastrow (PZ): When I went home, I guess the chapter of VVAW in Cincinnati, which at that point was just getting started, must have gotten my name that I had joined. They phoned me and told me they were having a meeting in a church basement. They were planning a march at that point to a military supply facility in Indiana. So I went to the meeting and listened.

How would you describe the political line, or the political approach, of the Cincinnati chapter?

PZ: Naively antiwar and, among more conscious elements, consciously anti-imperialist—without hardly being able to define it. We couldn't quote Lenin on what imperialism was. Some of us could, but most of us couldn't. I think we had a sense of history because we very much saw ourselves as patriots, to be able to go back and point out where the United States had done this time and time again—and as Vietnam veterans, saying, "Look, we're atoning for something our government did there and which we did again in Vietnam."

We had a pretty rousing chapter in Cincinnati; we were all over the place. We would do things constantly. The meetings, which were held weekly, were attended by about 25 people, which was a very good size, because we could draw on a lot more than that. We got involved with the whole antiwar peace movement in the city.

One of the first things I ever did was: They asked me to be the representative for this organization called the Cincinnati Peace Coalition. I became chairman of that coalition. The Peace Coalition actually turned into kind of the heads of all of the major antiwar groups in the city. It became influential in being able to turn out fairly large numbers of people.

Did people have any anger toward you as a veteran?

276

PZ: No. It was something quite different: "We were so glad to have you on our side, because you could tell us the truth, or you could tell other people the truth. What a wonderful thing that is, that you're going to come to our meetings," and so forth.

It was a remarkable experience for me. It made you feel very good. Respect was part of it, but it was more than that. It was kind of feeling that you got from other people because here you are representing that organization [VVAW].

I remember feeling the same way the first time I gave one of these big outdoor public speeches—it was an antiwar rally, and it would have been a relatively early one—getting up there and speaking to all these people as a Vietnam vet, because VVAW had not been in Cincinnati, basically, before then. All these people were so excited. They loved it. The response was just so great. I'm sure it didn't come from anything I said, but because of what I was representing. Boy, was that ever a shot of adrenaline. That kind of thing inspires one. That's pretty good impetus to keep doing it.

We had an [irrefutable] sort of position, which says something about truth. It was hard to beat the credibility of all these veterans; it's so much the key to where VVAW comes from. People could never beat that back, and even in those cases where we would be put on a program with an ROTC recruiter, who had also been to Vietnam, they could not say, "Oh, yes, the Vietnamese really like to have us here and we're fighting in the name of truth or justice." They couldn't. We were good enough at debating to score point after point after point. So after a while they just stopped coming, and we ended up always talking by ourselves.

Besides that, we did all kinds of things. We did things like go to the veterans' hospital and take people in wheelchairs to a baseball game—that sort of thing. We organized and demonstrated, mostly around the war.

We were telling them about the war. That's what we knew about. That's what we could talk to people about.

Was it a moral commitment that kept you going, or was it a political commitment?

PZ: I don't think you could disconnect those. It was a social commitment, too. We did become friends. We partied together. We did pretty near everything together.

We grew. We made money. We bought a huge printing press. Nobody was working. I still had money from Vietnam. Other people were on the GI Bill. It was a different period of time. We might get a part-time job to make a few bucks, but people didn't have families. You somehow didn't feel that you had to earn a living, and you got by pretty cheaply. If you ate rice and beans for a week, so what?

We were everywhere. I'm not joking. That was our life. That's what we did. It was full-time. Everything we thought about was what we could do for the organization. Just going to the meetings was damn near a full-time commitment. We had all the regular VVAW meetings, and the Peace Coalition meetings, and committee meetings in each of those; and then you had to go off and speak at other meetings, which was a major part of our work.

VVAW had the bodies and the commitment and the people who were willing to devote huge amounts of time and energy. We would go off to the county fair in Hamilton County, which is Cincinnati, and spend five days with a booth. We had to raise the money, and we did. We sold our newspapers and buttons and talked to people.

We'd spend immense hours at the unemployment office, talking to people, handing things out, working with a group called Unemployed Workers Organizing Committee and the October League. We worked with both of them because we were nonpartisan. We had one of these large industrial areas where we would go at five or four-thirty in the morning and dodge the cars as they came to the intersection, to hand out leaflets about something or other.

Our biggest event was actually getting arrested for marching in a Memorial Day parade in 1971 or 1972, because we wouldn't take down our VVAW banner. This was North College Hill, a Cincinnati suburb, and the parade organizers said, "If you carry that banner, we'll call the police." We had made the right applications. We had done it pretty much by the book. I think there were six of us who were eventually arrested for that. Of course the ACLU got on the case immediately. It was a big deal, and we made headlines all over the place. I guess it was "Four Antiwar Veterans Arrested."

I think we spent all of half an hour in the North College Hill jail. We went through a preliminary hearing, and eventually it was dropped. But shortly thereafter, we had bought a booth at a local fair. It was a fairly good-sized fair. Anyhow, we had our newspapers, and what we found was that many many people had heard about this. Our name had gotten out as a result of this. So we had all these people who wanted to sign up, or get our information. It was in a lot of ways the best thing that happened to us. For the organization, it was tremendous.

They [the establishment press] kept making stupid mistakes. There was a columnist in Cincinnati—Frank Weigle, I think, was his name—who was just really a redneck, right-wing dog, who picked up on this kind of stuff and started giving us this kind of publicity. Negative, but it was still the publicity we needed. "These sissy veterans are going to hold a parade at such and such. . . . " OK, fine, we'll take it any way we can get it.

We kind of, I guess, respected one another. He would say, "Tell me when you're going to do something. I may attack it, but at least I'll write about it." He used to argue with me about, you know, "You're doing things all wrong." We were covered fairly extensively in his column. It actually became a very good publicity device, and he knew that, I'm sure. He was a stupid dog, but a good stupid dog.

You were, then, aware of the fact that you could use the press, that kind of information.

PZ: Oh, sure. Absolutely. VVAW has, I think, historically been pretty damn good, in our own small way, at manipulating the media. We got it [coverage] time and time again. Of course, at the same time we say how the media ignores us and on and on and on, but they don't. If the people who run the media had had the sense to say in the first place, "Don't even pay any attention to these people," of course we never would have gotten any notice. They could have, because we were never hundreds of thousands.

Bill Davis grew up in Columbus, Ohio, in a working-class family. He joined the Air Force in August 1966 and remained on active duty until August 1970. For a year—from February 1968 to February 1969—he was in the Tactical Airlift Squadron, stationed at Vung Tau Army Airfield in Vietnam, where among his other duties he was assigned to play football. The following year (February 1969 to February 1970), he was stationed in Thailand. He joined VVAW in June 1970. He was interviewed in his home in Oak Park, Illinois, a suburb of Chicago.

Bill Davis (BD): I fell in with the GI paper and stuff in Ohio with Mark Rovic from Columbus, who was an antiwar activist and by and large liberal by his analysis, which wasn't a bad thing. I was just filled with this pent-up rage and anger and frustration. I was more of a "Let's attack and burn everything and snatch everything" sort of guy.

In Columbus, Ohio, we were more homogeneous. We worked together much better than any other place. We were under a state of siege there. We were fighting for our lives every minute there.

Why?

BD: Columbus was a very unique place in that it had state police training barracks; regional Army reserve center; the state National Guard facility; a military side to the airport; and then the Air Force base of course, the Strategic Air Command, and all the security and stuff that went with that; and a defense supply construction center—just an endless array of military suppliers, just an incredibly huge concentration of military and police forces there. So what you had there, basically, was this huge concentration of police and military force and very conservative town. They lynched union organizers right up to the 1950s. They'd been in the grip for years and years of a single mayor who was a fatherlike authoritarian figure, not nearly as progressive as Daley.

Two views of Bill Davis in Vietnam.

In 1972, I wasn't in any real leadership position. That summer, with the Republican convention and stuff, we had to step forward when [Bill] Crandle and some other guys declared the [Columbus] organization dead. Crandle had been in the national office when it was like this large group of people who worked with each other off and on in the New York area. He was also the regional coordinator of Ohio. He went to the Columbus papers and said the VVAW was no longer a functioning organization. He started to work organizing Vets for McGovern. To this day he claims that they did that just to motivate us.

We objected. We didn't agree. We had to kick the organization in the ass. We attended the meeting in Cincinnati in the late spring of 1972. That was the first time I met Zastrow. I got to know some of the people from around the state who I'd never met before.

So we pulled together shards of the old organization and moved forward to a more militant organization, recruiting more vets and new people and stuff. We are becoming more and more left in 1972, 1973. At this point you're looking at a core of 35 to 40 people, with a real active membership of 150 to 175 people for big events.

We moved out of the campus area, because at that point we were less and less a campus organization and more and more a community organization. It was a mile or so from the university area and still close enough for us to be connected to the university. We were still an organization on campus, pulling thousands and thousands of dollars out of the university. We were very solvent. All of it was accountable; nothing illegal was done with it. People didn't go on extravagant trips. Trips to the national meetings were always paid out of pocket. Expenses that were incurred were documented. We were sending a lot of money to the national organization at that point. We were paying for the printing of the papers.

We were talking to everyone. We couldn't make enough churches, high schools, suburban gatherings. We moved out and established chapters in Athens, Lima, and made connections all over the state. We were responding to people who came forward to us. There were people in those areas who began to organize.

We had always done guerrilla theater. The guerrilla theater actually started under the more liberal groupings of VVAW. It played well on the campuses, but occasionally we'd do it down by the state capital. Some poor person would be standing at a bus stop and suddenly a bunch of vets would jump him and beat him to the ground and drag him off, as a suspected communist.

We were denied entrance in the Fourth of July parade in Arlington, Ohio, which was one of the whoop-de-do suburbs. We'd always tried to get in and got a lot of publicity, because we were always denied access to the parade. There were a lot of people saying, "They were vets. They deserve to be here"; on the other hand, they were saying, "These guys are radicals. They're going to disrupt the parade." We said, "No, just let us in; we won't disrupt it." They wouldn't let us in, so we really disrupted it . We kept disrupting every year until they finally said, "Jesus, let these guys in the parade." So we were finally allowed in the parade.

Even more than the west coast, we were leading the country in GI work, direct organizing and counseling. We did Lockhorn. We had commercials on all the rock stations, "If you're AWOL, or you're going through town, stop and see us; maybe we can help you." We had hundreds of walk-ins on a monthly basis: "Hey, I'm AWOL. What can you guys do for me?"

And what did you do?

BD: Made it clear that they had to go back and then start the paperwork on various kinds of discharges. After we did like an induction sort of interview, we'd try to see what they were more suited for. More left people in the organizations were opposed to the CO stuff, but it was the best one. I'd tell guys straight out: I don't care if you are or not—just lie, if that's what it takes to get out.

There were obvious people who were hardship. There were people who for mental or physical reasons never should have got into the military. We were looking at McNamara's "One Hundred Thousand." [This program increased the pool of draftees by lowering the requirements for enlistment.] It was active duty initially; and then, as the war was winding down, then it became National Guardsmen, ROTC people, reservists—it was just a flood.

We worked a lot with the Guard and reserve. The reserve and Guard units wouldn't meet every weekend, there'd be different ones, but we had enough info: we knew which ones were meeting at what time, and we'd be there leafleting [at] four o'clock in the morning. We had a new counselor at the counseling center, and we'd have press releases out—you know, "VVAW Expands Counseling." All it took was two ROTC recruits, and it was, "VVAW Undermining the ROTC Program at OSU," which brought us a flood of ROTC people.

We started branching out into more class-oriented strike support. That had to do with the members who came into the chapter. A lot of us had been students, but we had to get jobs. The bulk of the guys were working-class. We supported striking workers at Borden's. The Borden strike was a natural; there were a lot of vets there.

We had a whole committee on turning out publicity and press releases. We made a lot of contacts in the local media, primarily with the rock stations. The newspapers were pretty conservative, and the TV; they didn't like us worth a damn, but they couldn't ignore us. Some of the stuff we did was just too good, whether they liked it or not.

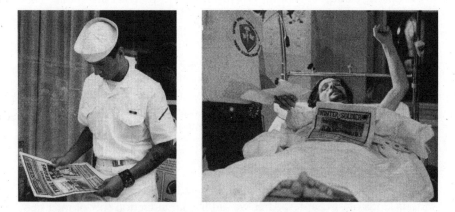

A Marine Corpsman in the Great Lakes and a hospitalized Vietnam veteran (probably in Detroit or Long Beach) reading VVAW's newsletter, *Winter Soldier,* 1973.

We worked in the VA hospitals. We did the papers and leaflets whenever necessary—demos, confrontations, visiting, whatever we could to get inside.

Were you successful in any respects?

BD: We broadened the organization. We brought a lot more guys who were vets into the organization. We gained a rep as a militant organization with realistic goals.

We had all the guards disarmed [in the VA hospitals]. Even though they were federal protective service, they were little better than rental cops. They were dangerous. These guys went berserk, Maced whole waiting rooms when they were trying to get us out. Fights and brawls were breaking out right inside on the wards of the VA.

Columbus chapter was very successful in the various things that it did.

Kansas

RON SABLE

My first contact with VVAW was seeing the broadcast of their going to Washington, throwing away the medals, Kerry testifying, and all that. I said, Boy, this is the organization for me—and I immediately found the Kansas City people after they returned from Washington. For the next year I spent nearly all my active free time with VVAW.

There were dozen or so core, key people. One of the interesting things about VVAW is that you had people all over the political spectrum. Kansas City mirrored that. Some people had political experience and political insights into the war; you had Reagan or Nixon supporters. There was one guy who had a lot of CIA-type experience before having served in Vietnam . . . assassination stuff and that sort of thing.

How would you classify yourself politically?

It shifted much farther to the left. . . . Nixon came to Kansas City at one point. . . . We organized a demonstration. We didn't have that many people, but let me tell you, the number of cops that were out and the response we got demonstrating against the president was startling. To me, as a middle-class kid, you grow up thinking the police are your friends. . . . This was the first time I was on the other side of that, and it was a revelation about what the experiences of many many people are with the police.

There was a VVAW delegation early in the summer of 1972 to Paris. I was one of those people. We were from all over the country. There were about 16 of us. This was a thing the Russell War Crimes Tribunal people had put

First peace meeting between VVAW and the NLF, Paris, 1971.

together. It was clearly a propaganda thing. We were getting together with all the veterans of the conflict to make peace because the peacemakers couldn't make peace.

The American government put a lot of pressure on the French government not to give visas to a lot of the other veterans. I don't think there were any Laotion or Cambodian veterans who participated in this. We met with the PRG and DRV delegations. [Respectively, the Provisional Revolutionary Government, formed by the NLF in 1969; and the Democratic Republic of Vietnam—that is, North Vietnam.] This was the first time that I had met people from all over the country. There are people from California who are Maoists . . . had the Red Book. . . . This was quite something to me. I came to understand that VVAW included people with a lot more political diversity than our Kansas City group.

The most important thing about the trip for me . . . was the realization that the government lies to you at official levels. The Vietnamese showed us pictures of the dikes that were bombed and literally on television, at that moment, Nixon was denying this. Later, he recanted, but it was this startling thing. . . . I mean, the president of the United States is lying publicly.

What we did for the year was a combination of demonstrations, public presentations—talking to high school civics classes, Lion's Club breakfasts about what it was all about. It was an educational function. We took over the city hall and hung the flag upside down. . . . Our demand there was a city council hearing, which we got. There wasn't that much political activity in Kansas City, so we were it.

The other thing was Cairo, Illinois. More than once that year, we gathered supplies together and trucked these down to southern Illinois. It was a very poor, depressed community. Here was the rhetorical community literally under siege by the police department. You could see the gunshot holes in the dwellings of these people. This was a war zone. It felt like that.

Cairo is a small town in southern Illinois, at the junction of the Ohio and Mississippi rivers; it was a poor community in which African-Americans suffered under what they perceived to be institutionalized racism. In April 1969, these African-Americans began a nonviolent boycott of white-dominated businesses; the white community reacted against the boycott, and some whites harassed blacks and even attacked them with firearms. VVAW members became involved in this conflict in 1971 by providing food, clothing, and medical supplies to the black citizens of Cairo. This support began as a midwestern project but was quickly adopted by the national office in New York. Cairo is one example of many projects that were initiated by a chapter or region and then taken on by the organization as a whole.

You also mentioned Cairo. It's not a veterans' issue; it's not a Vietnam issue. Why do anything in Cairo?

Sheldon Ramsdell: In Cairo, the issue was oppressed people doing something to help themselves by boycotting. . . . It related to the war and what we were doing to the Vietnamese. We saw direct connections. It was a minority community in distress. . . . The veterans felt the same way. I even felt it, for Christ's sake, as privileged as I am. It was very important that we were bonding with the black community. It made a lot of sense to go there with clothing and medicine. We loaded up trucks and joined a caravan and got down there and saw the oppression . . . the sheriff types and the rednecks with their guns, and they're watching us.

It was really an education for me and a lot of the media types.

The growth of VVAW in these states was reflected in other regions across the country. Chapters were formed in every state of the nation; the most active chapters were in cities with a strong antiwar movement and a history of left-wing activity. Although differences emerged among the various chapters over the goals of the organization and the role of members, these difference remained submerged while the war continued to rage.

285

VVAW not only grew nationally but also attracted members stationed at military bases around the globe as well as in Vietnam. In fact, the influence of VVAW in Vietnam contributed to the collapse of the American fighting forces there.

VVAW in Vietnam

JOE URGO, ANNIE LUGINBILL, DANNY FRIEDMAN,
BOB HANSON, LEE THORN

Joe Urgo (JU): The organization had grown very big in Vietnam over 1971. The *Playboy* ad [in February 1971] made it grow bigger. We were trying to reach the GIs. We were trying to encourage the resistance, and we were mailing letters in batches to these guys. We would try to send them as much literature as they asked for and anything else; but we didn't in some places—we were so busy organizing vets.

Annie Luginbill: You'd be surprised how many pieces of illicit information managed to make their way into various barracks and ships and everywhere else. CAMP [Chicago Area Military Project] used to send bundles of newspapers to ships [and] to constellations, and they'd get there. We'd get letters from GIs and it was like, "I got this copy from my neighbor who got it from this person." It works.

JU: I had this experience meeting a black guy in the vet center who told me his entire air rescue unit in Vietnam was in VVAW. We had one guy spend his whole year there doing nothing but working on some VVAW chapters. There was another guy who was doing full-time organizing, going around in an aircraft; but we didn't know about him until he came back and told us this.

While I was on the trip to North Vietnam in August of 1971, I was given a statement the Front [DRV and NLF] had sent to all its commanders in the field: instructions that any American soldier who wears a button or any physical display of a button of a rifle turned upside down, or carries his rifle in the down position, should not be shot at.

People started to wear the VVAW emblem as big as their T-shirt. We saw pictures of the logo as large as the shirt. They were having the mama-sans sew the VVAW emblem on their fatigue shirts. A guy came back and told us that you can actually go down and buy the patch [VVAW] in the markets.

Danny Friedman: We were getting a lot of mail coming in from guys still in Vietnam. Whole units, companies, and platoons [were] signing up. Firebase Pace signed up. They were responding to us en masse. Vietnamization was

In the last ten years, over 335,000 of our buddies have been killed or wounded in Vietnam. And more are being killed and wounded every day. We don't think it's worth it.

We are veterans of the Vietnam War. We have fought and bled from the swamps and hills of Vietnam to the plains of Cambodia. We have seen our buddies die there. And we can no longer remain silent.

We have seen the Vietnam War for ourselves. And from what we have seen, we believe that it is wrong, unjustifiable and contrary to the principle of self-determination on which our nation was founded.

We believe that the Vietnam War is a civil war—a war in which the United States has no right or obligation to intervene. We believe that the Saigon Government must stand or fall on its own. And we have seen the type of government it really is. A military dictatorship in which there are no free elections and some 40,000 people are held as political prisoners. We don't think that is the kind of government worth fighting for.

We have seen what the war is doing to Vietnam. The country is being physically destroyed by bombing, defoliation, and the killing of its civilian population. (Civilians in Vietnam are being killed and wounded at the rate of 200,000 a year, 60% of them children. And 80% of them as a result of American firepower.) And we don't think that that's worth it.

We have seen what the war is doing to our own country. We are being torn apart. Our young people are being alienated. Our most pressing domestic problems are being neglected for lack of funds while the war which has already cost us $130 billion goes on at $800 a second...$48,000 a minute...$2,880,000 an hour. Meanwhile the value of our dollar is being destroyed by inflation. And we don't think that that's worth it.

We have seen what the war is doing to our buddies and their families. Over 43,000 have already been killed and another 292,000 wounded—many of us maimed for the rest of our lives. And more are being killed and wounded every day. And we don't think that that's worth it.

We believe that the basic problems of Vietnam are not military but social, economic, and political. We believe that there is no military solution to the war. We believe that, in any case, we cannot win a land war in Asia. And we believe that in this nuclear age our national security does not require us to win it.

Therefore, we believe that the best way to support our buddies in Vietnam is to ask that they be brought home, now, before anyone else dies in a war that the American people do not understand, did not vote for, and do not want. And we think that that's worth fighting for.

If you're a Vietnam veteran and feel the same way we do we ask you to join us. If you're a concerned citizen we ask you to support us by filling out the coupon below. But we ask you to please do it now. The lives of a great many of our friends depend on it.

Vietnam Veterans Against the War
156 Fifth Avenue, Room 508, N.Y., N.Y. 10010

VVAW's ad in *Playboy,* February 1971.

going on then. So they'd say, "We ain't going on no goddamned patrols and get killed. We're just sitting here. Everybody knows this war is bullshit. We're waiting for it to end." Everybody had that basic understanding.

Bob Hanson: Joe Urgo was the guy who was responsible for all the nuts-and-bolts stuff, like keeping track of the membership. Poor Joe used to get letters from guys who had become members, months later, saying "Person deceased." That happened a lot.

JU: It was not until years later that I really understood how powerful we were in Vietnam . . . how seriously we were contributing to the collapse of morale. I don't think we actually knew how to do what we wanted to do, and we didn't understand how much we were actually doing.

> *Organizing in Vietnam proved to be very difficult, not only because of a lack of understanding on the part of national leaders, but also because those who were still in the armed forces and were caught organizing GIs were often harassed, jailed, or dishonorably discharged. Despite these setbacks, VVAW's contributions to the antiwar effort in Vietnam were significant.[21]*

Lee Thorn: The kind of expansion that happened on the west coast, happened all over the country. It was frantic. There was lots and lots of activity. There was a lot of active-duty work and international work. So we were politically growing, as well as organizing in Vietnam, as well as organizing on bases in Japan, North Africa, and Germany, as well as bases here in this country. It was great. It was fun, but we didn't know how to take care of ourselves. We exhausted ourselves.

Interlude: Vietnam Revisited

JOE URGO

As a result of Dewey Canyon III, VVAW had attracted the attention of international peace organizations and was asked to participate in various international meetings dealing with issues of war and peace. The first trip by a representative of VVAW to such a conference took place in August 1971: VVAW was invited to send someone to Japan to commemorate the anniversary of atomic bombing of Hiroshima and Nagasaki. During that trip, VVAW was invited to send a representative to North Vietnam. Joe Urgo was the first Vietnam veteran to visit North Vietnam, and the experience had a profound impact on his view of the war and American society. It also affected other vet-

erans, who read about it in The 1st Casualty, *the original name of VVAW's newsletter. Joe Urgo exemplifies the changes veterans underwent as a result of their antiwar activities.*[22]

I went on the trip very much afraid of what responsibility I was carrying. After the winter soldier investigation [in Detroit in 1971] and after meeting everybody in Dewey Canyon, I now had a real down-to-earth grasp of what VVAW was about. I felt like: I'm going there representing all of these guys; I'm going to the people who we were killing. It was a very intimidating kind of thing.

I remember being in Hiroshima before a panel of Hiroshima survivors—here's all these people sixty, seventy, eighty years old, recounting the horrors of what the United States did to them in the bombing—and being moved by it and listening intently and thinking . . . my God, we've done this to more than just the Vietnamese.

I turned like this, and there's three Vietnamese crying. These are delegates to this conference. It's so incredible. I'm sitting here watching these Vietnamese cry at what the United States did to the Japanese, and we're still doing that.

I landed [in Vietnam] and got off the plane. I was astounded that they greeted me as a brother, in a friendly and warm way, and it was not just public relations.

They took us out, and [we] saw a few bombed villages, and then they took me through the Museum of the Revolution. That was astounding. You go through a museum in Hanoi that is the history of their 2,000 years of resistance to oppression. You walk into the museum—the first room they take you into is a whole room that is filled with posters from all around the world against the war, and in a glass case they have their most honored gifts from around the world. They take you into a room where they show you statues of the Trung sisters, who led Vietnamese in resisting Chinese invaders.

Holy shit! You go through the rooms, and it just hits you. You realize the international support for Vietnam that you didn't get before. You go through this history and you realize: Of all the people in the world to pick, the United States goes and picks the one people with whom resistance is a national identity, you know? These are the people we are trying to beat down? Everything is tied into the resistance. It was an experience I was just tremendously moved by.

Everywhere I go, the kids are mobbing me, the Vietnamese hug me. My mind is being blown every day. The thing I learned . . . is: Once you say to the people, I'm on your side, they will excuse anything you do. That's what the Vietnamese did.

They took me up to High Point Harbor and showed me the coast off Haiphong. They took a boat out to the caves. The time that the Haiphong was being bombed, they moved the civilian population into the caves. They took me to those caves, and they would say things like, "Someday American tourists will be here. The American people are not our enemy; the government is our enemy." They would constantly say that.

They took us through churches to see the Catholics going to church, to make sure that we understood that it was not this religious persecution. They tried to take on all the myths that we were told.

Then they sat me down with—I think—some of their intelligence people and picked my brain. They didn't say, "What secrets can you tell us?" Do you know what that question was? "Why are your people so brutal? Why do they rape? Why do they do this?" They would try to understand the psychology.

What did you say?

I did the best that I could based on what I understood at the time about basic training and racism. I think they understood that I was sincere. My attitude was that I'll tell you anything you want to know. You're not my enemy. I'm on your side.

Was this the point where you began to feel that you were on their side, or was that already something you felt before?

That was the point I understood that concretely.

So I'm like absolutely astounded by this thing; and they asked us for statements, and I wanted to write as strong a statement as possible supporting them. VVAW always stood on that. Maybe that's why some of the vets resented some of the leadership, but that was a given in the organization. We weren't worried about being called traitors. The government just tried to kill us, and we are going to use our right to speak and we will say anything we want—I don't give a shit what you're called. They are right; that's their country.

I came back in August, and things were confusing. VVAW was never an organization that on a daily to weekly basis summed up what the political lines and questions were and then, on that basis, figured out policy. It was a little bit of this and a little bit of that; go here, go there.

The radicals started recognizing that we had to consciously take this someplace. We can't rely spontaneously on going from one high thing to another high thing to doing something more outrageous. There is just nothing you can do on that level anymore; you've got to settle down and stick your feet in the ground real seriously and decide how to organize. That's the challenge, and that's what the leadership was starting to feel.

Creating a National Structure

BARRY ROMO, JOHN LINDQUIST, ANNIE BAILEY,
PETE ZASTROW, MIKE McCAIN

While all these actions were taking place across the country, the national office in New York, which had not been elected by the general membership, tried to maintain its control of the organization. The members at large, however, demanded that a democratic process be put into place, to ensure that their interests would be reflected in VVAW's national agenda.

How did the organization absorb all of these people? How did the organization function?

Barry Romo: [We] divided the country up into 26 regions. We don't have presidents; we have coordinators. That was more than a name. It was our politics. People led by leading, not by having titles. There was a total rejection of the military style—that confining sort of thing.

John Lindquist (JL): We were small-unit-oriented because that's the way we fought. VVAW reflects the communities it's in. You'll start to notice that Milwaukee will be peculiar in its own way. Chicago and Milwaukee aren't the same. They're good and nice, but they're different.

So each group was fairly autonomous? Did the groups get to do what they wanted?

Annie Bailey (AB): Well, no. You couldn't put on a VVAW button and go out and bust up a bar, beat your chest, and get away with it. We'd get on your case about that.

Pete Zastrow (PZ): The focus of different chapters was very different, but on major issues, we agreed. We did hammer out a basis of unity at national meetings. We were having three or four national meetings every year. They would be three- or four-day meetings held all over the country.

We had 10 organizational objectives, and the theory was that you could have a chapter of the organization if you met certain qualifications. There was a membership requirement, but that changed from time to time; and you had to send in some dues; and you had to do things which promoted those objectives. Well, damn near anything you did could be said to promote those objectives.

AB: We had objectives that we fought over and reworded and added to and subtracted from. That's where all the political discussion came in, but when it came to working together, we would decide, democratically, what we were going to do. Everyone would vote on it, and the people who lost the vote always stuck around and participated in what we decided to do, and that is what held us together. It was true democracy. It really was. It was total chaos and I loved it.

Mike McCain: It was ultrademocratic, which led to some of its problems. There was a lot of folks and every one of them had an attitude. Every one of them had an agenda and felt that their opinion had a right to be heard. Meetings would go on and on and on. Women and other nonveterans had joined the organization, and they demanded a right to be heard.

JL: We were never closed. You had some left-wing dudes quoting Mao and you'd have dudes from down south talking about "fucking niggers" at the same meeting. You had a whole bunch of right-wing dudes and you had a bigger group in the middle. . . . That's how mass this organization was.

AB: There was a big fight over everything. We had some people who were constant obstructionists. We had some people that were really backward. I remember a national meeting in Chicago. Bill Marshall had been elected as a regional coordinator from Michigan. He's this black guy who was excellent. Oh, he was excellent. We got a bunch of people at the table. There's a big clump of us from the midwest sitting together, and [on] the other side of the table were all these guys from Texas, Florida, and Georgia and shit. Some fucking asshole from Georgia says, "What's niggers doing at our meeting?"

What did you do?

AB: It caused political struggle. We struggled over that shit, but we didn't go to blows or anything. We won him over. Now, some of those rednecks never came back to the meetings. Some of the best antiracist raps came from people like John Kniffin from Texas, who had this unique southern Texas drawl and this long red hair, and he was such a fucking redneck. He was a maniac, but he was good. I grew to love him.

PZ: I remember in my own mind being amazed the first time I saw an election, because it was the first time I had seen an election where somebody wasn't telling people how to vote. I mean, this was my peers, so to speak. People more or less my age, sitting around making decisions on their own, and picking some pretty good people. I was very impressed with some of the first people I met who were in the national office.

These were people who were articulate, who often had different points of view, but could articulate these points of view very well. These are people who had been in political arguments now, for some of them, years. I was someone who hadn't been. While I had a whole lot more education than most of them did, that wasn't where my education was. I was really impressed that here were people that were picked out a group of people by the people involved, and they had come out with some pretty damn good folks.

JOHN KNIFFIN, TERRY DuBOSE, SHELDON RAMSDELL, LINDA ALBAND, BARRY ROMO

In the fall of 1971, tensions over the direction in which the organization was heading, as it spread out into various community activities and took on a more consciously anti-imperialist position, were becoming more evident. In November, an emergency meeting of the steering committee was held in Kansas City. This meeting was a result of the growing friction among members of the steering committee, and between new members and the old leadership.

John Kniffin (JK): There was a schism going on then between Al Hubbard and John Kerry.

Terry DuBose (TDB): What they were trying to do was keep the credibility before the media, because the media was saying we weren't veterans. John Kerry felt like he had to tell the regional coordinators that Al Hubbard had not served in Vietnam and that he had not been an officer.

Sheldon Ramsdell (SR): John was also very anticommunist. He made it very clear one night in the office.

I do these photo spreads for the Liberation News Service. . . . I just give it away like to the New York Press Service, and so there was a spread on VVAW in the *Daily World,* an American communist newspaper, and my shit got in there. We pinned it up on the wall. At that same time, Al Hubbard received a peace award from the Soviets. John went off. He says, "That's a communist newspaper. Isn't that prize a communist prize that Al Hubbard got there?" He's got his feet up on the desk and he's a little nervous, which is making him think, "Maybe I should leave this radical organization." But we had no political philosophy; it was just a mixed bag of rednecks all the way to Maoists.

What did you think of Kerry and his contributions to the organization?

SR: Kerry was to me a mainstream politician basically. He was kind of using us. I said, "Go for it—you're welcome to take our venue and go for it."

Linda Alband: It was mutual use. There was a lot of validity that John brought to the organization: being a Yale graduate, his looks, and he had access to a lot of people we wouldn't necessarily get in [with]. It was good for both him and the organization. I always heard all the guys that I worked with talking about him. It wasn't anything bitter. They didn't think he used anybody any more than he got used, so it was like this mutual proposition. No one resented that.

Barry Romo: We didn't dislike him. He's an equivocator. He's a liberal. He's a politician. He was liberal, he was rich, he was from Massachusetts, he talked like a Kennedy, he had people cleaning his house that could have been our parents.

JK: More and more enlisted people were coming in, and they were viewing John Kerry as some kind of elitist. It degenerated into a black-white thing and into an officer versus enlisted man kind of thing.

There was a sort of an elitism in that the national steering committee, and the regional coordinators were the only ones who could discuss this. Everyone else had to go out, and they had a closed session. This kind of upset a lot of people. We're supposed to have this democratic organization and a bunch of kings say, "Go out in the livery and wait while we decide your fate."

The whole thing boiled down to: Where does the power of the organization lay? I had a mandate from Texas that we would fight for regional autonomy and a bottom-up power structure. The power of the organization lays with the membership. The power flows from the bottom up, not the top down. From that point on, my mandate from Tom, Rick, and Jim—and Wayne and the rest—was that when I went to the steering committee, I didn't go by myself. We went as a delegation. If we voted on something, we would caucus and we would arbitrate, and then we would vote.

Another one of the issues was an accounting of where all the money was going in the organization. The national office had raised all this money, but they didn't seem to know where it went. We sort of felt that the role of the national office, since they were raising all this money, was to distribute it to chapters and to use it as seed money to get more chapters started, to get the organization built. They seemed to feel that we were responsible for raising our own money, and moreover that any dues money we raised should be forwarded to the national office to further enrich their coffers. It got to the point where I was so pissed off at the national office when I took over as regional coordinator that I had all these membership applications laying on my table and my cat pissed on them. I guess the righteous thing to do would have been to recopy them all, but I decided the hell with it; I just bundled them all up and shipped them to the national office.[23]

TDB: The Kansas City meeting was the beginning of the end for me. After the Dewey Canyon III thing, the media attention became so intense [and] we were getting so many members that it got to the point where all we were doing was compiling a membership list. There was a practical discussion that developed in the organization about what was more important, using energy to build a membership or spending energy to do anything that would protest the war. It was turning into this bureaucracy of building membership lists and keeping records. It felt like we weren't protesting anymore.

That was also where there was actually some discussion of assassinating some senators during the Christmas holidays. They were people who I knew from the organization with hotheaded rhetoric.

They had a list of six senators . . . Helms, John Tower, and I can't remember the others, who they wanted to assassinate when they adjourned for Christmas. They were the ones voting to fund the war. They approached me about assassinating John Tower because he was from Texas. The logic made a certain amount of sense because there's thousands of people dying in southeast Asia. We can shoot these six people and probably stop it. Some of us were willing to sabotage materials, but when it came to people . . . I mean, there were a lot of angry people. They had been in Vietnam, they had lost friends. This had gone on for years; some of them had been protesting for five or six years. They were cynical, nihilistic, and some of them did talk real tough rhetoric, but nobody ever got shot by any of these people. It was just talk.

When I got back from that meeting, I couldn't get up the enthusiasm any more.

The meeting in Kansas City brought in a new steering committee. John Kerry, Craig Scott Moore, Mike Oliver, and Skip Roberts resigned from their leadership positions and were replaced by several new members. Al Hubbard and Joe Urgo remained in office and were joined by John Birch, Lenny Rotman, and Larry Rottman.

At the meeting, a motion was passed to change the structure of the executive committee, making it elective: the committee members would now be elected by regional coordinators. Also, the title of those who were elected to the committee was changed: they would now be called national coordinators. Furthermore, the term of a national coordinator would be limited to one year.[24]

This meeting foreshadowed future tensions within VVAW. As new members flooded in, the political direction of the organization changed. The new steering committee wanted to raise the stakes by confronting the United States government more directly: staging sit-ins and takeovers of national monuments and veterans administration offices, as veterans across the nation had already begun to do. In that sense, they were in tune with the more radical members of the local chapters. They were not, however, aligned with any single political ideology, nor were they ready to let their plans be overruled by democratic processes within VVAW. Some of the new leaders had been involved in VVAW activities for several years and had felt that they had a firm grasp on the role of the organization and its goals.

Despite these changes, many members of VVAW still distrusted the leadership. Eventually, new members would take over the national office through democratic processes. However, before that happened the new steering committee was able to coordinate one more national action: "Operation Peace on Earth."

Operation Peace on Earth

JOHN LINDQUIST, JACK McCLOSKEY, TERRY DuBOSE,
MIKE GOLD, DAVE CLINE, LEE THORN, BOB HANSON

When the new members of the steering committee took over in the fall of 1971, they prepared for the final coordinated VVAW action of the year. Actually, there was no cohesive overall plan. It was decided that each region could engage in its own activities, and a new wave of bombings at Christmas set off a variety of spontaneous actions by veterans, including takeovers of several symbolic sites across the nation.

The decision to carry out actions more or less independently across the nation had not been unopposed. Several chapters of VVAW had called for a return to Washington, D.C., after the Christmas holidays—that is, in January 1972—to press Congress to take immediate action to end the war. The most vociferous advocates of this approach were members of the chapters in Pennsylvania and Florida; they thought that returning to Washington would be significant and proposed that VVAW should not leave Washington until the war was over.

This proposal was voted down by the new steering committee, and its vote in favor of coordinated activities across the nation during the holiday season was in turn contested by various VVAW chapters that supported a return to Washington. In fact, the committee's unilateral decision caused a serious rift in VVAW, a rift that was evidently regional: leaders in the south and the midwest seemed more supportive of the proposal.[25] As a result of this controversy, veterans in various areas began to drop out of VVAW.

John Lindquist: We got to the point where we were doing so many things together in one place, we couldn't fucking afford it. So we said, Why not do a national demo regionally? First time we tried one of those was in December 1971. We had strong chapters in Texas. Killeen, Texas, had a VVAW chapter in Fort Hood. They did a thing there. We did a thing in Chicago, since it was more apt than Milwaukee. . . . Both teamed up . . . the midwest, basically. The east coast did the taking over the Statue of Liberty, the Betsy Ross house in Philadelphia, and all that stuff. The west coast and Bay Area tried taking over the drug ward in Travis Air Force Base. There's probably all kinds of little bullshit too. But that was the main five. That was the way it was envisioned at the national meeting. We picked these places. This is where you can go if you live in that area.

Jack McCloskey (JMC): They were takeovers by Vietnam vets' groups that had served in Vietnam and saying we were tired of our brothers and sisters getting killed. We're tired of this bullshit going on. We're tired of being lied to. We're tired of this— [Points to his skin; Jack McCloskey had a serious case of chloracne, affecting much of his body.] At the time we didn't even know about Agent Orange, except we knew a lot of us were becoming sick. We saw all these things and we started to get tired of all these things.

Why not write to a congressman, or lobby more?

JMC: [Laughter.] We felt that we had to take action. By that time, VVAW became sophisticated enough to know that writing your congressman don't mean diddly. This war had to be taken to the American public by Vietnam veterans that served and came back with their arms off, their legs off, their minds blown away on dope. That's why we did it.

Terry DuBose (TDB): Everybody agreed at the Saint Louis meeting to have a Christmas action. Our stated press release said, "Our brothers in Vietnam are not coming home for Christmas, so we're not going home for Christmas." Nobody went home to their families.

In New York, a handful of veterans started the activities by taking over the Statue of Liberty.

Mike Gold (MG): The guys in the national office didn't know about it. Guys from Maryland, Ohio, and Pennsylvania came to do that. It was a reaction to Nixon's Christmas bombings. Our feeling was that Nixon's gone nuts, he's bombing Vietnam into the stone age. They were just making mincemeat of this land.

The statue meant something to them. They thought it was an important symbol. They figured to hang the flag upside down and give the world an SOS. No one else had done that. It was coming from patriotism. It was a "from the head, from the heart" thing, a unique Vietnam Veterans Against the War thing.

Dave Cline: There's symbolism of the Statue of Liberty representing American freedom. We were saying that the so-called image of freedom had a lot more image to it than reality. We were operating out of the view that there is the promise of America and there's the reality of America. You fight for the promise, but you have to recognize the reality. . . . That's what it's about.

VVAW's takeover of the Statue of Liberty, 1976.

MG: It was on the front page of just about every newspaper in the world. It was an incredible act. I don't remember the polls tipping against the war until 1971. So there was a tremendous response to those things.

Lee Thorn (LT): We were trying to figure out something really spectacular to do . . . just after the vets in New York had taken over the Statue of Liberty. It was like the next day. I said, "We have to do something spectacular too, otherwise we won't get national publicity and this fucking [organizing] strategy won't work." So I was at this house with a friend of mine, and he says, "You guys take the South Vietnamese embassy." So I said, "That's a great idea."

I took the idea to a meeting that night. I said, "How about this idea?" Everybody said, "Wow!" These three or four guys went to the building and checked it out. We were really concerned about security because it was never done before. We thought it would bring every kind of law in the world.

We wanted to get arrested. We were just worried that somebody was going to find out. So what we did was, we said, Anybody who is going to be involved in these discussions, you can't leave. We're going to do it tomorrow morning, and nobody can leave, which was lucky, because one of the guys that went in there with us was a cop. [Laughs.] But he couldn't get to a telephone to call, so they didn't know about it.

JMC: This is in the embassy area. It's in the Flood Building here in San Francisco. We just went in, barricaded the doors, and told them, "We're Vietnam Veterans Against the War and we are here because we want to bring our brothers and sisters home and we don't want to see any more killing." We politely asked the Vietnamese to leave. We had all the doors barricaded.

How many people were inside?

JMC: Seventeen of us. All vets, with a cop. The cop was definitely a member of VVAW. The cop was a veteran.

Did you know he was a cop?

JMC: Fuck no; we didn't know he was a cop. We found out in the trial.

LT: They had a teletype. We barricaded ourselves into the offices and sent messages to fucking Saigon. [Laughs.] . . . "Stop the war." . . . They cut off the teletype and then cut off the telephone. We were calling the press and shit. In the meantime, Mike Oliver was back in our office. This had been set up. He called all the press, and then called the Lawyers' Guild to send a lawyer over. John Gladstone climbed in through the transom, so he was inside with us. Then they sent the tac squad and we were totally surrounded.

Did you think they were going to attack you?

LT: Oh, yeah. We were always nonviolent, so we wouldn't have hit the cops, but we would have gone into a nonviolent position. Mainly it was a tactical decision. If you're going to be violent, you've got to win. We knew we were taking a risk in terms of physical harm, but it was no risk like we had just taken—you know, being in Vietnam. And then they busted us.

JMC: They took us to trial. They tried to get us for treason and they tried to get us for trespassing. They had us dead to rights. We took in food; we took in sleeping bags.

We had an Asian judge. We had a racially mixed jury. The foreman of the jury was a retired Navy captain. We were able to show in the trial a film called *Only the Beginning,* with the veterans throwing their medals on the White

House lawn. We were able to get people like Sidney Peck [and] George Solomon to come in and testify, saying we were sane. We were able, each one of us, to get up in the stand and tell why we did what we had to do. The jury deliberated for about a day and a half. We were found innocent.

After we were found innocent, I'd say eight of the jurors came to our victory party. The captain of the jury joined VVAW, started doing research on the air war part of Vietnam and the Navy's participation.

LT: That [action] went around the world in terms of publicity. That really helped our organizing. It's an amazing organizing story. We developed organizing packets. Whenever we got in communication with somebody, we sent somebody with the organizing packet to the guys, and they lived there for a couple weeks or so. We had two chapters in San Francisco, the Berkeley chapter, Oakland, Freemont, Redwood City, Marin, Contra Costa, Concord, Fresno, Stockton. Eureka, Mendocino—just in northern California. The southern California area had LA, Orange County, San Diego, San Bernardino, Santa Barbara . . . all over the fucking place.

Bob Hanson (BH): The most effective action I was ever involved in was during the time I was with the chapter here in San Francisco. The heroin problem from late 1968 on became greater and greater each year in Vietnam, until about 1971. What they were doing was: In order to go home, you had to take a piss test. If you failed the piss test, you were forced to go into a military hospital before you could go home.

We got this call, a day or two after the Statue of Liberty had been taken over, from these guys who had been shackled in their seats from Ton Son Nhut back to here [and] were stuck in this ward in the hospital. These guys had taken over a wing on their own of Travis Air Force Base hospital and wanted some help in deciding what to do next.

LT: I get a call from Hanson or Oliver and they say we just got a call from these guys at Travis Air Force Base who barricaded themselves in their room. They were all heroin addicts who had been told that as soon as they got back, they were going to get out. But instead they weren't letting them out. They were sending them to Texas. Their enlistment was up, but they were being kept in.

A bunch of us got in cars, and we're zooming up there. I got in somebody's van. Hanson and Oliver had taken another car, and they had gotten there first. They got in and were able to barricade themselves in. None of the rest of us could get in.

BH: Three of us—myself, Mike Oliver, and this guy Shelly—made our way out to the base and got into the hospital. We talked with these guys all night long.

LT: We got all these congressional people involved. We had all the media there, local and national. They negotiated.

BH: After negotiations with various Air Force and Army officers, they were told that they would be allowed to go home. All of this resulted in the military stopping this process of preventing people from going straight home if they tested positive on these piss tests. We were barred, obviously, from Travis forever. [Laughs.] It was amazing.

LT: We broke that story in San Francisco. There's a guy who had been up in the mountains around Seattle. He had heard about us. He had been involved in the heroin thing with the CIA in Laos. We sent people back with him to organize the Seattle chapter.

So that whole story of heroin links in Laos came through VVAW?

LT: We broke the story in the spring of 1972, right after we got out of the trial.

In addition to carrying out such media events in their effort to stop the war and to support returning veterans, VVAW members in San Francisco and across the country began to engage in activities to help veterans in other ways.

MIKE McCAIN

Jill [his wife] and I started the discharge upgrading project in San Francisco. There was a huge number of vets with less than honorable discharges. They were kicking people out for drug addiction, and the drugs they were addicted to had come through the military. We were saying that you don't blame individuals, but you have to see their actions in context. It became a national project of Vietnam Veterans Against the War. Hundreds and thousands of bad discharges got upgraded to general at least, as a result of our work.

While all of these activities went on, around the holiday season and later, on the west and east coasts; veterans in Texas took on projects that were more relevant for their region, which had so many military bases.

TERRY DuBOSE, JOHN KNIFFIN, DAVE CLINE

Terry Dubose (TDB): We all went to Killeen. We went to the Oleo Strut and had a prayer breakfast for the GIs, did a winter soldier investigation-type thing, went into the hospital with books and just handed them out.

Mike McCain *(center, holding Nora Kate Dolly)* at his VVAW chapter in Oakland, California, in 1974 or 1975. The others are *(left)* Bob Traller, *(second from left)* David Pollack, and *(right)* Jeannie Dolly.

We decided what we wanted to do and went and did it. We didn't ask anybody permission in them days. We broke up into pairs of twos and passed out the books until the MPs came and picked us all up. They took us back to the police station and gave us barring orders. They were letters that said: You can never come on this base again.

John Kniffin (JK): There was a jewelry store chain in Texas called Tyrell's that had set up operations near some of the military bases. They were scamming guys who were departing for Vietnam, getting them to buy overpriced jewelry for their loved ones, girlfriends, and wives.

Dave Cline: They would be out on the streets hustling shit. Tyrell's would be out there saying, "Hey, GI, don't you want to get a ring for your girlfriend?" They had a thing that was really offensive, that if you got killed in Vietnam and owed them money, they would eat the rest of the debt. They would hang your name in the window as part of Tyrell's role of honor.

We started [a] boycott campaign, picketing the store. Our demands were: "End sidewalk solicitation; no garnish of wages if you didn't pay for what you bought; and the removal of the role of honor, because it was an insult to those who got killed. This thing spread throughout the country. It became a national boycott. They even came to the servicemen's fund headquarters in New York and wanted to negotiate.

They arrested people during the boycott, but we definitely fucked up their business.

JK: My wife was handling the media back in Austin. We're getting all these messages all the time—national office wants to know what's going on in Texas. They don't hear anything from the press. They've taken over the Vietnamese consulate in San Francisco, they occupied the Betsy Ross house in Philadelphia and occupied the Statue of Liberty in New York. "What are you doing in Texas?" We're doing our thing. We're doing fine; leave us alone.

TDB: It wasn't a hot media thing.

> *Thus Operation Peace on Earth revealed new cleavages in the organization. The Texas contingent, which had concentrated most of its activities on supporting active-duty GIs, felt slighted when the national office questioned its level of activity. In addition, there had been an earlier disagreement between the national office and the coordinator in Florida, Scott Camil. The rift between the north and the south would widen during the coming year—1972.*
>
> *With the departure of John Kerry and other original leaders, VVAW's connections with liberal financial supporters also began to weaken. The organization had carried out another series of media-grabbing events, but the war did not end.*

JOE URGO

1971 was the year of the veteran. So that was the end of the year—all these different actions going on—and it was more of a letdown than it was a breakout. There was a sense that we had done one thing after another that reached new peaks, and what we were looking for was another thing to do, to take it to another peak. But the problem was that we were now in a decline; the money was beginning to dry up.

The New Leadership Takes Over

JOHN KNIFFIN, LINDA ALBAND, BARRY ROMO, MIKE McCAIN

John Kniffin (JK): After John Kerry left, we elected a pretty good group of folks. This was in February of 1972 in Denver. There was two people from Texas in the national office, Rusty Branaugh and Alvin Glick. There was Dave and Diane Rosen from Colorado, [and] a guy from California, Mike McCain. We sent them off to New York as the new steering committee.

Rottman, Hubbard, and the rest of them [these were previous coordinators who had taken over briefly in November 1971] felt that it was their organization. Everything was in their name. They weren't going to turn over anything to the new steering committee. When the next steering committee meeting came up in Houston . . . we had to go all over that stuff again. We're still redoing what we had done in Denver in February. There was so much weird stuff going on.

Linda Alband: There were very different agendas for different people. I think one of the important things about Al [Hubbard] was he was older than a lot of people. He really used that to be a kind of an uncle or father figure, and that gave him stature over these people and he really didn't want to share the power he thought he had with anyone else. He didn't even go to Denver.

People go to New York from Denver and try to do what they were elected to do, and Al basically shuts them out. So there's this whole power play going on, although it could've probably been avoided if he'd gone to Denver. I don't think anyone wanted to see him out of the national office, but after he did that, you had to do it. It was like bringing in a grassroots group of elected national officers to do what people wanted them to do, rather than Al being able to make any decision unilaterally.

Barry Romo: I was elected to the national office [in 1972]. Two things were occurring within the organization. One, an ego thing was going on. People thought they should be the leaders, and their egos were just blown up. Another thing was liberalism versus a more radical world viewpoint. The other thing was a feeling that the national office was unresponsive to the organization's needs. The organization had now grown beyond the initial people that had organized it. It went beyond New York.

If you were accepting a leadership position, then you were accepting the fact that you had a responsibility. Your own life wasn't your own. You didn't get to go out and be an individual. People that couldn't live with that left. And the people that would do that, the organization loved, because they were submitting themselves to real democracy.

Mike McCain: I was elected to the national office in 1972. There was no way that the general membership was going to allow anybody to tell them what to do. Everybody had this knee-jerk reaction to top-down leadership. The feeling that I got was that here we had these guys in New York that were telling us what to do and they didn't know shit, so we had to do it for ourselves. They had an analysis of what the role of the organization was to be, which was very much like it had been: "Well, we've got a few things we can say," but it was not an active organization that they were proposing. They were wrong. The alternative, which was put forth by other veterans, which I was a part of, felt that we had a major role to take in the movement and the way to get there was by advocacy. We had to do things. People wanted to do something.

We knew what was going on. It was a traditional organizing attitude. It wasn't telling people what to do, or providing the ideological or philosophical leadership; it was task-oriented, to coordinate activity amongst all of these people who are each doing things on a local level. They had their own local conditions to deal with, but we tried to organize a few things on a national level. Every now and then there would be a day, or series of days, when activities would be coordinated throughout the country.

JK: During this committee meeting, when all of this kind of stuff was being discussed, we were getting information from the GIs about troop movements and buildup to counter the North Vietnamese offensive. Nixon was saying, "We'll do anything to stop the invasion of South Vietnam, short of the reintroduction of ground troops and nuclear weapons." We had evidence that they were doing both from the active-duty GIs.

Some of us felt that the issue of the troop buildup was much more important than these petty-ass little political struggles within the organization, and that's what we ought to be doing. In fact, I think [Gary] Staiger [a regional coordinator from Ohio] was the one who made the motion that what we need to do is go back to our regions, make the contacts, and keep this information coming out. Screw all this national organization stuff. The national, of course, is saying, "No, no, we've got to settle this now. We can't have two steering committees."

It caused a lot of friction between us.

The Last Patrol: 1972

ANN HIRSCHMAN, DANNY FRIEDMAN, BARRY ROMO, ANNIE BAILEY, BILL DAVIS

Despite the growing tensions within the organization, VVAW continued to expand its activity. In the summer of 1972, the Democrats and Republicans held their nominating conventions in Miami, Florida. VVAW planned to attend both conventions in order to pressure the parties to bring the war to an end. Although the Republicans continued to resist VVAW, the Democrats proved to be much more amenable to its demands. For one thing, by that time the Democratic Party had become much more inclusive, having broadened its base among antiwar liberals as well as among African-Americans and other groups that had once been kept on its periphery. Also, of course, the Democrats were now the opposition party, trying to regain the presidency. The Vietnam war had definitely become a liability for the Nixon administration, which had been promising to end it since 1968, and the Democrats now hoped that VVAW, with its perceived legitimacy, could help them win.

Ann Hirschman: We got invited to the Democratic convention. The Democratic Party at that point was making overtures that indicated that they wanted to be progressive. There was a clear perception that some of the Democrats, particularly the black caucus, seemed to have a very clear notion that the Democrats were not looking good on defense, and that perhaps working with a progressive veterans' group would shine them up.

We went in, and the first thing they did was search everybody but me. I was carrying the first aid pack, and it was forty-nine vets and me. Ron Dellums came over with Barry's birthday present from home. Some California delegate brought us pizza and Kentucky Fried Chicken. We watched the convention. People were taking us seriously. It was hot shit.

Danny Friedman: The bottom line was that we were the honored guests of the Democrats. We were treated like royalty everywhere we went. We were applauded. We were welcomed onto the floor of the convention. Jim Bouton, who was a former pitcher of the Yankees and a delegate from New Jersey, sent us up a whole ton of fried chicken.

Barry Romo (BR): We had four organizations: there was National Tenants Rights Organization, the Welfare Rights Organization with Beulah Sanders, the Southern Christian Leadership Conference with Ralph Abernathy, and VVAW. The four of us formed a leadership to put pressure on the Democratic convention to demand an antiracist platform with social justice. I was on the executive committee. I had a floor pass. I was allowed to go anywhere I fucking wanted.

There was a zillion good people there because they had beat fucking Daley, they had sat the black delegates, they nominated McGovern, they came out against the goddamned war. They put in a thing before the convention to pass a resolution in defense of the Vietnam Vets Against the War being attacked by the Nixon administration. The whole convention passed it. We won a lot.

The attack on the veterans had taken the form of indictments against eight VVAW leaders. See Chapter 5 for details.

Annie Bailey: We didn't lose a lot of people in those early days—we just kept getting more and more—but we had an exodus of vets who were working on the presidential campaign. Vets for McGovern. They really wanted us to take on Vets for McGovern as a national thing, but we wouldn't do it. That was something that we couldn't abide. We don't endorse candidates: democracy, yes; but candidates, no.

Bill Davis: I'd made one of the appearances [at a McGovern rally], and it just nauseated me. We had to take off our VVAW shit. It was like a wave of liberals left. Some went to work for McGovern.

BR: We didn't realize the allies and the depth of organizing that we could have expanded on with the people that were there. [We] didn't understand what we should have done in terms of networking with them, working from the base of that convention. It wasn't a question of rejecting it; it was a question of just ignorance. We were just too young. I'm a twenty-five-year-old national coordinator running around with Ralph Abernathy, not a graduate of a goddamned college, and only been out of the service four years.

We only had a small demonstration there, maybe 50 to 75 VVAW members. Everything was going for the confrontational one, which was with Nixon, what we called the Last Patrol—with three car caravans going to the thing; 1,500 to 2,000 VVAW members.

With the end of the Democratic convention, VVAW members converged on Miami for the Republican convention. Veterans began to arrive in Miami Beach on August 19 and 20 to prepare for the convention, which was to take place between August 21 and August 24.

ANN HIRSCHMAN, JOHN KNIFFIN, LEE THORN, TOM WETZLER,
BARRY ROMO, JACK McCLOSKEY, SHELDON RAMSDELL,
BOBBY MULLER, DANNY FRIEDMAN, LINDA ALBAND

Ann Hirschman (AH): First we got the land opened up. The day we opened the land was a day before the vets' convoy came.

John Kniffin: These convoys [were] coming from three different parts of the country—the northeast, west, [and] midwest—all converging on Miami. They were so massive that at one point they completely blocked the Tamiami freeway when some cop was rash enough to tell the lead car to pull over for going below the speed limit. So the lead car pulled over to one of these cop stations and everybody started following him. They ended up filling up the substation parking lot and blocking up all four lanes of the Tamiami freeway before the cop says, "Get out of here."

"Last Patrol": Convoy arriving in Miami Beach, 1972.

Lee Thorn: Coming down the east coast, they stopped off at all these military bases. Every time they got to a military base, the doors opened, the guys went in, there'd be cheering and shit. They'd bring them beer. I think we inspired them. It was OK to resist. It was OK to get organized. We supported them. They knew that when we said we'd do something, we did it. It was like we were still in Vietnam.

Tom Wetzler: It really was a wonderful convoy in a lot of ways. I remember I was in Flamingo Park when the main convoy came in. I had gone early to pick up a friend of mine. It looked like a scene from the liberation of Paris. You hear this rumbling in the background and people are saying, "The vets are coming!" They all ran to the fence, and coming down the street is this convoy. The convoy had met at Daytona Beach, and then from there it was one massive convoy. I seem to remember "When Johnny Comes Marching Home" whistled somewhere. There was someone with a helmet full of joints, passing them out. It was real exciting.

AH: After we had the land set up, the Nazis goose-stepped in.

Barry Romo (BR): The Nazis grabbed the stage in the middle of Flamingo Park. I saw them getting on the stage. So I run up on the stage to fight them and they fucking knocked me and threw me off, just in time for 1,500 vets to land. [Laughs.]

AH: I watched the ring of guys close in around the Nazis. Steve and Danny were on the stage. One of the Nazis made the stupid mistake of picking up a chair and hitting Steve. Danny picked up the chair and hit the Nazi. The chair exploded on the Nazi's head. They never did find the rest of the chair. He's doing some real dramatic bleeding and Danny says, "Four vets on each Nazi."

BR: We got up there and formed a cordon around them so that the demonstrators couldn't kill them. We gave them a minute to leave. They said no. We rushed them and kicked the shit out of them, drug them with their faces down on the concrete. The police stood by and laughed, because this is Miami Beach police.

AH: You have to understand, we are in south Miami Beach, where every Jewish working-class person from the entire eastern half of the northern tier of the United States retired. A bunch of them were Holocaust survivors.

At first, they were not happy with this encampment in their park, real unhappy with the counterculture, and terrified out of their sweet little old brains of anyone that looked wild. The vets looked wild and weren't the happiest crew in the world because they had to baby-sit for the yippies.

BR: After we kicked the Nazis' butts, it was hilarious, because then the Jewish women who wouldn't support us in Flamingo Park before were over there, "You need lights? We'll get lights. You need toilets? We'll get toilets. You guys kicked Nazis' ass!" Yeah, right, we're not fascists; we're antifascists.

AH: It was the dream of their life. This little old guy comes up to me and says, "We're very grateful." [She simulates an eastern European accent.] I said, "They're really very good boys. They really won't hurt you and they're not here to mess up the neighborhood. If we can help . . . " "Darlink, you've already helped more than you could realize." One of the ladies said, "What can we do for you?" Suddenly, we're drowning in chicken soup. The vets like to eat. We were up to our sweet little ears in soup.

I made the stupid mistake of mentioning that they had a passing fondness for beer. For the next two days we almost had enough beer. They sent trucks. They were just incredibly grateful. It cemented our relationship. Nobody could hurt these vets.

BR: We're in Flamingo Park, but we're separate, because there was just too much insanity with the other groups [yippies, zippies, etc.]. People just didn't feel secure; and we're vets, and vets like to feel secure no matter where they're at. So we set up our own camp with our own security, and people couldn't walk through unless we said.

Jack McCloskey (JKC): People were trying to come in trying to sell us heroin . . . every kind of dope you can think of.

We had walkie-talkies. People couldn't come in unless we cleared them first, and then they had to go with someone. It was like a military base in Vietnam. We knew that we would be infiltrated by people. We also knew we wanted to separate ourselves from political crazies, no matter what organization they came from.

Sheldon Ramsdell (SR): We were kicking informants off the campground at Flamingo Park every day. The media came in, and some of them weren't media at all.

How did you know?

SR: They didn't know how to behave. They didn't know how to fit in. You just knew there was something off here. He's taking photographs and he's got a microphone and he's only turning the machine on when you're giving your name, address, and serial number—that kind of thing. Obviously, you're not there to help us in any way. Maybe you are, but we're not convinced and you really have to leave. We take a picture and two guys would escort him off. He would be very upset. It only happened two or three times, but once was enough.

Once VVAW had set up camp and had dealt with the harassment from right-wing groups intent on disrupting the proceedings, and with apparently pointless protests such as those by the yippies (whom most members of VVAW detested), the veterans began to engage in their own series of demonstrations, which lasted three days.

SR: We marched silently from Flamingo Park to the Doral Hotel, where Nixon was. Pete McCloskey [a congressman from California] came up with bottles of Coca-Cola and handed them out; and I remember Mary McGrory wrote, "This terrorist group had bottles in their hands and no one threw a Molotov cocktail that day." [Laughs.]

On Tuesday, August 22—the second day of the convention—the veterans held what was to be its most dramatic protest. VVAW members once again marched silently, this time to the Fontainebleu Hotel, the center of the convention activities. As the journalist Hunter S. Thompson recalled, "The silence of the march was contagious, almost threatening. . . . The only sounds I remember hearing were the soft thump of boot leather on hot asphalt and the occassional rattling of an open canteen top." This march, however, received no other attention from the media.

SR: I was up at the Fontainebleu Hotel with Peggy Kerry [John Kerry's sister] and Hunter Thompson and all these other types [in an exaggeratedly deep voice], listening as the march was beginning. I was going to get down there with the unit.

I went down and Rocky Pomerance, the chief of police in Miami Beach, was among the heads of the National Guard [and] Secret Service—all these military and police officials of the brass standing in a circle—and I overheard him saying, "Well, there's some people in this march throwing things and breaking windows."

I just went right over there. . . . He already knew who I was. "This is Shelly Ramsdell, the PR dude with the Vietnam Veterans Against the War." I says, "I want to tell you this is going to be a peaceful march. There's going to be no trouble. If anyone causes trouble, isolate them—I don't care what you do. This has got to be peaceful; everything counts on this."

He was wonderful. He says, "Look, all right. Everybody get into the car." I don't know if I want do this, but I get into the car. We get near the march, and I say, "Let me out here. [Laughs.] I don't want them to see me getting out of your car." Rocky, [who] was our pal, says, "Well, we'll isolate them."

I says, "What you going to do?"

"Well, we'll pick them up. We got these U-Hauls—no windows, no ventilation—we'll stick them in there."

I said, "Oh, shit." [Laughs.]

Bobby Muller (BM): We went to the Fontainebleu Hotel, and we demanded a meeting with Nixon. We had all the VVAW people out there in the streets. We had an awful lot of people. They wouldn't let us in.

At the Fontainbleu, 500 heavily armed police officers confronted the marchers. No violent confrontation took place on that day; the veterans dispersed peacefully. However, on the next day—the day Nixon was to accept his party's renomination—they returned en masse to the convention site. Once again, they were confronted by the police.

BM: Myself, [Ron] Kovic, Bill Wyman—a double amputee—and I think a couple of other guys made it into the lobby of the hotel. We read a statement to the press. Somebody called in a bomb threat. It was just getting an excuse to get us out. So they kicked us out.

I remember we were in the front. The cops were several deep with the batons and masks. The guys like [Ed] Damato and others were saying these guys had volunteered for this duty, they wanted to crack heads, that there would be bloodshed. I said, "I'm not leaving."

Danny Friedman: The state police took over duties from the Miami Beach police because they thought the Miami police were too sympathetic. They

At the Republican convention, Miami, 1972. *Left to right, in wheelchairs:* Bobby Muller, Bill Wyman, and Ron Kovic.

had a Democratic mayor but a Republican governor, and he ordered the state police in and they were like storm troopers.

SR: In the beginning I guess there were a few anarchists wearing masks . . . who threw the smoke bombs and then burned the police barricades. I said, "This is it," you know.

BR: Then the demonstrations happened. People would sit down in the street, and they would be arrested nonviolently. Some people would go out and trash.

VVAW has never believed in trashing. We always thought it was counter-productive. We always believed that all it is a bunch of little children acting out their own frustration, and you can't win people over by setting fires to their stores. We made tons of mistakes but never made the mistake of thinking that setting a trash can on fire could change the world.

The police assaulted; it was a police riot. The police were beating people up and gassing people and everything else. We went out dragging people off the street who had been hurt real bad or who had been Maced, getting them to hospitals and stuff.

Linda Alband: I was back like behind the lines and we got teargassed anyway. The tear gas got lobbed in the wrong direction. I was with a bunch of senior citizens who were very severely damaged by the tear gas and choking. I thought some of them would have heart attacks. So I went to the police who, it had been advertised, would have water and stuff like that. I tried to get them to give me some so we could wash these people's faces off. They wouldn't even talk to me. They were just standing there.

JMC: I got teargassed. . . . I was treating an old man that got teargassed and I remember yippies coming up, saying, "What the fuck are you doing? This guy's your enemy." I'm saying, "Hey, I'm treating this man; he's dying from the tear gas." They took my hand, put it in a car door, and slammed the car door, breaking my two fingers.

BM: At that time, Congressman McCloskey from California had aides that were there. They gave me passes to go in as a delegate because McCloskey, who had run for president, had been denied through the RNC [Republican National Committee], the ability to use the forum of the Republican Convention to make an antiwar statement. They procedurally shut him out. He was very pissed. So Wyman, myself, and some walking guy [that is, not in a wheelchair] went in as alternate delegates.

We had been gassed and all that stuff approaching the convention. It was bedlam, but we had our alternate delegate passes and we got in. Somehow, while we were inside, Kovic showed up. I don't know how Kovic got in, but he ended up joining us.

We just sat there and waited for Nixon. When Nixon came on, we waited for the place to get silent and did what I consider the bravest thing that I've done, which is: took a deep breath, leaned back in the chair, and just shouted at the top of my lungs, "Stop the bombing; stop the war." Then we picked it up as a chant, "Stop the bombing; stop the war." The Secret Service was right around us, because we were dirtbags. We were wearing camouflage and stunk to high heaven. They said, "What do we do, what do we do?" While they're trying to figure out what to do, we're just steady screaming. They finally said, "Throw them out." Delegates spit on us and went a little crazy. They threw us out a back door. Thank God they shut the door, because the delegates wanted to kill us.

I remember, in traditional VVAW fashion, we reconvened at the city dump in Miami. That was the rendezvous point, the garbage dump. Can you imagine? I went to the garbage dump and said, "That's it. I'm out of here. Get me to the airport." [Laughs.]

Miami 1972 was really my last political action, because I realized I wasn't able to do this anymore. I was so angry and so confrontational. I could see it was going to go up in flames like me.

5

THE ATTACK ON THE WINTER SOLDIERS

*One of the lessons I learned from that period is that when you're doing
something right—really right, way down deep inside of you—
then it's going to just freak out people. So we freaked the cops,
the FBI, the CIA, and each other.*

Lee Thorn

*My own sense was that most of the things I saw us doing in the organiza-
tion were quite legal, quite aboveboard. . . . OK, go ahead and arrest us, but
try to prove that we were doing something illegal.*

Pete Zastrow

A National Security State

When the United States became a superpower at the end of the Second
World War, its efforts to maintain that status contributed to the growth of a
national security state; in the process, democracy at home and abroad was
compromised. The national security apparatus, which carried out foreign and
domestic policy initiatives outside public view, was erected in several stages
during the postwar years. Its scope and functions were formalized and fully
delineated in 1950, in a highly secret National Security Council document
known as NSC-68, which included various provisions for winning the cold
war. One such provision called on the National Security Council and the
agencies under its control to ensure a "government-created consensus"
among the American people for the nation's cold war policies.[1]

The national security apparatus sought to create consensus by engaging
several branches of the intelligence community in a campaign to warn the
American public of the dangers of communism, both foreign and domestic,
and to silence critics of American foreign and domestic policies. In addition
to clandestine operations, each president during the cold war—and Con-

gress—waged a public campaign against "dissidents" by branding them as unpatriotic and a danger to the nation.

Truman, for example, initiated a policy that required federal employees to sign loyalty oaths and assigned the FBI to uncover subversion within the government.[2] Congress, for its part, passed a series of laws restricting freedom of speech (including the Taft-Hartley Act of 1947 and the McCarran Internal Security Act of 1950); more important, through the House Committee on Un-American Activities, it conducted a series of public hearings whose purpose was to discredit and destroy opposition to the nation's cold war agenda.[3] These hearings are now, of course, infamous—they are typically described as witch-hunts that ruined any number of lives and undermined the Constitution without finding any real evidence of subversion—but at the time they were, to a considerable extent, effective.

The most potent and most dangerous weapon of the national security apparatus was the intelligence community. During the early years of the cold war, and later, in the 1960s—as a result of civil rights and antiwar activism— the various branches of the intelligence community were expanded greatly in size and scope. The FBI's Counter Intelligence Program (COINTELPRO) was the widest-ranging effort to infiltrate and destroy organizations that challenged American foreign and domestic policies. In the words of Ward Churchill and Jim Vander Wall:

> COINTELPRO efforts were marked—in varying degrees of intensity—by the utilization of the following methods against the Bureau's political targets: Eavesdropping . . . Bogus Mail . . . Disinformation . . . Harassment Arrests . . . Infiltrators and Agent Provocateurs . . . Fabrication of Evidence . . . and Assassinations.[4]

Through clandestine and often unconstitutional means, this program and others played a significant role in disrupting many organizations, including left-wing parties, civilian antiwar movements, and the Black Panther Party.

As the war in Vietnam intensified, the FBI was joined by other clandestine agencies in efforts to stifle dissent. The CIA, in an operation code-named CHAOS, engaged in domestic surveillance—overstepping its mandate, which restricted its activities to the international arena. Branches of military intelligence were also used against dissenters. Local "red squads" were formed by police departments in cities across the nation and became involved in the same kinds of activities as their counterparts in Washington. Right-wing groups were also enlisted in the government's attacks on dissenters, or were allowed to carry out their own attacks on left-wing groups and civil rights activists, even when their intention was to commit violence and the government was aware of that intention.

Vietnam Veterans Against the War became a target of the national security apparatus partly because of VVAW's efforts to warn the public of the corruption it perceived, and partly because it was seen as conferring legitimacy on the antiwar movement. And VVAW came under attack even though it consistently expressed its opposition to the war nonviolently. Evidently, the establishment saw these dissenting veterans as a threat because they spoke with the authority of experience: antiwar veterans, perhaps more than any other segment of the American population, were able to reveal the truth about Vietnam.

During 1971, as VVAW grew and its members expanded their critique of the war and American society, the Nixon administration stepped up the efforts to topple the organization. Across the nation, VVAW had drawn the attention of the media and thus was no longer isolated from the vast majority of the American public. By gaining the spotlight, however, VVAW also opened itself to attacks by its opponents. Attacks came from the White House, right-wing media pundits, much of the press, clandestine governmental agencies, and the courts. Essentially, VVAW—like other organizations and individuals who objected to national policies during the cold war— became an enemy of the national security state.

The assault in the press was led by right-wing editorialists such as William F. Buckley, J. F. Ter Horst, and Nick Thimmesch, who supported the Nixon administration's Vietnam policies. In particular, these columnists repeatedly attacked John Kerry, who was VVAW's leading public figure after Dewey Canyon III. Ter Horst seems to have fired the first shot, on May 2, 1971, in an article in the *Detroit News* entitled "2 Vets with Medals, 1 with Silver Spoon." He drew a contrast between Kerry, whose plea for immediate withdrawal from Vietnam had captured the attention of the nation, and another Vietnam veteran, Melville L. Stephens, who was arguing against withdrawal. In testimony before the Senate Foreign Relations Committee, Stephens had said that "the United States could not morally pull out so fast as to endanger the lives of those thousands of South Vietnamese who had trusted the American promise of deliverance from the Communist enemy." Ter Horst depicted Kerry as "wealthy, a product of the best Eastern schools" and noted that "Stephens grew up in Akron, Ohio, and is out of work."[5]

Ter Horst's focus on social class was signficant; he was, of course, playing on a long-standing phenomenon: there is a real tendency for the working class to distrust the elite, and this antagonism had often been used by right-wing demagogues, such as Senator Joe McCarthy. Ter Horst, then, clearly meant to drive a wedge between VVAW on the one side and the majority of working-class veterans and working-class Americans in general on the other. It is important to realize that this distinction was at best dubious: most of the veterans who supported immediate withdrawal were from working-class backgrounds; and although Kerry was from an upper-class family, he actually represented the more moderate faction of VVAW.

William F. Buckley, writing in the *Washington Star* and the *Boston Globe*, also attacked Kerry, but from another angle: though Buckley too mentioned

Kerry's upper-class background, he focused on the speech itself. Kerry had asked Americans to reassess the values and the obsession with communism that underlay the nation's tragic policies in Vietnam; Buckley responded by calling him "an ignorant young man," and contended, sarcastically, that Kerry's critique went "too deep to be bleached out by conventional remorse or resolve; better the destruction of America."[6]

Buckley's comments reflected the seriousness of the debate. VVAW was asking Americans to do something radical—to reconsider their concept of patriotism. By discussing Kerry's plea in terms of the "destruction of America," Buckley was exploiting a widespread fear that the nation was careening out of control. It is true that at this point most Americans were tired of the war, but it is also true that they were tired of the revolutionary rhetoric, and the actual violence, of some fringe groups in the antiwar movement, such as the Weather Underground. Accordingly, Buckley implied that the antiwar movement was itself a danger to the nation. Buckley's closing words were: "I shall not listen, ever, to those who say that [the Vietnam war] was less than the highest tribute to the national motivation, to collective idealism and to international rectitude."

This was to be expected from right-wing journalists, but VVAW was also misrepresented by the liberal, or relatively liberal, media. For example, when the steering committee met in Denver in the spring of 1972, one contingent of veterans moved that VVAW adopt a more consciously revolutionary agenda. This proposal was rejected by a large majority; nevertheless, the *New York Times,* which had acquired a copy from an unidentified source, ran a story claiming that the revolutionary agenda represented VVAW's actual polices.[7]

In addition, the Nixon administration used its access to the media to challenge the dissenting veterans: during the summer and fall of 1971, the White House staged numerous events to offset VVAW's antiwar messages. In October 1971, for instance, the White House held a press conference at which 10 Vietnam veterans who supported Nixon's policies were presented to the press; they were introduced as young men whose "dedication is in the highest tradition of the American spirit of volunteering." After their tour of duty, the adminstration had arranged for them to go back to South Vietnam, where they had helped "build housing developments in the town of Cat Lai, near Saigon, for men attending vocational training schools."[8] The press conference was staged after their return to the United States, and its purpose was apparent in a memo to Nixon from his aide Charles Colson: "These veterans are very strong supporters and most have been active in some anti–John Kerry activities." Colson advised the president to emphasize, as a "talking point," that these men were "outstanding examples of the young people in this country who are often overshadowed by their more radical peers." Actually, this episode revealed the extent to which VVAW had captured the moral high ground, since the press conference was designed to highlight the 10 veterans' compassion, and by association the administration's compassion, for the Vietnamese.

In any case, though, Nixon did not rely on presenting his counterarguments through the press; the administration was at the same time intensifying its extralegal attacks on VVAW. The tactics the administration used were not new, but it took them to new extremes.

For one thing, the antiwar veterans became a target of the intelligence community. The FBI had begun keeping files on VVAW in the fall of 1967, shortly after the organization was formed.[9] Agents monitored VVAW's activities and gathered information on individual members, hoping to leak "incriminating" information to news agencies. The FBI examined antiwar veterans' military records and their personal lives and tried to find links between VVAW and communist or radical organizations. (In this regard, it is worth pointing out that, then as now, membership in left-wing, even communist, organizations is protected under the Constitution.) Even when the FBI failed to uncover any "evidence that the CP [Communist Party] directs, dominates, or controls VVAW," agencies continued to monitor and harass antiwar veterans and shared information about individual members among themselves.[10]

Furthermore, the dissenting veterans became a target for powerful individuals in the administration. To cite just one example, when VVAW placed an ad in the *New York Times* on November 19, 1969, denouncing the war, Secretary of Defense Robert McNamara requested information on VVAW from the FBI. According to William C. Hunt, who was director of security in the Office of the Secretary of Defense, McNamara had become "very incensed" after seeing the ad and planned to "discuss it with the president."[11]

The activities undertaken by the intelligence agencies reached disturbing proportions. These agencies carried out observations of VVAW and harassed its members, presumably as a means of intimidation. Some members were followed and contacted, surveillance of VVAW offices was initiated, and phone taps were installed with little if any effort at concealment. Eventually, some of the veterans' families were questioned and harassed. Barry Romo's mother, for example, was repeatedly approached by FBI agents seeking to elicit information regarding her son "during pretext conversation[s]," although the FBI's own files reveal that Romo was never involved in any activities that would endanger Americans.[12]

Romo himself was arrested on August 20, 1971, for using "loud and profane" language at a dedication ceremony for a new VA hospital in Loma Linda, California, at which President Nixon spoke. Romo was sentenced to two years' probation. The probation would later be overturned on appeal, but while it was still in effect the FBI attempted to "discreetly explore the possibility" of having it "revoked and sentence imposed."[13] This occurred when Romo had been chosen to travel to North Vietnam sometime in 1972 as part of a VVAW delegation; the FBI was trying to have Romo jailed in order to remove him from the delegation. The attorney general of California (citing the state's penal code), refused the FBI's request, and Romo ultimately did go to North Vietnam in December of that year.[14]

VVAW and the Security Apparatus

The following narratives give brief but troubling glimpses into the kinds of clandestine activities that were used against VVAW and its members. Some of the FBI's records have been declassified, and these corroborate the veterans' charges of harassment, intimidation, and infiltration. However, a full accounting of such activities is still not possible, since today—more than 20 years after the events—many of the files remain classified.

"We're Watching You"

Did you experience any harassment or intimidation?

JAN BARRY

We knew we were going to be infiltrated. We knew we were going to have people trying to make us look like we were there to do things that we weren't there to do. I assumed military intelligence, at a minimum. I have seen some of my Army intelligence files, and I have seen enough of the activity that went on. They had everybody activated—Naval Intelligence, Air Force Intelligence, everybody.[15]

At Dewey Canyon, as we were marching the first day from the far end of the Mall past the White House to the Capitol, I stayed at the tail end. . . . One of the things about the military is road security. You have someone at the end of what you're doing so you don't have somebody plow into the back of what you're doing. There was this car with a couple or three people in it immediately behind the end of the march, which also had a huge truck that said Vietnam Veterans Against the War. There was another veteran there who said, "I know somebody in that car; he was in military intelligence." He walks over, starts pounding on the hood and says, "What are you fuckers doing here?" They didn't answer. They stayed right there behind the march.

SHELDON RAMSDELL

In Dewey Canyon we threw some people off the grounds because they . . . had phony credentials. We had our own credentials; they forged them, and they looked forged. We're saying, "Who put this together? [Laughs.] This is a joke. How much are they paying you for this shit? Get out of here. We love you and everything, but you've got to go." I mean, they were there to make mischief.

Was that a concern of yours—that people would come in to destabilize or infiltrate VVAW?

Well, not really. I mean, we weren't that vulnerable, really. There were individuals that were vulnerable, but most of us weren't at all. Working with the Secret Service with Eugene McCarthy for months . . . [and] my father was a policeman in Maine . . . I mean, you know how these mentalities kind of work, and they're really not all that efficient.

PETE ZASTROW

I remember I was on my way to a demonstration in Cincinnati. I had taken a bus, and this man came up and introduced himself—somebody-or-other Sherman, I think. He said he was the head of the FBI here in Cincinnati and could he sit down and have a cup of coffee with me.

I had no idea who this guy was. There was no reason he should have known who I was. Nor should he have had any idea that I was walking by here at such and such a time.

How did you react? Was it frightening?

No, it didn't frighten me at the time. I didn't frighten very easily. You know, fuck them. It's probably misplaced and stupid faith in the system. If you're not really doing anything wrong, you're all right. It's stupid, but what can I tell you?

Cincinnati, I should say, is a very right-wing town. But it's a Taft right-wing town. That means they play things very much by the rules. It's a genteel, conservative town. While the police didn't like us, it would have seemed amazing if the police had actually ever brutalized people. No matter how much they disagreed with what we were doing, that was just not how they functioned. Unlike Chicago police, who were quite willing to break the law in order to attack demonstrators, Cincinnati police, in those days, would have never done that, but they did keep pretty close track of us.

We found out later that they were paying $5 and $10 to people to go around and collect the leaflets we had distributed. God, we would have given them 50 for a nickel.

BILL DAVIS

Jane Fonda stayed at my place [in Columbus, Ohio] one time at the end of the Indo-China Peace Campaign tour. There were so many different undercover cops and agents and shit. . . . You get 20 cars with guys wearing ties, guys pretending to fix the electricity. You're going like, "Hi, how're you doing?"

The neighbors were pounding on my door complaining that there was no place to park on the street. I said, "Look, I'm sorry; there's some people staying here and there's all these cops and pigs here and there's nothing I can do about it." So then they'd go up and down the street, saying, "Why don't you leave these people alone? Why don't you get the fuck out of here? We don't have anyplace to park on the street."

Some of these people were so embarrassed they had to leave.

ANN HIRSCHMAN

In general, the police didn't attack VVAW all that often. VVAW's pretty daunting. There was one particular police officer in New York, though, who loved to attack us—myself, Danny Friedman, and Pete Mahoney very specifically. His name was John Finnegan. He was the head of the New York red squad.16

They didn't like the Peace Parade committee—"they" were the anticommunist, anti–left wing group in the New York City Police Department. They were rabid. They were there to eliminate us and to eradicate us and to get us out of New York.

John [Finnegan] didn't like me from way back because I used to blow his cover. He's gorgeous. His moonlighting job was he was the banker . . . in the Irving Trust ads. He's silver-haired, blue-eyed, straight-nosed, and looked so trustworthy. He used to get a CBS camera and get on buses and pretend to be a CBS reporter. I used to say, "This is not a reporter; this is a cop." He used to get all crazy.

About 1968 or 1969, a group called Newsreel did a movie called *Red Squad* about the Chicago and New York versions of the red squad. John was featured and I was one of the people in the film. After that, I was persona non grata. John tried to get me on felony counts for years.

I at the time was also working with the Black Panther Party, which interestingly enough had a fairly significant contingent of vets. I taught first aid to the Panther defense committee in 1966 and 1967. I wrote a first aid course specifically for demonstration of first aid. John Finnigan came in and literally would not allow us to distribute the first 50,000 copies of this.

In 1970, he busted me for practicing medicine without a license. He was real upset when Fitzy Mullen came in and said, "I'm a doctor. She's not practicing medicine; she's my nurse." Fitz, of course, had on a cutoff jeans jacket, love beads, and a beard down to his navel and didn't look like an average GP, but he had an MD degree. [Laughs.]

John busted me for riot, resisting, obstructing. He busted Danny Friedman numbers of times.

DANNY FRIEDMAN

I didn't spend much time at home with my parents—I was sleeping around, staying at the VVAW office—but the FBI [and] the police red squad came around and would talk to my neighbors and parents. "Did you know that the guy next to you is a communist?" and "What was he like as a kid?"

What did your parents think about all this?

Actually, they kind of supported me. They wished I was around more. They didn't like when I was on TV with my head bloodied and shit; but other than that, it was OK.

There were also phone taps. People talked about a lot of shit on the phone. We were very naive. We thought what we were doing was cool and OK.

Danny Friedman after being assaulted by the police during actions by the VVAW/WSO in Washington, D.C., July 3, 1974..

There was nothing illegal about it. It was just, so it had to be right, you know? There can't be anything illegal about something that's right.

LEE THORN

We were hassled during Vets for Peace—me personally. At the action at Fort Ord [California], I coordinated the legal backup, so I stayed at the Berkeley campus. On that day we were going to have this little overflight with an MDM [Movement for a Democratic Military] banner at Fort Ord. We told this ex-lifer who had this little airplane company the MDM stood for Morale and Discipline in the Military.

I was on the phone arranging this deal. We sent this guy over with cash to pay this guy who was going to put the banner on his plane. I told him to stay around and make sure the guy takes off. Our guy gave him the money. He went up above him on a hill, looks down, and the FBI swooped down—plainclothes guys in government cars. So the guy never takes off.

Then I call Fort Ord to tell them, and I'm using somebody else's phone. Somebody gets on the phone and says, "I'm sorry, Mr. Thorn; I disconnected you. I'll reconnect you." There's no way anyone should have known who I was. So I go down the hallway, with this guy, to call on the pay phone. As soon as I dial in, I say "Hello," and the phone would go dead. It happened three times, so I said, Fuck this. Then these cops came around. . . . This is during the time when cops were shooting.

I went home and took off all my clothes [so that no one could say he was carrying a concealed weapon], called my lawyer, and said, "I have all my clothes off. If you hear anything's happened to me, this is what's going on."

They cut off my phone at home. This scared the shit out of my wife. That was 1970. That was pre-VVAW. That shit went on for three years. That was trying.

By 1972, the cops had set up across the street from us. They had these microphones on top of the roof. You could see them. They had a guy 24 hours a day on a goddamned camera in a window across the way. Our phones weren't just tapped; they'd go off. We had to use different phones because those fucking phones weren't reliable.

One of the lessons I learned from that period is that when you're doing something right—really right, way down deep inside of you—then it's going to just freak out people. So we freaked the cops, the FBI, the CIA, and each other.

What impact did such surveillance have on the organization?

The cops were effective in the sense that when we started asking guys for DD-214s [military discharge forms]—and not even accepting that, doing

323

actual background investigations on new guys in order for them to become a member of a chapter—that was the beginning of the end.

It creates a kind of atmosphere of paranoia that makes it difficult to grow. It gets you on edge, having yourself photographed anytime you went into your own office. In that atmosphere, then these kinds of conspiratorial thinking—that people like RU [Revolutionary Union] were adept at and articulated—seemed true. We were vulnerable to it. We assumed every goddamned chapter was infiltrated by the police.

JOHN KNIFFIN

We were getting intense surveillance by local red squad people, the Houston police department, and federal agencies. Killeen and Houston were bad. Dallas was bad. Austin was an oasis of sanity in an otherwise right-wing reactionary state.

In general, the police and local cop red squads were giving us more grief than they were in other areas. If a political organizer in the south got too effective, then he'd get arrested for something.

The heat was serious and visible. You would go out and walk down the street to eat, and they're following you with a guy snapping pictures of you. They weren't even subtle about it. They were outright blatant about it. Crazy things were happening. Buildings we would already have access to were all of a sudden no longer available. All kinds of stuff, and just incredible paranoia.

ANNIE LUGINBILL

I could talk about tapped telephones. There were some days when we could neither make nor receive phone calls. One of our people very foolishly made an appointment to meet an AWOL GI at the office over the telephone, and somewhere about half an hour before the GI is due to show, the Office of Naval Intelligence is sitting outside our front door. It's a good thing the kid decided to take a pass and go somewhere else for a little while.

MIKE McCAIN AND JILL McCAIN

Mike McCain (MMC): VVAW was going to the Republican convention in 1972 because that's where Nixon was going to be. The convention was supposed to be in San Diego. Because I had been in southern California, I was scouting in San Diego as a VVAW representative. The first political bust of my life occurred because that's what I was doing.

I was living in Van Nuys at the time. I was going to college. The red squad came in and raided my apartment, with me in it. They came up to the door and said that they had a report of a disturbance in the neighborhood: "Mind if we come in?" I said, "Yeah, sure. What's going on? There's nothing happening here." I was being like a concerned citizen. I was ignorant and naive. They surrounded the place. They came screaming in. That place was filled with cops in like five seconds. Myself and my roommate are spread-eagled on the ground. We're in jail in minutes.

They went through my apartment. They ransacked the place. They stole everything. They took the typewriters; they took every single piece of paper, every book, my grandfather's shotgun. I had no idea what was going on.

What did you think you were being arrested for?

MMC: We found out very quickly. It didn't take long to figure out. They kept asking us, "Where's the guns? Where's the grenades?" Shit like that. We said, "What the fuck are you talking about?" I spent three days in jail without any charges being filed. We were so naive. We didn't have any clue as to what our rights were or anything.

Jill McCain: We were followed by the red squad when they had the national steering committee meeting here in 1972. They staked out the apartment across the street. We saw them with the cameras and stuff, and we're waving and stuff.

MMC: In 1976, we got information from some people high up in politics in San Francisco in the police department that the leadership was all going to be busted for various things, the biggest being possession and use of marijuana, which was probably the only reality that existed—nobody was trafficking in guns; nobody was dealing drugs. I spent a few days at our attorney's home— one of the National Lawyers Guild attorneys, a woman who's now a judge in San Francisco. I walked around with two attorneys with me all the time. Until probably 1977 or 1978, I was under constant surveillance. My phone was constantly tapped.

Did this kind of harassment scare people or curtail activities?

MMC: Oh, no. We already knew what the best was. The worst they could do was kill us. That's what I used to get in trouble for. I used to tell people, "We already been through hell; they can't do anything to us any more." Some people got very upset with my polemic: "You can't say that. They'll think you're advocating picking up the gun!" I didn't say that. You just have to be ready for them to kill you. I mean, look at the Black Panthers; look what they're doing to the Native American movement.

Infiltrators and Agents Provocateurs

PETE ZASTROW, JILL McCAIN, MIKE McCAIN, ANNIE LUGINBILL,
BARRY ROMO, BILL DAVIS, DAVID EWING

Pete Zastrow (PZ): I remember being told by someone at some very early date that if you had five people in your chapter, one of them was going to be an agent. I've never seen anything to make that untrue. I did enough stuff, particularly when I got into the national office, of going around and doing the interrogations . . . that I don't find that amazing. I guess I was hatchet man for a while.

Whom did you interrogate? Were these people who wanted to join VVAW?

PZ: No, no. These were people who we suspected were agents and later found out were agents and were willing to tell us what they had been doing.

What made you suspect someone was an agent?

PZ: I think you were constantly suspicious. You'd have to look at a specific case. They usually weren't vets. They were usually [romantically] attached.

Jill McCain: The state used women as agents. Many of the groupies that were around were agents. That was one of the easiest things to do, because guys would talk. The more difficult ones were the guys who were posing as veterans.

PZ: The closest example I can think of is the woman who is now head of Save the Lakefront in Chicago, Sheli Lulkin, who was the head of Labor Union Women in Chicago [Chicago Coalition of Labor Union Women]. She was very much involved in VVAW and part of the Chicago red squad. I mean she went everywhere with us. She was a very good friend. She was never in the middle of organization because she wasn't a vet, but she was involved in almost everything we did.[17]

In 1974, Pete Zastrow went to Buffalo, New York, to interview someone else who had been uncovered as an agent within the organization.

PZ: They just had a major FBI informant turn up there. She was on national television. She testified. She was both in VVAW and the Attica Support Group. Mary Ann . . . I can't remember her name anymore. It was a pretty big thing at the time, and they needed to have somebody go out and find out what she had told the FBI we were doing.

I talked to her at length, tedious length, and listened to all these sad stories about why she had done all these horrible things. We only had to beat confessions out of people occasionally. [Laughs.] But I do remember the bright lights in Milwaukee. [Laughs.] Somebody stuck in a closet with bright lights shining on them.[18]

What were your feelings when she was telling you this stuff? I mean, what was she telling you?

PZ: It was the kind of stuff where she would sell them the national minutes of the organization. . . . The stuff that they were being told was so essentially insignificant, it seemed to me. I guess I cared less about some of these conspiracies than other people did. My own sense was that most of the things I saw us doing in the organization were quite legal, quite aboveboard. . . . OK, go ahead and arrest us, but try to prove that we were doing something illegal.

So we're going to hold a demonstration? Demonstrations by and large are legal. You go through the formalities and you get your permits and all of that kind of crap, and OK—people don't like it, and they may try to break it up, but still, what you're doing is basically legal. The fact that the FBI knows you're going to hold it. . . . Who cares? The newspapers would tell them we're going to hold it anyhow. It's not to say that the FBI was not around. They were around constantly. They were constantly asking people things. There certainly were at national meetings, where people turned up with guns. They were grossly illegal. All this kind of stuff was going on. Of course VVAW had its loose cannons. Of course the media or the FBI or whoever would try to use these to cast aspersions on the organization, and they might be very successful. I'm sure in various localities they were successful. I guess from the inside, I never saw us as much of a threat as the bourgeoisie saw us.

Did you take any precautions as an organization to weed out informants?

PZ: We had our own special FBI report that anybody was supposed to turn in to the national office if they were approached or if there were suspicious things going on.

Mike McCain: We were prepared to deal with agents. We used to compare notes. We ended up identifying some 20 or 30 agents on a national level. We knew that's what they were and put out the word to let everybody know.

What impact did infiltration and provocation have on the organization?

PZ: The vast majority of the people in the organization were pretty sensible. Again, there were some strange people, and many of them went into other organizations and probably did many of the strange things that they used to occasionally talk about in VVAW. As far as I know, under VVAW auspices, there has never been a bombing. There has never been an assassination. I don't think we ever shot at a presidential candidate, although Sarah Jane Moore was a leading VVAW associate in the Bay Area when she shot at Ford[19] And there was Joe [Ramiro], . . . an ex-chapter member in Oakland who went off and ended up in jail for life.[20]

David Ewing: This woman named Sarah Jane Moore who shot at Ford was in the [Oakland] chapter. She called herself Sally. She was like fifty-five years old or something—a matronly old lady, a liberal woman. [Her actual age was forty-five.]

She joined as an FBI informant. She went in at the Hearsts' bequest. She joined VVAW because the secret police identified that as a group where the [Symbionese Liberation Army] terrorists were. That was how to get Patty back, because those people did it. They were right on that.

She was giving reports to the FBI about what was happening in the chapter. Then she became convinced that actually they [VVAW members in Oakland] were right, and [she] regretted working for the FBI. She had a change of heart.

She wanted to confess to Jeanne [Friedman] that she was wrong and stuff, but she didn't dare because she would have been exposed as a police agent. Meanwhile, they had become suspicious of her—Jeanne and the others—but they didn't tell us that they were suspicious of her. They searched her car and found some incriminating things or something. I had never been informed of any of this. So, the last meeting we all attended before the split, I gave her my telephone number. I didn't know this was the last meeting. I didn't know she was working for the police or anything.

A short time after that, she tried to assassinate President Ford while he was in the San Francisco area. She tried to make amends. She had this sudden change of heart and became a revolutionary. She was arrested.

My phone was tapped for two years after that. When I was in Chicago for an RSB [Revolutionary Student Brigade] convention, the FBI came to my door and harassed my wife. That caused years and years of problems for me.

Annie Luginbill (AL): In terms of police harassment, the Chicago chapter had its own particular infiltrator, at least during the period that I remember. There was a man named Robert Oxley who said he was a security guard somewhere. Bob came in and said he was very interested in doing vets' work. We said, "Fine." He came to our meetings. He came to our rallies. He leafleted. He sold newspapers.

There was a demo in Chicago in January of 1975 around deportation of immigrants and Antoine Pauley, who was a black kid who had been shot by a cop in Rogers Park. The themes was tied together, about oppression.

We were on 18th Street, down in the barrio. We marched. We went off the sidewalk and onto the street. The police wanted us back on the sidewalk. This was a Saturday and everybody was busy shopping. There was no way they were going to get us back onto the sidewalk. It was a very uneasy peace, until Bob Oxley jumped out of line and started beating on a police officer. Well, all hell broke loose. We were attacked by the police. They arrested 15 people in the demo. I was one of them. Most of the people they arrested were in VVAW.

I was up in Sheli Lulkin's apartment reading the *Chicago Daily News,* the Mike Royko column. The Mike Royko column was about our court case, which had just happened that morning, and about Robert Oxley, [who] was a police agent. He was a student at the police academy. He brought it out publicly. I had not known before.

I find it very ironic now, looking back on it, to learn about Bob Oxley in Sheli Lulkin's apartment, because approximately one year later Sheli Lulkin was exposed as a police agent.

Did you take precautions?

AL: Absolutely. One of the signs outside the national office door was: "No drugs. No guns. Leave bad attitudes at the door and don't bring them in." It's just standard kinds of things that people have always done on the left. Don't be stupid. If you're going to be stupid, don't do politics.

We in fact expelled someone from the Chicago chapter, a man named Rex, because he packed [a gun] all the time. We said, "Don't do this. If you're going to pack, don't come around us, because that not what we're about. We don't need weapons."

Why no guns?

AL: Easy setup. Why get busted for guns when that's not what we're about? So don't jeopardize the organization.

Barry Romo (BR): We were infiltrated heavily, and police repression was extremely heavy. We had a wonderful guy in the chapter. He was an Irish guy—sensible, everybody liked him, no ultraleftist.

[Ron] Kovic got beat up by the cops and put in the back of a police car, and they shoved him facedown and he was suffocating because [he had] no stomach muscles and [his] hands were handcuffed behind his back. This guy fought his way, along with a pacifist priest or minister . . . through the cops to save his life, to pull him back up so Ron could breathe. Great guy.

I get a phone call at the LA office. . . . "Is this VVAW?" . . . "Yes." . . . "Do you allow cops to belong to your organization?" . . . "No." . . . "Well, yes you do. My next-door neighbor, Sergeant Such-and-Such, is a member of VVAW. Are you sure you don't allow cops to belong?" We said, "We don't know anybody by that name, but could you give us the address of that neighbor?" Fucking went out and watched his house, and it ended up being this guy. He was a sergeant in the LAPD [Los Angeles Police Department] whose main job was to infiltrate the IRA support group, and he was using the VVAW as his cover. So he did absolutely nothing to VVAW. He had basically saved Kovic's life.

How did you deal with this infiltration?

BR: There was nothing we could do. If you're an open organization doing legal activity, you have to take the police busts when they come. Your safety is openness. We held meetings in Miami Beach with cops. I'm not telling you we didn't have secret meetings, but we had open meetings where we actually planned stuff out.

If you turn paranoid, then you destroy yourself. In fact, you've done the government's job. We took security extremely seriously. You treated people who were disruptive as agents. We had lots of people who were agents and disruptive, but we had lots of people who were disruptive and not agents. If you find someone's a cop, you don't keep him.

Bill Davis (BD): When VVAW was first organized in Columbus, the VP [vice president] of the organization was a military intelligence agent, Army. He'd been a former sergeant and he was with the chapter for two years . . . very instrumental in focusing what we were doing, seeing to all the administrative duties of the chapter, contacting people, keeping things going, making sure all the leaflets were printed. He was just pouring money and time and energy into keeping it going. The guy was good. We had no idea. It wasn't discovered for a very long time.

In 1972, when [Bill] Crandle and [Art] Flesh were getting ready to leave the organization, Art Flesh goes, "Hey, you'll never guess who was a pig." I said, "Who?" "The guy that used to be VP—Neil."

How did you discover him?

BD: His wife divorced him, and she'd been friends with Flesh and Crandle's wives. She called them up [and] said, "Hey, I divorced So-and-So."
"Really? What's he doing now?"
"He's a first lieutenant in Germany now." She goes, "You probably never knew it; he was undercover military intelligence."
Crandle and Flesh go, "Yeah, right, we never knew it. He did his job well. If you ever see him, thank him because he really kept us going for a while when things weren't going too well."
That was my first known case. We had people who would come to like one meeting and advocate we should storm this National Guard facility, get weapons and stuff like that; and I would say, "Geez, I don't think that's very

good idea. That's kind of counterproductive." They wouldn't say anything else, and we wouldn't see them again. They were agents provocateurs and shit. Whenever we would have a big demo, people would show up suddenly who were from out of state or weren't with VVAW, and we wouldn't have time to check them out—but we'd say, "Watch this guy and watch him carefully," and we'd put a couple of guys on him.

It was really scary—not to us, to the police. . . . But they were very polite to us. There was never any break-ins of any living quarters, but everyplace was monitored.

The Case of William Lemmer

JOHN KNIFFIN, TERRY DuBOSE, SHELDON RAMSDELL, LINDA ALBAND

When agents were uncovered, they were rarely found to have been successful in disrupting VVAW. Nevertheless, numerous local law enforcement agencies and the FBI paid informants and provocateurs to infiltrate VVAW, especially in the south. The southern chapters were highly infiltrated—more than any other chapters in the nation. The most widely publicized case was that of William Lemmer, who held the post of regional coordinator from Arkansas. He played a key role in the federal government's efforts to discredit and destroy VVAW. His activities contributed to an indictment of eight VVAW members in 1972.

Lemmer had joined VVAW in the summer of 1971, after having attended Dewey Canyon III. He quickly became known as a hothead, prone to violent rhetoric. Although he was a student, apparently with little income, by the fall of 1971 he began to spend money lavishly—an indication that he was being paid by the government. In February 1972, at the meeting of the steering committee in Denver, Lemmer assumed leadership of the Arkansas-Oklahoma region. He then tried to incite violence among the veterans.

Lemmer's case reveals the lengths to which the Justice Department and the FBI were willing to go in their attempts to discredit VVAW.[21]

John Kniffin (JK): Lemmer was the coordinator from Arkansas. He had elevated himself to coordinator, which wasn't real hard in those days because coordinators burned out real fast. Whoever was silly enough to continue, fine, you can do it.

Informants live by having enough truth to say to make them credible and then having a whole lot of bullshit to confuse the issue, and Lemmer was a master at that.

Terry DuBose (TDB): He was basically a flake. It wasn't this grand conspiracy on his part to indict anybody or anything like that. He was just playing it by ear, a day at a time, and telling them anything that popped into his mind.

JK: He was getting paid for it. So basically, when you look at it from that point of view, you've got an informant whose pay scale depends on how much information he's giving them. He's going to tell him what they want to hear. If he tells them something real outrageous, they're going to pay him more. He had a vested interest in trying to change things around, do things, provoke things, influence things.

TDB: Lemmer had this idea of taking over the Alamo at Christmas. [In 1971, during Operation Peace on Earth.] . . . Lemmer's circulating around through the GIs. . . . He says, "Look what's going on there. [That is, in San Francisco, New York, and other cities where VVAW members had taken over public sites.] We're not doing anything, so let's get out of here." He got a bunch of them together and took off for the LBJ Library. They wanted to occupy the replica of the Oval Office in the LBJ Library.

This was very disruptive, because we had made all these other plans and it was happening. We also didn't want to do anything that would jeopardize the safety of the GIs who we were working with. They would have been the ones to feel the heat for such activities.

Sheldon Ramsdell: Oh, Lemmer was a badass. I knew him in Saint Louis. We were going on to Cairo, Illinois, with the food, clothing, and medicine we collected. We're in Saint Louis in this apartment, and he sets us up on his porch. He's got these old antique guns and we're all standing like idiots, posing, and he's taking pictures. He set us up in Saint Louis—holding guns, for Christ's sake! They did everything in their power to make us look bad and threatening.

In Cairo, I photographed inside the church. We got back to Saint Louis and Bill Lemmer stole all my videos I took in Cairo, Illinois. They wanted my video really bad. They thought we were transporting guns, but we weren't.

I called New York and talked to Al Hubbard and said, "Get me the hell out of here. This guy can't be trusted. He's photographed us with guns. He's taken my tapes." So they gave me bus fare. I took a Greyhound bus. I had a lot of time to think. I got to New York and said, "We got a problem." I said, "I'm not afraid, but I don't like what's going on."

Linda Alband: I knew in Houston [where the steering committee held a meeting in the spring of 1972] that Bill Lemmer was an agent. . . . He had an FBI telephone billing code that he gave everybody.

Repercussions of Being Affiliated with VVAW

JAN BARRY

I had worked as a newspaper researcher. At some point, Hubbard says to me, "They're looking for a researcher at CBS News. Why don't you call this person?" I did. I had an interview. They said, "Great; we'll hire you."

I was introduced, taken around all the various departments at CBS News as one of those veterans involved in that demonstration [Dewey Canyon III]. People all through *Sixty Minutes,* the sports department, and Walter Cronkite's crew said, "Isn't that wonderful?" I worked there all through the summer of 1971 in the research department, covering everything. I covered a moon shot, *Sixty Minutes,* sports, the nightly news, the weekend news.

In the fall, I started on what they had hired me to focus on, which was the military aspects of the war. They had hired another person, who had been in Vietnam with a civilian group, to cover the civilian side of the Vietnam War. Then I'm hearing the scuttlebutt about how in the old days they got rid of people through the blacklist situation. They were gone like this [snaps his fingers], with their reputations totally besmirched. I thought, this is interesting, but this is 1971—what have I got to worry about?

All of a sudden one day, I get called in on the carpet. "You're in big fucking trouble," my supervisor says; "You know where it's coming from." He didn't say where it was coming from. I'm thinking, Why doesn't he say where it's coming from? How do I know where it's coming from? What became clear is that it didn't go to the news division; it went to the top of CBS Corporation to get rid of this $160-a-week researcher.

Nobody accused me of screwing up what I was doing. I was the person who checked to see that all those names were spelled right and when they put facts on the screen, that those were the facts. At one point I'm doing this, and somebody says to me, "You get one word wrong and you're screwed." I'm doing the job. All of a sudden I'm yanked into the office of a vice president who starts hollering and screaming and claiming that I have a conflict of interest in covering the Pentagon. I said, "That's interesting. If you want to switch me to something else, like the environment, how am I going to get away from the Army Corps of Engineers? If I cover the economy, how do I get away from the military-industrial complex of the economy?" As far as having a conflict of interest, Walter Cronkite has been beating the drum for the space program for years. He starts getting bluer and bluer and redder and redder. I said, "Furthermore, if you're going to press this issue, I'm going to have to think about a discrimination lawsuit." The guy practically choked to death.

During this time, I said, "I am considering going down to Washington and testifying before the congressional committee that once a year goes through the review of television licenses." "Oh, no, no, don't do that." I said, "Then what I want is a meeting with the president of CBS News. I want to hear from him." All this was subterfuge. Nobody said anything directly.

Even before I got a meeting with him, I start hearing, "Would you like to do a history of the Vietnam War, coauthored with CBS News?" This is a big thing being held out to me, right? But I'm also thinking, Yeah, but there's a whole lot of strings attached to it. Whose version of the history is this going to be, theirs or mine? When I meet with this guy, he in essence says, well, I handled myself pretty well. Would I consider being a special assistant to address their critics? I thought their critics most of the time were right on target. I said to him, "I don't want to work for an organization that treats people like this." That was it. He said, "We'll give you severance pay," which was six weeks and at those times was an enormous amount of money.

MIKE McCAIN

The FBI constantly harassed us. Hell, my first wife spilled her guts to them. My mother and father both refused to talk to them.

My father lost his job. After he retired from the Air Force, he went to work for the Department of Defense and at the time was working on the SAGE system, which is the semiautomatic ground environment control, an all-weather landing system. He was working on the SR-71. They pulled his security clearance because of me. He couldn't even enter the building. They just brought him his personal effects and that was it. They almost ruined my mother's life. It had a major effect on my family. We didn't speak for 10 years.

They were threatening to take people's children away because many were having children who weren't married. We had friends of ours who were subpoenaed before a grand jury, refused to testify, and had their children taken away by the state.

The Trial of the Gainesville Eight

BARRY ROMO, SHELDON RAMSDELL, ANN HIRSCHMAN,
JOHN KNIFFIN, MIKE McCAIN, PETE ZASTROW, DANNY FRIEDMAN

The most damaging attack on VVAW took place between July 1972 and August 1973, when the federal government accused eight members of conspiring to attack local and national law enforcement agencies during the Republican convention in Miami Beach, Florida. These members, who came to be known as the "Gainesville Eight" (they had met in Gainesville and were

The Gainesville Eight. *Left to right. Back row:* John Briggs, Peter Mahoney, Bill Patterson, Stan Michelsen, Don Perdue. *Front row:* Scott Camil, Alton Foss, John Kniffin.

tried there), were indicted in July 1972, shortly after the Republican convention and just at the start of the Democratic convention. Their trial lasted a year, and VVAW had to spend a great deal of time and money on their defense. This case exacerbated existing tensions within VVAW, raised further suspicions of infiltration, and essentially destroyed VVAW's southern region. It was only one of many such trials initiated by the Nixon administration to destroy critics of its policies in Vietnam.[22]

What was Gainesville about, in your mind?

Barry Romo (BR): It was the police trying to frame and destroy VVAW, to discredit VVAW and destroy our organizing. We were the only people out there who were vets who were speaking against the war, and it was to take our time and money away. I mean, they were so scared of us—utterly afraid of us—because we were combat vets. We were better trained than most of the police force, and we were still young and stupid. We were certainly given to Marxist jargon, if not content. We probably scared the pants off them.

Sheldon Ramsdell (SR): We had people in Vietnam, people in Europe; we supported GI resistance; there were elements that were Maoist and Marxist—all in there, mixed together, so that's why we looked so terrible and radical. The truth of the matter is that we were so credible that Nixon couldn't tolerate us any longer and he had to set up the Gainesville Eight. After we got the credibility, then we were in serious trouble, because then they were really going to destroy us. It was as clear as the nose on your face.

Ann Hirschman (AH): You have to remember that this was a time when you could hear John Mitchell stating in public on the radio that the Vietnam Veterans Against the War were the single most dangerous group in the United States. We scared a lot of people. There had been certain threats on people's lives. Hubbard had had a threat. The threats were clear and very real.

> *John Kniffin, a VVAW coordinator from Texas, was one of the defendants in the trial of the Gainesville Eight.*
> *What were the charges brought against you?*

John Kniffin (JK): We're being accused of a plot to attack the Republicans, 82nd Airborne, Secret Service, federal marshals, and the Miami and Miami Beach police departments with slingshots, fried marbles, and crossbows. Give me a break. What am I going to do? I missed. Please don't shoot me, police officer, with your .357 while I reload my crossbow. [Laughs.]

> *What led up to Gainesville?*

JK: The Democratic and Republican conventions were going to be held in the summer [of 1972]. We had a steering committee meeting in Houston in February [1972], where we discussed the issue of whether or not to relate to one convention or both. At that time, the Republican convention was scheduled to be in San Diego. The Democratic convention was scheduled to be in Miami. We had a southern organizational meeting in San Antonio, as I recall, where it was decided that we would go to the Democratic convention and not the Republican convention.

A lot of us, particularly in the south, figured: What's the point of relating to the Republican convention? It's going to be a coronation for King Richard. There's nothing to be served. At the Democratic convention, we might be able to do some education and mobilization.

There was also a financial issue. How do you go to one convention here and then across the country to another convention? We don't have that kind of money, despite the fact that the press claimed we were being funded by Moscow. I guess the government intercepted our checks. [Laughs.]

There was also this north-south paranoia. Were the southern coordinators trying to take over the leadership of the organization? The issue came up on a national level, and Scott [Camil] asked for a meeting of the southern coordinators in Florida and he asked Pete [Mahoney] to be there as a representative of the national office. So Pete was asked to come as a representative of the national office to make sure that we were discussing the convention and not taking over the organization. [This meeting of southern coordinators took place in Gainesville, Florida, on May 23, 1972.]

Lemmer had just come from a demonstration in Washington, D.C., and he was all hyped up about these troopers in black jumpsuits beating up women and bashing people and, "This is going to happen in Florida, and what are we going to do about it?" That's how it all started.

Sheldon Ramsdell (SR): Bill Lemmer, the infiltrator, was setting us up with weapons and all this bullshit. Bill Lemmer was trying to give them the guns from Cubans. It was very complicated; [it] even attaches itself to Watergate, for Christ's sake.

> *William Lemmer and a number of other agents and informants were trying to incite VVAW members to violence. Nothing came of this. Many of the veterans did not take this kind of talk seriously; they had heard it before, and in general they dismissed it as the overblown rhetoric of a few hotheads, or simply as (in Mike McCain's words) "talking shit." Actually, many of the veterans used such hyperbole themselves, as a way to blow off steam, not knowing that their comments were being monitored.*

Mike McCain (MMC): We were sitting under a tree in Houston at the national steering committee meeting. . . . Scott [Camil] was there, John Kniffin, me. . . . There were 10 or 12 of us who were there. We're all stoned out of our fucking minds on acid, smoking dope, drinking beer, talking shit. We're going, "All right, what can we do?" We got all these guys who know all of this stuff. . . . We could use silent gliders. We could come in under the radar and parachute out onto the convention center. We could cut the power! That's it!

That's the basis of this whole trial . . . these fucking freaks sitting around goofing. There was no way in hell we were going to do any of that shit. It was this whole fantasy. Somebody there was an agent. . . . His name was Emerson Poe. He was with Scott Camil who was from Gainesville, Florida.

JK: You have to understand, whenever you get two or more vets together, you're going to have some crazy conspiracy come out.

I remember one at my house. We would wrap the military records center in Saint Louis with wire, energize it, and then that would black out all the computer records from the entire military. All the GIs would get pissed off because they wouldn't get paid, so they'd just go home. Great idea! That kind of rhetoric went on all the time. Nobody thought too much about it. So some of that was going on at Gainesville.

While these kinds of discussions were going on—some serious, as with William Lemmer, but most simply "talking shit"—the Republicans changed the site of their convention from San Diego to Miami. Given this change in location, VVAW planned to attend both conventions. Meetings were held in Florida during several months before the conventions, preparing for demonstrations at both. The meetings were coordinated by Scott Camil and southern regional coordinators. They were attended by Barry Romo, who represented the national staff. He was assigned to oversee the planning.

BR: The reason they were able to do it [indict the eight veterans] was because people like Scott Camil were loudmouth, macho, violence-spouting assholes. He was a regional coordinator in the south. At first, I liked him. Very personable and charismatic. But then, when you got to know him, arrogance replaced humility, bravado replaced substance. In other words, he was a loudmouth.[23]

I'm not saying Scott was FBI, but I went to a meeting in Miami. . . . Some PL people are at the meeting, some zippies, and Cubans.[24] Scott Camil brings out 10 maps and says, "OK, we got three things on this map. You got all the police stations circled, you got bridges with access to Miami circled, and then something on the parkway circled. Now, if the police attack, what we'll probably do is maybe we'll have assaults on police stations, and maybe we'll close these things off. . . . We've ordered wrist rockets and slingshots. You can get them from me for so much money, and if you fry my marbles, when it hits people it will hurt them."

I said, "All that stuff's fine, but we're not going to do any of that. We're just here to demonstrate; that's all." No big argument. He's just playing a macho game. This guy ain't going to go up against a fucking police station with marbles. I'm not that dumb. I do know he's a vet who's a big-talking asshole, but he ain't that stupid. [Camil said,] "Yeah, you're right, you know, but we should think about it and be prepared or something."

He collects all the goddamn maps, and one's missing. Two of the people there are salt and pepper. White guy and black guy infiltrate VVAW and testify against him at the trial. The maps disappeared that were there. I don't know. Maybe they lost it. Maybe someone else kept the map. Maybe one of the people from PL kept the map. Tell me, if you were a cop infiltrating VVAW, that you would have let one of those go? No, no, I don't believe it. They never surfaced at the trial. That was my bloody secret that I kept for 20 years, and now I'm finally telling people—because I don't know if they would have gone after us or not, if Camil hadn't ordered these slingshots and made the maps.

The only person they could have convicted on those maps was Scott Camil. Nobody else was there from the Gainesville Eight. The stuff that they had to prove—that they were going to attack the convention—was the stuff that Camil did. Without that, there wouldn't have been any of it.

JK: Scott had a reputation for pretty heavy-handed rhetoric. One of the first things I had heard about Scott from Terry was that he had had a regional conference in Florida and had M-60s on the wire guarding the perimeter against southern cops and stuff like that. That's pretty heavy, some real flaky stuff.

The Gainesville indictments had come down just before the Democratic convention. As it turned out, we were subpoenaed to appear before the grand jury and we were held during the entire period of the Democratic convention. We were released at the end of the Democratic convention from subpoena, and then they issued warrants for our arrests that night. Originally it was six of us, all Vietnam combat veterans.

My theory is that Nixon may have had something heavy going on. It's consistent with the stuff on the Huston Plan [see Chapter 3] that's come out.

I suspect the problem they had was they didn't know how many vets they had involved. They saw these convoys coming from three different parts of the country, all converging on Miami. The northeast, west, midwest—all converging and coming down here.

What was your reaction to the indictments?

SR: I basically thought, first of all: We're innocent. We're going to win. We're going to come out on top. We're not doing anything wrong. . . . That's how much belief I had in the organization. There were a few people in the crowd that wanted to do something crazy, but you couldn't control that. None of the Gainesville Eight were very radical except Scott, who thought he was the greatest things since Che Guevera. So we were very vulnerable.

JK: It was a joke. We're sitting in the grand jury playing jacks in the hall, putting banners out the window, giggling and laughing. It was just harassment to keep us away from the convention. The indictment is a total fabrication.

Pete Zastrow (PZ): Nobody was really happy about it, for a lot of reasons. I think a lot of us just thought they were guilty and they were nitwits. I mean, what they were charged with was so stupid, so what if they were guilty? Conspiring to fry marbles or whatever. In retrospect, it's such absolute silliness, but at the same time it was going to send these people off to jail for long periods of time. Some of us felt pretty strongly that it was the government consciously trying to get us off what was our real issue, which was the war, and sidetrack us into something else. We were sidetracked, and while we kept trying to use meetings and rallies about the Gainesville Eight to talk about the war, that never turned into the focus of them. Of course, the focus was repression.

Mike McCain was an unindicted coconspiritor in the case of the Gainesville Eight.

Mike McCain (MCM): William Kunstler and Allen Dershowitz were our lawyers. . . . It was the Center for Constitutional Rights in New York. They were the best of the best, but they cost a pretty penny. We raised and spent $500,000 on legal fees. We knew that it was a fallacious attack on the organization, but we had to deal with it.

JK: Our lawyers took it much more seriously than we did. They're sitting there saying, "This is serious shit; they can put you away for twenty years." We said, "Bullshit. I don't even think they can get a jury in north Florida, the only state to give you LeMay and Wallace, to convict us on this kind of crap." The lawyers were influenced by the Center for Constitutional Rights, who, as far as I was concerned, were a bunch of damn Yankees and I didn't trust them. I didn't know what their motivation was. All I knew was that they talked about how much money they could raise on this case.

SR: I went down to do the pretrial hearings in Gainsville. I said, "You know I'm here to help you. . . . Obviously they're trying to destroy VVAW nationally, and you guys have gotten caught up in this thing. We support you. I'm down here to defend the organization and you people—keeping you people the hell out of prison."

I photographed the evidence in the jury room where they had the police helmets with the arrows stuck through, bows and arrows. . . . Where in the hell did you think they bought all this shit? In some sporting goods store. It wasn't evidence. This is a joke. I laughed.

Judge Winston Arnow, a retired lieutenant-colonel in Pensacola, said we're dead. But he got pissed off at [John] Mitchell because Mitchell wouldn't honor a subpoena that Doris Peterson presented to him in Washington. The judge threatened to arrest him and bring him down. Mitchell wouldn't even take the fucking oath. The judge had to make him put his hand on that Bible. You could see the fighting. The animosity was great. John Mitchell was on the stand, perjured himself 13 times, went to Watergate, answered the same questions, lied again, committed perjury.

He sent his lawyer down. Guy Goodwyn was the prosecutor, who was an absolute asshole. . . . Goodwyn was a jerk. I mean nobody liked him.[25] The whole thing was working against the government from the beginning, and I could see that. They were accusing us of being involved with McGovern. . . . in the Watergate! I was sitting there and I thought: Man, they don't have a case here.[26]

I had in my hands a photograph taken by a local newspaper of the group. They looked like a rock group: pieces of uniform, long hair. [This is the photo shown on page 335.] They looked great; it was beautiful; but they did not want their picture in the paper, quite frankly. Scott probably did, but the rest of them did not. So I said, "Screw it, this image is too good." Then I wrote this press release on the Mitchell testimony: "Bullshit, Bullshit, Bullshit." I put it out to the AP and everybody else, in red-white-and-blue folders. The guy from AP in Miami, *Miami Herald,* called me up and went after me. He said, "Why are you using these Madison Avenue techniques and this red-white-and-blue folder and this photo that makes them look like a wonderful rock group and all this?" I said, "If Nixon can get elected this way, why can't we?" I'm not a Madison Avenue slicko bullshitter, but I came out of that world and I knew how to do it. It wasn't hard. We've got to win this. I said, "I'll use your tactics anytime."

I lived in the house with Scott Camil and his lady friends and his weapons and his dope, which I found out about later. I didn't see it in the first few days, but later on they laid it on me. Camil one night put some guns on a bed. . . . They weren't illegal, I don't think. On the banister of the staircase they're holding a scale and weighing little marijuana bags. This is not my scene.

I got the hell out of town. I got very frightened. I just didn't want any part of it, but I did what I had to do. . . . I got the stories in the paper and did the interviews.

The pretrial hearings took place during the rest of 1972 and into 1973. The case was not tried until the summer of 1973. During that time, VVAW was preoccupied with raising money for the defense and preparing for the trial. Some of the members were becoming disillusioned with the defendants but felt they had to support them to save the integrity of the organization.

PZ: We all went down and demonstrated at the beginning of the trial. The Gainesville defendants all were staying together in a house someplace in Gainesville. They all had to be together because they were doing this stuff for the trial. My own little recollection is simply going into the house and seeing these huge piles of dope in the middle of the table in this house just before the trial started.

VVAW got started around drugs; it was a pretty big thing. When you came home from the war, . . . this was another part of your rebellion. . . . You grew your hair long and you smoked dope or whatever. But many of us had understood at that point, that the politics of the organization were more important than drugs. Not only had we given it up, but we were pretty adamantly against even being in places where drugs were, recognizing what kinds of problems this had caused and could cause. I said, "Somebody is watching over these people. [Laughs.] It's not God."

The flagrant use of marijuana by some of the codefendants led some of the leaders in VVAW to suspect that they might be agents. The leaders in the national office who began to harbor this suspicion felt wary about throwing too much support behind the defendants. But as the proceedings dragged on, other members across the country, who were not aware of that suspicion, became angered because the national organization did not seem to be providing the eight with enough help.

MCM: Scott [Camil] was already on the outs. Scott was totally opposed to the movement of the organization to this pre-party formation. [At that time, several members of the national office were trying to persuade VVAW to become a broader anti-imperialist organization.] There was a meeting we had on Newport, where they were just going to throw Scott to the wolves. I said, "No, you can't do that." You don't just get rid of him because it's politically expedient and he doesn't agree with you. I had a couple of people threaten to kill me right then. Bill Branson wanted to kill me right on the spot. We fronted each other off at the time, and within days the decision was made that I had to leave. They had a secret vote or something. That was one of the last straws with me and the rest of the national coordinators.

Despite the growing animosity caused by the trial, VVAW members continued to support the defendants publicly .

AH: I always felt that the best I could give Scott was that he was entirely self-centered. That led immediately to, Who the fuck is paying him to do this? Since seven of the eight were people that I came to know and like and trust and feel very strongly positive about, it was physically painful that Camil was not. There was a lot of talk about, Don't attack Camil because he's one of the eight and he was a vet and we don't wash our dirty laundry in public. Many moral tenets of the left came into play. . . . During the trial nobody attacked Camil.

JK: We were pissed off at our lawyers, who were telling us this was serious and you guys are guilty, and they hadn't been doing any preparation on the case—not interviewing any witnesses, not trying to find out what was going on. All they were doing was trying to build a record for appeal.

My feeling was, I didn't care about appeal. I wanted to win it in the courtroom the first go-around, because if I didn't, then every newspaper in the country would say "Radical Vets Convicted in Florida." Maybe five or 10 years later, after appeal, somewhere on the back pages of the want ad section it would say, "Veterans' Conviction Overturned on Appeal."

As the trial was getting under way, the Gainesville Eight uncovered efforts by the FBI to undermine the defense strategies by bugging the defendants' meetings with their lawyers in the courthouse.

JK: They had these little offices in the courthouse and one of them was assigned to us. It had a telephone company centrex [central exchange] that was adjacent to it. There was a vent in the wall. We're in there discussing jury selection. We had a guy named Jay Schulman, a body-language expert, to determine what would be the best kind of jury person. We were discussing this, and all of a sudden somebody noticed that there were feet and legs under there [the vent]. So one of us very quietly walked down the hall and grabbed this marshal, Billy Joyce, and says, "There's somebody next door listening to us." So Billy Joyce and two other marshals unlocked the door, and lo and behold, there's two FBI agents in there.

One of them I know was Agent Eckblath. I know that because he issued me my subpoena. Apparently they were both wire experts. Their claim was that they had suspicion that we had bugged the FBI office by going through that centrex to the other side of the building. They were there to make sure we weren't bugging them. [Laughs.]

Judge Arnow ruled that our claim that the FBI was harassing us and interfering with the attorney-client privilege by eavesdropping on jury selection was irrelevant. The outcome of that was that if you defendants can't trust the FBI, who can you trust? [Laughs.]

During the course of those hearings, we attempted to put Tom Hayden on the stand because apparently a similar occurrence had occurred in Chicago. The judge ruled it was irrelevant, that what happened in Chicago had no bearing on our case.

One of our codefendants in the case, Bill Patterson, had a theory that we should tell the people that, yeah, these things were discussed as contingency plans, if there was this assault on the demonstrators—but that we conspired to start a riot, no; that we had any plans to assassinate anyone, no; that we planned to blow up bridges and causeways, no. That was never discussed. Jay Schulman said, "No, that theory might work in a banana republic, but if you try it here, you might be looking at 20 years, so we'll just counter their testimony and not say what we were about at all." That's basically what we ended up doing.

Lemmer was their star witness. Everything Lemmer said was a fabric of lies. He wasn't this super-heavy Green Beret that he claimed to be. He wasn't with the 173rd Airborne on operations so secret that he didn't even know what he was doing. None of that was true. We ended up getting his medical records during the trial; and his first tour in Vietnam, he complained of chronic asthma and was brought back to a field hospital triage in the rear area and stayed there until rotation. Before he went on his second tour, he went over the hill.

Emerson Poe came forward as a witness. He was Scott's best friend, and he testified against Scott. Carl Becker came forward. It turns out he was with some sheriff's department in some parish in Louisiana.

Danny Friedman: He [Becker] testified that the whole Bush affair was an example of our violence. That's why the whole trial was a joke.

JK: I don't know who all was involved. I don't even know to this day whether any of my codefendants was an agent or not. It never came to that point where they had to put them on trial to testify. I don't know why.

At this point, John Kniffin pulled out a photograph taken at the meeting of the steering committee in Denver in February 1972. The photograph was of a group of perhaps a dozen men, presumably veterans, some standing and some sitting. The faces of several men were circled, including William Lemmer and Emerson Poe, two of the informers who played a pivotal role in the indictments—but the photo was taken before the informers had been revealed. No one looked out of place; everyone looked as though he belonged. It is hard not to wonder if any of the others in the photograph may also have been agents or informers.

JK: I represented myself. So did Bill; so did Scott.

After the government made their case, I get up and make my summation to the jury and I says, "Ladies and gentlemen of the jury, as far as I'm concerned, my best defense is the government's case. I see no point in boring you any further and I rest." The jury stayed out for about four and a half hours and came back with acquittal on all counts on all defendants.

How did you feel after the trial was over?

JK: I felt I had no support from the official organization; I felt I had been abandoned. From individuals—John Lindquist, Annie Bailey, Terry, Tom—I had a lot of support.

I felt like a professional windup rhetoric machine. They'd call me to all of these regions; I'd get up there, babble some shit, and they'd pass the hat; and I'd go fly off somewhere else. [John Kniffin and VVAW raised $684,000 in this way.]

What effect did the trial have on the organization?

PZ: They killed off VVAW in the southern half of the United States. They got the whole leadership and scared off a bunch of other people.

During the course of the Gainesville proceedings, the Watergate hearings had begun. In the first round of questioning on Watergate, John Dean and James McCord claimed that the plot to gather information on the Democrats had in part been meant to find links between VVAW and the Democratic Party. Apparently, the administration reasoned that if VVAW was shown to be a terrorist organization (the contention of the prosecutors in Gainesville) and was shown to have ties to the Democratic party (which by then had become more progressive and more firmly opposed to the war), the Republican

Party would surely win the election in the fall. Thus VVAW had become part of CREEP's plans—the target of one of its notorious "dirty tricks."[27]

SR: I met McCord at Watergate. I had my [VVAW] button on. He had just testified. I walked up to him and I said, "You don't really believe that we're terrorists. We're just ordinary veterans that organize." He puts his arm around me, hugs me, and says, "Don't worry about it, don't worry about it." Oh, he was a gentleman; he couldn't have been nicer. McCord knew the real story all along.

6

THE SPLINTERING OF VVAW

We had attracted a lot of people, but we had no center that said, "This is a veterans' antiwar organization." We were unable to develop that understanding for a long time, and that led to problems.

Bill Branson

The war was over. We were all tired by that time. There sure as hell wasn't any peace—personally, politically, or worldwide. The wounds that had remained in the background and not bothered any of us, particularly the vets, for all those years when we were living at a high pitch of intensity, began keeping people up nights. They wanted to sleep. They wanted some peace.

Ann Hirschman

The End of Protest

In the year after the political conventions of 1972, VVAW was fighting off the attempts by the Nixon adminstration to destroy it, and Vietnam was receding further and further from the national consciousness. On October 26, 1972, two weeks before the presidential elections, Henry Kissinger announced to the world that "peace is at hand" in Vietnam. Although Nixon had no intention of carrying through on Kissinger's proclamation before to the election, it helped to give him a landslide victory over George McGovern in November.[1]

On December 18, Nixon began Operation Linebacker Two against North Vietnam. This was the most savage bombing campaign of the war, a reign of terror that lasted several weeks. During its first week alone, more than 100,000 tons of explosives (the equivalent of five atomic bombs like the one dropped on Hiroshima) poured down on Hanoi, Haiphong, and other military and civilian targets in North Vietnam. As Operation Linebacker Two proceeded, destroying Bach Mai hospital and numerous other civilian facilities, the Nixon administration remained silent, refusing either to acknowledge the destruction or to answer critics—such as the columnist Anthony Lewis of the *New York Times,* who characterized the attacks as a "crime against humanity."[2]

Although many American and world leaders condemned the bombing, there were no large-scale protests by the antiwar movement, perhaps because the antiwar activists were spent, or benumbed by this new onslaught. At any rate, the activists could not know how long the operation would continue, and so the movement prepared for an intense effort against Nixon during his second inauguration on January 20, 1973. More than 60,000 activists came to Washington for a "counterinaugural," a silent protest against the ongoing brutality of the war.

Within a week of the inauguration, a peace agreement was signed by Le Duc Tho of North Vietnam and Henry Kissinger. This was essentially the same document that negotiators had hammered out in October of 1972, and its provisions were essentially what the Vietnamese had been seeking since 1962. Opertation Linebacker Two had had no effect on the outcome of the war other than to terrorize the Vietnamese population.

By May of 1973, all remaining American troops and POWs in Vietnam had been withdrawn. That month, President and Mrs. Nixon gave a gala party for the returned POWs. Nixon told the assembled guests that they were free because "the brave men that took those B-52s" into North Vietnam in December "did the job." The signing of the agreement and the return of the POWs signaled the end of almost 20 years of direct American involvement in Vietnam. It also signaled the end of activism for the majority of the antiwar movement.

Although most Americans assumed that their own involvement in Vietnam was now over, Nixon had secretly assured President Thieu of South Vietnam that the United States would "respond with full force" if the North Vietnamese and their South Vietnamese allies in the Provisional Revolutionary Government (PRG) escalated their attacks against his regime.[3] However, Nixon was never able to fulfill this promise: his plans were thwarted by Congress. In the summer of 1973, Congress passed a series of bills cutting off American funding for the Thieu regime in South Vietnam; in November, it passed the War Powers Act, which restricted the president's ability to wage war without its consent. Also, the Watergate investigations had begun in the fall of 1972, and Nixon was becoming increasingly involved in efforts to save his presidency.

In May 1973, the Senate began to hold televised hearings to uncover the full extent of the Watergate scandal. Throughout the summer of 1973, new revelations emerged from the ongoing investigation, implicating some of Nixon's top advisors in the illegal activities that had taken place the previous year, and also revealing the extent to which the president himself had been involved in the subsequent cover-ups. Millions of Americans were glued to their television screens as more and more evidence of Nixon's complicity in the affair became public. By the summer of 1974, the House Judiciary Committee had voted to recommend impeachment. Rather than subject himself to this humiliation, Nixon resigned from office on August 9, 1974—thus ending what may have been the most corrupt presidential administration in American history.

Although the Watergate hearings had revealed the degree to which Nixon had used the power of the White House to undermine the Democratic Party, they did not uncover the full extent of his use of intelligence agencies to restrict freedom of speech and to damage the antiwar movement; for example, the hearings did not cover the administration's atttacks on VVAW. Nor—to take another, particularly prominent example—did the hearings go into the administration's role in Chile. For several years, the CIA had been attempting to undermine the democratically elected president of Chile, Salvadore Allende. In September 1973, Allende was deposed in a coup d'état and killed, along with thousands of other Chileans, and the country fell into the hands of a miltary dictatorship that would remain in power for a decade.[4] This episode was to have a strong effect on the thinking of some antiwar veterans.

The Nixon administration had continued its clandestine actions after its involvement in Vietnam had presumably ended; but most Americans, happy that the war seemed to be over, were once again focusing their attention on their unstable economy. Throughout the 1970s, inflation continued to soar, as a result of military spending and a series of global events that adversely affected American economic hegemony. In 1973, for instance, the war in the middle east and the formation of OPEC contributed to a rise in oil prices, rocking the American economy. Also, the United States' economic power in Asia and Europe was weakened by a reemergence of global competitors.

Thus Americans were uneasy, and despite Nixon's ignominious exit, the right wing took advantage of this unease and slowly began to tighten its hold on the electorate. It spoke to issues that concerned most Americans: rising crime, economic instability, and social chaos. Right-wing politicians and pundits saw a national decline, and they blamed this decline on the changes in government policies brought about during the 1960s. They also used thinly veiled racist themes to attract larger segments of the working class away from the Democratic Party.

In reaction, the Democrats, who had lost—devastatingly—to Nixon in 1972, abandoned the base of support that had typically elected them between the 1930s and the 1960s. Democratic leaders now wanted to win back the "silent majority" that had turned to Nixon in the past two elections. As a result, a growing segment of the American electorate felt abandoned by the Democratic Party, and much of this segment withdrew from the political process: during the 1970s, barely half of all eligible voters turned out for presidential elections.

Although antiwar activism virtually ceased after "peace with honor" was declared in January 1973, the influence of the New Left was still evident in American society. In the early 1970s, an environmental movement emerged, which addressed the degradation of the environment caused by industrialization and the profit motive. Women continued to agitate for greater economic equality, and Native Americans, Latinos, gays, and a number of other groups fought for inclusion in the mainstream and asked Americans to redress years of injustice. In the early 1970s, for instance, the American Indian Movement (AIM) carried out a series of protests and takeovers of government properties, culminating at Wounded Knee, South Dakota—an episode in which some of the antiwar veterans were involved.

The town of Wounded Knee had been the site of a massacre of the Sioux Indians by the American cavalry in 1890. In the 1970s, the Pine Ridge reservation, which surrounded the town, was rife with social and economic problems: 50 percent of its families were on welfare, alcoholism was prevalent, and most children failed to complete high school. Leaders of the AIM staged a takeover to dramatize this and to ask the United States to honor its treaties with Native Americans. Thereupon, several hundred American military and paramilitary personnel, with automatic weapons, grenade launchers, and armored vehicles, surrounded Wounded Knee, in effect holding it under seige. AIM held out for 71 days and then reached a truce with federal officials. Then, for the next two years, federal agencies continued to pursue the leaders: federal law enforcement officials and the intelligence community, which classified AIM as one of the most dangerous organizations in the United States, harassed Native Americans in South Dakota, where AIM was strongest. The efforts to destroy AIM included a fabricated indictment and prosecution of one leader, Leonard Peltier, for the murder of two FBI agents.[5] Peltier was convicted and at the time of this writing was still serving two life terms in a federal penitentiary.

While Native Americans, women, Latinos, and others sought justice, the more radical elements of the antiwar movement had become frustrated by their inability to stop the war, which was still going on—or to clean up the corruption of the American political system that Watergate had revealed. This radical wing had fragmented into a variety of Maoist and Marxist-Leninist groups, hoping to foment a working-class revolution in the United States. One example is Students for a Democratic Society (SDS) and its ramifications. Numerous splinter groups had emerged from the convention of SDS in 1969, when SDS was taken over by the Maoist Progressive Labor Party (PLP, or PL). The leaders of PL tried to steer SDS away from student-centered activism into class-based organizing.[6] When PL made its move on SDS, members of SDS who called themselves the Revolutionary Youth Movement

(RYM-I) stormed out: although they too considered themselves Marxist-Leninists, they saw the Black Panther Party and students—not the working class—as the vanguard of revolution. Shortly thereafter, they formed the Weathermen (later the Weather Underground) and began on a bombing campaign against the American military-industrial complex. Out of these two tendencies, other splinter groups emerged during the late 1960s and 1970s. The Venceremos Brigade and Prairie Fire, two sects that, like RYM-I, emphasized third world leaders for the global revolution, split off from the original Weathermen. The Revolutionary Union (RU), which later changed its name to the Revolutionary Communist Party (RCP), followed in the footsteps of the PL. Thus the left wing of the antiwar movement was as fragmented as the rest of the movement.

Meanwhile, the war in Vietnam continued. Between January of 1973 and the end of April 1975, it took several hundred thousand more Vietnamese lives. On April 30, 1975, the communists took control of the South Vietnamese capital, Saigon. At roughly the same time, the five-year war in Cambodia, which had started with bombing by the United States, was brought to a tragic end when the Khmer Rouge took over, unleashing a holocaust against the Cambodian people.

Meanwhile, also, Vietnam veterans continued to suffer the effects of their tours of duty in Vietnam. In 1977, unemployment among white combat veterans was 39 percent; unemployment among black combat veterans was 48 percent. About one-third of the veterans were divorced; 41 percent had problems with alcohol.[7] In addition, veterans and their children began to have unexplained health problems. They developed skin rashes and cancers; their children were born with a disproportionate number of deformities. Despite these growing problems, the Veterans Administration continued to hold veterans at arms' length.

VVAW: Seeking New Directions in a New Context

Amid these developments, VVAW tried to maintain its viability. Its members tried to keep the war in the forefront of the national consiousness, and also to address the economic and social ills of veterans and the public. The following narratives reveal the degree to which they became caught up in the general turmoil while still speaking out against American aggression in Indochina and elsewhere and trying to help their former brothers-in-arms.

Where to Go From Here?

BARRY ROMO

After the 1972 convention in Miami . . . we were trying to figure out what to do next. The war was winding down compared to what it was before. We aren't always going to have the war; this isn't forever. How should we organize? What should we be organizing? We had to deal with the question of combining social justice with antiwar work.

MIKE McCAIN

There are still problems that need to be addressed. Racism still exists. We were active in the boycott at Cairo. We were very active in Wounded Knee.[8] We were active in the domestic workers' strike in Sacramento, the farm workers struggle. . . . All this stuff I'm talking about is all the same, which is: How do people live? What is this society supposed to be about?

BILL BRANSON

As the war wound down, it was very confusing. Where do we go from here? By this point, a lot of us had really expanded our concept of what was going on. We started broadening our viewpoint.

We were really identifying with the Vietnamese, as not only people who were being oppressed, but they were the ones who were right. We liked them.

We started to get an understanding of imperialism. We became anti-imperialist. We started to see that there was a rich class that was behind this. We saw that it wasn't just going on in Vietnam. It was going on in the United States. We would go to any rallies in the struggle against the rich.

The thing that taught us a lot of lessons was the state. We had agents trying to infiltrate in various parts of the country. They were very nasty. They were always fucking with people at demonstrations. They taught us a lot about who the enemy was.

We read about veterans way back to the Revolutionary War and saw how they had been treated. We compared what we were getting to what World War II vets got. We started demanding better benefits.

A lot of us really admired the Black Panther Party. They wouldn't take shit, and a lot of them were vets. We felt that there was no way to take on the state and be a pacifist. You couldn't just turn the other cheek. They were being nasty, and we could be just as nasty if we had to.

Veterans in Search of a Program

MIKE McCAIN, BARRY ROMO, ANNIE LUGINBILL, BILL BRANSON,
DAVE CLINE, JOE URGO, BILL DAVIS, PETE ZASTROW

Mike McCain (MMC): By 1972–1973, we could basically do or say whatever we wanted to in the political left. We had become the darlings of the political left at that point. We understood that everyone wanted to be with us because we had such credibility.

Barry Romo: VVAW was it. If you were a vet, you wanted to be with VVAW. A number of people without organization gravitated toward VVAW—independent leftists that weren't vets, as well as people that were vets. People from Venceremos gravitated toward VVAW. People were in the PL. People were in the CP.

Annie Luginbill: We took everybody. VVAW has always been open. We've never been exclusionary organization. It did not matter to us if you were a Vietnam vet, if you're male or female, provided you work around what VVAW is geared to work around.

Bill Branson: We had attracted a lot of people, but we had no center that said, "This is a veterans' antiwar organization." We were unable to develop that understanding for a long time, and that led to problems. At this time of spreading of interest, there was the question of where we should go; there was a number of groups that tried for control of VVAW.

Dave Cline: VVAW suffered . . . from becoming the darlings of the movement. . . . I mean, the best way to get laid was to be a VVAW guy. . . . To a certain degree, a number of people got their ego overblown. You go off, meeting with international this and international that, and your opinion becomes more than just your opinion. There was a certain tendency, at least in the national office, to think that they could tell people what was happening, that they knew everything. If you're motivated by a sense of mission about what you do, you don't work together. It becomes fragmentation. It leads to a lot of individual animosity. People dropped away off of that.

Joe Urgo: Other people held revolutionary philosophies. I was listening to what they were saying. I went to different meetings, and then I got involved in a Marxist-Leninist study group. I read everything by other people. I read what was the October League at that time. I read different Troskyite things. I studied the Prairie Fire book.

All of that to me was both rich and confusing. It was debates and talk. Sometimes I'd figure something out, and sometimes I'd just leave it a mass of things, but it was the process. We had to do it that way because there was no other way to do it. We had to figure out how to get new tools.

The political struggle over which direction to take was getting concentrated up in the leadership. It is very interesting that when you actually look at who became the revolutionaries, it was most of the leadership. That has a lot more to do with the amount of analysis, exposure, and depth of struggle that they were part of that made them revolutionaries. It was they who actually had the responsibility to figure things out, and so they took on that responsibility—and the more they took it on, the more they were grappling in Marxism-Leninism. I reached the limits of what I was capable of doing, and what was required was a more scientific approach. It was on the basis of that we began to seek out some more philosophy.

Pete Zastrow at the conference on Agent Orange in Chicago, 1980.

MMC: What happened to the leadership is: We sat down with the chairmen of these various organizations, who would come to our houses and sit down and talk to us and invite us to talk to their groups. We'd get invited to be in a study group. The group was historical political economics. An analysis of history is what was being put forward. We did this with a whole bunch of different people.

What did you think about these discussions?

MMC: Hey, this was really cool, man. I like this.

Bill Davis: I'd had my associations and flirtations with just about every group on the left.

Pete Zastrow (PZ): There were two of us who were leading the chapter in Cincinnati. We were being romanced by every group. We both were taking RU study groups and October League study groups. We knew the Weather Underground, the "Revolutionary Bathroom Bombers." [Laughs.] We got their private communiqués: "The Manifesto of the Weather Underground." They would be delivered to the door secretly at night. There were special ways that you could get information to them.

What did these groups want you to do?

PZ: To be consciously revolutionary, I think, more than anything else.
I don't want to make it sound like a problem, because it wasn't. We had told each other that we were going to keep the organization independent, which we did. Because we were single-issue, pretty much, we didn't have to get involved in some of the political debates that these organizations got involved in. We went to all of them and listened to all of them.

MMC: The subtext was that we were being hustled, but we didn't realize that. I didn't realize that until much later, and at that point I left politics. We were getting hustled by every political formation in the country everywhere, starting with the Democratic Party, the RU, the CPUSA, SDS, Weather Underground, Prairie Fire, the Trotskyists, Progressive Labor Party—everybody wanted us to be in activities with them. Everybody wanted us in their pocket. People were actively recruiting the leadership of the organization to be in these various pre-party organizations.

Many VVAW members—like Barry Romo, Pete Zastrow, Bill Davis, Bill Branson, and Joe Urgo—grappled with revolutionary ideology in an effort to find a way to make VVAW into a consciously anti-imperialist mass organization which would address the core problems of American society. By 1972, they had come to see the war in Vietnam as a symptom of more fundamental issues, such as nationalism, imperialism, and racism. Some others, who had also become conscious of these issues, left VVAW and participated in a number of efforts to bring about change.

JOEL GREENBERG

In about 1972, I decided that if I was going to be serious about politics, it was not going to be done in upstate New York. I moved back to the city and checked out a variety of different groups. By that time, my attitude was that it was a question of the system. The system had to be changed, and I did not feel that VVAW was the vehicle for that change.

Why not?

VVAW was an antiwar organization. It was not a political party. I did not believe in changing that organization from what its function was. In my opinion, that was a common mistake that a lot of people made in assessing the antiwar movement. A lot of people felt the antiwar movement was more than what it was, because they wanted it to be. They wanted it to be a pre-revolutionary situation, to take up a multitude of issues, but the fact remains that it was an antiwar movement.

I wound up joining the SWP [Socialist Workers Party]. I had virtually no contact with VVAW after that.

Working for the Revolution

BOBBY MULLER

VVAW totally spun out because of the fact that it was the kind of organization that it was. Everybody who wanted a chance to speak was given a chance to speak. When you have a sense of participatory democracy like that, you would start a meeting on Friday and it would wind up being a continuous meeting until Sunday. The only ones left were the guys totally pumped up on speed and the really disciplined cadre like the RU that came in and knew how to bide their time, had gone through this before, and had a very specific objective. They would increasingly be the ones with the stridency and the ones left over at the end of the meetings. Everybody else had gone to sleep or gone home.

They would pass these absurd resolutions, further spinning the organization out into la-la land. Guys wanted to come and hear about what we were doing in Vietnam; and we would tell them about the Catholic church, about the school system; and it was—Whoa, wait a minute, wait a minute. One guy said to me, "You know, you guys remind me of the end of the Second World War when people went into the concentration camps. They had the best of intentions, but they wound up killing the people that they were there to help. What they did was, they gave them milk, and milk was too rich for them to be able to digest." He said, "You're coming at people with maybe too much for what people seem to be able to absorb or digest."

JILL McCAIN

All of a sudden these people are arguing macroeconomics at the damn steering committee meeting, and people are going, "What the hell is going on here?" People were leaving in droves. There were a lot of guys who were just working-class vets who saw no place for themselves. They were left behind. There was this huge strata of this organization, people who threw up their hands and said, "Fuck you. I don't care what economic system the United States has."

MIKE McCAIN

Yeah, "I just want to find out what's going on next Saturday." All you argued about was ideology at steering committee meetings. We got to the point where there was these cliques being formed. . . . If people had been carrying guns, they would have been shooting each other. We were turning into what we were fighting against.

LEE THORN

There was a meeting here, a regional coordinators' meeting, in the summer of 1972. . . . It was Palo Alto. We were talking about two things at that meeting. One was what we were going to do when they declare the war over. That was when we came up with the notion of Winter Soldier [the Winter Soldier Organization]. Secondly, we talked about the move to Chicago and what is the need in terms of structure, and how we could set up a structure that would meet the needs of the local chapters, which were basically to be as autonomous as possible.

We didn't want to set Chicago up as some kind of special place. We needed a national headquarters because we needed somebody to deal with fundraising on a national level, we needed communication on a national level; but those people had to respond to the regional coordinators. The regional coordinators had to be accountable to the locals, and the locals had to be independent. We put restrictions on them. The only thing was to do the paper [VVAW's newsletter] and to coordinate membership roles. They couldn't make statements about VVAW.

We were real concerned about centralization, because our whole organizing style was based on decentralization. That's how you could get guys to come together, because they would only have to be worried about their backs, or the guys around them, which they can deal with. But if they had to watch their backs in terms of somebody halfway across the country, they weren't going to stick around.

I was real concerned about structure because I was an Alinsky-style organizer. [Saul Alinsky wrote *Reveille for Radicals,* 1969; and *Rules for Radicals,* 1972.] It was really important. . . . Power to the people, as far as I was concerned, was the key to the organization.

There was also the issue of something about imperialism. It probably had a lot to do with some fight between one form of Maoism over another, but I didn't know what the hell they were talking about. . . . There was this guy named Sam Shorr out of LA, who we were having a lot of trouble with. He was RU, and we didn't know that. . . . We just thought he was an asshole. So we figured we'd just get rid of this guy. We'll kick him upstairs. We kicked all these guys from all these places we were having trouble with upstairs, together with a couple of guys who deserved to go upstairs.

Well, when these guys went to the national, they didn't pay attention to any of the rules. They just did whatever they thought because they had this grand purpose, which was the revolution. They acted like cops. Now, I always thought that RU types, if they weren't cops, the cops should have invented them.

ANN HIRSCHMAN

That was a particularly vulnerable time for everybody. There were lots of temptations. I was vaccinated against cults at a young age, but most of these guys weren't.

Interlude: Hanoi Revisited

The VVAW members who were turning more toward Marxism-Leninism in its various manifestations were those who, before their enlistment, had a strong ideological commitment to cold war doctrine or had already formulated an antiwar analysis. They were also among the most educated; typically, after their service they had gone on to college, where they studied the nature of the war and American foreign policy in some detail. As a result, they were on the whole more inclined than many other members to engage in political dialogue and examination.

Their focus was also sharpened by actual experience. First, these were men who had participated in or seen some of the worst fighting in Vietnam. Sec-

ond, their disillusionment and anger were further fueled by the reception they received as antiwar veterans. Third, they were influenced greatly by their own visits to Hanoi or by reports of visits in the VVAW newsletter, Winter Soldier. *This experience, along with their view of American imperialism, convinced them that their activism should not end as Americans withdrew from Vietnam. They came to believe that although the war might end, the United States would continue to carry out policies that oppressed millions of people across the globe—unless they themselves acted against those policies.*

In December 1972, Barry Romo went to North Vietnam—the third such trip by a VVAW member. His experiences there reveal a great deal about the changes these men underwent as a result of their activities in VVAW. Barry Romo witnessed the Christmas bombings firsthand and received a strong impression of the American government's deceptiveness—and its willingness to "bomb Vietnam back to the stone age."

BARRY ROMO

What was the purpose of your trip?

To see what was going on there and be able to break the United States' media embargo. We could cut through all of the lies of the Nixon administration. We also brought packages and letters for 500 POWs.

We left New York, and on the plane was Telford Taylor, who was the chief prosecutor at Nuremberg; Joan Baez; and Reverend Michael Allen, assistant dean of theology at Yale.

I got there [Hanoi] three days before the Christmas bombing in December of 1972. They dropped more than [the equivalent of] a nuclear bomb a day on Hanoi. In a 24-hour period, there would be two waves of B-52 strikes. They would lead with F-111s, who would come in below the radar. Then they would be followed by a combination of B-52s and Phantoms doing both strategic and tactical bombing. That was a freak, because in October they had ended the bombing. Kissinger had said "peace was at hand."

We had to go down into the bunkers. I couldn't stand being underground. I think after the third time we went down into the bunkers, I talked to the Vietnamese and said, "I can't handle being underground." They said, "OK. Go to the bunkers, and after you've gone underground, then you can go back up—but you have to help and make sure all the other Americans get down there, because it would be an embarrassment if they were to die." So I would go help them get down in the bunkers, and then I would come back up.

Agence France-Presse was at the hotel we stayed at and they had a teletype machine. We would immediately see what the United States was saying. We would go visit someplace that was totally bombed and destroyed and see on the teletype machine the exact lie. It was like that. [Snaps his fingers.] Then we would issue a statement.

We went to Bach Mai hospital several times. The Vietnamese said that Bach Mai hospital was bombed; and Kissinger said there was no such thing as Bach Mai hospital—this is communist propaganda—despite the fact that Bach Mai was the largest hospital in Vietnam. It had been a hospital since French colonial days in the 1930s. We issued a statement that we had been there and it had been bombed. It was bombed more than three times. I got pictures of it. Then Kissinger changed twice. He said, well, it was an aid station. Then he said it was a hospital bombed by accident because there was military stuff around it. He went through all these changes.

We met with survivors of Con Son Island. We met with a group of women who had been tortured and raped on the island. They showed us their cuts and burns and physical problems and would tell us what it was like to be raped and tortured in American-built tiger cages.

Con Son, off the southern coast of South Vietnam, was used as a detention center by the South Vietnamese government; "tiger cages" were 4- by 5-foot cells in which political prisoners were held. The women Barry Romo met had peacefully protested against the war.

We visited POWs who had been bombed. They were incredibly freaked out because they thought the war was coming to an end and they were going home. All of a sudden, the bombing started again. "Am I going to be here five or six more years?" They may have come home and said one thing, but it was real interesting what they said while we were talking.

There was a committee of antiwar POWs. I put in a specific application to meet with them. We weren't allowed to meet with them. We only could meet with right-wing POWs. I think that they said, "If we let you meet with the antiwar people, they'll say it's a total propaganda trip. If we let you meet with people who aren't antiwar, they can't say that."

The Vietnamese were very leery of the humanitarian stuff, because at first they allowed the United States to send all kinds of goods to the POWs. They had this whole display of stuff that the United States, through humanitarian aid, had tried to send. Inside the toothpaste tubes they had monitors and electronic devices and razor blades and hidden wire saws. Very crude and stupid things, but it didn't surprise me because they [the United States military] were so racist: "Oh, these silly little gooks won't never know what's going on." They let stuff be sent if it was sent through the antiwar movement. We constantly got stuff in.

We could go walking totally free every day. In fact, our Vietnamese guides emphasized that they wanted us to go walk the streets alone, so that no one could say that we were guarded. One time, we were walking and a little kid saw my VVAW button and flashed a smile, riding his little bike. Someone on a past trip had given him a VVAW button. He waved and showed it, and Baez freaked out: "Look, he's got a VVAW button."

Then we went to the Army Museum in the center of Hanoi. There was a glass case full of international gifts, and right in the center of the case was a Vietnam Vets Against the War button. That was pretty incredible.

What effect did all of these experiences have on you?

I was freaked out because here I am in the center of Hanoi, and I killed Vietnamese, and now not only that but the United States is trying to kill me. So where do you go from there? I also didn't feel like other people saw what I saw. When we saw the POWs, Telford Taylor, Joan [Baez], and Michael Allen showed more compassion and love for the Americans than they did for the Vietnamese who were getting bombed. It really bothered me—not that I like to see a POW. I was a former soldier; my God, my nephew was killed in Vietnam. I knew what it was to cry over dead Americans. Seeing live Americans didn't bother me. If I had seen dead Americans, maybe that would have been too much.

What bothered me was that I was watching Vietnamese being slaughtered by our government. Going into workers' quarters where pieces of bodies were lying all over the place was a lot worse than seeing a person totally well walking to a press conference and feeling disoriented.

One day they held a party for us, and there were government ministers who came. They had made all this food and we were eating and drinking, and finally I had the equivalent of a mental breakdown. I started to cry. The Vietnamese stole me from the Americans and took me over to a corner. They calmed me down. They surrounded me like mother hens around a baby chick and started talking to me and told me that I was working off the question of guilt and hate and that they were destructive emotions—I had to start working off of love—and that the United States government had used me and taken my precious idealism and used that to get me to go to Vietnam and kill Vietnamese, and I had seen that was wrong. And that now I had taken the correct political stance, but I had to deal with it emotionally as well. If I didn't change, I would become self-destructive. I had to see that it wasn't my fault. When the war would end and there would be a great victory, the victory would not only be theirs but would be mine as well. Unlike any other American, I would be able to join in their victory because I had seen the war from both sides. It was a transformation time for me. Unbelievable.

What do you mean by "transformation time"?

That's where my love for the Vietnamese comes from. Here were people who had never gone to college. Here were people who owned one suit. Here were people who were having the equivalent of a nuclear bomb dropped on them every single day. Here were people who could cry, because I was crying, who could reach out and be that much of a human being. What they truly and genuinely were concerned with was me. My God, this is unbelievable. So the question of loving and respecting the Vietnamese grew out of that.

Nixon was pulling out GIs and turning it into an air war. I knew what B-52s could do. There ain't no precision bombing. A worldwide effort stopped Agent Orange from being used in Vietnam by the United States. We just gave it to the Vietnamese, our surrogate, to keep dropping on the Vietnamese. We knew that 6 percent, or whatever it was, of the population was being born deformed. The more the war became technological, the more the war became clean for America, the dirtier it became for the Vietnamese, the bigger blot it was on the United States.

I had to deal with the innocence of the Vietnamese. If I invade their country, then I have to have a reason. The reason is they're vicious, evil, rotten communists, right? They're out for worldwide destruction, and if I don't defeat them in Vietnam they'll be here; but if I went over there and slaughtered them, killed people, and bombed them, and they were never going to come to the United States, they become innocents. They didn't become equally wrong for living in their own country. You can't allow them to die. That became the imperative. We knew we were fighting for little kids being born deformed and we knew we were fighting against people who were bombing dikes.

I came back and I was an absolute maniac because the stress had been too much, despite the fact that I had gone through this little catharsis with the Vietnamese. I have just relived in my dreams every firefight in Vietnam. I've been bombed, seen bodies ripped apart, and been through the most intense two weeks in North Vietnam. Now I had come home and the war wasn't over!

[I] got back on New Year's Eve to New York. I'm getting up in the morning the next day, I think at three, to do CBS morning news with Walter Cronkite. I debated the head of the Conservative Party.

I would say, "Con Son Island. I met these people who were tortured." He would say, "Well, these aren't young Republicans on Con Son Island." I'd say, "Quite the contrary. Truong Dinh Dzu, who was number two in the last election, was arrested afterward, and he's there."[9]

This woman from the POW families kept saying, "We want our relatives home." I said, "Well, if you expect them to come home before the war is over, then you're expecting a first-time event. We didn't let Germans go and Germans didn't let Americans go. POWs get released at the end of a war. If you think they're going to release pilots who then can come back and bomb them a month later, this is not going to happen. If you want them back, peace. There's no other alternative."

If I do say so, I smashed the guy. Afterward he shook my hand and said, "Oh, you're a really good debater." I says, "Truth. It's not debate; it's truth."

Then I went on the road because we were building for the counterinaugural. So I went on a God knows how many states' tour. I would give five, six, seven speeches a day in building for the January 20 counterinaugural. I was just burned to a crisp.

The peace movement was alive and well. A million people went.[10] We had 15,000 from VVAW. We met at the Arlington cemetery and where we had camped. We signed the People's Peace Treaty and another agreement, and then we joined the larger demonstration. This was probably our strongest point.

> *Before he won his second term in office, Nixon turned his attention to other matters of foreign policy. He opened dialogues with China and struck new deals with the Soviet Union; and he and Kissinger felt that they could rely on these new friends to pressure their North Vietnamese allies into signing a lopsided peace accord, which would favor the South Vietnamese government.*
>
> *For Nixon, Vietnam became more and more of a distraction that he wished to be rid of.[11] After the Christmas bombings in 1972, he accelerated the peace process. An accord was finally signed on January 27, 1973, only a few days after the inauguration. This agreement was basically the same one that Nixon had rejected in October 1972; evidently, the earlier rejection had been calculated to ensure his reelection by prolonging the peace negotiations until after the voting.*
>
> *In the months following the accord, POWs were released and the withdrawal of American troops was completed. The war was now in the hands of the United States' proxies in South Vietnam.*
>
> *From this point on, the American press, and the public, virtually ignored Vietnam; but VVAW members who had been educating themselves knew that the war raged on, funded by the United States. Since many of them, like Barry Romo, had come to sympathize with North Vietnam, seeing the war as a struggle by the Vietnamese for independence, they remained committed to their antiwar crusade. For many in VVAW, however, the end of direct American involvement brought an end to activism.*

BOB HANSON

That was the end of an era for our organization. It really lost a lot of steam after the POWs were released. I remember being in the office, and nobody really knew what to do next after that happened. This sort of signaled the end of our involvement, and Americans have the attention span of a flea. VVAW really faded away after the POWs returned.

ANNIE BAILEY

When they declared the war over in 1973, we had a mass exodus.

The Winter Soldier Organization

Those who remained active in VVAW saw an opportunity to turn the organization into a mass-based anti-imperialist movement. Some of the leaders, like Barry Romo and Joe Urgo, both of whom had visited North Vietnam, had been courting civilian left-wing organizations.

New members, including many civilians and women, had joined VVAW since 1971, seeking a way to carry on anti-imperialist activities after many of the left-wing movements had splintered during the last years of the war. As a result of this influx of new members, the ideological battles within the organization were heightened. Thus two issues—the new members and the direction of VVAW—became closely intertwined.

The first major battle took place in 1973, when several members moved to change the name of VVAW to the Winter Soldier Organization (WSO) and make it a consciously anti-imperialist umbrella organization, which would . take the place of SDS, the Weather Underground, and other left-wing revolutionary organizations that had gone underground or disintegrated.

JOE URGO, BARRY ROMO, JEANNE FRIEDMAN, PETE ZASTROW,
SUKIE WACHENDONK, MIKE McCAIN

Joe Urgo: Brian Adams came up with the Winter Soldier Organization. . . . A whole section of vets thought that was right, including me, because what that said was: We can bring in all these people, all these nonvets.

Barry Romo (BR): The left had totally fallen apart. There was no SDS; no Black Panthers; no this, that, and the other; there was nothing. Maybe VVAW should be this group.

Jeanne Friedman (JF): By this time . . . I was teaching a class on Vietnam and Cuba. I was teaching, by the book, anti-imperialism classes, cultural history, Native American struggles. I was calling myself a Marxist-Leninist, and I did believe that centralized party was the way to go.

From my point of view, what was being built here was an honest-to-god working-class mass organization with some leadership from veterans but open to all. VVAW was going to be an anti-imperialist mass organization. That's what I thought was happening. . . . Who better than a veteran to say, "I know about United States imperialism. I fought for imperialism. I served it. Here's why we have to end it." My politics were very much anti-imperialist politics.

Pete Zastrow: Frankly, a lot of this had to do with the fact that leadership in a lot of these places was coming from women who saw much better than we did that there were vital issues that, while they weren't direct veterans' issues, were issues that veterans damn well ought to be interested in: child care, the rights of women, today it would be homelessness.

> *Sukie Wachtendonk and her husband Jim, of Madison, Wisconsin, were among many who became VVAW activists in reaction to the issue of Agent Orange. Jim Wachtendonk, a veteran, was exposed to Agent Orange during his tour of duty in Vietnam. They were interviewed at home in Madison.*
> *What was the role of women in VVAW?*

Sukie Wachtendonk: The difference between VVAW and every other veterans' organization is that women are allowed to be strong, have voices, and have equal membership. Every other traditional veterans' organization, including the DAV [Disabled American Veterans], would not allow women to have an equal voice.

JF: Women were doing a lot of the work. Women were paying attention to taking care of business.

BR: We were always primarily vets, because we were a vets' organization, but we refused to have an auxiliary. Women were absolute full members. We saw the inherent sexist nature of having a group who did not belong to the organization and who did work. They wanted to belong to VVAW. They couldn't stand up and tell about their experiences in Vietnam, but they could get up at a VVAW meeting and say what they thought we should be doing.

It caused problems with certain macho people but it wasn't a big problem, because we fought it and the times were against sexism. People weren't there for a macho trip to join VVAW to begin with.

Mike McCain: The women taught us boys a whole lot. They were mostly our girlfriends who ended up being some of the most valuable, the most dedicated, the most active, the most disciplined people in the organization. Jill and I supported that [WSO].

> *Other members of the organization, however, did not feel comfortable about changing its name.*

ANNIE BAILEY, JOHN LINDQUIST, DAVE CLINE

Annie Bailey (AB): What they [the supporters of WSO] were saying was, "Look, the backbone of the organization is not veterans. Look around at the chapters—who's doing the work? The wives, girlfriends, non-Vietnam veterans, people who were veterans but didn't go to Vietnam." I mean, how could you call it VVAW when it wasn't made up of Vietnam Veterans?

They tried to use me a couple of times. . . . "Hey, you've got to recognize Annie's work." . . . Bullshit. I don't care. Don't use my name, because I didn't agree on the WSO thing.

Why not?

AB: I was more into the politicalness of VVAW; and I was more understanding of the factions that were promoting this shit—some people from outside the organization, some cadre people. . . . WSO was a little bit of Venceremos, a little bit of Prairie Fire and Weather Underground, and honest elements thinking we should do anti-imperialist work.

John Lindquist (JL): I disagreed with adding the Winter Soldier Organization. The whole principle came from very valid people. . . . Bart Savage from Chicago [was] a genuine dude. Sure, he read some Marx and all that bullshit, but his heart was in the right place and there was a genuine feeling that we should just switch over to anti-imperialist work. I came to understand it later, but was pretty hot about it in the beginning. There's a whole bunch of people that aren't ready to take that step, didn't want to take that step, or just want to do vets' work.

Dave Cline (DC): There were some people saying it should become the Winter Soldier Organization and be a general anti-imperialist type of thing. I was pushing for keeping a veterans' focus—veterans' rights and those types of things.

Why did you push for that perspective?

DC: I felt that if you're going to be a relevant organization, you had to address the needs that were out there. I felt that the whole idea was moving away from a veterans' focus. . . . Look, in VVAW, one of the dynamics that took place was: Guys got involved; their girlfriends got involved; women's liberation came along; they didn't want to be second-class citizens. I can understand that—that's all good. But the idea that you make sexism be the principal slogan of a GI organization, when you got a bunch of guys whose only relationship with women is commercial, prostitution, it's just not dealing with the contradictions people were confronting.

The strength of VVAW was that it was a veterans' group. We went and fought in the war and are against sending other people to go and to deal with those who are suffering from it. I felt that when it was taken into a general anti-imperialist thing, it was drifting off into the political stratosphere and not dealing with concrete issues.

JL: We were in Placitas, New Mexico [in the spring of 1973], . . . at the actual formal vote for WSO to join the name. The name was supposed to be VVAW/WSO for a year, and then drop VVAW. We were able to get a compromise voted on and passed. . . . We had to formally vote again to drop VVAW, in two years. Wisconsin brought it up because we were bananas over this. We won that battle. . . . It was a compromise . . . but I didn't like using VVAW/WSO. In fact, I had to force myself to write it or say it, but I did it.

VVAW/WSO: Building an Anti-Imperialist Organization

Under the new title, VVAW/WSO members continued to involve themselves in organizing veterans and GIs. Also, the national office adopted many of the issues and programs that had been carried out by local chapters. Members were encouraged to become involved in their communities, and more ties were made with other groups on the left. In an editorial in the May 1973 issue of Winter Soldier, *VVAW's monthly newsletter, the national office said, "In April 1973, VVAW added WSO to its name. The primary reason was not to change direction, but to recognize the work of many nonveterans in the organization. This addition allows us to broaden our base and also allows for women and nonveterans to assume leadership positions. . . . VVAW/WSO will remain as a Veteran/GI oriented organization. . . . As we demand basic benefits for veterans, we will also demand more for other citizens. . . . We will continue to demand a change in the government's foreign and domestic policies that will result in a better America for all Americans."* 12

JEANNE FRIEDMAN

When it became WSO, some of the people in the national office wanted me to run for the California regional coordinator. Their thinking—Barry [Romo] and Eddie [Damato]—was that this would really make clear the change in VVAW.

The other thing that was going on was that there were differences emerging between the Los Angeles–Long Beach leadership of VVAW and the national office. The Long Beach crowd wanted no part in the national office leadership. The big fight was about the national office coordinating action and doing all kinds of things. . . . I also think the Long Beach branch was anti-ideological; they didn't like to see that ideology growing, the talk about anti-imperialism . . . that's not where they were at.

They [the national office] wanted the regional office out of Long Beach and they wanted it in northern California. Northern California was very strong; there were some wonderful leaders in East Bay; there was a thriving San Francisco chapter. . . . That's why I ran.

Although antiwar organizing slacked off in 1974 . . . there's still a lot of war resisters in Canada and Sweden. VVAW was doing work with them. . . . There were GI projects to support—everybody wanted to do that—and working with veterans on upgrading bad discharges [bad-conduct discharges and dishonorable discharges]. . . . I did a lot of work as VVAW/WSO brought the military law office into VVAW/WSO. It had originally started as a National Lawyers Guild project.

MIKE McCAIN

There was also a lot of stuff for veterans and universal unconditional amnesty. Jill [McCain] testified before Congress on the universal unconditional amnesty question. I was one of the cowriters of the political analysis, the political document which was the basis of granting unconditional amnesty—which the Congress eventually did.

Why pursue amnesty?

Because of all the deserters who had gone to Canada. We felt they were our brothers. The only difference between them and us was that they got to Canada and we didn't. It was my own ignorance. I didn't even know that option existed at the time that I was drafted. They had done what was the right kind of thing to do. Each of us in a democracy should have a right to decide whether or not we are going to participate in any activity.

PETE ZASTROW

We turned out a prison newsletter, which was quite extensive, and sent it into prisons every month. We recognized that was where a lot of vets were headed. A lot were already there. We were trying to keep in contact with vets in prison. We tried to build chapters. We did in a couple of places, but they got squashed pretty quickly. It was tough to do.

As the national office branched out into work on amnesty and prison work, the struggle between it and the Long Beach chapter was reflected in several other regions, such as Milwaukee. For those like John Lindquist, the change to WSO moved the organization farther away from the veterans' issues that the Wisconsin chapter had been pursuing. For some others, who were involved with groups such as the Revolutionary Union, the establishment of WSO threatened their own organizational objectives.

The struggle over the direction of the organization was very pronounced in California, where numerous civilians with strong anti-imperialist credentials, such as Jeanne Friedman, had joined VVAW. Women like Jeanne Fried-

man played a decisive role in advocating WSO and were supported by the vet-
erans who worked closely with them.

The argument over WSO was conducted on several fronts. On the one
hand, new members of VVAW—women, civilians, and people who had affili-
ations with underground left-wing groups like the Weather Underground—
wanted VVAW to become the leading anti-imperialist umbrella organization
in the United States and wanted it to attract more left-wing civilians. On the
other hand, veterans like John Lindquist wanted to avoid such a broad-based
approach; instead, they wanted VVAW to concentrate on veterans' issues.
This approach, ironically, fit in with one goal of the Revolutionary Union
(RU): to subsume VVAW under its own united front. Between 1973 and
1975, the RU began to win over more members of the national leadership.

ANNIE BAILEY

A lot of the more political people in VVAW became close to the RU because
they helped smash that whole thing [WSO]. [They argued that] vets are
important; we have to do vets' work. But in the end, that's what their thing
was about too—they wanted to dissolve VVAW and make it anti-imperialist.

JOHN LINDQUIST

The Revolutionary Union and the RCP—who first tried to infiltrate in 1973,
real strong in 1975—made their attempt with guns to take the organization
over in 1977. They've still fucked around with us ever since.

Secret members plotted to do what the communist central committee of
the RU told them to do. They picked up on the struggle that we're having
with the VA. . . . That came from Milwaukee; it came from VVAW. It was a
positive thing. It didn't come from them.

At the same time that they're recruiting, they're holding study groups. . . .
It was just a progression. I mean I went to a couple and I says, "Fuck this
bullshit. I'm not going to listen to this crap." But there's an honest element,
good VVAW people, that do not see these people as the enemy.

Barry [Romo] was recruited in the RU . . . a very strong member. He's still
a communist. He's an honest individual. Bill Davis studied Marx and Lenin.
. . . Maybe he's a communist. . . . Who the fuck knows? Pete [Zastrow] was
active. Eddie Damato. Those guys honestly went over and do some stuff.
They were starting to see the contradictions.

DAVID EWING

The RU was trying to set up chapters everywhere. When I was still in Baltimore, this guy met me and he said, "Stay here, David, and help us do this.

We'll start a VVAW chapter and get things going." I helped start a VVAW chapter in Baltimore in 1972, in July.

Why was the RU manipulating VVAW?

They saw that the way to make a revolution in this country was to mobilize different interest groups. The key was the working class. . . . But to make a broad challenge to the system, you can't have just the working class. You have to mobilize intellectuals when you can, students when you can, veterans, the unemployed. . . . A small part of their overall picture was the veterans' movement, of which they identified VVAW as the best portion of it. So they recruited people like Barry, who were the best people in VVAW, the most determined people, people who were minorities. The goal of the national office and RU leadership was to get rid of these leftists that we disagreed with.

I had no Vietnam service, and it didn't seem like the right thing for me. I wanted to be in San Francisco. I needed to be someplace where there was more exciting politics happening. I gave my girlfriend's car to SDS, and we moved to California in my van. I got involved in politics here, which is a much bigger scale. I came here in July after setting up VVAW in Baltimore.

DANNY FRIEDMAN

The RU was slick. I mean they came on like: "We like to drink beer and party like you guys." They'd take us out and stuff. They would feel out the more intellectual of the people. They apparently made a run at me. A couple of their guys took me out for beers and this and that. I didn't realize it at the time. They realized that I was like too working-class for them. I was never considered an intellectual. I was considered like a grunt.

Jim Duffy was my roommate, and they made a big run at him. It turned out that he was a secret member for many, many months before he admitted it.

BILL DAVIS

The RU wasn't very much in Columbus and they were looking to win VVAW over politically, so they sent a couple of kids over from Antioch College in Yellow Springs up to Columbus. By and large their base was mostly students. They came up to a meeting to speak, and there were a lot of guys there. Most all of them were working-class sort of guys.

The two kids from Antioch, with all the best intentions, launched into a description of what the working class was, working-class values, the dictatorship of the proletariat, and blah blah blah. They finished and we had more business to attend to in the meeting, so we thanked them for coming and we would be in touch with them. We weren't antagonistic or anything. They left.

I asked a couple of guys, "What was your impression of that?" One guy goes, "Why, that wasn't too bad. They had a lot of good things to say. But," he said, "did you see that one motherfucker? He was wearing earth shoes! Why would anybody want to wear something with no heels? It looks like they're going to fall over. How do they keep from falling over backwards?" The guys looked at them like kids. A lot of those people who we worked with on a regular basis were very anti-RCP and RU.

They sent some of their Ohio leadership people out to take me for a ride. I imagine that was kind of a screening thing. We drove to Athens and back and talked the whole time. It was very cordial. I was a straight-out dupe simply because I agreed with a lot of things that they said in meetings.

We were working in conjunction with them, more or less, in the Columbus chapter; but I can't think of one person who was actively recruited into the RU or the RCP. Eventually, we got the label of being under the sway of the RU.

PETE ZASTROW

After I'd been there for some time [Cincinnati], they [RU] invited me to join one of their study groups. They invited others too. I had no problem with that. It was good, and I learned a lot of things.

I think they were trying, as much as possible, to make sure that we were an organization that focused on veterans' affairs . . . to keep us focused on that as opposed to becoming a wider umbrella organization, which, in various parts of the country, the organization was becoming: Buffalo, California, Saint Louis.

BARRY ROMO

For a while [I] thought that VVAW should be this united front organization [WSO], but turned away from it because it didn't make sense. You can't organize people on the basis of ideology. You want a party, OK, you form a party or join a party. You don't try to turn a mass organization into a party. Let's fight for VVAW to be a vets' organization.

BILL BRANSON

I don't think the line the RU had, at least that I saw in California, was a bad one. The line that I saw coming out of the RU was that we should be a veterans' organization.

I knew them in California. . . . They were guys that were vets who had joined. . . . I didn't see any problems with them. I liked them. They were guys who had balls and had distinct ways of analyzing stuff.

370

DAVE CLINE

I was working with the RU at the time and I believed that they were promoting a positive direction, although sometimes they would be very narrow. I thought that they were pushing for a direction that would try to link up with real issues—unemployment and things like that. Also, at that time, the government was beginning to implement programs, because of groups like VVAW. They were trying to provide services, but also to try to deradicalize the veteran community. The veteran community was a radical force at that time.

JOE URGO

The RU was the one group that had the clearest revolutionary analysis and vision of American society and what needed to be done. These are the only folks whose vision is really belief in the masses, that the masses are the makers of history, so we have to organize ourselves to organize the masses.

I'd say the biggest impact on me was not Vietnam but, in the fall of 1973, the overthrow by the CIA of Allende in Chile. I listened to that on the news that night. I waited for the Congress to condemn and nobody said a word, and then I listened to the massacre of 40,000 people as the Chilean police massacred people in the stadium. It was the first time that I said to myself, OK, it's no longer a question of how and when.

ANN HIRSCHMAN

Most of the Mother Cabrini Brigade wound up in RU. If you look at the Mother Cabrini Brigade, they were serious Catholics. [This was the name these "serious Catholics" in VVAW—including Barry Romo, Joe Urgo, Ed Damato—had given themselves.] They had all been acolytes and altar boys. We're talking about a relatively authoritarian religion with rigid rules to live by. Then came the 1960s, Vietnam, then they're in leadership positions, there's a lot of threats from the outside, and things seem to be falling apart. Thinking has become increasingly difficult and painful. There's no parameters.

The war was over. We were all tired by that time. There sure as hell wasn't any peace—personally, politically, or worldwide. The wounds that had remained in the background and not bothered any of us, particularly the vets, for all those years when we were living at a high pitch of intensity, began keeping people up nights. They wanted to sleep. They wanted some peace. Some people found it in religion; some of the guys, like Bill Erhardt [a well-known veteran poet], got more and more involved in writing; and guys who were bent that way and exposed to it got involved with not only RU but several partisan groups that had a central leader who would tell you what to think. It was a real place of refuge. I never thought people had to feel guilty for that. They needed some crutches because emotionally they were crippled.

MIKE McCAIN

I didn't have a clue as to why, but for some reason I thought this was bad for the organization. . . . I thought we should be a mass organization of people, not ideology. We had a defined ideology for the organization, which was that we were opposed to the Vietnam war, we were critical of particular parts of the way our government worked, and that's all that we could do. We were not in a position to make an analysis of the entire culture, the economic system of capitalism, and stuff like that. Individuals could, but as an organization, I did not feel that that was our function or our role. . . . To do so would destroy the effectiveness of the organization.

By the summer of 1974, most of the leadership in the national office of VVAW had joined the RU, either openly or secretly. As the national office of VVAW came under its sway, the leadership sought to bring local chapters into line with the goals of the RU. As a result, veterans across the country who were not closely linked to the national office became disillusioned.

The struggle over the domination of the national office by RU was exacerbated by members who were competing with RU and wanted VVAW to remain a mass-based anti-imperialist organization. Through open letters to the membership at large, they exposed those who had joined RU. During the latter half of 1974 through 1975, a great deal of time was spent drafting position papers and arguing about the "correct line."

PETE ZASTROW

I got elected to national office in May of 1974. We lived on two floors of 827 Newport [in Chicago]. The first floor was vacant. We lived on the second floor and had the offices on the third floor. Everything we did was pretty much together. We met daily. The vast majority of us belonged to the RU. We were learning from all these revolutionaries—they knew everything. They could give us great political guidance.

We coordinated everything through the newspaper, primarily. We put out at least a 16-page newspaper every month. We did all the articles. . . . We would go in and we would have these meetings with the RCP delegate to VVAW. We'd go through what articles should be in the newspaper . . . debating them for days on end. We'd write them, go over them. . . . It did make sense in its own perverted way at the time. Some of it sure as hell doesn't make sense in retrospect, I tell you.

If you look at *The Veteran* [this was the title of VVAW's newsletter after 1975] or the *Winter Soldier* [the earlier title] of the time, you'll see that the RU's influence becomes greater and greater and greater. We would stop covering people who were doing things that we didn't agree with.

We were the ones that were pushing the veterans' base and focus. God—I mean there were some massive papers that were written about this at that time. I hate to think about the number of hours we spent doing ours.

Did you see yourselves as a revolutionary organization?

We were going to seize control of the country and run it.

How did you see this happening if it didn't involve violence or some activities that were illegal?

Well, because we would have such mass support that "legal" or "illegal" would be irrelevant. I can remember the big debates about fighting in the streets and how do you take on a tank, *Anarchist Cookbook* [by William Powell, 1971], and all that stuff; but we often felt rather nervous when organizations that we knew or organizations that were vaguely associated with us were arrested for explosives or things like that.

BILL DAVIS

I was elected to the national office of VVAW [in December 1974] and moved to Chicago. Everyone was already RU; at least, that was my impression. Maybe some of them were still being brought into the party or at various stages. I was a single person who was not, but everyone suspected I was a secret RU member.

So we'd have a national meeting and then they'd have a meeting I couldn't be at, which was fine with me. I'd go watch the Cubs, I'd wander off on my own; and they'd be arguing or pounding out some line or something.

ANNIE LUGINBILL

There were chapters of the VVAW that didn't relate to the VVAW when the RU was in power, like Wisconsin. I had had some experience with the RU back when I dealt with the Movement for a Democratic Military, and they upset me at first. I fell in with the national office and the Chicago people because they were people I knew and agreed with; but if I had been somewhere else and working with someone else, it could have easily been that I would have voted a different way. I suppose a lot of people looked at the national office as being hardcore Stalinists.

JACK McCLOSKEY

I think there was a certain element that took over. I think it was an element that was very sharp and very good but lost a lot of membership; I think a lot of people that came from the gut-level place dropped out because it was too left-wing. It hurt VVAW tremendously.

They were very slick in saying things that were very believable, but pushing it more and more toward the edge of violence. That's when I started saying, "Fuck you, I can't go that way." I grew up with a dogmatic line, "Kill a commie for Christ"—why should I buy into another one? So when people started saying, "This is the way you've got to do it; you have to have arms," well, fuck you, man. I've experienced that. I don't need that. That's why I still think to this day, RCP was government-made.

LEE THORN

We decided to stay in as long as we could, but it was tough because we were losing membership like crazy. It self-destructed, but I don't blame it on any one factor. It was true that we got taken over at the national office. It was true that associates of Venceremos had taken over San Jose, Oakland. . . . But in the San Francisco area it was pretty much the same people. We still were having meetings, but we were tired.

I'll tell you what, I was so drunk in those days. I broke up with my wife in 1972 . . . when the SLA [Symbionese Liberation Army] stuff hit. . . . I was harassed so much that I split for Kansas City in 1973 for six months and worked on this thing called the Leavenworth Brothers Defense Committee, which was a VVAW thing too. By the time I came back, which was like the middle of 1973, the chapter pretty well had been taken over. They were talking bullshit as far as I was concerned. The only legit people were in Milwaukee as far as we were concerned.

RON SABLE

There was all this factional political stuff going on in VVAW at the time. . . . That was before I had come out, but I was pretty sensitive to the fact that a lot of the left was homophobic. I didn't want any part of that. It seemed like that was the group in ascendance in VVAW at the time.

As the people in the national office found the RU's position more in line with where they wanted to take VVAW, they dropped the idea of keeping VVAW/ WSO as the new title—and the idea of making VVAW into an anti-imperialist party. As a result, new struggles ensued between those who supported the concept of WSO and those who wanted to use the RU's party structure.

As the national leadership became more closely associated with the RU, the organization began to promote a revolutionary line consistent with RU's ideology. The connections with the RU became apparent in1974, during a demonstration in Washington, D.C., over the Fourth of July. This demonstration had been coordinated by VVAW and the RU.

BARRY ROMO

We've got a demonstration in Washington in 1974. We brought several thousand people. It was the last major antiwar demonstration before the war ended

July Fourth protest in Washington, D.C., 1974.

. . . July Fourth. . . . We had demands, which included "end all aid to Thieu, decent benefits, single type of discharge, jobs," or something like that. Big demonstration, lots of people . . . I think there were 4,000 on the last day. . . . [Ron] Kovic goes there with 100 people—including a bunch of what we call "vet pimps," who brought their people—and he doesn't talk about the war.

Ron Kovic had left VVAW and formed an organization called the American Veterans Movement.

LEE THORN

Kovic had a meeting with Joan Baez and told her he had this vision: there'd be another American Bonus March. . . . Joan at that time had donated a lot of money, so Joan asks Kovic who to get in touch with up here. She got in touch with Jack [McCloskey].

We had dropped out, but they said come back in. Joan said she'd pay us a little something. Kovic said we have people in Florida and all these places. Hundreds of thousands of people were going to show up. We didn't have jobs, so we said OK. So they hire us. So we go to fucking D.C. VVAW's attending the same demo.

The first night we're there, we go on a demo with VVAW because we know all these people and it sounded like it was a good demo. They pulled some violent bullshit. Of course, our people got busted. All the RU types split. Our guys were out there getting their heads beaten.

Then we go and work. . . . It turned out that all the stuff Kovic said he had together wasn't together. They were just dreams, fantasies. So I liaison with Joan. Jack's doing the hand-holding with Kovic, and I'm doing the liaison with New York and Florida. Well, I called Florida and there's nothing happening. I called New York and this guy wants to see me. So I fly up to New York. He takes me to his house in the projects. He says, "You give us lunch, you give us buses and *x* number of dollars per person, and I'll get as many people down there as you want." [Laughs.] I said, "I'll talk to people." Kovic says, "OK, sure." So I call Joan and get the money and buses. Meantime, Jack and I are going back and forth between VVAW and fucking Kovic. They're all nuts as far as I'm concerned. They didn't want to deal with Kovic. I can't stand it and tell Jack that I can't do this shit.

So I went in Dellums's office and started organizing on the Hill [Capitol Hill] with Rusty Lindly, who had been D.C. liaison with VVAW in the old days and who at that time was working on legislation for the vets' centers. I worked with him on the language of vets' centers and then I said, "There's got to be some vets on the Hill."

At that time, there were no Vietnam vets on the Hill in office, but there were Vietnam vets working on the Hill as congressional aides. So we put together the Vietnam veterans' caucus during that same few weeks in order to get the vets' centers stuff together.

Then we come to the day of this event. We worked out this deal that AVM [American Veterans Movement] would come from one side and VVAW from the other, but of course they didn't tell us: fucking Kovic shows up with all these fucking flags. We're supposed to carry these American flags. Kovic wants to wheel to the bathroom of the White House and lock himself in. That's how crazy it was. That was his politics.

I tell Jack [McCloskey] that I can't go on this march. He said, "We'll get some Jack Daniels." It was a mess. It was totally splintered.

JOHN KNIFFIN

The Fourth of July in Washington was the last thing I went to with VVAW. I was disappointed by some of the crap that was going on by then. The way decisions were handled . . . the people in the camp who were generally not veterans who didn't know what we were about and didn't have the discipline that we had. They were like a bunch of kids that came in with one of the organizations.

I had a distinct feeling, particularly with folks like Barry, that what they were saying was: "We want to free you from the oppressors so we can oppress you." Why should I join with a group of people that say, "We're going to free you from a government that's trying to teach you how to think, but we're going to teach you how to think"?

In the early days, VVAW was such a bunch of anarchists. We had the hard-line commie ideologues and we had the hard-line anarchist ideologues and we had people who had no ideology whatsoever. They were all getting together and having all these incredible arguments, but there was an awful lot of love in the organization. That's what was missing in D.C.

DANNY FRIEDMAN

After we did this Washington thing in 1974, they [RU members] co-opted the whole thing. It was really revealed what they were, that they were out to take over the organization. I felt really betrayed by the guys like Ed [Damato] and Joe Urgo; these were the intellectuals of the group. I said, "Can't you guys see what they were doing?"

A month later, they had this thing, "Honor Vietnam Veterans at Shea Stadium." The Yankees were playing at Shea Stadium; Yankee Stadium was closed for renovation. It was free tickets if you prove you're a veteran. We all went down there. Basically, what we wanted to do was sit in the stands, watch the ball game, and hold up a couple of banners and posters. So I made the only tactical mistake I ever made. It was all done over my love of the Yankees.

377

I wanted to get great seats for the game. We had these seats all the way up with the veterans. What would happen if we wanted box seats at field level? It was an afternoon game. The Yankees weren't going anywhere. The stadium was mostly empty. They said, "Yeah, if you pay $4, you got box seats." Wow, box seats. I never sat in box seats before, and I wanted to do this. I talked the whole New York group into doing this. We got these box seats right behind third base, and it was great. All the other veterans were all the way up there.

The stadium police came around saying, "You guys got banners. You can't hold up no banners." So, sure enough, as soon as "The Star-Spangled Banner" starts, we hold up a banner: "Vietnam Veterans Against the War—Jobs for Veterans." The cops came over and attacked us. Nobody could help us. There was this whole rumble going on. I was kicking ass. I got my ass kicked. Then they dragged us into a room. They handcuffed us, worked us over. There were six of us that got arrested, the "Shea Stadium Six."

They got rid of the five other guys. They just dropped charges on them. I was charged with felonious assault. They charged me with felony assault because I fucked up one of the cops. They also cracked my head open and broke my ribs. The case went on for about a year. At first, it was really high-profile, "Shea Stadium Six"—and then the "Shea Stadium One."

My first hearing, the courtroom was full of VVAW/RCP types. [In 1975, RU had changed its name to Revolutionary Communist Party, RCP.] When the charges were eventually dropped to an ACD [adjournment in contemplation of dismissal] a year later, it was just me and my lawyer. That was the last thing I ever had to do with VVAW for a long time. I didn't speak to them for years.

As 1974 wound down, the battle lines within VVAW were clearly drawn. Some members from across the nation knew that the national office was dominated by RU and tried to disengage VVAW from its control; others simply dropped out.

JOHN LINDQUIST, ANNIE LUGINBILL, JEANNE FRIEDMAN, DAVID EWING, LEE THORN, BARRY ROMO, BILL BRANSON, PETE ZASTROW, JOE URGO

John Lindquist (JL): You got me saying, "Hey, let's pass a motion. You can't be a member of VVAW if you're a member of the RU, or any other party-building or party group." I democratically lost the motions.

I didn't run for reelection in October of 1974. They took over the chapter and we stepped out of leadership and became general members.

Annie Luginbill: People literally sat down and figured out: Well, if half a vote is over here and half a vote is over here and 15 are over here, how many votes are we going to have for and how many are going to be against?—and really it got into some pretty backroom kind of politics, except that it was in front of everybody.

Up to 1974, you and the national office agreed. What happened?

Jeanne Friedman (JF): I think what we started to not agree on is raising other anti-imperialist issues vis-à-vis veterans' issues. Some people, at least in our chapter, were talking about Ireland; some people were talking about South Africa; but I remember they were talking about veterans' issues. That's the way split started to emerge.

I didn't know, back then, that the RU was involved.

You didn't know that by 1974, Barry Romo and others in the national office were in the RU?

JF: They were hiding it pretty well for a long time. . . . Actually, I did sort of know because the national office people started saying that they were talking to these other people who were so helpful. I was nervous about it, but part of me said: They're studying Marxism-Leninism; that's good. They're getting a more theoretical framework; that's good. They were sharpening their own understanding of imperialism and really beginning to say they were Marxist-Leninist cadres. That part was OK with me, except that I hated the RU. I didn't like those people at Stanford.

I came from Palo Alto, where they had started, with Venceremos and the Revolutionary Union. . . . Originally, there was the Red Guard, and it split into Venceremos and the RU. It was my friends who were with the Venceremos side, although I never joined Venceremos. I did a lot of work with them on the Stanford campus.

I didn't get that they wanted to change the nature of VVAW/WSO until it was too late. I didn't see the damage until it was too late.

What do you mean by damage?

JF: The damage was that they had slotted VVAW to be a particular kind of organization in their firmament. They already had a party. That wasn't what I wanted. I wanted an anti-imperialist organization with a very heavy working-class composition and a heavy composition of veterans. The fights didn't come up until it was veterans' issues and it was clear they were soft-pedaling WSO. The first time we knew is when they put out an issue of the paper that dropped WSO.

What was ironic is that they [the previous leadership in the Long Beach area] were all on the side of veterans' issues. . . . It didn't make sense. . . . Here were these people, who a year earlier they wanted out, and now they were right? I also think there was a lot of egos. . . . Frankly, there was a lot of personality stuff going on.

The RU sent in their mole, a guy named Steve. It's clear he's the RU person. He opens his mouth and we all know it. He's just parroting everything they were saying. He won over two other people. None of us cared.

David Ewing (DE): I went to school at City College in San Francisco and immediately joined with the RU people. I immediately began working with them and joined a youth group [Revolutionary Student Brigade, RSB], which I stayed in from 1972 to 1976.

The people I worked with were incredibly incompetent, the worst organizers I had ever seen, ill-trained but very dogmatic. Just really miserable people. I was constantly at war with them and they intensely disliked me, but they needed me. I was really a political infighter; that's what I did. They assigned me to the Oakland Chapter. I was an ideal candidate to go into this very dangerous situation in Oakland.

Lee Thorn: I would go to meetings there [Oakland] about once every month or once every two months, and they were different from any other VVAW meetings I had been to; and I'd been at VVAW meetings all over the place—from Seattle, Kansas City, Chicago, New York, everywhere—but I'd never been to meetings like these. For one thing, it was over half nonvets. It turns out that at some point the entire SLA membership was in this Oakland chapter at one time or another. I knew all of them, but I didn't know that.

DE: By the time I got in, in 1975, the people in Oakland were terrorists and were hostile to us. The people who did the Patty Hearst kidnapping were members of the chapter. It was a real crazy thing.

The chapter had maybe 30 people. It was very polarized—three RU people and 27 of them—but only five or six of them spoke. The other people were hanger-ons, hippie people. The RU people were determined opponents. We were there at every meeting, objecting, fighting our line versus their line. It was a battle: for hours and hours, we fought them tooth and nail on every issue.

I was only in for about six months. The terrorist people decided that I was a secret member of the RU. They had a trial in absentia. I found this out from a friend of mine who was at the trial. They sentenced me to death. I went to a couple of meetings and the last meeting I attended, they said, "Dave, we want to inform you that we had tried you in absentia for being a secret member of the Revolutionary Union. You were expelled from the chapter and you are sentenced to death."

How did you react?

DE: On the one hand, it was funny, you know. I had very little to say. If they had killed me, people promised that they would retaliate and kill them. They certainly would have been killed.

It got that serious?

DE: Oh, yeah. I really thought my chances of dying were probably 50-50. It was that bitter and serious in Oakland because we were just destroying them. We were only two or three people and we completely fucked up everything they believed in.

What were their goals for VVAW as opposed to what the RU wanted to do?

DE: First and foremost, they wanted to get rid of the manipulators from RU, who were totally manipulating everything. It's true that they were. VVAW in the past was a very tolerant group. The RU made it a very intolerant group. So they reacted very strongly to our attempt to seize control of what had been an authentically mass organization and turn it into just an instrument of what was our grand scheme. They were rightfully angry about that because it was so antidemocratic. For them, I think the ideals of democracy were key. They wanted a democratic organization. Who can blame them?

The left was very polarized then. We saw them as RYM-I people, as Weathermen. We saw them as our enemies from 1969. We knew who they were and we hated their line. We had a very backward position on homosexuality, and we hated them for defending gay rights. There was a social gap. We all had short hair and were in the working class. They were all kind of hippies with no jobs.

Barry Romo: Their concept [that is those opposed to RU's domination] of what a vet should do is if you got a bonus, you should mail it to Vietnam. Vets should organize to support the Vietnamese and build things in Vietnam.

They tended to be better educated. They tended to be nonvets; and if they were vets, they tended to be non-Vietnam vets. They weren't struggling for a living and they hadn't grown up like that. If they had grown up in it, they hated the working class for the petty-bourgeois outlook. There's a whole group of people that hated the working class.

Bill Branson: Prairie Fire was trying to take us over at the time. [It is not clear that members opposed to the RU were part of Prarie Fire.]

[Jeanne] Friedman, Dolly [Jeannie Dolly, another member], and some others were spearheading this whole thing of making us this amorphous thing—which we saw as death. I opposed it. I saw them manipulating people and drawing them in against the center. They always had this thing of "they're all in the RU," instead of saying what policy they disagreed with. They disagreed with our tending to keep a focus around veterans' stuff.

DE: In order to fight the battle, they created chapters of their own. . . . There was only a chapter in Oakland, so they divided the Oakland chapter and made a San Francisco chapter out of it. Now they had two chapters. One had one RU person in the Oakland chapter and now only one in the San Francisco chapter, so they pretty well isolated us. Plus, they doubled the number of delegates for the pending national conference. They were just getting ready for the convention, for the battle. We had them outnumbered like 10 to one. They were really desperate.

Was there a meeting of the national steering committee where this really came to the fore?

Pete Zastrow (PZ): Yes—Saint Louis. We sat down days and days ahead of time and figured out where the votes were going to go. We had all these little shenanigans we could pull if necessary, to disqualify this state or get rid of that one if we had to. But the vote was never going to be all that close.

DE: We fucked with them amazingly when they got there. We were ready for them. We manipulated everything, so there was no democracy. It was horrible what we did to them; it was really unfair.

We controlled the national office, so we were in a position to know everything that was going on, to count the votes, make challenges to their delegates. I mean we had people right in the midst of their leadership, and they didn't have anybody in our leadership. They had nobody willing to go to the RU chapters. None of their people were cut out for that shit. We did that to them. We were democratic centralists, really tightly controlled. It was a really well-organized group. They were very vulnerable.

JL: When the WSO vote came up in October 1975, and WSO lost, 35 chapters walked out en masse.

JF: We're gone. I went down to the office and took all the files out of the regional office and moved it to my basement. We became VVAW/WSO Anti-Imperialist. We were the first ones in that, which makes it even more bizarre. Now there's an RCP contingent [VVAW Anti-Imperialist].

How long did the anti-imperialist branch last?

JF: At least a year. This was our organization. Then we just died. We just couldn't sustain a regional organization. San Jose folded. Santa Cruz was clear that they were going to stay intact as a veterans' group. The Santa Cruz vets' chapter was extraordinary. They run the Santa Cruz County veterans' building today. They took over the building. They didn't need us. Some of the people went into Seize the Time. I hung in there until the end.

PZ: Almost every one of the chapters that moved away from the organization were people with a very strong community organization because they branched out into a lot of other things. It's heresy, but they were much more correct than we were.

I guess it was the last time that the organization as an organization really had a chance to vote on anything. After that, votes were pretty much dictated by the various political organizations, or maybe I shouldn't say it that way. . . . There was no longer any need for votes. We never had anything else we needed to vote on.

I guess my own feeling—and I don't remember how clearly I voiced it—was the thought that it should have been a lot easier to coexist. I have never been one of the organization's hard-liners. But that's not the way it turned out.

Joe Urgo: Basically, what's happening around the country is that within this context of agents, suspicions, political lines, friends, confusion . . . everybody begins to identify with a little grouping; to set itself off and trying to figure out why we can't trust these people. I don't like the people in this city, but I like the people in that city; and sometimes, if there is a basis to unite people, you could deal with that.

During the infighting of 1974, many individual members had already left VVAW; but in 1975, when entire chapters were expelled or walked out, the organization was left in the hands of a small cadre of people from RU. At that point, its activities became increasingly associated with RU's goals, and funding dried up. Some of the remaining members began to fight with the RU leadership, which then tried to effectively dismantle VVAW.

PETE ZASTROW, BILL BRANSON, BILL DAVIS, JOE URGO, JOHN LINDQUIST, ANNIE BAILEY, DAVE CLINE

Pete Zastrow (PZ): We went bankrupt in 1975. We moved out of the building on Newport and we moved down to the south side of Chicago in 1976. In a lot of ways people got older and people had to work for a living. Their freedom to pop off all over the country became more restricted.

Bill Branson: The real problems started occurring when the RCP was formed. It was an incredibly centrist, undemocratic organization. At that point in time, there had been a raid on the VVAW cadre. They were developing a cult, Avakian [Bob Avakian, leader of RU/RCP] and that bunch, who manipulated this whole thing.

Bill Davis (BD): One of the main objections I always had with the RCP is that they were pulling a lot of people out of VVAW, recruiting them into the RCP, making them cadre, and taking them out of vets' work and putting them into other places.

Roland Cordero was a Vietnam vet but who was right-hand man to Bob Avakian on the west coast, who was given the responsibility to break down VVAW in the city and integrate them into the other organizations—in effect, dissolve the chapters and the national office. My wife Joan at the time was doing workplace organizations with the RCP and telling me how disgusting all these people were.

They were continually trying to send people out of town, and they did. They sent Brian [Adams] here, they sent Sam [Shorr] there, but Branson refused. They tried to send me to Detroit and leave Joan here. I said, "No, I won't do that." Christ, we were living together at that time, but we were working different shifts, not seeing each other.

My loyalty remained with VVAW, and that was another reason they wouldn't take me into the RCP. I was more concerned and loyal to VVAW and frequently said things like, "Why are you gutting our organization?"

The national office was not broken down and put into their various cells or different groups, and that was a continuing ongoing battle. We had our own office and facilities and security, and they needed us badly. They needed us for security whenever they did anything so they didn't get their ass kicked.

PZ: The RCP sponsored a great workers' convention in Chicago to build the National Workers' Organization [in 1977]. They set up little offices around the city to bring in more people. I would go to one of those offices and man it night after night with the two black kids who were living with me at the time. I ended up doing the printing. We would run off thousands and thousands of pages of propaganda.

At one point Barry came back with this thing that he said I had to mimeograph, but he said I had to do it very quietly and very secretly and I couldn't let anybody see it. I couldn't have this eleven-year-old who was living with me at the time help me with it, which was utterly ridiculous. The kid was dyslexic; he couldn't even read. But this had come down from on high. So I ran off this thing, and of course I immediately read it and hid copies of it away.

It was the paper that said we had found counterrevolutionaries in the RCP and here they are, this is what they think. Essentially what happened was the RCP, which it was at that point, split pretty close to even. Some areas of the country went entirely with the split side and other areas went entirely with the RCP. Chicago was pretty much divided.

Joe Urgo (JU): The split in the RCP was over the question of China, in which one-third of the central committee was ejected because they had clearly given up the vision. . . . They didn't want revolutionaries. People here begin to split

384

off because they are not that dedicated to revolution. The same struggle was going on in the RCP.

The question in VVAW became: How radical a change do we really want, and are we willing to fight for it? Are we going to use the experience we found in Vietnam to work for defeat of America in its wars? I felt that many vets were trying to make peace with the United States and to work for a few changes from within. The national office in Chicago was beginning to take the focus off of being anti-imperialist. They weren't being revolutionary. Are we going to be revolutionary or not?

I couldn't go back on what I had seen and learned after listening to the winter soldier investigation—the atrocities and guys breaking down. . . . But there was an appeal on both sides that was correct. I was able to figure out, more or less, which side I wanted to be on.

BD: Barry, the paragon of security and democratic centralism, won't tell us shit. He's fighting these people [those who wanted to remain in the RCP] tooth and nail day and night on high levels, totally at odds with them.

PZ: There was never any question among those of us in the national office which way we were going to go with it. I don't think we ever sat down and debated it. Those of us in the national office looked at this stuff and said, "This is asinine. The hell with these people."

The people from the RCP in Chicago, and some from actually out of town, came with guns to try to take over the national office. We were having a chapter meeting at the time. One person in the chapter was there at their request, and he was carrying a weapon. At this point, all of us were armed constantly. We wouldn't walk the streets without a sizable armament. [Laughs.]

Why?

PZ: We didn't know what was going to happen with these people. There were stories about poor little girls getting hit with baseball bats by huge men at various meetings in this city. . . . I mean it was pretty nasty. Anyhow, there was a chapter meeting going on. As soon as we heard someone at the door, someone in the chapter meeting immediately got out a weapon and disarmed the one person they suspected. The rest of us had our little stations around the house. I was in the second floor window.

They came up and beat on the door for a while. I think Barry talked to them through the door and told them that if they didn't leave we were going to kill them. They left.

John Lindquist (JL): Walter [Klim, who was in the house on Fielding when the takeover attempt took place] freaks out and turns over the chapter records in our back door.

Annie Bailey (AB): We get up in the morning and sitting outside our back door of our apartment is the mailing list, all the active files, and no note or nothing.

JL: You had people within VVAW that quit. Joe Urgo, Rich Bangert, Sammy Shorr, Marla Watson, past national office members of VVAW went out and actually quit VVAW, joined the RU and became cadre members. Any group that they're involved with—Unemployed Workers Organizing Committee [UWOC], Revolutionary Student Brigade, or whatever the fuck it is—as far as they're concerned, they control us.

There's an article printed in their national paper, not our paper, their paper: "We [VVAW] are the RCP." I read it. It blew my mind. After I read that thing, when they actually put it in print that they were us, that was the straw that broke the camel's back. I called and said, "How dare you say that?" Someone said, "Who the fuck are you?" I said, "I'm John Lindquist; I've been here since 1970. Who the fuck are you?" They were all freaked out. They tried to run this Marxist crap. I said, "Don't give me that Marxist crap."

JU: We had a vote in the summer of 1978 to decide whether to stay with VVAW, Inc., or to go with VVAW/AI. [VVAW/Anti-Imperialist was the name proposed by those who remained with the RCP.] More vets voted for AI, but the national office was controlled by those who opposed it. We formed VVAW/AI in 1979.

PZ: The RCP went on its merry way and turned into some strange cult. I mean, it's stupidity. . . . If they can't get attention any other way, they burn a flag because that will outrage people and that way get attention.

AB: I didn't like what was happening. I sympathized with what Bill and Pete and Barry were trying to do. I trusted them. I knew that they were VVAW guys. John wasn't quite so sure. He thought they were commies first and VVAW second.

JL: It could have gone one way or another, but when push came to shove, they stuck with the veterans, and I respect that. They actually came out and tell me, "We fucked up. The RCP's fucked up."

AB: I knew that when push came to shove, they would come down on our side. I knew it. Otherwise I wouldn't have kept beating my head against the wall, going down there every couple of weeks, sitting at the typewriter.

Dave Cline: After the split in the RCP, people started examining the shit more closely. I mean, I believe in socialism; I believe that capitalist system is a system that is as corrupt as the communists were—but eventually people have to come to some cooperative system. But you're also not the conveyor belt to recruit someone to nirvana in Marxist-Leninist heaven. We spent a lot of time, after the RCP thing, getting the shit off our shoes.

BD: A lot of people who originally went with them [RU/RCP] said, "Fuck you," separated, and stayed VVAW. They just couldn't control us. One thing about us: Whatever kinds of infiltrators and police and whatever we had, we shed ourselves of a lot of them.

There were enough people who were still in VVAW around the country who were not RCP and were not about to be RCP. John and Annie in Milwaukee wanted to continue to work with VVAW.

PZ: Milwaukee stayed. They kept them together during a period when the organization said politics are absolutely primary and all this—what we called at the time touchy-feely—has to go. Other places were driven out of the organization because they didn't have the same kind of base that Milwaukee does. They didn't have the organizational strength that John and Annie brought to it. People who didn't have that said, "VVAW isn't my organization and I'll have to do something else."

BD: After that, the Agent Orange shit broke.

Agent Orange: Back to the Front Lines

Agent Orange was a chemical defoliant (herbicide) that contained dioxin, the most toxic human-made substance ever developed. Using airplanes, the United States sprayed more than 12 million gallons of Agent Orange over 5 million acres of jungle and farmland in South Vietnam between 1961 and 1970. In addition to denuding the land and destroying crops, fish, and animals, Agent Orange killed uncounted Vietnamese peasants; it also increased miscarriages, birth defects, and other complications of childbirth. Moreover, because Agent Orange was sprayed indiscriminately from the air, it affected American military personnel. For some time, United States dismissed Vietnamese accounts of the effects of Agent Orange as "communist propaganda"; but a study completed by the Deparment of Defense in 1967 confirmed the dangers associated with dioxin.

JOHN LINDQUIST, SUKIE WACHTENDONK, ANNIE BAILEY, RON SABLE, JIM WACHTENDONK

John Lindquist (JL): Within a year, I was in the national office and Annie was regional coordinator.

It turns out that Maude DeVictor's thing breaks out the weekend that we're having a national meeting, March of 1978.[13] The Agent Orange stuff was on. It was a natural. It was a revitalization for the whole organization.

The whole agenda of the national meeting went right into Agent Orange. We came up with our demands: testing, treatment, and compensation for Agent Orange. Let's go. What do we need? Research.

VVAW spearheaded the efforts to get the issue of Agent Orange into the public arena. As a result, new veterans and their families became associated with VVAW. Some were part of the class-action suit filed by veterans to have the government acknowledge its role in covering up the known danger of Agent Orange, and to compensate veterans who had been exposed to it and who continued to suffer its effects.

Why did you become active over the issue of Agent Orange?

Sukie Wachtendonk (SW): I found out that they poisoned veterans. They had to cut my kids out of my belly. [She had to deliver by cesarean section because

Maude DeVictor at the first veterans' conference on Agent Orange, February 1979.

Annie Bailey *(center)* and Sukie Wachtendonk *(at right, behind the banner)* at the first demonstration against Agent Orange, Milwaukee, 1978.

the children were already at risk prenatally.] They had chromosome damage. They're ill a lot of the time. They can't ride the city buses, they can't go in the city parks, they can't go to the lakes surrounding the city. There are so many restrictions on them, and their constitutional rights have been trampled. I'm really disgusted that these corporations are able to continue to produce these chemicals that send my children into grand mal seizures. We have no constitutional rights to protect them. It goes against everything I was brought up to believe about this country. It really pisses me off the way we've been treated, and the way thousands of people have been treated.

The Agent Orange struggle reactivated VVAW. There were three or four of us in the midwest; and of course there were people, our counterparts, just like us—wives, friends of veterans—who were doing it on the east coast, the west coast, and the south. There were basically maybe 20 people nationwide. We did a lot of really good work and went on to getting involved in the class-action suit and signing the vets up and networking that way.

Annie Bailey (AB): Even though they didn't have an active chapter in New York, we had good contacts with Dave Cline, Mike Gold, Annie Hirschman, and those people. A lot of vets came back together, representing other vets' groups or little local Agent Orange groups. It turned out half of them were old VVAW members. Whenever the colors needed to be paraded out, they did it.

SW: A lot of them formed new organizations with their own names because they met the VVAW stigma and could not deal with it. So they broke off and formed their own organizations so they wouldn't have to deal with that, but they were still VVAW people.

AB: The center for all the research for the whole organization was right here in Milwaukee. It was done right here, right in this spot on that square table [in John Lindquist and Annie Bailey's home, where our interview took place].

SW: Doing the Agent Orange work, the research part of it was very important for Annie Bailey from Milwaukee and myself. We went to libraries. Muriel [Hogan] was a librarian at the time and had access to a lot of information. We compiled all of the dioxin studies that were available worldwide, in a book about six inches thick. We shot to hell their premise that there was no information on dioxin or Agent Orange as far as adverse side effects.

The VA first said that they never sprayed chemical defoliants in Vietnam. Then they said yes they did, but it was only done sparingly and no troops were exposed. Then as years went by, it came out that guys were exposed and, yes, it was a massive kind of exposure, but they can't do anything about it. We found a compilation of all the spraying missions carried out in Vietnam, dated, and what areas were covered. Beth, in California, also got the information and put together the Vietnam Network, where you could lay out on a map where you were and how much chemical exposure you had had. The VA maintained that there was no way to do this.

JL: We held the first winter soldier investigation on Agent Orange.

Ron Sable: I participated in one of those. At one point here, I got the occupational program and department here [Cook County Hospital in Chicago] to agree to do some evaluations of people and incorporate that into their program—at a time when you couldn't get the VA to do anything.

Were there any confrontations over your work on Agent Orange?

AB: Mostly it was chemical company goons fucking with people.

JL: Fucking with Sukie, mostly. They didn't fuck with us much around here.

SW: Our phones were tapped. They broke into our house.

At the beginning of the class-action suit, the chemical companies tried to obtain all of the medical records of everyone in the class. Judge Pratt, the first judge, said, "No, you can't have that before we go to trial." So two days after the judge ruled, there were break-ins across the country in plaintiffs' homes, and ours was one of them. There's a pattern there. I think that they were looking for the documents. They were in the files, and that's the only thing they touched when they broke in. They tried to get our records, but luckily, with VVAW training in security, we had foreseen the problems. There are documents buried all over the state of Wisconsin for safety.

Jim Wachtendonk was in Vietnam in 1970, as a dog handler with the 212th and the 595th Divisions of the Army. He patrolled the perimeter of bases and areas of military installations where cannisters of Agent Orange were stored. He was discharged in May 1971.

Jim Wachtendonk (JW): We were infiltrated twice. I've also been approached a couple of times at gigs. One guy one night tried to get me drunk and started asking questions about the national office and all this.

SW: And he ended up spilling his guts about a lot of stuff. [Laughs.] It was really good; we learned a lot from that guy.

What happened when you went to trial?

SW: We had a lawyer, Victor Yanakow, who was the original class-action attorney who filed the first case in 1978. We were the first family in Wisconsin to join in 1979. He was very capable, but also extremely radical. He would bring up points that the judge did not want to be heard, and Victor would press the point. He was very abrasive toward the second judge after the first judge was dropped. I don't know why.

The second judge totally changed the direction of the case and refused to admit documents and depositions that had been brought up, so we had to start basically anew. Victor was trying to fight the moves, but that costs money. So he brought in financial backing from other law firms from around the country, who then wanted more money and did not agree with Victor's tactics either. They undercut him.

The day before we were to go into court they withdrew the financial backing, and Victor walked into court with no money in this multimillion-dollar lawsuit. The judge didn't like Victor to begin with and chided him for daring to come into court without any financial backing. He proceeded to remove him from the case and appointed six corporate lawyers to represent us for one year on the case. The case was settled out of court the day the jury was being selected, for $180 million. They settled out of court for a pittance that nobody could collect on.

They rejected any research. You have to have chloracne rash documented within one year of your return from Vietnam, which most guys cannot do. You have to have soft tissue sarcoma and non-Hodgkin's sarcoma before you get anything. The kids were totally cut out, but there was some money set aside for them in trust to do psychological counseling.

JL: We worked on Agent Orange for six years before we lost the lawsuit.

AB: We really got fucked.

SW: We realized that it was over, that we had really gotten screwed; but we had to continue working to make this a safer place for us here. In Washington they weren't going to do anything to keep our kids safe and alive. We turned more into a community-based organization. We set up a pesticide policy here in Madison and began challenging all the chemical spraying that was going on here—on people's lawns by Chemlawn, and spraying along the lake.

JW: Monsanto would send their agronomist into the hearing [and] they paid millions of dollars to the UW [University of Wisconsin] Agronomy Department.

SW: Their scientists and lawyers and I would be there.

JW: There would be Sukie, "chemical phobic" mother [according to these experts].

SW: These are the guys who at these meetings were calling me a communist.
I'd written grants to get the Agent Orange settlement money. I spent months and months getting this really good grant together as a VVAW grant. I was told that I should bring it to the Madison community of veterans to get their support so it would be more community-based, which I did. They ripped the whole thing apart and dissected it; and they got VA officials in on this, discussing what should be done with this money.
I was talking treatment and testing: Here's the type of testing and here's the type of treatment we need to do; here are the programs our kids need. They continually set up roadblocks. So I just finally said, "I can't deal with this bullshit. I object to you being here [pointing, as if to a person], I object to you being here, and I object to you being here, and I object to being called a communist, and I'm leaving. You assholes have done this to me for too fucking long. I said I'd work with you, I've tried to work with you, and you can all get fucked," and out the door I went. So they sent in this piece of shit of a grant—which was part of what I had slaved and labored over, and part of what they wanted in—and took all of the political stuff out . . . just saying

the veterans and their families had done all the work initially through the years and had not been helped by the VA—period.

I never realized when we began this in 1978 that it would take 12 years with such losses. So many deaths of veterans. So many deaths of kids. Having all the documents from the class-action suit reveal all the dirty shit that went on between the chemical companies and the government, who knew everything as early as 1965. The judge sealed all the documents until the year 2025. Nobody is going to know about this.

Parting Shots: The Legacy of VVAW

*People began to realize, at least by the early 1980s, "Who's going to tell the
history of the Vietnam war? Are we going to leave it to just the usual
sources, or are we going to get involved?" So what a lot of people did, in
various regional groupings, is this process of speaking in schools, making
themselves available to be part of whatever process . . . says this is our history. This isn't Schlesinger's history; this isn't someone else's version—this
is our version of what the Vietnam war was about.*

Jan Barry

*VVAW brought a lot of people together. . . . It raised the political awareness
and understanding of a lot of people, radicalized them. It gave expression to
that collectively, I think, in a very impressive way at the time, but has been
sustained in the lives of people in countless ways in all sorts of avenues of
life. A lot of these guys have gone into all sorts of different areas with the
same learning of lessons in various ways from what we went through.*

Bobby Muller

The Cold War Revisited

Although the war in Vietnam had faded from the nation's consciousness by
the late 1970s, the United States continued—as in some ways it still continues—to wage an economic war against the Vietnamese. Foreign policy makers from the Carter administration to the present have refused to establish full
diplomatic relations with Vietnam. The United States has also used its economic clout to keep other nations from assisting the Vietnamese. In 1977,
for example, when India planned to send a hundred water buffalo to Vietnam, the United States threatened to withhold Food for Peace from India.[1]
The World Bank and the International Monetary Fund have refused to provide financial support to Vietnam, devastated by thirty years of fighting. If

the United States had lost the hot war in Vietnam, it seemed intent on winning the economic war.

During the late 1970s, American foreign policy makers also became preoccupied with a series of revolutionary movements around the globe. In Iran in 1979, students and Islamic militants overthrew a regime that had been backed by the United States, seized the American embassy, and held 52 Americans hostage for more than a year. Rebellious left-wing movements became active in Africa, Central America, and other parts of the third world. Bloody civil wars between American-backed governments and leftist revolutionaries broke out in El Salvador, Guatemala, and Nicaragua, threatening to undermine the United States' control of the region. The Sandinistas' victory over the Somoza's 45-year dictatorship in Nicaragua especially caused American foreign policy makers to fear that the United States was losing its grip.[2]

The Carter and Reagan administrations responded by increasing economic and military aid to "client" nations that were under siege, by stepping up clandestine operations in these war-torn regions, and by instituting a new military buildup at home. Although President Nixon had discontinued the draft at the end of the Vietnam war, President Carter reestablished draft registration in order to create a pool of conscripts for the possibility of increased military activity in the third world. However, with the memory of Vietnam still fresh in their minds, Americans were reluctant to undertake any such involvement. A Gallup poll in 1982, for instance, found that 89 percent of the American public opposed intervention in El Salvador.[3] This attitude on the part of Americans began to be described as the "Vietnam syndrome."

President Reagan and his advisers considered the "Vietnam syndrome" a serious impediment to their ability to deal forcefully with presumed international threats, and to cure the syndrome they developed a new version of the cold war. This had been foreshadowed in Reagan's campaign speeches when he was running for his first term in 1980; he described the Soviet Union as an "evil empire" and blamed it for all global disorder. Reagan also castigated the antiwar movement of the Vietnam era, saying that it had led to permissiveness and had caused Americans to lose their nerve; and he called on the nation to take pride in its military heritage and its status as world leader. When Reagan took office, his administration forged ahead with plans to reestablish American supremacy. In September 1982, American troops were sent into Lebanon. In 1983, the United States invaded Grenada. In 1986, the United States bombed Libya.

George Bush, as Reagan's successor, continued the military buildup; the Bush administration undertook an invasion of Panama in 1989 and, of course, the Gulf War in 1991. With the Gulf War, Bush announced, the United States had sent out the message that it had shed the "Vietnam syndrome."

These military adventures and the heightened cold war rhetoric were, in the words of Eric Hobsbawm, "designed as a therapy for the U.S.A. rather than as a practical attempt to reestablish a world balance of power. This had, in fact, been done quietly in the later 1970s"—that is, when the United States and its allies in Europe had begun a massive increase of armaments, along with more covert actions.[4]

There was also a cultural crusade: a concerted attempt to convince Americans that the United States' foreign policy was just, and that it was congruent with their traditional democratic values. For one thing, right-wing historians and editorialists reinterpreted the Vietnam war for a younger generation of Americans: the war was now said to have been just, but strategically flawed. Also, significant American filmmakers contributed to this interpretation by producing movies—starring, among others, Sylvester Stallone and Chuck Norris—in which the nation was allowed to refight the war and win it. In addition, veterans of the Vietnam war were rehabilitated: parades were held in their honor, and the Vietnam Veterans Memorial was built in Washington, D.C. (It is worth noting that the memorial—popularly known as "the wall"— was paid for with money raised by Vietnam veterans' organizations.)

While politicians, historians, and filmmakers aggrandized the United States, the majority of Americans were sinking into an economic morass. The national deficit had spiraled upward as a result of the military buildup of the 1980s (between 1979 and 1990, the annual defense budget increased from $200 billion to $300 billion), which had been accompanied by tax cuts.[5] To offset the increased deficit, federal funding for education, welfare, and numerous other social programs was sharply reduced. While the wealthiest 1 percent of the population doubled its income during the 1980s, most Americans struggled to make ends meet. In the words of Kevin Phillips, a conservative political analyst, "The 1980s were the triumph of upper America—an ostentatious celebration of wealth . . . and the glorification of capitalism, free markets and finance."[6]

Thus the United States' open-door policy and the cold war were very much alive during the 1980s; and both continue to have an impact in the 1990s, when the cold war has officially ended. In fact, the foreign policy elite learned valuable lessons from the Vietnam war. For the past twenty years much of the nation's foreign policy has been carried out covertly. When the United States deploys its military forces, it does so swiftly, using high-tech hardware and professional personnel. The rightist economic programs of the 1980s, which have adversely affected the majority of the American people, have also created a pool of young men and women for the professional armed forces, and many of these men and women were strongly influenced by the revisionism accompanying this economic philosophy. The new high-tech weaponry and the strategists' heavy reliance on air power provide assurance that few Americans will experience the devastation of war firsthand, as those who went to Vietnam experienced it. It is probable, then, that without access to alternative perspectives on the past, fewer and fewer Americans will raise any serious objections.

VVAW Revisited

In the following pages, men and women of Vietnam Veterans Against the War discuss its impact on their lives, after the war and into the present. They also discuss how their experiences during the Vietnam era shaped their responses to the renewed cold war. Finally, they respond to the question, "What do you see as the major legacy of VVAW?" What is evident from their narratives is a continuing commitment to peace, justice, and the duty of citizens in a democracy.

JACK McCLOSKEY

Jack McCloskey died of heart failure on February 15, 1996, at age fifty-three. Perhaps more than any other member of VVAW, he had spearheaded the efforts

Jack McCloskey: celebrating his fiftieth birthday; and *(second from left)* at a VVAW campout in Wisconsin, with John Lindquist *(left)* and others.

to create a community to which Vietnam veterans could return when they came home. He was instrumental in the development of rap groups, the recognition of posttraumatic stress disorder, and the establishment of vets' centers around the nation that provided, and still provide, counseling, drug rehabilitation, job placement, and many other programs for the walking wounded returning from combat.[7] His friends remember him as "Wacky Jacky," a man who embraced life with great gusto; they remember him, also, for his unflagging devotion to veterans, his love for his brothers, and his commitment to nonviolent social change. However, his service in Vietnam never left him: he suffered psychically from severe stress and physically from chloracne—he was among the many veterans who had been exposed to Agent Orange.

To add a personal note, I feel honored to have known Jack McCloskey. His human warmth became very clear to me on his last visit to Chicago in the fall of 1995, when he came to my home to meet my family and share a meal with us. He could not swallow more than a few bites of food—eating caused him a great deal of discomfort—but despite his pain, he spent most of the evening chasing my three-year-old son around the house, holding him on his knees to tell him stories, and making him laugh. By the end of the evening, he was "Uncle Jack."

I think VVAW saved more fucking lives just by its existence. Because without VVAW, a lot of these veterans had no place to go to. No place. A lot of them, I think, would have committed suicide. The rap groups started for Vietnam vets by VVAW were the model for the whole veterans' program that is existing today, the whole posttraumatic stress programs.

SHELDON RAMSDELL

Sheldon Ramsdell—Shelly—died of AIDS on March 25, 1996, at age 60. He had been the founding vice president of VVAW, coordinating its media campaigns. He was very proud of his work with the organization; when I met him in 1992, he still carried his VVAW identification. During the 1980s, he had fought for better research and treatment for AIDS and for the right of avowed gays and lesbians to serve in the armed forces. He always remained an active advocate of social justice. At the time of this writing, a book of his photographs was being prepared for posthumous publication.

RON SABLE

Ron Sable died—also of AIDS—shortly after our interview, on December 30, 1993, age forty-eight. After his involvement with VVAW, he had gone to medical school; he had then worked at Cook County Hospital in Chicago until his death. He devoted himself to providing good health care for Chicago's poor; to exposing the deadly effects of Agent Orange and other environmental health hazards; and, through most of the 1980s, to providing medical and psychological support for victims of AIDS.

I think it adds to the body of historic data that war is not a thing that people enter into lightly, that killing people that you don't have anything against is a horrible experience for people. You do this as an absolute last resort, to defend yourself. It's in the line of testimonies: *All Quiet on the Western Front* and [Dalton Trumbo's] *Johnny Got His Gun.* War is hell and people should know that. People should not be allowed to forget that.

LINDA ALBAND

Linda Alband lives in San Francisco. She was Randy Shilts's business associate for the last five years of his life, and she did primary research for his book Conduct Unbecoming *[1993; the subtitle is* Lesbians and Gays in the U.S. Military*]. At this writing she was on the board of directors of the Restitution Project and was working with Woman Vision, a nonprofit production company for educational media. Woman Vision produced* Straight from the Heart, *which was nominated for an Academy Award, and at the time of our interview had just completed* All God's Children.

ANNIE BAILEY AND JOHN LINDQUIST

John Lindquist and Annie Bailey still live in Milwaukee. They are both active members of VVAW and continue to work for veterans' rights in the midwest.

John Lindquist *(right)* with John Kettenhoffen, preparing food at a VVAW stand-down for the homeless in Chicago, 1995.

According to Annie, "The Vietnam War has colored everything we do, from the way we vote to what we eat. The most important thing we learned was to never trust the government, but to trust the people." Along with other VVAW members in Wisconsin, they have been instrumental in providing assistance to homeless veterans and have given much time and energy during yearly "stand-downs" for homeless veterans in Milwaukee and Chicago—weekend-long events that provide food, clothing, and medical care to homeless veterans. The Wisconsin region has continued to be a "family"; various functions are held, including an annual camp-out for veterans from across the midwest and the nation. John Lindquist and Annie Bailey have also been active in local politics, unions, and neighborhood organizations. When he walks his dog, John often takes along a can of paint to clean up graffiti.

Annie Bailey: The more political vets in the 1970s, who were more firmly against the war, would join VVAW, and through working with a chapter where they were, would meet other groups of people doing other things in the community. Once they got over their "veteranness" and started blending back into the community, got a job, got married, and started having a family, their priorities would change. They were still against the war, but they were active in their unions, they were into the food co-ops—you know—so in that way VVAW was a transitional organization. Thousands and thousands of guys came through the organization and readjusted in VVAW and went on to other organizations.

We just had a friend who hasn't been active for a long time. He's been on the Board of Directors of Jobs for Peace for years. He just got elected as county supervisor. He's a perfect example of someone who comes to meetings and does some big demos and starts to feel normal again and then gets out there and starts his own life.

JAN BARRY

Jan Barry, one of the founding members of VVAW, now lives in Montclair, New Jersey, with his wife Paula and their family. He is a journalist and the editor of three collections of poetry by Vietnam veterans, including Winning Hearts and Minds, *which was published in 1972 and received critical acclaim. He has worked to promote nonviolent conflict resolution projects, ranging from citizen-exchange and sister-city links with the Soviet Union to community activities countering violence at home.*

I think, in hindsight, VVAW was a civil rights movement for veterans. It gave the veterans a sense that they have real rights, not just what the government says are your rights. When I got out, I got this booklet that said, "Your Rights as a Veteran." . . . Nothing in there said that you had civil rights in the sense, as a citizen, to speak your own mind, to say what your experience was, not to let Nixon or Johnson say what your experience was. You've got a right as a veteran to work on changing these things without being labeled a troublemaker and having the government attack you—which was a lot of what was going on.

VVAW provided an introduction to the larger society. It broadened the perspective of lots of people. Many Vietnam veterans never thought about anybody else's issues as being important, or something to even think about or take seriously. By working in coalition, lots of people said, "Hey, you know, we ought to help this other group. This is also important."

Vietnam veterans coming out of VVAW identified something that needed to be addressed on behalf of a much larger group of people—rape victims and accident victims and cops and firemen who have to deal with all of that—and now I'm routinely reading about posttraumatic stress counseling. It did not even exist until VVAW helped put the finger on what needed to be focused on. It was a few people who decided this was important.

As it continued, VVAW has addressed the Central America insanity and the Persian Gulf craziness. Vietnam veterans have had a tremendous impact on Afghanistan veterans in Russia. A number of VVAW people continue to work with them.

People began to realize, at least by the early 1980s, "Who's going to tell the history of the Vietnam war? Are we going to leave it to just the usual sources, or are we going to get involved?" So what a lot of people did, in various regional groupings, is this process of speaking in schools, making themselves available to be part of whatever process . . . says this is our history. This isn't Schlesinger's history; this isn't someone else's version. This is our version of what the Vietnam war was about.

Much of what we were doing in VVAW had more to do with art . . . what you could do in a short period of time to have a big impact on somebody, to make them rethink everything, whether it was a short speech or quick demonstrations or the poetry and other literature. . . . This was not a long campaign; this was not massive numbers of people. It was often one person, one voice, one point that just hit people in such a way that they had to rethink what their assumptions were. That's not the usual way people think about politics or movement organizing. You have to think much more in the way actors, writers, and poets think. How do I convey this succinctly in such a way that people really say, Wow! That creative element was really the energy of VVAW.

One of the things that I think is difficult for people to grasp is: This is an organization that has no power. It has no power to compel anybody to do anything, in it or outside of it. The only thing it has is the power of ideas. You got a good idea? Do you have the energy and time to organize it and demonstrate that it was a good idea? Run with it. That's pretty much what it has been as an organization.

BILL BRANSON

Bill Branson lives and works in Chicago. He is an analyst for the Chicago Transit Authority. He is still an active member of VVAW; he continues to promote veterans' concerns and is actively involved in organizing the yearly stand-downs for homeless veterans in Chicago. His activism has also included abortion rights.

DAVE CLINE

When this book was being prepared, Dave Cline continued to live in Jersey City, New Jersey. He had been an active member of VVAW ever since he first joined, educating young people about the nature of the war as he experienced it and—during the 1980s—speaking out against American involvement in Central America.

I think one of the key factors in the shifting of the public opinion against the war was the fact that soldiers started coming home and saying it was wrong. The main prop that any government has in conducting any war is that people are going to support their children who are being sent to fight it. When their children come home and say their government is lying to you, people say, "Wait a minute—this ain't bunch of eggheads." They were able to discredit a certain strain of the antiwar movement, but when the soldiers started coming home and speaking against it, middle America begin to look at it.

Veterans became a major force in the antiwar movement. I don't doubt that people spit on people's uniforms and all that stuff, but some of that shit I hear about it is nonsense. I think there is a myth that was created about trying to put protestors against the veterans. As far as I'm concerned the only people that cared about us were the people that tried to end the war.

VVAW created a culture of resistance. There was a culture of resistance developing in the military and among veterans. The military was getting to the point of collapse.

Throughout the 1980s we began the schools program—where any military recruiters go in; we go in. I've spoken to over 100,000 students. I've spoken all over New York and New Jersey. We have a whole cadre that do it.

In 1982, we started looking at the Vietnam memorials and said we had to be there putting out an antiwar message as well. Today, a large percentage of the veterans buy into that shit . . . noble cause, POWs, MIAs, and all that. . . . Reagan and them took it to the max. We participate in Veterans Day parades. We have our message as part of the veterans' community as well. Veterans of the last war are always used to convince young people to fight the next war. We want to offer them an alternative.

We became involved in the efforts around opposing the war in Central America. We sent a truck with the veterans' peace convoy to Nicaragua. Then the Persian Gulf war broke. I was the national representative to the national coalition activities. I spoke for VVAW at the march on Washington on January 26, 1991.

BILL DAVIS

Bill Davis lives in Oak Park, Illinois, with his wife Joanie and their two children. He is still an active member of VVAW who has numerous speaking engagements in schools and other forums. He has been employed by United Parcel Service for the past 20 years and is the chief steward for Local 701 of the International Association of Machinists and Aerospace Workers. He is also president of the Shetland League of Oak Park Youth Baseball.

We established a relationship with the VA. They set up nationwide in-house organizations to review their policies and procedures with Vietnam vets. The first thing they attempted to do was to keep us outside. Independent guys and even vets who were more of a right-wing bent insisted that if they were going to have this thing, they had to have VVAW be a part of it. Some of the guys who worked in the vet centers when they first opened liked us. They wouldn't work with us, endanger their careers and stuff, but they liked us. Some of them had probably been VVAW members a long time ago. A lot of good things came out of it. Vet centers were opened.

Bill Davis speaking in Chicago on Memorial Day 1983, with *(center)* Mayor Harold Washington and *(far right)* Barry Romo.

TERRY DuBOSE

After his active involvment with VVAW, Terry DuBose returned to school and received a degree in radiographic technology. He said, "I wanted to earn my living in a constructive, humane way." He received a master's degree in health professions from Southwest Texas State University in 1996. He now lives in Little Rock, Arkansas. At the time of this writing he had recently been appointed director of the Diagnostic Medical Program at the University of Arkansas for Medical Sciences in Little Rock. He channels most of his energy into health-care issues, although he "still writes a letter once in a while to the editors of newspapers to express my concerns about the environment, the globalization of economics, oppression of minorities, and to just encourage folks to keep on keeping on."

DAVID EWING

David has remained active in veterans' issues and politics. He is the managing attorney for Swords to Plowshares in San Francisco, employing a staff of three lawyers who handle disability appeals for Vietnam veterans. He won Jack McCloskey's suit against the VA only a few weeks before Jack's death. In 1993, David Ewing filed an amicus curiae brief with the Supreme Court in the case of the Radiation Survivors, who were challenging a law that denied veterans access to attorneys. At the time of writing, he was working on a civil

Dave Ewing in his office at Swords to Plowshares, San Francisco, 1997.

rights case involving the American Legion's treatment of progressive and gay and lesbian veterans in San Francisco.

DANNY FRIEDMAN

Danny Friedman lives in Brooklyn, New York, where he is working as counselor for the U.S. Department of Labor Veterans' Program. He continues to be a strong advocate for veterans' rights and actively supports efforts to curb militarism in American society.

We gave legitimacy to the antiwar movement. The antiwar movement were considered a bunch of commies and peaceniks until the veterans got involved. To say that we didn't have an impact is like saying the sun doesn't have an impact on the temperature of the earth. It totally took the antiwar movement from a bunch of radical college kids, who people thought were terrorists, to the sons of America, and America started noticing. We were working-class kids who fought the war and came back. That was the bottom line. America, your sons have come home and are telling you, Hey, wake up and smell the roses. This is what really happened over there. We're not no college professors or commies. We're the guys that were there.

JEANNE FRIEDMAN

Jeanne Friedman still lives in California—in the Bay Area—but she is no longer a college teacher. The last class she taught was a veterans' reentry class at San Jose City College in 1976: "Too many drugs, too little politics." Since then she has worked for several nonprofit organizations involved in disability rights, protecting California's redwood forests, and supporting community-based organizations.

After the final split with the RU, I felt as though I had lost dozens of my best friends all at once. It took me several years to realize that I wasn't going to find that same kind of organizational camaraderie again. VVAW/WSO was an extraordinary organization. While it was on the front lines of the antiwar movement, it was internally trying to come to grips with the hardest questions of class, race, and sexism. Its self-appointed task was nothing less than the refashioning of the moral compass of the American military. The political splits were all the harder because we had had so much respect and love for one another.

MIKE GOLD

Beginning in 1975, Mike Gold was the director of Veterans Affairs for the City University of New York (CUNY); but at the time of this writing he had been released because of cuts in the university's budget. During his years at CUNY, he was "organizing veterans, trying to make them progressive and community-oriented." He created a network of support services for veterans enrolled in the university and in the process created one of the largest veterans' programs in a college setting in the United States. He has continued to work with VVAW and has been active in a variety of veterans' issues in New York City and New York state.

We have a speaking program. We speak in schools. We still work on Agent Orange. I'm doing a lot of projects on homeless veterans. . . .We established a vets' shelter in Queens, the first one in the country. . . . It's the best shelter in New York City. It shines. We've been doing this other thing in San Diego, San Francisco, and other places: the stand-down. . . . The core guys in a lot of these programs are old VVAW guys.

I feel that VVAW is still living. On the twenty-fifth anniversary you could really see that. There were lots and lots of people who came here and really wanted to be a part of it again.

JOEL GREENBERG AND ANNIE LUGINBILL

Joel Greenberg and Annie Luginbill live together in Chicago. They are both still active members of VVAW, taking part in antiwar work and the yearly stand-downs as well as other events sponsored by VVAW. Their involvement, however, is "more social than political" They have the "same beliefs as before, but we're not as active."

Joel Greenberg: All your Johnny-come-lately vets groups, as far as Vietnam veterans' organizations, didn't come out of the woodwork until after Iran. It was almost in a negative [way], as a response to the welcome home the hostages got, that these guys came out and a lot of these groups were formed. Prior to that, you might have a half dozen Vietnam vets' organizations across the country, and VVAW was the only national organization.

The question of drugs and addiction was addressed by VVAW in 1970 and 1971. Rap groups were taking place back then as precursors to the vet centers. The testimony of winter soldier and the testimony on dioxin and Agent Orange played a major role in waking people up to the actions of our government.

BOB HANSON

Bob Hanson still remains active in the veterans' community. He has the most demanding job at Swords to Plowshares in San Francisco: as a reception worker for the agency, he sees 1,000 homeless veterans a month, helping with

Bob Hanson at Swords to Plowshares in 1997.

referrals and emergency services. At this writing, he was planning to take time off to do screenwriting.

ANN HIRSCHMAN

Ann Hirschman lives in Cranbury, New Jersey, with her husband and their ten-year-old son. She took her son to Washington on June 1, 1996, for the "Promise the Children" march. She works as a nurse practitioner and loves her work "but hates what is happening to the system." She also works with the Peace Caucus of the American Public Health Association. She still keeps in touch with VVAW, especially with two other Annies—Annie Bailey and Annie Luginbill.

I see the legacy of VVAW when I look at the Gulf War vets who came back and started talking with VVAW people. The atomic vets from World War II were able to take themselves more seriously because VVAW was up front about Agent Orange. We were the first people, with Maude DeVictor [a clerk in the VA hospital in Chicago], to blow that up.

I see John Kerry going to Vietnam and say, "Hey, we're part of that." I see my husband who was in his bookstore one day and, having been exposed to VVAW, saw a vet and after a couple of times said, "You need to talk to somebody; call my wife." This guy finally got desperate. He was totally on edge. He had never come home. I said to him after about two and a half hours on the phone, "You're in law enforcement; you got an early out—right? So you never got a chance to talk about this with anyone, because it wasn't exactly kosher in law enforcement circles to say, 'I have a PTSD problem.'" The next

Left to right: Annie Luginbill, Ann Hirschman, and Annie Bailey, with Ann Pine in New York, 1992.

day he sent me flowers and a note. He knew from our conversation that I was VVAW. He's finally coming home.

I go to American Public Health Association [APHA], a 100,000-member organization of doctors and public health people. The ex-president of the organization is a Vietnam vet and went back to Vietnam. That had been made possible by the paving the way by the guys from VVAW who had gone back. He's finally come home.

I went to a Vietnam caucus at the APHA meeting, and all of a sudden we're having a plenary session at this organization because some guys who were very happy to say that they were directly affected by VVAW and the peace caucus got together. A plank went through in their organization two years ago for recognition of Vietnam. Where did that come from? The only organization that started that was us.

JOHN KNIFFIN

John Kniffin lives in Brenham, Texas, where he works for an electronics firm. He lives in a woods with his wife, their dogs and cats, and a couple of horses.

Our main role was in helping to end the war and helping to generate a little awareness of what exposing the human organism to long periods of stress will do to anybody—a rape victim, a guy in prison, a GI in combat. Insofar as inflicting any moral code on this country, pretty obviously we failed in that. We didn't succeed in getting them to question, on any kind of long-term basis, whether or not the United States should pursue this gratuitous violence.

MICHAEL McCAIN AND JILL McCAIN

Michael McCain is an independent television and film producer who has won numerous awards for his work. At this writing, Jill McCain, after working in law and real estate, was about to complete a degree in nursing and planned to pursue a medical career. They both remain active in their community.

BOBBY MULLER

Bobby Muller has been active in the veterans' community since his days with VVAW. After having completed a law degree, he worked to set up Vietnam Veterans of America (VVA) in 1978, to work on Capitol Hill for veterans' rights and benefits. He also set up the Vietnam Veterans of America Foundation, which has been instrumental in advocating normalization of relations between the United States and Vietnam. Bobby Muller was one of the first veterans to return to Vietnam after the war had ended. He went to begin the process of normalizing relations and was also involved with providing medical and technical assistance and a variety of other activities that have sought to heal the wounds of the war. VVA now runs a clinic in Hanoi. VVA also played a leading role in the international campaign to eradicate antipersonnel land mines.

VVAW brought a lot of people together. . . . It raised the political awareness and understanding of a lot of people, radicalized them. It gave expression to that collectively, I think, in a very impressive way at the time, but has been sustained in the lives of people in countless ways in all sorts of avenues of life. A lot of these guys have gone into all sorts of different areas with the same learning of lessons in various ways from what we went through.

Those of us who started VVA were guys like myself that came out of VVAW. When we had our first convention in 1983, . . . I argued that obviously we needed to address the issues of war and peace, because the whole purpose of us, in part, was to be an alternative to the veterans' groups, the existing groups out there, which are all knee-jerk supporters of the military and right-wing elements.

I really came to recognize—under Reagan—that we were losing the battle for political control, with all of this revisionism and heralding and rehabilitating the concept of service and veterans, making them heroes and all that crap. As we rolled out in this open membership process, without any filters or screens, just taking Vietnam vets who were coming into these chapters that were proliferating like mushrooms out there, we were losing.

Guys who were coming in were more and more resembling traditional veterans. I remember we had a front-page article in our publication, *The Veteran*—the title was "Fools Rush In"—a big article about Vietnam vets as mercenaries working with the Contras in Nicaragua. Instead of getting letters saying, "This is unbelievable!" "How can they be suckered again?" "We're in another bogus war," we got more letters from guys wanting to know how to join up as mercenaries to go fight with the Contras.

This had a lot to do with the revisionism and a whole changing of the sense of history, and the needs of guys when they are twenty-one years old and fresh out of an insane war are different from the needs of guys that are in their forties who have kids asking them, "Were you in the war, Daddy? What did you do?" They want to be latter-day heroes.

You have all the years of Reagan basically rehabilitating the Vietnam vet, giving them parades and dinners and heralding them and saying, "Look— look at Indochina; all the boat people risking their lives. Look at the reeducation camps. Look at Vietnam's invasion of Cambodia. Look at how they're holding our guys prisoners. All of that is proof that ours was a just war to prevent that legacy." That's why this POW issue is such total propaganda, because they used it as a hate issue, fanning the emotions of the American people, trying to justify, after the fact, our war, by portraying the Vietnamese as the most vile, evil, rotten people on the face of the planet.

One thing I just wanted to let you know is that I did have the privilege of leading the first group of Vietnam veterans back to Vietnam since the war had ended. That was in December of 1981. As the president of the Vietnam Veterans of America in this country, I went to the Vietnamese, presented myself, explained who I was and what I wanted to do; and after some negotiations, they agreed. We had a wreath laid at Ho Chi Minh's mausoleum in Hanoi. The *New York Times* broke it as a front-page story. Before I left, I did the *Today Show* [and] *Good Morning America*. [I] came back, did *Nightline*, all the talk shows, Donahue. It was a tremendous story. I got probably between 300 and 400 death threats when I got back.

How did it feel to be back?

It was stunning. It was the basis of our real commitment to reconciliation, our commitment to ending the war with Vietnam, which still goes on politically and economically. You know—working on behalf of lifting the embargo, establishing diplomatic relations, and providing assistance to the people of Indochina. It's an outrage that we're holding a nation of 70 million people, the majority of which weren't even alive when we had our war there, hostage to this propanganda campaign.

BARRY ROMO

Barry Romo lives in Chicago, where he works for the United States Postal Service. He is an active member of VVAW, serving as a national coordinator. He continues to be speak out against American military intervention across the globe, and for social justice in the United States and abroad. He helps to put out VVAW's newsletter, The Veteran; *speaks at schools and other organizations throughout Illinois and across the country about his experiences in Vietnam and VVAW; helps to coordinate the annual stand-downs in Chicago; and remains a tireless advocate for veterans' rights. In addition to his VVAW activities, he is an active union member and who is devoted to his teenage daughter, Jessi.*

LEE THORN

Lee Thorn lives in San Francisco with his wife, Bernadette McAnulty. He has three sons: at the time of this writing Brendan was an infant, John was seven, and Jesse was fifteen. Since his days with VVAW in the early 1970s, Lee Thorn has remained an advocate for peace and veterans' concerns. He has also been involved, as an organizer or consultant, with other organizations—these include Flower of the Dragon, Swords to Plowshares, Veterans for Draft

Lee Thorn at his fiftieth birthday party, 1993, with his wife, Bernadette McAnulty.

411

Resistance, Veterans Speakers Alliance, and the Vietnam Veterans Project. He teaches ethics and writing in the M.B.A. program at the University of San Francisco, from which he received his own degree. He says,"I occassionally drag my creaking old bones to a rally or demonstration. I keep the faith."

VVAW people are all over the place. I would love us to be able to pass on that there's a strength. . . . We were an angry bunch of guys, but we channeled that to positive social change and we told anybody who would listen to us our truth, over and over again. We consciously cultivated warrior mentality. . . . I mean warrior as a spiritual kind of thing. We have been good examples to our kids.

JOE URGO

After his years with VVAW, Joe left in 1975 to work at automobile plants in Detroit, where he also organized for the RCP. Joe now lives and works in New York City. He is a "revolutionary communist" and a member of VVAW/AI (Anti-Imperialist).

In September 1990, Joe Urgo and his friend Shawn Eichman were arrested and prosecuted in federal court for terrorism and felonious destruction of government property; they had climbed to the roof of the armed forces recruiting office at Times Square in New York and had hung antiwar banners and attempted to burn an American flag, as a protest against the preparations for the Gulf war. Joe Urgo was represented by William Kunstler. Both defendants were acquitted of terrorism, but they were convicted on the second charge, destruction of government property. (The sentence involved community service in a veterans' center.)

Joe Urgo believes that "burning the flag will be a personal and political rite of passage in the future—a valuable weapon in the tool bag of every radical and revolutionary as we destroy the American empire of imperialism, exploitation, and war." His goal is to build a new society "in which common people live in common for the common good."

VVAW and Vietnam had set me on a different course in life. I learned about imperialism during my trip to Hanoi, reading books like those by [the historian Howard] Zinn, and Mao's Red Book. These experiences and debates had brought me to the point where, by 1975, I was a communist revolutionary.

In 1980 or so I began to notice that there had been a significant debate in the ruling class about what to do with Vietnam vets. That led to the building of the monument and the parade. VVAW/AI planned a demonstration at the dedication cermony for the wall. When a representative of the American Legion said, "We're proud of what we did and we'll do it again," we stood up, turned our backs, put our fists in the air, and said, "We will never do it again."

The government was using veterans to honor the war. We said, "There is no honor. You're only honoring us to use people for other wars." There were lots of independent vets there who protested against the ceremony in their own ways.

During the rest of the 1980s, we organized against the Rambo films, passing out flyers at movie theaters along with a coalition of other veterans' groups. We opposed the United States' intervention in Central America and continue to oppose American interference in other countries.

JIM WACHTENDONK AND SUKIE WACHTENDONK

Jim and Sukie Wachtendonk live in Madison, Wisconsin, where they continue to try to cope with the effects of Agent Orange on Jim and on their family. Jim Wachtendonk works for the city of Madison, installing and repairing traffic signs. He is also a musician who has composed and performed numerous songs about the Vietnam war and its impact on veterans; he performs in a variety of settings, including a number of benefit performances each year for groups involved with veterans' issues and other social issues.

Jim Wachtendonk at Dewey Canyon IV, 1981.

Jim Wachtendonk (JW): We got all the recruiters kicked out of all the high schools in town. They could only be there twice a year now.

Sukie Wachtendonk (SW): We found an obscure policy written in 1968 that said there would be no active recruiting in Madison schools.

JW: The question became: What was active? So we would say: The guidance office has three-quarters of its walls covered with "BE ALL THAT YOU CAN BE"; there's "I WANT YOU" posters down the hallway. And then we used the Freedom of Information Act to get all the trip tickets for all the government vehicles used by the recruiters to go to the schools, to see how many times they were there. One hundred and forty times a year. Is that active?

Then I was fixing a sign—the kids had taken Chadborn and Ash and they had climbed the pole and spray-painted an H in front of Ash. So I'm there and there are a couple of kids coming by shooting the breeze, and I asked the kids if they had seen any recruiters in the schools. This kid said, "Well, yeah, I was talking to this recruiter"; and he was telling me this story about how he was really seriously thinking about going into the Army, but his mom wasn't really too sure if it was right for him. She was kind of saying: You have options; there was college and all this. He was still seventeen, and he said the recruiter would call the house. That's another form of harassment they do. They call and call and call.

So he said this recruiter told him, "Well, what you do is you tell your mom you got a friend in Milwaukee. Tell her you're going to see your friend in Milwaukee and going to a Bucks game. I'll get you a ticket; and while we're there, we'll get you a physical, get all that done—because you'll be eighteen in six months, you can decide all that on your own."

This kid loved his mom, and obviously he had never lied to her. So he tells me this story and I said, "Holy shit. Can I have your phone number?"

He gave me his phone number, and I called his mom. . . . Introduced myself and told her what we were trying to do, and she had never done anything political in her life, never taken a stand for anything. She said, "This man would call and call and harass us. It was like he was trying to drive a wedge between my son and I." He was told to lie.

I said, "You know something? There's hearings this coming Wednesday; we're going to be dealing with this issue and the recruiters are going to be there. If I just tell this story, they could just say it happened or didn't happen, but if you were to be there to tell this story, I think that would really do it."

She did come to the meeting and told her story, and the school board . . . all their fucking mouths were open. . . . The recruiters didn't know what to say. We told the board how many times they were at the school, how much of the guidance material is all that; it's not colleges, technical schools, all that—it's not equal. So after the whole thing was done, the shooting match was done, they got kicked off the campus, except for career day twice a year;

and the counseling office now has an equal amount of trade school, technical school, and college material, and they can't have posters up and shit like that.

TOM WETZLER

Tom Wetzler lives in San Antonio, Texas, where he is still an active member of VVAW.

PETE ZASTROW

Pete Zastrow lives in Chicago with his family. He continues to be an advocate for peace and lends his time and energy to VVAW activities when he can.

Other people have a view that says the organization was more significant than in my heart of hearts I think it was or is.

In retrospect, I think we probably had our little effect, and I think maybe the impact came most in the people who were involved in the organization, particularly in some of the early days. We had to have some way to release the energy, which was pretty fierce, that came from having been involved in Vietnam—hating what we had done, why we were sent there, the people that sent us there, at whatever level we understood that—and VVAW being a place initially to use that energy and at the same time learn a lot about how

Pete Zastrow *(second from left in back row)*, Barry Romo *(third from left in back row)*, and Tom Wetzler *(second from right, wearing the vest)* in Ho Chi Minh City, 1987, as part of a VVAW delegation.

the political system works . . . because these are the people who then went on to the vet centers and little groups all over the country. We still get letters from the Black Lung Association of West Virginia, which is Vietnam vets who got this started to try to get benefits for the miners. It's that kind of thing. I mean that's a real influence.

I like to think that my own little contribution was in trying to explain to people that . . . Look, the time is going to come when just having been there is not going to be enough. You'd better learn a little bit about why we were there.

We continue to be very independent. I don't think we have a major role to play in the revolution, which isn't going to come in the next 150 years anyhow. When something like Iraq happens, suddenly I think we become very important as a left voice for antimilitarism. Who knows when it will happen the next time? . . . When we invade Yugoslavia, then it will be a lot of Gulf vets who will do the speaking. But we do have an experience which is unique. At this point, I don't think there is much we're going to do, except talk to schools, continue to put out information, get involved in any political issues that are vaguely concerned with veterans. . . . The world's changed; what can I say? Probably for the better, but I don't know.

Epilogue

An imperial power, whether or not it is interested in establishing colonies . . .
must bear the burden of minor wars to save clients, fill vacuums of power,
or protect some larger economic interests. It must do so in order to maintain
a world order that it believes it is responsible to protect.

Eliot Cohen, Citizens and Soldiers [1]

The spirit, the policy, and the methods of Imperialism are hostile to the
institutions of self-government, favouring forms of political tyranny and
social authority which are deadly enemies of effective liberty and equality.

J. A. Hobson, Imperialism [2]

My own involvement in this oral history of the Vietnam Veterans Against the War began during a later war—the Persian Gulf war. On January 17, 1991, the day after the United States had launched an attack on Iraqi forces in Kuwait, Barry Romo, a Vietnam veteran who was a national coordinator for the VVAW, was arrested as he approached an antiwar rally near the Kluczynski Federal Building in Chicago, where he had been scheduled to speak. As he crossed Dearborn Street to reach the rally, Romo was suddenly surrounded by half a dozen officers of the Chicago Police Department who threw him to the pavement, subdued him when he tried to get up, and then whisked him away in a paddy wagon. Actually, Barry had done nothing to provoke his arrest, but he was charged with assaulting a police officer and was held in custody for the duration of the rally before being released. Then, while he was awaiting trial, he was forbidden to travel outside a hundred-mile radius around Chicago; he was, therefore, unable to appear at other antiwar demonstrations across the country where he had also been scheduled to speak. He was never tried: three months after his arrest, the charges against him were dropped.

I had been present at the rally on that cold winter evening in Chicago and had witnessed Barry Romo's arrest, although I did not yet know who he was. I learned of his identity the next day, from a local radio broadcast. Because I had felt that his arrest was unjust, I looked up his telephone number and called him to give my support, and to offer to testify in his defense. This incident was the beginning of my relationship with the narrators of *Winter Soldiers.*

Barry Romo's arrest, which seemed obviously designed to keep him from speaking out against the escalation of American involvement in the Persian Gulf, piqued my interest in finding out more about the VVAW. I was then a graduate student in American history, with—I assumed—a solid background in the history of the Vietnam war, but I realized that I knew very little about VVAW. I had seen its name mentioned in several books on the war and the antiwar movement, but the accounts of its activities were generally very brief and were limited to descriptions of a few major episodes during the height of the war. I was particularly interested in finding out who the men and women of VVAW were. Why had they decided to oppose the war in Vietnam after serving in the armed forces? What had happened to them? And now, two decades later, why would a veteran like Barry Romo feel the need to speak out against a war in which he was not a combatant? One of my purposes in creating this oral history was to find answers to these questions. However, I also wanted to consider a broader question: what these veterans' experiences, in the Vietnam war and afterward, might tell us about American society, and the American military, in the latter half of the twentieth century. In this Epilogue, I offer my conclusions about that larger issue—and about the speakers themselves and the organization they represent.

The narratives and analyses of the men and women in this oral history, and the tragedy of the Vietnam war itself, can be best understood, I think, within their historical context. To many observers, myself among them, that context was essentially the rise of the United States to global hegemony after World War II and the efforts of its foreign policy makers to maintain hegemony at any cost. These efforts were in large part motivated by economics—specifically, a commitment to free trade—and carried out in terms of economics, and the attempt to create a new world order based on these principles increasingly undermined democracy at home and abroad.[3] When the right to self-determination of any other nation, such as Vietnam, conflicted with the efforts of the United States to sustain or expand its economic domination, then that right was sacrificed at the altar of "open doors." This was an ideological contradiction, and though for most Americans it remained hidden from the view, it became glaringly clear to those men who were asked, or required, to advance the cause of American ascendancy in Vietnam by serving as foot soldiers.

This is not meant to imply that the international policies and actions of the United States had been free of contradictions before it became a superpower.

On the contrary, throughout its history the nation had engaged in actions incompatible with its proclaimed mission of supporting democracy and self-determination. What was different after World War II was the scope of its involvement, and the consequent level of deception. When dominance came to mean *global* dominance, the United States had to expand its military forces enormously to protect the nation's vital interests worldwide. For the first time in American history, citizen-soldiers were drafted in peacetime, essentially to achieve the imperial aspirations of the nation's leaders.

The American crusade to create a continental empire "from sea to shining sea" dated back to the beginning of the nineteenth century. Historians disagree about how to interpret this crusade; but on one interpretation at least, during that century the United States wrested territory from its native inhabitants by means of a genocidal policy that nearly annihilated them and confined the survivors to an early form of concentration camps. On this analysis, American expansionism was motivated by a desire for land and for the mineral resources beneath it.

The Americans who fought to build this continental empire were not conscripts but professional soldiers and volunteers from the lower ranks of society. They were immigrants, farmers, and laborers who saw military service as their way of achieving the American dream. This small standing army of professional soldiers and volunteers, who were well trained and relied on the military for their livelihood, was sufficient to defeat the poorly armed native populations, already weakened by disease and by prolonged struggles with earlier settlers.[4]

Thus most Americans did not have to participate in this genocide—but they reaped its harvest. The territory acquired by conquest provided rich material rewards for Americans, who equated ownership of private property with independence and were therefore, in general, land-hungry. After soldiers had blazed a trail through the frontier, settlers followed in their footsteps and filled the "empty" land. The settlers built homesteads and sang the praises of the nation that allowed them all this freedom. Industrialists and speculators also benefitted greatly from the abundant natural resources, which fueled the nation's economic and industrial expansion in the latter half of the nineteenth century.

Americans justified these policies with the concept of "manifest destiny." Given that concept, resistance by their victims was often characterized as aggression, as standing in the way of an enterprise ordained by God. The national conscience—for all but a few—was also soothed by racism: the adversary was viewed as inherently inferior. Americans felt assured that their own actions were defensive, and were consistent with their democratic ideals, because they could see the enemy as wild savages who threatened their hearths and homes.[5]

By the turn of the century, the United States had succeeded in creating a continental "city upon the hill." But even within its borders, its industrialists and politicians were still not at ease. Cyclical depressions continued to disrupt the economy, causing widespread unrest among workers and uncertainty in the markets. Moreover, European competitors had, during the same period of time, expanded their empires across the seas and had created spheres of influence that severely circumscribed the access of American companies to markets and raw materials deemed necessary for the continued industrial expansion and the economic well-being of the nation.

The American economic and military elite viewed this situation with trepidation and concluded that if they themselves and—presumably—the nation were to prosper, the United States would also have to expand its interests beyond its borders. Thus the "open door" policy was developed during the McKinley administration, replacing manifest destiny and supplementing racism as the guiding principle behind American foreign policy. It would remain the guiding principle throughout the twentieth century.

The proponents of the open-door policy, as latecomers in the scramble for overseas territories, argued that the development of spheres of influence contradicted laissez-faire capitalism and threatened the economic well-being of the United States and other industrialized nations. American foreign policy makers, therefore, argued that the world's markets and natural resources should be available to all comers.[6] To prepare the United States for its expanded role, the foreign policy elite committed the nation to a rapid buildup of its naval forces and its standing army. The policymakers also unleashed a series of attacks against their competitors, arguing that other nations' imperialism was inconsistent with liberal democracy. With their open-door mandate in hand, American leaders had few qualms as they embarked on their new, global enterprise; they were secure in the knowledge that this new mission was consistent with the traditional American principles of anti-imperialism and the recently adopted principles of free trade. That, then—on this analyis— was the situation as the nineteenth century neared its end.

American leaders then set out to implement their policy by acquiring Cuba, Puerto Rico, and the Philippines from the faltering Spanish empire. American politicians, and the American press, characterized the Spanish-American war as a defensive war, waged against an imperial power that had challenged the sovereignty of the United States. Americans viewed themselves as liberators, freeing dark-skinned masses from a colonial oppressor much as they had freed themselves a century before.

Despite such grandiose proclamations, American foreign policy makers had no intention of granting independence to their newly acquired territories. These territories were considered vitally important as outposts for the Navy, which was expanding and had been charged with ensuring American access to Latin America and the Pacific. As a result, the United States granted Puerto Rico and Cuba only limited autonomy, reserving the right to intervene in their internal affairs if these seemed to be in conflict with its own foreign interests. The United States opened Puerto Rico and Cuba to American investors, appointed and supported governing bodies who cooperated with its demands, and squelched any local dissent—with force when necessary. The status of these two nations changed very little during the first half of the twentieth century.[7]

The Philippines proved much more difficult to tame. Unlike Cuba or Puerto Rico, the Philippines is not a single island but an extensive archipelago. Also, the Filipinos engaged in five years of guerrilla warfare when they realized that the United States did not intend to give them independence. Seventy thousand American military personnel were required to put down this insurrection, and in the process, American soldiers often used brutal tactics; in fact, public revelations of atrocities led to an anti-imperialist movement in the United States, challenging its policy for the Philippines. This movement, however, was small, short-lived, and plagued by ideological inconsistencies and was never able to attract a strong following among the American middle class—which remained largely unaffected by the war.[8] Nor did this movement influence the makers of foreign policy, who did not, of course, see their own actions as imperialistic. Proponents of the war in the Philippines often argued that those who resisted American aid were savages who needed to be dragged out of the darkness and into the light of day; the United States was seeking only to bring them civilization. For many Americans, this kind of argument, combined with racism and the open door doctrine, provided a justification for policies that might otherwise have seemed inconsistent with the nation's ideals.

Throughout the first half of the twentieth century, the United States continued to expand its influence throughout the Caribbean, Central America, and Mexico. Since most of the countries in this region lacked the financial and military resources to put up much resistance, the United States was able to prevail with relatively little effort. Its efforts were carried out primarily by the Marine Corps, and out of public view. Most Americans, of course, never saw any of these foreign interventions firsthand; typically, when Americans were apprised of the interventions at all, it was only in the context of national defense and of the national mission to spread democracy and free trade across the globe.

Although the United States relied on professional military forces for these ventures, the ideal of the citizen-soldier did not lose its currency among national leaders or the public. Later, when professional forces were insufficient to achieve the goals of foreign policy, that ideal was used by politicians to compel Americans to "serve their country." Woodrow Wilson, for example, declared at the outset of American participation in World War I, "The spirit of every profession is different from the spirit of the country. . . . We want men whose occupation is peace, because they are the only men who can carry into the field the spirit of America as contrasted with the spirit of the professional soldier."[9] During World War II, the concept of the citizen-soldier had a very strong influence, particularly in conjunction with the fact that Japanese had actually attacked the United States at Pearl Harbor. Also, in World War II the line between good and evil was clearly demarcated: Americans saw the Axis powers as vicious aggressors, the war itself as a noble undertaking, and the United States as democracy's first line of defense. The decisive victory reaffirmed their belief that their nation, above all others, had been chosen to lead the world. It also gave the nation's policy makers an opportunity to construct a new world order based on the doctrine of free trade.

But during the ensuing cold war, in order to prepare the American public, and especially young Americans, for the nation's new global role, the state, its national security apparatus, and its allies in nongovernmental institutions—such as the media and religious bodies—carried out a propaganda campaign, presenting all American international activity, present and past, as just and defensive. If the United States was to succeed in its mission, this kind of propaganda campaign was necessary. Very soon after World War II, the nation's leaders had already encountered resistance to their plans from American occupational troops; some troops and their families, for instance, protested that their role in the former Asian colonies was inconsistent with their role during the war itself and demanded to be sent home.[10] These protesters too appealed to the concept of the citizen-soldier: they had taken up arms to defend their country against fascism, not to become caretakers of an empire.

By this time, then, Americans had to be convinced that military, diplomatic, and economic actions undertaken for the purposes of hegemony were consistent with the image of the United States as peaceful, freedom-loving, and committed to democracy and the rule of law. Therefore, they had to be convinced that the world, including the United States, was facing a threat—an international communist conspiracy. When President Truman was about to promulgate the "Truman doctrine," Senator Arthur Vandenberg, chairman of the Senate Foreign Relations Committee, urged him to "scare the hell" out of the American public.[11] Truman—and each of his successors—took this advice to heart. The Truman doctrine, it might be argued, inaugurated the cold war by casting the Soviet Union and its presumed proxies as a direct threat to American sovereignty.

This attempt to persuade the American public of the dangers facing it need not be construed as a grand conspiracy. It can be seen, rather, as the result of a consensus among the political, cultural, and economic elite about the nature of American society and its role in the world. Godfrey Hodgson coined the term "imperial liberalism" to describe this consensus. Hodgson has argued that the nation's leaders "believed the American system worked at home and must be strong abroad."[12] They were managers of an increasingly technocratic industrial society that believed in the sanctity of private property and subscribed, in a sense, to social Darwinism, believing that it could diagnose and prescribe treatments for the world's social and economic problems.

It is within the context of the cold war that the war in Vietnam was waged. Vietnam, on this view, became a thorn in the side of American foreign policy makers who wanted to build a global empire of free trade. The United States had undertaken various imperialistic wars in the nineteenth century and the early twentieth century; but the war in Vietnam was, above all, ideological: it was fought to preserve the sanctity of the open door doctrine. Also, it was fought against a people who had a long history of resistance to colonialism and had acquired the skill and willingness to carry out a protracted war of independence. The United States began its foray into Vietnam as a clandestine operation, much like some of its other international operations: creating a puppet regime in South Vietnam and then propping it up with financial and military support. But gradually, the operation escalated into total war waged by the United States. As a result, larger and larger numbers of citizen-soldiers were required to take up arms.

The foregoing analysis is, of course, an interpretation with which some readers may disagree. However, I believe that it provides a context for understanding the nature of the Vietnam war—a war that has often seemed incomprehensible—and the response of the dissenting veterans.

The seeds of these veterans' discontent and dissent had been sown during the most intense period of the cold war. When they went to war as citizen-soldiers, the nation was still, to some extent, basking in its victory in World War II, but it was also preoccupied with the threat of communism. The United States was proud of its military heritage and was convinced that it should lead the world, but it was feeling the rumblings of social discontent. When these men decided to go to war, or to acquiesce in being sent to war, their decision was influenced by those somewhat contradictory factors, as well as by personal factors; some of them, after all, were teenagers who were grappling with their own identity and were seeking direction in life.

Like the majority of young men who served in the armed forces during the Vietnam war, the antiwar veterans came from predominantly working-class backgrounds; but they had grown up in a time of economic vigor that propelled a significant segment of the working class upward into the middle class. Thus they were not part of an underclass that held few illusions about the American dream or the role of the United States in the world. Also, they were not enrolled in Robert McNamara's "One Hundred Thousand Program," which was designed to widen the pool of draft-eligible men and did so by lowering enlistment standards to include men in category IV on the armed forces' battery of intelligence tests. Of the 3 million men who served in Vietnam, about 500,000 (250,000 with an IQ of less than 85) were brought into the armed services under that program,[13] but the men who would eventually become part of VVAW were not from this sector: they were generally well-educated working-class and middle-class Americans.

Some of the men whose voices have been heard in this oral history—especially those who served before 1967, when the antiwar movement began to capture public attention—initially "bought the program." They had grown up in a society that seemed to be providing them, and most of their fellow citizens, with the American dream—and Watergate was still in the future. They had, as a rule, no special reason to be cynical or even doubtful, and many of them enlisted with the idea that they would be defending democracy against communism. As Barry Romo remembered it, "I thought I was going to Vietnam to save my Catholic brothers and kill communists, who were the new Nazis in the world."

It is true that some were reluctant to jump into the fray and eventually volunteered mainly because they were about to be drafted anyway. As Danny Friedman commented, "Even though I was as patriotic as I was, I wasn't right wing gung ho or anything, I considered myself a cool dude and everything, but also going to college and going out with girls was cool too. It seemed like more fun." When Friedman dropped out of college, he became eligible for the draft—a typical situation. But many of these men too were influenced by the dominant ideology of the cold war and by heroic images of warfare in the popular media.

Working-class boys often became eligible for the draft when they completed their high school education; and some of those who went on to college, like Danny Friedman, found themselves either inadequately prepared for it or bored with it. Many working-class students attended community colleges where they were being trained to become low-ranking functionaries in a high-tech society.[14] Although such work was thought of as a step up the corporate ladder, in reality it was not all that different from the work of the previous generation—repetitive tasks in factories, for example, with little opportunity for advancement—and such a life, for some young men, could not compete with the glamour of the military.

Thus many young men, then as always, yearned for adventure and saw the military as a way to find it. Danny Friedman, for instance, said, "I was like off on this grand adventure. I had no fear, no anxiety. I was oblivious to what the reality of it was. It was just like I was going to play war, except this time, I got real guns. This is going to be fun." For him, and for many others, military service was seen as an escape from a boring life. Boredom, in fact, is a constant theme running through several of the narratives. To be a soldier, moreover, meant a brief chance—perhaps a young man's only chance—to win something that eluded most of the American working class: respect, or even glory. And so, often, these men went to war with visions of John Wayne and Audie Murphy before their eyes.

There were also more practical motives, though. Some of those who were waiting to be called up by the draft hoped that by volunteering, they would have a better opportunity to choose their assignments. By the early 1960s, the armed forces were considered an opportunity for technical training—

training that would provide a more secure future in a society that was rapidly deindustrializing and thus was offering fewer opportunities for high-wage employment in industry. Young men, in particular, were affected by this restructuring and were experiencing higher rates of unemployment than their fathers, partly because employers were often reluctant to hire draft-age men.[15] Also, many young men did not see their fathers as role models who might help them navigate in the rapidly changing American economy: they were aware that their fathers had little education and little autonomy in the world of work.[16]

Finally, many men, although they may have been troubled by the contradictions of the war and by the revelations of the antiwar movement, went to war because they saw no other feasible alternative to being drafted. Refusal to serve carried heavy sanctions, which most were unwilling to bear. And many had little confidence in their own ability to understand the real nature of the situation in Vietnam: they felt isolated in a society preoccupied with the cold war.

But although their motives were varied, these men tended to have several characteristics in common. In general, they represented the best and the brightest of their generation of working-class youth. Most of them had excelled in school and hoped to continue their education beyond high school. They had participated in extracurricular activities, both in school and in their communities. They were on the whole model citizens who took seriously the idea of participating in the democratic process.

They also shared, for the most part, a commitment to what they saw as traditional American values: social justice and equality. This commitment had been shaped by their families and their own everyday experience. They had been encouraged to respect others regardless of racial, religious, or ethnic differences. They had grown up in multiracial, multiethnic communities. Most of them describe their support for the civil rights movement, expressing a sense that African-Americans' struggle for equality was consistent with traditional American values. Often, their parents were union activists and supporters. And nearly all of the men who went off to this war, for whatever reason, believed in the cold war ideology that sanctified the United States and demonized its enemies. The influence of this ideology is evident when they note that their parents felt quite differently: parents often tried to discourage them from enlisting, or advised them not to cooperate with their draft boards. In heeding their nation's call to arms—in becoming citizen-soldiers and accepting their new status—these men hoped that in Vietnam they would, as Tom Wetzler put it, "find something to justify [their] faith that what the United States was doing was right and just and good, that the people in Vietnam would like us being there."

The transformation from citizen-soldier to "winter soldier" was, of course, an individual, personal process. For many, though, it was clearly a result of contradictions perceived between American ideals and reality: the nature of the armed forces and the way the war in Vietnam was being conducted. As Jan Barry's narrative attests, some citizen-soldiers had begun to doubt the official justifications for American involvement in Vietnam even before the major escalation of troops began in 1965; and a consistent theme that runs throughout the narratives in this book is the veterans' feeling of having been betrayed by the government that had sent them off to fight.

Many who served in the armed forces in Vietnam and later joined VVAW developed—through their own experiences in boot camp or shortly after their arrival in Vietnam—a sense that they were not there to save the Vietnamese people. Those who believed, as Mike McCain did, that "the military is always supposed to be in the service of the people," were disturbed, for one thing, by the racist attitudes some of their commanders held toward the Vietnamese. Those who believed that this was a war to preserve democracy began to develop a sense that they were actually, as Jan Barry put it, a "palace guard" for a police state—a task they considered abhorrent and incompatible with the ideal of the citizen-soldier. Thus many came to feel that their allegiance belonged not to their commanders or even to the armed forces but rather to the democratic principles they had been raised to respect and uphold.

Moreover, in Vietnam many soldiers also developed a sense that the military command was incompetent and was needlessly endangering the lives of American soldiers. As Joe Urgo says, "What I realized is that nobody actually believed in what they were doing, but they were doing it because this is what they were trained to do. It was filled with all this macho power and authority, but they would never figure out what the problem was, and solve it." Many of the commanding officers these soldiers encountered fell short of the idealized image of a military hero: courageous, omniscient, and dedicated to truth and justice. Needless to say, this is a common experience in all wars—perhaps even a universal experience—but some of these men, especially the young men, may not have realized that; and even if they had, it would probably have been no less disturbing. Also, soldiers in Vietnam came to believe, more specifically, that their lives were being needlessly jeopardized by officers who were inexperienced and inadequately trained to deal with guerrilla warfare. Enlisted men were required to spend one year in Vietnam, but an officer's tour of duty in the field was only six months. By the time an officer had learned to wage guerrilla warfare, he would be sent to the rear and replaced with a novice. "Grunts" who had learned through experience that certain tactics would risk their lives for no discernable military advantage naturally resented officers who used such tactics.

Because this was supposed to be an ideological war—a war for the "hearts and minds" of the Vietnamese people—the taking of territory was often meaningless. Soldiers might engage in heavy combat, suffering heavy casualties, in order to take a hill or village; then their commanding officers would pull them back, returning the territory to the NVA or the NLF forces; and still later, the "grunts" would have to retake the position. The people who were managing this war seemed to look on the soldiers as dispensable, inter-changeable parts in a military machine that relied heavily on technology.

In addition to their developing sense of wrongness with regard to the armed services and the conduct of war, these men also developed a realization that the American public was not being told the truth. As Jan Barry states, "It became clear that what was being claimed in Washington and out of Saigon headquarters had nothing to do with what we could see for ourselves."

Once these soldiers began to doubt the veracity of their leaders, they sought and found alternative sources of information—information that would more closely resemble their own experiences in Vietnam. They read antiwar literature and began to be more open to the arguments of civilian protesters. And many white soldiers began to listen intently to their African-American comrades, who tended to hold few illusions about the war.

For many, then, as their tours of duty wound on, all of the presumed reasons for American involvement were stripped away, layer by layer, until all they were left with was the will to survive—and in some cases, to seek revenge for the deaths of their buddies. Despite their growing misgivings, they had little time for reflection: they were stationed in an alien environment thousands of miles from home, and they were often in the line of fire from the Vietnamese they had come to protect. Their ability to express their grow-ing unease was also circumscribed by the military structure, which, of course, is hierarchical and rigid and does not allow for democratic deliberations con-cerning tactics. Frequently, therefore, these citizen-soldiers resorted to covert acts of resistance to authority: desertion, fraggings, disobedience, and drug abuse. Such acts became more commonplace as the war wound on.[17]

And those who survived their tour of duty had further cause for unease. First, they found that their military obligations had not yet been fulfilled. After they left Vietnam, many veterans were once again subjected to the kind of "chickenshit"—meaningless drills and harassment by commanding offi-cers—that had no relevance to their ability to carry out their actual duties. And when they were finally discharged, many veterans found themselves back in a world that seemed alien to them. Rather than being greeted with parades, they found that they were often treated as pariahs by the media and by the government that had sent them to fight. They had returned to a coun-try that would rather have forgotten them.

Veterans, especially those who returned after 1968, also returned to a nation that was in the midst of an economic decline. Inflation and rising unemploy-ment affected every segment of the American workforce, and unemployment was even worse among veterans than their civilian counterparts. Furthermore, veterans' benefits were sorely inadequate and were sometimes difficult to obtain at all.[18] These factors made their reintegration into society more diffi-cult and contributed to their growing sense that they had been used.

Most of the narrators here, though, did not immediately speak up. At first, some of them actually concealed their status as veterans from their peers; and some—like many other veterans who were trying to forget what they had experienced in Vietnam—engaged in self-destructive behavior. They could not, however, escape a gnawing sense that what they had just lived through was wrong.

Several factors, in addition to their military service, contributed to these men's conversion from silent citizen-soldiers to winter soldiers who felt a need to speak out against the war in order to bring it to an end. First, most of those who participated in antiwar activities were college-educated or went on to college after their release from military duty.[19] In fact, some returned to school partly to gain a better understanding of what they had just experienced. In school, veterans encountered perspectives which legitimized their belief that this war contradicted the democratic ideals of the nation.

Second, as I noted in the Introduction, typically these veterans returned to cities and college towns where vibrant antiwar communities existed. Their experiences with civilian antiwar activists were mixed; but for the majority of returning veterans, the antiwar community provided a safe haven where veterans could express their feelings and find support. This antiwar community allowed veterans to voice their misgivings about the war, challenged them when they continued to rely on pro-war propaganda (as some still did) to make sense of their experience, and provided them with an alternative analysis of the conflict that came closer to their firsthand knowledge. Without such support, these veterans might have succumbed to despair and confusion, as many others did; in numerous studies of the effects of this war on veterans, there is considerable evidence of posttraumatic stress disorder—high rates of unemployment, divorce, suicide, and other indices.[20]

Third, most of the antiwar veterans felt compelled to act because of two episodes that took place as their awareness of the history of the war was expanding: President Nixon's invasion of Cambodia was revealed, and student protesters at two universities—Kent State and Jackson State—were killed. The invasion was announced at a time when the United States was supposedly withdrawing its troops from Vietnam and seeking a just and honorable peace. Nixon's announcement of the invasion and his administration's response to the protests gave credence to veterans' growing concern that the war was not ending, that more Americans would be put in the line of fire for no clear reason, and that the government was willing to kill its own citizens at home in order to continue pursuing the war.

The antiwar veterans believed strongly that speaking out against the war was an act of patriotism—an expression of their commitment to democracy and their concern for their fellow Americans. They believed that those who spoke for the Johnson and Nixon administrations were lying, and that they themselves, by speaking the truth, could affect the course of the war. As John Kniffin says, "Nixon kept on talking about the silent majority. . . . I think a lot of us felt that the silent majority was an unenlightened majority, that if they knew what was going on, and they knew that it was wrong, then the people of the United States would stop it."

These antiwar veterans did not think of themselves as radicals; they believed in the democratic system and felt that they were acting in consonance with their predecessors in the abolitionist movement of the nineteenth century, the labor movement, the civil rights movement, the women's movement, and other earlier efforts to make American democracy a living reality. Thus initially the VVAW focused on exposing hypocrisy and appealing to the nation's leaders to uphold democratic principles. Its methods were also meant to be consistent with other movements for social, political, and economic justice by those who lack power. James Scott has observed that such movements "originate in critiques within the hegemony—in taking the values of the ruling elites seriously, while claiming that they (the elites) do not. To launch an attack in these terms is to, in effect, call upon the elite to take its own rhetoric seriously."[21] The VVAW, then, was asking the Washington establishment to live up to its own cold war rhetoric.

However, by using the channels for discourse created by those in power—politicians and the media—the VVAW was engaging in an unequal battle. As is true of most social movements, the establishment, in this case the foreign policy elite, used its access to the media to condemn its opponents; accordingly, the antiwar veterans were accused of being radicals or even communists. This was an old story in the United States, where the establishment had often defined the acceptable limits of political discourse; citizens who become activists for social justice have often been accused of radicalism. Throughout this oral history, it seems evident that the nation's leaders were able to sway a considerable portion of the American public, especially those who had no real familiarity with the military or with the war in Vietnam. The narrators recount numerous instances of being "chased out of town," derided, and attacked for their views.

The VVAW was further impeded by the national security apparatus. Various means were used by the national security establishment to discredit and destroy VVAW; and although the state's attack on VVAW did not succeed in silencing the antiwar veterans, it did sometimes foment distrust among members, and it often forced them to shift their attention away from antiwar activism to defending the organization itself.

As these veterans came up against the power of the state to define the nature of the conflict in Vietnam and to stifle their dissent, and as they became involved in the process of organizing, they eventually did become more radicalized. As they reached out to other veterans and to civilian antiwar activists, their perspective on the war and American society was broadened. Thus a large segment of the veterans' movement came to believe that the war was a symptom of more profound problems—though they did not all agree on how to deal with these deeper problems to achieve a more just and more peaceful society.

This radicalization tended to move the antiwar veterans farther away from the government, from whatever media still remained uncritical of the war, and from whatever portion of the public still remained committed to it. Also, it made some of the veterans uneasy about the direction in which VVAW was headed. Some, like Jan Barry, who had been engaged in the antiwar struggle for years, felt "burned out." Barry's disagreement actually had to do mostly with how best to reach out to the public. He and many others dropped out of leadership positions in VVAW and chose instead to continue the struggle for the "hearts and minds" of the American public through the written word. In this, they were similar to numerous civilian dissidents who wanted to find new avenues for changing the attitudes of intransigent political leaders and of those citizens who were still apathetic or still pro-war.

Frustration like that felt by Jan Barry led to a changing of the guard in the national office of the VVAW. Some members aligned themselves with more militant veterans whose perspective on the war was consciously anti-imperialistic and who wanted to expand the VVAW's activities. Their ideological critique of the war had struck a chord with many young veterans and a significant segment of the antiwar community. Many of the men who became leaders during this period of VVAW's development were veterans who had served during the year of the Tet offensive, when the war had been at its most intense and most brutal—and when discontent among GIs on active duty was growing rapidly. By this time it seemed obvious that neither the Democrats nor the Republicans were willing to act to end the war. These new leaders had also experienced the efforts by the Nixon administration to undermine VVAW. Their radicalism grew out of these experiences and was, they felt, consistent with the democratic principles they had grown up with.

Under this leadership, VVAW grew for a brief time; its membership increased from 8,000 in the spring of 1971 to 50,000 by the summer of 1972. Civilians and veterans alike became members, expanding the organization's activities. Its new leaders, however, could not contain the various political and tactical divisions that developed along with this growth. They had hoped to transform VVAW into a mass-based anti-imperialist movement, but they ran into resistance from a number of quarters. By 1971, most Americans and a significant proportion of veterans had turned against the war, but this opposition was not necessarily based on anti-imperialism. The inability of VVAW's leaders to control its direction during this phase was typical of social movements in the United States: it is not easy to build a nationwide organization in a country divided by race, region, and class and committed to individual autonomy. Veterans who had rebelled against conformity in the armed forces were, as members of VVAW, unwilling to sacrifice their individuality for what its leaders considered the good of the whole. In addition, some—frustrated in their attempts to change the nation's Vietnam policies by working within the system—began to advocate violence against those who were prosecuting the war.

For these reasons, VVAW was plagued by internal dissension. But many veterans saw that as part of their commitment not only to ending the war but also to what they considered true democracy. For some young people, this was their first taste of democracy in action; and although divisions within the organization often led to lengthy national meetings (some of which lasted for several days at a time), some veterans and their supporters were actually exhilarated by this "chaos."

In this anarchistic climate, VVAW's more revolutionary contingent—which was its best-organized component—took control. Its acquisition of power was facilitated by the signing of peace accords in 1973; as a result of those accords, the organization lost many members, both veterans and civilians, who were not committed to the leaders' anti-imperialist position. As the organization turned farther to the left, with the leaders affiliating themselves with the Revolutionary Union (RU)—later to be the Revolutionary Communist Party (RCP)—it became more and more marginal and less and less relevant to the vast majority of veterans and civilians.

For several years, the revolutionary cadre of veterans who had gained control of the national office tried to work for change within RU and RCP. They came to feel, however, that—just as they had been used in Vietnam—they were being used for the communist revolution. By 1977, the VVAW had broken off its affiliations with all left-wing sectarian groups. Thereafter, those who have remained active within the organization refocused their energies, speaking out on issues that continued to affect veterans and once again working within the system for changes in American foreign policy.

Thus VVAW moved from early efforts at speaking out against the war to efforts to expose the hypocrisy of national leaders to a more radical critique of the war which included a call to revolution, and then back to a more pragmatic approach, concentrating on concrete issues that affected its constituency. This reflected a process undergone by many social movements led by minorities. In a society where the limits of acceptable political discourse are narrowly defined, as was the case in the United States during the cold war—and where the majority of citizens do not share the same experiences as those who are calling on them to act, as was the case with VVAW—change is likely to be incremental and is often imperceptible to those involved.

Nonetheless, the VVAW did have an impact on the war, and on the lives of all veterans. By reaching out to those who were still in the service, the antiwar veterans hampered the ability of the armed forces to wage war. The disintegration of the fighting forces in Vietnam played a significant role in ending direct American participation on the ground.[22] It is true that for some time the VVAW had difficulties reaching the general public, but the antiwar veterans were welcomed by people who were still serving in Vietnam and across the globe. They provided GIs on active duty with programs to assist them in their resistance and, more important, helped them become aware of the rights they were entitled to as citizens of the United States.

Also—and perhaps even more important—the VVAW built a community of healing for veterans. Its members, along with some mental health profes-

431

sionals, recognized the psychological impact of the war on returning veterans well before the Veterans Administration acknowledged the existence of such problems. They coined the term "post-Vietnam syndrome" and worked hard to address the needs of their fellow veterans. In 1980, ten years after their pioneering efforts had begun, posttraumatic stress disorder (PTSD) among combat veterans was formally recognized by the American Psychiatric Association.[23]

It is worth saying a few words about PTSD. According to some estimates, perhaps as many as one-fourth of all Vietnam veterans, and more than half of the combat veterans, suffer from this syndrome.[24] Veterans with PTSD are now entitled to benefits, but red tape at the Veterans Administration makes it difficult for them to get assistance; some have to wait for months or even years before they receive their benefits and are given appropriate treatment. The VVAW led the way in providing assistance to veterans with PTSD. It formed rap groups in which veterans gathered together informally to discuss the traumas they had experienced. These early forms of therapy led to the formation of programs like Twice Born Men and Swords to Plowshares in San Francisco, which were precursors of veterans' centers now found throughout the country. The federal government had not acknowledged the need for such facilities until 1979, when Congress appropriated $12 million for the development of 90 centers. By 1983, 135 "vet centers" had been opened across the country, and 4,000 Vietnam veterans come through their doors each month seeking assistance.[25] By now, these programs have assisted several hundred thousand Vietnam veterans and other victims of trauma.

A similar issue was Agent Orange, used as a defoliant during the Vietnam war. This herbicide contains dioxin, a contaminant; and members of VVAW worked to reveal the effects of dioxin on veterans who had been exposed to it. They conducted research that linked Agent Orange to various physical afflictions suffered by Vietnam veterans, accused the government and chemical companies of colluding to hide this link from veterans and the public, and initiated a class-action lawsuit that won some compensation for veterans. (As with PTSD, however, veterans sometimes still have to wade through the bureaucracy of the Veterans Administration before they are eligible for benefits.)

One consequence of the class action over Agent Orange was to make the American public more aware of callousness, and potential callousness, in its industrial and political establishment. Another consequence was to energize other veterans who had undergone analogous experiences. These included veterans who had served during the 1950s and had been exposed to dangerous levels of radiation during the testing of nuclear weapons, and veterans of the Persian Gulf war who had been exposed to chemical agents. Although the effects of such exposure in the Gulf war are not yet fully known, the government has responded more quickly to veterans' concerns—a result of VVAW's having paved the way.

In addition to veterans' causes, antiwar veterans who became affiliated with VVAW branched out to address many other national and community issues. Indeed, this is perhaps the greatest legacy of the VVAW. Young men came home from the war, demonstrated, talked, studied, and sought to influence the political process. Former and current members of VVAW continue to take seriously their role as citizens in a democracy. They continue to speak out in the hope that their voices will be heard and that in some way their actions and words will have an effect on the political process.

The long-term achievements of the activism represented by VVAW, however, are perhaps not all that could have been desired. The assessment that follows is highly personal, but I think it would be shared by many of the antiwar veterans.

In April of 1971, during Dewey Canyon III, John Kerry, who was then a national spokesperson for VVAW, addressed the Senate Foreign Relations Committee. He ended his speech with the following plea to the American people:

> We wish that a merciful God could wipe away our memories of that service as easily as this Administration has wiped away their memories of us. But all that they have done and all that they can do by this denial is to make more clear than ever our own determination to undertake one last mission—to search out and destroy the last vestige of this barbaric war, to pacify our own hearts, to conquer the hate and fear that have driven this country these last ten years and more, so when thirty years from now our brothers go down the street without a leg, without an arm, or a face, and a small boy asks why, we will be able to say "Vietnam" and not mean a desert, not a filthy obscene memory, but mean instead the place where America finally turned and where soldiers like us helped it in the turning.[26]

Twenty-five years have passed since John Kerry asked Americans to turn away from a foreign policy that had wreaked such havoc. It seems, however, that rather than turning away from the "hate and fear that have driven this country," the nation has sunk deeper into the quagmire that brought about the Vietnam war and the civil strife associated with it. The United States' military failure in Vietnam did not spell the end of imperialism. On the contrary, it seems that American leaders have learned some cynical lessons from their mistakes in southeast Asia. They have replaced the citizen-soldier with the professional and have successfully waged clandestine economic wars against nations that stray away from the new American world order. During the 1990s, American foreign policy makers have also relied more heavily on a high-tech arsenal. It can surely be argued that this transformation has further denigrated the nation's democratic heritage. In the words of Rousseau, "As soon as public service ceases to be the main business of the citizens, and they prefer to serve with their pocketbooks rather than with their persons, the State is already close to ruin."27

If it seems that the foreign policy elite can exercise its will unchecked, perhaps that is because its actions are clandestine and because it is able to control national dialogue through the media and to define the history of American foreign policy in general and the Vietnam war in particular. For most Americans, Vietnam is almost ancient history. What they know of Vietnam is, on the whole, what they hear from political leaders and what they see in films, on television, and in print. Since the end of the war, much of the popular discourse about it has been dominated by right-wing pundits and politicians who have sought to portray it as a noble cause, flawed only strategically. What many Americans see and hear is conveyed largely by a few media conglomerates, and these have traditionally supported American military ventures.28 And this is not merely a matter of history. For the generation of Americans who came of age after Vietnam, what they know about the war and how they perceive it will in part determine their reaction to their nation's present and future military efforts and goals.

For the men and women whose voices have filled these pages, then, the war is not over. Veterans continue to suffer from the physical and emotional wounds of the war and contine to fight for redress of their grievances. And the men and women of VVAW also struggle, against a conservative tide, to keep the lessons they learned in Vietnam alive in the American conscience. They often see themselves as having grown up in a time of ideological conformity, and they know that such an atmosphere can influence behavior—that it can allow, or compel, individuals to engage in activities that conflict with their ethical and political ideals. In schools, in houses of worship, and in many other forums, they continue to describe their military experiences and to speak out against American military policies in Central America, the Persian Gulf, and elsewhere. In short, they continue to act as "winter soldiers." Present as well as former members of VVAW across the country are still telling their stories. As Dave Cline said, "Veterans of the last war are always used to convince kids to fight the next war." The VVAW is trying to provide young Americans with an alternative perspective on the past, so that they will not be so easily persuaded to fight the next war.

In conclusion, I think it will be appropriate to state explicitly my own perception of these antiwar veterans—which by now, in any case, must have become fairly apparent.

To begin with, I see their protest as an act of courage and conscience: they had done their duty and survived, and it would have been much easier for them simply to have returned home and carried on with their private lives as civilians. In speaking against the war, they acted essentially out of patriotism, perhaps the highest form of patriotism. The Vietnam veterans who opposed the war were heroes not only because they had served their nation in a war but even more because they returned home from it to engage in another battle, a struggle to save lives and to preserve democracy. Their outspoken attacks on the nature of the war, on its impact for American GIs and for the Vietnamese, and on the danger it represented for American society were consistent with the nation's democratic principles and institutions.

Second, I would argue, as they argued, that the real threat to American democracy was not in Vietnam, but at home; the Washington establishment and the military leaders who prosecuted the war were undermining the ideals and institutions they had been charged to protect. To take just one example, the efforts made by the Nixon administration to silence the antiwar veterans—who were using only words to effect a change in the nation's foreign policy—was an indirect attack on the nation's democratic heritage, which is also a revolutionary heritage. The antiwar veterans' experiences in the war at home as well as in Vietnam revealed the degree to which the nation's leaders

At the site of the Vietnam Veterans' Memorial in Washington: "No more Vietnams."

had abandoned American ideals as they sought to expand their reach across the globe.

Their organization, the Vietnam Veterans Against the War, gave much to its members as well as to the nation. To the veterans who created and, later, became part of VVAW, it was a source of strength and healing. These veterans were confronting their own awakening, and that confrontation intensified as the war became increasingly brutal and the Nixon administration increased its efforts to conceal its policies from the American public and to silence the antiwar movement. The VVAW helped veterans to move beyond their own confusion and bitterness to a new understanding of the war and of the role they could play in bringing it to an end. Over the years, although these veterans have suffered from the trauma of war, they have not allowed that to override their interest in reaching out to their fellow citizens or their hope that the United States can live up to its lofty ideals

For the nation, the history of the VVAW provides an important perspective on the war in Vietnam, and an important lesson for the future. At any time, citizen-soldiers might be called on to serve their country's imperial aspirations. The young men and women who may be called, and the leaders who may call them, would be wise to learn from the stories these veterans tell. Perhaps their efforts, and their history, will help to bring about their goal: "No more Vietnams."

Notes

Introduction

1. Mark Gerzon, *A Choice of Heroes: The Changing Faces of American Manhood* (Boston, Mass.: Houghton Mifflin, 1982). Gerzon discusses the extent to which young men are exposed to a heroic image of soldiers in American society, and the impact of this image on their desire to serve their nation.

2. John Helmer, *Bringing the War Home: The American Soldier in Vietnam and After* (New York: Free Press, 1974), p. 161.

3. For example, Helmer, op. cit., argues that 14 percent of Vietnam veterans saw combat regularly. Eliot Cohen contends that 25 percent were combat veterans, in *Citizens and Soldiers: The Dilemmas of Military Service* (Ithaca, N.Y.: Cornell University Press, 1985), p. 65. Others have given numbers that fall within this range. Part of the problem in determining the exact percentage lies in how one defines "combat." Despite the discrepancies, however, it is safe to say that the vast majority of Vietnam veterans had seen little if any combat while they were in-country.

4. John Shay, *Achilles in Vietnam* (New York: Atheneum, 1994), p. 11.

5. Robert Heinl, "The Collapse of the Armed Forces," *Armed Forces Journal* (June 1971). See also David Cortright, *Soldiers in Revolt* (New York: Anchor, 1975).

6. Numerous studies have been written on the psychological casualties of the war. Two of the best are Shay, op. cit.; and Robert J. Lifton, *Home from War* (New York: Simon and Schuster, 1973). Shay, in particular, describes a sense of betrayal of ideals among veterans who served in Vietnam.

7. For more detailed information on resistance within the military, see Helmer, op. cit.; Cortright, op. cit.; and Richard Moser, *The New Winter Soldiers: GIs' and Veterans' Dissent during the Vietnam Era* (New Brunswick, N.J.: Rutgers University Press, 1996).

8. Cohen, op. cit., p. 124.

9. Press release announcing the "winter soldier" investigation (January 11, 1971). From Barry Romo's personal VVAW archive.

10. Nelson Adkins, ed., *Thomas Paine: Common Sense and Other Political Writings,* American Hertage Series (New York: Macmillan, 1953), p. 55.

Chapter 1

1. Tim O'Brien, *Going After Cacciato* (New York: Dell , 1975), p. 234.

2. Quoted in John Helmer, *Bringing the War Home: The American Soldier in Vietnam and After* (New York: Free Press, 1974), p. 91. Al Hubbard was an active member of VVAW's national steering committee from 1969 to 1972.

3. Quoted in Gabriel Kolko, *Confronting the Third World: United States Foreign Policy,* 1945–1980 (New York: Pantheon, 1988), p. 41.

4. Thomas Paterson, *On Every Front: The Making of the Cold War* (New York: Norton, 1979), p. 36.

5. Marty Jezer, *The Dark Ages: Life in the United States, 1945–1960* (Boston: South End, 1982), pp. 75–76.

6. Lawrence Wittner, *Cold War America: From Hiroshima to Watergate* (New York: Praeger, 1974), p. 259.

7. Kolko, op. cit, p. 55.

8. Quoted in Paterson, op. cit, pp. 78–79.

9. John Patrick Diggins, *The Proud Decades: America in War and Peace, 1941–1960* (New York: Norton, 1988), pp. 98–99.

10. Ibid., p. 133.

11. William Graebner, *Coming of Age in Buffalo: Youth and Authority in the Postwar Era* (Philadelphia, Pa.: Temple University Press, 1990), pp. 14–15; and Grace Palladino, *Teenagers* (New York: Basič, 1996), p. 194.

12. Walter LaFeber, *America, Russia, and the Cold War, 1945–1984* (New York: Knopf, 1985), pp. 96–98.

13. Numerous books have been written on the cold war at home. For example, see Victor Navasky, *Naming Names* (New York: Viking, 1980); David Caute, *The Great Fear: The Anti-Communist Campaign under Truman and Eisenhower* (New York: Simon and Schuster, 1978); and Stanley Kutler, *The American Inquisition: Justice and Injustice in the Cold War* (New York: Hill and Wang, 1982).

14. A. P. Thornton, *Imperialism in the Twentieth Century* (Minneapolis: University of Minnesota Press, 1977), p. 261.

15. Eliot Cohen, *Citizens and Soldiers: The Dilemmas of Military Service* (Ithaca, N.Y.: Cornell University Press, 1985), p. 155; Arthur Ekirch, *The Civilian and the Military* (New York: Oxford University Press, 1956), p. 288.

16. Kolko, op. cit., pp. 50–52. For specific cases of clandestine activities, see Richard Immerman, *The CIA in Guatemala: The Foreign Policy of Intervention* (Austin: University of Texas Press, 1982); and Walter LaFeber, *Inevitable Revolutions: The United States in Central America* (New York: Norton, 1984).

17. Godfrey Hodgson, *America in Our Time: From World War II to Nixon, What Happened and Why* (New York: Vintage, 1976), p. 9.

18. Stanley Aronowitz, *False Promises: The Shaping of American Working Class Consciousness* (New York: McGraw-Hill, 1973), pp. 95–97; Hodgson, op. cit., p. 140.

19. Edward Pessen, *Losing Our Souls: The American Experience in the Cold War* (Chicago: Ivan Dee, 1993), pp. 46–47. For more on the complicity of the media, see the following. Noam Chomsky and Edward Herman, *Manufacturing Consent: The Political Economy of the Mass Media* (New York: Pantheon, 1988). Clarence Wyatt, *Paper Soldiers: The American Press and the Vietnam War* (Chicago, Ill.: University of Chicago Press, 1995), on the print media and American policy in Vietnam. J. Fred McDonald, *Television and the Red Menace: The Video Road to Vietnam* (New York: Praeger, 1985), on television coverage of the Vietnam war.

20. Lawrence Suid, *Guts and Glory: Great American War Movies* (Boston: Addison-Wesley, 1978), p. 7. On the popularity of westerns and war programs on television, see McDonald, op. cit., chap. 3.

21. Loren Baritz, *Backfire: Vietnam—The Myths That Made Us Fight, the Illusions That Helped Us Lose, the Legacy That Haunts Us Today* (New York: Ballantine, 1985), p. 37.

22. Vincent Nobile, "Political Opposition in the Age of Mass Media: GIs and the Veterans Against the War in Vietnam" (Ph.D. dissertation, University of California at Irvine, 1987), pp. 100–105.

23. Frances Fitzgerald, *America Revised: History Schoolbooks in the Twentieth Century* (Boston, Mass.: Little, Brown, 1979), p. 128.

24. Ibid., pp. 188–220.

25. William Graebner, *The Engineering of Consent* (Madison: University of Wisconsin Press, 1987), p. 143.

26. Sara Diamond, *Roads to Dominion: Right-Wing Movements and Political Power in the United States* (New York: Guilford, 1995), p. 61.

27. Mary Perkins Ryan, "Catholic Education, and War and Peace" in Thomas Quigley, ed., *American Catholics and Vietnam* (Grand Rapids, Mich.: Eerdmans, 1968), p. 56. For more detail on the Catholic church and the cold war, see Kenneth Wald, *Religion and Politics in the United States* (Washington D.C.: CQ, 1992). For a discussion of Francis Cardinal Spellman, who was probably the nation's most prominent Catholic cold warrior, see Eric Hanson, *The Catholic Church in World Politics* (Princeton, N.J.: Princeton University Press). For more detailed analysis of the role of evangelicals in the cold war, see Diamond, op. cit.

28. Hodgson, op. cit., p. 11.

29. Palladino, op. cit., p. 162.

30. Ibid., pp. 162–172.

31. Todd Gitlin, *The Sixties: Years of Hope, Days of Rage* (New York: Bantam 1987), pp. 1–3.

32. Thomas (Tom) Dooley was a doctor and missionary who worked in Indochina, like many other Christians involved in parachurch organizations.

Chapter 2

1. Quoted in Lawrence Wittner, *Cold War America: From Hiroshima to Watergate* (New York: Praeger, 1974), p. 244.

2. For a broad view of American foreign policy objectives in the third world, see Gabriel Kolko, *Confronting the Third World: United States Foreign Policy, 1945–1980* (New York: Pantheon, 1988). For an analysis of the United States' activities in specific regions, such as Latin America, see Walter LaFeber, *Inevitable Revolutions: The United States in Central America* (New York: Norton, 1984). For American involvement in specific nations, see, for example, Richard Immerman, *The CIA in Guatemala: The Foreign Policy of Intervention* (Austin: University of Texas Press, 1982).

3. For a detailed analysis of Vietnamese history, see David Marr, *Vietnamese Tradition on Trial, 1920–1945* (Berkeley: University of California Press, 1981); and Frances Fitzgerald, *Fire in the Lake: The Vietnamese and Americans in Vietnam* (New York: Random House, 1972).

4. Quoted in George Donelson Moss, *Vietnam: An American Ordeal* (Englewood Cliffs, N.J.: Prentice Hall, 1990), p 27.

5. Loren Baritz, *Backfire: Vietnam—The Myths That Made Us Fight, the Illusions That Helped Us Lose, the Legacy That Haunts Us Today* (New York: Ballantine, 1985), p. 46.

6. George Herring, *America's Longest War: The United States and Vietnam, 1950–1975* (New York: Knopf, 1979), p. 10.

7. Walter LaFeber, *America, Russia, and the Cold War: 1945–1984* (New York: Knopf, 1985), pp. 8–28.

8. Moss, op. cit., pp. 71–72; Herring, op. cit., pp. 43–48.

9. The undemocratic nature of the South Vietnamese government has been documented by numerous historians, including Herring, op. cit., chap. 2; Marylin Young, *The Vietnam Wars, 1945–1990* (New York: Harper Perennial, 1991), pp. 60–65; and Gabriel Kolko, *Anatomy of a War: Vietnam, the United States, and the Modern Historical Experience* (New York: Pantheon, 1985), pp. 88–91.

10. Truong Nhu Tang, *A Viet Cong Memoir: An Inside Account of the Vietnam War and Its Aftermath* (New York: Vintage, 1986), pp. 63–80. See also Young, op. cit., pp. 69–71; Kolko, op. cit., chap. 8.

11. Wittner, op. cit., p. 226. For an analysis of the views of American intelligence agents, see Neil Sheehan, *John Paul Vann and America in Vietnam* (New York: Random House, 1988).

12. Quoted in Baritz, op. cit., p. 101.

13. Moss, op. cit., pp. 104–131.

14. The Johnson administration had drafted a statement legitimizing an increased American military presence in Vietnam well before the Gulf of Tonkin incident. The United States had also been provoking the North Vietnamese, who until that point had not been involved in military sense in the South Vietnamese resistance movement, to respond aggressively. Events in the Gulf of Tonkin provided

Johnson with an opportunity to portray his escalation as defensive. Young, op. cit., 114–121.

15. Ibid., p. 240.

16. Compared with veterans of World War II, Vietnam veterans returning home received a pittance for education and other services. For details, see Sar Levitan and Joyce Zickler, *Swords into Plowshares: Our GI Bill* (Salt Lake City, Utah: Olympus, 1973).

17. I have been unable to identify this work.

Chapter 3

1. The growth of the antiwar movement in the United States is documented in numerous studies. Among the best is Charles DeBenedetti, *An American Ordeal: The Antiwar Movement of the Vietnam Era* (Syracuse, N.Y.: Syracuse University Press, 1990); chaps. 4 and 5 are especially useful. An excellent account of the scope of the movement can be found in Nancy Zaroulis and Gerald Sullivan, *Who Spoke Up? American Protest Against the War in Vietnam, 1963–1975* (New York: Holt, Rinehart and Winston, 1984). Accounts of the student movement can be found in James Miller, *Democracy Is in the Streets: From Port Huron to the Seige of Chicago* (New York: Simon and Schuster, 1987); and Todd Gitlin, *The 60s: Years of Hope, Days of Rage,* (New York: Bantam, 1989).

2. DeBenedetti, op. cit.; chaps. 4 and 5 describe antiwar activity before 1965.

3. Ibid., p. 199. The march in Washington in October 1967—characterized by the Yippies, especially Abbie Hoffman, as an effort to "levitate" the Pentagon—led to a confrontation with troops and hundreds of arrests. Analyses in the media were typified by David Brinkley, who described the march as a "coarse, vulgar episode." According to polls taken shortly afterward, a vast majority of Americans (70 percent), felt that such behavior "hurt the antiwar cause."

4. See Mitchell Hall, "CALCAV and Religious Opposition to the War in Vietnam," in Melvin Small and William Hoover, eds., *Give Peace a Chance* (Syracuse, N.Y.: Syracuse University Press, 1992), p. 49; and George Herring, *America's Longest War: The United States and Vietnam, 1950–1975* (New York: Knopf, 1986), p. 173.

5. Herring, op. cit., pp. 176–177.

6. Ibid., pp. 182–183.

7. Because many of the files of intelligence agencies remain classified, the full extent of clandestine activity has yet to be revealed; but several studies have been made using the material that is available. This research has found considerable illegal activity by the various branches of the intelligence community, including infiltration of movements, break-ins at offices and homes, wiretaps, and assasinations. See Frank Donner, *The Age of Surveillance* (New York: Knopf, 1980) and *Protectors of Privilege: Red Squads and Police Repression in Urban America* (Berkeley: University of California Press, 1990); and Ward Churchill and Jim Vander Wall, *Agents of Repression: The FBI's Secret War Against the Black Panther Party and the American Indian Movement* (Boston: South End, 1990).

8. Herring, op. cit., pp. 182–183.

9. A thorough description of deceit by the Nixon White House is found in Seymour M. Hersh, *The Price of Power: Kissinger in the Nixon White House* (New York: Summit, 1983). The impact of the antiwar movement on Nixon's secret plan to escalate the war is evident in Hersh's account of the Moratorium's antiwar rally in October 1969; Hersh states, "Nixon came out of the crisis convinced that the protestors had forced him to back down" (p. 130). See also Jonathan Schell, *The Time of Illusion* (New York: Vintage, 1976). Schell summarizes his analysis as follows: "What the Nixon men thought was unconnected to what they said. What they said was unconnected to what they did" (p. 6).

10. The United States had already bombed Laos during Johnson's presidency; Nixon used ARVN forces to invade Laos in February 1971. Cambodia was also a target: the Nixon administration began a secret air war against Cambodia in 1970. See Marylin Young, *The Vietnam Wars: 1945–1990* (New York: Harper Perennial, 1991), pp. 232–253.

11. Quoted in Schell, op. cit., pp. 56–57.

12. Ibid., pp. 111–112.

13. Athan Theoharis, *Spying on Americans: Political Surveillance from Hoover to the Huston Plan* (Philadelphia, Pa.: Temple University Press, 1978), pp. 13–39.

14. David Cortright, *Soldiers in Revolt: The American Military Today* (Garden City, N.Y.: Anchor Doubleday, 1975); chap. 3 analyzes alienation among GIs in Vietnam. See also Richard Moser, *The New Winter Soldiers: GIs' and Veterans' Dissent during the Vietnam Era* (New Brunswick, N.J.: Rutgers University Press, 1996), chaps. 3 and 4.

15. DeBenedetti, op. cit., p. 175.

16. Sheldon Ramsdell discusses Ball's donation in his interview (San Francisco, Calif., December 17, 1991).

17. Jan Barry Crumb to Dave Dellinger (October 6, 1967), in VVAW Archives, box 1, file 2, State Historical Society of Wisconsin, Madison (hereafter cited as SHSW). The Mobilization to End the War in Vietnam (MOBE) corresponded with VVAW in the fall of 1967 to get VVAW's endorsement for the march on Washington, which took place in October.

18. Nonviolence is consistently emphasized in the narratives; it was a point of pride with these veterans.

19. James Boggio to Carl [Rogers] and Steve [unidentified] in the national office (October 27, 1968), in VVAW Archives, box 1, file 4, SHSW.

20. DeBenedetti, op. cit., p. 249. Sam Brown and David Hawk were student leaders in the liberal wing of the antiwar movement. Brown had been president of the Young Republicans and an active member of NSA before becoming an antiwar activist while studying in Harvard's Divinity School.

21. DeBenedetti, op. cit., p. 255.

22. Gabriel Kolko, *Anatomy of a War: Vietnam, The United States, and the Modern Historical Experience* (New York: Pantheon, 1985), p. 346.

23. The incident on Wall Street took place on May 8, 1970. Danny Friedman was one of the veterans involved in it; see his narrative in Chapter 2. See also DeBenedetti, op. cit., p. 283. Seymour Hersch, op. cit. (p. 427n.), relates a discussion between Nixon and Haldeman on May 5, 1971 (a year later), in which they considered using "thugs" from the Teamsters Union to beat up antiwar activists; thus it is conceivable that someone in the White House had been involved in the earlier episode.

24. In the armed forces, and particularly in Vietnam, African-Americans were much more activist than the majority of whites. As veterans, African-Americans tended to gravitate more toward the Black Panther Party than toward VVAW; this can be explained in terms of their disillusionment with the political process. See Cortright, op. cit., pp. 39–49.

25. See Herring, op. cit., for a brief description of the invasion of Cambodia.

26. For analyses of the changing nature of the war, see (among numerous accounts), Ronald Spector, *After Tet: The Bloodiest Year in Vietnam* (New York: Vintage, 1993).

27. The antiwar veterans' effect on the breakdown of control in the armed forces is documented in Cortright, op. cit., pp. 34, 80.

28. Movement for a Democratic Military (MDM) was led predominantly by African-Americans and was influenced by the Black Panthers, an organization known for its militancy toward the war and civil rights. For more on MDM, see Larry Waterhouse and Mariann G. Wizard, *Turning the Guns Around* (New York: Praeger, 1971), pp. 136–137.

29. The majority of the veterans I interviewed, including Barry Romo, were highly decorated for their service in Vietnam; they had received Purple Hearts, Silver Stars, and numerous other awards.

30. It was at this time that the story of My Lai broke in the press. The media tended to portray soldiers as the murderers; that is, men like William Calley—rather than the military and civilian leaders who were prosecuting the war—were blamed for the massacre. The earliest Hollywood films about the war also showed alienated killers who, as veterans, posed a threat to society. See Rick Berg, "Losing Vietnam: Covering the War in an Age of Technology," in John Carlos Rowe and Rick Berg, eds., *The Vietnam War and American Culture* (New York: Columbia University Press, 1991), pp. 115–147. See also George Dionisopoulos, "Images of the Warrior Returned: Vietnam Veterans in Popular American Film," in Richard Morris and Peter Ehrenhaus, eds., *Cultural Legacies of Vietnam: Uses of the Past in the Present* (Norwood, N.J.: Ablex, 1990), pp. 80–98.

31. The GI movement (like most movements) began with acts of individual resistance. The Fort Hood Three, privates James Johnson, Dennis Mora, and David Samas, refused orders to Vietnam on June 30, 1966, on the basis that the war was immoral. Similarly, in October 1966, Dr. Howard Levy refused to train Green Beret medics. Such actions led to increased ties between civilian antiwar activists and military dissenters. These young men planted the seeds for a much larger GI movement, which emerged in 1967. See Cortright, op. cit., p. 52; and DeBenedetti, op. cit., p. 155.

32. Hersh, op. cit., pp. 192–193.

33. VVAW Archives, box 1, files 1–4, SHSW.

34. VVAW Newsletter (no. 1, March 1971), p. 3. The newsletter was included in an FBI memorandum to the Nixon administration regarding VVAW's march on Washington (Federal Bureau of Investigation, Bureau File 100-448092, April 12, 1971), in VVAW File, FBI Archives, Washington, D.C.

35. Dewey Canyon I was the code name for a secret invasion of Laos that took place in January–February 1969. Dewey Canyon II was another invasion of Laos, in February 1971. See John Kerry and VVAW, *The New Soldier* (New York: Collier, 1971), p. 26.

36. Federal Bureau of Investigation, teletype (serial no. 448092-71, April 13, 1971), in VVAW File, FBI Archives.

37. Scott Armstrong and Bob Woodward, *The Brethren* (New York: Avon, 1979), pp. 154–157.

38. *Washington Daily News,* front-page headline (April 22, 1971).

39. John Dean, internal White House memorandum to H. R. Haldeman and John Ehrlichman (April 21, 1971). White House Staff File, John Dean, Public Papers of the Presidents of the United States (Office of the Federal Register, National Archives and Records Service, College Park, Md.)

40. This demonstration was the first of its kind, and before it took place, members of the Nixon administration had discussed ways of blunting its effect and playing down its significance. They came up with several schemes, such as offering to have the medals retrieved by an "appropriate Mail Room employee." See, for example, John Dean, White House memorandum to H. R. Haldeman and John Ehrlichman (April 22, 1971). White House Staff File of John Dean, box 83 (National Archives, College Park, Md.)

41. The Nixon administration had leaked the information regarding Al Hubbard's status to the press. Department of Defense, Directorate of Defense Information, Press Division: response to query from Lloyd Norman of *Newsweek* and Roger Peterson of ABC News (April 21, 1971). VVAW File, FBI Archives.

Chapter 4

1. This number includes everyone who signed a membership card and supported the organization financially, civilians as well as veterans. Several interviewees indicated that somewhere between 20,000 and 30,000 members were veterans. Interviews with Mike McCain (Chicago, Ill., October 20, 1992); Joe Urgo (New York, December 10, 1992); Barry Romo (February 2 and September 18, 1992).

2. Quoted in Charles DeBenedetti, *An American Ordeal: The Antiwar Movement of the Vietnam Era* (Syracuse, N.Y.: Syracuse University Press, 1990), p. 304.

3. Ibid., p. 305.

4. Ibid., p. 310.

5. Ibid., p. 315.

6. Ibid., p. 323.

7. George Herring, *America's Longest War: The United States and Vietnam 1950–1975* (New York: Knopf, 1979), p. 240.

8. Quotation and polling data in DeBenedetti, op. cit., p. 322.

9. Jonathan Schell, *The Time of Illusion* (New York: Vintage, 1975), p. 173.

10. DeBenedetti, op. cit., p. 333.

11. For a detailed account of this escalation, see Herring, op. cit., p. 249.

12. DeBenedetti, op. cit., p. 331.

13. Ibid., 341–342.

14. Schell, op. cit., p. 174.

15. This phrase is attributed to G. Gordon Liddy; quoted in DeBenedetti, op. cit., p. 315.

16. For an account of the efforts by the Nixon administration to discredit Ellsberg, see Schell, op. cit., pp. 161–168.

17. Ibid., especially chaps. 4 and 5, for an account of illegal activities by the White House.

18. Interviews with Danny Friedman (New York, December 4, 1992) and Ann Hirschman (Cranbury, N.J., December 2, 1992.)

19. Gary Lawton was a veteran who had been arrested for the alleged murder (in April 1971) of two police officers in Riverside, California. He was an activist in various organizations in southern California, and many leftists assumed that he had been framed. His case dragged on for years before he was finally acquitted. A Federal Bureau of Investigation memorandum (Los Angeles, Calif., July 27, 1972) briefly discusses the Lawton case. (From Barry Romo's FBI files; Romo obtained the memorandum through the Freedom of Information Act.)

20. Student Mobilization Committee to End the War in Vietnam (SMC) was created by the Young Socialist Alliance (YSA) in the fall of 1967. Throughout its existence, VVAW had been a target of socialist groups who sought to co-opt it; as a result, the national office kept such groups at arm's length. For a discussion of SMC's role in the antiwar movement, see DeBenedetti, op. cit., pp. 163–170.

21. David Cortright, *Soldiers in Revolt: The American Military Today* (Garden City: Anchor Doubleday, 1975), p. 34. Cortright discusses the influence of VVAW in the armed forces during the fall of 1971. For example, at one point soldiers circulated a petition among troops stationed in Vietnam, and in the Navy; this petition expressed their "opposition to further United States military involvement by air, sea, or land forces in Vietnam, Laos, Cambodia, or other countries of southeast Asia." Two of the men who were responsible for circulating the petition were arrested, and one of these two was discharged for "substandard personal behavior."

22. Joe Urgo's account of his trip is in *1st Casualty* (vol. 1, no. 2, October 1971).

23. John Kniffin's growing distrust of the national office in New York is echoed in much of the correspondence between that office and regional leaders during this period (summer and fall of 1971). See, for example, letter from Gary Staiger et al. (Dayton, Ohio, November 1971). VVAW Archives, box 5, file 2, SHSW.

24. Notes from emergency meeting of the steering committee (November 12 and 15, 1971). VVAW Archives, box 8, file 2, SHSW.

25. Numerous letters were written, in response to the proposed action and its rejection, between the national office in New York and regional coordinators. See, for example, Jon Birch, Larry Rottman, Joe Urgo, and Al Hubbard to Scott Camil (undated), VVAW Archives, box 2, file 12; Scott Camil, "Open Letter to All Vets" (undated), VVAW Archives, box 2, file 12; Dave Rosen and Gary Mundt of Colorado VVAW to national office (December 19, 1971), VVAW Archives, box 2, file 8, SHSW.

Chapter 5

1. Walter LaFeber, *America, Russia, and the Cold War: 1945–1984* (New York: Knopf, 1985), p. 97.

2. Ibid., pp. 67–69. Stanley Kutler, *The American Inquisition: Justice and Injustice in the Cold War* (New York: Hill and Wang, 1982), pp. 36–39.

3. There are numerous accounts of such congressional actions. See Kutler, op. cit.; Victor Navasky, *Naming Names* (New York: Viking, 1980); David Caute, *The Great Fear: The Anti-Communist Campaign Under Truman and Eisenhower* (New York: Simon and Schuster, 1978).

4. Ward Churchill and Jim Vander Wall, *Agents of Repression* (Boston, Mass.: South End, 1990), pp. 36–62. (The methods listed in this passage are chapter titles.) See also Athan Theoharis, *Spying on Americans: Political Surveillance from Hoover to the Huston Plan* (Philadelphia, Pa.: Temple University Press, 1978); Frank Donner, *Age of Surveillance* (New York: Knopf, 1980).

5. J. F. Ter Horst, "2 Vets with Medals, 1 with Silver Spoon," *Detroit News* (May 2, 1971).

6. William F. Buckley, "The Self-Indictment of an Anti-War Veteran," *Washington Star* (June 14, 1971); and "John Kerry's Speech—II," *Boston Globe* (June 15, 1971).

7. John Helmer, *Bringing the War Home: The American Soldier in Vietnam and After* (New York: Free Press, 1974), p. 96.

8. Charles Colson, memorandum for the president (October 22, 1971). White House Staff File, Charles Colson, National Archives, College Park, Md.

9. SAC, New York, United States government memorandum to director, FBI (100-160644, September 20, 1967). FBI Archives, Washington, D.C. (SAC is the designation of a special agent.)

10. See SAC, New York, United States government memorandum to director, FBI (100-160644, October 26, 1967). FBI archives. There is no evidence in the files—including those on individual members such as Pete Zastrow, Michael McCain, and Barry Romo—of connections to the Communist Party or of violent or destructive behavior.

11. D. J. Brennan, United States government memorandum to W. C. Sullivan (November 19, 1967). White House Staff File, John Dean.

12. ADIC, Los Angeles, United States government memorandum to director, FBI (100-77940, July 15, 1976). This is one of several visits FBI agents made to Mrs. Romo. Memoranda are in Barry Romo's personal FBI file.

13. Teletype to director from Los Angeles (100-77703, April 28, 1972). Personal FBI file of Barry Romo.

14. Teletype to director (100-448092) from Los Angeles (100-77703, May 2, 1972). Personal FBI file of Barry Romo.

15. Jan Barry's claim that "everybody" was "activated" is confirmed by communications between the White House and intelligence agencies. See, for example, Federal Bureau of Investigation Bureau File 100-448092 (April 12, 1971), which was provided to the White House staff. It describes the Dewey Canyon III action planned by VVAW and concludes: "Copies of this document are being disseminated locally to the 108th Military Intelligence Group, the Naval Investigation Service Office, the Office of Special Investigations of the United States Air Force, the Secret Service," and various other agencies.

16. "Red squads" operated in every major city where there was antiwar or left-wing activity. For a detailed account, see Frank Donner, *Protectors of Privilege: Red Squads and Police Repression in Urban America* (Berkeley: University of California Press, 1990).

17. Ibid., pp. 127–128. Donner documents the identity of this informant and her participation in numerous left-wing groups.

18. A tape was made of the interrogation of one FBI informant, on which he reveals his activities to VVAW members. This tape is in the possession of John Lindquist (Milwaukee, Wis.); I have listened to it.

19. Sarah Jane Moore was originally paid as an FBI informant to infiltrate VVAW in the Bay Area in California. Members in the Bay Area remember her as "strange" and "troubled." Her attempted assassination of Ford took place on September 22.

20. Joe Ramiro was a Vietnam veteran who joined VVAW and was also a member of the Symbionese Liberation Army. He was implicated in the murder of a school superintendent in Oakland, California; his life reflects much of the frustration and anger experienced by vets. See John Bryan, *This Soldier Still at War* (New York: Harcourt Brace Jovanovich, 1975).

21. See John Kifner, article in *New York Times* (August 14, 1972).

22. For other cases brought against antiwar protestors, see Donner, op. cit., pp. 353–385.

23. Among VVAW members, Scott Camil remains a controversial figure. Some believe he was an agent; some think he was simply one of many veterans whose anger increased as the war wound on. Camil grew up in a right-wing family, joined the Marines, volunteered for service in Vietnam, and served two tours there, receiving nine medals. For more information about Camil, see Bud Schultz and Ruth Schultz, *It Did Happen Here: Recollections of Political Repression in America* (Berkeley: University of California Press, 1989), pp. 319–333.

24. Cubans were hired by the FBI and the Miami police department to infiltrate and disrupt VVAW activities before the Republican convention, in order to "embarass

George McGovern," whose antiwar position threatened the Nixon administration. *Gainsville Sun* (May 23, 1973).

25. Goodwyn was the lead attorney in a number of conspiracy cases brought against antiwar groups during the late 1960s and early 1970s. For more information, see Donner, op. cit.

26. The Nixon administration knew that VVAW was supported by several leading Democrats during Dewey Canyon III; these Democrats had given VVAW $50,000 for the demonstration. The Nixon administration wanted—before the elections of 1972—to infiltrate VVAW, find (or possibly instigate) violence, and expose links between VVAW and the Democratic Party. This plan backfired as the Gainesville trial began and the initial Watergate break-in became public; nevertheless, Robert Dole tried to insinuate that there was a link between antiwar protesters and McGovern: Dole made a public appeal to McGovern "to get in touch with his antiwar supporters and let us have our convention in peace." Quoted in *New York Times* (July 16, 1972).

27. See Mary McGrory, "McCord Creates a Desert," *Washington Star* (May 23, 1973). See also Jack Anderson, "Nailing the Vets," *New York Post* (July 11, 1973).

Chapter 6

1. Seymour Hersch, *The Price of Power: Kissinger in the Nixon White House* (New York: Summit, 1983), pp. 589–609.

2. Quoted in Nancy Zaroulis and Gerald Sullivan, *Who Spoke Up? American Protest Against the Vietnam War, 1963–1975* (New York: Holt, Rinehart, and Wilson, 1984), p. 398.

3. Ibid., p. 404.

4. Hersch, op. cit., pp. 267–296.

5. For details on Wounded Knee and the FBI's actions against AIM, see Ward Churchill and Jim Vander Wall, *Agents of Repression: The FBI's Secret War Against the Black Panther Party and the American Indian Movement* (Boston: South End, 1990). For details on the Peltier case, see Peter Matthiessen, *In the Spirit of Crazy Horse* (New York: Viking, 1991).

6. David Caute, *The Year of the Barricades: A Journey Through 1968* (New York: Perennial Library, 1988), pp. 440–443; Zaroulis and Sullivan, op. cit., pp. 251–255; James Miller, *Democracy Is in the Streets: From Port Huron to the Seige of Chicago* (New York: Simon and Schuster, 1987), p. 311.

7. Myra MacPherson, *Long Time Passing: Vietnam and the Haunted Generation* (New York: Anchor, 1984), p. 580.

8. VVAW was asked to support the Native Americans in Wounded Knee in 1973. Several of those inside the besieged compound were Vietnam veterans. VVAW organized support, including sending medicine, food, and other aid. Ann Hirschman was able to get into the encampment, where she provided medical aid. Interview with Ann Hirschman (Cranbury, N.J., December 2, 1992).

9. For more information on Truong Dinh Dzu, see Marylin Young, *The Vietnam Wars: 1945–1990* (New York: Harper Perennial, 1991), pp. 184–187.

10. "A million" is an exaggeration; about 60,000 people attended this event.

11. Hersch, op. cit., pp. 610–635.

12. *Winter Soldier* (June 1973).

13. Maude DeVictor had been working at the West Side Veterans Administration hospital in Chicago when she discovered that the VA was covering up data on Agent Orange and its effects on veterans. She subsequently turned over the material she had compiled to a local television station in Chicago, which broadcast a special report. Maude DeVictor was never fully credited for her role in initiating this issue, although she was warmly received by VVAW and continues to work with the organization.

Chapter 7

1. Noam Chomsky, "Visions of Righteousness," in Carlos Rowe and Rick Berg, eds., *The Vietnam War and American Culture,* (New York: Columbia University Press, 1991), p. 39.

2. For an overview of revolutionary activity in the third world, see Eric Hobsbawm, *The Age of Extremes: A History of the World, 1914–1991* (New York: Vintage, 1994), chap. 15. For Central America in particular, see Walter LaFeber, *Inevitable Revolutions: The United States in Central America* (New York: Norton, 1984). For American responses to the Sandinista revolution in Nicaragua, see Thomas W. Walker, ed., *Nicaragua: The First Five Years* (New York: Praeger, 1985).

3. Polling data in Myra MacPherson, *Long Time Passing: Vietnam and the Haunted Generation* (New York: Doubleday, 1984), p. 170.

4. Hobsbawm, op. cit., p. 248.

5. Holly Sklar, *Chaos or Community: Seeking Solutions, Not Scapegoats, for Bad Economics* (Boston: South End, 1985), p. 143.

6. Ibid., p. 5.

7. VVAW's central role in gaining recognition of PTSD as a "legitimate" disorder has recently been acknowledged even by those who oppose its inclusion in the Veterans Administration list of covered illnesses. Jack McCloskey, in particular, has become the target of revisionists. See Phoebe S. Spinrad, "Patriotism and Pathology: Anti-Veteran Activism and the VA," *Journal of Vietnam Veterans Institute* (vol. 3, no. 1, 1994).

Epilogue

1. Eliot Cohen, *Citizens and Soldiers* (Ithaca, N.Y.: Cornell University Press, 1985), p. 31.

2. J. A. Hobson, *Imperialism* (Ann Arbor, Mich.: Ann Arbor Paperbacks, 1965), p. 152.

3. For an analysis of the open-door doctrine, see William Appleman Williams, *The Tragedy of American Diplomacy,* (New York: Dell, 1972). For a more recent description of its impact, see Gabriel Kolko, *Confronting the Third World* (New York: Pantheon, 1988).

4. In 1897, the standing army numbered 25,000 men. There were also 114,000 men in state militias, which provided the second line of defense. Cohen, op. cit., p. 94.

5. Numerous historians and other analysts discuss racism, manifest destiny, and the destruction of native peoples. See, for example, Richard Drinnon, *Facing West: The Metaphysics of Indian Hating and Empire Building* (New York: Schocken, 1980); Vine Deloria, *Custer Died for Your Sins* (New York: Avon, 1970); Dee Brown, *Bury My Heart at Wounded Knee* (New York: Bantam, 1976); John Niehardt, *Black Elk Speaks* (New York: Morrow, 1932).

6. W. A. Williams, op. cit., pp. 48–57. See also Walter LaFeber, *The New Empire: An Interpretation of American Expansion, 1860–1898* (Ithaca, N.Y.: Cornell University Press, 1963).

7. There are many accounts of American military forays into Latin America. On the Caribbean in general, see David Healy, *Drive to Hegemony: The United States in the Caribbean, 1898–1917* (Madison: University of Wisconsin Press, 1988). On Puerto Rico, see Raymond Carr, *Puerto Rico: A Colonial Experiment* (New York: Vintage, 1984). On Cuba, see Hugh Thomas, *Cuba, or the Pursuit of Freedom* (New York: Harper and Rowe, 1971).

8. Walter L. Williams, "United States Indian Policy and the Debate over Philippine Annexation: Implications for the Origin of American Imperialism," *Journal of American History* (vol. 66, no. 4, March 1980), pp. 810–831. Richard Severo and Lewis Milford, *The Wages of War: When America's Soldiers Came Home, From Valley Forge to Vietnam* (New York: Touchstone), pp. 211–227.

9. Quoted in Cohen, op. cit., p. 124.

10. Arthur Ekirch, *Civilian and Military* (New York: Oxford University Press, 1956), p. 272.

11. Walter LaFeber, *America, Russia, and the Cold War, 1945–1984* (New York: Knopf, 1985), p. 53.

12. Godfrey Hodgson, *America in Our Time: From World War II to Nixon, What Happened and Why* (New York: Vintage, 1976), p. 12. Hodgson expands on this theme in chap. 6.

13. Christian Appy, "A War for Nothing: A Social History of American Soldiers in the Vietnam War" (Ph.D. dissertation, Harvard University, 1987), pp. 28–30; and John Helmer, *Bringing the War Home: The American Soldier in Vietnam and After* (New York: Free Press, 1974), p. 9.

14. Samuel Bowles and Herbert Gintis, *Schooling in Capitalist America: Educational Reform and the Contradictions of Economic Life* (New York: Basic, 1976), pp. 203–223.

15. On the economic factors that motivated young men to enlist, see Helmer, op. cit., pp. 106–111.

16.   For a discussion of socioeconomic changes in the United States as a factor undermining family life, see Richard Sennett and Jonathan Cobb, *Hidden Injuries of Class* (New York: Knopf, 1972).

17.   See Robert D. Heinl Jr., "The Collapse of the Armed Forces," *Armed Forces Journal* (June 1971), pp. 38–45; Appy, op. cit., chap. 7; David Cortright, *Soldiers in Revolt: The American Military Today* (Garden City, N.Y.: Anchor Doubleday, 1975), chaps. 3 and 4.

18.   Sar Levitan and Joyce Zickler, *Swords into Plowshares: Our GI Bill* (Salt Lake City, Utah: Olympus, 1973).

19.   Hamid Mowlina and Paul Geffert, "Vietnam Veterans Against the War: A Profile Study of the Dissenters," in David Thorne and George Butler, eds., *John Kerry and the Vietnam Veterans Against the War: The New Soldier* (New York: Collier, 1971), pp. 172–174.

20.   For an analysis of veterans' problems with reintegration into American society, see Robert J. Lifton, *Home from War: Neither Victims nor Executioners* (New York: Simon and Schuster, 1973); John Shay, *Achilles in Vietnam* (New York: Atheneum, 1994); and Ellen Frey-Wouters and Robert Laufer, *Legacy of a War: The American Soldier in Vietnam* (New York: Sharpe, 1986).

21.   James Scott, *Domination and the Arts of Resistance* (New Haven, Conn.: Yale University Press, 1990), p. 106.

22.   Cortright, op. cit., argues in detail that soldiers' resistance affected the ability of the armed forces to prosecute the war.

23.   Myra MacPherson, *Long Time Passing: Vietnam and the Haunted Generation* (New York: Doubleday, 1984), p. 187.

24.   Ibid., p. 191.

25.   Ibid., p. 230.

26.   John Kerry and the Vietnam Veterans Against the War, *The New Soldier* (New York: Collier, 1971), p. 24.

27.   Cohen, op. cit., p. 117.

28.   Benjamin Barber, *Jihad versus McWorld* (New York: Ballantine, 1995), pp. 118–128. See also Ben Bagdikian, *The Media Monopoly* (Boston: Beacon, 1992).

Bibliography

INTERVIEWS

Note: Tapes of the interviews are in VVAW Archives, Madison, Wisconsin State Historical Society.

Alband, Linda. San Francisco, Calif. August 29, 1992.

Bailey, Annie. Milwaukee, Wis. July 1, 1992; April 8, 1993.

Barry, Jan. Montclair, N.J. December 5, 1992.

Blecker, Michael. San Francisco, Calif. August 27, 1992.

Branson, Bill. Chicago, Ill. October 17, 1992.

Cline, David. Jersey City, N.J. December 4, 1992.

Davis, Bill. Oak Park, Ill. October 12, 1992.

DuBose, Terry. Austin, Tex. December 10, 1994.

Ewing, David. San Francisco, Calif. August 27, 1992.

Gold, Mike. New York, N.Y. December 2, 1992.

Friedman, Danny. New York, N.Y. December 3, 1992.

Friedman, Jeanne. Chicago, Ill. September 23, 1995.

Greenberg, Joel. Chicago, Ill. October 20, 1992.

Hanson, Bob. San Francisco, Calif. August 26, 1992.

Hirschman, Ann. Cranbury, N.J. December 2, 1992.

Kniffin, John. Austin, Tex. December 10, 1994.

Lindquist, John. Milwaukee, Wis. July 1, 1992; April 8, 1993.

Luginbill, Annie. Chicago, Ill. October 20, 1992.

McCain, Michael, and Jill McCain. Chicago, Ill. November 15, 1994.

McCloskey, Jack. San Francisco, Calif. August 26, 1992.

Muller, Bobby. Washington, D.C. December 8, 1992.

Ramsdell, Sheldon. San Francisco, Calif. August 29, 1992.

Romo, Barry. Chicago, Ill. February 2 and September 18, 1992.

Sable, Ron. Chicago, Ill. October 20, 1992.

Thorn, Lee. San Francisco, Calif. August 30, 1992.

Urgo, Joe. New York, N.Y. December 10, 1992.

Wachtendonk, Jim, and Sukie Wachtendonk. Madison, Wis. June 28, 1992.

Wetzler, Tom. San Antonio, Tex. December 9–11, 1994.

Zastrow, Pete. Chicago, Ill. July 12 and September 11, 1992.

DOCUMENT COLLECTIONS

Papers of Vietnam Veterans Against the War (VVAW) and the civilian and GI antiwar press. Madison: Social Action Collection, Wisconsin State Historical Commission.

Personal files and archives. John Lindquist and Annie Bailey; Michael McCain; Barry Romo; Pete Zastrow.

VVAW and COINTELPRO FBI files. Washington, D.C.: Headquarters, Federal Bureau of Investigation.

White House Special Files of the Nixon administration. Alexandria, Va.: Nixon Project, National Archives.

BOOKS

Adkins, Nelson, ed. *Thomas Paine: Common Sense and Other Political Writings,* American Heritage Series (New York: Macmillan, 1953).

Appy, Christian. "A War for Nothing: A Social History of American Soldiers in the Vietnam War" (Ph.D. dissertation, Harvard University, 1986).

Aron, Raymond. *The Century of Total War* (Boston, Mass.: Beacon, 1954).

Aronowitz, Stanley. *False Promises: The Shaping of American Working Class Consciousness* (New York: McGraw-Hill, 1973).

Bagdikian, Ben. *The Media Monopoly* (Boston, Mass.: Beacon, 1992).

Barber, Benjamin. *Jihad versus McWorld: How Globalism and Tribalism are Reshaping the World* (New York: Ballantine, 1995).

Baritz, Loren. *Backfire: Vietnam—The Myths That Made Us Fight, the Illusions That Helped Us Lose, the Legacy That Haunts Us Today* (New York: Ballantine Books, 1985).

Barnes, Peter. *Pawns: The Plight of the Citizen-Soldier* (New York: Knopf, 1972).

Barry, Jan. *Peace Is Our Profession: Poems and Passages of War Protest* (Montclair, N.J.: East River Anthology, 1981).

Baskir, Lawrence M., and William Strauss. *Chance and Circumstance: The Draft, the War, and the Vietnam Generation* (New York: Random House, 1978).

Berkowitz, William. "The Impact of Anti-Vietnam War Demonstrations Upon National Public Opinion and Military Indicators," *Social Science Research* (vol. 2, March 1973), pp. 1–14.

Bowles, Samuel, and Herbert Gintis. *Schooling in Capitalist America: Educational Reform and the Contradictions of Economic Life* (New York: Basic, 1976).

Boyle, Richard. *GI Revolts: The Breakdown of the U.S. Army in Vietnam* (San Francisco, Calif.: United Front, 1973).

Bryan, John. *This Soldier Still at War* (New York: Harcourt Brace Jovanovich, 1975).

Carr, Raymond. *Puerto Rico: A Colonial Experiment* (New York: Vintage, 1984).

Caute, David. *The Great Fear: The Anti-Communist Campaign Under Truman and Eisenhower* (New York: Simon and Schuster, 1978).

————. *Sixty-Eight: The Year of the Barricades* (London: Hamish Hamilton, 1988).

Chambers, John Whiteclay. *To Raise an Army* (New York: Free Press, 1987).

Chomsky, Noam, and Edward S. Herman. *The Washington Connection and Third World Fascism* (Boston: South End, 1979).

Churchill, Ward, and Jim Vander Wall. *Agents of Repression: The FBI's Secret War Against the Black Panther Party and the American Indian Movement* (Boston, Mass.: South End, 1990).

Cohen, Eliot A. *Citizens and Soldiers: The Dilemmas of Military Service* (Ithaca, N.Y.: Cornell University Press, 1985).

Cortright, David. *Soldiers in Revolt: The American Military Today* (Garden City, N.Y.: Anchor Doubleday, 1975).

————, and Max Watts. *Left Face: Soldier Unions and Resistance Movements in Modern Armies* (New York: Greenwood, 1991).

DeBenedetti, Charles. *The Peace Reform in American History* (Bloomington: Indiana University Press, 1980).

————, with Charles Chatfield. *An American Ordeal: The Antiwar Movement of the Vietnam Era* (Syracuse, N.Y.: Syracuse University Press, 1990).

Diamond, Sara. *Roads to Dominion : Right-Wing Movements and Political Power in the United States* (New York: Guilford, 1995).

Diggins, John Patrick. *The Proud Decades: America in War and Peace, 1941–1960* (New York: Norton, 1988).

Divine, Robert. "Historiography: Vietnam Reconsidered," *Diplomatic History* (no. 12, Winter 1988), pp. 79–93.

Donner, Frank. *The Age of Surveillance* (New York: Knopf, 1980).

————. *Protectors of Privilege: Red Squads and Police Repression in Urban America* (Berkeley: University of California Press, 1990).

Drinnon, Richard. *Facing West: The Metaphysics of Indian-Hating and Empire-Building* (New York: Schocken, 1990).

Dunaway, David K., and Willa K. Baum, eds. *Oral History: An Interdisciplinary Anthology* (Nashville, Tenn.: American Association for State and Local History, 1984).

Duncan, Donald. "The Whole Thing Was a Lie," *Ramparts* (no. 13, February 1966), pp. 12–24.

Ehrhart, W. D. *Passing Time: Memoir of a Vietnam Veteran Against the War* (Jefferson, N.C.: McFarland, 1989).

———. *Vietnam Perkasie: A Combat Marine's Memoir* (New York: Zebra/Kensington, 1983).

Ekirch, Arthur. *The Civilian and the Military* (New York: Oxford University Press, 1956).

Frey-Wouters, Ellen, and Robert Laufer. *Legacy of a War: The American Soldier in Vietnam* (New York: Sharpe, 1986).

Fitzgerald, Frances. *America Revised: History Schoolbooks in the Twentieth Century* (Boston, Mass.: Little, Brown, 1979).

———. *Fire in the Lake: The Vietnamese and Americans in Vietnam* (New York: Random House, 1972).

Frisch, Michael. *A Shared Authority: Essays on the Craft and Meaning of Oral and Public History* (Albany: State University of New York Press, 1990).

Fussell, Paul. *Wartime: Understanding and Behavior in the Second World War* (New York: Oxford University Press, 1989).

Gardner, Lloyd. *Approaching Vietnam: From World War II through Dienbienphu* (New York: Norton, 1988).

Gerzon, Mark. *A Choice of Heroes: The Changing Faces of American Manhood* (Boston, Mass.: Houghton Mifflin, 1982).

Giglio, Gerald. *Days of Decision: An Oral History of Conscientious Objectors in the Military During the Vietnam War* (Trenton, N.J.: Broken Rifle, 1989).

Gitlin, Todd. *The Sixties: Years of Hope, Days of Rage* (New York: Bantam, 1987).

Graebner, William. *Coming of Age in Buffalo: Youth and Authority in the Postwar Era* (Philadelphia, Pa.: Temple University Press, 1990).

———. *The Engineering of Consent* (Madison: University of Wisconsin Press, 1987).

Grele, Ronald. *Envelopes of Sound* (Chicago, Ill.: Precedent, 1975).

Hall, Mitchell K. *Because of Their Faith: CALCAV and Religious Opposition to the Vietnam War* (New York: Columbia University Press, 1990).

Hallin, Daniel. *The Uncensored War* (New York: Oxford University Press, 1986).

Hanson, Eric O. *The Catholic Church in World Politics* (Princeton, N.J.: Princeton University Press, 1987).

Hayes, James R. "The Dialectics of Resistance: An Analysis of the GI Movement" *Journal of Social Issues* (vol. 31, no. 4, 1975), pp. 125–137.

Healey, David. *Drive to Hegemony: The United States in the Caribbean, 1898–1917* (Madison: University of Wisconsin Press, 1988).

Heinl, Robert D., Jr. "The Collapse of the Armed Forces," *Armed Forces Journal* (June 1971), pp. 38–45.

Hellman, John. *American Myth and the Legacy of Vietnam* (New York: Columbia University Press, 1986).

Helmer, John. *Bringing the War Home: The American Soldier in Vietnam and After* (New York: Free Press, 1974).

Herman, Edward, and Noam Chomsky. *Manufacturing Consent: The Political Economy of the Mass Media* (New York: Pantheon, 1988).

Herr, Michael. *Dispatches* (New York: Avon, 1977).

Herring, George. *America's Longest War: The United States and Vietnam, 1950–1975* (New York: Knopf, 1986).

Hersh, Seymour. *The Price of Power: Kissinger in the Nixon White House* (New York: Summit, 1983).

Himmelstein, Jerome. *To The Right: The Transformation of American Conservatism* (Berkeley: University of California Press, 1990).

Hobsbawm, Eric. *The Age of Extremes: A History of the World, 1914–1991* (New York: Vintage, 1994).

Hodgson, Godfrey. *America in Our Time: From World War II to Nixon, What Happened and Why* (New York: Vintage, 1976).

Huntington, Samuel. *The Soldier and the State* (Cambridge, Mass.: Belknap, Harvard University Press, 1957).

Jezer, Marty. *The Dark Ages: Life in the United States, 1945–1960* (Boston, Mass.: South End, 1982).

Kaplan, Amy, and Donald Pease, eds. *Cultures of United States Imperialism* (Durham, N.C.: Duke University Press, 1993).

Kerry, John, and VVAW. *The New Soldier* (New York: Collier, 1971).

Kissinger, Henry. *White House Years* (Boston, Mass.: Little, Brown, 1979).

Kolko, Gabriel. *Anatomy of a War: Vietnam, The United States, and the Modern Historical Experience* (New York: Pantheon, 1985).

———. *Confronting the Third World* (New York: Pantheon, 1988).

Kovic, Ron. *Born on the Fourth of July* (New York: McGraw Hill, 1976).

Kutler, Stanley. *The American Inquisition: Justice and Injustice in the Cold War* (New York: Hill and Wang, 1982).

LaFeber, Walter. *America, Russia, and the Cold War: 1945–1975* (New York: Wiley, 1976).

———. *The New Empire: An Interpretation of American Expansion, 1860–1898* (Ithaca, N.Y.: Cornell University Press, 1963).

———. *Inevitable Revolutions: The United States in Central America* (New York: Norton, 1984).

Levitan, Sar, and Joyce Zickler. *Swords into Plowshares: Our GI Bill* (Salt Lake City, Utah: Olympus, 1973).

Lewy, Guenter. *America in Vietnam* (New York: Oxford University Press, 1978).

Lifton, Robert Jay. *Home From the War: Neither Victims Nor Executioners* (New York: Simon and Schuster, 1973).

Lipsitz, George. *Rainbow at Midnight: Labor and Culture in the 1940s* (Urbana: University of Illinois Press, 1994).

Lyttle, Bradford. *The Chicago Anti-Vietnam War Movement* (Chicago, Ill.: Midwest Pacifist Center, 1988).

MacPherson, Myra. *Long Time Passing: Vietnam and the Haunted Generation* (New York: Doubleday, 1984).

Marwick, Arthur. *Total War and Social Change* (New York: St. Martin's, 1988).

Marr, David. *Vietnamese Tradition on Trial, 1920–1945* (Berkeley: University of California Press, 1981).

McDonald, J. Fred. *Television and the Red Menace: The Video Road to Vietnam* (New York: Praeger, 1985).

McWethy, Jack, ed. "Problems in the Ranks: Vietnam Disenchantment, Drug Addiction, and Racism Contribute to Declining Morale," in *The Power of the Pentagon* (Washington, D.C.: Congressional Quarterly, 1972).

Miller, James. *"Democracy Is in the Streets": From Port Huron to the Seige of Chicago* (New York: Simon and Schuster, 1987).

Moser, Richard. "From Deference to Defiance: America, The Citizen-Soldier and the Vietnam Era" (Ph. D. dissertation, Rutgers University, 1989).

———. *The New Winter Soldiers: GI and Veterans Dissent During the Vietnam Era* (New Brunswick, N.J.: Rutgers University Press, 1996).

Moskos, Charles. "The American Combat Soldier in Vietnam," *Journal of Social Issues* (vol. 31, 1984).

Moss, George Donelson. *Vietnam: An American Ordeal* (Englewood Cliffs, N.J.: Prentice Hall, 1990).

Navasky, Victor S. *Naming Names* (New York: Viking, 1980).

Nobile, Vincent. "Political Opposition in the Age of Mass Media: GIs and Veterans Against the War in Vietnam" (Ph.D. dissertation, University of California at Irvine, 1987).

O'Brien, Tim. *Going After Cacciato* (New York: Dell, 1975).

Paterson, Thomas. *On Every Front: The Making of the Cold War* (New York: Norton, 1979).

Pentagon Papers, The, as Published by the New York Times (New York: Bantam, 1971).

Perret, Geoffrey. *A Country Made by War: From the Revolution to Vietnam—The Story of America's Rise to Power* (New York: Vintage, 1990).

Pessen, Edward. *Losing Our Souls: The American Experience in the Cold War* (Chicago, Ill.: Ivan Dee, 1993).

Portelli, Alessandro. *The Death of Luigi Trastulli* (Albany, N.Y.: State University of New York Press, 1991).

Prados, John. *The Hidden History of the Vietnam War* (Chicago, Ill.: Ivan Dee, 1995).

Rowe, John Carlos, and Rick Berg, eds. *The Vietnam War and American Culture* (New York: Columbia University Press, 1991).

Ryan, Mary Perkins. "Catholic Education, and War and Peace," in Thomas Quigley, ed., *American Catholics and Vietnam* (Grands Rapids, Mich.: Eerdmans, 1968).

Sale, Kirkpatrick. *SDS* (New York: Random House, 1973).

Scheer, Robert. "Hang Down Your Head, Tom Dooley," *Ramparts* (January 1965).

Schell, Jonathan. *The Time of Illusion* (New York: Vintage, 1976).

Schultz, Bud, and Ruth Schultz. *It Did Happen Here: Recollections of Political Repression in America* (Berkeley: University of California Press, 1989).

Scott, James. *Domination and the Arts of Resistance* (New Haven, Conn.: Yale University Press, 1990).

Sennett, Richard, and Jonathan Cobb. *Hidden Injuries of Class* (New York: Knopf, 1972).

Severo, Richard, and Lewis Milford. *The Wages of War: When American Soldiers Came Home—From Valley Forge to Vietnam* (New York: Simon and Schuster, 1989).

Shay, John. *Achilles in Vietnam* (New York: Atheneum, 1994).

Sheehan, Neil. *A Bright Shining Lie: John Paul Vann and America in Vietnam* (New York: Random House, 1988).

Shor, Ira. *Culture Wars: School and Society in the Conservative Restoration, 1969–1984* (Boston, Mass.: Routledge and Kegan Paul, 1986).

Shy, Richard. *A People Numerous and Armed: Reflections on the Military Struggle for American Indepenence* (Ann Arbor: University of Michigan Press, 1990).

Small, Melvin, and William D. Hoover, eds. *Give Peace a Chance: Exploring the Vietnam Antiwar Movement* (Syracuse, N.Y.: Syracuse University Press, 1992).

Spector, Ronald. *After Tet: The Bloodiest Year in Vietnam* (New York: Vintage, 1993).

Stapp, Andy. *Up Against the Brass* (New York: Simon and Schuster, 1970).

Suid, Lawrence. *Guts and Glory: Great American War Movies* (Boston, Mass.: Addison-Wesley, 1978).

Terry, Wallace. *Bloods: An Oral History of the Vietnam War* (New York: Random House, 1984).

Theoharis, Athan. *Spying on Americans: Political Surveillance from Hoover to the Huston Plan* (Philadelphia, Pa.: Temple University Press, 1978).

Thomas, Hugh. *Cuba, or the Pursuit of Freedom* (New York: Harper and Row, 1971).

Thornton, A. P. *Imperialism in the Twentieh Century* (Minneapolis: University of Minnesota Press, 1977).

Vietnam Veterans Against the War. *The Winter Soldier Investigation: An Inquiry into American War Crimes* (Boston, Mass.: Beacon, 1970).

Wald, Kenneth. *Religion and Politics in the United States* (Washington, D.C.: CQ, 1992).

Waterhouse, Larry G., and Mariann G. Wizard. *Turning the Guns Around: Notes on the GI Movement* (New York: Praeger, 1971).

Williams, William Appleman. *The Tragedy of American Diplomacy* (New York: Dell, 1972).

Wittner, Lawrence. *Rebels Against War: The American Peace Movement, 1933–1983* (Philadelphia, Pa.: Temple University Press, 1984).

——. *Cold War America: From Hiroshima to Watergate* (New York: Praeger, 1974).

Wood, Gordon. *The Creation of the American Republic* (New York: Norton, 1972).

Woodward, Bob, and Scott Armstrong. *The Brethren: Inside the Supreme Court* (New York: Avon, 1979).

Wyatt, Clarence. *Paper Soldiers: The American Press and the Vietnam War* (Chicago: University of Chicago Press, 1995).

Yergin, Daniel. *Shattered Peace: The Origins of the Cold War and the National Security State* (Boston, Mass.: Houghton Mifflin, 1977).

Young, Marilyn. *The Vietnam Wars: 1945–1990* (New York: Harper Perennial, 1991).

Zaroulis, Nancy, and Gerald Sullivan. *Who Spoke Up? American Protests Against the War in Vietnam, 1963–1975* (Garden City, N.Y.: Doubleday, 1984).

FILMS

Different Sons. Video; director, Jack Ofield; producer, Arthur Littman (Bowling Green Films, 1970).

It's Only the Beginning. Video (Vietnam Veterans Against the War, 1972).

The Winter Soldier. Video (20/20 Productions, 1972).

Credits for Photographs

Page 1: Ted Reich, Chicago Daily News.

Page 33: Barry Romo.

Page 42: Terry DuBose.

Page 45: Danny Friedman.

Page 55: Lee Thorn.

Page 68: VVAW.

Page 87: Jan Barry.

Page 105: Terry DuBose.

Page 113: Barry Romo.

Page 131: Joel Greenberg.

Page 143: Official Marine Corps photograph by Pfc. M. J. Coates.

Page 153: Danny Friedman.

Page 167: John Lindquist.

Page 196: VVAW.

Page 199: Sheldon Ramsdell.

Page 213: Lee Thorn.

Page 224: Photo by Barbara Rothkrug / LNS.

Page 226: Terry DuBose.

Page 234: Photo by Sheldon Ramsdell.

Page 241: From John Kerry, *The New Soldier* (New York: Macmillan, 1971); photo by Michael Abramson.

Page 263: Danny Friedman.

Page 274: VVAW.

Page 280: Bill Davis.

Page 282: VVAW.

Page 284: Jean Lattes / Le Vésinet.

Page 287: *Playboy* (vol. 18, no. 2), p. 65.

Pages 298, 302, 308, 312: VVAW.

Page 322: VVAW/WSO.

Page 335: VVAW/GCDC.

Page 353: Pete Zastrow.

Page 375: VVAW/WSO; photo by Rich Klein.

Page 388: VVAW.

Page 389: *Milwaukee Journal* Photo.

Page 397: Jack McCloskey.

Page 399: John Lindquist.

Page 403: Photo provided by Barry Romo.

Page 404: Photo by Bob Hanson, provided by David Ewing.

Page 407: Photo by David Ewing, provided by Bob Hanson.

Page 408: Photo provided by Barry Romo.

Page 411: Lee Thorn.

Page 413: Photo by Ralph Weege.

Page 415: Photo from Barry Romo and VVAW.

Page 435: Photo from Barry Romo's collection.

Index

Also from Haymartket Books

Winter Soldier: Iraq and Afghanistan
Eyewitness Accounts of the Occupations
Iraq Veterans Against the War with Aaron Glantz, foreword by Anthony Swofford • In March 2008, veterans of the Iraq and Afghanistan occupations gathered to present firsthand accounts of the brutality and injustice they witnessed. This book preserves the testimonies of hundreds of veterans on the U.S. military's changing "rules of engagement," torture of detainees, gender and sexuality within the military's ranks, and the crisis in veterans' health care. ISBN: 978-1-931859-65-3

Beyond the Green Zone
Dispatches from an Unembedded Journalist in Occupied Iraq
Dahr Jamail with a foreword by Amy Goodman • As one of the only U.S. journalists to spend time unembedded in Iraq, Jamail has filed indispensable reports chronicling the unfolding disaster there—from the siege of Fallujah to prison torture and the raids of Iraqi homes. Now available in an updated paperback edition. ISBN: 978-1-931859-47-9

Road from ar-Ramadi:
The Private Rebellion of Staff Sergeant Camilo Mejía
Camilo Mejía • A courageous personal account of rebellion within the ranks of the U.S. military in wartime—written by the first soldier to publicly refuse to return to fight in Iraq. Mejía's story has been called the classic account of military resistance among the Iraq War generation. ISBN: 978-1-931859-553-0

War Without End: The Iraq War in Context
Michael Schwartz • Schwartz's comprehensive analysis argues that U.S. policy in Iraq is circumscribed by an interest in long-term regional influence. This perspective contextualizes the role of torture, oil, and elections in Iraq, and the roots of Iraq's civil conflict. ISBN: 978-1-931859-54-7

Vietnam: The (Last) War the U.S. Lost
Joe Allen • As the United States faces a major defeat in its occupation of Iraq, the history of the war in Vietnam—and the true story of how it was stopped—take on a fresh importance. This history from below examines the relationships between the era's antiwar movement, GI rebellion and the rebesistance of the Vietnamese which together brought the war to an end. ISBN: 978-1-931859-49-3

Soldiers in Revolt: GI Resistance During the Vietnam War
David Cortright with a new introduction by Howard Zinn • "An exhaustive account of rebellion in all the armed forces, not only in Vietnam but throughout the world."—*New York Review of Books*. ISBN: 978-1-931859-27-1

The Democrats: A Critical History
Lance Selfa • This book demonstrates the Democratic Party's historic alignment with business interests, their frequent support for wars, and reluctance to grant reforms, tracing the material circumstances that place the party at odds with rhetorical commitments to minorities, workers, and the poor. ISBN: 978-1-931859-55-4

About Haymarket Books

Haymarket Books is a nonprofit, progressive book distributor and publisher, a project of the Center for Economic Research and Social Change. We believe that activists need to take ideas, history, and politics into the many struggles for social justice today. Learning the lessons of past victories, as well as defeats, can arm a new generation of fighters for a better world. As Karl Marx said, "The philosophers have merely interpreted the world; the point, however, is to change it."

We take inspiration and courage from our namesakes, the Haymarket Martyrs, who gave their lives fighting for a better world. Their 1886 struggle for the eight-hour day, which gave us May Day, the international workers' holiday, reminds workers around the world that ordinary people can organize and struggle for their own liberation. These struggles continue today across the globe—struggles against oppression, exploitation, hunger, and poverty.

It was August Spies, one of the martyrs who was targeted for being an immigrant and an anarchist, who predicted the battles being fought to this day. "If you think that by hanging us you can stamp out the labor movement," Spies told the judge, "then hang us. Here you will tread upon a spark, but here, and there, and behind you, and in front of you, and everywhere, the flames will blaze up. It is a subterranean fire. You cannot put it out. The ground upon which you stand is on fire."

We could not succeed in our publishing efforts without the generous financial support of our readers. Many people contribute to our project through the Haymarket Sustainers program, where donors receive free books in return for their monetary support. If you would like to be a part of this program, please contact us at info@haymarketbooks.org.